Data-Centric Systems and Applications

More information about this series at http://www.springer.com/series/5258

Carlo Batini • Monica Scannapieco

Data and Information Quality

Dimensions, Principles and Techniques

 Springer

Carlo Batini
Università degli Studi
di Milano-Biccoca
Milan, Italy

Monica Scannapieco
Istituto Nazionale di Statistica-Istat
Rome, Italy

ISSN 2197-9723   ISSN 2197-974X   (electronic)
Data-Centric Systems and Applications
ISBN 978-3-319-24104-3   ISBN 978-3-319-24106-7   (eBook)
DOI 10.1007/978-3-319-24106-7

Library of Congress Control Number: 2016933451

This Springer imprint is published by Springer Nature
The registered company is Springer International Publishing AG Switzerland

To my father Curzio Batini
Carlo

To Giulio, Valerio and Massimo
and to my enriched "Ernania" world
Monica

Preface

Motivation for the Book

This book is the result of a study path that started in 2006, when the two authors of this book published the book *Data Quality: Concepts, Methodologies and Techniques*. After 8 years, *Data and Information Quality* is a book that adds significantly new contents to the previous one.

In this preface, we recall the motivations for the first book and the evolution of research and application issues that led us to move from the data quality (DQ) concept to the information quality (IQ) one.

Motivation for Data Quality

Electronic data play a crucial role in the information and communication technology (ICT) society: they are managed by business and governmental applications and are fundamental in all relationships between governments, businesses, and citizens. Because electronic data is so widely diffused, the "quality" of such data and its related effects on every kind of activity of the ICT society are more and more critical.

The relevance of data quality in both decisional and operational processes is recognized by several international institutions and organizations. As an example, the importance of data quality in decisional processes is clearly stated in the quality declaration of the European Statistical System [209], in which its mission is identified as follows: "We provide the European Union and the world with high quality information on the economy and society at the European, national, and regional levels and make the information available to everyone for decision-making purposes, research, and debate."

Furthermore, quality of data is also a significant issue for operational processes of businesses and organizations. In [432], published in 2013, the economic value of open data across different sectors is estimated from 3 to 5 trillion dollars per year,

and the importance of the role of the quality of open data is stated as follows: "One
of the biggest barriers to using open data in transportation is the extent and quality
of the available data."

The "Year 2000 problem" has been a data quality problem. In that case, it was
necessary to modify software applications and databases using a two-digit field to
represent years, and the costs of such operations have been estimated to be around
1.5 trillion US dollars (see [202]).

Some disasters are due to the presence of data quality problems, among them
the use of inaccurate, incomplete, out-of-date data. For example, the explosion
of the space shuttle Challenger is discussed in [234] according to a data quality
perspective; the analysis reports more than ten different categories of data quality
problems having a role in the disaster.

Such problems caused by poor data quality are the motivations at the basis of
the several initiatives that are being launched in the public and private sectors, and
in standardization bodies, with data quality having a leading role, as detailed in
Chap. 1; the initiatives include, for instance, the Data Quality Act promoted by the
US government in 2002 [478].

Electronic data are only to a certain extent of better quality than data stored
in paper documents. Indeed, electronic data benefit from a defined and regulated
representation, but processes that originate such data are often out of control, and
consequently errors in data proliferate.

The fundamental technology used in information systems for the last 40 years
has been databases. In the last decades, information systems have been migrating
from a hierarchical/monolithic to a network-based structure, where the potential
data sources that organizations can use for the purpose of their businesses are
dramatically increased in size and scope. Data quality problems in databases
have been further worsened by this evolution. In networked information systems,
processes are involved in complex information exchanges and often operate on input
obtained from other external sources, frequently unknown a priori.

As a consequence, the overall quality of the data that flow between information
systems may rapidly degrade over time if both processes and their inputs are not
themselves under strict quality control. On the other hand, the same networked
information systems offer new opportunities for data quality management, including
the possibility of selecting sources with better quality data and of comparing sources
for the purpose of error localization and correction, thus facilitating the control and
improvement of overall data quality.

Due to the above-described motivations, researchers and organizations need to
increasingly understand and solve data quality problems and thus need to answer the
following questions: What is, in essence, data quality? Which kind of techniques,
methodologies, and data quality issues are at a consolidated stage? What are the
well-known and reliable approaches? Which problems are open? This book attempts
to answer all these questions.

From Data Quality to Information Quality

The evolution of ICT technologies in the last 40 years has been overwhelming.

The related evolution of information systems has been characterized by the advent of distributed architectures and networks. In centralized systems, information flows have a common and shared format, and information quality control is facilitated by the homogeneity and the centralization of procedures and management rules. A distributed information system allows the distribution of resources and applications across a network of geographically distributed systems. Problems of information management are more complex than in centralized systems, and heterogeneities and autonomies usually increase with the number of tiers and nodes. A cooperative information system interconnects various information systems of different and autonomous organizations, which share common objectives. The relationship between cooperative information systems and the quality of data is double faced: on the one hand, it is possible to profit from the cooperation between agents in order to choose the best quality sources. On the other hand, information flows are less controlled than in centralized systems, and the quality of information may rapidly decrease in time.

More recently, information systems have evolved toward Web information systems, adopting a variety of Web technologies, where single data producers are highly autonomous and heterogeneous and have no obligation for the quality of the information produced, and no producer has a global view of the system. Accordingly, these systems are extremely critical from the point of view of information quality.

In parallel with the evolution of information systems, information managed in the system has evolved across a variety of *information types*, emphasizing on the one hand the *sensory perceptual character* of information and on the other the *linguistic character* of information. Each information type organizes information in a specific way and has a (more or less formal) syntax and semantics. As to the sensory character, we have drawings, maps, images, sounds, videos, and flavors. As to the linguistic character of information, we can distinguish several types of information such as:

1. *Structured information*, i.e., information represented in terms of a set of instances and a schema, which are tightly coupled, as the schema binds the semantic interpretation and properties of instances with features such as types, domains, integrity constraints, etc. (e.g., relational tables in databases).
2. *Semistructured information*, i.e., information that is either partially structured or has a descriptive rather than prescriptive schema [5, 97, 109]. An XML record is an example of semistructured information, where a schema can be defined that binds only a part of the contained information.
3. *Unstructured information*, i.e., any sequence of symbols, coded in natural language or any other symbolic language with no semantics induced by an explicit schema.

The Web has been in the last years an extraordinary vehicle of production, diffusion, and exchange of information. We can classify types of Web information according to a second coordinate that refers to their structure, usage, or localization in the Web, thus resulting in:

- Open data
- Linked open data
- Deep Web
- Surface Web, i.e., data available in "static" HTML
- Social data
- Big Data

Open data are freely available machine-readable data. The philosophy behind open data has been long established in public bodies, but the term "open data" itself is recent, gaining popularity with the rise of the Internet and World Wide Web and, especially, with the launch of open data government initiatives. Bauer and Kaltenböck [48] adopt the following set of properties for being open data: data must be complete, primary, timely, accessible, machine processable, nondiscriminatory, with nonproprietary format, and license free.

Open data become *linked open data* when [60]:

1. Information is available on the Web (any format) under an open license.
2. Information is available as structured data (e.g., Excel instead of an image scan of a table).
3. Nonproprietary formats are used (e.g., Comma-separated values (CSV) instead of MS Excel).
4. URI identification is used so that people can point at individual data.
5. Data is linked to other data to provide context.

The term *Big Data* has been forged to express data that exceed the processing capacity of conventional database systems, i.e., data are too big, move too fast, or do not fit the structures of organization database architectures. Big Data is gaining more and more attention both in academic and business sectors. Notwithstanding in the data engineering and information system communities, (very) large databases are not a new research topic; nowadays it is frequently observed that the main unmatched challenges in Big Data concern the so-called 3Vs—variety, volume, and velocity—(see Chap. 14 for a deeper discussion on these issues).

The reader would have noticed that so far we have used the terms data (and data quality) and information (and information quality) interchangeably, without a precise distinction. For the sake of clarity, in the remainder of the book, we will use:

- The term *data* when we make reference to structured data in a database and also when the term is a part of a compound term when it is homogeneously and universally adopted in the literature, as in the cases of, e.g., data source, data model, data integration (technology), linked open data, Web data, and Big Data
- The term *information* when we make reference to all other information types (with the exception of linked open data and Big Data mentioned above)

- The term *data quality* (or DQ) when we refer to dimensions, models, and techniques strictly related to structured data
- In all other cases, when dimensions, models, and techniques refer to a wider spectrum of information types, we use the term *information quality* (or IQ)

Goals

The goal of this book is to provide a systematic and comparative description of the vast number of research issues related to quality of data and information and thus to illustrate the state of the art in the area of data and information quality. Dealing with the quality of all types of information introduced in the motivation section requires tremendous effort. So, we decided to focus in this book on:

- Maps
- Loosely structured texts (texts that are halfway been unstructured and semistructured information, see Chap. 3 for further discussion on this point)
- A particular but relevant type of loosely structured texts, namely, laws
- Linked open data
- Images
- Web data in general
- Big Data

With reference to Web data in general and Big Data, these types of information are of growing importance in modern societies and economies. At the same time, the research so far on Web data and Big Data quality cannot be considered at a mature stage, so we decided to deal with these topics in a final chapter, more closely related to open problems.

While being a real problem in a vast number of activities in the private and public sectors, IQ resulted recently in a significant number of contributions to the research community. From 1995 to 2008, three information quality journals have been launched so far: the *Data Quality Journal* in 1995, the *International Journal of Information Quality* in 2007, and the *ACM Journal of Data and Information Quality* in 2008.

There are several international conferences promoted by the database and information system communities that have IQ as their main topic. Among them, the International Conference on Information Quality (ICIQ) [325], promoted by the MIT Total Data Quality Management (TDQM) Program, has been taking place since 1996.

On the practical side, many IQ software tools are advertised and used in various data-driven applications, such as data warehousing, and to improve the quality of business processes. Frequently, their scope is limited and domain dependent, and it is not clear how to coordinate and finalize their use in data quality processes.

On the research side, the gap, still present between the need for techniques, methodologies, and tools and the relatively limited maturity of the area, has led so far to the presence of fragmented and sparse results in the literature and the absence of a systematic view of the area.

Furthermore, in the area of IQ, we highlight the existence of a dichotomy, typical of many other research areas that have a deep impact on real life, between practice-oriented approaches and formal research contributions. This book tries to address such a dichotomy, providing not only comparative overviews and explanatory frameworks of existing proposals but also original solutions that combine the concreteness of practical approaches and the soundness of theoretical formalisms. By understanding the motivations and the different backgrounds of solutions, we have figured out the paradigms and forces contributing to the IQ environment.

Focusing first on data quality, our main concern is to provide a sound, integrated, and comprehensive picture of the state of the art and of future evolutions of data quality in the database and information system areas. This book includes an extensive description of techniques that constitute the core of data quality research, including record linkage (also called object identification), data integration, error localization, and correction; such techniques are examined in a comprehensive and original methodological framework. Quality dimension definitions and adopted models are also analyzed in depth, and differences between the proposed solutions are highlighted and discussed. Furthermore, while systematically describing data quality as an autonomous research area, we highlight the paradigms and influences deriving from other areas, such as probability theory, statistical data analysis, data mining, knowledge representation, and machine learning. Our book also provides very practical solutions, such as methodologies, benchmarks for the most effective techniques, case studies, and examples.

The rigorous and formal foundation of our approach to data quality issues, presented with practical solutions, makes this book a necessary complement to books already published. Some books adopt a formal and research-oriented approach but are focused on specific topics or perspectives. Specifically, Dasu and Johnson [161] approach data quality problems from the perspective of data mining and machine learning solutions. Wang et al. [649] provide a general perspective on data quality, by giving a heterogeneous collection of contributions from different projects and research groups. Jarke et al. [341] describe solutions for data quality issues in the data warehouse environment. Wang et al. [651] survey research contributions, including new methods for measuring data quality, for modeling quality improvement processes, and for organizational and educational issues related to information quality.

Some other books give much more room to practical aspects rather than to formal ones. In particular, leading books in the practitioners' field are Redman [519] and [521] and English [202]. The two Redman books provide an extensive set of data quality dimensions and discuss a vast set of issues related to management methodologies for data quality improvement. English's book provides a detailed methodology for data quality measurement and improvement, discussing step-by-step issues related to data architectures, standards, process- and data-driven improvement methodologies, costs, benefits, and managerial strategies.

Moving on to information quality, to the best of our knowledge, this is the first book on the quality of data that coherently extends the dissertation on quality from data to information. We discuss in the following the structure of the book focusing on new chapters and extensions with regard to the Data Quality book [37]:

1. Beyond Chap. 2, which discusses data quality dimensions in structured relational data, three new chapters, Chaps. 3–5, are focused on dimensions, with Chap. 3 dealing with quality of maps, quality of semistructured texts, and quality of law texts, Chap. 4 with quality of linked open data, and Chap. 5 with quality of images. In Chap. 4, languages and models typical of linked open data are briefly introduced (in particular, Resource Description Framework).
2. With reference to Chap. 8 on object identification, also present in [37], a new chapter has been added, Chap. 9 that discusses recent advancements and novelties in the literature on this topic.
3. Chapter 11 on information quality in use bridges a gap of the previous book, dealing with IQ in its relationships with the quality of business processes and with the quality of decisions, seen from the point of view of utility, especially economic utility. The section on cost-benefit classifications, which in the previous book was placed in Chap. 7 on activities, has been moved to this chapter.
4. Chapter 12 on methodologies for IQ assessment and improvement has been enriched with two new sections: the first deals with a methodology that extends data considered from relational data to more general types of information, while the second compares 12 main methodologies for IQ assessment and improvement according to several criteria.
5. Chapter 13 deals with the domain of health information systems, characterized by a great variety of information types and of information usages.
6. The final Chap. 14 on open problems completely renews the old one focusing on Web data in general and on Big Data; we discuss several research results that provide a first picture of the research in the two areas.

To complete the comparison with the old book, the chapter on tools has been deleted, due to their high volatility.

Organization

The book is organized into 14 chapters. Figure 1 lists the chapters and details interdependencies among them.

We initially (Chap. 1) provide basic concepts and establish coordinates to explore the area of data and information quality. Subsequently Chap. 2 focuses on dimensions that allow for the measurement of data quality in databases, both for

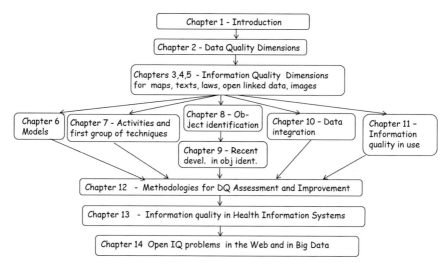

Fig. 1 Interdependencies among chapters

values and for schemas. The chapter also introduces a classification of the huge number of data and information quality dimensions in terms of several clusters of dimensions with similar meanings. The first two chapters are preparatory to the rest of the book. The following three chapters discuss information quality and information quality dimensions. Three coordinates are introduced referring to the different information types considered in the book:

- Quality of perceptual information, focusing in Chap. 3 on quality of maps and in Chap. 5 on quality of images
- Quality of linguistic information, focusing in Chap. 3 on quality of semistructured data in general and more specifically on quality of law texts
- Quality of linked open data, discussed in Chap. 4

Models to express the quality of data and semistructured information are investigated in Chap. 6. Subsequent chapters are dedicated to activities and techniques especially (but not exclusively, see later) conceived for the quality of structured data. Chapter 7 introduces the main activities for measuring and improving data quality. Activities, such as error localization and correction, are discussed in Chap. 7; the three subsequent chapters are dedicated to the most important family of techniques and related research areas, namely:

- Object identification, discussed in its basic phases in Chap. 8 and in its recent advancements in Chap. 9; in Chap. 9 we also extend the discussion on object identification from structured data to other types of information, namely, maps and images.
- Data integration (Chap. 10).

The third part of the book moves to issues related to information quality in use. Chapter 11 discusses all the issues related to quality in use, from contextual quality dimensions to the relationship between quality and utility of information, cost-benefit analysis of IQ improvement initiatives, and relationship between IQ and decision quality.

Dimensions, models, activities, and techniques are the ingredients of any methodology for data quality measurement and improvement; methodologies are the subject of Chap. 12. Specifically, in this chapter existing methodologies are examined and compared, and an original, comprehensive methodology for IQ is proposed, with an extensive case study.

Chapter 13 considers specific issues in IQ in the domain of health information systems. Finally Chap. 14 discusses several open issues that are on the edge of recent research contributions in Web data quality and Big Data quality.

Carlo Batini and Monica Scannapieco are the main authors of the book. Some chapters are due to the contribution of other authors. Chapter 4 has been written by Anisa Rula, Andrea Maurino, and Carlo Batini. Chapter 5 has been written by Gianluigi Ciocca, Silvia Corchs, Francesca Gasparini, Carlo Batini, and Raimondo Schettini. Chapter 13 has been written by Federico Cabitza and Carlo Batini. Chapter 14 has been written by Monica Scannapieco and Laure Berti.

Intended Audience

The book is intended for those interested in a comprehensive introduction to the wide set of issues related to data and information quality. It has been written primarily for researchers in the fields of databases and information management interested in investigating properties of data and information that have an impact on the quality of processes and on real life. This book introduces the reader to autonomous research in the field of information quality, providing a wide spectrum of definitions, formalisms, and methods enriched with critical comparisons of the state of the art. For this reason, the book can help establish the most relevant research areas in data quality, consolidated issues, and open problems.

A second category of potential readers are data and information system administrators and practitioners, who need a systematization of the field and practical methods in the area. This category also includes designers of complex cooperative systems and services, such as e-Business and e-Government systems, that exhibit relevant data quality problems.

A third category of readers are professionals such as physicians, nurses, health-care assistants, and, more generally, stakeholders who are involved in hospital treatment policies and operations that interact with health information systems and who should be aware of issues related to health information quality.

Figures 2, 3, and 4 suggest possible paths, which can be followed by the above audiences.

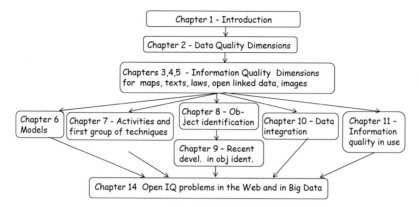

Fig. 2 Reading path for the researcher

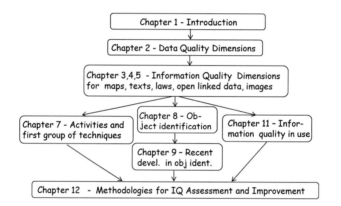

Fig. 3 Reading path for the chief information officer

The *researcher path*, for researchers interested in the core research areas in data quality, skips the chapter on methodologies (Chap. 12). The *information system administrator path* skips models (Chap. 6), data integration issues (Chap. 10), and health information quality (Chap. 13), and finally the healthcare professional path skips models (Chap. 6) and data integration issues (Chap. 10).

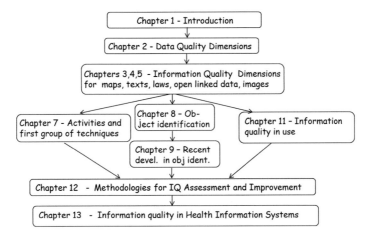

Fig. 4 Reading path for the healthcare professional

Guidelines for Teaching

To the best of our knowledge, IQ is not a usually considered topic in undergraduate and graduate courses. Several PhD courses include mainly data quality issues, while the market for professional, often expensive courses is rapidly increasing. However, recent initiatives are in the direction of introducing data quality in undergraduate and graduate courses.[1]

With the advent of Big Data, several data science courses are being organized (see, e.g., Coursera "Data Science" specialization). Most of them include dedicated sessions on (1) cleaning data in order at a preprocessing stage and (2) evaluating quality in input and in output to data analysis processes.

We have organized the book to be used in an advanced course on the quality of databases and information systems. The areas of databases and information systems are currently lacking consolidated textbooks on data quality; we have tried to cover this demand. Although this book cannot be defined as a textbook, it can be adopted, with some effort, as basic material for a course on IQ. Due to the undeniable importance of these topics, what happened in the 1980s for other database areas, e.g., database design, could happen for IQ: the plethora of textbooks which favored the introduction of this area in university courses.

---

[1] As an example, in 2005 the University of Arkansas at Little Rock promoted a Master of Science in information quality (MS IQ).

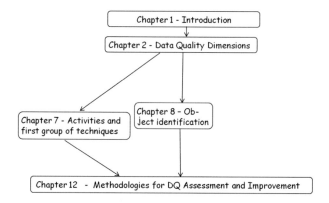

Fig. 5 Teaching path for a basic course on data quality

IQ can be the topic of self-contained courses or else of cycles of seminars in courses on databases and information systems management. Data integration courses would also benefit from data quality seminars. With regard to information systems management, IQ can be taught in connection with topics such as information management, information economics, business process reengineering, process and service quality, and cost and benefit analysis. IQ techniques can also be offered in specific courses on data warehousing and data mining.

The material of this book is sufficiently self-contained for students who are able to attend a course on databases. As students' prerequisites, it is useful, but not mandatory, to have notions of mathematics and, to some extent, probability theory, statistics, machine learning, and knowledge representation.

The book provides enough material to cover all the necessary topics without the need for other textbooks. In the case of a PhD course, the references are a good starting point for assigning students in-depth analysis activities on specific issues.

In Figs. 5, 6, and 7, we show possible reading paths for a basic and advanced course on data quality and for a basic course on information quality. The whole book can be considered for an advanced course on information quality.

In terms of exercises, a useful approach for students is to develop a complex IQ project that can be organized into three parts. The first part could be devoted to the assessment of the quality of two or more databases jointly used in several business processes of an organization. The second part could focus on the choice and application of methodologies and techniques described in Chaps. 7–9, 11, and 12 to improve data quality levels of the databases to a fixed target. The third part, which considers Chaps. 4 and 5, could deal with databases extended with images plus a dataset of linked open data. This approach gives students a taste of the problems that they are likely to face in a real-life environment.

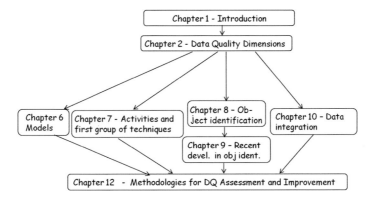

Fig. 6 Teaching path for an advanced course on data quality

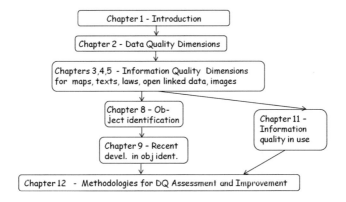

Fig. 7 Teaching path for a basic course on information quality

Acknowledgments

We would like to thank Ralf Gerstner of Springer-Verlag, who initially had the idea of considering data quality as a consolidated issue to be described in a book. We thank the data and information quality community for supporting us with references and discussions and in particular our coauthors on some of the chapters of this book. A special thanks also to our families for being patient during weekends spent on revisions.

Milan, Italy   Carlo Batini
Rome, Italy   Monica Scannapieco
May 2015

Contents

Chapter 1
Introduction to Information Quality

1.1 Introduction

The Search query "data quality" entered into Google returns about three million pages, and searching similarly for the term "information quality" (IQ) returns about one and a half million pages, both frequencies showing the increasing importance of data and information quality. The goal of this chapter is to show and discuss the perspectives that make data and information (D&I) quality an issue worth being investigated and understood. We first (Sect. 1.2) highlight the relevance of information quality in everyday life and some of the main related initiatives in the public and private domains. Then, in Sect. 1.3, we show the multidimensional nature of information quality by means of several examples. In Sect. 1.4, we discuss information quality and its relationship with several classifications proposed in the literature for information. Section 1.5 analyzes the different types of information systems for which IQ can be investigated. In Sect. 1.6, we address the main research issues in IQ, application domains in which it is investigated, and related research areas. The research issues (Sect. 1.6.1) concern dimensions, models, techniques, and methodologies; together, they provide the agenda for the rest of the book. The specific application domains for which D&I is relevant can be several, since data and information are fundamental ingredients of all the activities of people and organizations. We focus (Sect. 1.6.2) on three of them that we identified as particularly relevant—e-Government, life sciences, and the World Wide Web—highlighting the role that IQ plays in each of them. Research areas related to IQ will be examined in Sect. 1.6.3.

© Springer International Publishing Switzerland 2016
C. Batini, M. Scannapieco, *Data and Information Quality*, Data-Centric Systems
and Applications, DOI 10.1007/978-3-319-24106-7_1

1.2   Why Information Quality Is Relevant

The consequences of poor quality of information can be experienced in everyday life but, often, without making explicit connections to their causes. Some examples are: the late or mistaken delivery of a letter is often blamed on a dysfunctional postal service, although a closer look often reveals data-related causes, typically an error in the address, which can be traced back to the originating database. Similarly, the duplicate delivery of automatically generated mails is often indicative of a database record duplication error.

Information quality seriously impacts on the efficiency and effectiveness of organizations and businesses. The report on information quality of the Data Warehousing Institute (see [162]) estimates that IQ problems cost US businesses more than 600 billion dollars a year. The findings of the report were based on interviews with industry experts, leading-edge customers, and survey data from 647 respondents. In the following, we list further examples of the importance of IQ in organizational processes:

- *Customer matching.* Information systems of public and private organizations can be seen as the result of a set of scarcely controlled and independent activities producing several databases very often characterized by overlapping information. In private organizations, such as marketing firms or banks, it is not surprising to have several (sometimes dozens!) customer registries, updated by different organizational procedures, resulting in inconsistent, duplicate information. Some examples are: it is very difficult for banks to provide clients with a unique list of all their accounts and funds.
- *Corporate householding.* Many organizations establish separate relationships with single members of households or, more generally, related groups of people; either way, they like, for marketing purposes, to reconstruct the household relationships in order to carry out more effective marketing strategies. This problem is even more complex than the previous one, since in that case, the information to match concerned the same person, while in this case, it concerns groups of persons corresponding to the same household. For a detailed discussion on the relationship between corporate householding information and various business application areas, see [650].
- *Organization fusion.* When different organizations (or different units of an organization) merge, it is necessary to integrate their legacy information systems. Such integration requires compatibility and interoperability at any layer of the information system, with the database level required to ensure both physical and semantic interoperability.

The examples above are indicative of the growing need to integrate information across completely different data sources, an activity in which poor quality hampers integration efforts. Awareness of the importance of improving the quality of information is increasing in many contexts. In the following, we summarize some of the major initiatives in both the private and public domains.

1.2.1   Private Initiatives

In the private sector, on the one hand, application providers and systems integrators and, on the other hand, direct users are experiencing the role of IQ in their own business processes.

With regard to application providers and systems integrators, IBM's (2005) acquisition of Ascential Software, a leading provider of data integration tools, highlights the critical role data and information stewardship plays in the enterprise. The 2005 Ascential report [665] on data integration provides a survey that indicates information quality and security issues as the leading inhibitors (55 % of respondents in a multi-response survey) to successful data integration projects. The respondents also emphasize that information quality is more than just a technological issue. It requires senior management to treat information as a corporate asset and to realize that the value of this asset depends on its quality.

In a research by the Economist Intelligence Unit [617] in 2012 on managers' perception of the most problematic issues in the management of Big Data, "access the right data" (a kind of data quality dimension related to relevance of data) ranks first, while accuracy, heterogeneity reconciliation, and timeliness of data rank, respectively, second, third, and fourth.

The awareness of the relevance of information quality issues has led Oracle (see [481]) to enhance its suite of products and services to support an architecture that optimizes information quality, providing a framework for the systematic analysis of information, with the goals of increasing the value of information, easing the burden of data migration, and decreasing the risks inherent in data integration.

With regard to users, Basel2 and Basel3 are international initiatives in the financial domain that require financial services companies to have a risk-sensitive framework for the assessment of regulatory capital. Initially published in June 2004, Basel2 introduced regulatory requirements leading to demanding improvements in information quality. For example, the Draft Supervisory Guidance on Internal Ratings-Based Systems for Corporate Credit states (see [239]): "institutions using the Internal Ratings-Based approach for regulatory capital purposes will need advanced data management practices to produce credible and reliable risk estimates" and "data retained by the bank will be essential for regulatory risk-based capital calculations and public reporting. These uses underscore the need for a well defined data maintenance framework and strong controls over data integrity."

Basel3, which was agreed upon by the members of the Basel Committee on Banking Supervision in 2010, proposes further policies for financial services companies (see [295]), by means of fine-tuning their risk-weighted asset models, improving their information quality in terms of improved rating coverage and transparency on underlying assets, and optimizing their asset segmentations. Based on the observation that Basel3 would require even more transparency into the risk positions taken by financial institutions, a novel approach to the evaluation and improvement of information quality in the financial sector is proposed in [172], and the Business Process Modeling Notation is used to represent bank business processes, to identify where information elements enter the process, and to trace the various information outputs of processes.

1.2.2 Public Initiatives

In the public sector, a number of initiatives address information quality issues at international and national levels. We focus in the rest of the section on two of the main initiatives, the Data Quality Act in the United States and the European directive on reuse of public information.

In 2001, the President of the United States signed into law important new Data Quality legislation, concerning "Guidelines for Ensuring and Maximizing the Quality, Objectivity, Utility, and Integrity of Information Disseminated by Federal Agencies," in short, the Data Quality Act. The Office of Management and Budget (OMB) issued guidelines referred for policies and procedures on information quality issues (see [478]). Obligations mentioned in the guidelines concern agencies, which are to report periodically to the OMB regarding the number and nature of information quality complaints received and how such complaints were handled. The OMB must also include a mechanism through which the public can petition agencies to correct information that does not meet the OMB standard. In the OMB guidelines, information quality is defined as an encompassing term comprising utility, objectivity, and integrity. Objectivity is a measure to determine whether the disseminated information is accurate, reliable, and unbiased and whether that information is presented in an accurate, clear, complete, and unbiased manner. Utility refers to the usefulness of the information for its anticipated purpose by its intended audience. The OMB is committed to disseminating reliable and useful information. Integrity refers to the security of information, namely, protection of the information from unauthorized, unanticipated, or unintentional modification, to prevent it from being compromised by corruption or falsification. Specific risk-based, cost-effective policies are defined for assuring integrity.

The European directive 2003/98/CE on the reuse of public information (see [206] and its revision published in 2013 [207]) highlights the importance of reusing the vast information assets owned by public agencies. The public sector collects, produces, and disseminates a wide range of information in many areas of activity, such as social, economic, geographical, meteorological, business, and educational information. Making public all generally available documents held by the public sector, concerning not only the political process but also the legal and administrative processes, is considered a fundamental instrument for extending the right to information, which is a basic principle of democracy. Aspects of information quality addressed by such a directive are the accessibility to public information and availability in a format which is not dependent on the use of specific software. At the same time, a related and necessary step for public information reuse is to guarantee its quality in terms of accuracy and currency, through information cleaning campaigns. This makes it attractive to new potential users and customers.

1.3   Introduction to the Concept of Information Quality

Quality, in general, has been defined as the "totality of characteristics of a product that bear on its ability to satisfy stated or implied needs" [331], also called "fitness for (intended) use" [352], "conformance to requirements" [156], or "user satisfaction" [657].

From a research perspective, *information quality* has been addressed in different areas, including statistics, management, and computer science. Statisticians were the first to investigate some of the problems related to information quality, by proposing a mathematical theory for considering duplicates in statistical datasets in the late 1960s. They were followed by researchers in management, who at the beginning of the 1980s focused on how to control information manufacturing systems in order to detect and eliminate information quality problems. Only at the beginning of the 1990s computer scientists began considering the problem of defining, measuring, and improving the quality of electronic information stored in databases, data warehouses, and legacy systems.

When people think about information quality, they often reduce quality just to accuracy. For example, let us consider the surname "Batini"; when this is spelled during a telephone call, several misspellings are reported by the other side, such as "Vatini," "Battini," "Barini," and "Basini," all inaccurate versions of the original. Indeed, information is normally considered to be of poor quality if typos are present or wrong values are associated with a concept instance, such as an erroneous birth date or age associated with a person. However, information quality is more than simply accuracy. Other significant dimensions such as completeness, consistency, and currency are necessary in order to fully characterize the quality of information. In Fig. 1.1, we provide some examples of these dimensions for structured data, which are described in more detail in Chap. 3. The relational table in the figure describes movies, with title, director, year of production, number of remakes, and year of the last remake.

In the figure, the cells with data quality problems are shaded. At first, only the cell corresponding to the title of movie 3 seems to be affected by a data quality problem.

Id	Title	Director	Year	#Remakes	LastRemakeYear
1	Casablanca	Weir	1942	3	1940
2	Dead poets society	Curtiz	1989	0	NULL
3	Rman Holiday	Wylder	1953	0	NULL
4	Sabrina	null	1964	0	1985

Fig. 1.1 A relation Movies with data quality problems

In fact, there is a misspelling in the title, where Rman stands for Roman, thus causing an accuracy problem. Nevertheless, another accuracy problem is related to the exchange of the director between movies 1 and 2; Weir is actually the director of movie 2 and Curtiz the director of movie 1. Other data quality problems are a missing value for the director of movie 4, causing a completeness problem, and a 0 value for the number of remakes of movie 4, causing a currency problem because a remake of the movie has actually been proposed. Finally, there are two consistency problems: first, for movie 1, the value of LastRemakeYear cannot be lower than Year; second, for movie 4, the value of LastRemakeYear cannot be different from null, because the value of #Remakes is 0.

The above examples of dimensions concern the *quality of data values* represented in the relation. Besides data, a large part of the design methodologies for the relational model addresses properties that concern the *quality of the schema*; for example, several normal forms have been proposed with the aim of capturing the concept of good relational schema, free of anomalies and redundancies. Other data quality and schema quality dimensions will be discussed in Chap. 3.

The above examples and considerations show that:

- Data quality is a multifaceted concept, to the definition of which different dimensions concur
- Quality dimensions, such as accuracy, can be easily detected in some cases (e.g., misspellings) but are more difficult to detect in other cases (e.g., where admissible but not correct values are provided)
- A simple example of a completeness error has been shown, but like happens with accuracy, completeness can also be very difficult to evaluate (e.g., if a tuple representing a movie is entirely missing from the relation Movie)
- Consistency detection does not always localize the errors (e.g., for movie 1, the value of the LastRemakeYear attribute is wrong)

The above example concerned a relational table of a database. Problems change significantly when other *types of information* different from structured relational data are involved. Let us focus on Fig. 1.2, showing an image representing a flower. Instinctively, the image on the right-hand side is considered of better quality in comparison to the image on the left-hand side. At the same time, it is not immediate to identify the dimension(s) that we are considering to come to such a conclusion.

In the preface, we provided a list of different information types. In the next section, we introduce several classifications of information relevant to quality issues, while issues related to information quality in several *types of information systems* will be considered in Sect. 1.5.

Bad quality   Good quality

Fig. 1.2 Two images of the same flower with intuitively different image quality levels

1.4   Information Quality and Information Classifications

Structured data represent real-world objects, with a format and a model that can be stored, retrieved, and elaborated by database management systems (DBMSs). The process of representing the real world by means of structured data can be applied to a large number of phenomena, such as measurements, events, characteristics of people, environment, sounds, and smells. Structured data are extremely versatile in such representations but are limited by their intrinsic characteristics.

The types of information introduced in the preface strongly enhance the property of structured data to represent phenomena of the real world. Since researchers in the area of information quality must deal with a wide spectrum of possible information types, they have proposed several classifications for information. The first classification discussed in the preface refers to the perceptual vs. linguistic character of the information, and, among linguistic types of information, we can distinguish among structured, semistructured, and unstructured information.

A second point of view sees information as a product. This point of view is adopted, for example, in the IP-MAP model (see [563]), an extension of the Information Manufacturing Product model [648], which will be discussed in detail in Chap. 6; the IP-MAP model identifies a parallelism between the quality of information and the quality of products as managed by manufacturing companies. In this model, three different types of information are distinguished:

- *Raw data items* are considered smaller data units. They are used to construct information and component data items that are semi-processed information.

- While the raw data items may be stored for long periods of time, the *component data items* are stored temporarily until the final product is manufactured. The component items are regenerated each time an information product is needed. The same set of raw data and component data items may be used (sometimes simultaneously) in the manufacturing of several different products.
- *Information products*, which are the result of a manufacturing activity performed on data.

Looking at information as a product, methodologies and procedures used over a long period for quality assurance in manufacturing processes can be applied to information, with suitable changes having been made to them. This issue will be discussed in Chaps. 6 and 12.

The third classification, proposed in [446], addresses a typical distinction made in information systems between elementary data and aggregated data. *Elementary data* are managed in organizations by operational processes and represent atomic phenomena of the real world (e.g., social security number, age, and sex). *Aggregated* data are obtained from a collection of elementary data by applying some aggregation function to them (e.g., the average income of tax payers in a given city).

Dasu and Johnson in [161] investigate new types of data that emerge from the diffusion of networks and the Web. They distinguish several new types of data; the following among them are relevant in this book:

- *Federated data*, which come from different heterogeneous sources and, consequently, require disparate data sources to be combined with approximate matches
- *Web data*, which are "scraped" from the Web and, although characterized by unconventional formats and low control on information, more often constitute the primary source of information for several activities

Previous classifications did not take into account in the time dimension of information investigated in [85]. According to its change frequency, we can classify source information into three categories:

- *Stable* information is information that is unlikely to change. Examples are scientific publications; although new publications can be added to the source, older publications remain unchanged.
- *Long-term-changing information* is information that has a very low change frequency. Examples are addresses, currencies, and hotel price lists. The concept of "low frequency" is domain dependent; in an e-trade application, if the value of a stock quote is tracked once an hour, it is considered to be a low-frequency change, while a shop that changes its goods weekly has a high-frequency change for clients.
- *Frequently changing information* is information that has intensive change, such as real-time traffic information, temperature sensor measures, and sales quantities. The changes can occur with a defined frequency or they can be random.

For this classification, the procedures for establishing the time dimension qualities of the three types of information, i.e., stable, long-term-changing, and frequently changing information, are increasingly more complex.

1.5   Information Quality and Types of Information Systems

Information is collected, stored, elaborated, retrieved, and exchanged in *information systems* used in organizations to provide services to business processes. Different criteria can be adopted for classifying the different types of information systems and their corresponding architectures; they are usually related to the overall organizational model adopted by an organization or the set of organizations that make use of the information system. In order to clarify the impact of information quality on the different *types of information systems*, we adopt the classification criteria proposed in [486] for distributed databases. Three different criteria are proposed: distribution, heterogeneity, and autonomy.

Distribution deals with the possibility of distributing the data and the applications over a network of computers. *Heterogeneity* considers all types of semantic and technological diversities among systems used in modeling and physically representing data, such as database management systems, programming languages, operating systems, middleware, and markup languages. *Autonomy* has to do with the degree of hierarchy and rules of coordination, establishing rights and duties, defined in the organization using the information system. The two extremes are (1) a fully hierarchical system, where only one subject decides for all and no autonomy at all exists, and (2) a total anarchy, where no rule exists and each component organization is totally free in its design and management decisions. For the three criteria, we adopt for simplicity a <yes, no> classification, warning the reader that there is a continuum among extreme solutions.

The three classifications are represented together in the classification space in Fig. 1.3. Six main types of information systems are highlighted in the figure: Monolithic, Distributed, Data Warehouses, Cooperative, Cloud, and Peer to Peer.

- In a *monolithic information system* , presentation, application logic, and data management are merged into a single computational node. Many monolithic information systems are still in use. While being extremely rigid, they provide advantages to organizations, such as reduced costs due to the homogeneity of solutions and centralization of management. In monolithic systems, data flows have a common format, and data quality control is facilitated by the homogeneity and centralization of procedures and management rules.
- A *data warehouse* (DW) is a centralized set of data collected from different sources, designed to support several tasks, including business analytics and management decision making. The most critical problem in DW design concerns the cleaning and integration of the different data sources that are loaded into

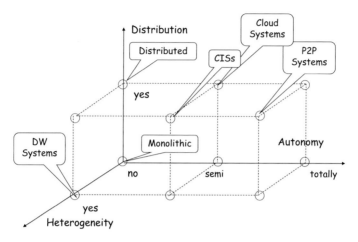

Fig. 1.3 Types of information systems

the DW, in that much of the implementation budget is spent on data cleaning activities.

- A *distributed information system* relaxes the rigid centralization of monolithic systems, in that it allows the distribution of resources and applications across a network of geographically distributed systems. The network can be organized in terms of several tiers, each made of one or more computational nodes. Presentation, application logic, and data management are distributed across tiers. The different tiers and nodes have a limited degree of autonomy; data design is usually performed centrally, but to a certain extent, some degree of heterogeneity can occur, due to the impossibility of establishing unified procedures. Problems of data management are more complex than in monolithic systems, due to the reduced level of centralization. Heterogeneities and autonomy usually increase with the number of tiers and nodes.

- A *cooperative information system* (CIS) can be defined as a large-scale information system that interconnects various systems of different and autonomous organizations while sharing common objectives. According to [170], the manifesto of CISs, "an information system is cooperative if it shares goals with other agents in its environment, such as other information systems, human agents, and the organization itself, and contributes positively toward the fulfillment of these common goals." The relationship between CISs and information quality is double-faced. On the one hand, it is possible to profit the cooperation between agents in order to choose the best quality sources and thus improve the quality of circulating information. On the other hand, information flows are less controlled than in monolithic systems, and the quality of information, when not controlled, may rapidly decrease in time. Integration of data sources is also a relevant issue in CISs, especially when partners decide to substitute a group of databases that have been independently developed with an integrated in-house database. In *virtual data integration*, a unique virtual integrated schema is built to provide unified access. This case is affected by information quality problems, because inconsistencies in information stored at different sites make it difficult to provide integrated information.

- *Cloud information systems* consist of groups of remote servers that are networked to allow centralized data storage and online access to computer services or resources.[1] For these systems, autonomy and heterogeneity are partial due to the presence of a logically centralized data storage.
- *Peer-to-Peer information systems* are based on equal roles with respect to network communications (differently from client-server communication). These systems do not need a central coordination and hence exhibit the maximum level of autonomy as well as of heterogeneity.

The above illustrated typologies do not take into account the fact that there are several "domain/specific" information systems. As a significant example, it is worth mentioning another type of information system largely used in hospitals and clinics: healthcare information systems. These systems are characterized by usage of a vast amount of different types of information, from structured data to semistructured blood test outcomes, handwritten documents, and images as the result of radiographies or ultrasound scans, and exhibit challenging objectives in the integrated analysis of such heterogeneous types of information. Healthcare information systems will be discussed in Chap. 13.

1.6 Main Research Issues and Application Domains

Due to the relevance of information quality, its nature, and the variety of information types and information systems, achieving information quality is a complex, multidisciplinary area of investigation. It involves several research topics and real-life application areas. Figure 1.4 shows the main ones.

Research issues concern first of all techniques , to some extent models, and two "vertical" areas that cross the first two, i.e., dimensions and methodologies. We will discuss them in Sect. 1.6.1. Three of the application domains mentioned in Fig. 1.4, namely, e-Government, life sciences, and the World Wide Web, in which IQ is particularly relevant, are discussed in Sect. 1.6.2.

Research issues in IQ originate from research paradigms initially developed in other areas of research. The relationship between information quality and these related research areas will be discussed in Sect. 1.6.3.

---

[1]Wikipedia definition available at http://www.en.wikipedia.org/wiki/Cloud_computing# Architecture.

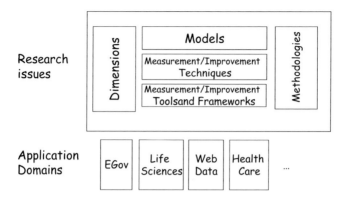

Fig. 1.4 Main issues in information quality

1.6.1   Research Issues in Information Quality

Choosing *dimensions* to measure the level of quality of information is the starting point of any IQ-related activity. Though measuring the quality of ICT technologies, artifacts, processes, and services is not a new issue in research, for many years, several standardization institutions have been operating (e.g., ISO; see [327]) in order to establish mature concepts in the areas of quality characteristics, measurable indicators, and reliable measurement procedures. Dimensions are discussed in Chaps. 2–5, 13, and 14. Dimensions are applied with different roles in techniques and models.

Models are used in databases to represent data and data schemas. They are also used in information systems to represent business processes of the organization; these models have to be enriched in order to represent dimensions and other issues related to information quality. Models are investigated in Chap. 6.

Techniques correspond to algorithms, heuristics, knowledge-based procedures, and learning processes that provide a solution to a specific IQ problem or to an *information quality activity*, as defined in Chap. 7. Examples of IQ activities are identifying if two records of different databases represent the same object of the real world or not and finding the most reliable source for some specific information. IQ activities are defined in Chap. 7, and techniques are discussed in Chaps. 7–10, and 14.

Methodologies provide guidelines to choose, starting from available techniques, the most effective IQ measurement and improvement process (and hopefully, most economical for comparable results) within a specific information system. Methodologies are investigated in Chap. 12.

1.6.2   Application Domains in Information Quality

In this section, we analyze three distinct application domains of IQ, shown in Fig. 1.4: e-Government, life sciences, and the World Wide Web. Their importance has been growing over the last few years, because of their relevance in the daily lives of people and organizations. A fourth domain, healthcare, will be discussed in detail in a dedicated chapter, namely, Chap. 13.

1.6.2.1   e-Government

The main goal of all e-Government projects is the improvement of the relationship between the government, agencies, and citizens, as well as between agencies and businesses, through the use of information and communication technologies. This ambitious goal is articulated in different objectives:

1. The complete automation of those government administrative processes that deliver services to citizens and businesses and that involve the exchange of information between government agencies
2. The creation of an architecture that, by connecting the different agencies, enables them to fulfill their administrative processes without any additional burden to the users that benefit from them
3. The creation of portals that simplify access to services by authorized users

e-Government projects may face the problem that similar information about one citizen or business is likely to appear in multiple databases. Each database is autonomously managed by the different agencies that historically have never been able to share data about citizens and businesses.

The problem is worsened by the many errors usually present in the databases, for many reasons. First, due to the nature of the administrative flows, several citizens' information (e.g., addresses) are not updated for long periods of time. This happens because it is often impractical to obtain updates from subjects that maintain the official residence information. Also, errors may occur when personal information on individuals is stored. Some of these errors are not corrected, and a potentially large fraction of them is not detected. Furthermore, information provided by distinct sources differ in format, following local conventions, that can change in time and result in multiple versions. Finally, many of the records currently in the database were entered over years using legacy processes that included one or more manual data entry steps.

A direct consequence of this combination of redundancy and errors in information is frequent mismatches between different records that refer to the same citizen or business. One major outcome of having multiple disconnected views for the same information is that citizens and businesses experience consistent service degradation during their interaction with the agencies. Furthermore, misalignment brings about additional costs. First, agencies must make an investment to reconcile records using clerical review, e.g., to manually trace citizens and businesses that cannot be correctly and unequivocally identified. Secondly, because most investigation techniques, e.g., tax fraud prevention techniques, rely on cross-referencing records of different agencies, misalignment results in undetected tax fraud and reduced revenues.

1.6.2.2   Life Sciences

Life sciences information and specifically biological information are characterized by a diversity of information types, very large volumes, and highly variable quality. Data are available through vastly disparate sources and disconnected repositories. Their quality is difficult to assess and often unacceptable for the required usage. Biologists typically search several sources for good-quality information, for instance, in order to perform reliable in silico experiments. However, the effort to actually assess the quality level of such information is entirely in the hands of the biologists; they have to manually analyze disparate sources, trying to integrate and reconcile heterogeneous and contradictory information in order to identify the best information. Let us consider, as an example, a gene analysis scenario. Figure 1.5 shows an example of a simple information analysis pipeline. As the result of a microarray experiment, a biologist wants to analyze a set of genes, with the objective of understanding their functions.

In Step 1, the biologist performs a Web search on a site that is known to contain gene information for the particular organism under consideration. Once the information is obtained, the biologist must assess its reliability. Therefore, in Step 2, the biologist performs a new Web search in order to check if other sites provide

Fig. 1.5 Example of biological information analysis process

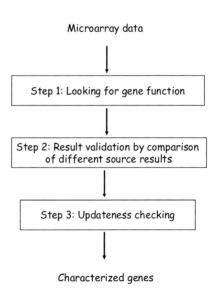

the same gene information. It may happen that different sites provide conflicting results. Then (Step 3) the biologist also has to check that the provided results are up to date, i.e., if a gene is unknown in the queried sites or no recent publication on that gene is available, e.g., through PubMed (see [619]). The described scenario has many weaknesses:

1. The biologist must perform a time-consuming manual search for all the sources that may provide the function of the interested gene. This process is also dependent on the user having personal knowledge about which sites must be queried.
2. The biologist has no way of assessing the trustworthiness of a result.
3. In Step 2, the biologist has no way of evaluating the quality of the results provided by different sites.
4. In Step 3, a new Web search must be performed which again can be very time consuming.

In order to overcome such weaknesses, life sciences and biology need robust information quality techniques.

1.6.2.3 World Wide Web

Web information systems are characterized by the presentation of a large amount of information to a wide audience, the quality of which can be very heterogeneous. There are several reasons for this variety. First, every organization and individual can create a Web site and load every kind of information without any control on its quality and sometimes with a malicious intent. A second reason lies in the conflict between two needs. On the one hand, information systems on the Web need to publish information in the shortest possible time after it is available from information sources. On the other hand, information has to be checked with regard to its accuracy, currency, and trustworthiness of its sources. These two requirements are in many aspects contradictory: accurate design of information structures and, in the case of Web sites, of good navigational paths between pages and certification of information to verify its correctness are costly and lengthy activities. However, the publication of information on Web sites is subject to time constraints.

Web information systems present two further aspects in connection to information quality that differentiate them from traditional information sources: first, a Web site is a continuously evolving source of information, and it is not linked to a fixed release time of information; second, in the process of changing information, additional information can be produced in different phases, and corrections to previously published information are possible, creating, in such a way, further needs for quality checks. Such features lead to a different type of information than with traditional media.

As a final argument, in Web information systems it is practically impossible to individuate a subject, usually called *information owner*, responsible for a certain information category. In fact, information are typically replicated among the different participating organizations, and one does not know how to state that an organization or subject has the primary responsibility for some specific information.

All previously discussed aspects make it difficult to certify the quality of data sources and, for a user, to assess the reputation of other users and sources. Information quality for Web and Big Data is discussed in Chap. 14.

1.6.3 Research Areas Related to Information Quality

Information quality is fairly a new research area. Several other areas (see Fig. 1.6) in computer science and other sciences have in the past treated related and overlapping problems; at the same time, such areas have developed in the last decades (in the case of statistics, in the last centuries), paradigms, models, and methodologies that have proved to be of major importance in grounding the information quality research area. We now discuss such research areas.

1. *Statistics* includes a set of methods that are used to collect, analyze, present, and interpret information. Statistics has developed in the last two centuries a wide spectrum of methods and models that allow one to express predictions and formulate decisions in all contexts where uncertain and imprecise information is available for the domain of interest. As discussed in [410], statistics and statistical methodology as the basis of information analysis are concerned with two basic types of problems: (a) summarizing, describing, and exploring information and (b) using sampled data to infer the nature of the process that produced the

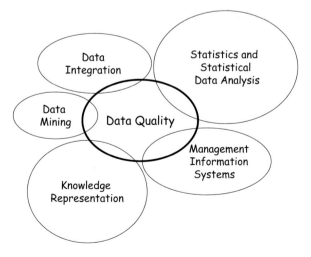

Fig. 1.6 Research areas related to information quality

information. Since low-quality information are an inaccurate representation of the reality, a variety of statistical methods have been developed for measuring and improving the quality of information. We will discuss some statistical methods in Chaps. 7–9.

2. *Knowledge representation* (see [166, 467] for insightful introductions to the area) is the study of how knowledge about an application domain can be represented and what kinds of reasoning can be done with that knowledge (which is called *knowledge reasoning*). Knowledge about an application domain may be represented procedurally in the form of program code or implicitly as patterns of activation in a neural network. Alternatively, the area of knowledge representation assumes an explicit and declarative representation, in terms of a *knowledge base*, consisting of logical formulas or rules expressed in a representation language. Providing a rich representation of the application domain, and being able to reason about it, is becoming an important leverage in many techniques for improving information quality; we will see some of these techniques in Chaps. 8 and 9.

3. *Data and information mining* (see [294]) is an analytic process designed to explore usually large sets of data in search of consistent patterns and/or systematic relationships between attributes/variables. *Exploratory data mining* is defined in [161] as the preliminary process of discovering structure in a set of data using statistical summaries, visualization, and other means. In this context, good-quality information is an intrinsic objective of any data mining activity (see [63]), since otherwise the process of discovering patterns, relationships, and structures is seriously deteriorated. From another perspective, data and information mining techniques may be used in a wide spectrum of activities for improving the quality of data; we will examine some of them in Chaps. 7–9.

4. *Management information systems* (see [164]) are defined as systems that provide the information necessary to manage an organization effectively. Since information and knowledge are becoming relevant resources both in operational and decision business processes, and poor-quality information result in poor-quality processes, it is becoming increasingly important to supply management information systems with functionalities and services that allow one to control and improve the quality of the information resource.

5. *Data integration* (see [397]) has the goal of building and presenting a unified view of data owned by heterogeneous data sources in distributed and CISs. Data integration will be considered in Chap. 7 as one of the basic activities whose purpose is improving information quality and will be discussed in detail in Chap. 10. While being an autonomous and well-grounded research area, data integration will be considered in this book as strictly related to data quality, regarding two main issues: providing query results on the basis of a quality characterization of data at sources and identifying and solving conflicts on values referring to the same real-world objects.

1.7   Standardization Efforts in Information Quality

ISO has enacted in 2008 the standard ISO/IEC 25012:2008 (see [330]), for what in the standard is defined as data quality, that is, "the degree to which the characteristics of data satisfy stated and implied needs when used under specified conditions," and provides "a general data quality model for data retained in a structured format within a computer system." The document presents:

- A set of terms and definitions for concepts involved
- Two perspectives that can be adopted when considering data quality characteristics (or dimensions in the following of this book): the inherent perspective and the system-dependent one.

In Fig. 1.7, we see all dimensions defined in the ISO standard.

When we look at the definitions of data and information proposed in the document, we discover that:

1. Data is defined as "reinterpretable representation of information in a formalized manner suitable for communication, interpretation, or processing"
2. Information is defined as "information-processing knowledge concerning objects, such as facts, events, things, processes, or ideas, including concepts, that within a certain context have a particular meaning"

DQ characteristic	Definition (all definitions except for completeness and accessibility begin with: the degree to which data has attributes that...")
Correctness	correctly represent the true value of the intended attribute of a concept or event in a specific context of use
Completeness	subject data associated with an entity has values for all expected attributes and related entity instances in a specific context of use
Consistency	are free from contradiction and are coherent with other data in a specific context of use
Credibility	are regarded as true and believable by users in specific context of use.
Currentness	are of the right age in a specific context of use
Accessibility	data can be accessed in a specific context of use, particularly by people who need supporting technology or special configuration because of some disability
Compliance	adhere to standards, conventions or regulations in force and similar rules relating to data quality in a specific context of use
Confidentiality	ensure that it is only accessible and interpretable by authorized users in a specific context of use
Efficiency	can be processed and provide the expected levels of performance by using the appropriate amounts and types of resources in a specific context of use
Precision	are exact or that provide discrimination in a specific context of use
Traceability	provide an audit trail of access to the data and of any changes made to the data in a specific context of use
Understandability	enable it to be read and interpreted by users, and are expressed in appropriate languages, symbols and units in a specific context of use
Availability	enable it to be read and interpreted by users, and are expressed in appropriate languages, symbols and units in a specific context of use
Portability	enable it to be installed, replaced or moved from one system to another preserving the existing quality in a specific context of use
Recoverability	enable it to maintain and preserve a specified level of operations and quality, even in the event of failure, in a specific context of use

Fig. 1.7 ISO standard data quality dimensions

This choice is different from our choice in the Preface, and it is also specular to the usual one in textbooks and scientific papers, where information is defined in terms of data (see, e.g., [241]).

The ISO effort shows several limitations, such as follows:

- The flat classification adopted among characteristics that is not coherent with, e.g., the classification provided in the document "ISO/IEC 9126 Software engineering—Product quality, an international standard for the evaluation of software quality," where quality characteristics are expressed in terms of sub-characteristics.
- Several characteristics (e.g., completeness) depend on the model adopted for data representation, even though this dependence is not explicitly discussed.
- Data organized in models that neatly distinguish between instances and schemas are considered, e.g., the relational model, while schemaless types of information, such as textual documents, are ignored.
- There is no attempt to distinguish between different types of data and information, from structured data to texts and images.

1.8 Summary

In this chapter, we have perceived that information quality is a multidisciplinary area. This is not surprising, since information, in a variety of formats and with a variety of media, is used in every activity and deeply influences the quality of processes that use information. Many private and public organizations have perceived the impact of information quality on their assets and missions and have consequently launched initiatives of large impact. At the same time, while in monolithic systems information is processed within controlled activities, with the advent of networks and the Web, information is created and exchanged with much more "turbulent" processes and needs more sophisticated management.

The issues discussed in this chapter introduce the structure of the rest of the book; dimensions, models, techniques, and methodologies will be the main topics addressed. While information quality is a relatively new research area, other areas, such as statistical data analysis, have addressed in the past some aspects of the problems related to information quality; with statistical data analysis, also knowledge representation, data and information mining, management information systems, and data integration share some of the problems and issues characteristic of information quality and, at the same time, provide paradigms and techniques that can be effectively used in information quality measurement and improvement activities.

Chapter 2
Data Quality Dimensions

2.1 Introduction

In Chap. 1, we provided an intuitive concept of information quality and we informally introduced several data quality dimensions, such as accuracy, completeness,
currency, and consistency.

   This chapter investigates information quality in greater depth, in particular with
reference to structured data, typical of relational databases, and presents multiple
associated *dimensions*. Due to this focus, in this chapter we will adopt the term
data quality and the acronym DQ for it. Each dimension captures a specific
aspect included under the general umbrella of data quality. Both data and schema
dimensions are important. Data of low quality deeply influence the quality of
business processes, while a schema of low quality, e.g., an unnormalized schema
in the relational model, results in potential redundancies and anomalies during the
life cycle of data usage. Data dimensions can be considered more relevant in real-life
applications and processes than schema dimensions.

   More specifically, quality dimensions can refer either to the *extension* of data,
i.e., to data values, or to their *intension*, i.e., to their schema. Both data dimensions
and schema dimensions are usually defined in a qualitative way, referring to general
properties of data and schemas, and the related definitions do not provide any
facility for assigning values to dimensions themselves. Specifically, definitions do
not provide quantitative measures, and one or more *metrics* are to be associated
with dimensions as separate, distinct properties. For each metric, one or more
measurement methods are to be provided regarding (see [521]) (1) where the
measurement is taken, (2) what data are included, (3) the measurement device, and
(4) the scale on which results are reported. Based on the literature, at times we will
distinguish between dimensions and metrics, while at other times we will directly
provide metrics.

   The quality of conceptual and logical schemas is very important in database
design and usage. Conceptual schemas are typically produced within the first

© Springer International Publishing Switzerland 2016   21
C. Batini, M. Scannapieco, *Data and Information Quality*, Data-Centric Systems
and Applications, DOI 10.1007/978-3-319-24106-7_2

phase of the development of an information system (IS). Erroneous conceptual schema design strongly impacts the system development and must be detected as soon as possible. Logical schemas are at the base of the implementation of any database application. Methods and techniques for assessing, evaluating, and improving conceptual schemas and logical schemas in different application domains is still a fertile research area.

Despite such recognized importance, the prevalent attention to the definitions of DQ dimensions has been devoted to data values, which are used, more extensively than schemas, in business and administrative processes. As a consequence, in this chapter we deal especially with data dimensions, but we also discuss some of the most relevant schema dimensions.

In the following sections, we describe in detail data dimensions in order to understand the different possible meanings and metrics. As a terminological note, when we refer to the relational model, we use the term *tuple* to indicate a set of *fields* or *cell values*, corresponding usually to different *definition domains* or *domains*, describing properties or *attributes* of a specific real-world object; we use interchangeably the terms *relational table* or *table* or *relation* to indicate a set of tuples. When we refer to generic data, we use the term *record* to indicate a set of fields, and we use interchangeably the terms *file* or *dataset* to indicate a set of tuples. As a consequence, *tuple* can be used in place of *record* and *table/relation* can be used in place of *structured file*.

The chapter is organized as follows. In Sect. 2.2, we introduce a classification framework of data and information quality dimensions grouped in clusters of "similar" dimensions. In Sects. 2.3–2.6, we focus on specific clusters, namely, accuracy, completeness, accessibility, and consistency.

Some proposals of comprehensive classifications of dimensions are first illustrated and then compared in Sect. 2.7. Section 2.8 deals with schema dimensions, briefly describing correctness, minimality, completeness, and pertinence and, in more detail, readability and normalization.

2.2 A Classification Framework for Data and Information Quality Dimensions

Dimensions for data quality introduced in this chapter and dimensions for information quality discussed in subsequent chapters of the book can be characterized by a common classification framework that allows us to compare dimensions across different information types. The framework is based on a classification in clusters of dimensions proposed in [45] where dimensions are included in the same cluster according to their similarity. Clusters are defined in the following list, where the first item in italics is the representative dimension of the cluster, followed by other member dimensions. In this section, dimensions will be introduced informally and their meaning will be left to intuition:

1. *Accuracy*, correctness, validity, and precision focus on the adherence to a given reality of interest.
2. *Completeness*, pertinence, and relevance refer to the capability of representing all and only the relevant aspects of the reality of interest.
3. *Redundancy*, minimality, compactness, and conciseness refer to the capability of representing the aspects of the reality of interest with the minimal use of informative resources.
4. *Readability*, comprehensibility, clarity, and simplicity refer to ease of understanding and fruition of information by users.
5. *Accessibility* and availability are related to the ability of the user to access information from his or her culture, physical status/functions, and technologies available.
6. *Consistency*, cohesion, and coherence refer to the capability of the information to comply without contradictions to all properties of the reality of interest, as specified in terms of integrity constraints, data edits, business rules, and other formalisms.
7. *Usefulness*, related to the advantage the user gains from the use of information.
8. *Trust*, including believability, reliability, and reputation, catching how much information derives from an authoritative source. The trust cluster encompasses also issues related to security.

The first six clusters will be considered in this chapter and in Chaps. 3–5. The usefulness cluster will be considered for images (Chap. 5) and for information in general in Chap. 11. The trust cluster will be discussed in Chap. 14 dedicated to Web data and Big Data.

In the following part of the book, dimensions will be introduced and discussed based on the above classification.

2.3   Accuracy Cluster

Accuracy is defined as the closeness between a data value v and a data value v', considered as the correct representation of the real-life phenomenon that the data value v aims to represent. As an example if the name of a person is John, the value $v' =$ John is correct, while the value $v =$ Jhn is incorrect.

The world around us changes, and what we have called in the above definition "the real-life phenomenon that the data value v aims to represent" reflects such changes. So, there is a particular yet relevant type of data accuracy that refers to the rapidity with which the change in real-world phenomenon is reflected in the update of the data value; we call *temporal accuracy* such type of accuracy, in contrast to *structural accuracy* (or, simply, *accuracy*), that characterizes the accuracy of data as observed in a specific time frame, where the data value can be considered as stable and unchanged. In the following, we will consider first structural accuracy and later temporal accuracy.

2.3.1 Structural Accuracy Dimensions

Two kinds of (structural) accuracy can be identified, namely, a syntactic accuracy and a semantic accuracy.

Syntactic accuracy is the closeness of a value v to the elements of the corresponding definition domain D. In syntactic accuracy, we are not interested in comparing v with the true value v′; rather, we are interested in checking whether v is any one of the values in D, whatever it is. So, if v = Jack, even if v′ = John, v is considered syntactically correct, as Jack is an admissible value in the domain of persons' names. Syntactic accuracy is measured by means of functions, called *comparison functions*, that evaluate the distance between v and the values in D. Edit distance is a simple example of a comparison function, taking into account the minimum number of character insertions, deletions, and replacements to convert a string s to a string s′. More complex comparison functions exist, for instance, taking into account similar sounds or character transpositions. In Chap. 8, a detailed description of the main comparison functions will be provided.

Let us consider the relation Movies introduced in Chap. 1, shown in Fig. 2.1.

The value Rman Holiday in movie 3 for Title is syntactically inaccurate, since it does not correspond to any title of a movie. Roman Holiday is the closest movie name to Rman Holiday; indeed, the edit distance between Rman Holiday and Roman Holiday is equal to 1 and simply corresponds to the insertion of the char o in the string Rman Holidays. Since 1 is the edit distance, the measure of syntactic accuracy is 1. More precisely, given a comparison function C, we may define a measure of syntactic accuracy of a value v with respect to a definition domain D, as the minimum value of C, when comparing v with all the values in D. Such a measure will be in the domain $[0, \ldots, n]$, where n is the maximum possible value that the comparison function may have.

Semantic accuracy is the closeness of the value v to the true value v′. Let us consider again the relation Movies in Fig. 2.1. The exchange of directors' names in tuples 1 and 2 is an example of a semantic accuracy error: indeed, for movie 1, a director named Curtiz would be admissible, and thus it is syntactically correct.

Id	Title	Director	Year	#Remakes	LastRemakeYear
1	Casablanca	Weir	1942	3	1940
2	Dead Poets Society	Curtiz	1989	0	NULL
3	Rman Holiday	Wylder	1953	0	NULL
4	Sabrina	NULL	1964	0	1985

Fig. 2.1 A relation Movies

Nevertheless, `Curtiz` is not the director of `Casablanca`; therefore a semantic accuracy error occurs.

The above examples clearly show the difference between syntactic and semantic accuracy. Note that while it is reasonable to measure syntactic accuracy using a distance function, semantic accuracy is measured better with a `<yes, no>` or a `<correct, not correct>` domain. Consequently, semantic accuracy coincides with the concept of *correctness*. In contrast with what happens for syntactic accuracy, in order to measure the semantic accuracy of a value v, the corresponding true value has to be known, or, else, it should be possible, considering additional knowledge, to deduce whether the value v is or is not the true value.

From the above arguments, it is clear that semantic accuracy is typically more complex to calculate than syntactic accuracy. When it is known a priori that the rate of errors is low and the errors result typically from typos, then syntactic accuracy tends to coincide with semantic accuracy, since typos produce values close to the true ones. As a result, semantic accuracy may be achieved by replacing an inaccurate value with the closest value in the definition domain, under the assumption that it is the true one.

In a more general context, a technique for checking semantic accuracy consists of looking for the same data in different data sources and finding the correct data by comparisons. This latter approach also requires the solution of the *object identification problem*, i.e., the problem of understanding whether two tuples refer to the same real-world entity or not; this problem will be discussed extensively in Chaps. 8 and 9. The main issues to be addressed for solving the object identification problem are:

- *Identification*: Tuples in one or several sources may not have unique identifiers, and thus they need to be put in correspondence by means of appropriate *matching keys*.
- *Decision strategy*: Once tuples are linked on the basis of a matching key, a decision must be made to state whether it corresponds to the same entity or not.

The accuracy discussed above is referred to a single value of a relation attribute. In practical cases, coarser accuracy definitions and metrics may be applied. As an example, it is possible to calculate the accuracy of an attribute called *attribute* (or *column*) *accuracy*, of a relation (*relation accuracy*), or of a whole database (*database accuracy*).

When considering accuracy for sets of values instead of single values, a further notion of accuracy can be introduced, namely, duplication. *Duplication* occurs when a real-world entity is stored twice or more in a data source. Of course, if a primary key consistency check is performed when populating a relational table, a duplication problem does not occur, provided that the primary key assignment has been made with a reliable procedure. The duplication problem is more relevant for files or other data structures that do not allow the definition of key constraints. A typical cost of duplication is, for example, the additional mailing cost that enterprises pay for mailing customers, when customers are stored more than once in the their database. An indirect cost must be added to this direct cost, which consists of the loss of reputation of the enterprise in the eyes of its customers who may be bothered by having to receive the same material more than once.

For relation and database accuracy, for both syntactic and semantic accuracy, a *ratio* is typically calculated between accurate values and the total number of values. For instance, the accuracy of a relation can be measured as the ratio between the number of correct cell values and the total number of cells in the table. More complex metrics can be defined that consider comparison functions; for instance, as we said before, a typical process for syntactic accuracy evaluation is to match tuples from the source under examination with tuples of another source which is supposed to contain the same but correct tuples.

In such a process, accuracy errors on attribute values can be either those that do not affect the tuple matching or those that can stop the process itself, not allowing the matching. For instance, an accuracy error on an attribute `SocialSecurityNumber` (SSN) value can seriously affect the matching attempt; instead, given that SSNs are used for matching, an accuracy error on an attribute with a minor identification power, such as `Age`, cannot prevent the identification process from being carried out correctly. In the rest of this section, we illustrate a few metrics (see [222]) taking these aspects into account.

Let us consider a relational schema R consisting of K attributes and a relational table r consisting of N tuples. Let q_{ij} ($i = 1 \ldots N, j = 1 \ldots K$) be a Boolean variable defined to correspond to the cell values y_{ij} such that q_{ij} is equal to 0 if y_{ij} is syntactically accurate; otherwise it is equal to 1.

In order to identify whether or not accuracy errors affect a matching of a relational table r with a reference table r′ containing correct values, we introduce a further Boolean variable s_i equal to 0 if the tuple t_i matches a tuple in r′, otherwise equal to 1. We can introduce three metrics to distinguish the relative importance of value accuracy in the context of the tuple. The first two metrics have the purpose of giving a different importance to errors on attributes that have a higher identification power, in line with the above discussion.

The first metric is called *weak accuracy error* and is defined as

$$\sum_{i=1}^{N} \frac{\beta((q_i > 0) \bigwedge (s_i = 0))}{N},$$

where $\beta(.)$ is a Boolean variable equal to 1 if the condition in parentheses is true, 0 otherwise, and $q_i = \sum_{j=1}^{K} q_{ij}$. Such metric considers the case in which for a tuple t_i accuracy errors occur ($q_i > 0$) but do not affect identification ($s_i = 0$).

The second metric is called *strong accuracy error* and is defined as

$$\sum_{i=1}^{N} \frac{\beta((q_i > 0) \bigwedge (s_i = 1))}{N},$$

where $\beta(.)$ and q_i have the same meaning as above. Such a metric considers the case in which accuracy errors occur $(q_i > 0)$ for a tuple t_i and actually do affect identification $(s_i = 1)$.

The third metric gives the percentage of accurate tuples matched with the reference table. It is expressed by the degree of syntactic accuracy of the relational instance r

$$\sum_{i=1}^{N} \frac{\beta((q_i = 0) \bigwedge (s_i = 0))}{N}$$

by actually considering the fraction of accurate $(q_i = 0)$ matched $(s_i = 0)$ tuples.

2.3.2 Time-Related Accuracy Dimensions

A relevant aspect of data is their change and update in time. In Chap. 1 we provided a classification of types of data according to the temporal dimension, in terms of stable, long-term-changing, and frequently changing data. The principal time-related dimensions proposed for characterizing the above three types of data are currency, volatility, and timeliness.

Currency concerns how promptly data are updated with respect to changes occurring in the real world. As an example in Fig. 2.1, the attribute #Remakes of movie 4 has low currency because a remake of movie 4 has been done, but this information did not result in an increased value for the number of remakes. Similarly, if the residential address of a person is updated, i.e., it corresponds to the address where the person lives, then the currency is high.

Volatility characterizes the frequency with which data vary in time. For instance, stable data such as birth dates have volatility equal to 0, as they do not vary at all. Conversely, stock quotes, a kind of frequently changing data, have a high degree of volatility due to the fact that they remain valid for very short time intervals.

Timeliness expresses how current the data are for the task at hand. The timeliness dimension is motivated by the fact that it is possible to have current data that are actually useless because they are *late* for a specific usage. For instance, the timetable for university courses can be current by containing the most recent data, but it is not timely if it is available only after the start of the classes.

We now provide possible metrics of time-related dimensions. Currency can be typically measured with respect to *last update* metadata, which correspond to the last time the specific data were updated. For data types that change with a fixed frequency, last update metadata allow us to compute currency straightforwardly. Conversely, for data types whose change frequency can vary, one possibility is to calculate an average change frequency and perform the currency computation with respect to it, admitting errors. As an example, if a data source stores product names that are estimated to change every 5 years, then a product with its last update metadata reporting a date corresponding to 1 month before the observation time can be assumed to be *current*; in contrast, if the date reported is 10 years before the observation time, it is assumed to be *not current*.

Volatility is a dimension that inherently characterizes certain types of data. A metric for volatility is given by the length of time (or its inverse) that data remain valid.

Timeliness implies that data not only are current but are also in time for events that correspond to their usage. Therefore, a possible measurement consists of (1) a currency measurement and (2) a check that data are available *before* the planned usage time.

More complex metrics can be defined for time-related dimensions. As an example, we cite the metric defined in [31], in which the three dimensions currency, volatility, and timeliness are linked by defining timeliness as a function of currency and volatility. More specifically,

1. Currency is defined as

$$Currency = Age + (DeliveryTime - InputTime),$$

   where *Age* measures how old the data unit is when received, *DeliveryTime* is the time the information product is delivered to the customer, and *InputTime* is the time the data unit is obtained. Therefore, currency is the sum of how old data are when received (*Age*), plus a second term that measures how long data have been in the information system, (*DeliveryTime − InputTime*).
2. Volatility is defined as the length of time data remains valid.
3. Timeliness is defined as

$$\max\left\{0, 1 - \frac{currency}{volatility}\right\}.$$

   Timeliness ranges from 0 to 1, where 0 means bad timeliness and 1 means good timeliness.

Observe that the relevance of currency depends on volatility: data that are highly volatile must be current, while currency is less important for data with low volatility.

2.4 Completeness Cluster

Completeness can be generically defined as "the extent to which data are of sufficient breadth, depth, and scope for the task at hand" [645]. In [504], three types of completeness are identified. *Schema completeness* is defined as the degree to which concepts and their properties are not missing from the schema. *Column completeness* is defined as a measure of the missing values for a specific property or column in a table. *Population completeness* evaluates missing values with respect to a reference population.

If focusing on a specific data model, a more precise characterization of completeness can be given. In the following we refer to the relational model.

2.4.1 Completeness of Relational Data

Intuitively, the completeness of a table characterizes the extent to which the table represents the corresponding real world. Completeness in the relational model can be characterized with respect to (1) the presence/absence and meaning of null values and (2) the validity of one of the two assumptions called *open world assumption* (OWA) and *closed world assumption* (CWA). We now introduce the two issues separately.

In a model *with* null values, the presence of a null value has the general meaning of a missing value, i.e., a value that exists in the real world but for some reason is not available. In order to characterize completeness, it is important to understand *why* the value is missing. Indeed, a value can be missing either because it exists but is unknown or because it does not exist at all or because it may exist but it is not actually known whether it exists or not. For a general discussion on the different types of null values, see [30]; here we describe the three types of null values, by means of an example.

Let us consider a Person relation with the attributes Name, Surname, BirthDate, and Email. The relation is shown in Fig. 2.2. For the tuples with Id equal to 2, 3, and 4, the Email value is NULL. Let us suppose that the person represented by tuple 2 has no e-mail: no incompleteness case occurs. If the person represented by tuple 3 has an e-mail, but its value is not known, then tuple 3 presents an incompleteness. Finally, if it is not known whether the person represented by tuple 4 has an e-mail or not, incompleteness may not be the case.

In logical models for databases, such as the relational model, there are two different assumptions on the completeness of data represented in a relational instance r. The CWA states that only the values actually present in a relational

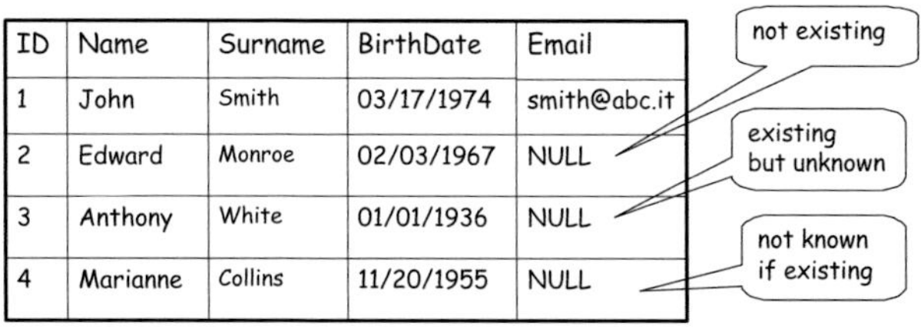

Fig. 2.2 The Person relation, with different null value meanings for the e-mail attribute

table r and no other values represent facts of the real world. In the OWA we can state neither the truth nor the falsity of facts not represented in the tuples of r.

From the four possible combinations emerging from (1) considering or not considering null values and (2) assuming OWA or CWA, we will focus on the following two most interesting cases:

1. Model without null values with OWA
2. Model with null values with CWA

In a model *without* null values with OWA, in order to characterize completeness, we need to introduce the concept of *reference relation*. Given the relation r, the reference relation of r, called ref(r), is the relation containing all the tuples that satisfy the relational schema of r, i.e., that represent objects of the real world that constitute the present true extension of the schema.

As an example, if Dept is a relation representing the employees of a given department and one specific employee of the department is not represented as a tuple of Dept, then the tuple corresponding to the missing employee is in ref(Dept), and ref(Dept) differs from Dept in exactly that tuple. In practical situations, the reference relations are rarely available. Instead their cardinality is much easier to get. There are also cases in which the reference relation is available but only periodically (e.g., when a census is performed).

On the basis of the reference relation, the completeness of a relation r is measured in a model without null values as the fraction of tuples actually represented in the relation r, namely, its *size* with respect to the total number of tuples in ref(r):

$$C(r) = \frac{|r|}{|ref(r)|}.$$

As an example, let us consider the citizens of Rome. Assume that, from the personal registry of Rome's municipality, the overall number is six million. Let us suppose that a company stores data on Rome's citizens for the purpose of its business; if the cardinality of the relation r storing the data is 5,400,000, then $C(r)$ is equal to 0.9.

In the model with null values with CWA, specific definitions for completeness can be provided by considering the granularity of the model elements, i.e., value, tuple, attribute, and relations, as shown in Fig. 2.3. Specifically, it is possible to define:

- A *value completeness*, to capture the presence of null values for some fields of a tuple
- A *tuple completeness*, to characterize the completeness of a tuple with respect to the values of all its fields
- An *attribute completeness*, to measure the number of null values of a specific attribute in a relation
- A *relation completeness*, to capture the presence of null values in a whole relation

Fig. 2.3 Completeness of different elements in the relational model

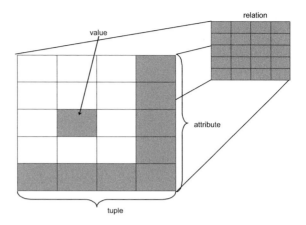

As an example, in Fig. 2.4, a Student relation is shown. The tuple completeness evaluates the percentage of specified values in the tuple with respect to the total number of attributes of the tuple itself. Therefore, in the example, the tuple completeness is 1 for tuples 6754 and 8907, 0.8 for tuple 6587, 0.6 for tuple 0987, and so on. One way to see the tuple completeness is as a measure of the information content of the tuple, with respect to its maximum potential information content. With reference to this interpretation, we are implicitly assuming that all values of the tuple contribute equally to the total information content of the tuple. Of course, this may not be the case, as different applications can weight the attributes of a tuple differently.

The attribute completeness evaluates the percentage of specified values in the column corresponding to the attribute with respect to the total number of values that should have been specified. In Fig. 2.4, let us consider an application calculating the average of the votes obtained by students. The absence of some values for the Vote attribute simply implies a deviation in the calculation of the average; therefore, a characterization of Vote completeness may be useful.

The relation completeness is relevant in all applications that need to evaluate the completeness of a whole relation and can admit the presence of null values on some attributes. Relation completeness measures how much information is represented in the relation by evaluating the content of the information actually available with respect to the maximum possible content, i.e., without null values. According to this interpretation, completeness of the relation Student in Fig. 2.4 is 53/60.

Fig. 2.4 Student relation
exemplifying the
completeness of tuples,
attributes, and relations

StudentID	Name	Surname	Vote	ExaminationDate
6754	Mike	Collins	29	07/17/2004
8907	Anne	Herbert	18	07/17/2004
6578	Julianne	Merrals	NULL	07/17/2004
0987	Robert	Archer	NULL	NULL
1243	Mark	Taylor	26	09/30/2004
2134	Bridget	Abbott	30	09/30/2004
6784	John	Miller	30	NULL
0098	Carl	Adams	25	09/30/2004
1111	John	Smith	28	09/30/2004
2564	Edward	Monroe	NULL	NULL
8976	Anthony	White	21	NULL
8973	Marianne	Collins	30	10/15/2004

2.4.2 Completeness of Web Data

Data that are published in Web information systems can be characterized by evolution in time. While in the traditional paper-based media, information is published once and for all, Web information systems are characterized by information that is continuously published.

Let us consider the Web site of a university, where a list of courses given at that university in the current academic year is published. At a given moment, the list can be considered *complete* in the sense that it includes all the courses that have been officially approved. Nevertheless, it is also known that more courses will be added to the list, pending their approval. Therefore, there is the need to apprehend how the list will evolve in time with respect to completeness. The traditional completeness dimension provides only a static characterization of completeness. In order to consider the temporal dynamics of completeness, as needed in Web information systems, we introduce the notion of completability.

We consider a function $C(t)$, defined as the value of completeness at the instant t, with $t \in [\texttt{t\_pub}, \texttt{t\_max}]$, where $\texttt{t\_pub}$ is the initial instant of publication of data and $\texttt{t\_max}$ corresponds to the maximum time within which the series of the different scheduled updates will be completed. Starting from the function $C(t)$, we can define the *completability* of the published data as

$$\int_{t\_curr}^{t\_max} C(t),$$

where $\texttt{t\_curr}$ is the time at which completability is evaluated and $\texttt{t\_curr} < \texttt{t\_max}$.

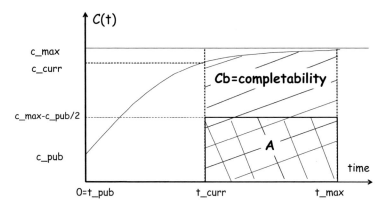

Fig. 2.5 A graphical representation of completability

Completability, as shown in Fig. 2.5, can be graphically depicted as an area Cb of a function that represents how completeness evolves between an instant `t_curr` of observation and `t_max`. Observe that the value corresponding to `t_curr` is indicated as `c_curr`; `c_max` is the value for completeness estimated for `t_max`. The value `c_max` is a real reachable limit that can be specified for the completeness of the series of elements; if this real limit does not exist, `c_max` is equal to 1. In Fig. 2.5, a reference area A is also shown, defined as

$$(t\_max - t\_curr) * \frac{c\_max - c\_pub}{2},$$

that, by comparison with Cb, allows us to define ranges [High, Medium, Low] for completability.

With respect to the example above, considering the list of courses published on a university Web site, the completeness dimension gives information about the current degree of completeness; the completability information gives the information about how fast this degree will grow in time, i.e., how fast the list of courses will be completed. The interested reader can find further details in [498].

In Chap. 14, we will describe the impact that low quality resulting from temporal variability of Web data has on the object identification problem.

2.5 Accessibility Cluster

Publishing large amounts of data in Web sites is not a sufficient condition for its availability to everyone. In order to access it, a user needs to access a network, to understand the language to be used for navigating and querying the Web, and to perceive with his or her senses the information made available. *Accessibility* measures the ability of the user to access the data from his or her own culture, physical status/functions, and technologies available. We focus in the following on causes that can reduce physical or sensorial abilities and, consequently, can reduce accessibility, and we briefly outline corresponding guidelines to achieve accessibility. Among others, the World Wide Web Consortium [637] defines the individuals with disabilities as subjects that

1. May not be able to see, hear, move, or process some types of information easily or at all
2. May have difficulty reading or comprehending text
3. May not have to or be able to use a keyboard or mouse
4. May have a text-only screen, a small screen, or a slow Internet connection
5. May not speak or understand a natural language fluently

Several guidelines are provided by international and national bodies to govern the production of data, applications, services, and Web sites in order to guarantee accessibility. In the following, we describe some guidelines related to data provided by the World Wide Web Consortium in [637].

The first, and perhaps most important, guideline indicates provision of equivalent alternatives to auditory and visual content, called *text equivalent content*. In order for a text equivalent to make an image accessible, the text content can be presented to the user as synthesized speech, braille, and visually displayed text. Each of these three mechanisms uses a different sense, making the information accessible to groups affected by a variety of sensory and other disabilities. In order to be useful, the text must convey the same function or purpose as the image. For example, consider a text equivalent for a photographic image of the continent of Africa as seen from a satellite. If the purpose of the image is mostly that of decoration, then the text "Photo of Africa as seen from a satellite" might fulfill the necessary function. If the purpose of the photograph is to illustrate specific information about African geography, such as its organization and subdivision into states, then the text equivalent should convey that information with more articulate and informative text. If the photo has been designed to allow the user to select the image or part of it (e.g., by clicking on it) for information about Africa, equivalent text could be "Information about Africa," with a list of items describing the parts that can be selected. Therefore, if the text conveys the same function or purpose for the user with a disability as the image does for other users, it can be considered a text equivalent.

Other guidelines suggest:

• Avoiding the use of color as the only means to express semantics, helping daltonic people appreciate the meaning of data
• Usage of clear natural language, by providing expansions of acronyms, improving readability, a frequent use of plain terms
• Designing a Web site that ensures device independence using features that enable activation of page elements via a variety of input devices
• Providing context and orientation information to help users understand complex pages or elements

Several countries have enacted specific laws to enforce accessibility in public and private Web sites and applications used by citizens and employees in order to provide them effective access and reduce the digital divide.

Chapter 14 will further discuss accessibility of Web data with a focus on system-dependent features, e.g., session identification problems, robot detection and filtering, etc.

2.6 Consistency Cluster

The consistency dimension captures the violation of semantic rules defined over (a set of) data items, where items can be tuples of relational tables or records in a file. With reference to relational theory, *integrity constraints* are an instantiation of such semantic rules. In statistics, *data edits* are another example of semantic rules that allow for the checking of consistency.

2.6.1 Integrity Constraints

The interested reader can find a detailed discussion on integrity constraints in the relational model in [30]. The purpose of this section is to summarize the main concepts, useful in introducing the reader to consistency-related topics.

Integrity constraints are properties that must be satisfied by all instances of a database schema. Although integrity constraints are typically defined on schemas, they can at the same time be checked on a specific instance of the schema that presently represents the extension of the database. Therefore, we may define integrity constraints for schemas, describing a schema quality dimension, and for instances, representing a data dimension. In this section, we will define them for instances, while in Sect. 2.8, we will define them for schemas.

It is possible to distinguish two main categories of integrity constraints, namely, *intrarelation constraints* and *interrelation constraints*.

Intrarelation integrity constraints can regard single attributes (also called *domain constraints*) or multiple attributes of a relation.

Let us consider an Employee relational schema, with the attributes Name, Surname, Age, WorkingYears, and Salary. An example of the domain constraint defined on the schema is "Age is included between 0 and 120." An example of a multiple attribute integrity constraint is "If WorkingYears is less than 3, then Salary could not be more than 25.000 Euros per year."

Interrelation integrity constraints involve attributes of more than one relation. As an example, consider the Movies relational instance in Fig. 2.1. Let us consider another relation, OscarAwards, specifying the Oscar awards won by each movie and including an attribute Year corresponding to the year when the award was assigned. An example of interrelation constraint states that "Year of the Movies relation must be equal to Year of OscarAwards."

Among integrity constraints, the following main types of *dependencies* can be considered:

- *Key dependency.* This is the simplest type of dependency. Given a relational instance r, defined over a set of attributes, we say that for a subset K of the attributes, a key dependency holds in r, if no two rows of r have the same K-values. For instance, an attribute like SocialSecurityNumber can serve as a key in any relational instance of a relational schema Person. When key dependency constraints are enforced, no duplication will occur within the relation (see also Sect. 2.3 on duplication issues).
- *Inclusion dependency.* Inclusion dependency is a very common type of constraint and is also known as *referential constraint.* An inclusion dependency over a relational instance r states that some columns of r are contained in other columns of r or in the instances of another relational instance s. A *foreign key constraint* is an example of inclusion dependency, stating that the referring columns in one relation must be contained in the primary key columns of the referenced relation.
- *Functional dependency.* Given a relational instance r, let X and Y be two nonempty sets of attributes in r. r satisfies the functional dependency $X \rightarrow Y$, if the following holds for every pair of tuples t_1 and t_2 in r:

$$\text{If } t_1.X = t_2.X, \text{ then } t_1.Y = t_2.Y,$$

where the notation $t_1.X$ means the projection of the tuple t_1 onto the attributes in X. In Fig. 2.6, examples of relations respectively satisfying and violating a functional dependency $AB \rightarrow C$ are shown. In the figure, the relation r_1 satisfies the functional dependency, as the first two tuples, having the same values for the attribute A and the attribute B, also have the same value for the attribute C. The relation r_2 does not satisfy the functional dependency, since the first two tuples have a different C field.

Fig. 2.6 Example of functional dependencies

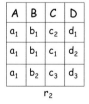

2.6.2   Data Edits

In the previous section, integrity constraints were discussed within the relational model as a specific category of consistency semantic rules. However, where data are not relational, consistency rules can still be defined. As an example, in the statistical field, data coming from census questionnaires have a structure corresponding to the *questionnaire schema*. The semantic rules are thus defined over such a structure in a way very similar to relational constraints. Such rules, called *edits*, are less powerful than integrity constraints because they do not rely on a data model like the relational one. Nevertheless, data editing has been done extensively in the national statistical agencies since the 1950s and has revealed a fruitful and effective area of application. *Data editing* is defined as the task of detecting inconsistencies by formulating rules that must be respected by every correct set of answers. Such rules are expressed as *edits*, which denote error conditions.

As an example, an inconsistent answer to a questionnaire can be to declare

```
marital status = "married", age = "5 years old".
```

The rule to detect this kind of errors could be the following:

```
if marital status is married, age must not be
less than 14.
```

The rule can be put in the form of an edit, which expresses the error condition, namely,

$$\text{marital status} = \text{married} \wedge \text{age} < 14.$$

After the detection of erroneous records, the act of correcting erroneous fields by restoring correct values is called *imputation*. The problem of localizing errors by means of edits and imputing erroneous fields is known as the *edit-imputation problem*. In Chap. 7 we will examine some issues and methods for the edit-imputation problem.

2.7   Approaches to the Definition of Data Quality Dimensions

In this section we describe some general proposals for dimensions. There are three main approaches adopted for proposing comprehensive sets of the dimension definitions, namely, theoretical, empirical, and intuitive. The *theoretical approach* adopts a formal model in order to define or justify the dimensions. The *empirical approach* constructs the set of dimensions starting from experiments, interviews, and questionnaires. The *intuitive approach* simply defines dimensions according to common sense and practical experience.

In the following, we summarize three main proposals that clearly represent the approaches to dimension definitions: Wand and Wang [640], Wang and Strong [645], and Redman [519].

2.7.1   Theoretical Approach

A theoretical approach to the definition of data quality is proposed in Wand and Wang [640]. This approach considers an information system (IS) as a representation of a *real-world system* (RW); RW is *properly represented* in an IS if (1) there exists an exhaustive mapping $RW \rightarrow IS$ and (2) no two states in RW are mapped into the same state in the IS, i.e., the inverse mapping is a function (see Fig. 2.7).

All deviations from proper representations generate deficiencies. They distinguish between *design deficiencies* and *operation deficiencies*. Design deficiencies are of three types: *incomplete representation, ambiguous representation,* and *meaningless states.* They are graphically represented in Fig. 2.8.

Only one type of operation deficiency is identified, in which a state in RW might be mapped to a wrong state in an IS; this is referred to as *garbling*. Garbling with

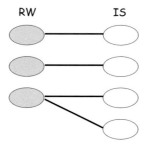

Fig. 2.7 Proper representation of the real-world system in the theoretical approach from [640]

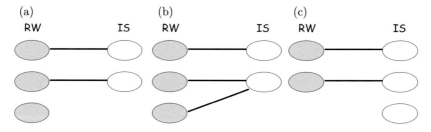

Fig. 2.8 (**a**) Incomplete, (**b**) ambiguous, and (**c**) meaningless representations of the real-world system in the theoretical approach

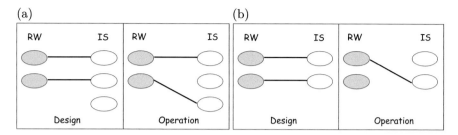

Fig. 2.9 Garbling representations of the real-world system from [640]. (**a**) Not meaningful. (**b**) Meaningful

a map to a meaningless state is dangerous, as it will preclude a map back to a real-world state (see Fig. 2.9a). Garbling to a meaningful but wrong state will allow the user to map back to a real-world state (see Fig. 2.9b).

A set of data quality dimensions are defined by making references to described deficiencies. More specifically, the identified dimensions are (the quoted text is from [640]):

- *Accuracy*: "inaccuracy implies that the information system represents a real-world state different from the one that should have been represented." Inaccuracy refers to a garbled mapping into a wrong state of the IS, where it is possible to infer a valid state of the real world though not the correct one (see Fig. 2.9b).
- *Reliability* indicates "whether the data can be counted on to convey the right information; it can be viewed as correctness of data." No interpretation in terms of data deficiencies is given.
- *Timeliness* refers to "the delay between a change of the real-world state and the resulting modification of the information system state." Lack of timeliness may lead to an IS state that reflects a past RW state.
- *Completeness* is "the ability of an information system to represent every meaningful state of the represented real-world system." Completeness is of course tied to incomplete representations.
- *Consistency* of data values occurs if there is more than one state of the information system matching a state of the real-world system; therefore "inconsistency would mean that the representation mapping is one-to-many." This is captured by the representation, so the inconsistency is not considered a result of a deficiency.

2.7.2 Empirical Approach

In the proposal discussed in Wang and Strong [645], data quality dimensions have been selected by interviewing data consumers. Starting from 179 data quality dimensions, the authors selected 15 different dimensions, represented in Fig. 2.10

Category	Dimension	Definition: the extent to which ...
Intrinsic	Believability	data are accepted or regarded as true, real and credible
	Accuracy	data are correct, reliable and certified free of error
	Objectivity	data are unbiased and impartial
	Reputation	data are trusted or highly regarded in terms of their source and content
Contextual	Value-added	data are beneficial and provide advantages for their use
	Relevancy	data are applicable and useful for the task at hand
	Timeliness	the age of the data is appropriate for the task at hand
	Completeness	data are of sufficient depth, breadth, and scope for the task at hand
	Appropriate amount of data	the quantity or volume of available data is appropriate
Representational	Intepretability	data are in appropriate language and unit and the data definitions are clear
	Ease of understanding	data are clear without ambiguity and easily comprehended
	Representational consistency	data are always presented in the same format and are compatible with the previous data
	Concise representation	data are compactly represented without behing overwhelmed
Accessibility	Accessibility	data are available or easily and quickly retrieved
	Access security	access to data can be restricted and hence kept secure

Fig. 2.10 Dimensions proposed in the empirical approach

with their definitions. A two-level classification is proposed, in which each of four *categories* is further specialized into a number of *dimensions*. The four categories are:

- *Intrinsic data quality*, capturing the quality that data has on its own. As an example, accuracy is a quality dimension that is intrinsic to data.
- *Contextual data quality* considers the context where data are used. As an example, the completeness dimension is strictly related to the context of the task.
- *Representational data quality* captures aspects related to the quality of data representation, e.g., interpretability.
- *Accessibility data quality* is related to the accessibility of data and to a further nonfunctional property of data access, namely, the level of security.

2.7.3 Intuitive Approach

Redman [519] classifies DQ dimensions according to three categories, namely, conceptual schema, data values, and data format. *Conceptual schema* dimensions correspond to what we called schema dimensions. *Data value* dimensions refer specifically to values, independently of the internal representation of data; this last aspect is covered by *data format* dimensions. Our focus here is on data

Dimension Name	Type of dimension	Definition
Accuracy	data value	Distance between v and v', considered as correct
Completeness	data value	Degree to which values are present in a data collection
Currency	data value	Degree to which a datum is up-to-date
Consistency	data value	Coherence of the same datum, represented in multiple copies, or different data to respect integrity constraints and rules
Appropriateness	data format	One format is more appropriate than another if it is more suited to user needs
Interpretability	data format	Ability of the user to interpret correctly values from their format
Portability	data format	The format can be applied to as a wide set of situations as possible
Format precision	data format	Ability to distinguish between elements in the domain that must be distinguished by users
Format flexibility	data format	Changes in user needs and recording medium can be easily accommodated
Ability to represent null values	data format	Ability to distinguish neatly (without ambiguities) null and default values from applicable values of the domain
Efficient use of memory	data format	Efficiency in the physical representation. An icon is less efficient than a code
Representation consistency	data format	Coherence of physical instances of data with their formats

Fig. 2.11 Dimensions proposed in the intuitive approach [519]

extension; therefore, in Fig. 2.11, we provide the definitions for data value and format dimensions only.

2.7.4   A Comparative Analysis of the Dimension Definitions

According to the definitions described in the previous section, there is no general agreement either on which set of dimensions defines DQ or on the exact meaning of each dimension. In fact, in the illustrated proposals, dimensions are not defined in a measurable and formal way. Instead, they are defined by means of descriptive sentences in which the semantics are consequently disputable. Nevertheless, we attempt to make a comparison between the different definitions provided with the purpose of showing possible agreements and disagreements in the different proposals. In order to cover a larger number of proposals, besides those previously described by Wand and Wang [640], Wang and Strong [645], and Redman [519], we also consider Jarke et al. [341], Bovee et al. [86], Naumann [461], and Liu [408]. Hereafter we will refer to the proposals with the name of the first author of the work.

Reference	Definition
Wand 1996	<u>Timeliness</u> refers only to the delay between a change of a real world state and the resulting modification of the information system state
Wang 1996	<u>Timeliness</u> is the extent to which age of the data is appropriate for the task at hand
Redman 1996	<u>Currency</u> is the degree to which a datum is up-to-date. A datum value is up-to-date if it is correct in spite of possible discrepancies caused by time-related changes to the correct value
Jarke 1999	<u>Currency</u> describes when the information was entered in the sources and/or the data warehouse. <u>Volatility</u> describes the time period for which information is valid in the real world
Bovee 2001	<u>Timeliness</u> has two componenents: age and volatility. Age or <u>currency</u> is a measure of how old the information is, based on how long ago it was recorded. <u>Volatility</u> is a measure of information instability-the frequency of change of the value for an entity attribute
Naumann 2002	<u>Timeliness</u> is the average age of the data in a source
Liu 2002	<u>Timeliness</u> is the extent to which data are sufficiently up-to-date for a task

Fig. 2.12 Time-related dimension definitions

With regard to time-related dimensions, in Fig. 2.12, definitions for currency, volatility, and timeliness by different authors are illustrated. In the figure, Wand and Redman provide very similar definitions but for different dimensions, i.e., for timeliness and currency, respectively. Wang and Liu assume the same meaning for timeliness, Naumann proposes a very different definition for it, and Bovee only provides a definition for timeliness in terms of currency and volatility. Bovee's currency corresponds to timeliness as defined by Wang and Liu. Volatility has a similar meaning in Bovee and Jarke. The comparison shows that there is no substantial agreement on the names to use for time-related dimensions; indeed, currency and timeliness are often used to refer to the same concept. There is not even agreement on the semantics of a specific dimension; indeed, for timeliness, different meanings are provided by different authors.

With regard to completeness, in Fig. 2.13, different proposals for completeness definitions are shown. By comparing such definitions, it emerges that there is substantial agreement on what completeness is, although it often refers to different granularity levels and different data model elements, e.g., information system in Wand, data warehouse in Jarke, and entity in Bovee.

Reference	Definition
Wand 1996	The ability of an information system to represent every meaningful state of the represented real world system.
Wang 1996	The extent to which data are of sufficient breadth, depth and scope for the task at hand
Redman 1996	The degree to which values are present in a data collection
Jarke 1999	Percentage of the real-world information entered in the sources and/or the data warehouse
Bovee 2001	Deals with information having all required parts of an entity's information present
Naumann 2002	It is the quotient of the number of non-null values in a source and the size of the universal relation
Liu 2002	All values that are supposed to be collected as per a collection theory

Fig. 2.13 Completeness dimension definitions

2.7.5 Trade-Offs Between Dimensions

Data quality dimensions are not independent, i.e., correlations exist between them. If one dimension is considered more important than the others for a specific application, then the choice of favoring it may imply negative consequences for the other ones. In this section, we provide some examples of possible trade-offs.

First, trade-offs may need to be made between timeliness and any one of the three dimensions: accuracy, completeness, and consistency. Indeed, having accurate (or complete or consistent) data may need checks and activities that require time, and thus timeliness is negatively affected. Conversely, having timely data may cause lower accuracy (or completeness or consistency). A typical situation in which timeliness can be preferred to accuracy, completeness, or consistency is given by most Web applications: as the time constraints are often very stringent for Web data, it is possible that such data are deficient with respect to other quality dimensions. For instance, a list of courses published on a university Web site must be timely though there could be accuracy or consistency errors and some fields specifying courses could be missing. Conversely, when considering an administrative application, accuracy, consistency, and completeness requirements are more stringent than timeliness, and therefore delays are mostly admitted in dimensions other than timeliness.

Another significant case of trade-off is between consistency and completeness [33]. Here the question is "Is it better to have less but consistent data, i.e., poor completeness, or to have more but inconsistent data?" This choice is again very domain specific. As an example, statistical data analysis typically requires a significant and representative amount of data in order to perform the analysis; in this case, the approach is to favor completeness, tolerating inconsistencies or adopting techniques to solve them. Conversely, when considering the publication of a list of votes obtained by students as the result of an exam, it is more important to have a list of consistency checked votes than a complete one, possibly deferring the publication of the complete list.

2.8 Schema Quality Dimensions

In the previous sections, we provided an in-depth characterization of DQ dimensions. In this section, the focus is on schema quality dimensions. However, there is a strict relationship between quality of schemas and quality of data, as highlighted in the next example. Let us suppose we want to model residence addresses of people; in Fig. 2.14, there are two possibilities to model such a concept. Specifically, in Fig. 2.14a, the residence addresses are modeled as attributes of a relation `Person`, while in Fig. 2.14b, the residence addresses are modeled as a relation `Address`, with the fields `Id`, `StreetPrefix`, `StreetName`, `Number`, and `City`, and a relation `ResidenceAddress` storing the address at which the person lives. The solution in Fig. 2.14a has some problems. First, representing addresses as a single field creates ambiguity on the meaning of the different components; for instance, in tuple 3 of the `Person` relation, is 4 a civic number or the number of the avenue (it is actually part of the name of the square)? Second, the values of the attribute `Address` can also contain information that is not explicitly

(b) **Person**

ID	Name	Surname
1	John	Smith
2	Mark	Bauer
3	Ann	Swenson

(a) Person

ID	Name	Surname	Address
1	John	Smith	113 Sunset Avenue 60601 Chicago
2	Mark	Bauer	113 Sunset Avenue 60601 Chicago
3	Ann	Swenson	4 Heroes Street Denver

Address

ID	StreetPrefix	StreetName	Number	City
A11	Avenue	Sunset	113	Chicago
A12	Street	4 Heroes	null	Denver

ResidenceAddress

PersonID	AddressID
1	A11
2	A11
3	A12

Fig. 2.14 Two ways of modeling residence addresses

required to be represented (e.g., the floor number and zip code of tuples 1 and 2 of the `Person` relation). Third, as the `Person` relation is not normalized, a redundancy problem occurs and hence further errors on the `Address` attribute may be potentially introduced (see the same address values for tuples 1 and 2 of the `Person` relation). On the other hand, the solution in Fig. 2.14b is more complex. In real implementation there is often the need to manage trade-offs between the two modeling solutions.

A comprehensive proposal on schema dimensions is described in the book of Redman [519] and includes six dimensions and 15 subdimensions referring to schema quality.

Here, we focus on dimensions related to the accuracy, completeness, redundancy, and readability clusters introduced in Sect. 8.5.3. In the definitions we are going to provide, we assume that the database schema is the result of the translation of a set of requirements, expressed usually in natural language, into a set of conceptual (or logical) structures, expressed in terms of a conceptual (or logical) database model.

2.8.1 Accuracy Cluster

Accuracy, or better correctness in this context, is of two types:

1. *Correctness with respect to the model* concerns the correct use of the constructs of the model in representing requirements. As an example, in the Entity Relationship (ER) model, we may represent the logical link between persons and their first names using the two entities `Person` and `FirstName` and a relationship between them. The schema is not correct with respect to the model since an entity should be used only when the concept has a unique existence in the real world and has an identifier; this is not the case with `FirstName`, which would be properly represented as an attribute of the entity `Person`.
2. *Correctness with respect to requirements* concerns the correct representation of the requirements in terms of the model constructs. Assume that in an organization each department is headed by exactly one manager and each manager may head exactly one department. If we represent `Manager` and `Department` as entities, the relationship between them should be one-to-one; in this case, the schema is correct with respect to requirements. If we use a one-to-many relationship, the schema is incorrect.

2.8.2 Completeness Cluster

Completeness measures the extent to which a conceptual schema includes all the conceptual elements necessary to meet some specified requirements. It is possible that the designer has not included certain characteristics present in the requirements

in the schema, e.g., attributes related to an entity Person; in this case, the schema
is incomplete. *Pertinence* measures how many unnecessary conceptual elements are
included in the conceptual schema. In the case of a schema that is not pertinent, the
designer has gone too far in modeling the requirements and has included too many
concepts.

Completeness and pertinence are two faces of the same issue, i.e., obtaining at
the end of the conceptual design phase a schema that is the *exact* correspondence in
the model of the reality described by requirements.

2.8.3 Redundancy Cluster

In this section we deal with *minimality* and *normalization*.

A schema is minimal if every part of the requirements is represented only once
in the schema. In other words, it is not possible to eliminate some element from
the schema without compromising the information content. Consider the schema
in Fig. 2.15, which represents several relationships between concepts Student,
Course, and Instructor. We represent also minimum and maximum cardinal-
ities of entities in relationships, except in one case, where we indicate the maximum
cardinality with the symbol "?". The schema is redundant in the case in which the
direct relationship Assigned to between Student and Instructor has the
same meaning as the logical composition of the two relationships Attends and
Teaches; otherwise, it is nonredundant. Notice that the schema can be redundant
only in the case in which the unspecified maximum cardinality of the entity Course
is "1" since only in this case does a unique instructor correspond to each course and
the composition of the two relationships Attends and Teaches may provide the
same result as the relationship Assigned to.

Fig. 2.15 A possibly
redundant schema

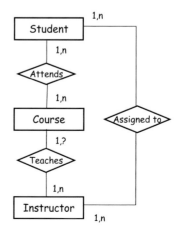

The property of *normalization* has been deeply investigated, especially in the relational model, although it expresses a model-independent, general property of schemas.

In the relational model, normalization is strictly related to the structure of functional dependencies. Several degrees of normalization have been defined in the relational model, such as first, second, third, Boyce Codd, fourth, and other normal forms. The most popular and intuitive normal form is the *Boyce Codd normal form* (BCNF). A relational schema R is in BCNF if for every nontrivial functional dependency X `->` Y defined on R, X contains a key K of R, i.e., X is a superkey of R. For more details on the BCNF and other normal forms, see [30, 198].

To exemplify, a relational schema R is in BCNF if all nontrivial functional dependencies have a key on the left-hand side of the dependency, so, all non-key attributes depend on a unique key. The interpretation of this property is that the relational schema represents a unique concept, with which all nontrivial functional dependencies are homogeneously associated and whose properties are represented by all non-key attributes.

We have placed normalization in the redundancy cluster since an unnormalized schema presents a set of anomalies with respect to a corresponding normalized schema.

As already mentioned, normalization is a property that can be defined in every conceptual or logical model; as an example of normalization not applied to the relational model, Fig. 2.16 shows an unnormalized schema in the Entity Relationship model. It is made of a unique entity `Employee-Project`, with five attributes; two of them, the underlined ones, define the identifier of the entity. Following [38], we can define the concept of normalized ER schema by associating the functional dependencies defined among the attributes of the entity and adapting the above definition of BCNF to the entities and the relationships. We define the following functional dependencies in the schema:

- `EmployeeId` → `Salary`
- `ProjectId` → `Budget`
- `EmployeeId,ProjectId` → `Role`

that lead to a violation of BCNF. With the objective of normalizing the schema, we can transform the entity `Employee-Project` into a new schema (see Fig. 2.17) made of two entities, `Employee` and `Project`, and one many-to-many relationship defined between them. Now the entities and the relationship are in BCNF, as is the whole schema.

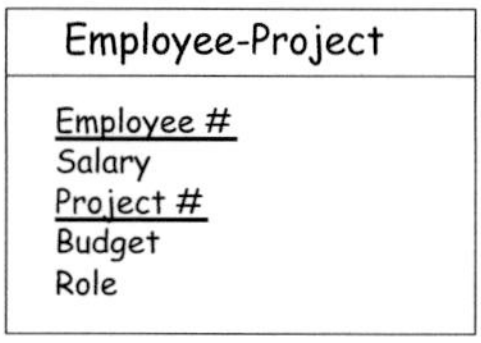

Fig. 2.16 An unnormalized
Entity Relationship schema

Fig. 2.17 A normalized schema

2.8.4   Readability Cluster

Intuitively, a schema is readable whenever it represents the meaning of the reality represented by the schema in a clear way for its intended use. This simple, qualitative definition is not easy to translate in a more formal way, since the evaluation expressed by the word *clear* conveys some elements of subjectivity. In models, such as the Entity Relationship model, that provide a graphical representation of the schema, called *diagram*, readability concerns both the diagram and the schema itself. We now discuss them.

With regard to the diagrammatic representation, readability can be expressed by a number of *aesthetic criteria* that human beings adopt in drawing diagrams: crossings between lines should be avoided as far as possible, graphic symbols should be embedded in a grid, lines should be made of horizontal or vertical segments, the number of bends in lines should be minimized, the total area of the diagram should be minimized, and, finally, hierarchical structures such as generalization hierarchies among, say, a parent entity E1 and two-child entities E2 and E3 should be such that E1 is positioned at a higher level in the diagram in respect to E2 and E3. Finally, the child entities in the generalization hierarchy should be symmetrical with respect to the parent entity. For further discussion on aesthetic criteria, see [47, 601].

The above criteria are not respected in the case of the Entity Relationship diagram of Fig. 2.18. We can see in the diagram many crossings between lines. Most objects are placed casually in the area of the schema, and it is difficult to identify the group of entities related by generalization hierarchy. The schema, in a few words, has a "spaghetti style."

Following the aesthetic rules described above, we may completely restructure the diagram, leading to the new diagram shown in Fig. 2.19. Here, most relevant concepts have a larger dimension, there are no bends in lines, and the generalization hierarchy is more apparent.

The second issue addressed by readability is the *compactness* of schema representation. Among the different conceptual schemas that equivalently represent a certain reality, we prefer the one or the ones that are more compact, because compactness favors readability. As an example, on the left- hand side of Fig. 2.20, we see a schema where the represented entity City is related to the three-child entities in the generalization hierarchy. Due to the inheritance property [198], which states that all concepts related to the parent entity are also related to all the child entities, we can drop the three occurrences of relationships involving the entity

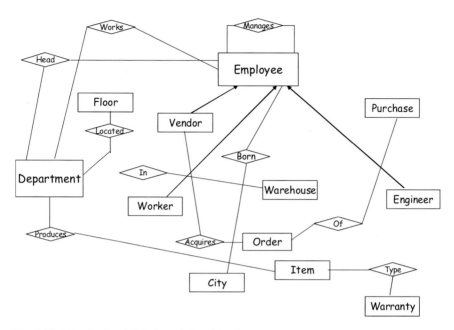

Fig. 2.18 "Spaghetti style" Entity Relationship schema

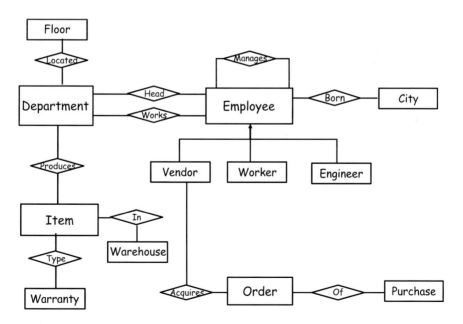

Fig. 2.19 An equivalent readable schema

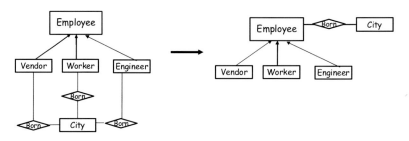

Fig. 2.20 A schema transformation that improves compactness

`City` and change them into a single relationship with the entity `Employee`, resulting in a more compact and readable schema.

2.9 Summary

In this chapter we have seen a variety of dimensions and metrics that characterize the concept of information quality for the case of structured data. These dimensions provide a reference framework to those organizations interested in the quality of data and allow them to characterize and to some extent measure the quality of datasets. Furthermore, fixing and measuring DQ dimensions allow comparison with reference thresholds and values that may be considered target quality values to be achieved in the organization. As a consequence, quality dimensions are at the basis of any process of measurement and improvement of DQ in an organization. As an example, in contracts related to sale of data, the issue of quality of service is crucial, expressing precisely and unambiguously the demand for quality data. Finally, dimensions may be mentioned in laws and rules concerning data usage in government for citizen/business relationships.

Moreover, we have seen general proposals for sets of dimensions that aim to fully specify the DQ concept in a general setting (see Sect. 2.7). However, there further exist proposals that are related to specific domains that need *ad hoc* dimensions in order to capture the peculiarities of the domain. Examples of proposals for data quality dimensions come from:

1. The *archival domain* (see [380, 677] and the InterPARES project [328]), which makes use of dimensions such as *condition* (of a document) that refers to the physical suitability of the document for scanning.
2. The *statistical domain*: National Statistical Institutes and international organizations such as the European Union or the International Monetary Fund define several dimensions for statistical and scientific data (see [326]). As an example, the notion of *integrity* is related to the fact that statistical systems should be based on adherence to the principle of objectivity in the collection, compilation, and dissemination of statistics.

Dimensions are the core of any investigation in data and information quality, and they will be used in the rest of the book. From the next chapter, we will explore several types of information and will discover the characteristics of data and information quality that are invariant and the characteristics that instead change according to the information type.

Chapter 3
Information Quality Dimensions for Maps and Texts

3.1 Introduction

In Chap. 2, we have considered quality dimensions for structured data. In this chapter, we move from data quality dimensions to information quality dimensions. We will consider two coordinates for the types of information, respectively, the *perceptual coordinate* and the *linguistic coordinate*. From one side, we will explore how dimensions change according to the coordinate and to the type of information, considering as to the perceptual coordinate the case of maps and as to the textual coordinate the case of semistructured texts. From the other side, we will deal with a better detail a topic that has been introduced in Chap. 2, related to how dimensions change or evolve when specific domains are considered. In particular, we will consider a special kind of semistructured texts, namely, law texts.

The chapter is organized as follows. Section 3.2 considers the different coordinates involved in shifting our focus from structured data to all other types of information. Section 3.3 deals with maps. We will introduce the general map conceptual structure in the representation of space and time, leading to identify spatial and temporal characteristics involved in quality dimensions. As to the spatial conceptual structure, three different issues are considered, related to topological, geometrical, and thematic characteristics of maps. Section 3.4 discusses quality of semistructured texts, focusing on the quality dimensions specific of texts, from readability to comprehensibility, cohesion, and coherence, together with metrics to measure such dimensions. Section 3.5 deals with texts in the domain of laws, addressing quality dimensions for the three cases of individual laws, of law legal frameworks in a single country, and of law legal framework in a set of associated countries.

© Springer International Publishing Switzerland 2016   53
C. Batini, M. Scannapieco, *Data and Information Quality*, Data-Centric Systems
and Applications, DOI 10.1007/978-3-319-24106-7_3

3.2   From Data Quality Dimensions to Information Quality Dimensions

Dimensions discussed in Chap. 2 are defined for structured data. An unbelievable vast amount of realities is instead represented by types of information that are not structured data. Reality is represented by a piece of information either in its realistic inherent character (let us think of a photo of a landscape or a photo of a group of students in a class or a map and a descriptive text in a travel guide) or in other ways, e.g., in novels and poetry as a virtual representation of reality itself (let us think of the novel *The Hobbit* by John Ronald Reuel Tolkien with respect to semistructured texts or, as to maps, of the *Atlas of Remote Islands* by Judith Schalansky).

Dimensions for structured data are closely related to inner characteristic and properties of the underlying data model. An example is given by the different types of completeness, defined with and without the open world assumption for the different types of structures of the relational model, namely, the tuple, the column, the table, and the set of tables.

In this chapter, we start to examine the evolution of dimensions along the three perspectives defined for information in the preface, i.e., the linguistic perspective, the perceptual perspective, and the Web perspective; see Fig. 3.1, where we have labeled the types of information with the chapter in the book where they are discussed.

This chapter is focused on maps for perceptual type of information and semistructured texts and law texts for linguistic types; we will see that also in these cases, dimensions tend to specialize to the intrinsic conceptual properties of the type of information, such as space and time, and to the specific domain they aim to represent, such as law texts.

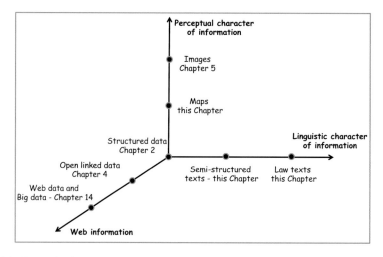

Fig. 3.1 Types of information considered in the book according to the perceptual, linguistic, and Web coordinates

3.3 Information Quality in Maps

A map can be defined as a representation, usually on a flat surface, of the features of an area of the earth or of a portion of the heavens, showing them in their respective forms, sizes, and relationships (according to some convention of representation) and in their evolution in time. Maps have been for long used for a vast amount of human activities such as sailing, driving, and walking where, depending on the decision and actions to be taken, the user requested to the map different degrees of approximation in the representation of the related territory. Properties of information used to represent maps can be classified in terms of the following categories: (a) space, (b) time, and (c) characteristics or themes of the real world in their space localization and in their time evolution. As to space, we can distinguish at least two types of properties of spatial objects: (a) topology and (b) geometry.

Topology is defined (see [667]) as the study of qualitative properties of certain objects (called topological spaces) that are invariant under a certain kind of transformation (called a continuous map), especially those properties that are invariant under a certain kind of equivalence (called homeomorphism). Topology is a major area of mathematics concerned with the most basic properties of space, such as connectedness, continuity, and boundary. Geometry is the branch of mathematics concerned with issues of shape, size, relative position of figures, and the properties of space.

As a consequence of the above discussion, we will adopt for quality dimensions of objects represented in maps the (a) space-topological, (b) space-geometric, (c) space-thematic, and (d) temporal classification. For what concerns space, the different concepts and related primitives involved in topological and geometrical characteristics can be represented by means of conceptual schemas, called *application schemas* in the geographical information system (GIS) literature. With reference to topological primitives, we show in Fig. 3.2 their application schema as referenced in [570].

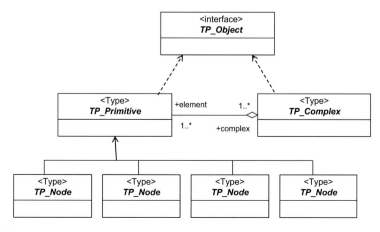

Fig. 3.2 Schema of topological primitives specified by ISO 19107 (from [570])

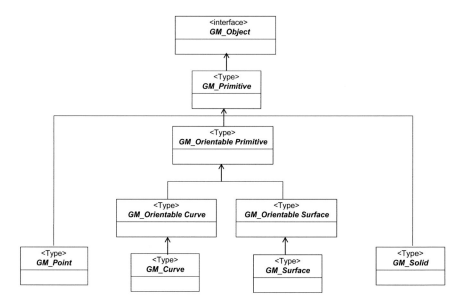

Fig. 3.3 Schema of basic geometric primitives specified by ISO 19107 (from [570])

As to geometry, in the ISO standard 19107, geometric characteristics are of three types: primitive, aggregate, and complex. In Fig. 3.3, we show ISO 19107 basic geometric primitives. Geometric primitives as above provide all components needed to depict the shape and the location of user artifacts such as buildings, roads, intersections, roundabouts, bridges, networks of roads, railway networks, and electricity networks or else natural phenomena, such as rivers, lakes, seas, and mountains.

For each set of such characteristic of the territory, a map provider can adopt further sets of symbols or text that result in wider sets of rules that can be enforced for the set; such characteristics can be represented in terms of further application schemas. Some of the application schemas have been standardized in ISO 19107, such as the one in Fig. 3.4, representing roads and bridges of a road network. Other domains have not been standardized so far; in this case, the provider of the map may introduce, explicitly or implicitly, new objects and relationships by means of new user-defined conceptual schemas.

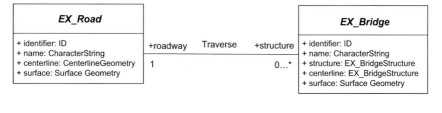

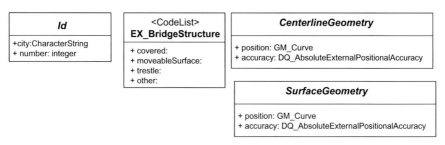

Fig. 3.4 Application schema for representing roads and bridges compliant with ISO 19109 rules (from [570])

3.3.1 Conceptual Structure of Maps and Quality Dimensions of Maps

In the discipline of GISs, the quality of maps has been investigated for a long time, and standardization bodies have produced several standards focused on maps quality. In Fig. 3.5, we show a list of dimensions for the different clusters introduced in Chap. 2, where the references are the ISO standard 19100 and the Spatial Data Transfer Standard, SDTS (see [573]). For each dimension, we provide an informal definition borrowed from the reference source.

In Fig. 3.6, we classify the dimensions according to the spatial/temporal/thematic coordinates introduced above. We clearly see the evolution of dimensions with respect to structured data influenced by the map coordinates. As to accuracy, syntactic accuracy and semantic accuracy are differentiated according to all relevant topological, geometric, temporal, and thematic coordinates.

In the following, we focus on describing some of the dimensions mentioned in Figs. 3.5 and 3.6 (see also [285, 328, 485] for a general introduction to this issue).

3.3.1.1 Accuracy Cluster

Accuracy describes the degree of adherence of geographic data to the most plausible corresponding true value. We focus here on *relative positional accuracy* and *absolute positional accuracy.*

Cluster	Dimension	Source	Definition
Accuracy	Positional	Iso 19100	Accuracy of the position of features
Accuracy	Relative positional	Iso 19100	Closeness of the relative positions of features in a dataset to their respective relative positions accepted as or being true
Accuracy	Absolute positional	Iso 19100	Closeness of reported coordinate values to values accepted as or being true
Accuracy	Horizontal positional	SDTS	Accuracy of the horizontal position in the data set
Accuracy	Vertical positional	SDTS	Accuracy of the vertical position in the data set
Accuracy	Gridded data position	Iso 19100	Closeness of gridded data position values to values accepted as or being true
Accuracy	Thematic	Iso 19100	Accuracy of quantitative attributes and the correctness of non quantitati-ve attributes and of the classifications of features and their relationships
Accuracy	of quantitative attributes	Iso 19100	Accuracy of quantitative attributes
Accuracy	Temporal validity	Iso 19100	Validity of data with respect to time
Accuracy	of a time measurement	Iso 19100	Correctness of the temporal references of an item (reporting of error in time measurement)
Accuracy	Correctness of non quantitative attributes	Iso 19100	Correctness of non-quantitative attributes
Correctness	Correctness of classifi-cation	Iso 19100	Comparison of the classes assigned to features or their attributes to a universe of discourse (e.g. ground truth or reference data set)
Completeness	-	Iso 19100	Presence or absence of features, heir attributes and relation-ships
Completeness	Pertinence (or Commis-sion)	Iso 19100	Excess data present in a dataset
Consistency	Logical	Iso 19100	Degree of adherence to logical rules of data structure, attri-bution and relationships
Consistency	Conceptual	Iso 19100	Adherence to rules of the application conceptual schema
Consistency	Domain	Iso 19100	Adherence of values to the value domains
Consistency	Format	Iso 19100	Degree to which data is stored in accordance with the physical
Consistency	Topological	Iso 19100	Correctness of the explicitly encoded topological characteri-stics of a dataset
Consistency	Temporal	Iso 19100	Correctness of ordered events or sequences, if reported

Fig. 3.5 Quality dimensions of maps in the ISO 19100 geographic information quality standards and in the spatial data transfer standard

Conceptual issue → Dimension Cluster ↓	Space -topological	Space - geometric	Space -thematic	Temporal
Accuracy		1. Positional 2. Absolute position acc. 3. Relative position acc. 4. Gridded data pos.acc. 5. Horizontal acc. 6. Vertical acc. 7. Geometric precision	1. Thematic acc. 2. Accuracy/corr. of quantitative attributes 3. Accuracy/corr. of non quantitative attributes 4. Classification accuracy/correct-ness 5. Thematic precision	1. of a time measurement 2. Temporal validity 3. Temporal precision
Completeness			1. Completeness 2. Pertinence	
Consistency	1. Conceptual 2. Topological	Conceptual	1. Logical 2. Conceptual 3. Domain 4. Format	Temporal

Fig. 3.6 Quality dimensions of maps classified by map conceptual characteristics

Fig. 3.7 Example of relative
positional accuracy

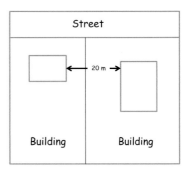

Relative positional accuracy, which has traditionally been used to indicate the positional accuracy of maps, is defined as the difference of the distance between two defined points in a geospatial dataset and the true distance between these points within the overall reference system. See an example of relative positional accuracy in Fig. 3.7.

Satellite navigation technology, such as GPS, introduced the possibility of obtaining a point coordinate directly without relating to neighboring features. Therefore, another accuracy definition is needed; absolute positional accuracy is defined as the distance between a defined point in geospatial dataset and its true position in the overall reference system; see Fig. 3.8.

Precision (or *resolution*) refers to the amount of detail that can be discerned in space (geometric precision), time, or theme (thematic precision). Precision is always finite because no measurement system is infinitely precise and because databases are intentionally generalized to reduce detail [624].

Fig. 3.8 Example of absolute
positional accuracy

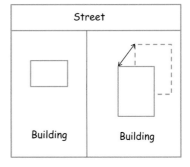

Precision is linked with accuracy, since the level of precision affects the map specification against which accuracy is assessed. Two maps with the same overall accuracy levels but different levels of precision do not have the same quality; the map with the lower precision has weaker accuracy requirements. For example, thematic accuracy will tend to be higher for general land use/land cover classes like urban than for specific classes like residential.

Correctness refers to the degree of adherence of existence of geographic data (features, attributes, functions, relationships) to corresponding elements of the universe of discourse. An accurately located feature which is incorrectly coded has a problem with correctness. A threshold bottom value of correctness for acceptance should be set depending from the relevance of individual datasets. It is not acceptable, in fact, to have even a single error in the coding of the country boundary polygons, while a limited number of errors in soil coverages might be tolerated.

3.3.1.2   Completeness Cluster

Completeness is the degree of adherence of the entirety of geographic data (features, their attributes, and relationships) to the universe of discourse. Completeness is an assessment of the dataset's existing features against what should currently be located within the dataset. Completeness is also related to the attribute data to assess whether all of the pertinent attributes are accounted for. A reasonable requirement for the bottom limit of dataset completeness is that not more than 1 % of the features and attributes existing in the source data are missing in the map.

3.3.1.3   Consistency Cluster

Consistency is the degree of adherence of geographic data to semantic specification (data structure, their features, attributes, and relationships) to the models and schemas (application model, application schema, and data model); it can be measured by the percentage of geographic data that are consistent. *Topological/geometric consistency* are quality dimensions that can be measured in terms of the percentage of adherence to the explicitly encoded topological/geometric characteristics of the dataset.

3.3.2   Levels of Abstraction and Quality of Maps

Maps allow us to address, with reference to the representation of the territory, one of the most relevant issues in computer science, the abstraction issue, in its relationship with data quality. Database conceptual models can be seen as representations that abstract objects and phenomena of a reality of interest from details that are considered not relevant, focusing only on specific characteristics. While abstracting from the real world we omit information, so we inevitably produce an approximation and, potentially, a loss of quality in the representation of phenomena. The effects of abstraction and the relationships between abstraction and quality are particularly intriguing in maps, where abstractions affect all characteristics of maps, such as topology, geometry, time, and symbolic and textual themes. As an example, in our experience of visiting a city or making a travel by car, we need maps at different levels of detail. *Cartographic generalization*, a well-known process in GIS, involves symbolizing data and applying a set of techniques that convey the salient characteristics of that data. These techniques seek to give prominence to the essential qualities of the feature portrayed, e.g., that buildings retain their anthropogenic qualities, such as their angular form. In Fig. 3.9, we show a list

Operator	Before	After
(a) **Smoothing** Reduce angularity of the map object.		
(b) **Collapse** Reduce dimensionality of map object (area to point, linear polygon to line).		
(c) **Displacement** Small movement of map objects in order to minimise overlap.		
(d) **Enhancement** Emphasize characteristics of map feature and meet minimum legibility requirements.		
(e) **Typification** Replacement of a group of map features with a prototypical subset.		
(f) **Text Placement** Non overlapping unambiguous placement of text.		
(g) **Symbolization** Change of symbology according to theme (pictorial, iconic), or reduce space required for symbol.		

Fig. 3.9 A list of cartographic generalization operators from [570], Encyclopedia of Geographic Information Systems ©Springer 2008

of possible cartographic generalization operators that apply some of the above techniques.

As said in [570],

> different combinations, amounts of application, and different orderings of these techniques can produce different yet aesthetically acceptable solutions. The focus is not on making changes to information contained in the database, but to solely focus upon avoiding ambiguity in the interpretation of the image. The process is one of compromise reflecting the long held view among cartographers that making maps involves telling small lies in order to tell the truth!.

3.4 Information Quality in Semistructured Texts

A general, unspecific structure for textual information is composed by the following items:

- Word: atomic element; words separated by space delimiters
- Sentence: grammatical unit of one or more words
- Text: set of sentences considered as unitary
- Collection of texts: group of texts grouped for some specific purpose

When we use natural language, the sentences we write or pronounce are characterized by a *lexicon* that considers words, a *grammar* that establishes a set of structural rules for word composition in sentences, and a *semantics* that provides the meaning of sentences, texts, and collection of texts. Further, *rhetoric* is the use of language that brings forth a literary effect, and *pragmatics* is the way in which context contributes to meaning. Besides grammar, the term syntax is also used to refer to the rules and principles that govern the sentence structure of any individual language.

Lexicon, syntax, semantics, rhetoric, and pragmatics can be considered as kinds of *linguistic structures*, since from one side, they provide an organization of the text that allows us to recognize concepts and relationships among concepts in the text and from the other side, they do not organize precisely the text as data embedded in relational tables.

It is not so common to find texts that are fully unstructured. An example is shown in Fig. 3.10, which represents the last chapter of James Joyce's masterpiece, *Ulysses*. This famous text has no punctuation mark, but, apart from some poetic license, the sentence respects the rules of the English grammar. The absence of the type of structure created by punctuation marks is as a literary artifice used by Joyce to simulate the experience that every one of us does when every night moves from wakefulness to sleep, when thoughts and their verbal expressions slowly fade.

We can classify relevant dimensions for texts according to lexicon, syntax, semantics, rhetoric, and pragmatics coordinates. In Fig. 3.11, we see the quality

I saw them not long ago I love flowers Id love to have the whole place swimming in roses God of heaven theres nothing like nature the wild mountains then the sea and the waves rushing then the beautiful country with the fields of oats and wheat and all kinds of things and all the fine cattle going about that would do your heart good to see rivers and lakes and flowers all sorts of shapes and smells and colours springing up even out of the ditches primroses and violets nature it is as for them saying theres no God I wouldnt give a snap of my two fingers for all their learning why dont they go and create something I often asked him atheists or whatever they call themselves go and wash the cobbles off themselves first then they go howling for the priest and they dying and why why because theyre afraid of hell on account of their bad conscience ah yes I know them well who was the first person in the universe before there was anybody that made it all who ah that they dont know neither do I so there you are they might as well try to stop the sun from rising tomorrow the sun shines for you he said the day we were lying among the rhododendrons on Howth head in the grey tweed suit and his straw hat the day I got him to propose to me yes first I gave him the bit of seedcake out of my mouth and it was leapyear like now yes 16 years ago my God after that long kiss I near lost my breath yes he said I was a flower of the mountain yes so we are flowers all a womans body yes that was one true thing he said in his life and the sun shines for you today yes that was why I liked him because I saw he understood or felt what a woman is and I knew I could always get round him and I gave him all the pleasure I could leading him on till he asked me to say yes and I wouldnt answer first only looked out over the sea and the sky I was thinking of so many things he didnt know of Mulvey and Mr Stanhope and Hester and father and old captain Groves and the sailors playing all birds fly and I say stoop and washing up dishes they called it on the pier and the sentry in front of the governors house with the thing round his white helmet poor devil half roasted and the Spanish girls laughing in their shawls and their tall combs and the auctions in the morning the Greeks and the jews and the Arabs and the devil knows who else from all the ends of Europe and Duke street and the fowl market all clucking outside Larby Sharons and the poor donkeys slipping half asleep and the vague fellows in the cloaks asleep in the shade on the steps and the big wheels of the carts of the bulls and the old castle thousands of years old yes and those handsome Moors all in white and turbans like kings asking you to sit down in their little bit of a shop and Ronda with the old windows of the posadas 2 glancing eyes a lattice hid for her lover to kiss the iron and the wineshops half open at night and the castanets and the night we missed the boat at Algeciras the watchman going about serene with his lamp and O that awful deepdown torrent O and the sea the sea crimson sometimes like fire and the glorious sunsets and the figtrees in the Alameda gardens yes and all the queer little streets and the pink and blue and yellow houses and the rosegardens and the jessamine and geraniums and cactuses and Gibraltar as a girl where I was a Flower of the mountain yes when I put the rose in my hair like the Andalusian girls used or shall I wear a red yes and how he kissed me under the Moorish wall and I thought well as well him as another and then I asked him with my eyes to ask again yes and then he asked me would I yes to say yes my mountain flower and first I put my arms around him yes and drew him down to me so he could feel my breasts all perfume yes and his heart was going like mad and yes I said yes I will Yes.
·   Trieste-Zurich-Paris 1914-1921

Fig. 3.10 A famous example of fully unstructured text

Conceptual issue → Cluster ↓	Lexicon	Syntax	Semantics	Rhetoric	Pragmatics
Accuracy	Lexical accuracy	Syntactic accuracy			
Readability	Readability				
	Text comprehension Closer-to-text base comprehension Closer-to-situation model level comprehension				
Consistency	Coherence Referential Cohesion – local co-reference Referential Cohesion – global co-reference				
Accessibility					Cultural accessibility

Fig. 3.11 Dimensions for semistructured texts and related classification criteria

dimensions we will consider in this section related to texts in natural language. Notice the change of perspective with respect to both structured data and to maps; here, the emphasis is on the fact that the text has to be read by a human being, whose goal is to understand the piece of real, artificial, or imaginary world the text describes.

We now consider the different dimension clusters.

$$\text{Lexical accuracy} = \frac{\sum_i^K \text{closeness}\,(w_i, V)}{K}$$

Fig. 3.12 Formula for lexical accuracy

3.4.1 Accuracy Cluster

Lexical accuracy deals with the closeness of words in the text to a reference vocabulary. In order to measure the closeness, we can adopt any of the metrics that we introduced in Chap. 2 for the syntactic accuracy of structured alphanumeric data. The formula in Fig. 3.12 shows that for a text of K words, the closeness has to be measured for each word w_i against the vocabulary V used in the text.

Syntactic accuracy deals with the adherence of the text to the syntactic rules defined in the corresponding natural language the text refers to. We will not go into detail on this dimension.

3.4.2 Readability Cluster

In this section, we will consider two dimensions, readability and text comprehension.

3.4.2.1 Readability

Readability is defined as reading easiness. Readability is also defined as what makes some texts easier to read than others [184]. Klare [370] defines readability as "the ease of understanding due to the style of writing." This definition focuses on writing style as separate from issues such as content, coherence, and organization. Readability is then concerned with the relative difficulty of reading written text. Readability should not to be confused with *legibility*, which is concerned with typeface and layout.

Readability research largely traces its origins to an initial study by Kitson [369] that demonstrates tangible differences in sentence lengths and word lengths, measured in syllables, between two newspapers and two magazines. See also [689] for a historical perspective of readability. The majority of metrics proposed for readability are based on factors that represent two broad aspects of comprehension difficulty: (a) lexical or semantic features and (b) sentence or syntactic complexity. According to [114], formulas that depend on these variables are popular because they are easily associated with text simplification.

As a consequence of the above perspective, readability is usually measured by using a mathematical formula that considers syntactic features of a given text, such

$$0.4 * \left[\left(\frac{words}{sentence} \right) + 100 * \left(\frac{complexwords}{words} \right) \right]$$

Fig. 3.13 Formula for the Gunning Fog index

as word length and sentence length. Over 200 formulas have been reported for readability in the English language [184] from the 1920s to the 1980s, among them being Gunning Fog index [283], automated readability index (ARI) [560], Flesch reading ease [225, 240], and Flesch-Kincaid grade level [368]; we discuss in some detail Gunning Fog and ARI.

The Gunning Fog index produces an approximate grade level required to understand the document. The basic idea in the index is that the longer sentences are and the greater is the complexity of words used in them, the higher is the difficulty to read the text. The formula for the Gunning Fog index is shown in Fig. 3.13.

An example of evaluation of the Gunning Fog index from [494] is the text in Fig. 3.14. This passage has seven sentences and 96 words. The average sentence length is 13.7. There are nine difficult words (in **boldface**). The Gunning Fog index is $= 0.4 * (13.7 + 9.375) = 9.23$.

ARI is a readability measure designed to represent the US grade level needed to comprehend the text. Unlike the other indexes, ARI relies on a ratio characters per word, instead of the usual syllables per word. See the formula for the ARI index in Fig. 3.15, where:

- Characters is the number of characters in the text.
- Words is the number of words in the text.
- Sentences is the number of sentences in the text.
- Complex words are difficult words defined as those with three or more syllables.

In **describing** the humpback whale song, we will adhere to the **following designations** . The shortest sound that is **continuous** to our ears when heard in "real time" will be called a "unit." Some units when listened to at slower speeds, or **analyzed** by machine, turn out to be a series of pulses or **rapidly** sequenced, discrete tones. In such cases, we will call each discrete pulse or tone a "subunit." A series of units is called a "phrase." An **unbroken** sequence of **similar** phrases is a "theme," and **several** distinct themes combine to form a "song."
{From "Songs of Humpback Whales." 1971. Payne, R. S. & S. McVay. Science 173: 585-597.}

Fig. 3.14 Example of evaluation of the Gunning Fog index

$$ARI = 4{,}71 * \frac{characters}{words} + 0{,}5 * \frac{complex\ words}{sentences} - 21{,}43$$

Fig. 3.15 Formula for the ARI index

3.4.2.2   Text Comprehension

Traditional readability formulas are generally not based on theories of reading or comprehension building, but on tracing statistical correlations. At the beginning of the 1960s, new developments transformed the study of readability, including new tests of reading comprehension and the contributions of linguistics and cognitive psychology. An example of the evolution of the readability concept is in [433] that defines readability as "the degree to which a given class of people find certain reading matter compelling and comprehensible." This definition stresses the interaction between the text and a class of readers of known characteristics such as reading skill, prior knowledge, and motivation.

The shortcomings of traditional formulas also become evident when one matches them against psycholinguistic models of the processes that the reader brings to bear on the text. Psycholinguists regard reading as a multicomponent skill operating at a number of different levels of processing: lexical, syntactic, semantic, and discoursal [372]. A psycholinguistically based assessment of text comprehensibility must go deeper than surface readability features to explain how the reader interacts with a text. It must include measures of text cohesion and meaning construction and encode comprehension as a multilevel process [372].

Due to the wider scope of such studies, we adopt the term *text comprehension* or *comprehensibility* to characterize the corresponding quality dimension. Comprehensibility is the ability to be understood and intelligible. Comprehension is also the ability to grasp something mentally and the capacity to understand ideas and facts; comprehension skills are related to the ability to use context and prior knowledge to aid reading and to make sense of what one reads and hears. As a consequence, comprehension is based on readers' prior knowledge, information presented in the text, and the use of context to assist recognition of words and meaning.

Another area that influenced studies on readability has been rhetoric structure theory (RST) [426], a linguistic method for describing natural texts, characterizing their structure primarily in terms of relations that hold between parts of the text. RST identifies hierarchical structure in text, describes the relations between text parts in functional terms, and provides a general way to describe the relations among clauses in a text, whether or not they are grammatically or lexically put in evidence.

A first set of elements proposed in [184] to evolve from readability to text comprehension is shown in Fig. 3.16.

Although the terms in Fig. 3.16 are not explained in the text, we recognize (a) among design elements aesthetic and symbolic features that extend the legibility dimension introduced above, (b) new structural items such as chapters and headings, and (c) content items such as organization and coherence that will be considered soon.

Content Proposition Organization Coherence	Style Syntactic and Semantic elements
Structure Chapters Headings Navigation	Design Typography Format Illustrations

Fig. 3.16 Basic elements for ease reading in [184]

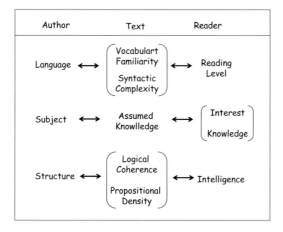

Fig. 3.17 Matches needed for easy reading identified in [469]

A more advanced model that enhances readability toward text comprehension appears in [469]; here, the motivation of the enhancement lies in the observation that in writing a document, an author has to be mindful of the needs of the anticipated audience, and there must be some matchings across three principal aspects of the text: the language adopted, the subject, and the logical or narrative structure; see Fig. 3.17. The audience can be defined by their degree of interest in the subject, how much they already know about it, their reading ability, and their general intelligence.

As an example of subject and assumed knowledge to increase comprehension, in several detective novels, Agatha Christie introduces a preamble with the main characters of the novel. Let us consider *The Mysterious Affair at Styles*; see Fig. 3.18. This is an example of knowledge that the reader will use as a priori knowledge to improve the comprehension of the text, resulting in an increase of comprehensibility.

Characters in "The Mysterious Affair at Styles"
Captain Hastings, the narrator, on sick leave from the Western Front.
Hercule Poirot, a famous Belgian detective exiled in England; Hastings' old friend
Chief Inspector Japp of Scotland Yard
Emily Inglethorp, mistress of Styles, a wealthy old woman
Alfred Inglethorp, her much younger new husband
John Cavendish, her elder stepson
Mary Cavendish, John's wife
Lawrence Cavendish, John's younger brother
Evelyn Howard, Mrs. Inglethorp's companion
Cynthia Murdoch, the beautiful, orphaned daughter of a friend of the family
Dr. Bauerstein, a suspicious toxicologist

Fig. 3.18 Example of comprehensibility

Finally, two kinds of measure are suited to appraising text structure: logical coherence and propositional density. *Logical coherence* is the extent to which one statement is ordered according to a chain of reasonings, a sequence or chain of events, a hierarchy, or a classificatory system. *Propositional density* is closeness, measured by intervening words, between one crucial idea and the next.

3.4.3   Consistency Cluster

The consistency cluster is discussed with reference to cohesion and coherence that will initially be introduced in general and subsequently separately in the section.

3.4.3.1   Cohesion and Coherence

Recent contributions in the literature show how text comprehension is intrinsically related with the other two dimensions that we discuss in this section, cohesion and coherence. Contributions appearing in [275, 434], and [273] testify an impressive path for enhancing the investigation on models and tools for discourse comprehension, underlying the evolution from the text item to the more complex discourse concept. The definition of discourse in the above papers includes both oral conversation and printed text. The utterances in oral conversation and the sentences in printed text are composed by the speaker-writer with the intention of communicating interesting and informative messages to the listener-reader. Since there are times when discourse communication breaks down, a model of discourse comprehension should handle instances when there are communication breakdowns in addition to successful comprehension.

Multiple levels of comprehension have been identified by numerous researchers over the years. The taxonomy proposed in [273] includes five levels, detailed in Fig. 3.19, namely, the surface code; the explicit text base; the situation model, also called the mental model; the discourse genre and rhetorical structure (the type of

Surface code
        Word composition (graphemes, phonemes, syllables, morphemes, lemmas, tense, aspect)
        Words (lexical items)
        Part of speech categories (noun, verb, adjective, adverb, determiner, connective)
        Syntactic composition (noun-phrase, verb-phrase, prepositional phrases, clause)
        Linguistic style and dialect
Textbase
        Explicit propositions
        Referents linked to referring expressions
        Connectives that explicitly link clauses
        Constituents in the discourse focus versus linguistic presuppositions
Situation model
        Agents, objects, and abstract entities
        Dimensions of temporality, spatiality, causality, intentionality
        Inferences that bridge and elaborate ideas
        Given versus new information
        Images and mental simulations of events
        Mental models of the situation
Genre and rhetorical structure
        Discourse category (narrative, persuasive, expository, descriptive)
        Rhetorical composition (plot structure, claim + evidence, problem + solution, etc.)
        Epistemological status of propositions and clauses (claim, evidence, warrant, hypothesis)
        Speech act categories (assertion, question, command, promise, indirect request, greeting, expressive
        evaluation)
        Theme, moral, or point of discourse
Pragmatic communication
        Goals of speaker / writer and listener / reader
        Attitudes (humor, sarcasm, eulogy, deprecation)
        Requests for clarification and backchannel feedback (spoken only)

Fig. 3.19   Levels of discourse in [273]

discourse and its composition); and the pragmatic communication level between speaker and listener or writer and reader. The *surface code* preserves the exact wording and syntax of clauses. The *text base* contains explicit propositions that preserve the meaning, but not the exact wording and syntax. The *situation model* is the content or microworld that the text is about. The situation model for an expository text refers to the reader's prior knowledge about the text's subject matter. The text genre is the category of text, such as a technical scientific text versus a mystery novel. The *rhetorical structure* is the use of language that brings forth a literary effect. *Pragmatics* is the way in which context contributes to meaning. Figure 3.19 elaborates on these five levels by identifying the codes, constituents, and content associated with each level. Comprehension can misfire at any of the five levels depicted in Fig. 3.19. The cause of the misfire may be attributed to either deficits in the reader (i.e., lack of knowledge or processing skill) or the discourse (e.g., incoherent text, unintelligible speech). The consequence of a misfire can range from a complete breakdown in comprehension to a modest irregularity that captures the comprehender's attention.

Readability, comprehensibility , and cultural accessibility are all related to the problem of measuring the difficulty of a text; although being properties of the whole text, they lack the ability to capture focus on relationship among words and concepts in different sentences, properties that are instead captured by text cohesion and coherence.

A distinction is made between cohesion and coherence in [274]. Cohesion consists of characteristics of the explicit text that play some role in helping the reader mentally connect ideas in the text. Coherence is a cognitive representation that reflects the interaction between linguistic discourse characteristics and world knowledge.

When the focus is on the text as an object of investigation, coherence can be defined as characteristics of the text (i.e., aspects of cohesion) that are likely to contribute to the coherence of the mental representation.

Both cohesion and coherence represent how words and concepts conveyed in a text are connected on particular levels of language, discourse, and world knowledge. Cohesion is considered an *objective* property of the explicit language and text and is achieved by means of explicit linguistic resources that allow to express connections (relations) between words, sentences, etc. These cohesive resources give hint to the reader on how to form a unitary representation of concepts expressed by the text.

Coherence results from an interaction between text cohesion and the reader. The coherence relations are constructed in the mind of the reader and depend on the skills and knowledge that the reader brings to the situation. Coherence is considered a characteristic of the reader's mental representation and as such is considered *subjective*. A particular level of cohesion may lead to a coherent mental representation from one reader but an incoherent representation for another.

The literature (see [275]) distinguishes various kinds of cohesion and coherence. One common distinction is between local and global levels. Both cohesion and coherence are locally and globally structured. The reader finds local cohesion relations between adjacent clauses in the text and global cohesion links between groups of clauses and groups of paragraphs. Moreover, the following conceptual categories of cohesion and coherence can be distinguished: lexical, referential, temporal, locational, causal, and structural.

After this general introduction on cohesion and coherence together, we focus now on each one of the two dimensions.

3.4.3.2 Cohesion

Cohesion is defined in [291] as "the use of certain linguistic devices to link or tie together textual units." More specifically, *lexical cohesion* among two units of discourse is the use of lexical relations between words in the two units, such as identical word (reiteration), synonymy, hypernymy, and conjunction. Examples (from [291]) are:

1. Before winter **I** built a chimney, and **shingled** the sides of my **house**. **I** thus have a tight **shingled** and plastered **house**.
2. Peel, core and slice **the pears and the apples**. Add **the fruit** to the skillet.

Nonlexical cohesion corresponds to the use of nonlexical relations such as anaphora, i.e., the use of a linguistic unit, such as a pronoun, to refer to the same person or object as another unit, usually a noun. An example is the use of "his or her" to refer to Anne in the sentence: Anne asked Edward the salt; Edward passed the salt to his or her (example from [667]).

As to *referential cohesion*, a first metric for referential cohesion is *local coreference*, which occurs when a noun, pronoun, or a noun phrase refers to another constituent in the text. A simple measure of local coreference cohesion is the proportion of adjacent sentence pairs in the text that share a common noun argument:

$$\text{Local coreference cohesion} = \frac{\Sigma_{i=1}^{n-1} R_{i,i+1}}{n-1},$$

where $R_{i,i+1}$ is equal to 1 if adjacent sentences i and $i+1$ share a common noun argument, 0 otherwise. *Global coreference* includes all possible pairs of sentences where coreferential cohesion is computed. The metric is the proportion of pairs that have a coreferential connection:

$$\text{Global coreference cohesion} = \frac{\Sigma_{i-1}^{n} \Sigma_{j-1}^{n} R_{ij} : i < j}{nx\frac{n-1}{2}},$$

where R_{ij} refers to sentences i and j and has the same definition as the R before.

3.4.3.3 Coherence

Coherence is especially relevant to the research on text comprehension: authors should design a text in such a way that the addressee may detect the relationships linking individual text constituents and thus may build a coherent mental model of the text's content.

Text coherence can be reconstructed using a set of coherence relations, which relate the semantic constituents of a text to one another. The type of the relation can be made explicit, by means of connectives, e.g., the sentence "as she is sick, Laure stays home." Alternatively, the relation remains implicit and thus has to be inferred, via context clues and background knowledge, by the reader, e.g., the sentence "Jennifer is sick. She stays home." To reconstruct the relation between individual constituents, such inference may be based on quite a complex frame and script knowledge, e.g., the sentence "Barbara was invited to Carlo's birthday party. She wondered if he would like a kite. She went to her room and shook her piggy bank. It made no sound."

Since many coherence relations remain implicit and must be interpreted by the reader, one cannot determine the coherence structure of a text in a straightforward fashion. There are two main perspectives:

1. From the perspective of discourse production, coherence is a property of the mental representation of the content that the text composition is to convey. This property may be reconstructed as the author's coherence structure. This structure determines the author's strategies for composing the text and is reflected in the surface text by means of coherence cues.

2. From the perspective of discourse comprehension, coherence is a property of the mental representation that is built while reading the text. The coherence cues support in this case the text recipient in building a coherent, mental model of the text content. This property may be reconstructed as the reader's coherence structure.

3.4.3.4   The Coh-Metrix Tool

Coh-Metrix is a tool developed to analyze and measure text on levels one through four. The original purpose of the Coh-Metrix project was to concentrate on the cohesion of the text base and on discourse coherence.

The theoretical vision behind Coh-Metrix is to use the tool to:

1. Assess the overall cohesion and language difficulty of discourse on multiple levels
2. Investigate the constraints of discourse within levels and between levels
3. Test models of multilevel discourse comprehension

Coh-Metrix [275] represents an advance on conventional readability measures because it reports on detailed language and cohesion features. The system integrates semantic lexicons, pattern classifiers, part-of-speech taggers, syntactic parsers, shallow semantic interpreters, and other components that have been developed in the field of computational linguistics. This integration allows for the examination of deeper-level linguistic features of text that are related to text processing and reading comprehension.

The Coh-Metrix measures (i.e., indexes, metrics) cover many of the components in Fig. 3.19; we mention some of them related to surface code. As to word measures, Coh-Metrix computes scores for word frequency, ambiguity, abstractness, and parts of speech. For example, the ambiguity and abstractness of content words (e.g., nouns, main verbs, adjectives) are measured by calculating the values of polysemy and hypernymy with WordNet [227]. Polysemy refers to the number of senses that a word has; ambiguous words have more senses. Hypernymy refers to the number of levels deep a word appears in a conceptual, taxonomic hierarchy. A low score means the word tends to be comparatively superordinate in the hierarchy and is therefore more abstract.

With reference to syntax, Coh-Metrix has several indexes of syntactic complexity, among them:

• Modifiers per noun phrase: the mean number of modifiers per noun phrase is an index of the complexity of referencing expressions.
• Words before the main verb of the main clause: the number of words before the main verb of the main clause is an index of syntactic complexity because it places a burden on the working memory of the comprehender.

3.4.4 Other Issues Investigated in the Area of Text Comprehension

Several other issues are investigated in the literature on text comprehension. They are discussed in the following.

- Effects of poor knowledge and reading skill on comprehension—[487] explores the relative contribution of reading skill and prior knowledge to comprehension irrespective of text cohesion. There is ample evidence showing that prior knowledge has a large influence on expository text comprehension. Ozuru et al. [487] extend these findings by exploring whether, and how, the relative contribution of prior knowledge changes depending on the level of comprehension. Two levels of comprehension are considered, namely, (a) closer-to-text base and (b) closer-to-situation model. Closer-to-text base comprehension can be operationally defined as performance on comprehension questions that require minimal information integration (i.e., information explicitly stated within a sentence). On the other hand, closer-to-situation model level comprehension is defined by performance on comprehension questions that require more extensive information integration (i.e., bridging that involves integration of information across two or more sentences). Changes to the relative contribution of prior knowledge to text comprehension as a function of different types of comprehension questions are investigated in the paper.
- Text comprehension for English as the second language—Several studies have investigated the issue of text comprehension and text difficulty for second language (L2) learners. Also in this case, the most investigated language is English. Crossley et al. [157] investigate this problem for Japanese readers; experiments show that Coh-Metrix formulas yield a more accurate prediction of reading difficulty than did other traditional readability measures. The use of a cognitively based readability formula that is better suited to predict the readability of L2 texts could provide classroom teachers with a valuable resource for analyzing and selecting appropriate text for L2 learners.
- Text comprehension in specific domains—With reference to the health domain, [194] investigates a corpus-driven method for building a lexicon of semantically equivalent pairs of technical and lay medical terms. Such lexicon can be used in the context of a text-to-text generation system, where a technical text is edited to be more comprehensible to a lay reader. The key points of the approach are (a) the use of combined measures of association to identify pairs of semantically equivalent terms and (b) a knowledge-based heuristic that acts as a powerful filter for identifying semantically equivalent pairs.
- Text comprehension in languages different from English—An example of text comprehension investigation performed in a language different from English, namely, Portuguese, appears in [18]. A number of features of Coh-Metrix are adapted to Portuguese (called Coh-Metrix-PORT), along with a set of new features, including syntactic features to capture simplification operations and

```
Cognitively motivated features – basic
    Number of words
    Number of sentences
    Number of paragraphs
    Average number of words per sentence
    Average number of sentences per paragraph
    Average number of syllabes per word
Cognitively motivated features – complex
    Incidence of functional words
    Average number or verbs hyperonyms
    Number of person pronouns
    Number of negations
    Number of connectives
    Verb ambiguity ratio
    Nouns ambiguity ratio
Syntactic constructions considered in the text wimplification system
    Incidence of caluses
    Incidence of subordination
Features derived form n-gram language models (LM) plus out-of-vocabulary rate scores
    LM probability of unigrams
    LM probability of bibrams
    LM probability of trigrams
    Out-of-vocabulary words
```

Fig. 3.20 Feature set in [18]

n-gram language model features, where n-grams are the groups of n words used in a vast corpus of reference written documents.

The feature set adopted (see Fig. 3.20) consists of four groups of features. The first group contains cognitively motivated features; it is divided into a set of basic features, which consist of simple counts that do not require any linguistic tool or external resources to be computed, and a set of more complex features. The second group contains features that reflect the incidence of particular syntactic constructions which are targeted in the text simplification system. The third group contains features derived from n-gram language models built considering unigrams, bigrams, and trigrams probability plus out-of-vocabulary rate scores.

3.4.5 Accessibility Cluster

The notion of complex words, adopted in readability metrics, introduces a link to the notion of difficult words. While complex words are evaluated on the basis of shallow syntax (number of syllables), difficult words are related to the understanding of the word meaning by the reader. The notion of difficult word is then related to the dimension of linguistic (or cultural) accessibility of a text.

The more a text makes use of nondifficult words, the more it is linguistically accessible. Of course, the notion of difficult word is user (and then context) dependent. A possible measure of linguistic/cultural accessibility of a text is the proportion of difficult words with respect to total words in the text, where difficult may be defined as not included in a basic vocabulary.

Cultural accessibility concerns the diffusion among the users of the skills and capabilities required for an understanding of the text; so it can be measured with several metrics:

- In case of message written in a single language, a possible metrics is the percentage of words whose meanings can be understood by an average user. The percentage can be evaluated, e.g., checking how many words appear in a vocabulary that is assumed as understood by all people that achieved a certain instruction degree, such as a mandatory instruction degree. As an example, in Italy, a list of 5000 words has been constructed that are understood by those people that achieved the Italian mandatory instruction degree, corresponding to the tenth year of instruction.
- In case the message is written in a multiplicity of languages, a possible metrics is the percentage of the world population that it is assumed to speak natively at least one language in the list.

One of the authors of this book experienced the writing of an educational book whose topics were an introduction to most relevant issues in theoretical computer science. The author was committed to use only the 5000 words mentioned above. Every other term introduced in the book had to be defined in terms of the 5000 words, plus other defined terms. The initial draft version of the book started with the sentence "Everyone of us makes use daily of lot of different types of information"; such sentence was corrected as "Almost every day everyone of us makes use of lot of different types of information," since the word "daily" was not included in the basic vocabulary.

3.4.6 Text Quality in Administrative Documents

This section can be considered as a sidetrack between the part of the chapter on semistructured texts and the subsequent section on quality of law texts. We deal here with the quality of administrative documents such as letters sent by a public administration to citizens and businesses. More specifically, we focus on letters sent by a tax department to taxpayers, documents that can be considered less stringent than law texts from the point of view of accuracy, unambiguity, etc., but being administrative documents, they are to be written with care. Renkema [522] investigates the above domain, discussing a case study of the Dutch Tax Department. A model is proposed to be used to evaluate text quality. The model, shown in Fig. 3.21, is based on three quality categories called correspondence, consistency, and correctness, thus being called the CCC model.

Correspondence is the quality that is achieved when the text of the letter fits the goal of the sender. In this meaning, correspondence is very much similar to effectiveness, so it is a category that was not considered in Fig. 3.11, showing dimensions for semistructured texts. The reason for this is that letters are a very specific type of semistructured texts; they can be better considered as informative services to users,

	Correspondence	Consistency	Correctness
A. Text type	a. Appropriateness	2. Purity of genre	3. Application of genre rules
B. Content	4. Sufficient information	5. Agreement between facts	6. Correctness of facts
C. Structure	7. Sufficient coherence	8. Consistent structure	9. Correct linking words
D. Wording	10. Appropriate wording	11. Unity of style	12. Correct syntax and choice of words
E. Presentation	13. Appropriate lay-out	14. Layout adapted to text	15 Correct spelling and punctuation

Fig. 3.21 Quality dimensions considered in the CCC model

and, in this respect, effectiveness is indeed the most important quality when we consider such kind of services (see [631] for a detailed discussion on this point). Consistency and correctness have been previously examined in this section with reference to the consistency and accuracy clusters. As to their subdimensions, we refer the reader to [522] for a detailed discussion; here, we observe that a lot of attention in their choice is given to issues related to communication. In particular, [522] underlines that a motto of the Dutch Tax Department is "We can't make it more fun, but we can make it easier."

3.5   Information Quality in Law Texts

A law is a system of rules, enforced through a set of institutions, used as an instrument to underpin civil obedience, politics, economics, and society.

Laws can be enacted by legislative bodies that may govern the policies and behaviors of citizens, public administrations, and companies operating at national or subnational (e.g., municipalities, districts, states in the United States, regions, etc.) levels or operating at the level of groups of countries linked by some form of federation or association, such as the European Union. A law is typically organized in articles, which are in turn organized in commas (or paragraphs).

When we refer to the concept of quality of a law, we can refer to two very different meanings:

1. The effectiveness of the law, seen as a set of norms aiming to change the organization and rules of behavior in some aspect of a society, at the national, subnational, or federated level
2. The quality of the text expressing the law

Notice that the two above meanings are interrelated; as an example, a law that is expressed by means of ambiguous sentences can be interpreted in different ways, resulting in potential corruption or abuse of power, withdrawing in such a way its effectiveness. To deepen this point, see in Fig. 3.22 the five golden rules that are proposed in [513] to express the quality of law texts. Rule 1 refers to the text expressing the law. Rule 2 is related to the effectiveness of the law. Rule 3 addresses

1. **It is simply stated, succinct, and has a clear meaning** - It is imperative that those who enforce and interpret the law, and those who are subject to the law, are able to understand both the letter and the intent of the law.
2. **It is completely successful in achieving its objective** - Every law in a democracy has a problem-solving purpose, or objective, that serves the best interests of the people and reflects their highest aspirations. The ideal law is completely successful in attaining its objective.
3. **It interacts synergistically with other laws** - Laws often have an effect upon, and are affected by, other laws. The ideal law is designed so that its interaction with other laws is synergistic in the attainment of its problem-solving objective.
4. **It produces no harmful side effects** - All human-made products, including laws, have unintended side effects that may be beneficial, neutral, or detrimental. A law that accomplishes its problem-solving goal is not acceptable if its unintended side effects degrade the established living standards or quality of life of the people, or infringe upon human rights. Therefore, the ideal law produces no detrimental side effects upon the human rights, living standards, or quality of life of the people.
5. **It imposes the least possible burdens on the people** - The ideal law imposes the least possible costs and other burdens upon the people so that the maximum positive net benefit of its enforcement is attained. It is cost-efficient, safe, non-intrusive, and user friendly.

Fig. 3.22 Five golden rules for expressing the qualiy of law texts

both the quality of the law text and the law objectives, since the interactions among different law texts referring to a same matter depend both on how the text connects the law texts (see later the reference accuracy dimension) and the general semantic architecture of the law texts. Rules 4 and 5 address the first meaning introduced for quality of law, i.e., effectiveness again.

In the following, we are interested to discuss the second meaning, considering the law text as a specific type of text. In this respect, quality dimensions can be referred to three different contexts: (a) a single law, (b) a legal framework ruling a single country, and (c) a legal framework ruling a group of countries characterized by some form of political union or federation. Quality dimensions discussed in the following have a different relevance in such three contexts, as shown in Fig. 3.23.

As a general introduction to the discussion on dimensions, several countries have addressed the issue of quality of law texts through the identification of a list of drafting rules to be adopted in the process of law formation. We will now investigate the most relevant quality dimensions for law texts providing a definition and several drafting rules related to such dimensions. The examples in Fig. 3.24 are taken from [559]. See also [680] for European Union rules for legislative drafting.

Several tools have been proposed to guide a legislative drafter in planning a new bill. Biagioli et al. [72] present a model-driven tool that aims at helping the legislative drafter to build a new act starting from a conceptual model of the act. Using this module, the classical drafting process is inverted: the structure of a bill is constructed on the basis of its semantics. Gostojić et al. [272] present a formal model of legal norms modeled in OWL. It is intended for semiautomatic drafting and semantic retrieval and browsing of legislation. Gostojić et al. [272] observe that most existing solutions model legal norms using formal logic, rules,

Cluster	Quality dimension	Single law	Legal framework of a single country	Legal framework of a set of federated countries
Accuracy	Referential accuracy	Not relevant	x	x
Redundancy	Conciseness	Not relevant	x	x
Readability	Clarity Simplicity Unambiguity	x x x	x x x	x x x
Accessibility	Cultural accessibility	x	x	x
Consistency	Coherence Unambiguity	Not relevant x	x	x
Global quality index		x	Not defined	Not defined

Fig. 3.23 Quality dimensions of law texts and contexts in which they are relevant

Quality dimension	Example of rule
(reference) Accuracy	First version: Article 1 –This law repeals all previous laws on tax fraud Second version: Article 1 –This law repeals Law 122/2005 in the aspects related to tax fraud Third version: Article 1 –This law repeals Law 122/2005, whole Art. 1 and Art. 7, paragraphs 1 and 3
Unambiguity	- Do not use "and/or". Use "or" to mean any one or more. - Use "the" if the reference is unambiguous. Otherwise, use "this", "that", "these" or "those".
Conciseness	- Omit needless language. If a word has the same meaning as a phrase, use the word. - Use the shortest sentence that conveys the intended meaning - Administrative bodies should not use the phrase "in substantially the following form" or "substantially as follows", since the meaning of "substantially" is ambiguous.
Clarity	- ($\rightarrow$) from pertinence) A statement of purpose or occasional example may, however, be helpful to users, including courts interpreting the act. - A suggested order of arrangement of a bill is: a. Short title. b. Preamble; findings; purpose. c. Definitions. d. Scope, exceptions, and exclusions, if any. e. Creation of an agency or office. f. Administration and procedural provisions. g. Substance (state positive requirements in order of time, importance, or other logical sequence). h. Prohibitions and penalties. i. Repeals. j. Saving and transitional provisions to existing relationships, if any. k. Effective dates.
Simplicity	- Select short, familiar words and phrases that best express the intended meaning according to common and approved usage. The language should be dignified, not pompous. Examples: Use "after", instead of "subsequent to"; use "before" instead of "prior to".
Cohesion & Coherence	- Do not use both a word and its synonym. - Be consistent in the use of language throughout the bill. Do not use the same word or phrase to convey different meanings. Do not use different language to convey the same meaning

Fig. 3.24 The most popular quality of law text dimensions and related examples of drafting rules

or ontologies. Nevertheless, they were not intended as a basis for drafting, retrieval, and browsing of legislation. The proposed model formally defines legal norms using their elements and elements of legal relations they regulate.

We now consider each of the dimensions of Fig. 3.23.

3.5.1 Accuracy Cluster

In this section, we discuss two dimensions, accuracy and unambiguity.

3.5.1.1 Accuracy

Accuracy is important in its general sense in all types of texts and documents, but its enforcement is particularly relevant in law texts, which discipline the life of persons, organizations, and companies. A particular type of accuracy is reference accuracy, especially relevant in the context of a country legal framework. Every law disciplines specific issues of the life of a country, such as fiscal system, pollution and environment, and family duties. In all countries in the world, it happens that a new law suppresses, extends, or modifies one or more articles of one or more previous law texts. The syntactic structures (or reference mechanisms) chosen to express such changes strongly influence the accuracy of the law. *Reference accuracy* is the quality dimension that addresses this issue; we see in Fig. 3.25 three different sentences with increasing levels of reference accuracy. The sentence "This law repeals (cancels) all previous laws on tax fraud" is an example of implicit reference: if we want to understand which corpus of rules have to be suppressed, we have to investigate in a legal framework all the previous law texts that in part or on the whole address tax fraud, together with their implicit or explicit references. The improvement related to the second sentence "This law repeals Law 320/2005 in the aspects related to tax fraud" is in the fact that now the field of investigation is restricted to only one law. The third sentence "This law repeals Law 320/2005, whole Art 1 and Art 7, paragraphs 1 and 3" precisely identifies the articles in law texts and their parts that are no longer valid.

Notice that the above examples could also be associated with two other quality dimensions that we will discuss later, clarity and unambiguity. This confirms that the different dimensions are deeply related to each other, as we will also see in Sect. 3.5.6 on the Global Quality Index.

Fig. 3.25 Sentences in law texts with different levels of referential accuracy

First version
Article 1 – This law repeals (cancels) all previuos laws on tax fraud.

Second version
Article 1 – This law repeals Law 320/2005 in the aspects related to tax fraud.

Third version
Article 1 - This law repeals Law 320/2005, whole Art. 1 and Art 7, commas 1 and 3.

3.5.1.2 Unambiguity

Unambiguity is a form of accuracy; the more a set of norms is ambiguous, the more the certainty and the accuracy of the *Diritto* (Italian term for the entirety) are lost. In [483], it is noticed that

> regulatory requirements should be unambiguous; the potential for differing interpretation by regulatory officials and adjudicators should be minimised. Compliance with the rules should be discernible by observation of actions or conditions that are visible or that can be objectively established and that can be conclusively proved under applicable rules of evidence in legal proceedings. Information necessary to determine compliance should be available at minimal cost to enforcement authorities and regulated entities.

As another example, words with generic meaning should be avoided in law texts and rules. As an example, in [559], referring to rules enacted by municipalities, it is said that municipalities should not use the phrase "in substantially the following form" or "substantially as follows," since the meaning of "substantially" is ambiguous. This phrase may mean that no amendments of "substance" are allowed or that no "important" amendments are allowed.

With reference to member states of the European Union, [680] states that, at the date of study was published, unambiguity was required from Belgian, German, Italian, Portuguese, Spanish, and UK drafters.

Finally, [310, 337, 349] discuss the relationship between corruption and the quality of the legislation, seen according to its effectiveness and nonambiguity. In particular, [349] argues that there is a strong correlation between corruption and discretionary power, and more discretion for officials "...leads to a higher effective burden on business, more corruption, and a greater incentive to move to the unofficial economy."

3.5.2   Redundancy Cluster

Conciseness concerns single law texts referring to the number of words and sentences that are used to express the essence of the law. Conciseness is related to the lexicon of the natural language used to express the law; the more the language has specialized terms to express technical issues, the more the use of anaphoras can be avoided, and the law is concise. At the same time, the large use of technical terms creates a trade-off with clarity and simplicity. Conciseness refers also to legal frameworks; it has been estimated that the total number of national laws in Italy is at least one order of magnitude than the total number of national laws in France and Germany. Such form of conciseness can be improved with so-called testi unici that can be considered law texts that integrate laws enacted in a time period on the same matter into a single text. As an example, in Italy, every year a new fiscal law is enacted that changes some aspect of the fiscal duties of citizens and businesses.

3.5.3   Readability Cluster

Clarity and simplicity are particular types of readability. The examples in Fig. 3.24 allow us to understand the difference. Clarity is a global property of the law text; its goal is to give an order to the sentences expressing the law that may aid the reader to understand without further investigation the consequentiality among sentences and the core vision and aims of the ruler as expressed in the law text. Simplicity is a more granular quality and corresponds to use of a plain language both in words and in sentences.

Clarity is addressed in [21], where the role of verification of legal knowledge in improving the quality of legal decision making is analyzed and a knowledge-based environment is proposed that helps the ruler to find out semantic anomalies in the legislation. Semantic anomalies can occur if the rules used in the legislation or regulations lack clarity. Detected anomalies are reported to legislators. They can repair the anomalies in the legislation before the law is enforced. Thus, not only the quality of the legislation is improved but also its enforcement is also facilitated.

In [620], the process of translation from legal texts to a knowledge base is specified in terms of two steps, namely, (a) translation and (b) integration. During the translation step, the hierarchical structure of legislation is analyzed. This view of legislation contains sufficient detail for detecting structural defects that can be reported as focus points. Then, concept extraction (supported by a natural language parser) is used to identify the concepts used in each chapter, article, and section that are consequently put into a conceptual model. Finally, the norms within each block are described by a conceptual schema that represents the unique interpretation of a single article of legislation.

Integration results in combining the articles that use identical concepts to create an integrated conceptual schema. During this process, synonyms (different words, same meaning) are resolved as identical concepts, and homonyms (same word, different meanings) are distinguished as separate concepts. The structure of exceptions and extensions to the general rule is unraveled for each concept. At this point, the final conceptual model is produced.

3.5.4   Accessibility Cluster

We have seen in the discussion on referential accuracy that usually in legal frameworks, each law contains several references to other laws. The whole legislative corpus can be seen as a network, each law being a node linking toward (and linked by) several other nodes through natural language expressions. Manual activity is usually required in order to build the hypertext of a distributed legislative corpus. *Legal framework accessibility* is the property that holds when the set of law texts is organized so to allow citizens and businesses to friendly navigate in the network, in such a way to be able to know which is the norm in force on a given matter of their interest. Since law texts are usually represented in several document bases of the different institutions and public administrations in a country, the access and navigation mechanisms should be independent from the specific document base where the law is managed and stored. Therefore, also the term *interoperability* is used for this quality dimension.

In [71, 418, 419], an architecture is presented that offers a cooperative information service to citizens and businesses providing unified access to Italian and European Union legislation published on different institutional Web sites. The system is built upon a cooperative technological architecture, resulting in a federation of legislative databases developed with different platforms. Cooperation is achieved by means of suitable application gateways that provide "loose" integration by adopting two standards to identify the resources and to represent document structure and metadata by XML markup according to ad hoc DTDs. The adoption of these standards allows for automatic dynamic hyperlinking among law texts and semiautomatic building of legislation in force.

The architecture of the system (named with the acronym NIR, from the Italian "Norme in Rete" or Network of Norms) is shown in Fig. 3.26.

Other contributions to accessibility can be found in [9] where an OWL model of normative provisions is proposed and an example is shown of how this approach enables inference for supporting norms accessibility and reasoning. The approach is applied in a European Union Directive case study.

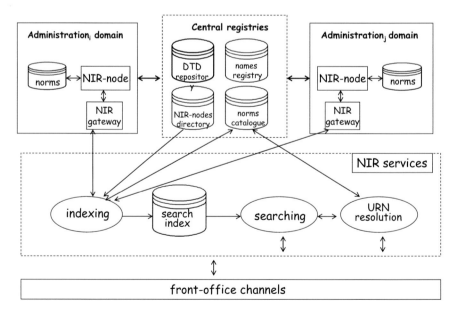

Fig. 3.26 Cooperative architecture of the NIR system

3.5.5 Consistency Cluster

A weak form of consistency and coherence holds for single law texts; consistency is achieved when the different articles and paragraphs are not contradictory (although this is a very rare case); for coherence , we refer to local coherence as discussed in Sect. 3.4.3. Consistency and coherence are more interesting in the case of country legal frameworks, both in case of laws enacted at different times on the same topics and in case of laws enacted by different authorities, as happens, e.g., in Italy when both the National Parliament and regions rule a same matter; in this case, the norms can be contradictory (lack of consistency) or else can be characterized by compatible but nonconsequential norms (lack of coherence). The same arguments apply to legal frameworks of federated countries.

The issue of coherence has been investigated in [542], which analyzes the multilingual language policy adopted in the European Union that establishes that:

- Regulations and official documents should be drafted in all official languages of the member states.
- All linguistic versions are to be considered original, thus implying a perfect equivalence between them, at least from the legal point of view.

Such rules are claimed to be in contrast with the principle of noncoincidence of any two linguistic systems. The awareness of such contrasting principles has given rise to a lively debate as to the possibility of a "perfect" translation of any legal text. The aim of [542] is not to argue for or against this possibility, but rather to analyze the methods, mechanisms, and criteria adopted by the translator in order to compare translational problems and to produce a text that is equivalent to the original source. In particular, a framework for interlinguistic translation has been introduced that allows analyzing two linguistic versions of a law according to (a) the criteria of differentiation, (b) the levels of equivalence, (c) the levels of difference, and (d) the value of differentiation.

We omit the first three aspects and focus on the value of the differentiation. Differences between the linguistic versions can be grouped according to the following categories:

- Specificity that can be of time, space, object, goal, domain, or language
- Emphasis that can be on the process (i.e., on the dynamic aspect of the action described), on the product (i.e., on the outcome of the action described), or on the agent (i.e., in relation to the use of a passive form)
- The linguistic quality of versions that can vary according to their different levels of accuracy/clarity (vs. vagueness), formality/rhetorical care (vs. informality), and figurativeness (vs. directness)

3.5.6   Global Quality Index

We conclude this section discussing a quality index, corresponding to an aggregated quality dimension. The Working Group of the Regional Council of Tuscany, a region in Italy (flanked by the Italian Interregional Law Observatory), has proposed an Index of Legislative Quality (see [148, 484]), where 100 % corresponds to maximum quality and 0 % corresponds to minimum quality. The quality evaluated by the index is intended as a measure of "how well the legislative text complies to the legislative drafting rules." Such rules for their technical nature can be applied directly by the regional legislative offices with no need for further interpretation. These rules regard the syntactic and structure-related level of the text, e.g., formatting constraints, naming and referencing conventions, and domain-specific expressions and terms. The Working Group identified 21 rules extracted from the 93 items contained in the "Rules and Suggestions for Legislative Drafting" and denoted them as "quality factors." Assumptions on the quality factors are as follows:

1. They are interdependent.
2. They have equal intrinsic relevance.
3. The more frequently the rule is applied properly (within the whole reference body of law texts), the higher is the factor's contribution to the overall quality of the single law; factors can be weighted according to the frequency of proper compliance of the corresponding rule.
4. Weights (W_i) go from 5 (very relevant) to 1 (not relevant). Therefore, these weights are relative to a specific time period, territorial level (a region), and legislative scope.

In Fig. 3.27, we list the factors together with synthetic definitions.

There is a many-to-many correspondence among factors and quality dimension clusters introduced at the beginning of this chapter; we show the correspondence in Fig. 3.28.

The evaluation of the Index proceeds as follows. For each law, it is calculated:

- A Qualitative Standard (QS) = $\Sigma\ W_i$ with i such that the rule R_i is properly applied within the law.
- A Qualitative profile (QP) = $QS - \Sigma\ W_i$ with i such that the R_i rule is not (properly) applied within the law.
- A Quality Index (QI) = QP/QS.
- An Improvement Index (II) $= 1 - QI$.

The Quality Index can be used to identify law texts and sections of law texts to be syntactically amended/replaced. Other indicators, such as indicators discussed in Sect. 3.4.2, can be used to identify law texts and sections to be made more readable.

3.5 Information Quality in Law Texts

Factor ID	Quality factor (scope of the rule)
R1	Use of Abbreviations (as few abbreviations as possible, capita letters, extended expression in glossary)
R2	Number formatting (latin figures, except for measures and percentages)
R3	Date formatting (dd month yyyy hour)
R4	Partition referencing (compliancy to the section hierarchy)
R5	Conventions on units of measurements (written in full, ISO standard)
R6	Act referencing (descending order, full absolute references)
R7	Reference and quotation drafting
R8	Excpetions to rule quotation
R9	Act partitioning
R10	Act partitioning: Sectioning
R11	Act partitioning: Numbering (Latin figures, i.e., letters)
R12	Item drafting
R13	Item numbering
R14	Paragraph drafting and numbering (Arabic figures, no line returns)
R15	Paragraph partitioning
R16	Reference to items or paragraphs
R17	Drafting of modification rules
R18	Numbering of additional items
R19	Numbering of additional paragraphs
R20	Additional letters and numbers (paragraph partitions)
R21	Expression of the definitive rule repeal

Fig. 3.27 Quality factors considered in the evaluation of the global quality index

Quality factor / Qdim Cluster	R1	R2	R3	R4	R5	R6	R7	R8	R9	R10	R11	R12	R13	R14	R15	R16	R17	R18	R19	R20	R21
1. Correctness, Accuracy, Precision		x	x		x	x	x	x		x			x	x	x	x		x	x	x	x
2: Completeness, Pertinence			x	x		x	x	x									x				
3: Minimality Redundancy, Compactness				x		x	x			x			x	x	x	x		x	x	x	
4: Consistency, Coherence, Compliance	x	x	x	x	x	x	x	x	x	x	x	x	x	x	x	x	x	x	x	x	x
5: Readability, Comprehensibility, Usability	x			x	x		x	x	x	x	x	x	x	x	x	x	x	x	x	x	x
6: Accessibility			x	x		x		x	x	x	x	x	x	x				x	x	x	x

Fig. 3.28 Quality factors and their relationship with quality dimensions

3.6 Summary

The concept of data and information evolves from structured data typical of relational databases to semistructured data, unstructured data, images, sounds, and maps, resulting in a continuous change of the concept of information quality. In this chapter, we have considered a variety of dimensions and metrics that characterize the concept of information quality, specialized to the cases of maps, semistructured texts in general and in the specific case of law texts.

We have seen that when we move from structured data to other types of information, the clusters of dimensions and the higher level of dimensions' definitions represent an invariant among the types of information. At the same time, for each type of information, depending on its nature, dimensions can be specialized accordingly. We have observed a similar phenomenon also in Chap. 2, e.g., in the case of completeness, where we have introduced several types of completeness for the different information structures in the relational model, such as tuple, attribute, and relation. As to maps, due to their nature of modeling a bidimensional or tridimensional space, we have defined different types of accuracy that are associated to the different space coordinates such as horizontal or vertical. Similarly, also metrics are tailored to the characteristics of the type of dimensions.

We have also seen that the relevance of dimensions for a specific type of information depends on the use of such type. For written semistructured texts that are used by human beings for communication purposes, most relevant dimensions refer to the readability cluster and the consistency cluster. Furthermore, while in databases data are represented at two different levels, the schema and the values and, consequently, different groups of dimensions have to be conceived; for other types of information, this distinction fades.

It is not surprising that there are many dimensions, since information aims to represent all kinds of spatial, temporal, and social phenomena of the real world. As long as ICT technologies will continue evolving and being applied to new sciences and applications, data quality dimensions will evolve as well and new dimensions will arise.

Chapter 4
Data Quality Issues in Linked Open Data

Anisa Rula, Andrea Maurino, and Carlo Batini

4.1 Introduction

The increasing diffusion of linked data as a standard way to share knowledge on the Web allows users and public and private organizations to fully exploit structured data from very large datasets that were not available in the past. Over the last few years, linked data developed into a large number of datasets with an open access from several domains leading to the linking open data (LOD) cloud.[1] Similar to other types of information such as structured data, linked data suffers from quality problems such as inconsistency, inaccuracy, out-of-dateness, incompleteness, and inconsistency, which are frequent and imply serious limitations to the full exploitation of such data. Therefore, it is important to assess the quality of the datasets that are used in linked data applications before using them. The quality assessment allows users or applications to understand whether data is appropriate for their task at hand.

The topic of linked data quality assessment has not yet received sufficient attention from the linked data community [692]. This chapter investigates information quality (IQ) in a linked data setting, which poses new challenges that were not handled before in other types of information. Adopting quality dimensions for the assessment of linked data is not a straightforward problem.

In this chapter, we focus on quality dimensions at the extensional level rather than the intensional level. The quality of the extensional level is more relevant than the intensional level in a linked data setting since linked data was envisioned to publish structured and interlinked data on the Web, without significant attention to the schema. Therefore, the prevalent focus to the definitions of IQ dimensions goes to instances, which are used more extensively than schemas in linked data.

---

[1] http://www.lod-cloud.net/.

© Springer International Publishing Switzerland 2016

C. Batini, M. Scannapieco, *Data and Information Quality*, Data-Centric Systems and Applications, DOI 10.1007/978-3-319-24106-7_4

We describe a set of IQ dimensions that are a consequence of unification and formalization of quality dimensions from three different areas: Web information systems, semantic Web, and relational databases. For each dimension cluster introduced in Chap. 2, we describe in detail IQ dimensions and their respective metrics. Along this line, we give a definition for each dimension adopted according to the linked data setting. The metrics associated with each dimension are also identified and reported.

In the following sections, we first provide an overview of linked data and the related semantic Web technologies used in this field (Sect. 4.2). In Sect. 4.3 we provide a detailed description of accuracy, completeness, redundancy, readability, consistency, and accessibility clusters. Section 4.4 discusses the relationships between dimensions.

4.2   Semantic Web Standards and Linked Data

Linked data applies to the general architecture of the World Wide Web (for simplicity Web) and engages semantic Web standards such as resource description framework (RDF), RDF schema (RDFS), Web ontology language (OWL), and simple protocol and RDF query language (SPARQL). This section presents the principles of linked data built upon the technologies and the standards provided by the Web and the semantic Web.

4.2.1   The Web and the Rationale for Linked Data

The Web is considered as an information global space where Web documents are interlinked to other related Web documents through hyperlinks which allow users to browse between related documents that are accessible through the Internet. Web documents rely on a set of standards, such as uniform resource identifiers (URIs) and hypertext markup language (HTML). A URI identifies globally a Web document; moreover, a URI as a globally unique identification mechanism is used to identify also other Web resources such as real-world objects (e.g., places, people, or images). The Web makes use of URIs to enable interaction with other documents through specific protocols such as the application-level protocol—hypertext transfer protocol (HTTP). The content of the Web documents that all computers may interpret is represented by the HTML which contains formatted natural language, digital images (e.g., in JPEG format), and other types of information.

Despite the benefits the Web provides, most of the Web's content is designed for humans to read. Machines are not able to understand information for their convenient consumption. Consider, for instance, one is interested to answer the following question: "Which is the world capital with the highest population in the world?" We can get an answer to such question from the Web if either someone has performed and published the result of the query or there exists a Web site having the data for download in a structured format which can be processed off-line. Machines can parse Web pages for layout or routine processing, but in general they cannot process the above query since no machine-readable structured data and semantics are made available by the respective sources such that they can subsequently be processed by machines. In general, data published on the Web are as raw dumps in formats such as CSV or XML, or marked up as HTML tables, sacrificing much of its structure and semantics. Further, Web documents as mentioned before connect to each other through hyperlinks that are not semantically processable by machines.

4.2.2 Semantic Web Standards

Semantic Web is conceived as an extension of the current Web, which enables sharing and reuse of data over the Web. Traditionally, the semantic Web is represented as a "semantic Web layer cake" where each layer represents a technical component needed for its construction (see Fig. 4.1). Here we shortly discuss some of the fundamental layers of the "cake," which are RDF, RDFS, OWL, and SPARQL.

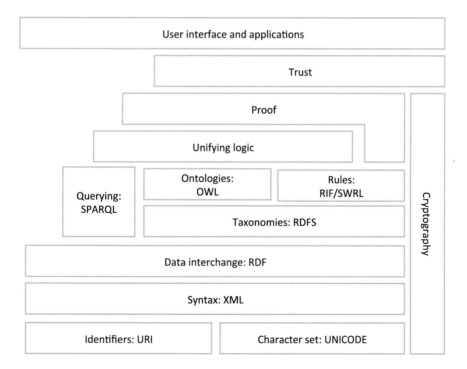

Fig. 4.1 Semantic Web layer cake

4.2.2.1 Resource Description Framework

In order to enable applications to process data on the Web, it is important to
represent contents expressed in a standard format; for this goal the semantic
Web adopts the RDF data model. The basic construct of the RDF data model is
statements about resources which can be exchanged among applications without
loss of meaning. A statement is represented by a *triple* containing three *RDF terms*
in the form of subject-predicate-object. An RDF term is an element that can be of
three types: URI, literal, and blank node.

There are two types of literals in an RDF data model: *plain* and *typed*. Both
plain and typed literals represent a literal value, like a string, number, or date.
The plain literal is a string associated with a language tag. A language tag (e.g.,
`"Lisbon"@en`) indicates the language of a string element such as English. The
typed literal is a string associated with a data type URI. A data type URI is
defined by an XML schema[2] and corresponds to dates, integers, and floating point
numbers, for instance, `"1985-02-05"^^xsd:date`. A blank node just denotes
the existence of some resources without a name. Blank nodes are used inside a
document that contains an RDF description and cannot be referenced outside their
originating scope. After defining the core elements of a triple, we now provide a
formal definition of *RDF triple*.

Definition 4.1 (RDF Triple). Given an infinite set $\mathcal{U}$ of URIs, an infinite set $\mathcal{B}$ of
blank nodes, and an infinite set $\mathcal{L}$ of literals, a triple $\langle s, p, o \rangle \in (\mathcal{U} \cup \mathcal{B}) \times \mathcal{U} \times (\mathcal{U} \cup \mathcal{B} \cup \mathcal{L})$ is called an *RDF triple* where s, p, o represent the subject, predicate, and
object, respectively, of the triple.

The use of blank nodes is discouraged for linked data since blank nodes do not
have consistent naming, i.e., a node with the same name in two different graphs
does not represent the same node. In the following we assume that the subject and
the predicate are URIs, while the object (also known as the property value) can
be either a URI or a literal. Based on the type of the object, RDF triples can be
distinguished in two types:

- *Literal triples* are RDF triples where the object is of type literal.
- *RDF links* are RDF triples where the object is of type URI.

Further, RDF links can be distinguished into internal and external. While in
the former case the link is provided between two resources belonging to the same
dataset, in the latter case the link is provided between two resources belonging to
two different datasets.

An RDF data model can represent information as a directed graph that consists
of nodes and edges where nodes refer to subjects or objects and edges refers to
predicates which provide links between nodes. The data type nodes are represented
by squares. The term *RDF graph* has been adopted from the World Wide Web

---

[2]An XML schema is a description of XML document.

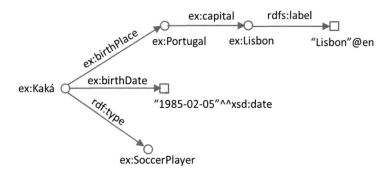

Fig. 4.2 Example of RDF

Consortium (W3C) Data Access Working Group [49, 93, 303] and is formally defined as follows.

Definition 4.2 (RDF Graph). An *RDF graph* $\mathcal{G} \subset (\mathcal{U} \cup \mathcal{B}) \times \mathcal{U} \times (\mathcal{U} \cup \mathcal{B} \cup \mathcal{L})$ is a finite set of RDF triples.

Figure 4.2 represents an example of an RDF graph containing five triples. The semantics of this graph is that the soccer player Kaka was born on 5 February 1985 in Portugal and that Lisbon is the capital of Portugal. Within the graph, Kaka, Portugal, Lisbon, and soccer player are identified by URI references. Date of birth and the label Lisbon are identified as literals and are represented by square nodes.

4.2.2.2 Syntax for RDF

The RDF data model represents information at an abstract level. A serialization makes RDF usage practical by providing a concrete format to the abstract model, where the concrete format allows the publication and exchange of RDF data among different information systems on the Web. There are several serialization formats such as RDF/XML, N-Triples, N3, and Terse RDF Triple Language (Turtle). Throughout this chapter, we will use Turtle to represent RDF triples and graphs. Turtle defines a textual syntax and a compact and natural text form, with abbreviations for common usage patterns and data types. URIs are enclosed with brackets and may be abbreviated when URIs are repeated by using the symbol `@prefix` and a qualified name to be used in the document. Literals are represented between double quotes and may be given either a language suffix or a data type URI by using the symbol @ followed by the language tag and the symbol `^^` followed by any legal URI, respectively. Blank nodes are represented by using the underscore prefix.

The RDF graph described in Fig. 4.2 is written in the Turtle syntax as shown in Listing 4.1.

Listing 4.1 Example of a set of RDF triples

```
@prefix  ex:  <http://example.org/ontology/>  .
@prefix  rdf:  <http://www.w3.org/1999/02/22−rdf−syntax−ns#>  .
@prefix  rdfs:  <http://www.w3.org/2000/01/rdf−schema\#>  .

ex:Kaka         rdf:type       ex:SoccerPlayer  .
ex:Kaka         ex:birthDate   "1985−02−05"^^xsd:date  .
ex:Kaka         ex:birthPlace  ex:Portugal  .
ex:Portugal     ex:capital     ex:Lisbon  .
ex:Lisbon       rdfs:label     "Lisbon"@en  .
```

4.2.2.3 Semantics for RDF

In this section we discuss two semantic aspects related to RDF, the RDF schema and the Web ontology language.

RDF Schema

RDF provides a way to model information but does not provide a way of specifying what information means, i.e., its semantics. To add meaning to RDF data, we need to define a vocabulary to describe classes of things and their relationships. This is the role of RDF vocabulary description language, RDFS, used to define resources. RDFS classifies resources as classes or properties. All resources of a class share the same characteristics determined by the class. Resources can be instances of multiple classes and classes can have multiple instances. The most popular property is rdf:type (for brevity we use the "rdf" prefix for <http://www.w3.org/1999/02/22-rdf-syntax-ns#>) which states a relation between a resource and its associated classes.

Some important resources in RDFS are as follows (for brevity we use the "rdfs" prefix for
<http://www.w3.org/2000/01/rdf-schema#>):

- *rdfs:Class.* Used to represent a resource that is of type RDF class.
- *rdf:Property.* Used to represent a property that is of type RDF property.
- *rdfs:subClassOf.* Used as a predicate to mean that the subject is a subclass of the object.
- *rdfs:subPropertyOf.* Used as a predicate to mean that the subject is a sub-property of the object.
- *rdfs:domain.* Used as a predicate when the subject is a property and the object is the class that is domain of this property.
- *rdfs:range.* Used as a predicate when the subject is a property and the object is the class that is range of this property.

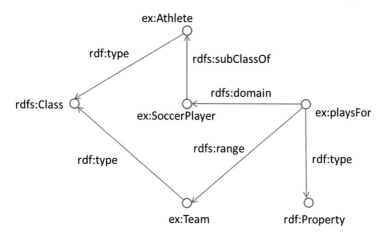

Fig. 4.3 Example of RDF schema

Listing 4.2 Example of the property definition "ex:playsFor"

```
@prefix ex: <http://example.org/ontology/> .
@prefix rdf: <http://www.w3.org/1999/02/22-rdf-syntax-ns#> .
@prefix rdfs: <http://www.w3.org/2000/01/rdf-schema\#> .

ex:playsFor rdf:type      rdf:Property .
ex:playsFor rdfs:domain   ex:SoccerPlayer .
ex:playsFor rdfs:range    ex:Team .
```

Figure 4.3 shows an RDF schema describing a soccer player that is a subclass of the class athlete. It is possible to notice the property ex:playsFor (instance of rdf:Property) with domain ex:SoccerPlayer and range ex:Team. The terms ex:Athlete and ex:Team are declared to be instances of the rdfs:Class.

By using these relational primitives, the author of an RDFS vocabulary implicitly defines rules that allow additional information to be inferred from RDF graphs. For instance, consider the following triple ex:Kaka rdf:type ex:SoccerPlayer. It is possible to infer ex:Kaka rdf:type ex:Athlete because of the rdfs:subClassOf property. Listing 4.2 illustrates a Turtle serialization of Fig. 4.3.

Web Ontology Language

Ontologies are the pillars of the semantic Web as well as of linked data which specify the knowledge that is shared and exchanged between different systems. The knowledge specified is defined through the semantics of the terms used for describing data and the relations between these terms. Ontologies enable humans and machines to interpret the meaning of data that is being exchanged.

Web ontologies are ontologies that make use of one of the standard Web ontology languages and are published on the Web, like RDFS and OWL. OWL can be used to extend RDFS to formulate more expressive schema and subclass hierarchies and additional logical constraints by enabling richer entailment[3] regimes. OWL is recognized by W3C Recommendation, and since 2008, OWL was extended to OWL2 which is also recognized by W3C.

In order to model knowledge about a domain of interest, OWL2 uses three ontology notions that are axioms, entities, and expressions.[4] An *axiom* is the elementary piece that an OWL ontology expresses and is often referred to as a *statement*. An example of statement is "Rome is the capital of Italy." In general, OWL statements can be either true or false given a certain state of affairs.

In OWL terms, we say that a set of statements A *entails* a statement a if in any state of affairs wherein all statements in A are true, also a is true. There exist reasoners which can automatically compute entailments. In this way, axioms that are subtle and difficult for people to understand are discovered by reasoners.

The constituents of statements in OWL2 are *individual names* (like "Rome," "Italy"), categories denoted as *classes* (like "city," "state"), or relations denoted as *properties* (like "is capital of") [453]. In this chapter, we mainly work with individual names which comprise RDF terms that run in the subject or object position of a triple to denote objects of the real world. We use the term *entity* as a short form for an individual name.

A *fact* is an instantiation (an axiom stating that an individual name has the type of a class expression), a relation, an attribute, or an individual equality (an axiom stating that two names refer to the same individual). In particular, we consider facts as relations which have the form $\langle s, p, o \rangle$ with s and o being entities and p being a property. Intuitively, this means that the property p relating s to o *holds*, i.e., the fact is considered true under an interpretation.

4.2.2.4 Query Language for RDF

SPARQL is the standard language for querying the RDF data model developed by the W3C Data Access Working Group in 2008 and is associated with the SPARQL protocol for formulating queries across diverse datasets through the Web. The results of SPARQL queries can be *result sets* or *RDF graphs*. We distinguish between graphs returned as answers to queries and graphs contained in documents by naming the former group of graphs as *answer graph*.

SPARQL queries may contain from one to many RDF graphs. Such graphs are called *basic graph patterns*. A basic graph pattern does not contain RDF triples but *triple patterns* where the subject, predicate, or object position may be a variable. The triples in the basic graph pattern match against triples in the RDF dataset, thus

---

[3]Draw consequences from existing knowledge.

[4]Entities can be combined into expressions by creating complex descriptions.

producing a solution mapping, i.e., a *result set*. The result set is a set of bindings of variables to RDF terms. Each binding applied to the triple pattern returns a triple present in the RDF graph.

Figure 4.1 shows that SPARQL lays over RDF and not over RDFS and OWL standards; thus, it does not provide direct support for inferencing. In the near future, an integration of RDFS and OWL entailment with SPARQL is likely to be built. SPARQL is similar to the database query language SQL with the difference that SPARQL operates over graph data represented as RDF triples, while SQL operates on structured relational data.

Consider the case we want to extract all the names and the appearances of the soccer players of the "AC Milan" team (see Listing 4.3).

The PREFIX statements define abbreviations for namespaces. The SELECT clause contains two variables preceded by "?", which retrieves the name and the appearances of a soccer player. The remainder of the query, starting WHERE, contains a list of RDF triple patterns. The WHERE clause has three RDF triple patterns, separated by a full stop. The first pattern matches resources of type dbo:soccer_player; the second and third patterns state that these resources have a name and the team ex:AC_Milan.

The response to a query, computed by a process known as *graph matching*, is shown in Fig. 4.4, where both query and dataset are shown as a result set specified in Turtle (to simplify, only part of the above dataset is included).

A SPARQL query can be executed through a program or Web site that serves as a SPARQL endpoint. A SPARQL endpoint is an HTTP server (identified by a given URL) which receives requests from SPARQL clients.

Listing 4.3 Example of a SPARQL query

```
PREFIX ex:  <http://example.org/ontology/> .
PREFIX rdf: <http://www.w3.org/1999/02/22-rdf-syntax-ns#> .

SELECT DISTINCT ?name ?appearance
WHERE {
  ?s rdf:type dbo:soccer_player ;
    ex:name ?name ;
    ex:team ex:AC_Milan
}
```

Fig. 4.4 Example of a result set of a SPARQL query

?name	?appearance
Mario_Balottelli	33
Kaká	20

4.2.3   Linked Data

In this section we address two issues, namely, the linked data principles and linked open data.

4.2.3.1   Linked Data Principles

Linked data is part of the semantic Web, and it is built upon semantic Web technologies. Linked data enables us to relate data by generating semantic connections among datasets. In 2006 Tim Berners-Lee coined the term *linked data* to refer to a set of principles for publishing and interlinking structured data on the Web:

1. Use URIs as names for things
2. Use HTTP URIs so those names can be dereferenced
3. Provide useful information by using the standards (RDF, SPARQL) upon dereferencing of those URIs
4. Include links using externally dereferenceable URIs to discover more things

The first linked data principle encourages the use of URIs to identify things. As in the Web of documents, in linked data, a URI is used to identify a document describing an entity. A document identified by a URI, which can return representations such as RDF descriptions, is called an *information resource*[5] (IR). On the other hand, in linked data, a URI identifies not only documents but also real-world objects or abstract concepts (places, people, images).

The second principle advocates the use of the identification mechanism (URIs) through specific protocols such as the application-level protocol, HTTP, to achieve interoperability between independent information systems. According to the third principle, we assume that each URI identifying an entity *e* is dereferenceable. The URI entities can be dereferenceable through the HTTP mechanism, known as *content negotiation*. This mechanism dereferences the URI that identifies the entity and returns the description of the entity in a specified data format and language indicated by a user agent. For short we call a description of an entity, an *entity document*.

Entity documents can be represented in the form of HTML pages when read by humans. Entity documents that are intended to be read by machines are represented as RDF documents in order to enable different applications to process the standardized content. Further, the applications should be aware of the difference between entities and their descriptions for further investigation. Some publishers (e.g., DBpedia) explicitly distinguish between a URI that denotes the entity and its description by assigning different URIs in order to make them unambiguous. For

---

[5]All the essential characteristics can be conveyed in a message and be transported over protocols such as HTTP.

example, http://www.example.org/resource/Milano represents the entity and http://www.example.org/data/Milano represents the entity document.
Note that the terms *entity document* and *document* will be used interchangeably in this chapter.

Linked data distributed across the Web apply a standard mechanism for specifying the connections between real-world objects (fourth principle). The mechanism of interlinking is provided through RDF links. Differently from the standard Web that connects documents, linked data connects entities. The RDF links enable the process of discovering, accessing, and integrating data in a straightforward way.

4.2.3.2   Linked Open Data

In 2007, the W3C linking open data (LOD) project began publishing existing datasets under open licenses based on linked data principles. According to the open data definition,[6] the datasets converted into RDF can be freely accessed, reused, and redistributed.

LOD can be considered as a new application domain. Its importance has been growing over the last few years. To encourage people to publish linked data, the initiator of the linked data paradigm, Tim Berners-Lee, proposed a five-star rating system.[7] In this way data publishers can evaluate how much their datasets conform to the linked data principles according to the rating system shown in Fig. 4.5.

Each additional star corresponds to an increased reusability and interoperability of the published data.

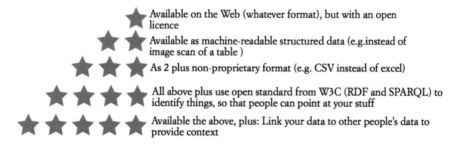

Fig. 4.5 The five-star rating system

---

[6]http://www.opendefinition.org/.

[7]http://www.opendefinition.org/http://www.w3.org/DesignIssues/LinkedData.html.

4.3   Quality Dimensions in Linked Open Data

The five-star rating system presented above measures the quality in terms of how much a dataset conforms to the linked data principles. In general, as we have seen in previous chapters, measuring the quality means evaluating a set of dimensions which capture specific aspects of IQ. Linked data quality dimensions definition poses a number of unique challenges. They are:

1. Linked data refers to a Web-scale knowledge base consisting of interlinked published data from a multitude of *autonomous* information providers. The quality of provided information may depend on the intention of the data provider. Among other issues, linked data providers may publish datasets with incomplete or inaccurate metadata that influence the quality of the datasets themselves.
2. The increasing diffusion of the linked data paradigm allows consumers to fully exploit vast amount of data that were not available in the past. Intuitively, as the size of data increases, it becomes more and more difficult to assess the quality of data.
3. Datasets in linked data may often be used by *third-party applications* in ways not expected by the original creators of the dataset.
4. Linked data provides *data integration* through interlinking data between hetero-geneous data sources. The quality of integrated data is related to the quality of original data sources, which is not straightforward to be modeled.
5. Last but not the least, relevant linked data can be considered as a dynamic environment where information can change rapidly and cannot be assumed to be static (velocity of data). Changes in linked data sources should reflect changes in the real world; otherwise, data can soon become outdated. Out-of-date information can reflect data inaccuracy problems and can deliver invalid information.

Quality of linked data includes a number of novel aspects, such as coherence via links to external datasets, data representation quality, or consistency with regard to implicit information. The structured nature of linked data makes them similar to relational databases which handle large quantities of heterogeneous and distributed data. In relational databases, as we discussed in Sect. 2.4 of Chap. 2, both the closed world assumption (CWA) and the open world assumption (OWA) can hold. This is also valid for linked data. While for relational data CWA is the usual assumption to hold, the interconnected nature of linked data makes OWA the natural assumption. OWA has an impact on the difficulty of defining and evaluating the compliance between data and schemas: a relation between two instances can hold even if the schema does not model such relation between the concepts the instances belong to; conversely, we cannot conclude that a relation between two concepts of different schemas does not hold because it is not represented in the data instances. Nevertheless, usually in the literature on linked data, the CWA is implicitly assumed to hold for the definition and assessment of quality dimensions, such as completeness and consistency.

Furthermore, database management systems (DBMS) based on RDF data such as Virtuoso [205] use a schemaless approach; namely, they allow users to publish first RDF data and subsequently (and optionally) to load the schema. The data representation model in relational databases uses expressive schema languages for defining the structure and the constraints on data ensuring in such a way the coherence between the database schema and the database instance. In linked data, as a result of the schemaless approach, the DBMS does not intrinsically prevent to add incorrect or inconsistent information to the datasets.

Therefore, to ensure the quality of RDF data in terms of accuracy and consistency quality dimensions, the linked data community proposes tools and techniques for the a posteriori validation of RDF data.

In the following sections, we provide a list of the most frequently used quality dimensions such as accuracy, completeness, redundancy, readability, accessibility, and consistency.

4.3.1 Accuracy Cluster

Accuracy refers to the extent to which entities and facts correctly represent the real-life phenomenon. Similarly to relational data, accuracy in linked data can be classified into syntactic and semantic accuracy.

4.3.1.1 Syntactic Accuracy

Syntactic accuracy is defined as the degree to which an entity document conforms to the specification of the serialization format and literals are accurate with respect to a set of syntactical rules.

Syntactic accuracy problems mostly refer to *literals incompatible with data type range* or *malformed data type literals*. For example, a property `ex:dateOfBirth` has the range `xsd:date`, but there are triples where `ex:dateOfBirth` in the predicate position have `xsd:integer`. In a second case, assume that the data type associated with a literal is `xsd:gYear` and it is possible to identify triples where `xsd:dateTime` literals are used instead. Misspelled literals can be considered as syntactic inaccurate data [312], for instance, the `Milano-Bicoca` is a misspelled literal with respect to `Milano-Bicocca`.

A metric for syntactic accuracy is the ratio between the number of incorrect values of a given property and the total number of values for the same property. Techniques that capture incorrect property values can be *distance based*, *deviation based*, and *distribution based* [78]. As an example, consider John to be the correct property value of `foaf:name` and Jack the incorrect property value; then it is possible to evaluate the distance between the correct and the incorrect values by employing a *comparison function*. With reference to software tools, validators [238, 312] are used to detect syntactic accuracy with respect to data types (measured in terms of correct/incorrect values for a given property), ranges (measured in terms of correct/incorrect value range for properties holding numerical values), and syntactic rules (correct/incorrect values with respect to given patterns) [249].

4.3.1.2   Semantic Accuracy

Semantic accuracy is defined as the degree to which data values correctly represent the real-world facts. Semantic accuracy refers to accuracy of the meaning. In order to capture the semantic inaccuracies, one needs to understand whether facts precisely capture the status of the real world. We consider two types of semantic accuracy issues: *inaccurate annotation* and *spurious annotation*.

Let us consider, for example, an RDF document written in the Turtle syntax describing a set of triples from a dataset as shown in Listing 4.4.

This example highlights the problem of a spurious annotation where the object ex:Milan in the first triple is spurious as it does not appear in the real world (since ex:Milan is not the capital of Italy). The entity ex:Italy, in the third triple, is classified as an instance of the class :Place rather than a more appropriate class ex:Country. This problem represents the situation of an *inaccurate classification* as the triple has been correctly represented but not accurately classified.

Semantic accuracy is more difficult to be assessed than syntactic accuracy because the vocabulary containing the definition of all terms in the syntactic accuracy is sufficient for the metric assessment. Here, there is the need of a real-world state representation which is usually given by a gold standard or a reference dataset.

However, some metrics proposed in the literature are (a) *validity of a fact* that checks the semantic accuracy of the fact against several sources or even several Web sites [393] and (b) *accuracy of the annotation, representation, labeling*, or *classification* that is detected as a value between 0 and 1 [395]. Additionally, the semantic accuracy of the dataset can be verified with the help of unbiased trusted third party (humans) [78].

Listing 4.4 The RDF triples describe the entity http://example.org/Milan

```
@prefix ex: <http://example.org/ontology/> .
@prefix rdf: <http://www.w3.org/1999/02/22-rdf-syntax-ns#> .

ex:Italy   ex:capital     ex:Milan  .
ex:Italy   ex:areaTotal        ''301338''^^xsd:double  .
ex:Italy   rdf:type        ex:Place    .
```

4.3.1.3 Currency

Datasets in linked data are considered to be dynamic.[8] Changes happen at both schema and instance levels to reflect the real-world state. Therefore, entity documents and links between entities can be added, removed, or updated [154, 615]. If the change is not timely with respect to the real world, the information consumed by users or applications becomes outdated. Out-of-date data may reflect invalid information (i.e., false information).

Currency concerns how promptly data are updated. Consider an example where the triples are retrieved from the Web as of May 2013. The first and third triple in Listing 4.5 has high currency, while the second triple does not represent a current result with respect to the real world at the time the data was retrieved. The object of the second triple is not updated to the current club which is Parma. In this case, currency is low.

Currency of data elements is a metric used to indicate whether data elements represent current values or not (i.e., valid values in the current state). This metric is hard to apply due to the fact that it is difficult to automatically associate real-world facts with RDF triples. Currency can be measured with respect to temporal annotations such as the *last update time*, which annotate documents or facts with a time point. Currency may be assessed at document and fact level as both documents and facts can be associated with temporal annotations. Measuring currency of arbitrary documents or facts in linked data presents several challenges: (1) it is unlikely that temporal annotations (e.g., the last modification date) are associated with facts; (2) temporal annotations are not always available; and (3) linked data is characterized by *autonomous providers* which use different vocabularies and different approaches for representing temporal annotations. Temporal annotations associated with facts or documents are considered to be scarce which negatively impact the assessment of currency [533]. Different methods are provided for measuring currency, which rely mainly on two components: (a) the time when the data was last modified and (b) the observation time; according to these two components, currency of a data element is defined as time period between the two components.

Listing 4.5 The triples present some of the RDF data referring to the current clubs

```
Ronaldinho          currentclub    Clube_Atletico_Mineiro
Antonio_Cassano     currentclub    Internacional
Cristiano_Ronaldo   currentclub    Real_Madrid_C.F.
```

---

[8]http://www.w3.org/wiki/DatasetDynamics.

4.3.1.4 Timeliness

Timeliness expresses how current the data is for the task at hand. The timeliness dimension is motivated by the fact that it is possible to have current data that is actually useless because it reflects a too old state of the real world for a specific usage. According to the timeliness dimension, data should ideally be recorded and reported as frequently as the source values change and thus never become outdated.

Consider a user checking the flight timetable for his or her flight from a city A to a city B. Suppose that the result is a list of triples comprising of the description of the entity A such as the connecting airports, the time of departure and arrival, the terminal, the gate, etc. This flight timetable is updated every 10 min (volatility). Assume there is a change of the flight departure time, specifically a delay of 1 h. This information is communicated to the control room with a slight delay and is sent to the system after 30 min. The timeliness constraint of updating the timetable within 10 min is not satisfied, which renders the information out-of-date.

The first step in developing timeliness of a data element can be to quantify currency and volatility. In the previous section, we introduced currency and here we give a short introduction about volatility and how it can be assessed. *Volatility* characterizes the frequency with which data is updated over time.

Volatility can be assessed at document and fact level. Based on the frequency of change of documents or facts, we distinguish two categories (see also the discussion in Chap. 1): (a) *stable data elements*, data elements that do not change over time, and (b) *volatile data elements*, data elements that change over time. As an example, the date of birth of a person can be classified as a stable data element. In contrast, a person working for a company is very likely to change company; then the property working for can be classified as a volatile data element.

Volatility is measured as the length of time between two updates (also known as the shelf life of the data element) during which the data element remains valid. This can be expressed by two components: (a) the expiry time (the time when the data becomes invalid) and (b) the input time (the time when the data was first published in linked data). Due to the challenges we listed in currency, the expiry time and input time are not always available. It is possible to estimate the expiry time of data elements given their change history [134].

In Listing 4.5 the facts about the soccer players can be considered as volatile facts. These facts cease to be valid if currency of these facts is not included in the shelf life of facts defined by their volatility. Volatility of facts is a surrogate metric used to indicate the validity of facts. For example, if we notice that Antonio Cassano changes team on average every 2 years, then we can deduce that after 2 years from the last change, the fact is likely to be not valid.

Although the combination of the two metrics, currency and volatility, seems the right approach for measuring timeliness, it does not represent a necessary condition for measuring timeliness. Other factors that are not reflected in the system can influence the judgment about the timeliness of the information.

Timeliness plays an important role in a data integration scenario. Linked data, differently from relational databases, can take advantage of the original data source and thus provide the assessment without the user's involvement. As we observed in volatility, datasets in linked data usually do not directly represent facts from the real world but from an existing information system which in turn is considered as the real-world representation. For example, consider having the same information represented in two different datasets A and B. We would like to integrate our dataset C to either the dataset A or the dataset B. It is obvious that we would like to integrate our dataset to the most updated one. Therefore, we measure the timeliness of each dataset based on their original data source by measuring the distance between last modified time of the data source and last modified time of the dataset.

4.3.2   Completeness Cluster

4.3.2.1   Completeness

Completeness refers to the degree to which all required information is present in a particular dataset. In terms of linked data, completeness comprises of the following aspects: (a) *schema completeness* refers to the degree to which the classes and properties of an ontology are represented. (b) *property completeness* refers to the degree of the missing values for a specific property. (c) *population completeness* provides the percentage of all real-world entities of a particular type that are represented in the datasets. (d) *linkability completeness*, which has to be considered only for linked data, refers to the degree to which instances in the dataset are interlinked.

As an example, let us consider a result set returned as a result of issuing a query. The triples contained in the result set have either the property ex:areaTotal or the property ex:populationTotal. These properties relate two arguments of type *country* and *literal*. The completeness of each property is given as the ratio between the number of entities of type country having the property and the total number of entities of type country.

In general, completeness can be measured in terms of:

1. Schema completeness—no. of classes and properties represented/total no. of classes and properties [78, 249, 436]
2. Property completeness—no. of values represented for a specific property/total no. of values for a specific property [78, 249]
3. Population completeness—no. of real-world objects represented/total no. of real-world objects [78, 249, 436]
4. Linkability completeness—no. of instances in the dataset that are interlinked/total no. of instances in a dataset [282]

It should be noted that in this case, users should assume a closed world assumption where a gold standard dataset is available and can be used to compare against the converted dataset.

Linkability completeness is only considered in LOD and not in relational data. Let us consider a set of entities and a network constructed for each of them. Optionally, a new set of edges can be added to each local network, and a set of new local networks around the original set of entities is created. Once the original local network is created, an analysis of completeness of the link for each node is computed. In order to measure the completeness of links, we first need to assess the linkability dimension according to network measures such as linkability degree, cluster coefficient, owl:sameAs chains, centrality, and description richness [282].

4.3.2.2 Relevancy

Relevancy refers to the provision of information which is in accordance with the task at hand and important to the users' query.

Relevancy is highly context dependent and is highly recommended in Web information systems since the process of retrieving the relevant information becomes complicated when dealing with a big flow of information. As an example of relevancy, we may consider a user is looking for flights between any two cities. He or she is looking for relevant information, i.e., departure and arrival airports and starting and ending time, duration, and cost per person should be provided. Some datasets, in addition to relevant information, also contain much irrelevant data such as car rental, hotel booking, travel insurance, etc., and as a consequence a lot of irrelevant extra information is made available. Providing irrelevant data distracts service developers and potentially users and wastes network resources. Instead, restricting the dataset to only flight-related information simplifies application development and increases the likelihood to return only relevant results to users.

The retrieval process of relevant data can be performed (a) using a combination of hyperlink analysis and information retrieval methods [78], (b) ranking (a numerical value similar to PageRank, which determines the centrality of RDF documents and facts [84]), and (c) counting the occurrence of relevant data within metadata attributes (e.g., title, description, subject) [78]. An alternative metric can be the coverage (i.e., number of entities described in a dataset) and level of detail (i.e., number of properties) in a dataset to ensure that there exists an appropriate volume of relevant data for a particular task [238].

4.3.3 Redundancy Cluster

4.3.3.1 Conciseness

Conciseness in a linked data setting refers to the presence of irrelevant elements with respect to the domain or the minimization of redundant schema and data elements.

Conciseness is classified into:

- *Intensional conciseness* (schema level) which refers to the case when the data does not contain redundant schema elements (properties and classes). Only essential properties and classes should be defined.
- *Extensional conciseness* (data level) which refers to the case when the data does not contain redundant objects (instances).

Intensional conciseness measures the number of unique schema elements (i.e., properties and classes) of a dataset in relation to the overall number of schema elements in a schema [436]. Extensional conciseness measures the number of unique entities in relation to the overall number of entities in the dataset [436]. Further, extensional conciseness can be measured as the total number of instances that violate the uniqueness rule in relation to the total number of relevant instances [249, 395].

An example of intensional conciseness would be a particular flight, say A123, being represented by two different properties in the same dataset, such as http://flights.org/airlineID and http://flights.org/name. In this case redundancy between airlineID and name can ideally be solved by fusing the two properties and keeping only one unique identifier. In other words, conciseness should push stakeholders to reuse as much as possible schema elements from existing ontologies rather than creating new ones since the reuse will support data interoperability.

4.3.3.2 Representational Conciseness

Representational conciseness refers to the extent to which information is compactly represented. Consider, for instance, a search engine that represents the URIs for the destination compactly with the use of the airport codes. For example, MXP is the airport code for Milano Malpensa; therefore, the URI is http://airlines.org/MXP. This short representation of URIs helps users share and memorize them easily.

Representational conciseness can be measured as (a) detection of long URIs or those that contain query parameters [313] or (b) detection of RDF primitives, i.e., RDF reification, RDF containers, and RDF collections [313].

The concise representation of data not only contributes to the human readability of that data but also influences the performance of data when queried. Keeping URIs concise and human readable is highly recommended for large scale and/or frequent processing of RDF data as well as for efficient indexing and serialization. Hogan et al. [313] associate the use of very long URIs (or those that contain query parameters) as an issue related to the representational conciseness of the data.

4.3.4   Readability Cluster

4.3.4.1   Understandability

Understandability refers to the ease with which data can be comprehended without ambiguity and be used by a human information consumer.

This dimension can also be referred to as the comprehensibility of the information where the data should be of sufficient clarity in order to be used [78, 238]. Semantic Web was mainly envisioned to provide information in machine-readable format such that the data can be processed by machines. Understandability contributes toward the usability of machine-readable data from humans. In linked data, data publishers are encouraged to provide human-readable labels and descriptions of entities. Consider a dataset about flight information given as follows:

Listing 4.6 Example of understandability
```
ex:m.049jnng      ex:departure     m.043j22x  .
ex:m.049jnng      ex:arrival       m.045j23y  .
m.049jnng         ex:label         ''American Airline ''@en .
m.043j22x         ex:label         ''Boston Logan Airport ''@en .
```

As one may see, the first two triples do not contain human-readable labels. These triples are not meaningful to the user. Then consider the last two triples which label each entity of the first triple. With the human-readable labels, one is able to interpret the first triple as the flight of the American Airline has departure from Boston Logan Airport.

Understandability can be measured as follows: (a) the completeness of human-readable labeling of entities [195, 313], (b) the engagement of URIs[9] that follow a conventional pattern [195], (c) the availability of SPARQL queries examples [238], and (d) the ratio between all entities having one label and all entities with any label [195].

4.3.5   Accessibility Cluster

4.3.5.1   Licensing

Licensing is defined as the granting of permission for a consumer to reuse a dataset under defined conditions.

Licensing is a new quality dimension not considered for relational databases but mandatory in an open data world such as LOD. A license enables information consumers to use the data under clear legal terms. Flemming [238] and Hogan et al. [313] both state that each RDF document should contain a license under which the content can be (re)used. Additionally, the existence of a machine-readable

---

[9]http://www.w3.org/Provider/Style/URI.

indication (by including the specifications in a VoID[10] description) as well as a human-readable indication of a license is important not only for the permissions a license grants but as an indication of which requirements the consumer has to meet [238]. Detecting whether the RDF dataset is attributed under the same license as the original one allows user to understand the compatibility of licenses [238]. Although both these studies do not provide a formal definition, they agree on the use and importance of licensing in terms of IQ. Some of the metrics identified for licensing are as follows: (a) the datasets are accompanied by a license; (b) the datasets are accompanied by a summary and a link to the full version of the license; and (c) the license sets out the conditions of attribution, reuse, redistribution, and commercialization. Additionally, [381] presents a semantic framework for evaluating Creative Commons (CC) ShareAlike recursive statements. Villata and Gandon [629] present an approach, similar to what is proposed by Gangadharan et al. [255], applied to the Web of data scenario using Web languages only. They consider only CC licenses compatibility and composition.

Providing licensing information increases the usability of the dataset as the consumers or third parties are thus made aware of the legal rights and permissiveness under which the pertinent data are made available. Consider a search engine that aggregates data from several existing data sources; a clear indication of the license allows the search engine to reuse the data. For example, the LinkedGeoData dataset is licensed under the Open Database License,[11] which allows others to copy, distribute, and use the data and produce work from the data allowing modifications and transformations. Due to the presence of this specific license, the flight search engine is able to reuse this dataset to pull geospatial information and feed it to the search engine.

4.3.5.2 Availability

Availability of a dataset is the extent to which data (or some portion of it) is present, obtainable, and ready for use. Availability of a dataset refers to the accessing methods of the entity documents. One method can be to dereference the HTTP URI of the entity document. In addition, it is possible to make datasets available through SPARQL endpoints or by downloading RDF dumps. Linked data search engines alternatively provide APIs for the crawled data.

Let us consider the case in which the user looks up a flight in a flight search engine. However, instead of retrieving the results, he or she receives an error response code 404 Not Found. This is an indication that a requested resource is unavailable. In particular, with this error code, he or she may assume that either there is no information present at that specified URI or the information is unavailable.

---

[10]http://vocab.deri.ie/void.

[11]http://www.opendatacommons.org/licenses/odbl/.

Thus, an apparently unreliable search engine is less likely to be used, in which case the user may not book flights from this search engine after encountering such issues.

Availability can be measured as follows:

- Checking whether the server responds to a SPARQL query [238].
- Checking whether an RDF dump is provided and can be downloaded [238].
- Detecting dereferenceable URIs (by checking for dead or broken links [312]. For instance, when an HTTP-GET request is sent, the status code 404 Not Found is not returned [238]. Detecting useful data (particularly RDF) may be another metric that is returned upon a lookup to a URI [312].
- Detecting whether the HTTP response contains the header field stating the content type of the returned file such as application/rdf+xml [312].

4.3.5.3 Linkability

Linkability refers to the degree to which entities that represent the same concept are linked to each other, be it within or between two or more data sources.

Linkability is a relevant dimension in linked data since the process of data integration is made possible through the links created between various datasets. Linkability is provided by RDF triples that establish a link between the entity identified by the subject and the entity identified by the object. Through the typed RDF links, data items are effectively interlinked. Moreover, the correct usage of the property is important to ensure proper representation of the type of relationship between the entities (e.g., owl:sameAs, skos:related skos:broader etc.) [292].

In order to overcome these problems, we need some metrics to assess the quality of links. The proposed metrics are based on network measures. The linkability can be given as the degree of how many hubs there are in a network[12] [282]. Other measures are clustering coefficient (how dense is the network) and centrality, which indicates the likelihood of a node being on the shortest path between two other nodes. The *owl:sameAs chains* and description richness through *owl:sameAs links* are alternative metrics based on the property owl:sameAs [282].

4.3.5.4 Interoperability

Interoperability is the degree to which the format and structure of data conform to previously returned data as well as data from other sources.

As an example, let us consider different airline datasets using different notations for representing the geocoordinates of a particular flight location. While one

---

[12]In [282], a network is described as a set of facts provided by the graph of the Web of data, excluding the blank nodes.

dataset uses the WGS 84 geodetic system, another one uses the GeoRSS points system to specify the location. This makes querying the integrated dataset difficult, as it requires users and the machines to understand the heterogeneous schema. Additionally, with the difference in the vocabularies used to represent the same concept (in this case the coordinates), consumers are faced with the problem of how the data can be interpreted and displayed.

Interoperability can be assessed by detecting whether the dataset reuses existing vocabularies or entities from existing established vocabularies. The reuse of well-known vocabularies, rather than inventing new ones, not only ensures that the data is consistently represented in different datasets but also supports data integration and management tasks. In practice, for instance, when a data provider needs to describe information about people, FOAF[13] should be the vocabulary of choice. Moreover, reusing vocabularies maximizes the probability that data can be consumed by applications that may be tuned to well-known vocabularies, without requiring further preprocessing of the data or modification of the application. Even though there is no central repository of existing vocabularies, suitable terms can be found in SchemaWeb,[14] SchemaCache,[15] and Swoogle.[16] Additionally, a comprehensive survey done in [556] lists a set of naming conventions that should be used to avoid inconsistencies.[17] Another possibility is to use LODStats [175], which allows to perform a search for frequently used properties and classes in the linked open data cloud.

4.3.6   Consistency Cluster

Consistency means that a knowledge base is free of (logical/formal) contradictions with respect to particular knowledge representation and inference mechanisms. For example, let us consider the following facts in Listing 4.7.

The OWL property `owl:disjointWith` is used to state that the classes are disjoint and no instance can be at the same time an instance of both classes. However, after reasoning on the dataset, it is possible to identify an inconsistency caused by the third triple since the instance John cannot be both a boy and a girl.

Listing 4.7   An example of axioms violating the dataset
```
:Boy  owl:disjointWith  :Girl  .
:John  a  :Boy  .
:John  a  :Girl  .
```

---

[13]http://www.xmlns.com/foaf/spec/.

[14]http://www.schemaweb.info/.

[15]http://www.schemacache.com/.

[16]http://www.swoogle.umbc.edu/.

[17]However, they only restrict themselves to only considering the needs of the OBO foundry community but still can be applied to other domains.

For assessing consistency, we can employ an inference engine or a reasoner, which supports the expressivity of the underlying knowledge representation formalism. In practice, scalable authoritative OWL reasoner (SAOR) can be employed in order to shed light on the reasoning issues related to the interpretation of RDF data on the Web. Alternatively, RDFS inference and reasoning with regard to the different OWL profiles can be used to measure consistency in a dataset. Some inconsistency issues can be given as follows:

- Detection of use of entities as members of disjoint classes using the formula:
  $\frac{\text{no. of entities described as members of disjoint classes}}{\text{total no. of entities described in the dataset}}$ [312]
- Detection of misplaced classes or properties[18] using entailment rules that indicate the position of a term in a triple [312]
- Detection of misuse of `owl:DatatypeProperty` or `owl:Object Property` through the ontology maintainer[19] [312]
- Detection of use of members of `owl:DeprecatedClass` or `owl:DeprecatedProperty` through the ontology maintainer or by specifying manual mappings from deprecated terms to compatible terms [312]
- Detection of invalid `owl:InverseFunctionalProperty` values by checking the uniqueness and validity of the inverse-functional values [312]
- Detection of the redefinition by third parties of external classes/properties (ontology hijacking) such that reasoning over data using those external terms is affected [312]
- Detection of negative dependencies/correlation among properties using association rules [83]
- Detection of inconsistencies in spatial data through semantic and geometric constraints [452]

4.4 Interrelationships Between Dimensions

The IQ dimensions discussed in the previous section are not independent from each other, but correlations exist among them. If one dimension is considered more important than the others for a specific application (or use case), then the choice of favoring it may imply negative consequences on the others. Investigating the relationships among dimensions is a relevant issue, as shown by the following examples of the possible interrelations between them. In this section, we describe the intrarelations between some of the dimensions.

First, consider the relationship between semantic accuracy and timeliness. The assessment of timeliness of facts or documents tells about their semantic accuracy. If

---

[18]For example, a URI defined as a class is used as a property or vice versa.

[19]For example, attribute properties used between two resources and relation properties used with literal values.

a fact or a document is outdated, then it is more likely to be inaccurate. Second, there exists a relationship between timeliness and the semantic accuracy, completeness, and consistency dimensions. Indeed, having semantically accurate, complete or consistent data may require time and thus timeliness can be negatively affected. Conversely, having timely data may cause low accuracy, incompleteness, and/or inconsistency.

Based on quality preferences given by the Web application, a possible order of IQ would be timely, consistent, accurate, and then complete. For instance, a list of courses published on a university Web site should be first of all timely, secondly consistent and accurate, and finally complete. Conversely, when considering an e-banking application, first of all it should be accurate, consistent, and complete as stringent requirements and only afterward timely since delays are allowed in favor of correctness of data provided.

The representational conciseness dimension and the conciseness dimension are also closely related to each other. On the one hand, representational conciseness refers to the conciseness of *representing* the data (e.g., short URIs), while conciseness refers to the compactness of the *data itself* (redundant attributes and objects). Both dimensions thus point toward the compactness of the data. Moreover, representational conciseness not only allows users to understand the data better but also provides efficient process of frequently used RDF data (thus affecting performance). On the other hand, Hogan et al. [313] associate performance to the issue of "using prolix RDF features" such as (1) reification, (2) containers, and (3) collections. These features should be avoided as they are cumbersome to represent information in triples and can prove to be expensive to support in data-intensive environments.

Additionally, the interoperability dimension is interrelated with the consistency dimension, because the invalid usage of vocabularies may lead to inconsistency in the data.

Versatility is related to the accessibility since it makes data available via different means (e.g., SPARQL endpoint, RDF dump) and inadvertently points toward the ways in which data can be accessed. Additionally, versatility allows users with different nationality to understand the information better, e.g., provides data in different languages. Furthermore, there exists an interrelation between the conciseness and the relevancy dimensions. Conciseness frequently positively affects relevancy since removing redundancies increases the proportion of relevant data that can be retrieved.

The linkability dimension is associated with the syntactic accuracy dimension. It is important to choose the correct similarity relationship such as *same, matches, similar*, or *related* between two entities to capture the most appropriate relationship [292], thus contributing toward the syntactic accuracy of the data. Additionally, linkability is directly related to the linkability completeness dimension. However, the linkability dimension focuses on the quality of the interlinks, whereas the linkability completeness focuses on the presence of *all* relevant interlinks in a dataset.

These examples of interrelations between dimensions highlight the interplay between them and show that these dimensions are to be considered differently in different IQ assessment scenarios.

4.5   Summary

In this chapter, we have presented a list of quality dimensions and metrics that characterize the concept of IQ in linked data. The goal of this chapter is to obtain a clear understanding of the quality dimensions and metrics available for linked data quality assessment. We analyzed the dimensions and metrics with respect to quality dimensions and metrics proposed in relational databases. These dimensions provide a reference framework to those organizations interested in the quality of linked data and allow them to characterize and, to some extent, measure the quality of datasets.

As this chapter reveals, most of the dimensions preserve the same definition but not the method of measuring their respective metrics. The metrics depends a lot on the data input which provides new challenges.

The number of publications regarding quality in LOD in the span of 10 years since 2005 [692] is rather low. One of the reasons for this could be the infancy of the research area or the possible reuse of research from mature, related domains. Additionally, in most of the existing works, the metrics were often not explicitly defined or did not consist of precise statistical measures. Moreover, only few approaches are actually accompanied by an implemented tool, and none of these tools is able to ensure an overall quality of the dataset. Only recently (2015), EU projects such as COMSODE[20] provide a framework that is able to assess the overall quality of the linked data based on the quality dimensions and metrics defined in this chapter.

Meanwhile, there is much research on IQ being done, and guidelines as well as recommendations on how to publish "good" data are currently available. However, there is less focus on how to use this "good" data. The quality of datasets should be assessed, and an effort to increase the quality aspects that are amiss should be performed thereafter. For a discussion on data and information in use, see Chap. 11.

---

[20]http://www.comsode.eu/.

Chapter 5
Quality of Images

Gianluigi Ciocca, Silvia Corchs, Francesca Gasparini, Carlo Batini, and Raimondo Schettini

5.1 Introduction

An image is the result of the optical imaging process which maps physical scene properties onto a two-dimensional luminance distribution; it encodes important and useful information about the geometry of the scene and the properties of the objects located within this scene [339, 611, 687].

Several approaches to the concept of image quality are proposed in the literature. Image quality is often understood as the subjective impression of how well image content is rendered or reproduced [527], the integrated set of perceptions of the overall degree of excellence of an image [199], or an impression of its merits or excellence as perceived by an observer neither associated with the act of photographing nor closely involved with the subject matter depicted [359]. In these definitions, image quality actually refers to the quality of the imaging systems used to acquire or render the images. Although suitable targets and studio scenes are often used for testing, we do not know in advance what objects/subjects will be actually acquired and processed. Depending on the applications, both scene contents and imaging conditions may range from being completely free (the common use of a consumer digital camera) to strictly controlled.

The Technical Advisory Service for Images proposes the following definition: "The quality of an image can only be considered in terms of the proposed use. An image that is perfect for one use may well be inappropriate for another" [604]. We will address the "fitness for use" issue in Chap. 11. According to the International Imaging Industry Association [321], image quality is the perceptually weighted combination of all visually significant attributes of an image when considered in its marketplace or application. We must, in fact, consider the application domain and expected use of the image data. An image, for example, could be used just as a visual reference to an item in the digital archive; and although image quality has not been precisely defined, we can reasonably assume that in this case, image quality requirements are low. On the contrary, if the image were to "replace" the original,

© Springer International Publishing Switzerland 2016

C. Batini, M. Scannapieco, *Data and Information Quality*, Data-Centric Systems and Applications, DOI 10.1007/978-3-319-24106-7_5

image quality requirements would be high. Another quality definition that considers an image as input of the vision stage of an interaction process is formulated in [340], where it is claimed that in order to answer the question what image quality is, the question has to be split in other three questions: (1) what are images, (2) what are images used for, and (3) what are the requirements which the use of images imposes on them. To begin with the answers to the first two questions, they observe that images are the carriers of visual information about the outside world and that they are used as input to human visual perception. Taking into account that images are not necessarily processed by a human observer, according to this definition, we can consider the quality of an image as the degree of adequacy to its function/goal within a specific application field.

Visual perception itself is part of the three processes perception, cognition, and action, which together constitute human interaction with the environment (see Fig. 5.1). Images, therefore, can be regarded as input to the perception stage of interaction. Using a technical view of perception, it can be defined as the stage of human interaction whose attributes of items outside the world are measured and internally quantified. The aim of this quantification is essentially twofold. First, items in the outside world can be discriminated from one another using their internally quantified attributes. The result of this process is an essential step toward the construction of higher-level abstract descriptions of scene geometry and object location, descriptions upon which later processes such as navigation in the scene are based. Second, items in the outside world can be identified by comparing their internally quantified attributes with quantified attributes, stored in memory, of similar items observed in the past. Identification of what is depicted in the image is an essential step in the interpretation of scene content, and this determines the semantic awareness of what is in the scene.

With respect to the third question, the authors conclude that the items depicted in the image should be successfully discriminable and identifiable. Summarizing, according to Janssen and Blommaert: the quality of an image is the adequacy of this image as input to visual perception, and this adequacy is given by the

Fig. 5.1 Schematic overview of the interaction process by Janssen and Blommaert [340]

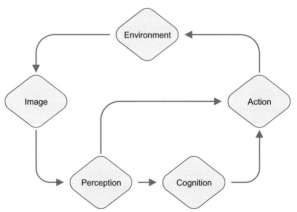

discriminability and identifiability of the items depicted in the image. In Fig. 5.1, their schematic overview of the interaction process is shown. The result of visual processing is used as *input to cognition* (for tasks requiring interpretation of scene content) or as *input to action* (e.g., in navigation, where the link between perception and action is mostly direct). Since action will in general result in a changed status of the environment, the nature of the interaction process is cyclic.

The chapter is organized as follows. In Sect. 5.2, we discuss factors that influence image quality, quality models, and related quality dimensions. In Sect. 5.3, we consider approaches to image quality assessment. In Sect. 5.4, the relationship between quality assessment and the image production workflow is examined. Section 5.5 is dedicated to quality assessment in high-quality image archives, while Sect. 5.6 focuses on video quality and video quality assessment.

5.2 Image Quality Models and Dimensions

Given a specific domain and task, there are several factors that may influence the perceived image quality; they may be:

- Intrinsic to the scene, e.g., scene geometry and lighting conditions
- Intrinsic to imaging devices, e.g., spatial resolution, geometric distortions, sharpness, noise, dynamic range, color accuracy, and color gamut
- Depending on imaging processing pipelines, e.g., contrast, color balance, color saturation, and compression
- Intrinsic to the human visual system, e.g., luminance sensitivity, contrast sensitivity, and texture masking
- Depending on human observers, e.g., previous experiences, preferences, and expectations

In previous chapters, we have discussed dimensions as classified in terms of clusters, introduced in Chap. 2. The literature on image quality (IMQ in the following) groups dimensions in terms of models, according to different criteria. A first example of the models is the fidelity-usefulness-naturalness (FUN) [527] that assumes the existence of three major dimensions: fidelity, usefulness , and naturalness.

Fidelity is the degree of apparent match of the image with the original (see Fig. 5.2). Ideally, an image having the maximum degree of fidelity should give the same impression to the viewer as the original. As an example, a painting catalogue requires high fidelity of the images with respect to the originals. *Genuineness* and *faithfulness* are sometimes used as synonyms of fidelity [321]. Dozens of books and hundreds of papers have been written about image fidelity and image reproduction, e.g., [565]. Fidelity can be located in the accuracy dimension cluster.

Usefulness is the degree of apparent suitability of the image with respect to a specific task. In many application domains, such as medical or astronomical imaging, image processing procedures can be applied to increase the image usefulness [270].

(a)   (b)   (c)

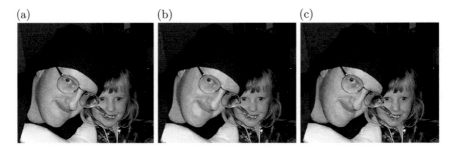

Fig. 5.2 Images exhibiting different fidelity degrees. (**a**) Original image. (**b**) Quantized image. (**c**) Compressed image

(a)   (b)

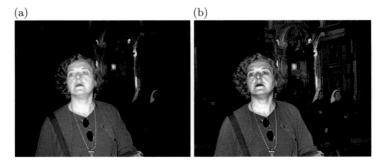

Fig. 5.3 Example of image usefulness. (**a**) A faithful image. (**b**) A contrast-enhanced image showing more details in the background

An example of image usefulness is shown in Fig. 5.3. The image to the left may be accurate with respect to the original, but the image to the right shows more details in the background due to a contrast enhancement algorithm applied. The enhancement processing steps have an obvious impact on fidelity.

Naturalness is the degree of apparent match of the image with the viewer's internal references. This attribute plays a fundamental role when we have to evaluate the quality of an image without having access to the corresponding original. Examples of images requiring a high degree of naturalness are those downloaded from the Web or seen in journals. Naturalness also plays a fundamental role when the image to be evaluated does not exist in reality, such as in virtual reality domains. Figure 5.4 shows three images with decreasing degrees of naturalness with respect to a mental reference of skin color.

Recently, Moorthy et al. [450] suggested extending the dimensions of image quality by considering also its *visual aesthetic* and *content*. We may refer to their model as the QAC model (quality, aesthetic, content).

Visual aesthetics is a measure of the perceived beauty of a visual stimulus (see Fig. 5.5). Aesthetics is intrinsically subjective; different users may consider an image to be aesthetically appealing for different reasons based on their backgrounds and expectations. Notwithstanding the subjective nature of this dimension, several

(a)   (b)   (c)

Fig. 5.4 Images with decreasing degrees of naturalness with respect to a mental reference of the skin color

(a)   (b)   (c)

Fig. 5.5 Examples of image aesthetic. The images are shown according to the aesthetic votes given by the community of the DPChallenge (http://www.dpchallenge.com) Web site. The subject refers to the "Fan" contest

(a)   (b)   (c)

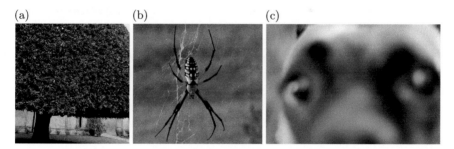

Fig. 5.6 How image content influences quality. (**a**) The image could be considered of poor quality because the tree was not fully captured. (**b**) For a person hating spiders, the image may be not considered of good quality. (**c**) A blurred image can be considered of good quality if the content is important for the photographer

works tackle the problem to estimate the aesthetics of an image by developing computational procedures. These procedures exploit visual properties and compositional rules trying to predict aesthetic scores with high correlation with human perception [70, 163, 474].

Semantic content has an important impact on the evaluation of the quality of an image, and thus, it cannot be discounted during assessment (see Fig. 5.6. Users'

Model →	Fun Model			QAC Model		
Dimensions	Fidelity	Usefulness	Naturalness	Quality	Aesthetics	Content
Accuracy	X objective		X subjective	X subjective		X subjective
Completeness				X subjective		X subjective
Redundancy				X subjective		X subjective
Readability				X subjective	X subjective	X subjective
Accessibility				X subjective		X subjective
Consistency				X subjective		X subjective
Trustworthiness				X subjective		X subjective
Usefulness		X fittness for use		X subjective		

Fig. 5.7 Correspondences between dimension clusters and image quality models

previous experiences influence the judgment of a good or bad image content. For example, an image can be considered of poor quality if it depicts offensive (to the user) content, but if the same image is evaluated on the other quality dimensions, it may receive a higher rating.

The above two models can be compared against the dimension clusters introduced in Chap. 2; see Fig. 5.7. It also represented the subjective/objective nature of dimension measurement.

With reference to the FUN model, fidelity and naturalness correspond to accuracy, fidelity being objective and naturalness being subjective. Usefulness is the dimension corresponding to fitness for use. The QAC model has two of the three dimensions, quality and content, that are orthogonal to dimensions and are subjective. The aesthetics dimension pertains to the readability cluster and is subjective. We have considered similar dimensions when we have discussed schema quality in Chap. 2.

We conclude the discussion on dimensions introducing other two IMQ dimensions:

• Figure 5.8 shows three different examples of lack of completeness, where the principal content of the image is partially hidden by other contents, due to (a) intentional, aesthetic; (b) unintentional, accidental; and (c) systemic causes. We can say that a digital image is *complete* if it depicts all the information it must convey.
• The second IMQ dimension we discuss is *minimality* that can be defined as the minimal amount of memory space such that the image still fits for use. In Fig. 5.9,

Fig. 5.8   Examples of incompleteness due to different motivations

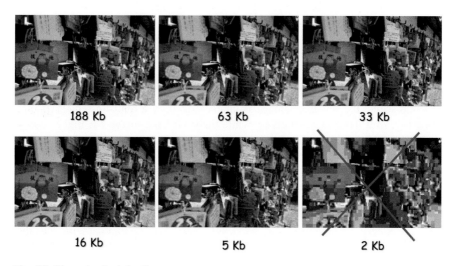

Fig. 5.9   Example of minimality

Fig. 5.10 Example of
trade-off between fidelity and
usefulness

we show several images of a scene crowded with objects. From left to right and
up to down, the images are characterized by decreasing memory space, the last
one being the first image whose associated memory space is too low to allow a
bright perception. Minimality is a dimension of the redundancy cluster.

A final issue concerns trade-offs between dimensions, an aspect that we
addressed in Chap. 2. Looking at Fig. 5.10, we see that the two images represent a
common scene; the left-hand image is characterized by a realistic rendering of a
dense fog, so it has a higher fidelity, while the right-hand image has higher utility
(and lower fidelity) due to the cleaner representation of the stop traffic signal and of
the bike route.

Summing up, the overall IMQ can be evaluated with metrics as a single number weighting the individual components. These weights depend on the specific image data type and on its function/goal. Furthermore, the approach of creating an IMQ model can be divided into three steps [36]:

- Identification of relevant quality attributes for the task at hand
- Determination of relationships between perceived quality values and objective measurements
- Combination of quality attribute measures to predict overall image quality

5.3 Image Quality Assessment Approaches

Image quality can be assessed either for an image seen in isolation or for an image seen together with a reference one [422]. Image quality assessment is usually performed with subjective approaches or objective approaches that we discuss in the following.

5.3.1 Subjective Approaches to Assessment

Subjective approaches exploit psychological experiments involving human observers. Standard psychophysical scaling tools for measuring subjective image quality are now available and described in some standards, such as ITU-R BT.500-11 [199, 334, 610].

Subjective test methods can be categorized into two main groups: methods that use explicit references and methods that do not use any explicit reference. *Single stimulus* (SS) methods belong to the first category, while *stimulus comparison* (SC) methods belong to the second one. In SS methods, a single image or sequence of images is presented and the assessor provides an index of the entire presentation, while in SC methods, two images or set of images are displayed, and the viewer provides a rating of the relation between the images. Each display of image or images to be rated is called *presentation*. For both SC and SS methods, different variants exist; the main difference is in the scale that the assessors use to evaluate the presentations.

Subjective image quality assessment makes it necessary to take into account the *human vision system* characteristics, the image rendering procedure, the subjects' characteristics, and the perceptual task [199]. The human vision system is specialized and tuned to recognize the features that are most important for human evolution and survival; there are other image features that humans cannot distinguish or that are easily overlooked [655]. These facts make quality assessment highly dependent on the image contents.

Fig. 5.11 Example of how the perceptual quality is influenced by the visibility of the distortion. Gaussian noise is applied to the top (*left-side*) and bottom (*right-side*) regions of the image. The image on the *right* is typically perceived as having higher quality than the image on the *left*

Consider, for example, Fig. 5.11. The same amount of Gaussian noise is applied to the image, first to the sky/clouds region (Fig. 5.11, left) and second to the sand/rocks region (Fig. 5.11, right). The perceived image quality is strongly influenced by the distortion visibility. When the distortion is applied to the sand/rock region, it is less noticeable. The noise is masked by the variations in the texture of the region. When the distortion is applied to almost uniform regions, as in the case of the sky/clouds region, it stands out prominently. This effect is called *texture masking* and is fundamental to take it into account when designing image quality metrics.

Subjective experiences and preferences may influence the human assessment of image quality; for example, it has been shown that the perceived distortions are dependent on how familiar the test person is with the observed image [322]. Image quality assessment is also affected by the user's task, e.g., [191, 417]: passive observation can be reasonably assumed when the observer views a vacation image, but not X-rays for medical diagnosis. The cognitive understanding and interactive visual processing, like eye movements, influence the perceived quality of images in a top-down way [654]. If the observer is provided with different instructions when evaluating a given image, he or she will give different scores to the same image depending on those instructions. Prior information regarding the image contents or fixation may therefore affect the evaluation of the image quality.

Although effective, the efficiency of subjective approaches is very low. This has led the research toward the study of objective image quality measures not requiring human interaction.

5.3.2   Objective Approaches

Objective approaches exploit suitable metrics computed directly from the digital image (see Fig. 5.12). These image quality metrics can be broadly classified in full reference, no reference, and reduced reference metrics [654].

5.3.2.1   Full Reference

Full reference (FR) metrics perform a direct comparison between the image under test and a reference or "original" in a properly defined image space. Having access to an original is a requirement of the usability of such metrics. Among the quality dimensions previously introduced, only image fidelity can be assessed. Different FR metrics are described and compared in [118, 654]. Among them, we can cite the *structural similarity index* [654], the *visual information fidelity index* [567], the *moment correlation index* [659], the *most apparent distortion index* [389], and the *gradient magnitude similarity deviation* [681].

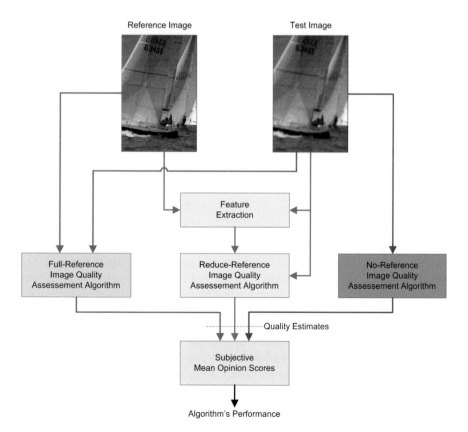

Fig. 5.12 Objective image quality assessment approaches

5.3.2.2 No Reference

No reference (NR) metrics assume that image quality can be determined without a direct comparison between the original and the processed images. Examples of NR metrics are those designed to identify the presence of specific processing *defects*. Among them are:

- *Colorfulness* [300], which means characterized by rich, vivid, and distinctive variety of colors
- *Contrast*, the difference in color and light between parts of the image or the separation between the darkest and brightest areas of the image
- *Blockiness* [598, 653], the characteristic of being made up of blocks or patches
- *Blurriness* [143, 429], the characteristic of being indistinct and without sharp outlines
- *Graininess*, the characteristic of being discontinuous in structure and shape
- Noise [153], namely, unwanted effects in the image that disturb people or make it difficult to perceive the image content
- *Quantization noise* [91], the error generated when a continuous signal is sampled in amplitude into discrete pixels
- *Zipper*, defect generated during the conversion of a raw image acquired with a single sensor array into an RGB image (demosaicing), some of whose borders are characterized by color misregistration
- *Sharpness* [150], is the contrast along edges in the image.

Figure 5.13 shows some of these defects; note that the defects have been accentuated for ease of readability. Defects introduced above cannot be considered as new image quality dimensions; however, they are correlated with quality dimensions discussed in Fig. 5.7; in Fig. 5.14, we show the most significant correlations, classified into positive, negative, and nonmonotonic, namely, both positive and negative, correlations.

5.3.2.3 Reduced Reference

Reduced reference (RR) metrics lie between FR and NR metrics. They extract a number of features from both the reference and the image under test (e.g., [111, 383, 541, 586, 652]). These features are used as a surrogate of all the information conveyed by images, and image comparison is based only on the correspondence of these features. Thus, among dimensions proposed in Sect. 5.2, only fidelity can be assessed.

The aforementioned image quality approaches assess the quality by directly taking into account the properties of the images themselves in the form of their pixel or feature values. Considering the usefulness dimensions of the QAC model, image quality can also be indirectly assessed by quantifying the performance of an image-based task or a set of tasks. This can be done manually by domain experts and/or automatically by a computational system. For example, in a biometrics system, an

(a) (b) (c)

(d) (e) (f)

Fig. 5.13 Examples of image defects detected by no-reference metrics. (**a**) Original. (**b**) Colorfulness. (**c**) Contrast. (**d**) Blockiness. (**e**) Blurriness. (**f**) Graininess

image of a face is of good quality if the person can be reliably recognized. This can be done by manually inspecting each image acquired and evaluating if the pose satisfies the application constraints (e.g., non-occluded face) or enforced by law requirements (e.g., open eyes). Image distortions that are irrelevant for the task can therefore go unnoticed or simply ignored by the observer. The quality evaluation could be done by a face recognition algorithm that automatically processes each image and assesses the fulfillment of the constraints and requirements [417].

Indirect assessment can be also performed by assessing the performance of the imaging/rendering devices. Using suitable sets of images and one or more direct methods (both objective and subjective), it is possible to assess the quality of the imaging and rendering procedures. In this case, image quality is related to some

Defect → Quality Dimension	Colorfulness	Contrast	Blocking	Blurriness	Graininess
Accuracy			High negative correlation		
Fidelity			High negative correlation		
Naturalness	High non monotonic correlation	High non monotonic correlation	High negative correlation		
Usefulness			High negative correlation	High negative correlation	High negative correlation

Fig. 5.14 Significant correlations between defects and image quality dimensions

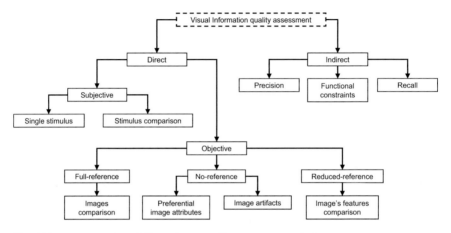

Fig. 5.15 Taxonomy of the different image quality assessment techniques

measurable features of imaging/rendering devices, such as spatial resolution, color depth, etc. These features can be quantitatively assessed using standard targets and ad hoc-designed software tools such as Imatest [322] and IQLab [149], but these measures alone are not sufficient to fully assess image quality. We finally notice that the camera phone image quality initiative of the International Imaging Industry Association suggests both objective and subjective characterization procedures [321]. Figure 5.15 graphically depicts the different image quality approaches.

A procedure typically followed to validate the IMQ methods evaluates the metrics on a database and performs subjective tests simultaneously using standard psychophysical scaling tools. The obtained perceptual quality ratings are averaged to obtain the mean opinion score. Both objective and subjective results are then compared through different performance metrics. Since the subjective quality score is a single numerical value, it should be noted that also the objective quality measure must be expressed using a single value. Typical measures of performance are related to prediction accuracy, prediction monotonicity, and prediction consistency with respect to the subjective assessments. Different databases are available to test the algorithms' performance with respect to the human subjective judgments. Among the most frequently used, we can cite LIVE [568], MICT [546], IVC [108], TID2008 [509], and the Toyama database [612]. Even though it is a rather small dataset, the A57 [117] database is also available.

5.4 Quality Assessment and Image Production Workflow

In Fig. 5.16, a generic image workflow chain with the indication of where the different IMQ assessment approaches are applied is shown. It starts with the source data (e.g., natural scene, phenomenon, measured values) to be captured by a digital image. The source can be specific of a narrow domain (e.g., resonance image) or broad domain (e.g., personal photo collections). Depending on the domain, acquisition constraints (e.g., semantic or environmental) are applied. The imaging block in Fig. 5.16 broadly refers to any imaging device, hardware or software, that transforms the source into a digital image. An example of a physical imaging device can be a camera, scanner, or tomograph, while a software device can be any application that is able to create a synthetic image (e.g., map, flow chart, diagram, etc.).

Once the image is created or acquired, imaging metadata can be automatically embedded in the image header (e.g., EXIF). They may include information such as maker, model of the camera, device settings, date and time, time zone offset, and GPS information. Other metadata are usually added both for catalogue and retrieval purposes. The overall metadata schema is usually set at the beginning of the digitalization stage and is based on application needs and the workflow requirements.

The digital image along with the metadata can be directly stored in an archive for further use or go through a validation phase that is aimed to have an initial assessment of the suitability and/or quality of the image with respect to the application needs. For example, a manual inspection can be performed in order to check if the whole scene has been correctly acquired or if it satisfies certain constraints. Validation constraints can be those related to the semantic of the image and can be evaluated either by human observers or automatically via computational algorithms (e.g., [554]). Images that do not pass the validation phase are rejected.

In the image quality literature, little attention is given to the scene contents. The scene is composed of the contents itself (e.g., a face) and the viewing/acquisition environment: geometry, lighting, and surrounding. We may call *scene gap* the lack of coincidence between the acquired and the desired scene. The scene gap should be quantified either at the end of the acquisition stage or during the validation stage (if any). The scene gap can be considered *recoverable* if subsequent processing steps can correct or limit the information loss or corruption in the acquired scene. It is *unrecoverable* if no suitable procedure exists to recover or restore it. The recoverability of the scene gap is affected by the image domain. When narrow image domains are considered (e.g., medical X-ray images), to achieve limited and predictable variability of the relevant aspects of image appearance, it is easier to

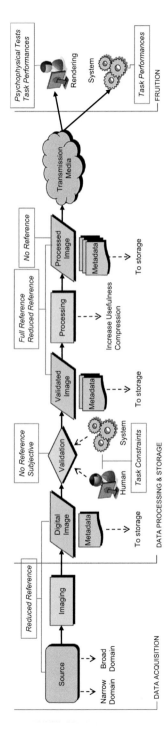

Fig. 5.16 Relationship between the image production workflow chain and the image quality assessment approaches

devise procedures aimed to automatically detect or reduce the scene gap. When broad image domains are considered, it is very difficult and, in many cases, impossible to automatically detect, quantify, and recover the scene gap.

The characteristics of the imaging device have an obvious impact on the quality of the acquired image. The hardware (e.g., sensors and optics) and/or software components (processing algorithms) of the device may be very articulated and complex. Their roles can be to keep image fidelity as much as possible and improve image usefulness, naturalness, or suitable combinations of these quality dimensions. We may call *device gap* the lack of coincidence between the acquired image and the image as acquired by an ideal device properly defined or chosen and used. The characteristics of the devices to be used must be carefully evaluated in order to limit the images rejected in the validation phase. To this end, RR and NR methods introduced in Sect. 5.3.2 can be used to evaluate the device. Only RR methods can be used to evaluate the digital image with respect to the source, because the source belongs to a different domain representation that makes it impossible a direct comparison. NR methods are used to detect the presence of defects in the imaging pipeline.

If required, the image can be further processed in order to increase its usefulness for the task at hand (e.g., through the contrast enhancement or binarization) or in order to allow more efficient transmission and storage. During this phase, any of the image quality assessment techniques can be applied. In particular, full reference assessment techniques can be used since two digital images (before and after the processing) are available. Extra information can be added (usually information about the enhancements and processing that have been applied). The image can now be delivered and finally used either by a human observer or by an application.

Finally, as an example, we cite a real case study where information quality assessment is applied within a printing workflow chain; see [151].

5.5   Quality Assessment in High-Quality Image Archives

In this section, we discuss how image quality assessment is addressed in high-quality image archives. Quality metrics and rules are suggested. It must be noted that some of the techniques that are described within this context may be applied for others as well.

Figure 5.17 illustrates an image workflow chain aimed for the population of a generic image archive for professional users such as institutional museums, photographic agencies, and, in general, any entity responsible for the management and distribution of high-quality image archives. Notwithstanding that, in this scenario, the main scope of the workflow chain is to collect images with the maximum fidelity in order to preserve the characteristics of the originals as much as possible; one of the major issues institutions should consider is the anticipated use of their digital image collections (i.e., the task). How will the images be made accessible, on a stand-alone workstation, via the Web, or via mobile devices? Will they be used for consultations or reproductions? Are there any access restrictions? These questions, among others, have to be answered *before* a digitization project

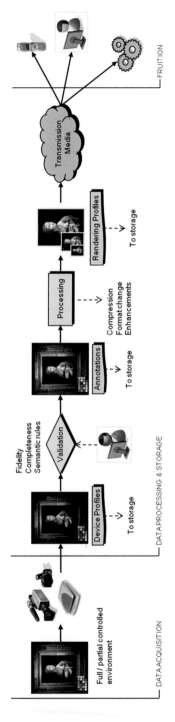

Fig. 5.17 Image workflow chain of a high-quality digital image archive

starts [246]. Depending on the final image usage, different quality issues must be addressed. Several files should be stored for every image to fulfill all requirements, mainly preservation and access. In general, images in a high-quality archive can be grouped into three main categories [618]: master, access, and thumbnail images.

Master images (or digital masters) are those with the highest quality. They can serve as surrogate for the original and as a long-term source for derivative files and print reproductions. They are stored in an uncompressed form, and their quality level is high. *Access images* are those used in place of master images, for consultation, for reference, and, in general, for public access (local or global). They generally fit within the viewing area of the average monitor and are compressed for speed of access. Their quality is acceptable for general research and depends on the level of fruition. To this end, copies of access images, each with a different level of quality, are needed. *Thumbnail images* are small images used for internal reference, indices, or bookmarks usually presented with the bibliographic record. They are designed to display quickly online (and thus are store compressed) and allow the user to determine whether they want to view the access images or not. They are also used for consultation in specific instances (e.g., devices with small displays) but are not always suitable for images consisting primarily of text.

The acquisition environment can be considered as only partially controlled. For example, in the case of an art gallery, the environment cannot be excessively tampered with to properly light the objects or move them in a better place to facilitate the acquisition procedures; further, paintings must be illuminated with lights that must not harm the colors, or the camera cannot be freely placed in front of the objects. The acquisition is performed by high-end acquisition devices. Special devices can also be used to acquire large surfaces at high resolution. Since the fidelity of the acquired image is of paramount importance, color charts are used to calibrate and characterize the acquisition devices [565]. They may be also acquired along with the objects constituting reliable references for RR IMQs and subsequent processing steps. In the validation phase, it is important to assess that the whole object has been completely and correctly acquired as in the case of the multi-view acquisitions of 3D objects or the surface tessellation of very large paintings.

Image quality can be assessed either by evaluating the fidelity of the colors in the color chart, by using any of the reduced reference methods, or by assessing if any image distortions introduced by the acquisition device is present (e.g., noise or blur on edges) using no reference metrics. For verified images, the color charts may be removed and only the objects of interest retained. Images are annotated with auxiliary information such as the title of the opera, author, and creation date. Since the images collected may be distributed and used in different ways, the processing phase may include resizing, thumbnail creation, digital image format changes, and compression in order to derive access and thumbnail images. For images that undergo processing steps, quality check is mandatory and, according to the type of processing FR, reduced reference or NR methods can be applied. For compression, FR methods such as SCIELAB [693] and SSIM [654] are useful. However, if the image is resized before compression, they cannot be applied and NR methods such as blockiness and quantization noise should be used instead. The images thus collected can be accessed by browsing by users or indexed and exploited within the framework of traditional information retrieval (IR) systems.

Metadata associated with the acquired images are of great importance in this application scenario. In [74], four types of metadata schemes are proposed that institutions can use to describe their artifacts: descriptive metadata, administrative metadata, structural metadata, and technical metadata. For advanced tasks, the ISO/IEC MPEG working group has defined the MPEG-7 standard [333], an XML-based multimedia content description interface that allows the storage of textual, numerical, or relational descriptions along with the multimedia data [578]. Since all the stored textual data are intertwined and can refer to the same conceptual entities in complex and complementary ways, the quality of the data stored into the database should be also taken into account with appropriate metrics (see [37, 39]).

Given a processed image, we may be interested in predicting the overall IMQ of the final printed document. The IMQ assessment of the image has to be evaluated before printing the document, so that the final product reaches the desired quality level. The processed image can be sent to a printer emulator software that taking into account all the characteristics of the hardware/software of the real printer, inks and paper, is able to generate an image of what the print will look like (soft proofing). This soft-printed image can be used to estimate the quality of the final printed document using FR, RR, and NR metrics or subjective judgments. Furthermore, the quality of the actual printed image can be assessed according to the specific task. In this case, the evaluation is mainly subjective since it must take into account the print usage (fliers, brochures, art catalogue, high fidelity reproduction, etc.) and possibly the creator intents and preferences. To assess the quality, care should be taken to set up properly viewing condition (light, background, etc.).

A similar approach can be used when printing composite documents with several images on a single page. In this scenario, quality can be independently assessed on each image using the above workflow, and then a coherence analysis could be performed to ensure that, for example, the color features of similar images are in agreement among each other or that all the images belong to a similar semantic class (e.g., indoor, outdoor, landscape, etc.).

During the fruition of the image, the perceived image quality is greatly affected by the rendering device and the viewing conditions. For a faithful reproduction of digital images, the rendering devices must be carefully calibrated and characterized [565]. A best practice is to employ a *color management system* based on the international color consortium (ICC) color management model. A device profile can be embedded into an image file which will enable the image to be automatically adjusted where necessary [332]. At this stage, image quality assessment can be carried out using subjective methods to evaluate the perceived image quality in the fruition environments. Some basic guidelines on how to acquire digital images of four different categories can be found in [74].

5.6   Video Quality Assessment

As in the case of images, digital video data, stored in video databases and distributed
through communication networks, is subject to various kinds of distortions during
acquisition, compression, processing, transmission, and reproduction. Most of the
contemporary video coding standards use motion compensation and block-based
coding schemes for compression. As a result, the decoded video suffers from one
or more of the compression artifacts, such as blockiness, blurriness, color bleeding,
ringing, false edges, jagged motion, chrominance mismatch, and flickering. Transmission errors such as damaged or lost packets can further degrade the video quality.
Furthermore, the preprocessing or post-processing stages in the video transmission
system, such as   domain conversion (analog to digital or vice versa), frame rate
conversion, and   de-interlacing degrade the video. Therefore, the methods for
evaluating video quality play a critical role in quality monitoring to maintain quality
of service requirements; performance evaluation of video acquisition and display
devices; evaluation of video processing systems for compression, enhancement, etc.

As in IMQ assessment, in video quality (VQ) assessment, two main approaches
can be distinguished: subjective and objective assessment. The video quality
expert group (VQEG) is the principal forum that validates objective video quality
metric models [632] that result in International Telecommunication Union [334]
recommendations and standards for objective quality models for both television
and multimedia applications. Similarly to the IMQ assessment, subjective tests for
VQA can be classified as double stimulus (continuous or impairment scale), single
stimulus (continuous or category rating), or pair comparison. Also in this case, the
performance of the objective model is evaluated with respect to its correlation with
the subjective data.

Among the most popular available video databases to be used as test bed, we can
cite the VQEG FRTV Phase I database [633] and the LIVE video Quality Database
[409]. The LIVE database includes videos distorted by H.264 compression, as
well as videos resulting from simulated transmission of H.264 packetized streams
through error-prone communication channels.

Following the survey article of Chikkerur et al. [131], the VQ assessment
methods can be classified as natural *visual characteristics-oriented* or *perceptual-
based metrics*. The natural visual characteristics refer to both statistical measures
(mean, variance, distribution) and natural visual features-based models (measure
blurring, blocking, edge detection, texture properties, etc.). Among the metrics
specifically designed for VQ assessment and belonging to the NVF group, we cite
the metric [499] and the video quality metric [502]. The video quality metric was
developed by the National Telecommunications and Information Administration
and provides several quality models like the *television model*, the *general model*,
and the *video conferencing model*. Some VQ assessment algorithms detect and
use motion information explicitly, taking into account the optical flow fields.
For example, the FR metric named motion-based video integrity evaluation [561]
combines two indices that capture spatial and temporal distortions explicitly. In the

case of RR methods for video, we can cite the metric by Soundararajan and Bovik [587].

In [131], several metrics are tested on the LIVE video database, and the authors conclude that the metric MS-SSIM [531] designed for still IMQ assessment and the metrics explicitly designed for the case of VQ assessment, VQM, and MOVIE are the best performing methods. Therefore, they also conclude that improved spatiotemporal modeling is needed for VQ assessment as current video quality metrics do not offer improved performance as compared to some existing still image quality metrics that are applied to video.

5.7   Summary

A challenge task in IMQ assessment is how to design a general purpose IMQ metric capable of assessing different artifacts simultaneously. It is not surprising that the major part of the IMQ metrics are designed to measure only a single distortion. The few that consider two distortions simultaneously are mainly concerned with the case of correlated noise and blur. A first idea could be to combine different IMQ assessment metrics into a single method. However, before considering different combination strategies, the normalization problem of the single metrics should be addressed. Both the normalization and combination of multiple metrics are still open problems within the IMQ assessment community. The same issue applies if we aim to increase the performance of detecting a given artifact by combining several metrics. To cope with this problem, recently general purpose metrics (or universal metrics) have been recently proposed by Tang and Kapoor [286], Mittal and Bovik [1], and Ye and Doermann [686]. Despite these methods showing promising results as generic metrics, they have been mainly tested only on the LIVE database where each corrupted image is affected by a single distortion. Recently a multi-distortion database [345] has been introduced where the multiple distortions consist of blur followed by JPEG and blur followed by noise. A preliminary study about the interaction between noise and JPEG distortions can be found in [152].

Objective image quality assessment is an active and evolving research area. In this chapter, we have given a compendium of the state of the art of the different IMQ assessment methods. To help users in the choice of IMQ metrics to be used within their image workflow chains, we have classified and summarized the different available metrics. We have also outlined the relationship between the image workflow chain and the image quality assessment approaches , how and when these different kinds of metrics can be applied within a generic image workflow chain and within three application scenarios. It should be now evident that the selection and usage of the different metrics depend on the semantic content of the image, the application task, and the particular imaging chain applied. In order to design more reliable and general purpose image quality metrics, an interdisciplinary approach is the challenge for the next years. Evidence from the biological studies will help us to understand how our brain works when involved in the quality assessment task. Computational models of the visual system that account for these cognitive behaviors could be integrated within the perceptual quality metric design [73]. Last but not least, semantic models coming from the image understanding community can certainly help us to improve the metrics' design and performance.

Chapter 6
Models for Information Quality

6.1 Introduction

In the previous chapters, we introduced several dimensions that are useful to describe and measure information quality in its different aspects and meanings. Focusing on structured data, database management systems (DBMSs) represent data and relative operations on it in terms of a *data model* and a *data definition and manipulation language*, i.e., a set of structures and commands that can be represented, interpreted, and executed by a computer. We can follow the same process to represent, besides data, their quality dimensions. This means that in order to represent data quality, we have to extend data models.

Models are widely used in databases for various purposes, such as analyzing a set of requirements and representing it in terms of a conceptual description, called *conceptual schema*; such a description is translated into a *logical schema* in terms of which queries and transactions are expressed.

Models are also used in the wider area of information systems to represent business processes of organizations; processes are described in terms of activities, their inputs and outputs, causal relationships between them, and functional/non-functional requirements. Such models are needed in order to help the analyst, e.g., to analyze and foresee process behavior, measure performance, and design possible improvements.

In this chapter, we investigate the principal extensions of traditional models adopted for structured relational data and semistructured data to deal with data quality dimension issues. In Sect. 6.2, we investigate proposed extensions of conceptual and logical database models for structured data. Logical models are considered both from the perspective of data description models and as related to data manipulation and data provenance. Then we discuss models for semistructured information, with specific attention to XML schemas (Sect. 6.3). In Sect. 6.4, we move on to management information system models; here, we investigate two "orthogonal" issues: (1) extensions of models for process descriptions to issues

© Springer International Publishing Switzerland 2016

C. Batini, M. Scannapieco, *Data and Information Quality*, Data-Centric Systems and Applications, DOI 10.1007/978-3-319-24106-7_6

related to quality of sources, users involved in data checks, etc., and (2) proposals for joint representation of elementary and aggregated data and related qualities. In all the models that we are going to describe, we will see that the extensions of models to data quality issues lead to structures characterized by significant complexity.

6.2 Extensions of Structured Data Models

The principal database models are the Entity Relationship model, the most common for conceptual database design (see [38]), and the relational model, adopted by a wide range of DBMSs.

6.2.1 Conceptual Models

Several solutions exist for extending the Entity Relationship model with quality characteristics (see [594, 595]). The different proposals focus on *attributes*, the unique representation structure in the model with which data values may be associated. A possibility is to model the quality of attribute values as another attribute of the same entity. For example, if we want to express a dimension (e.g., accuracy or completeness) for the attribute Address of an entity Person, we may add (see Fig. 6.1) a new attribute AddressQualityDimension to the entity.

The drawback of this solution is that now the entity is no longer normalized, since the attribute AddressQualityDimension is dependent upon Address, which is dependent upon Id. Another problem is that if we want to define several dimensions for an attribute, we have to define a new attribute for each dimension, resulting in a proliferation of attributes.

A second possibility is to introduce two types of entities, explicitly defined for expressing quality dimensions and their values: a data quality dimension entity and a data quality measure entity.

The goal of the DataQualityDimension entity is to represent all possible pairs of dimensions and corresponding ratings; the pairs <DimensionName, Rating> constitute the set of dimensions and possible corresponding values resulting from measurements. In the previous definition, we have implicitly assumed that the scale of rating is the same for all attributes. If the scale depends on the attribute, then we have to extend the properties of the DataQualityDimension entity to <Dimension-Name, Attribute, Rating>.

Fig. 6.1 A first example of quality dimension represented in the Entity Relationship model

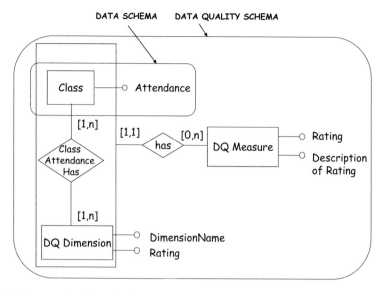

Fig. 6.2 An example of Data Quality Schema as proposed in [595]

In order to represent metrics for dimensions, and their relationship with entities, attributes, and dimensions, we have to adopt a more complex structure than the one shown in Fig. 6.1, in which we introduce the DataQualityMeasure entity; its attributes are Rating, in which the values depend on the specific dimension modeled, and DescriptionofRating. The complete *data quality schema*, which we show by means of the example in Fig. 6.2, is made up of:

1. The original *data schema*, made in the example of the entity Class with all its attributes (here, we represent only the attribute Attendance).
2. The DQ Dimension entity with a pair of attributes <DimensionName, Rating>.
3. The relationship between the entity Class, the related attribute Attendance, and the DQ Dimension entity with a many-to-many relationship ClassAttendanceHas; a distinct relationship has to be introduced for each attribute of the entity Class.
4. The relationship between the previous structure and the DQ Measure entity with a new representation structure that extends the Entity Relationship model and relates entities and relationships.

The overall structure adopted in Fig. 6.2 has been proposed in [595]. The above example shows how complex a schema becomes extended with the above structures to describe qualities.

6.2.2 Logical Models for Data Description

The relational model is extended in [647, 649] with quality values associated with
each attribute value, resulting in the *quality attribute model*. We explain the model
with an example, shown in Fig. 6.3.

The figure shows a relational schema Employee, defined on attributes
EmployeeId, DateofBirth, and others, and one of its tuples. Relational
schemas are extended, adding an arbitrary number of underlying levels of
quality indicators (only one level in the figure) to the attributes of the schema,
to which they are linked through a quality key. In the example, the attribute
EmployeeId is extended with three quality attributes, namely, accuracy, currency,
and completeness, while the attribute DateofBirth is extended with accuracy
and completeness, since currency is not meaningful for permanent data such
as DateofBirth. The values of such quality attributes measure the quality
dimensions' values associated with the whole relation instance (top part of the
figure). Therefore, completeness equal to 0.7 for the attribute DateofBirth
means that the 70 % of the tuples have a non-null value for such an attribute.
Similar structures are used for the instance level quality indicator relations (bottom
part of the figure); if there are n attributes of the relational schema, n quality tuples
will be associated to each tuple in the instance.

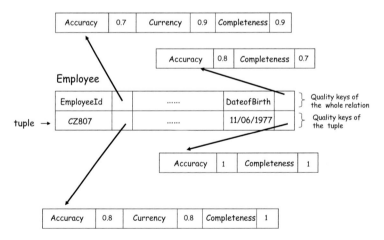

Fig. 6.3 An extension of the relational model

6.2.3 The Polygen Model for Data Manipulation

In principle, in every process of data collection and analysis, such as medical or biological experiments, data originating from different sources are manipulated in different stages; new data produced at each stage inherit the quality of ancestor data according to histories that depend on the execution plan. In Chap. 7, for several quality dimensions and relational algebra operations, we will investigate the functional relationships between the quality values of the input data and the quality values of the output data. In this section, we investigate an extension of the relational model, called *polygen model* [644, 649], proposed for explicitly tracing the origins of data and the intermediate sources. The model is targeted to heterogeneous distributed systems; the name of the model is derived from "multiple" "sources" (respectively, "poly" and "gen" in Greek). Now we briefly discuss the model, relevant for its pioneer role in the area. A *polygen domain* is a set of ordered triples composed of:

1. A datum drawn from a simple domain in a schema of a local database
2. A set of *originating databases* denoting the local databases from which the datum originates
3. A set of *intermediate databases* in which the data led to the selection of the datum

A *polygen relation* is a finite set of time-varying tuples, each tuple having the same set of attribute values from the corresponding polygen domains. A *polygen algebra* is a set of relational algebra operators whose semantics allows annotation propagation. The five primitive operators in the model are project, cartesian product, restrict, union, and difference. More precisely:

1. *Project, cartesian product, union*, and *difference* are extended from the relational algebra. The difference operator over two polygen relations r_1 and r_2 is extended as follows (for the remaining operators, see [644, 649]). A tuple t in r_1 is selected if the data part of t is not identical to those of the tuples of r_2. Since each tuple in r_1 has to be compared with all the tuples in r_2, it follows that all the originating sources of the data in r_1 are to be included in the intermediate source set produced by the difference operator.
2. The *restrict* operator is introduced to select tuples in a polygen relation that satisfy a given condition, and such tuples populate intermediate sources.
3. *Select* and *join* are defined in terms of the restrict operator, so they also involve intermediate sources.
4. New operators are introduced, e.g., *coalesce*, which takes two columns as input and merges them into one column (no inconsistency is admitted).

Note that in general in heterogeneous multidatabase systems, the values coalesced may be inconsistent. This issue is not considered in the polygen approach; it will be discussed in detail in Sect. 10.4.3 dedicated to instance-level conflict resolution techniques.

6.2.4   Data Provenance

The polygen model is a first attempt to represent and analyze the provenance of data, which has been recently investigated in a more general context. *Data provenance* is defined in [98] as the "description of the origins of a piece of data and the process by which it arrived in the database." We will provide a detailed discussion on provenance in the context of Web data in Chap. 14, while in this chapter, the focus is on structured data in a database.

The typical mechanism to trace the provenance is the use of *annotations* that can be exploited to represent a wide spectrum of information about data, such as comments or other types of metadata, and, in particular, data representing the quality of data. Annotations can be used in a variety of situations including:

1. Systematically trace the provenance and flow of data, namely, even if the data has undergone a complex process of transformation steps, we can determine the origins by examining the annotations.   .
2. Describe information about data that would otherwise have been lost in the database, e.g., an error report about a piece of data.
3. Enable the user to interpret the data semantics more accurately and to resolve potential conflicts among the data retrieved from different sources. This capability is useful in the field of data integration (see Chap. 10), where we are interested in understanding how data in different databases with heterogeneous semantics and different quality levels can be integrated.
4. Filter the data retrieved from a database according to quality requirements.
5. Improve the management of data trustworthiness through annotations referring to the reputation of a source or to a certification procedure.

Two types of provenance are defined in the literature, *why provenance* and *where provenance* (see [98, 158], and [133] as the main references in this area). We introduce them by means of an example. Assume we issue the following query:

```
SELECT StudentId, LastName, Sex
FROM Student
WHERE Age > SELECT  AVERAGE Age FROM Student
```
over the relational schema Student (StudentId, LastName, Sex, Age).

If the output is the tuple <03214, Ngambo, Female>, the provenance of the tuple can be related to two distinct data items:

1. The set of tuples in the input relation that contributed to the final result. In this case, all the tuples have to be selected as contributing tuples, since any modification in one tuple may affect the presence of <03214, Ngambo, Female> in the result. This kind of provenance is called *why provenance*, since we are looking for the tuples that explain the shape of the output.
2. The tuple(s) in the input relation that originated the values 03214, Ngambo, and Female in the output tuple. In this case, the set is made up of the unique tuple with StudentId = 03214. This kind of provenance is called

where provenance, since in this case, we are interested in finding from where annotations are propagated. In the case of a join between two tuples, both would be considered part of the input set.

The where provenance is particularly useful in the data quality context. In the case where annotations represent quality values, control of the process of quality dimension propagation is allowed by identifying the sources that are responsible for quality degradation. For the above reasons, in the following, we focus on the where provenance.

We will discuss the concept of the where provenance and its different meanings in the following context: given a relational database D, with a set of annotations associated with tuples in D, and a query Q over D, compute the provenance of an output tuple t in the result of Q.

If we think of possible meanings, i.e., methods to compute the where provenance (similar considerations can be made for the why provenance), two different approaches exist: the *reverse query* (or lazy) approach and the *forward propagation* (or eager) approach.

In the *reverse query approach* (see [98, 158]), a "reverse" query Q' is generated in which the result is the tuple or set of tuples that contribute, when Q has been executed, in producing it.

In the *forward propagation approach*, when applying Q, an enriched query Q* is generated and executed that computes how annotations are propagated in the result of Q. The approach is called *eager*, since provenance is immediately made available, together with the output of Q. The forward propagation approach, in turn, has three possible types of execution or *propagation schemes* [133], called the *default scheme*, the *default-all scheme*, and the *custom propagation scheme*. We introduce the three schemes by means of an example. Assume (see Fig. 6.4) we have a database of clients made up of two different tables, Client1 and Client2 and a mapping

Client1

Id	Description
071 [ann_1]	Cded [ann_2]
358 [ann_3]	Hlmn [ann_4]
176 [ann_5]	Stee [ann_6]

Client2

Id	Last Name
E3T [ann_7]	Nugamba [ann_8]
G7N [ann_9]	Mutu [ann_{10}]

MappingRelation

Id	Client1Id	Client2Id
1 [ann_{11}]	071 [ann_{12}]	E3T [ann_{13}]
2 [ann_{14}]	358 [ann_{15}]	G7N [ann_{16}]

Fig. 6.4 Two Client relations and a mapping relation

table between identifiers of clients in `Client1` and `Client2` (a typical situation in many organizations).

Intuitively, the default propagation scheme propagates annotations of data according to where data is copied from. Assume that the following query Q_1 is computed on the database of Fig. 6.4:

```
SELECT DISTINCT c.Id, c.Description
FROM Client1 c
WHERE c.Id = 071
```
The result of Q_1 executed against the relation `Client1` in the default propagation scheme is the unique tuple
$< 071[ann_1]; Cded[ann_2] >$

The semantics of the default scheme is quite natural, but it has a drawback, in that two equivalent queries (i.e., queries that return the same output for every database) may not propagate the same annotations to the output. Consider the two queries, Q_2:

```
SELECT DISTINCT c2.Id AS Id, c2.LastName AS LastName
FROM Client2 c2, MappingRelation m
WHERE c2.Id = m.Client2Id
```

and Q_3:

```
SELECT DISTINCT m.Id AS Id, c2.LastName AS LastName
FROM Client2 c2, MappingRelation m
WHERE c2.Id = m.Client2Id
```

The results of running Q_2 and Q_3 under the default propagation scheme are shown in Fig. 6.5. For Q_2, the annotations for the `Id` attribute are from the `Client2` relation, while for Q_3, the annotations for the `Id` attribute are from the `MappingRelation`.

The *default scheme* propagates the annotation for equivalent queries differently. We need a second propagation scheme, where propagations are invariant under equivalent queries. This scheme is called the *default-all propagation scheme* in [133]; it propagates annotations according to where data is copied from among all equivalent formulations of the given query. In case a user wants to bear the responsibility to specify how annotations should propagate, a third scheme can be adopted, the *custom scheme*, where annotation propagations are explicitly declared in the query.

Output of Q2

Id	Last Name
E3T [ann_7]	Nugamba [ann_8]
E3T [ann_9]	Muto [ann_10]

Output of Q3

Id	Last Name
E3T [ann_13]	Nugamba [ann_8]
E3T [ann_16]	Muto [ann_10]

Fig. 6.5 The output of two queries

The above schemes can be applied flexibly, whatever the type of the annotated information, i.e., it could be the source relation, the exact location within the source, or a comment on the data.

6.3   Extensions of Semistructured Data Models

In [548], a model for associating quality values to data-oriented XML documents is proposed. The model, called *data and data quality* (D^2Q), is intended to be used in the context of a cooperative information system (CIS). In such systems, the cooperating organizations need to exchange data with each other, and it is therefore critical for them to be aware of the quality of such data. D^2Q can be used in order to certify the accuracy, consistency, completeness, and currency of data. The model is semistructured, thus allowing each organization to export the quality of its data with a certain degree of flexibility. More specifically, quality dimension values can be associated with various elements of the data model, ranging from the single data value to the whole data source. The main features of the D^2Q model are summarized as follows:

- A *data class* and a *data schema* are introduced to represent the *domain* data portion of the D^2Q model, namely, the data values that are specific to a given cooperating organization's domain.
- A *quality class* and a *quality schema* correspond to the quality portion of the D^2Q model.
- A *quality association function* that relates nodes of the graph corresponding to the data schema to nodes of the graph corresponding to the quality schema. Quality associations represent biunivocal functions among all nodes of a data schema and all non-leaf nodes of a quality schema.

In Fig. 6.6, an example of a D^2Q schema is shown. On the left-hand side of the figure, a data schema is shown representing enterprises and their owners. On the right-hand side, the associated quality schema is represented. Specifically, two quality classes, `Enterprise_Quality` and `Owner_Quality` are associated with the `Enterprise` and `Owner` data classes. Accuracy nodes are shown for both data classes and related properties. For instance, `Code_accuracy` is an accuracy node associated with the `Code` property, while `Enterprise_accuracy` is an accuracy node associated with the data class `Enterprise`. The arcs connecting the data schema and the quality schema with the `quality labels` represent the quality association functions.

The D^2Q model is intended to be easily translated into the XML data model. This is important for meeting the interoperability requirements that are particularly

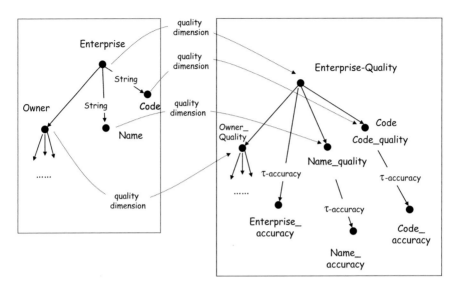

Fig. 6.6 Example of D^{2}Q quality schema

stringent in cooperative systems. Once translated into XML, the model can be
queried by means of an extension of the XQuery language that queries quality
values in the model. XQuery allows users to define new functions. Quality values
represented according to the D^{2}Q model can be accessed by a set of XQuery
functions, called *quality selectors*. Quality selectors are defined for accuracy,
completeness, consistency, and currency and for the overall set of quality values
that can be associated with a data node.

In Fig. 6.7, the implementation of the quality selector *accuracy*() is shown as
an example. Searchroot is a function defined to reach the root of a document
containing the input node.

The D^{2}Q model represents quality values to be associated with generic data.
XML is used as a language for modeling quality dimensions in a growing number of
contributions. For example, see in [428] a proposal for modeling quality of data by
means of six quality measures meaningful in the biological domain. Being domain
specific, such a proposal also includes metrics that allow the computation of node
quality values across the XML graph, by considering the interdependencies between
quality values of the various nodes in the graph.

```
define function accuracy($n as node*) as node* {
let $root := searchroot($n), qualitydoc:=document(string($root/@qualityfile))
for $q in $n/@quality
for $r in $qualitydoc//*[@qOID eq $q]/accuracy
return $r }
```

Fig. 6.7 Accuracy selector implementation as an XQuery function

6.4 Management Information System Models

In this section, we discuss management information system models in their relation to data quality issues. We discuss process models in Sects. 6.4.1 and 6.4.2, introducing the information production map (IP-MAP) model and its extensions. Issues related to data models are discussed in Sect. 6.4.3.

6.4.1 Models for Process Description: The IP-MAP Model

The IP-MAP model [563] is based on the principle that information can be seen as a particular product of a manufacturing activity, and so descriptive models (and methodologies) for information quality can be based on models conceived in the last two centuries for manufacturing traditional products. The IP-MAP model is centered on the concept of *information product (IP)*, introduced in Chap. 1.

An *IP-MAP* is a graphical model designed to help people comprehend, evaluate, and describe how an information product such as an invoice, customer order, or prescription is assembled in a business process. The IP-MAP is aimed at creating a systematic representation for capturing the details associated with the manufacturing of an information product. IP-MAPs are designed to help analysts to visualize the information production process, identify ownership of process phases, understand information and organizational boundaries, and estimate time and quality metrics associated with the current production process. There are eight types of construct blocks that can be used to form the IP-MAP. Each construct block is identified by a unique name and is further described by a set of attributes (metadata). The content of metadata varies depending on the type of construct block. In Fig. 6.8, the possible types of construct blocks are shown, together with the symbol used for their representation.

An example of IP-MAP is shown in Fig. 6.9. Information products (IP in the figure) are produced by means of processing activities and data quality checks on *raw data* (RD) and semi-processed information or *component data* (CD). In the example, we assume that high schools and universities of a district have decided to cooperate in order to improve their course offering to students, avoiding overlappings and being more effective in the education value chain. To this end, high schools and universities have to share historical data on students and their curricula. Therefore, they perform a record linkage activity (we will address in depth the issue of record linkage in Chaps. 8 and 9) that matches students in their education life cycle. To reach this objective, high schools periodically supply relevant information on students; in case it is in paper format, the information has to be converted in electronic format. At this point, invalid data are filtered and matched with the database of university students. Unmatched students are sent back to high schools for clerical checks, and matched students are analyzed; the result of the analysis on curricula and course topics are sent to the advisory panel of the universities.

Concept name	Symbol	Description
Source (raw input data)		Represents the source of each raw (input) data that must be available in order to produce the information product expected by the customer
Customer (output)		Represents the consumer of the information product. The consumer specifies the data elements that constitute the "finished" information products.
Data quality		Represents the checks for information quality on those data items that are essential in producing a "defect-free" information product.
Processing		Represents any calculations involving some or all of the raw input data items or component data items required to ultimately produce the information block.
Data Storage		It is any data item in a database.
Decision		It is used to describe the different decision conditions to be evaluated and the corresponding procedures for handling the incoming data items, based on the evaluation.
Business Boundary		Specifies the movement of the information product accross departmental or organization boundaries.
Information system boundary		Reflects the changes to the raw data items or component data items as they move form one information system to another type of information system. These system changes could be inter or intra business units.

Fig. 6.8   IP-MAP construct blocks

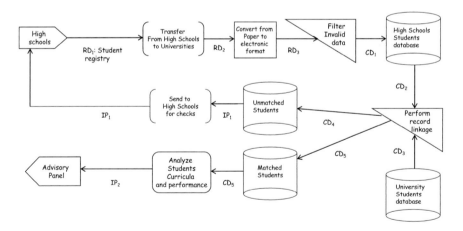

Fig. 6.9   An example of IP-MAP

6.4.2   Extensions of IP-MAP

The IP-MAP model has been extended in several directions. First, more powerful mechanisms have been provided in [501, 549], called *event process chain diagrams* representing the *business process overview*, the *interaction model* (how company units interact), the *organization model* (who does what), the *component model* (what happens), and the *data model* (what data is needed). This is done by modeling the following:

- The event that triggers the use of data by a process
- The communication structure between sources, consumers, and organizational groups
- The hierarchy of organizational groups/functions
- The relationship between products, storages, and other data components
- Logical relationships between events and processes

A modeling formalism is proposed in [549], called IP-UML, extending UML with a data quality profile based on IP-MAP. The use of UML instead of the IP-MAP formalism has the following advantages:

1. UML is a standard language, and computer-aided tools have been implemented for it.
2. UML is a language supportive of analysis, design, and implementation artifacts, so the same language can be used in all the phases of analysis and development.
3. The expressive power of UML is higher with reference to the process modeling constructs.

We briefly recall that in UML (see [192, 243]), the specification of analysis and design elements is based on the notion of a *model element*, defined as an abstraction drawn from the system being modeled; the principal model elements are *classes* and *relationships* between classes. A *constraint* is a semantic restriction that can be attached to a model element. A *tag definition* specifies new kinds of properties that may be attached to model elements. A *tagged value* specifies the actual values of tags of individual model elements. A *stereotype* is a new model element that extends previously defined model elements through a precise semantics. According to the UML specification [477], "a coherent set of such extensions, defined for a specific purpose, constitutes a *UML profile*".
The starting concepts of IP-UML are the ones defined in the IP-MAP framework; the result of the proposed extension is a UML profile called data quality profile. The *data quality profile* consists of three different models, namely, the data analysis model, the quality analysis model, and the quality design model.
   The *data analysis model* specifies which data are important for consumers, as its quality is critical for the organization's success. In the data analysis model information products, raw data and component data are represented as a stereotyped UML class. A *quality data class* is a class labeled with this stereotype generalizes information product classes, raw data classes, and component data classes. The

quality analysis model consists of modeling elements that can represent quality requirements of data, related to one of the dimensions typically defined for data quality. The set of dimensions proposed consists of four categories; for example, the *intrinsic information quality category* includes accuracy, objectivity, believability, and reputation. In order to model the overall set of dimension-related requirements, the following stereotypes are introduced:

1. A *quality requirement* class generalizes the set of quality requirements that can be specified on a quality data class.
2. A *quality association* class associates a quality requirement class with a quality data class. Quality requirements on data need to be verified so that, if they are not satisfied, improvement actions can be taken; therefore, a constraint is specifically introduced on the quality association.

The specification of a distinct stereotype for each quality requirement has the advantage of clearly fixing the types of requirements that can be associated with data.

The *quality design model* specifies IP-MAPs. The IP-MAP dynamic perspective, in which processes are described together with exchanged data, can be obtained by combining *UML!activity diagrams* with *UML object flow diagrams*. Activity diagrams are a special case of state diagrams in which the states are action or subactivity states and in which the transitions are triggered by completion of the actions or subactivities in the source states. Object flows are diagrams in which objects that are input or output from an action may be shown as object symbols. The following UML extensions need to be introduced, to represent IP-MAP elements:

- *Stereotyped activity*, to represent processing and data quality blocks
- *Stereotyped actor*, to represent customer, source, and data storage blocks
- *Stereotyped dependency relationship*, to give a precise semantics to the relationships between some elements

Notwithstanding the rich set of new structures introduced in the extensions of IP-MAP, such extensions suffer from different limitations, discussed in the next section, with new models that attempt to override such limitations.

6.4.3   Information Models

A first limitation of IP-MAP (and IP-MAP extensions) lies in the fact that it does not distinguish between or provide specific formalisms for *operational processes*, which make use of *elementary information*, and *decisional processes*, which use *aggregated data*. The information system of an organization is composed of both types of data that present different quality problems. So, it seems relevant to enrich models for management information systems to explicitly provide a uniform formalism to represent both types of information and their quality dimensions.

Fig. 6.10 Organizations, processes, and information flows in a cooperative information system

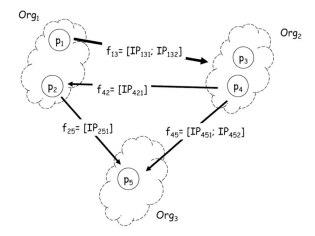

Secondly, IP-MAP does not take specific features of CIS into account. In a CIS, as Fig. 6.10 shows, an organization can be modeled as a collection of processes that transform input information flows into output information flows and that carry a stream of information products. In Fig. 6.10, three organizations are represented that exchange four information flows: two of them are composed of two information products each; the two remaining flows exchange one single information product. In the domain of a specific organization, an input flow to a process can be transformed into (1) an internal flow, (2) an input to another intraorganizational process, or (3) an output flow to one or more external organizations.

In [443–445], a comprehensive approach to overcome the above limitations is presented, discussed in the following sections.

6.4.3.1   Modeling Information Flows of an Organization

We first distinguish two different roles for organizations exchanging information flows in a CIS, namely, a *producer (organization)* when it produces flows for other organizations and a *consumer (organization)* when it receives flows from other organizations. Every organization usually plays both roles. Following traditional manufacturing practice, we characterize the quality of the individual items produced on the producer side; by extension, we associate a *quality offer profile* to a producer organization. Such a profile represents the quality that the organization is willing to offer to its customers, i.e., to other consumer organizations that require that information for use in a cooperative process. Symmetrically, on the consumer side, we define the notion of *quality demand profile* to express acceptable quality levels for the information items that consumers will acquire. Ultimately, we frame the problem of managing information quality within an organization as the problem of matching the quality profile offered by that organization to the quality requested by the consumers of the organization. At this point, we are able to define a framework for expressing quality offer and demand in a CIS context. The framework models both the structure of a cooperative organization (*information schema*) and its quality profiles (*quality schema*; see next section) in a uniform, hierarchical way.

We start by associating quality profiles with the elementary information items that the organization produces and consumes during the execution of processes (see Fig. 6.11 for the metaschema of the information schema, represented with a class diagram in UML).

An *information flow* f is a sequence of *physical information items* (PII) that are streamed from a producer process to one or more consumer processes. For instance, given a domain entity Address, and its instance 4 Heroes Street (suitably identified using keys defined for Address), a PII would be a specific copy of J. Smith's address, produced at a particular time t by a process p_1 and sent to a process p_2 over flow f. All PIIs produced by any process at any time, referring to the same data, homogeneous in meaning, are associated with a single *logical information item* 4 Heroes Street.

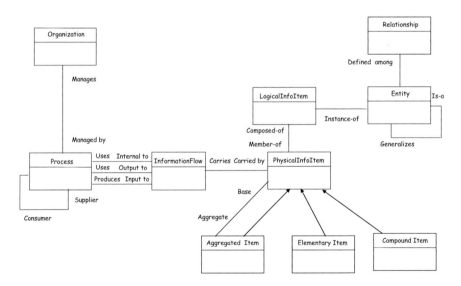

Fig. 6.11 Data, process, and organization schema

PII and logical information items describe *atomic* (or *elementary*) information items and their flow in time. As the metaschema in Fig. 6.11 shows, a *compound item* is obtained recursively from other compound or elementary items using composition functions, such as the record-type function (e.g., an `Address` is composed of `Street`, `City`, and `ZipCode`). An *aggregated item* is obtained from a collection of elementary and compound items by applying an aggregation function to them (e.g., the average income of taxpayers in a given town).

With the above representation structures, we are able to model both information flows made of elementary items and flows made of aggregated items. Finally, we associate information flows between processes and processes with organizations. Information flows are of three types: input to, output from, and internal to processes. We enrich the set of representation structures with other structures, typical of a conceptual model, such as *entity*, *relationship* among entities, and *generalization* among entities, as done in the schema in Fig. 6.11, with usual meanings in the Entity Relationship model.

6.4.3.2   A Quality Profile Model

In order to represent and compute quality profiles, associated with all the classes in the previous schema, we model the quality profile of an organization as a *data cube* on a given set of dimensions, using the *multidimensional database model* proposed in [10]. We view the quality profile of a single item as one point in a *multidimensional cube*, in which the axes include a hierarchy of entities consisting of physical and logical information items, flows, processes, organizations, and quality dimensions.

The information carried by each quality point in the resulting *quality cube* is the single quality measurement at the finest level of granularity, i.e., the quality descriptor associated with a single PII and for a single dimension. Figure 6.12 shows the *star schema*, according to the data warehouse modeling approach; it has the quality values as fact entity and the remaining ones as the dimension entities; attributes of fact and dimension entities are not shown.

The quality profiles for information flows, processes, and entire organizations are computed as appropriate aggregations from a base quality cube. Thus, once an appropriate set of *aggregation functions* (e.g., average) is defined over quality descriptors, quality profiles at each level of granularity in an organization are described within an established framework for multidimensional data. As an example, consider again Fig. 6.10, where two organizations, five processes, and four flows are defined. We may aggregate quality values along the following chain: (1) PII, (2) information flow, (3) process, and (4) organization; and, using aggregation functions, we may associate quality values with each one of the above information flows, processes, and organizations, according to the perspective we choose.

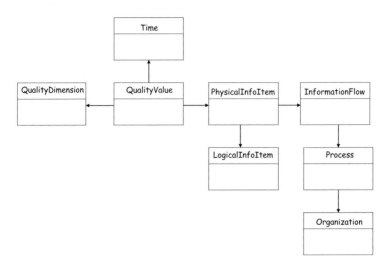

Fig. 6.12 Star schema of the data quality cube

6.5   Summary

In this chapter, we have seen several proposals for extending data, information, and process models, to provide them with structures for representing quality dimensions and for using them to measure and improve quality profiles of single information flows, processes, and entire organizations. In the following chapters, we will address the core topics of research in and experience with information quality, i.e., techniques and methodologies proposed for IQ measurement and improvement. We anticipate that such techniques and methodologies seldom rely on the proposals presented in this chapter on model extensions, with the distinctive exception of the IP-MAP model. Furthermore, only a few prototypical DBMSs have experienced the adoption of some of the approaches mentioned for data quality, among them [20]. This feeble connection is due to the complexity of the overall equipment of the representational structures proposed in the different approaches and the lack of consolidated tools and DBMSs to manage them. From an application perspective, rather than articulated data models, quality metadata descriptions can be used to document quality. As an example, in the Official Statistical domain, Eurostat provides guidelines for quality reports to be associated to datasets produced by National Statistical Institute. Such guidelines include the identification of specific quality metadata characterizing quality dimensions, i.e., accuracy and reliability, timeliness and punctuality, coherence and comparability, and accessibility and clarity [208].

The future of research on models appears to be in provenance and trustworthiness issues, as we will discuss in Chap. 14. In cooperative and Web information systems, knowing the provenance and the trustworthiness of data is crucial for the user, who may trace the history of data and increase his or her awareness in accessing and using them.

Chapter 7
Activities for Information Quality

7.1 Introduction

In Chap. 1 we noticed that information quality is a multifaceted concept, and the cleaning of poor quality information can be performed by measuring different dimensions and setting out several different activities, with various goals. An *information quality activity* is any process we perform directly on information to improve their quality. An example of "manual" information quality activity is the process we perform when we send an e-mail message and the e-mail bounces back because of an unknown user; we check the exact address in a reliable source, and we type the address on the keyboard more carefully to avoid further mistakes. An example of "computerized" information quality activity is the matching of two files in which inaccurate records are included, in order to find similar records that correspond to the same real-world entity. Other activities for improving information quality act on processes; they will be discussed and compared with information quality activities in Chap. 12.

Information quality activities are performed using different techniques that result in different efficiency and effectiveness for measuring and improving information quality dimensions. The final goal of this chapter, and of Chaps. 8–10, is to define the information quality activities and introduce the most relevant techniques proposed to support each of them. In this chapter we first define the activities (Sect. 7.2) and provide the reader a map of the book sections where the different activities are dealt with. The two most investigated information quality activities, namely, object identification and data integration, will be discussed in Chaps. 8–10. In this chapter, we discuss two of the activities, namely, quality composition (Sect. 7.3) and error localization and correction (Sect. 7.4). All of the above activities will be considered in the context of methodologies showing their possible usage in Chap. 12.

© Springer International Publishing Switzerland 2016
C. Batini, M. Scannapieco, *Data and Information Quality*, Data-Centric Systems and Applications, DOI 10.1007/978-3-319-24106-7_7

7.2   Information Quality Activities: Generalities

Although a large quantity of algorithms, heuristics, and knowledge-based techniques have been proposed that are classified as *information quality activities*, a limited number of categories can be identified. They are listed in the following, providing introductory definitions that will be detailed later in this chapter, as well as in Chaps. 8, 9, and 10:

1. *New information acquisition* is a process of information acquisition performed with the goal of refreshing the information at issue (e.g., a relation, an XML file, an image) with new quality data. The manual example discussed above falls in this category.
2. *Standardization* (or *normalization*) is the modification of information with new information according to defined standard or reference formats, e.g., change of Bob to Robert and change of Channel Str. to Channel Street.
3. *Object identification* (or *record linkage*, *record matching*, *entity resolution*), given one or more information sources, has the purpose of identifying those records in the sources that represent the same real-world object. When the information source is a single one, this activity is also called *deduplication*.
4. *Data integration* is the task of presenting a unified view of data owned by heterogeneous and distributed data sources. Data integration deals with quality issues mainly with respect to two specific activities:

   • *Quality-driven query processing* is the task of providing query results on the basis of a quality characterization of data at sources.
   • *Instance-level conflict resolution* is the task of identifying and solving conflicts of values referring to the same real-world object.

5. *Source trustworthiness* has the goal of rating sources on the basis of the quality of information they provide to other sources in an open or cooperative context, where no or little control exists on the quality of information.
6. *Quality composition* defines an algebra for composing information quality dimension values; for instance, given two sources in which the completeness values are known, and an operator, e.g., the union, computes the completeness of the union, starting from the completeness of the operand sources.
7. *Error localization* (or *error detection*), which, given one or more information sources and a set of semantic rules specified on them, finds records that do not respect such rules.
8. *Error correction*, which, given one or more information sources, a set of semantic rules, and a set of identified errors in records, corrects erroneous values in records in order to respect the overall set of rules.
9. *Cost optimization* has the goal to optimize a given target on information quality, according to a cost objective. For example, among different providers of information sources characterized by different costs and quality dimension metrics, one could be interested to select the provider with the optimal cost/quality ratio for a given information demand.

Other activities that more loosely pertain to information quality are:

- *Schema matching*, which takes two schemas as input and produces a mapping between semantically correspondent elements of the two schemas
- *Schema cleaning*, which provides rules for transforming the conceptual schema in order to achieve or optimize a given set of qualities (e.g., readability, normalization) while preserving other properties (e.g., equivalence of content)
- *Profiling,* which analyzes information in the source in order to compute (or infer) intensional properties, such as the number of records in the source and, in the case of structured relational data, the structure of the database, fields with similar values, join paths, and join sizes

Schema matching, schema cleaning, and schema profiling will not be considered in the following. Two of the activities, namely, object identification/record linkage and data integration, are of crucial importance in current business scenarios and have been widely investigated from a research and industrial perspective. Three specific chapters are dedicated to them; Chaps. 8 and 9 will discuss object identification and Chap. 10 will describe data integration. In addition:

1. New information acquisition will be dealt with in Chap. 12 in the context of information quality improvement methodologies.
2. Standardization is usually performed as a preprocessing activity in error localization, object identification, and data integration. However, as standardization is mostly included in object identification techniques, we will describe it in detail in Chaps. 8 and 9 as one of the steps of object identification.
3. Source trustworthiness is an emerging research issue in open and Web systems. When dealing with such systems, trust and information quality become two crucial concepts. We will discuss such issues in Chap. 14, dedicated to open research problems for Web data and Big Data.
4. Cost optimization covers three different aspects: (1) cost trade-offs between quality dimensions, discussed in Chap. 11; (2) cost and benefit classifications for characterizing information quality in business processes, addressed in Sect. 11.4.1; and (3) cost-benefit analysis of information quality improvement processes, discussed in Chap. 12.

In the rest of this chapter, we briefly describe the remaining activities. The following sections deal with quality composition (Sect. 7.2) and error localization and correction (Sect. 7.3).

7.3 Quality Composition

In several contexts, including e-Business and e-Government, especially when information is replicated across different sources (e.g., a relation, a map, etc.), it is usual to obtain new information by combining information extracted from one or more sources. In these contexts, it is important to be able to calculate a quality dimension or the set of qualities of the new resulting information, starting from the quality dimension values of the original sources, if available. Furthermore, in order to enhance the quality of data, it is often not enough to consider single sources and independently orchestrate improvement actions on them; instead, such actions should be properly complemented by composing information from different sources.

Let us consider a set of public administrations that cooperate with each other in an e-Government scenario, and let us focus on a specific information quality dimension, namely, the completeness dimension. In some countries, in every municipality the following registries are held: (1) a personal registry for home residents and (2) a separate registry for the civil status of the residents. At the regional level, we may assume that there are local income tax payer registries, while at central level there are usually national social insurance, accident insurance, and other registries. These sources usually have different levels of completeness in representing the corresponding reality of interest, and in many administrative processes, these sources are combined. It would be interesting to directly calculate the completeness of the combined result starting from the completeness of the sources, if known, without performing on the result a costly process of quality measurement. This is the goal of the information quality composition activity.

The general problem statement for the definition of the quality composition problem is represented in Fig. 7.1. The information source, or the set of information sources, X, is described according to a model M, e.g., for relational tables the relational model and for maps the conceptual model described in Chap. 3, and is processed by a generic composition function F. The composition function F is defined on a set of operators $O = [o_1, \dots, o_k]$ defined in the model M. Also, a function Q_D calculates the value of the quality dimension D for X, i.e., $Q_D(X)$, and the value of D for Y equals $F(X)$, i.e. $Q_D(Y)$. We aim to define the function $Q_D^F(X)$ that calculates $Q_D(Y)$ starting from $Q_D(X)$, instead of calculating such a value directly on Y by applying the function $Q_D(Y)$.

Fig. 7.1 The general problem of quality composition

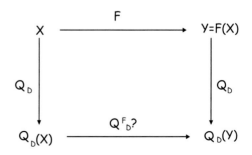

We will consider the case of this problem in which:

- *M* is the relational model.
- *O* corresponds to the set of relational algebraic operators, such as union, intersection, cartesian product, projection, selection, and join.
- *D* is a specific information quality dimension, e.g., completeness or accuracy.
- Q_D^F is a function that evaluates the quality of the relations under different hypotheses and for different relational operators.

The problem of defining a *composition algebra* for relational data quality dimensions has been considered in several papers in the literature, namely, Motro and Ragov [455], Wang et al. [649], Parsiann et al. [491–493], Naumann et al. [464], and Scannapieco and Batini [547]. In Fig. 7.2 these approaches are compared on the basis of (1) the variants of the adopted relational model and data architecture, (2) the quality dimensions considered, (3) the relational algebra operators taken into account, and (4) the specific assumptions on the sources. In the following section, we comment all the issues dealt with in Fig. 7.2; when describing the approaches, we will use the names of the authors in the first column of the table.

We recall that in Chap. 2 we have introduced the concepts of closed world assumption, open world assumption, reference relation, and the related dimension definitions of value completeness, tuple completeness, and relation completeness.

Paper	Model	Specific assumptions on the sources	Quality dimensions considered	Algebraic operators
Motro 1998	Relational model with OWA (implicit)	No assumption	Soundness Completeness	Cartesian Product Selection Projection
Parssiann 2002	Relational model with OWA (implicit)	Uniformely distributed errors in identifier attributes Error probabilites for all attributes independent of each other Uniformely distributed errors in non identifier attributes for mismember and other tuples	Accuracy Inaccuracy Mismembership Incompletness	Selection Projection Cartesian Product Join
Wang 2001	Relational model	Uniformly distributed errors	Accuracy	Selection Projection
Naumann 2004	Data integration system Set of data sources + Universal relation with CWA	Set relationships between sources - Disjointness - Quantified overlap - Independence (coincidential overlap) - Containment	Coverage Density Completeness	Join merge Full outer join merge Left outer join merge Right outer join merge
Scannapieco 2004	Relational model with OWA and CWA	Open world vs closed world assumption Set relationships between sources - Disjointness - Non quantified overlap - Containment	Completeness	Union Intersection Cartesian product

Fig. 7.2 Comparison between approaches to quality composition

7.3.1 Models and Assumptions

Motro and Parssian consider a relational model in which an ideal (called *conceptual* by Parssian) relation *r-ideal* and the corresponding real relation *r-real* can be constructively defined; as a consequence, they may distinguish common and non-common tuples between them. Motro defines dimensions in terms of the differences between r-ideal and r-real, measured considering, respectively, common tuples and uncommon ones. Parssian goes further, distinguishing, between the two types of tuples, pairs of tuples that differ in the primary keys (called *identifiers* in the Parssian approach and in the following) and tuples that are identical on the keys and differ on the non-key attributes (*non-identifier* attributes in the following). The assumptions dealt with by Parssian on error probabilities both on identifier and non-identifier attributes are described in Fig. 7.2. Wang is not interested in completeness issues. He or she does not consider tuples that are in the ideal relation and are not members of the real relation; furthermore, he or she assumes that the tuples that appear in the real relation are only there by mistake, called *mismember tuples*. Wang, within a simplified model, assumes uniform distribution of errors in the relation.

Naumann, differently from other authors, investigates quality composition in the context of a data integration system. Naumann adopts a model where data sources correspond to local relations and databases. A global source exists, called *universal relation*, that corresponds to the set of all tuples that can be obtained through the sources at hand. Naumann considers four different cases of set relationships between sources: (1) disjointness; (2) containment; (3) independence, corresponding to coincidental overlap; and (4) quantified overlap, where the number of common tuples among sources is known. In the following, we will describe the set of operators adopted by Naumann, both in expressing the relationship between the sources and the universal relation and in the characterization of quality composition. Naumann is interested in evaluating the quality of the process of composing sources, in order to put together information that is split into different sources. For this reason, he or she is interested in evaluating the behavior of join operators.

The *full outer join merge* operator is defined as a suitable adaptation of the full outer join operator of relational algebra (see [198]) to the context in which conflicts in tuples are taken into account. In the proposed model, it is assumed that tuples of different sources have been identified as corresponding to the same object of the real world. When we merge two tuples t_1 and t_2 referring to the same object, depending on the situations, common attributes can have (1) both null values; (2) t_1 a null value and t_2 a specified value; (3) the inverse, i.e., t_1 a specified value and t_2 a null value; (4) the same specified value; and (5) different specified values. In the last case, it is assumed that a *resolution function* is provided. Let us consider two given sources, corresponding to relations r_1 and r_2. The *join merge* operator may be defined as an extension of the join operator by further applying the resolution function. The *full* (and the *left/right) outer join merge* operators are defined as an extension of the outer join operators, where join merge is used instead of join. The *universal relation* is defined as the full outer join merge of r_1 and r_2. Within this model, Naumann

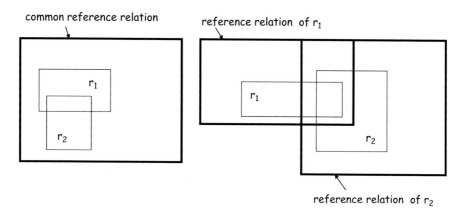

Fig. 7.3 Assumptions for reference relations

adopts the closed world assumption, since only tuples in the sources may exist in the universal relation.

Scannapieco adopts both closed world and open world assumptions; in this way, all the types of completeness discussed in Chap. 2 may be defined. Furthermore, in the open world assumption, given two distinct relations r_1 and r_2, two different hypotheses can be made on the reference relations: (1) the two reference relations of r_1 and r_2 are the same, and (2) the reference relations differ. This is due to the fact that when composing relations with composition operators such as union or join, we may give (see Fig. 7.3) two different interpretations to the operations, according to the following assumptions:

- If the two reference relations are the same (left-hand side of Fig. 7.3), incompleteness concerns the lack of objects with sources referring to the same reality of interest.
- If the two reference relations are different (right-hand side of Fig. 7.3), the interpretation of the composition results in the integration of different realities of interest.

In the two previous cases, the evaluation of the resulting completeness has to be different. With reference to set relationships between sources, Scannapieco considers overlap, containment, and a weaker notion of overlap, where the number of common tuples is not known.

7.3.2 Dimensions

In this section we first discuss dimensions comparatively, then we focus on two specific dimensions, namely, accuracy and completeness.

In Motro, given an ideal relation `r-ideal` and the corresponding real relation `r-real`, two dimensions are defined:

- *Soundness* measures the proportion of the real data that is true:

$$\frac{|\texttt{r-ideal}| \cap |\texttt{r-real}|}{|\texttt{r-real}|}.$$

- *Completeness* measures the proportion of the true data that is stored in the real relation:

$$\frac{|\texttt{r-ideal}| \cap |\texttt{r-real}|}{|\texttt{r-ideal}|}.$$

Parssian defines four different dimensions, depending on the pair of tuples considered in the relationship between the ideal relation and the real relation. More precisely:

- A tuple in `r-real` is *accurate* if all of its attribute values are accurate, i.e., are identical to the values of a corresponding tuple of `r-ideal`. We call S_{accurate} the set of accurate tuples.
- A tuple is *inaccurate* if it has one or more inaccurate (or null) values for its non-identifier attributes and no inaccurate values for its identifier attribute (or attributes); $S_{\text{inaccurate}}$ is the set of inaccurate tuples.
- A tuple is a *mismember* if it should not have been captured into `r-real`, but has been; $S_{\text{mismember}}$ is the set of mismember tuples.
- A tuple belongs to the *incomplete* set $S_{\text{incomplete}}$ if it should have been captured into `r-real`, but has not been.

In Fig. 7.4 we show an example of (1) an ideal relation `Professor`; (2) a possible corresponding real relation, with accurate tuples in white, inaccurate tuples in pale

Id	LastName	Name	Role
1	Mumasia	John	Associate
2	Mezisi	Patrick	Full
3	Oado	Nomo	Full
4	Rosci	Amanda	Full

(b) real relation *Professor*

Id	LastName	Name	Role
1	Mumasia	John	Associate
2	Mezisi	Patrick	Full
3	Oado	George	Full
5	Ongy	Daniel	Full

(a) ideal relation *Professor*

Id	LastName	Name	Role
5	Ongy	Daniel	Full

(c) Set of incomplete tuples for *Professor*

Fig. 7.4 Examples of accurate/inaccurate/mismember tuples and incomplete set in the Parssian approach

gray, and mismember tuples in dark gray; and (3) a set of incomplete tuples. Accuracy, inaccuracy, and mismembership of $\mathtt{r\text{-}real}$ are defined, respectively, as

$$\text{accuracy} = \frac{|S_{\text{accurate}}|}{|\mathtt{r\text{-}real}|},$$

$$\text{inaccuracy} = \frac{|S_{\text{inaccurate}}|}{|\mathtt{r\text{-}real}|},$$

$$\text{mismembership} = \frac{|S_{\text{mismember}}|}{|\mathtt{r\text{-}real}|}.$$

The completeness of $\mathtt{r\text{-}real}$ can be defined as

$$\frac{|S_{\text{incomplete}}|}{|\mathtt{r\text{-}real}| - |S_{\text{accurate}}| + |S_{\text{incomplete}}|}$$

since, when considering $\mathtt{r\text{-}real}$, we have to eliminate mismember tuples and add the set of incomplete tuples.

Wang, within the concept of accuracy, distinguishes between a *relation accuracy* and a *tuple accuracy*. In the hypothesis of uniform distribution of errors that cause inaccuracy, the tuple accuracy is defined as *probabilistic tuple accuracy*. It coincides numerically with the overall relation accuracy.

In Naumann, completeness is analyzed from three different points of views, corresponding to the coverage, density, and completeness dimensions:

1. The *coverage* of a source $\mathtt{s}$ captures the number of objects represented in the source $\mathtt{s}$ with respect to the total number of objects in the universal relation $\mathtt{ur}$ and is defined as

$$\frac{|\mathtt{s}|}{|\mathtt{ur}|}.$$

2. The *density* of a source captures the number of *values* represented in the source and is defined as the number of non-null values referred to by the attributes in the universal relation. More formally, we first define the *density of an attribute* $\mathtt{a}$ of $\mathtt{s}$ as

$$d(\mathtt{a}) = \frac{|(\mathtt{t} \in \mathtt{s} \mid \mathtt{t.a} \neq \text{null})|}{|\mathtt{s}|}.$$

The *density* of the source $\mathtt{s}$ is the average density over the set of all attributes $\mathtt{A}$ of the universal relation $\mathtt{ur}$:

$$\frac{1}{|\mathtt{A}|} \sum_{\mathtt{a} \in \mathtt{A}} d(\mathtt{a}).$$

Symbol	Meaning
r	input relation
$r_1, r_2, ..., r_n$	a set of n input relations
s	output relation
$\|r\|$	size of the relation r
acc	accuracy
inacc	inaccuracy
cov	coverage
compl	completeness

Fig. 7.5 Symbols used in the exposition

3. The *completeness* of a source s captures the number of values represented in the source, with respect to the total potential amount of values of the real world; it is expressed by the formula

$$\frac{|\ (a_{ij} \neq null\ |\ a_{ij} \in s)\ |}{|\ ur\ |\ \times\ |\ A\ |},$$

where a_{ij} is the value of the jth attribute of tuple t_i in s.

Scannapieco considers all the dimensions presented for completeness in Chap. 2 and also other ones (the interested reader can refer to [547]).

In the rest of the section, we provide various results on accuracy and completeness. Due to previously discussed heterogeneity of approaches, we will discuss each proposal separately. Due to the more significant contributions provided, in the following we focus on Wang, Parssian, Naumann, and Scannapieco. We adopt the symbols described in Fig. 7.5.

7.3.3 Accuracy

Wang provides several results for selection and projection operators. We analyze selection, while for the more complex formulas related to projection, we refer to [649]. Under the assumption that $|\ s\ |$, the size of the output relation, is available, the following formula easily derives from the hypothesis of uniform distribution of errors:

$$acc(s) = acc(r).$$

Other formulas are provided for the worst and best case scenarios; for instance, for the worst case, if $|r| \leq |s|$, then $acc(s) = 0$. See [649] for more details.

Results provided by Parssian are richer, due to the the larger set of dimensions defined for the input relations. We provide details for accuracy and inaccuracy in the case of cartesian product and selection operations.

For cartesian product, applied to two relations r_1 and r_2, the following formulas can be simply derived:

$$\mathrm{acc}(s) = \mathrm{acc}(r_1) * \mathrm{acc}(r_2)$$

and

$$\mathrm{inacc}(s) = \mathrm{acc}(r_1) * \mathrm{inacc}(r_2) + \mathrm{acc}(r_2) * \mathrm{inacc}(r_1) + \mathrm{inacc}(r_1) * \mathrm{inacc}(r_2).$$

Concerning the selection operation, four different cases apply according to the structure of the condition in the selection: the selection condition applies to an identifier/non-identifier attribute and the selection is an equality/inequality. We will examine two of them.

In the case where the condition is an inequality applied to an identifier attribute, due to the assumption of uniform distribution of errors, the accuracy, inaccuracy, mismembership, and completeness values for s are identical to the ones for r. This is because the status of the selected tuples remains unchanged.

In the case where the condition is an equality applied to a non-identifier attribute A, tuples are selected or not selected depending on their being accurate or inaccurate in the values of A. To estimate the size of the various components of s, we need to estimate the probability that an accurate/inaccurate/mismember tuple is in one of the parts of r related to non-identifier attributes appearing or not appearing in the condition. We call $P(t \in s)$ such probability. The formula for accuracy in this case is intuitively

$$\mathrm{acc}(s) = \mathrm{acc}(r) * \frac{|r|}{|s|} * P(t \in s).$$

For a formal proof of the previous formula and details on all remaining cases, see [493].

7.3.4   Completeness

In the following we focus on the contributions by Naumann and Scannapieco. First, in the Naumann approach, there is a functional relationship between completeness, coverage, and density of a relation r_1, namely,

$$\mathrm{compl}(r_1) = \mathrm{cov}(r_1) * \mathrm{density}(r_1).$$

Assumption/ operator	r_1 and r_2 disjoint	Quantified overlapping (= x)	r_1 contained in r_2
Join merge	0	$|x| / |ur|$	$cov(r_1)$
Left outer join merge	$cov(r_1)$	$cov(r1)$	$cov(r_1)$
Full outer join merge	$cov(r_1) + cov(r_2)$	$cov(r_1) + cov(r_2) -$ $|x| / |ur|$	$cov(r_1)$

Fig. 7.6 Coverage composition functions in Naumann

This relationship results directly from the definitions provided. Naumann characterizes the composition functions, in the case of binary operators on two relations r_1 and r_2, for the three dimensions, and all the previously defined operators under the assumptions defined in Sect. 7.3.1.

In Fig. 7.6 we show several cases for the coverage dimension, which we discuss here; for other cases, see [464].

Looking at Fig. 7.6, in the case of the join merge, the results of the operator under the different assumptions are, respectively, (1) no object, (2) only the common objects, and (3) only the objects of r_1, leading straightforwardly to the formulas. In the case of the left outer join merge, due to the property of the left outer join of maintaining all the tuples of the first source r_1 in the result, the coverage is independent of the assumptions and is equal to $cov(r_1)$. Similar considerations hold for the full outer join merge case. For all the other cases and properties not mentioned here, we refer to [464].

In the approach of Scannapieco, we consider the two cases of the open world assumption, in which given r_1 and r_2 input relations are defined, respectively, over (1) the same reference relation or (2) two different reference relations. Note that we assume to know the sizes of the reference relations themselves and not the reference relations themselves. We consider the evaluation of completeness for the union operator:

Case 1: Same reference relation. We suppose that

$$ref(r_1) = ref(r_2) = ref(s).$$

In the case in which no additional knowledge on relations is available, we may only express an upper bound:

$$compl(r) \geq max(compl(r_1), compl(r_2)).$$

Behind this inequality, we can distinguish three more cases:

1. Disjointness: if $r_1 \cap r_2 = 0$, then $\texttt{compl(s)} = \texttt{compl}(r_1) + \texttt{compl}(r_2)$.
2. Non-quantified partial overlap: if $r_1 \cap r_2 \neq 0$, then $\texttt{compl(s)} > \max(\texttt{compl}(r_1), \texttt{compl}(r_2))$.
3. Containment: if $r_1 \subset r_2$, then $\texttt{compl(s)} = \texttt{compl}(r_2)$.

For example, Fig. 7.7a, b shows the two relations `dept1` and `dept2`, each representing professors of a department and having the same reference relation, $\texttt{ref-dept} = \text{ref}(\texttt{dept1}) = \text{ref}(\texttt{dept2})$, corresponding to all the professors of the department. Notice that `dept1` represents only full professors. We have the following input data: (1) $|\texttt{dept1}| = 4$, (2) $|\texttt{dept2}| = 5$, and (3) $|\texttt{ref-dept}| = 8$. Hence, $\texttt{compl(dept1)} = 0.5$ and $\texttt{compl(dept2)} = 0.625$. From this information we can derive

$$\texttt{compl(dept1} \cup \texttt{dept2)} \geq 0.625.$$

Figure 7.7c shows relation `dept3`, the size of which is 4; this relation contains only associate professors; therefore, `dept3` $\cap$ `dept1` is $\emptyset$. In this case, we can easily compute

$$\texttt{compl(dept1} \cup \texttt{dept3)} = 0.5 + 0.5 = 1.$$

(a)

Id	LastName	Name	Role
1	Ongy	Daniel	Full
2	Mezisi	Patrick	Full
3	Oado	George	Full
4	Rosci	Amanda	Full

(b)

Id	LastName	Name	Role
1	Mumasia	John	Associate
2	Mezisi	Patrick	Full
3	Oado	George	Full
4	Gidoy	Nomo	Associate
5	Rosci	Amanda	Full

(c)

Id	LastName	Name	Role
1	Mumasia	John	Associate
2	Oymo	Vusi	Associate
3	Msgula	Luyo	Associate
4	Keyse	Frial	Associate

(d)

Id	LastName	Name	Role
1	Ongy	Daniel	Full
2	Oado	George	Full

Fig. 7.7 Examples of input relations. (**a**) dept1, (**b**) dept2, (**c**) dept3, (**d**) dept4

Figure 7.7d shows relation dept4, the size of which is 2; observe that dept4 ⊆ dept1. In this case, we have

$$\texttt{compl}(\texttt{dept1} \cup \texttt{dept4}) = 0.5.$$

Case 2: Different reference relations. We consider a case that can occur in real scenarios, i.e., the reference relations are a disjoint and complete partition of a domain. This is the case, for example, when we merge two disjoint sets of citizens resident in different cities. More specifically, we suppose that $\texttt{ref}(r_1) \cap \texttt{ref}(r_2) = \emptyset$ and $\texttt{ref}(s) = \texttt{ref}(r_1) \cup \texttt{ref}(r_2)$. In this case, it is easy to show that the completeness of s for the union is

$$
\begin{aligned}
\texttt{compl}(\texttt{s}) &= \frac{|r_1| + |r_2|}{|\texttt{ref}(r_1)| + |\texttt{ref}(r_2)|} \\
&= \frac{\texttt{compl}(r_1) * |r_1| + \texttt{compl}(r_2) * |r_2|}{|\texttt{ref}(r_1)| + |\texttt{ref}(r_2)|}.
\end{aligned}
$$

For other cases, related to intersection and cartesian product, we refer you to [547].

7.4   Error Localization and Correction

In the introduction of this chapter, error localization and error correction activities have been identified as information quality activities. Error localization and correction are useful every time information is collected from error-prone sources (e.g., those in which manual input has been performed) or acquired from sources whose reliability is not known at all.

In previous chapters we have seen that errors in information may be expressed in terms of a wide number of dimensions; for some of them, we have provided measures and, in the case of consistency, formal models to characterize the dimension. We argue that corresponding methods for error localization and correction depend on the quality dimension we want to control and achieve and on the type of information to be assessed. In this section we deal with questionnaires for statistical surveys, which can be seen as hierarchical semistructured data. The following sections are organized as follows:

1. Localization and correction of inconsistencies is discussed in Sect. 7.4.1.
2. Localization and correction of incomplete data in Sect. 7.4.2.
3. Localization of outliers, i.e., data values that are anomalous with respect to other data and usually are an indicator of incorrect data, in Sect. 7.4.3.

7.4.1   Localize and Correct Inconsistencies

Historically, the problem of localizing inconsistencies has occurred in statistical surveys carried out by processing answers obtained through a collection of questionnaires, and it is also typical of data collected in experiments and analyses (e.g., clinical) for medical diagnosis and care. Error localization and correction is becoming increasingly important when using sensor networks, e.g., for detection of harmful biological and chemical agents and in collecting data in monitoring environmental conditions. The error rate of these sensor networks is highly dependent on the current battery level of the device, interference, and other parameters. We will discuss this issue in more detail in Chap. 14.

A first formalization of the error localization problem appears in [228]; more recent contributions appear in several papers (see [95, 508, 673]). In the following, we will consider data collected through questionnaires as a reference case. As we will see, the approach can be generalized to other cases where more complex data models are defined, e.g., relational data model with integrity constraints.

When designing a questionnaire, the data provided as responses to the questionnaire must verify a set of properties, corresponding to the edits introduced in Chap. 2. In the statistical world, the set of all edits is called the *set of edit rules*, or *check plan*, or *compatibility plan*. Usually, such rules are known only to a certain extent, since collecting and expressing rules is a costly activity, and even a simple questionnaire can result in tens and hundreds of such rules. Errors, or inconsistencies between answers or out-of-range answers, can be due to low quality in the original design of the questionnaire or can be introduced during any later phase of data production, such as data input or conversion.

When edits are collected, it is crucial that they be proven to be *consistent*, i.e., without contradictions; otherwise, every conceivable procedure to use edits in order to localize errors will fail. Furthermore, they should be *nonredundant*, i.e., no edit in the set can be logically derived from other edits.

As an example of an inconsistent set of edits, assume a survey is performed on the employees of a company. Consider the three edits (here, and in the following, we informally introduce the syntax and the semantics of edits):

1. `Salary = false`, which means "every employee has a salary."
2. `Has a desk = false`, which means "every employee has a desk."
3. `(Salary = true)` and `(Has a desk = true)`, which means "an employee is not allowed to have a salary and to have a desk."

There is an evident contradiction among the three edits. This is an indication that one of the edits, most probably edit 3, is wrong. An example of a redundant set of edits is:

1. `Role = professor ∧ AnnualIncome < 100.000`
2. `AnnualIncome < 100.000`

where the redundancy concerns the constraint on `AnnualIncome`.

Once we have a *valid*, i.e., at least consistent, set of edits, we can use them to perform the activity of *error localization*. This may be done by checking if the truth assignments associated with the values in the questionnaire satisfy the logic formula corresponding to the set of edits. In this activity, it would be obviously preferable to have a *nonredundant* set of edits, because decreasing the number of edits while maintaining the same power of inconsistency detection can simplify the whole process.

After the localization of erroneous records, in order to correct errors, we could perform on them the activity called *new data acquisition* in Sect. 7.2. Unfortunately, this kind of activity is usually very costly, and, in all the contexts in which data are collected for statistical purposes, the use of edits is usually preferred to correct erroneous data. The activity of using edits to correct erroneous fields by restoring correct values is called *error correction* or *imputation*. The problem of localizing errors by means of edits and imputing erroneous fields is usually referred to as the *edit-imputation problem*. Fellegi and Holt in [228] provide a theoretical model for the edit-imputation problem. The main goals of the model are as follows:

- The data in each record should satisfy all edits by changing the fewest fields possible. This is called the *minimum change principle*.
- When imputation is necessary, it is desirable to maintain the marginal and joint frequency distribution of values in the different fields.

The above two goals may be in conflict, as the following example shows. Consider a questionnaire that collects several properties of people, such as `<Age, MaritalStatus, TypeofWork>`. A "true" record such as `<68, married, retired>` could result due to some error into `<6, married, retired>`. Such a record does not respect an edit such as

`Age < 15 ∧ MaritalStatus = married.`

We may correct 6 into 15, respecting the minimum change principle for the age, but if we apply the rule in all similar cases, we alter the distribution of values of `Age`. Even changing 6 (and analogous incorrect values) in order to respect the frequency distribution of correct values of `Age`, we could modify the joint distribution with `MaritalStatus` and `TypeofWork`. Thus, in general, we have to perform more complex and wide changes. Fellegi and Holt provide a solution to the edit-imputation problem that finds the minimum number of fields to change in order to respect all the edits, thus achieving the first goal. They make an important assumption in their method: that implicit edit is known. *Implicit edits* are those that can be logically derived from explicitly defined edits. In *error localization* they were considered redundant edits, and so they were minimized; during *error correction* they cannot be ignored, since they express properties that do not fail for a record but may fail as values are changed. The following example adapted from [673] provides intuition for computational issues. Consider a record

`<Age, MaritalStatus, Relationship-to-Head-of-Household>,`

and the following two edits:

```
edit1: Age < 15 ∧ MaritalStatus = married
edit2: MaritalStatus = not married ∧
Relationship-to-Head-of-Household = spouse
```

An implicit edit, as may easily be checked, is

```
edit3: Age < 15 ∧ Relationship-to-Head-of-Household
       = spouse
```

We initially assume that edit3 is hidden. Consider now a record r_1 = <10, not married, spouse>. The record fails for edit2; in order to correct the record, we may change the marital status to married, to obtain a new record r_2 that now fails for edit1. So, we have to make a second attempt that involves the value spouse. If we explicitly consider edit3, we immediately reach the conclusion that at least one of the two values <10, spouse> has to be changed.

Assuming availability of implicit edits, Fellegi and Holt formulate the problem as a set covering problem. Alternatively, if implicit edits are not available, then the edit-imputation problem can be solved by integer programming methods which are much slower. Probabilistic imputation methods have to be used to deal with the second goal, namely, to maintain the marginal and joint frequency distribution of variables. We refer to [95] for these issues.

7.4.2   Incomplete Data

In Chap. 2 we introduced completeness as a relevant data quality dimension, and we defined and provided metrics for it in the context of relational tables. Another type of incompleteness arises in the measurement of phenomena during a period of time, e.g., in time series. We consider now both cases of completeness.

With regard to relational tables, enforcing explicit values for an attribute A, or for a set of attributes A_1, A_2,..., A_n in place of missing ones, can be expressed as the problem of conformance to edits of the form

   A₁ = null or A₂ = null or ...or Aₙ = null.

In this case, the problem of finding the minimum number of values to be modified is trivial, since this number coincides with the set of missing values. Thus, the goal that becomes critical is to maintain the marginal and joint frequency distributions of the attributes. If the attributes to be considered are A_1, A_2,..., A_n, an assumption can be made that attributes are missing monotonically, that is, A_i is not missing only if A_{i-1}, A_{i-2}, ..., A_1 are not missing. In this case, a regression method can be performed recursively, generating valid values from A_1 to A_n.

With regard to time series, two types of incompleteness can be identified, namely, truncated data and censored data. *Truncated data* corresponds to observations that

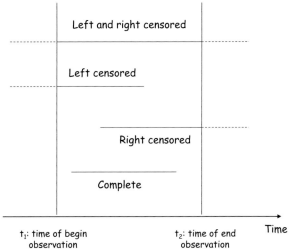

Fig. 7.8 Types of incomplete data in time series

are dropped from the analyzed dataset. For example, customers that take at the most one flight a year might not be included in an airline customer database. *Censored data* correspond to data that we know for sure have not been collected before a certain time t_1 (*left censored data*) or after a certain time t_2 (*right censored data*). As an example of left censored data, assume we are interested in measuring the *mean time between failures* of a computer; we could have only historical data available after a certain time t_1, and we might not know at what time $t_0 < t_1$ the computer started operating. The possible situations are shown in Fig. 7.8.

Note that truncated or censored data can also appear in relational tables with values not time stamped. For instance, a 64-bit integer cannot represent values higher than $2^{64} - 1$; so, integer overflows correspond to censored values. As another example, a sales invoice system may assign a default date for missing date invoices. As a consequence, invoices with missing values all have exactly the same data, which has a high frequency.

Truncated and censored data can be detected with the help of histograms and frequency distributions. For example, in the sales order system, corresponding to the default date, a spike appears in the frequency distribution of dates.

7.4.3 Discovering Outliers

A value that is unusually larger or smaller in relation to other values in a set of data is called an *outlier*. As an example, consider the following data:

$$2, 5, 6, 3, 8, 76, 4, 3, 7.$$

Intuition tells us that 76 is a suspicious value, because all the other data are numbers between 0 and 10. Typically, an outlier is attributable to one of the following causes in the measurement of data:

1. It is incorrectly observed, recorded, or entered in a dataset.
2. It comes from a different population, in relation to other Values.
3. It is correct, but represents a rare event.

In our example, 76 could be a simple typo, where the separating comma between 7 and 6 is missing. This is an example of temporary false or spurious value, sometimes called *data glitch*, that corresponds to causes 1 and 2. It is important to distinguish between outliers of type 3, correct but rare data, and outliers of types 1 and 2, i.e., data glitches. As a consequence of the above discussion, methods for managing outliers are characterized by two phases, (1) discovering outliers and (2) deciding between rare data and data glitches.

Outliers are detected by measuring the departure of values from what we expect them to be. We discuss the following methods that can be used for the detection of outliers: control charts, distributional outliers, and time series outliers. A comprehensive list of these methods is discussed in detail in [161].

- *Control charts* have been developed primarily by the manufacturing industry to measure the quality of products; several data samples are collected, and statistics, such as mean and standard error, are computed and analyzed. As an example, in Fig. 7.9, the region inside the rectangle represents values that are inside single attribute error limits, while the ellipse represents the joint control limits based on the joint distribution of the two attributes. Some points that are inside control limits of the single attributes are outliers when the elliptic control area corresponding to the pair of attributes is considered.

  Control charts are suitable for studying one or two attributes at a time. They cannot be used for capturing outliers based on interrelationships between attributes; it is possible that a value might be well suited in relation to any given attribute, but might be outside fixed error bounds in relation to the attributes taken together.

Fig. 7.9 Example of a control chart based on two attributes

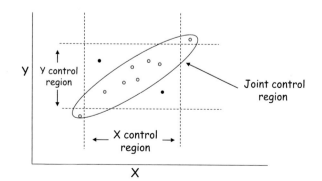

- *Distributional outliers.* According to this method, outliers are seen as points which are in a region of low density. Since these points are relatively isolated, they are "probable" outliers. The intuition is that outliers are likely to be at a large distance from the other data points. Starting from this intuition, distributional outliers can be found computing the value $F[d](x)$ for every point x in the set of values, which is the fraction of points in the set of values at distance d or more from x. The set of $F[p, d]$ outliers is the set of points x such that $F[d](x) > p$, where p is a threshold value. Note that outliers could be clustered, e.g., because of default or censored values for some of the fields. The threshold p should be adjusted to take these fields into account.
- *Time series outliers.* These methods analyze outliers in time series. They consider relevant properties of time series, such as the fact that data which are close in time tend to be highly correlated. They also consider the presence of cyclic patterns in the data, such as credit card payments that may have peaks at certain hours in the week. A technique for time series starts with partitioning the group of attributes measured in series (e.g., `<CreditCardNumber, Expense>`) into sections, using a space partitioning strategy. Each class of the partition is a state that a data point can have in time. A given time series is modeled as a trajectory of states, with transition probabilities between states. Thus transitions can be ranked by their likelihoods, and outliers correspond to low likelihood transitions.

Once the outliers are identified, we have to decide whether they represent an abnormal but legitimate behavior or a data glitch. In the time series methods, two different measures of deviation are considered for the decision. The *relative deviation* represents the movement of a data point relative to other data points over time. For instance, the data points may represent the history of credit card purchases of a customer, with some customers purchasing at a faster rate, while other customers continue at the same rate at which they started. The *within deviation* measures the dynamics of a data point in relation to its own expected behavior.

We briefly compare the two strategies. The relative deviation is more robust, since state changes require significant changes in attributes. The within deviation is sensitive to minor changes and is better for analyzing long-term changes; thus, it is more suitable for discriminating between rare data and glitches. In fact, genuine changes are usually persistent over time, whereas glitches appear and disappear unpredictably. A drop in revenues at a single point in time is more likely to be a data problem, such as missing data, rather than a downward trend. Patterns in glitches reveal systematic causes, such as data in particular missing intervals.

7.5   Summary

In this chapter we have introduced several information quality activities, discovering that the improvement of information quality in an organization can be performed with a variety of actions and strategies. All of the activities introduced apply to information and produce new information of improved quality according to a given process. Other improvement activities can rely on processes that manipulate data, modifying the process or introducing suitable controls in the process; we will discuss them in Chap. 12.

We have also started the discussion on activities while thoroughly analyzing (1) quality composition and (2) error localization and correction. For such activities we introduced a spectrum of techniques for several possible cases. In such a way, we provided a framework for analysis that allows the reader to choose the specific approach to adopt based on the context of use.

Chapter 8
Object Identification

8.1 Introduction

In this chapter we address object identification (IQ), the most important and the most extensively investigated information quality activity. Due to such an importance, we decided to dedicate two chapters of the book to object identification, this chapter focusing on consolidated techniques and the next one on recent advancements.

In order to introduce critical issues, let us describe an example related to an e-Government application scenario. In such a scenario, different agencies are in charge of administrative procedures related to businesses: storing information on businesses in their respective national registries, authorizing specific activities, and providing services, e.g., for collecting taxes. In each agency, the same set of businesses is represented, with some attributes common to all agencies and some others specific to an agency. We report in Fig. 8.1 a real example of the same business as represented in three national registries (some details, irrelevant in this context, have been changed for privacy reasons).

The three tuples present several differences:

1. Values of the identifiers are different due to different coding policies adopted by the three agencies; also, in the case in which they share a common domain and meaning (this is the case for agencies 1 and 3), they differ due to some data entry errors.
2. Names are different, although several common or similar parts exist (also, in this case, some data entry error can be recognized).
3. Types of activity are different; this difference may be due to several reasons, such as typos, deliberately false declarations, or data updated at different times.
4. Further differences appear in remaining `Address` and `City` attributes.

   Yet, the three tuples represent the same business!
   We call *object identification* the IQ activity needed to identify whether data in the same source or in different ones represent the same object of the real world.

© Springer International Publishing Switzerland 2016   177
C. Batini, M. Scannapieco, *Data and Information Quality*, Data-Centric Systems
and Applications, DOI 10.1007/978-3-319-24106-7_8

Agency	Identifier	Name	Type of activity	Address	City
Agency 1	CNCBTB765SDV	Meat production of John Ngombo	Retail of bovine and ovine meats	35 Niagara Street	New York
Agency 2	0111232223	John Ngombo canned meat production	Grocer's shop, beverages	9 Rome Street	Albany
Agency 3	CND8TB76SSDV	Meat production in New York state of John Ngombo	Butcher	4, Garibaldi Square	Long Island

Fig. 8.1 How three agencies represent the same business

As mentioned in Chap. 1, poor IQ in a single information source produces poor quality of services and economic losses. Poor IQ referring to the same types of objects (e.g., persons, businesses, and portions of territory) in different information sources yields poor results in all applications (e.g., queries, transactions, keyword-based searches, statistics) that access the same objects in the different information sources. This type of access is typical of many government(or business or citizen)-to-government(or business or citizen) interactions. For example, to discover tax frauds, different agencies can cross-check their databases in order to search for contradictions or correlations among data: this is possible only if data referring to the same object can be identified.

This chapter is organized as follows. In Sect. 8.2 we briefly provide a historical perspective of the object identification problem. In Sect. 8.3, we discuss the different types of information involved in the object identification process. In Sect. 8.4 we describe the general steps of the process that are detailed in Sect. 8.5. In Sect. 8.5.4 we introduce the specific object identification techniques that are detailed in the subsequent sections: Sect. 8.6 describes probabilistic techniques, Sect. 8.7 illustrates the empirical ones, and, finally, Sect. 8.8 details the knowledge-based techniques. The chapter ends with a comparison of the techniques in Sect. 8.9.

8.2   Historical Perspective

The term *record linkage* is mentioned for the first time in [186]. Since computer applications have been used to automate more and more administrative activities, demographic studies, health experiments, and epidemiological analyses, it has become clear that information often results from the merging of different sources, created and updated at different times and by different organizations or persons. Moreover, merging information produces new information of potentially higher value, since properties that are merged can be related with new types of aggregations, analyses, and correlations.

In the 1950s and 1960s, information was represented in *files*, *records*, and *fields*; this terminology justifies the original term *record linkage* as the activity that results in the integration of information from two or more independent sources. In those times, database management systems (DBMSs) adopted a variety of models for representing structured data, such as the hierarchical and the network data model. In the 1980s the relational model, proposed in Codd's seminal paper [144], was adopted in most of modern DBMSs.

In this chapter we will frequently use the *file/record/field* terminology whenever the techniques apply to the more general file structure. In other cases, we will adopt instead the *relation/tuple/attribute* terminology.

One of the first efforts for moving from empirical procedures to formal methods originates from the geneticist Howard Newcombe [470], who introduced frequencies of occurrences of values in strings and decision rules for matching and unmatching records. Such procedures were used in the development of health files of individuals. Later in time, Fellegi and Sunter [229] provided a mature formal theory for record linkage (see Sect. 8.6.1). A great number of subsequent experiments and theoretical improvements originated from the Fellegi and Sunter work, and record linkage was applied to other fields different from the health applications, such as administrative and census applications, characterized by a large amount of data and from sources with various degrees of trustworthiness and accuracy. In such applications, it is crucial to produce efficient computer-assisted matching procedures that can reduce the use of clerical resources and effective methods that can reduce errors in matching and unmatching. See [672] for a general discussion on the peculiarities of record linkage methods on administrative data.

In recent years, new techniques have been proposed that extend the linkage activity from files to more complex structures. At the same time, also in geographical information systems, the need arose to superimpose (or conflate) maps and images from different sources and with different formats, for maps the vector and raster formats. We will consider matching of maps and images in the next chapter, while in this chapter we focus instead on structured data and semistructured information. Such techniques also try to exploit knowledge on the application domain to produce more effective decision procedures. These topics will be examined in more detail in the following sections.

8.3   Object Identification for Different Data Types

Techniques developed for dealing with the object identification problem strictly depend on the type of information used to represent objects. Focusing on structured and semistructured data and refining the classifications provided in Chap. 1, we

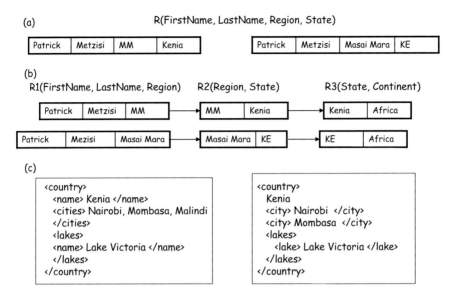

Fig. 8.2 Examples of matching objects of the three data typologies. (**a**) Two tuples, (**b**) two hierarchical groups of tuples, (**c**) two XML records

distinguish three main data types that refer to the same class of objects:

1. *Simple structured data,* that correspond to pairs of files or relational tables
2. *Complex structured data,* i.e., groups of logically related files or relational tables
3. *Semistructured information,* such as pairs of XML marked documents

In Fig. 8.2, data of the three different types are shown. In Fig. 8.2a, b, an object of type `Person` is represented, while a `Country` is represented in Fig. 8.2c.

In order to discover matching and unmatching objects within the three structures, we need different strategies. Historically, simple structured data correspond to traditional files, which have poor mechanisms to represent the semantics of data. With the advent of DBMSs, and specifically relational DBMSs, it has been possible to assign semantics to such structures, in terms of domains, keys, functional dependencies, and constraints. The advent of networks and the Web and the development of the XML standard have pushed the investigation of techniques for semistructured data. More recently, semantic Web standards have provided rich semantic models based on a graph structure, generalizing the tree structure of the XML data model; the reader can refer to Chap. 4 for a detailed discussion on such models.

In relation to the above discussion, two different terms are widely used in the literature: *record linkage* and *object identification.* Other terms used are *record matching* and *entity resolution. Record linkage* is used when the matching activity is performed on simple structured data, in our terminology, files or relations. Usually, it is known a priori that the two relations model the same entity of the real world, e.g., persons, businesses, or buildings. The goal of record linkage is to produce a new file where all the tuples of the two input files referring to the same entity of the real world (e.g., the same person, the same business) are merged into a single record; techniques may also simply produce the cluster of matching records without choosing the representative record. When a single file is considered, the goal of record linkage is to discover and unify the records in the file that refer to the same entity of the real world; in this case, it is called *deduplication* or *duplicate identification*.

Object identification is an evolutive term for record linkage and deals with complex structured data and XML documents where objects of the real world are represented, in general, with a wider spectrum of structures than simple structured data. For instance:

1. In data warehouses, objects used for dimensions in a star schema are represented with a group of relations related by foreign key constraints; this is the case of the tuples in Fig. 8.2b.
2. In normalized relational schemas, several relations are needed to represent an object.
3. In documents, objects are hidden in natural language descriptions, and their presence may be revealed by some schema specification (e.g., XML schemas).

These characteristics call for more sophisticated techniques when moving from simple structured data to complex structured data and semistructured data; at the same time, relational DBMSs and XML models, in comparison to files, provide richer mechanisms (e.g., keys) to reveal structural similarities between data, resulting in more complex but also more powerful techniques.

8.4   The High-Level Process for Object Identification

Although inspired by different general paradigms and tailored to the different types of information introduced in the previous section, consolidated techniques for object identification have a common structure, described in Fig. 8.3, where we assume for simplicity we have two files as input information.

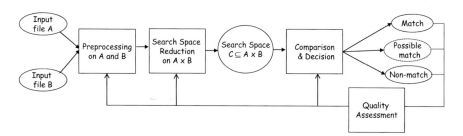

Fig. 8.3 Relevant steps of object identification techniques

In Fig. 8.3 the following activities are present:

1. A *preprocessing* activity that has the goal of working on data in order to standardize it and correct evident errors (see Sect. 8.5.1).
2. At this point we recognize that performing record linkage on the whole potential search space, consisting of the cartesian product of tuples in input files, results in a complexity $O(n^2)$, where n is the cardinality of each of the input relations. To make record linkage feasible, we have to produce a reduced search space (see Sect. 8.5.2).
3. Then, a decision model is used to decide if records in the reduced search space C correspond to the same object, do not match, or no decision can be made automatically and a domain expert has to be involved. This activity is made of two steps:

   • The *choice of a comparison function*, or in the following *comparison* between tuples, that chooses the distance function and/or the set of rules that express the distance between pair of records in C; such comparison function is evaluated for such pairs (distance functions are discussed in Sect. 8.5.3, while rules are considered in knowledge-based techniques in Sect. 8.8).
   • A *decision* is made among matching, unmatching, and possible matching based on the analysis of values of the comparison function (see Sect. 8.5.4).

4. Finally, a *quality assessment* activity can be performed, during which measures are evaluated to assess if the result is satisfactory. Minimization of *possible matches* is a typical goal of object identification techniques to reduce clerical involvement. At the same time, a further goal to be achieved is to minimize *false positives*, i.e., false assignments of pairs of tuples to the match decision, and the complementary *false negatives*. When the quality of the process is not satisfactory, it can be iterated, e.g., by adopting a new comparison function (see Sect. 8.9.1).

Another activity that is sometimes performed during object identification is *fusion*: given a cluster of records that have been matched, the fusion activity builds a single record as a representative of the whole cluster. We will consider fusion in Chap. 10.

Three major categories of techniques for the comparison and decision activities can be identified on the basis of the underlying research paradigms:

1. *Probabilistic techniques*, based on the extremely relevant set of methods developed in the last two centuries in statistics and probability theory, ranging from classical statistical inference to Bayesian networks to data mining approaches.
2. *Empirical techniques* that make use in the different phases of the process of algorithmic techniques such as sorting, tree traversal, neighbor comparison, and pruning.
3. *Knowledge-based techniques*, in which domain knowledge is extracted from the files involved and reasoning strategies are applied to make the process more effective.

Both in probabilistic and in knowledge-based techniques, the steps of the general procedure, described in Fig. 8.3, can be either performed independently of the domain (*domain-independent techniques*) or could be based on domain-specific information or knowledge (*domain-dependent techniques*).

Furthermore, in some applications it is useful to have a priori a sample of data for which it is known whether they match or not; such a sample is called *labeled data*, while *unlabeled data* are data for which the matching status is unknown. Labeled data can be used effectively to learn probabilities, distance functions, or knowledge used in the different techniques. Two different types of learning can be identified: *supervised learning*, when knowledge is available on matching/unmatching pairs, and *unsupervised learning*, when the source knowledge is of a different nature (e.g., integrity constraints on the domain).

Finally, in the case in which complex structured data and semistructured data are involved, further tree/graph traversal activity is needed in order to apply the strategy to all parts of the structure.

8.5 Details on the Steps for Object Identification

In this section, the first three steps described in Fig. 8.3, namely, preprocessing, search space reduction, and the issues related to comparison functions, will be illustrated in detail. The next sections deal with step 4, applying decision method. In the last section of the chapter, we will introduce metrics for step 5, quality assessment.

8.5.1 Preprocessing

The preprocessing step includes the following activities:

- *Standardization*, consisting of reorganization of composed fields, data type checks, and replacement of alternative spellings with a single one. A typical example of *reorganization* of a composite field is given by addresses. In many applications addresses are stored as a single string; the standardization activity may consider parsing the string into substrings corresponding, for instance, to StreetName, CivicNumber, City, and State. In the context of object identification, this type of reorganization has the purpose of making comparisons easier. However, it can be performed also to facilitate accuracy checks. Indeed, for fields derived from decomposition, dictionaries may be available for the use as lookup tables for correcting the data. *Data type checks* regard the standardization of formats. For example, dates must be expressed in the same format: 1 Jan 2001, 01-1-2001, and 1st January 2001 should be homogenized to a single format.

Replacement of alternative spellings includes abbreviations that can be replaced
by the corresponding complete word, e.g., `rd.` by `road`.

- *Conversion of upper/lower cases*, in which data to be compared corresponding
to alphabetic strings are transformed to be homogeneous in terms of upper and
lower cases. So, for instance, if names of companies are stored such that the first
character is upper case, then the corresponding strings are converted such that all
their characters are lower cases, e.g., `Hewlett Packard` is transformed into
`hewlett packard` and `Microsoft` into `microsoft`.

- *Schema reconciliation* is a more complex activity that must address all conflicts that can occur when data under consideration come from disparate data
sources. Examples of such conflicts are heterogeneity conflicts, semantic conflicts, description conflicts, and structural conflicts. More details on this can be
found in Chap. 10.

8.5.2   Search Space Reduction

The object identification problem has a search space dimension equal to the
cardinality of $A \times B$, given two sets of records A and B to be compared. The reduction
of the search space can be done by three different methods, namely, blocking, sorted
neighborhood, and pruning (or filtering).

Blocking implies partitioning a file into mutually exclusive blocks and limiting
comparisons to records within the same block. Blocking can be implemented by
choosing a *blocking key* and grouping into a block all records that have the same
values on the blocking key. Blocking can also be implemented by *hashing*. The
blocking key is used for hashing records in hash blocks. If b is the number of blocks
and n/b is the dimension of each block, then the total time complexity of blocking
is $O(h(n) + n^2/b)$ where $h(n) = n\log n$ if blocking is implemented by sorting or
$h(n) = n$ if blocking is implemented by hashing.

Sorted neighborhood (see [308]) consists of sorting a file and then moving a
window of a fixed size on the file, comparing only records within the window. The
number of comparisons is consequently reduced from n^2 to $O(wn)$, where w is the
size of the window; considering the sorting complexity $O(n\log)$, the method requires
a total time complexity of $O(n\log n + wn)$. See also Sect. 8.9.2 for a comparison
between blocking and sorted neighborhood methods (SNMs).

Pruning (or *filtering*) has the objective of first removing from the search space
all records that cannot match each other, without actually comparing them. As an
example, let us consider the case where two records are declared to be a match if a
given comparison function $f(r_i, r_j)$ is greater than a threshold τ. If an upper bound
for f is found, e.g., $f(r_i, r_j) <= \delta(r_i)$ for each j, then, if $\delta(r_i) <= \tau$, $f(r_i, r_j)$ will
be lower than τ for each r_j; therefore, r_i cannot have any record to be matched with
and can be removed from the search space.

8.5.3 *Distance-Based Comparison Functions*

Distance-based comparison functions, or distance functions in short, have been widely investigated, especially string-based distance functions, where the distance is evaluated on strings of characters (see surveys [289, 465]), and item-based distance functions, where the distance is evaluated on strings seen as lists of words (also called items) separated by blank characters. In the rest of this section, we review some of the most important functions, and we provide examples to show similarities and differences.

8.5.3.1 String-Based Distance Functions

Edit Distance. The edit distance between two strings is the minimum cost of converting one of them to the other by a sequence of character insertions, deletions, and replacements. Each of these modifications is assigned a cost value. As an example, assuming that the insertion cost and the deletion cost are each equal to 1, the edit distance between the two strings Smith and Sitch is 2, as Smith is obtained by adding m and deleting c from Sitch.

    n-Grams, Bigrams, and q-Grams. The n-grams comparison function forms the set of all the substrings of length n for each string. The distance between the two strings is defined as $\sqrt{\sum_{\forall x} |f_{s'} - f_{s''}|}$, where $f_{s'}$ and $f_{s''}$ are the number of occurrences of the substrings x in the strings s' and s'', respectively. Bigrams comparison ($n = 2$) is widely used and is effective with minor typographical errors. Positional q-grams are obtained by sliding a window of length q over the characters of a string s.

    Soundex Code. The purpose of the soundex code is to cluster together names that have similar sounds. For example, the pronunciations of Hilbert and Heilbpr are similar. A soundex code always contains four characters. The first letter of the name becomes the first character of the soundex code. The remaining three characters are drawn from the name sequentially, by accessing a predefined table. As an example, the soundex code of Hilbert and Heilbpr is H416. Once the four-character limit has been reached, all remaining letters are ignored.

    Jaro Algorithm. Jaro introduced a string comparison function that accounts for insertions, deletions, and transpositions. Jaro's algorithm finds the number of common characters and the number of transposed characters in the two strings. A *common character* is a character that appears in both strings within a distance of half the length of the shorter string. A *transposed character* is a common character that appears in different positions. As an example, comparing Smith and Simth, there are five common characters, two of which are transposed. The (scaled) Jaro string comparator is given by

$$f(s_1, s_2) = \frac{\frac{N_c}{\text{lengthS}_1} + \frac{N_c}{\text{lengthS}_2} + 0.5\frac{N_t}{N_c}}{3},$$

where s_1 and s_2 are strings of lengths lengthS_1 and lengthS_2, respectively, N_c is the number of common characters between the two strings (where the distance for common characters is half the minimum length of s_1 and s_2), and N_t is the number of transpositions.

Hamming Distance. The Hamming distance counts the number of mismatches between two numbers. It is used primarily for numerical fixed size fields like zip codes or social security numbers. For example, the Hamming distance between 00185 and 00155 is 1 because there is one mismatch.

Smith-Waterman. Given two sequences, the Smith-Waterman algorithm uses dynamic programming to find the lowest cost of changes that convert one string into another. Costs for individual changes, namely, modifications, insertions, and deletions, are parameters of the algorithm. The algorithm performs well for many abbreviations, taking into account gaps of unmatched characters, and also when records have missing information or typographical mistakes.

8.5.3.2   Item-Based Distance Functions

Edit distance and other measures that consider the data to be compared as alphabetic strings can lead to distance measures that do not match with our intuition and practical situations.

Let us consider Fig. 8.4. If we want to link the two tables in Fig. 8.4 using as distance function the edit distance and normalizing the distance with the length 16 of the longest string, in the comparison of string AT&T Corporation with the two strings of the first table, we have

$$\text{edit distance} < \text{AT\&T, AT\&T Corporation} >= 12 \div 16 = 0.75$$

$$\text{edit distance} < \text{IBM Corporation, AT\&T Corporation} >= 5 \div 12 = 0.4,$$

where "IBM Corporation" is closer than "AT&T" to "AT&T Corporation," leading to an unintuitive conclusion.

We can introduce a second metric that considers values no longer as alphabetic strings, but as groups of items, separated by blank characters, being in such a way a token-based distance function. This different view of data leads to a new distance

Fig. 8.4 Example of string comparison

...		...	...		...		...	...
AT&T		...	...		AT&T Corporation		...	...
IBM Corporation					IBM Corporation			
...		...	...					

called *Jaccard distance*, proposed in [335] more than one century ago, that can be evaluated with a two-step procedure:

1. Split strings s_i and s_j; in list of items, we call, e.g., LIT_i and LIT_j the lists of items corresponding to s_i and s_j.
2. The Jaccard distance between two values s_i and s_j is

$$\text{Jaccard distance}(s_i, s_j) = 1 - \frac{\left|LIT_i\right| \cap \left|LIT_j\right|}{\left|LIT_i\right| \cup \left|LIT_j\right|}.$$

In this case we have

$$\text{Jaccard distance} < \text{AT\&T, AT\&T Corporation} >= 12 \div 16 = 0.5$$

$$\text{Jaccard distance} < \text{IBM Corporation, AT\&T Corporation} >= 5 \div 12 = 0.66.$$

TF-IDF. The token frequency-inverse document frequency (TF-IDF) or *cosine similarity* is widely used for matching similar strings in documents. The basic idea is to assign higher weights to tokens appearing frequently in a document (TF weight) and to assign lower weights to tokens that appear frequently in the whole set of documents (IDF weight). For a term i in a document j, the weight $w_{i,j}$ is

$$w_{i,j} = (tf_{i,j}) \times \log\left(\frac{N}{df_i}\right),$$

where $tf_{i,j}$ is the number of occurrences of i in j, df_i is the number of documents containing i, and N is the total number of documents. The similarity between two documents is then computed as the cosine between their respective weighted term vectors. Specifically, being $V = \{w_1, \ldots, w_n\}$ and $U = \{w_1, \ldots, w_n\}$ the weighted term vectors, the cosine similarity is

$$\frac{V \cdot U}{|V| \cdot |U|}.$$

8.5.4 *Decision*

In Fig. 8.5, the set of object identification techniques that will be detailed in the rest of this chapter is shown. Each technique is described by a name, the technical area within which the technique was proposed (probabilistic, empirical, or knowledge based) and the type of data representing objects to be identified (pairs of files, relational hierarchies, or XML documents). Several object identification techniques

Name	Technical Area	Type of data
Fellegi and Sunter and extensions	probabilistic	Two files
Cost-based	probabilistic	Two files
Sorted Neighborhood and variants	empirical	Two files
Delphi	empirical	Two relational hierarchies
DogmatiX	empirical	Two XML documents
Intelliclean	knowledge-based	Two files
Atlas	knowledge-based	Two files

Fig. 8.5 Object identification techniques

are not described in the text, including [180, 394, 545]. The main criteria used to select the listed techniques are:

- Adoption: Fellegi and Sunter (and its extensions) is the first and by far the more established technique, and it is representative of probabilistic techniques. The SNM and its variants are also representative of empirical methods.
- Novelty: DogmatiX is among the first techniques dealing with object identification in XML documents, and Delphi is among the first ones dealing with complex structured data. Cost-based techniques have the originality of dealing with costs of linkage errors. Intelliclean and Atlas have been the first contributions on knowledge-based approaches to object identification.

8.6   Probabilistic Techniques

In this section we describe the probabilistic techniques based on the Fellegi and Sunter theory, providing the original model, subsequent extensions, and a cost-based technique.

8.6.1   The Fellegi and Sunter Theory and Extensions

The record linkage theory was proposed by Fellegi and Sunter in [229]. In this section, we summarize the proposed theory and briefly describe the subsequent extensions and refinements.

Given two sets of records A and B, let us consider the cross product $A \times B = \{(a, b) | a \in A \text{ and } b \in B\}$. Two disjoint sets M and U can be defined starting from

$A \times B$, namely, M= $\{(a,b)|a \equiv b, a \in A$ and $b \in B\}$ and U= $\{(a,b)|a!\equiv b, a \in$ A and $b \in B\}$, where the symbol $\equiv$ means that the records a and b represent the same real-world entity (and $!\equiv$ they do not). M is named the *matched set* and U is named the *unmatched set*. The record linkage procedure attempts to classify each record pair as belonging to either M or U. A third set P can be also introduced representing possible matches.

Let us suppose that each record in A and B is composed of n fields; a *comparison vector* γ is introduced that compares field values of records a_i and b_j (see Fig. 8.6), namely, $\gamma = [\gamma_1^{ij}, \ldots, \gamma_n^{ij}]$. γ is obtained by means of comparison functions, defined as $\gamma_k^{ij} = \gamma(a_i(k), b_j(k))$, denoted in the following for brevity as γ_k. Usually, only a subset of the fields of A and B is compared. γ is a function of the set of all $A \times B$ record pairs; with each couple of fields of each pair, it associates a specific level of agreement. As an example, given two files with fields Name, Surname, and Age, we may define a γ comparison function made of three predicates on each of the fields, namely, agree Name, agree Surname, and agree Age.

The functions γ_i can compute a binary agreement on values, i.e., $\gamma(v_1, v_2) = 0$ if $v_1 = v_2$, 1 otherwise, or else a three-value result, i.e., $\gamma(v_1, v_2) = 0$ if $v_1 = v_2$, 1 if either v_1 or v_2 is missing, 2 otherwise. The functions can also compute continuous attribute values; relevant comparison functions have been described in Sect. 8.5.3. The set of all comparison vectors is the comparison space Γ.

Given (a_i, b_j), the following conditional probabilities can be defined:

- $m(\gamma_k) = \Pr(\gamma_k|(a_i, b_j) \in M)$
- $u(\gamma_k) = \Pr(\gamma_k|(a_i, b_j) \in U)$

Fig. 8.6 The Fellegi and Sunter record linkage formulation

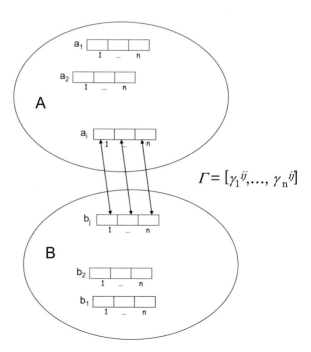

As an example, for the above files with fields `Name`, `Surname`, and `Age`, the probabilities `Pr(agree Name|M)`, `Pr(agree Surname|M)`, and `Pr(agree Age|M)` and `Pr(agree Name|U)`, `Pr(agree Surname|U)`, and `Pr(agree Age|U)` can be defined. Note that the size of Γ depends on its inner structure.

By considering all the fields, we define analogous formulas for γ:

- $m(\gamma) = \Pr(\gamma|(a_i, b_j) \in M)$
- $u(\gamma) = \Pr(\gamma|(a_i, b_j) \in U)$

The above probabilities are called *m-* and *u-probabilities*, respectively. In the case in which we are able to estimate such probabilities, they become crucial in a possible assignment decision procedure. Fellegi and Sunter introduced the ratio R among such probabilities as a function of γ, namely,

$$R = m(\gamma)/u(\gamma),$$

where γ ranges in the comparison space Γ, and, we recall, is a function of the set of all A × B record pairs. The ratio R, or the natural logarithm of such a ratio, is called *matching weight*. By composition, R is a function of the set of all A × B record pairs.

Fellegi and Sunter defined the following *decision rule*, where T_μ and T_λ are two thresholds (on which we will comment in the following):

- If $R > T_\mu$, then designate pair as a match.
- If $T_\lambda <= R <= T_\mu$, then designate pair as a possible Match.
- If $R < T_\lambda$, then designate pair as a unmatch.

The area $T_\lambda <= R <= T_\mu$ partitions the set of $\gamma \in \Gamma$, and corresponding record pairs, into three disjoint subareas, namely, D_1, including pairs declared as *match*; D_2, including pairs declared as *possible match*; and D_3, including pairs declared as *unmatch*.

We show in the following the Fellegi and Sunter original technique with some simplifying assumptions:

- Instead of considering the R ratio, we consider the probability of matching $m(\gamma)$.
- Probabilities are approximated by frequencies in an experiment.
- The comparison function is expressed in terms of a numeric distance function.

Given the universe U of pairs of records in A and B, we can practically apply the Fellegi and Sunter technique choosing a sample S of U, in which a reduced number of representative pairs is contained. We assume that for all pairs in S, we are able to label pairs as matching or unmatching.

In a second stage, for every possible distance among pairs, the frequency of matching and, under our assumptions, the complementary frequency of unmatching are evaluated, leading to the diagram in Fig. 8.7. In the diagram, distances are assumed for simplicity to correspond to the series of integer numbers up to a maximum distance, and percentages of matching are reported for each vertical region under the corresponding distance.

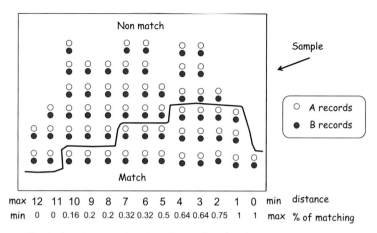

Vertical regions contain pairs of records ordered
according to decreasing values of distance

Fig. 8.7 Example distribution of match and unmatch in the sample as a function of distance among pairs

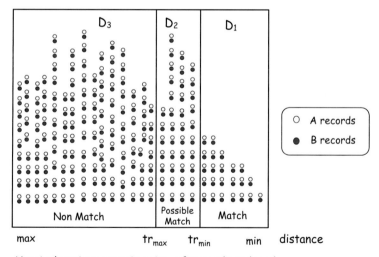

Vertical regions contain pairs of records ordered
according to decreasing values of distance

Fig. 8.8 Distribution of matching and unmatching applied to the universe U

At this point, we evaluate the distances among pairs on the whole universe U, leading to a diagram similar to the previous one; see Fig. 8.8. Now, we can evaluate

Fig. 8.9 The regions of the
Fellegi and Sunter decision
model [281]

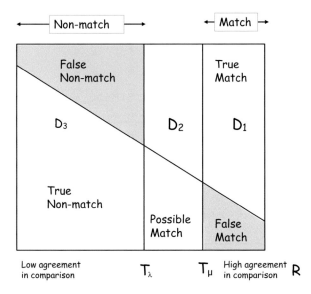

the error made for a given pair of threshold values, by evaluating, using percentages
as exemplified in Fig. 8.7:

- The weighted sum of percentages of records that are wrongly attributed as
  matching (matching records correspond to the right-hand side of the figure,
  area C1).
- The weighted sum of percentages of records that are wrongly attributed as
  unmatching (unmatching records correspond to the left-hand side of the figure,
  area C2).

In order to provide criteria to fix the two thresholds T_μ and T_λ, we have to decide
which are the rates of error we are willing to accept in the decision rule proposed
above; such error rates correspond to the two gray areas in Fig. 8.9. Once the error
rates are fixed, the two thresholds are consequently fixed. Fellegi and Sunter proved
that the above decision rule is optimal, where optimal means that the rule minimizes
the probability of classifying pairs as belonging to the area D_2 of possible matches.

8.6.1.1   Parameters and Error Rates Estimation

The Fellegi and Sunter theory is based on the knowledge of the u- and
m-probabilities. Several methods have been proposed to compute or estimate such
probabilities. First, Fellegi and Sunter proposed a method to compute the u- and
m-probabilities providing a closed-form solution under certain assumptions. More
specifically, considering that

$$\Pr(\gamma) = \Pr(\gamma|\mathrm{M})\Pr(\mathrm{M}) + \Pr(\gamma|\mathrm{U})\Pr(\mathrm{U}),$$

they observed that if the comparison vector γ regards three fields, among which a conditional independence assumption holds, then a system of seven equations and seven unknowns can be solved to find $\Pr(\gamma|\mathsf{U})$ and $\Pr(\gamma|\mathsf{M})$ (being $7 = 2^3 - 1$, where the subtracting term is due to the constraint that probabilities must be equal to 1).

Several parameter estimation methods for the theory have been proposed in the literature. Basically, such methods provide an *estimation* of the u- and m-probabilities rather than a computation of such parameters in closed form. The expectation-maximization (EM) algorithm and machine learning methods are the principal methods used for the estimation.

The *expectation-maximization* (EM) algorithm is used to find maximum likelihood estimates of parameters in probabilistic models, where the model depends on unobserved latent variables. EM includes an expectation (E) step, which computes the expected values of the latent variables, and a maximization (M) step, which computes the maximum likelihood estimates of the parameters, given the data and setting the latent variables to their expectation [174].

While continuing holding the conditional independence assumption, Winkler first showed how to estimate m- and u-probabilities by means of the EM algorithm in [669]. Jaro [343] proposed another method to compute the $m(\gamma)$, $\gamma \in \varGamma$ with the EM algorithm, which is implemented by commercially available software. Estimation methods have focused more recently on specific domains, such as persons and businesses, and specific fields, such as first names, last names, and street names (see [670] for a detailed discussion).

The conditional dependence assumption holds very rarely. Proposals for estimating m- and u-probabilities under the *conditional dependence assumption* have been made in various works that come from the areas of statistics, information retrieval, and machine learning (see [671] for a survey). Specifically, generalized EM methods can be used [668] for estimations of such probabilities. The methods of Larsen and Rubin [388] are based on Bayesian models. The probability estimation of such methods is not accurate enough to estimate the error rates in the record linkage. The proposal of Belin and Rubin [52] goes in the direction of addressing this limitation. Specifically, Belin and Rubin proposed a mixture model for estimating false match rates, for given threshold values. The method requires training data and works well in a few situations, i.e., when there is a good separation between weights for matching and unmatching. Also, training data are considered a problem with very large data files.

In machine learning applications, typically, labeled training data (see Sect. 8.4) are used, for which the true classification is known, allowing *supervised learning*. In [472], it is observed that the use of Bayesian networks makes it possible to straightforwardly combine labeled and unlabeled data during training, in order to obtain suitable decision rules. If only unlabeled data are used, then the decision rules may be very poor.

8.6.2   A Cost-Based Probabilistic Technique

In this section we describe a probabilistic technique [626] for performing record matching with the aim of minimizing the cost associated with misclassification errors, corresponding to false matches and false unmatches in Fig. 8.9.

As previously described, the Fellegi and Sunter model proves that the proposed decision rule is optimal with respect to the minimization of the area needing clerical review (possible matches), for any pair of fixed thresholds on the probabilities of false matches and false unmatches.

The perspective adopted in [626] is different, in that it aims to minimize the *cost* associated with the misclassification error. The cost is considered as constituted by two different components, namely, (1) the cost of the decision process, including, for instance, the number of comparisons needed for the decision, and (2) the cost of the impact of a certain decision. The comparison vector that, as introduced, corresponds to the attribute values of two given records that need to be compared is indicated by $\bar{x}$. In the following we provide an example showing the difference between error-based models and cost models. Given a comparison vector $(1,1,0)$ with the probability of 75 % of appearing among matches and 25 % of appearing among unmatches, a rule based on the minimum error would assign it to M. Conversely, assuming that the cost of misclassifying a record as a match is more than three times the cost of misclassifying a record as a unmatch, the comparison vector would be assigned to U.

Costs are domain dependent and are considered as known in the proposed model. Moreover, the matching probabilities of the comparison records are also considered as known. Given such inputs, the model produces as outputs the decision rule on the membership to M or U and the required thresholds.

In the model, the costs c_{ij} are considered, meaning the costs of making a decision D_i when the compared pairs of records have an actual matching status j (M = 0 or U = 1). Decisions correspond to assignments to the three areas D_1, D_2, and D_3 defined in Sect. 8.6.1, related, respectively, to matching, possible matching, and unmatching pairs. Therefore, a cost is assigned to each decision, as shown in the table in Fig. 8.10.

Fig. 8.10 Costs corresponding to various decisions

Cost	Decision	Actual Matching
c_{10}	D_1	M
c_{11}	D_1	U
c_{20}	D_2	M
c_{21}	D_2	U
c_{30}	D_3	M
c_{31}	D_3	U

The cost that has to be minimized is given by

$$
\begin{aligned}
c_m = & c_{10} * P(d = D_1, r = M) + c_{11} * P(d = D_1, r = U) \\
& + c_{20} * P(d = D_2, r = M) + c_{21} * P(d = D_2, r = U) \\
& + c_{30} * P(d = D_3, r = M) + c_{31} * P(d = D_3, r = U),
\end{aligned}
$$

where d is the predicted class of a pair of records and r is the actual matching status of a pair of records. The attribution of every point in the decision space constituted by the union of D_1, D_2, and D_3 is done in order to have the cost c_m minimized. Inequalities are imposed on a particular expression of c_m obtained by applying the Bayes theorem and a few other transformations to the formulation given above. Further details can be found in [626].

8.7 Empirical Techniques

The first proposal for a record matching technique based mainly on an empirical approach can be traced to 1983, to the work by Bitton and DeWitt [77] focused on deduplication. The idea is to detect *exact* duplicates in a table, first sorting the table and then checking the identity of neighboring tuples. This basic approach has been adapted and extended in subsequent works in order to detect *approximate* duplicates with the goal of achieving better accuracy and performance results. In this section, we will review some major empirical techniques, starting from the SNM (Sect. 8.7.1) and the related priority queue algorithm (Sect. 8.7.2), then describing a technique for matching complex structured data (Sect. 8.7.3), and concluding with a technique for matching XML data (Sect. 8.7.4) and some additional empirical approaches to search space reduction (Sect. 8.7.5).

8.7.1 Sorted Neighborhood Method and Extensions

The basic SNM was proposed in [309, 593] and is also referred to as the *merge-purge* method. Given a collection of two or more files, the sorted neighborhood method is applied to a sequential list of records built from such files. The method, which spans over the search space reduction, comparison, and decision activities, can be summarized in three phases, depicted in Fig. 8.11 (let x_i, y_i, and z_i denote a possible matching record i in three different sources):

- *Create keys.* Given the list of records derived from the union of available sources in a single file (see Fig. 8.11, left), a key is computed by extracting a subset of relevant fields or portions of fields. Indeed, the rationale is that similar data will have closely matching keys. If N is the total number of records in the list, the complexity of this step is O(N).

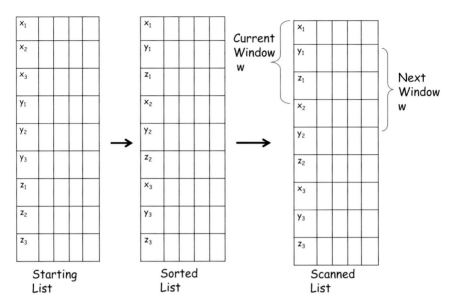

Fig. 8.11 Phases of the SNM method

- *Sort data.* On the basis of the key selected in the previous phase, records are sorted in the data list (see Fig. 8.11, middle). The complexity of this step is O($N\log N$).
- *Merge.* A fixed size window is moved through the sequential list of records, limiting the comparisons for matching records to those records in the window (see Fig. 8.11, right). If the size of the window is w records, then every new record entering the window is compared with the previous $w - 1$ records to find matching records. The decision about matching records is made according to domain-specific rules expressed in *equational theory*. The complexity of the merging phase is O(wN).

When the three phases are applied serially, the total time complexity of the method is O($N\log N$) if $w < \lceil \log N \rceil$, O(wN) otherwise.

In addition to the comparison performed in the merging phase, a *transitive closure step* is performed. Specifically, if records r_1 and r_2 are found to be similar and records r_2 and r_3 are also found to be similar, then r_1 and r_3 are marked to be similar as well. Note that while the couples (r_1, r_2) and (r_2, r_3) must be within the same window to be declared as similar, the inferred similarity between (r_1, r_3) does not require the two records to belong to the same window. This property can be exploited in order to have smaller sizes for the scanning window, with invariant accuracy of the result.

The effectiveness of the SNM depends highly on the key selected to sort the records, since only keys of good quality cause similar records to be close to each other in the window, after the sorting phase. As an example, the first names of person records can be selected instead of last names, since we may suppose (or know) that last names can be more frequently misspelled than first names, which are typically more familiar. The SNM assumes that a "key designer" chooses the most suitable key, based on considerations of the selectivity of the different attributes. In [64], the basic SNM is extended by making the choice of the key automatically. In order to choose a "good" key for matching instead of relying on key designers, the idea is to rely on a quality characterization of records and on an identification power criterion that captures the selectivity of the different attributes. Experimental validation of the proposed method shows that whenever the quality characterization is taken into account, such automatic choice outperforms the basic SNM.

So far, the basic SNM has been described running *once* on the list of concatenated source files. In the following, we describe two further versions: the *multi-pass approach*, which proposes several runs of the algorithm for more effectiveness, and the *incremental SNM*, which eliminates the need for the method to work on a single list of input data.

8.7.1.1 Multi-Pass Approach

The multi-pass SNM is based on the consideration that running the SNM on a single sorting key does not produce the most suitable results. For example, if a highly selective key is chosen as the matching key, such as `SocialSecurityNumber`, even a single digit error can compromise the final result. Therefore, the idea is to have several runs of the method, each with a different key and very small windows. Having different keys allows to reasonably ensure that if there are errors on some of them, the subsequent runs will compensate such errors. Also, running SNM with small windows corresponds to run less expensive steps instead of a single expensive one.

Each run of the multi-pass approach produces a set of pairs of records that can be merged. A transitive closure step is then applied to such pairs of records, and the result is the union of all pairs found in the independent runs, with the addition of pairs that can be inferred by transitive closure. The experimental evidence is that the multi-pass approach drastically improves the accuracy of the basic SNM with a single run on large varying windows, as also remarked in Sect. 8.9.

8.7.1.2 Incremental SNM

The incremental SNM is proposed for when it is too expensive to produce a single file of all input data. Typically, the step of producing a single file may be acceptable once; but, then, the problem occurs on how to deal with newly arrived data. The basic idea of the incremental SNM is to select a set of *prime representatives* of records for each cluster deriving from the application of the SNM. Once new data need to be merged, they will be concatenated with the set of prime representatives; the SNM will work on this concatenated set and new prime representatives will be selected for subsequent incremental phases. Each cluster can have more than one eligible prime representative, and the strategies for selecting them can be various. For example, a strategy could be to select the longest and most complete record. As another example, the prime representative could be selected as the record representing the most general concept within the cluster.

8.7.2   The Priority Queue Algorithm

The priority queue algorithm, first proposed in [448], is based on the same ideas of sorting and scanning as in the SNM. The main distinguishing issues are:

- The usage of a domain-independent strategy to perform duplicate record detection, based on the Smith-Waterman algorithm [584] (see Sect. 8.5.3)
- The usage of an efficient data structure, exploiting the union-find structure [603]
- The proposal of a heuristic method based on a priority queue for improving the performance of the SNM

The *union-find* data structure is used for detecting and maintaining the connected components of an indirect graph. The problem of detecting duplicates can be modeled in terms of determining the connected components of a graph, if considering the transitivity of equality. Specifically, each record of the file can be modeled as a node of a graph, where an undirected edge connects two nodes if they match.

The matching of a pair of records can be recursively verified by considering if they belong to the same connected component: if they do, a match is declared; if they belong to different components, a unmatch is declared; otherwise, they are compared to each other, and, in case of a matching, a new component is added to the graph. The two operations of the union-find structure are *union* (x, y), combining the set to which x belongs with the set to which y belongs (further, a representative for the union set is also chosen and the union set replaces the two initial sets), and find(x), returning the representative of the unique set containing x.

The algorithm considers a priority queue containing a fixed number of sets of records that are representatives of clusters. Only the most recently detected cluster members are stored in the queue. Given a record a, the algorithm first checks if it is a member of the clusters represented in the priority queue by comparing the cluster representative of a with the cluster representative of each set in the priority queue. This check is done by the *find* operation. If the check is successful, then a is already known to be a member of a cluster in the priority queue. If it is not successful, then a is compared with records in the priority queue by the Smith-Waterman algorithm. If a match is detected, the *union* function adds the a's cluster to the cluster of the matched record; otherwise, a must be a member of a cluster not present in the queue, and so it is saved with the highest priority as a singleton set in the queue.

The priority queue algorithm can perform considerably better than SNM for very large files and databases. For instance, the number of record comparisons can be reduced up to five times for a database of 900,000 total records (see [448]). In Sect. 8.9, further details on the experimental results are provided.

8.7.3 A Technique for Complex Structured Data: Delphi

A technique for complex structured data is described in [23], where the Delphi algorithm is proposed; complex structured data considered in Delphi are called *dimensional hierarchies*, they consist of a chain of relations linked by foreign key dependencies. Given a pair of adjacent relations in the hierarchy, we call *parent* the relation on the foreign key side and *child* the relation on the key side.

Dimensional hierarchies of relations are used typically (but not exclusively) in star schemas of data warehouses, where the chain of relations is composed of a relation representing the table of facts and one or more relations representing the dimensions of interest for the multidimensional analysis, organized with various normalization degrees. We adopt in the following a more general term for dimensional hierarchies, namely, *relational hierarchies*.

An example of relational hierarchy is shown in Fig. 8.12, where persons are represented in (1) the relation `Person`, (2) the `Administrative Region` of residence (e.g., district or region, according to country), and (3) `Country`. The relation `Country` is parent of the relation `Administrative Region` and is at the top of the hierarchy, while the relation `Person` is at the bottom. Note that `RegId` and `CtryId` are generated keys, used for an efficient link for pairs of tables.

In Fig. 8.12, three different types of objects are represented in the schema:

1. Persons, with region and country of residence
2. Regions, characterized by a set of resident persons and country
3. Countries, characterized by a set of regions, and for each region, a set of resident persons

Person

PId	First name	Last Name	RegId
1	Patrick	Mezisi	1
2	Amanda	Rosci	2
3	George	Oado	3
4	John	Mumasia	4
5	Vusi	Oymo	7
6	Luyo	Msgula	5
7	Frial	Keyse	8
8	Wania	Nagu	6
9	Paul	Kohe	7

Administrative Region

RegId	RegionName	CtryId
1	MM	1
2	MM	2
3	Masai Mara	1
4	Eastern Cape	3
5	Free State	3
6	FS	4
7	HHohho	5
8	Lumombo	6

Country

CtryId	CountryName
1	KE
2	Kenia
3	SOA
4	South Africa
5	SWA
6	Swaziland

Fig. 8.12 Three hierarchical relations

For each type of object, we may examine which are the duplicates in the relational hierarchy; e.g., we see that three different African countries are represented in the `Country` relational instance, with both the official name and an acronym.

The main idea of Delphi is to exploit the hierarchical structure of tuples, using both local (called *textual*) and global (called *co-occurrence*) similarity measures. Examine the tuples in the `Country` relation of Fig. 8.12. If we simply adopt a similarity measure local to the relation, e.g., the edit distance between names of countries, we can falsely conclude that `<SOA, SWA>` are duplicates and `<KE, Kenia>`, `<SOA, South Africa>`, and `<SWA, Swaziland>` are not duplicates. If in addition to the edit distance we adopt a second distance that looks at how such items co-occur with linked tuples in the child `Administrative Region` relation, then we can see that (1) KE and Kenia have the MM tuple in common and (2) for the three pairs `<KE, Kenia>`, `<SOA, South Africa>`, and `<SWA, Swaziland>`, we can find nonoverlapping groups of tuples linked with the pair.

The above example shows that in order to discover duplicates in relational hierarchies, we have to exploit the full structure of the hierarchy, or at least of adjacent relations. This strategy has two claimed advantages compared to "local" record linkage strategies:

1. It reduces the number of false matches, i.e., pairs of tuples incorrectly detected to be duplicates; this is the case with the pair `<SOA, SWA>`.
2. It reduces the number of false unmatches, i.e., pairs of tuples incorrectly detected as non-duplicates; this is the case with the pair `<KE, Kenia>`.

More formally, traditional textual similarity measures are extended with a *co-occurrence similarity function* defined as follows. In a relational hierarchy, a tuple in a parent relation R_i joins with a set, which we call its children set, of tuples in the child relation; the co-occurrence between two distinct tuples is measured by the amount of overlap between the children sets of the two tuples. An unusually significant co-occurrence (more than the average overlap between pairs of tuples in R_i or above a certain threshold) is a cause for suspecting that one is a duplicate of the other. The above duplicate detection procedure can be performed for all types of objects represented in the hierarchy (in our example, persons, regions, and countries). Two objects are considered duplicates if corresponding pairs of tuples in each relation of the hierarchy either match exactly or are duplicates, according to duplicate detection functions at each level. The complete Delphi algorithm is described in Fig. 8.13.

In order to make efficient the top-down traversal of the hierarchy and reduce the number of pairwise tuple comparisons, a potential duplicate identification filter is adopted to efficiently isolate a subset consisting of all potential duplicates and prune the tuples that cannot be duplicates. The pruning step corresponds to search space reduction in Sect. 8.5.2.

1. Process first the top most relation
2. Group relations below the top most relation into clusters of tuples
3. Prune each cluster according to properties of distance functions eliminating tuples that cannot be duplicates.
4. Compare pairs of tuples within each group according to two comparison functions and corresponding thresholds
   ✓ Textual similarity between two tuples
   ✓ Co-occurrence similarity between the children sets of the tuples
5. Decide for duplicates comparing a suitable combination of the two measures against a given threshold or a set of thresholds.
6. Dynamically update thresholds
7. Move one level down in the hierarchy

Fig. 8.13 The Delphi algorithm

The dynamic threshold update step has the goal of adapting thresholds used in step 5 to structural characteristics of different groups; the number of items of the definition domain may vary across groups, and names of regions in one country may be longer or constitute a wider set than they are in another country, thus influencing the thresholds. See Sect. 8.9.4 on decision methods comparison.

8.7.4 XML Duplicate Detection: DogmatiX

In this section we describe a technique for object identification for XML documents. Finding duplicates in XML data has two major additional challenges when compared to files or relational data, namely, (1) the identification of objects to compare and (2) the possibility that the same elements are defined with different structures due to the flexibility of XML as a semistructured data model. In [660], an algorithm called DogmatiX (Duplicate Objects Get Matched in XML) that explicitly considers these features is proposed. The algorithm has a preprocessing phase that consists of three steps:

- *Step 1: candidate query formulation and execution.* XML data are first queried to extract duplicate candidates. Duplicate candidates are considered with respect to a real-world type. For instance, Person and People can be considered as two representations of the same real-world type Individual. The candidate selection is not done automatically in DogmatiX.
- *Step 2: description query formulation and execution.* The descriptions of duplicate candidates are expressed by queries that select only some of the properties that are associated with objects, namely, the ones that are considered meaningful for object identification. As an example, while the Name and Surname of a Person can be considered as relevant for identifying it, information about the person's hobbies cannot be relevant to the scope. Two heuristics to determine the candidate's descriptions are proposed in [660]. The heuristics are based on a locality principle: given an element e, the farther some information is from e, the less related it is to it.

- *Step 3: object description (OD) generation.* A relation consisting of tuples OD(value, name) is generated, where value describes an instance of some information and name identifies the type of information by name. For instance, (Smith, Surname) is part of the object descriptor for a Person instance included in the duplicate candidates.

After such a preprocessing phase, three actual steps for duplicate detection are performed:

- *Step 4: comparison reduction.* First a filter is applied to reduce the number of duplicate candidates: the filter is defined as an upper bound to the similarity measure and does not require the computation of such a measure, but preliminarily removes objects from the set of possible duplicates. Then, a clustering phase is applied in order to compare only objects within the same cluster.
- *Step 5: comparisons.* Pairwise comparisons are performed on the basis of a similarity measure. Such a similarity measure is defined in a domain-independent way (see [660] for details). The similarity measure takes into account some important features like (1) relevance of data or their identification power, by means of the introduction of a variant of the inverse document frequency (IDF) metric, and (2) the distinction between nonspecified and contradictory data; e.g., the fact that two persons have several different preferences may be an indicator the two persons are distinct, while a missing preference should not penalize the similarity measure.
- *Step 6: duplicate clustering.* The transitivity of the relationship *is-duplicate-of* is applied to XML objects selected as duplicates in step 5.

The algorithm is a representative example of object identification for semistructured data.

8.7.5   Other Empirical Methods

The time efficiency of the record linkage process can be improved by the reduction of the search space, which can be performed by means of blocking and windowing strategies. For instance, instead of making detailed comparisons of all 10 billion pairs from two sets of 100,000 records representing all persons in a State, it may be sufficient to consider the set of pairs that agree on LastName and ZipCode in the address. Note that there is an implicit assumption that comparisons not made due to blocking are unmatch records. A good field to be chosen for blocking should contain a large number of values that are fairly uniformly distributed and must have a low probability of inaccuracy errors; specifically, this last property is due to the fact that errors in a field used for blocking can result in failure to bring linkable record pairs together.

When specific conditions hold, further techniques can be applied to optimize record linkage. In the following, we briefly describe the 1–1 matching technique that can be used when it is known that few duplications occur. Then, we describe the bridging file technique that can be used when a third source is available that links the two sources that are going to be matched.

8.7.5.1   1–1 Matching Technique

The basic idea of the 1–1 matching technique is to force each record of the set A to be matched with at most one record of the set B. The rationale behind this technique is that if there are few duplicates, it is sufficient to stop to the *best* matching record, which is the record having the highest agreement weight with the observed one. In [343] a technique to force 1–1 matching is proposed, in which the set of matching assignments is globally optimized.

8.7.5.2   Bridging File

Given the two files A and B, the bridging file includes a set of common identifying information for them. For instance, let us suppose that both A and B store personal information of citizens, namely, Name, Surname, and Address, but A stores, in addition, tax-related information, while B stores social service-related information. The information common to A and B can be available in a *bridging file*, as represented in Fig. 8.14. Notice that a record in A can be linked to several records in B, but typically *not to all*; therefore, the idea is that when a bridging file is available, record linkage efficiency can be improved. However, in order to have good matching results, it is very important to have high-quality bridging files.

Fig. 8.14 Bridging file example

A	A&B	B
$Tax_{1,1}$	$Name_1, Surname_1, Address_1$	$SocialService_{2,1}$
$Tax_{1,2}$	$Name_2, Surname_2, Address_2$	$SocialService_{2,2}$
...	...	...
...	...	...
$Tax_{1,n}$	$Name_n, Surname_n, Address_n$	$SocialService_{2,n}$

8.8   Knowledge-Based Techniques

In this section, we describe the details of three techniques that are classified as knowledge based. Specifically, Sect. 8.8.1 describes the Choice Maker system, Sect. 8.8.2 describes the Intelliclean system, and Sect. 8.8.3 describes the Atlas system.

8.8.1   Choice Maker

Choice Maker [96] is based on rules, called *clues*. Clues are domain-independent or domain-dependent relevant properties of data. They are used in two phases: offline (the system determines on a training set the relative importance of the various clues in an attempt to produce for as many examples as possible a decision that is consistent with the human marking, resulting in weight assignments to clues) and at runtime (the trained model is applied to the clues to compute a match probability that is compared with a given threshold). Several types of clues can be defined in Choice Maker, such as:

1. *Swaps of groups of fields*, e.g., swaps of first and last names, such as Ann Sidney with Sidney Ann.
2. *Multi-clues*, i.e., groups of clues that differ only by a parameter. For example, one may want to create clues that fire if the first names of records representing persons match and belong to one of the five name frequency categories; category 1 contains the very common names (such as "Jim" and "Mike" in the United States) and category 5 contains very rare names.
3. *Stacked data* describe data that store multiple values for certain fields. For example, current and old addresses may be stored in a relation so that a person can also be located when searching an old address.
4. *complex clues* that capture a wider set of properties of the application domain.

Complex clues are original types in Choice Maker. They are domain dependent. For an example of a complex clue, assume we have a database of US citizens, a small portion of which is represented in Fig. 8.15, and we want to eliminate duplicates from the relation. We can use a decision procedure based on attributes FirstName, LastName, and State. In this case, we probably decide that the pairs of tuples $<1,4>$, $<5,8>$ are unmatched, since values of attributes FirstName and LastName are distant, due probably to several typos. Let us assume that rich senior citizens usually live for one period of the year (around summer) in northern states and for another period (around winter) in southern states. Such a clue can be expressed in Choice Maker as a complex rule and leads to matched pairs of previously unmatched tuples $<1,4>$, $<5,8>$.

Record #	First Name	Last Name	State	Area	Age	Salary
1	Ann	Albright	Arizona	SW	65	70.000
2	Ann	Allbrit	Florida	SE	25	15.000
3	Ann	Alson	Louisiana	SE	72	70.000
4	Annie	Olbrght	Washington	NW	65	70.000
5	Georg	Allison	Vermont	NE	71	66.000
6	Annie	Albight	Vermont	NE	25	15.000
7	Annie	Allson	Florida	SE	72	70.000
8	George	Alson	Florida	SE	71	66.000

Fig. 8.15 A small portion of the registry of US citizens

The decision procedure can be overridden in special cases. For example, if we trust an identifier such as a social security number, we could use a rule that forces a unmatch decision if the two records have different identifier values.

8.8.2   A Rule-Based Approach: Intelliclean

The main idea of Intelliclean [416] is to exploit rules as an evolution of previously proposed distance functions; rules are extracted from domain knowledge and fed into an expert system engine, making use of an efficient method for comparing a large collection of rules to a large collection of objects. Rules are of two types, with different goals:

- *Duplicate identification rules*, specifying conditions according to which two tuples can be classified as duplicates. Duplicate identification rules include text similarity functions, but go further, allowing more complex logic expressions for determining tuple equivalence. An example of a duplicate identification rule is shown in Fig. 8.16, where duplicates are searched for in a `Restaurant` relation, with attributes `Id`, `Address`, and `Telephone`. For the rule in Fig. 8.16 to be activated, the corresponding telephone numbers must match, and one of the identifiers must be a substring of the other; furthermore, the addresses must also be very similar (similarity of addresses using the *FieldSimilarity* function must be higher than 0.8). Records classified as duplicates by this rule have a certainty factor (CF) of 80 %. A *certainty factor* (CF) represents expert confidence in the effectiveness of the rule in discovering duplicates, where $0 < \text{CF} < 1$. Specifically, we can assign a high certainty factor to a rule if we are sure that it will identify true duplicates. Analogously, we assign smaller values for rules that are less strict.

Define rule Restaurant_Rule
Input tuples: R1, R2
IF (R1.telephone = R2.telephone)
AND (ANY_SUBSTRING (R1.ID, R2.ID) = TRUE)
AND (FIELDSIMILARITY (R1.address = R2.address) > 0.8)
THEN
DUPLICATES (R1,R2) CERTAINTY = 0.8

Fig. 8.16 An example of the duplicate identification rule in Intelliclean

1. Preprocessing
Perform data type checks and format standardization
2. Processing
   2.1 The compared records are fed into an expert system engine together with a
   set of rules of the form IF <condition> THEN <action>.
   2.2 Check iteratively within a sliding window first Duplicate Identification rules
   and then Merge Purge rules using a basic production system to see which ones
   should fire based on the facts in the database, looping back to the first rule when
   it has finished.
   2.3 Perform transitive closure under uncertainty using an improved version of the
   multi-pass Sorted Neighborhood searching method
3. Human verification and validation stage
Human intervention to manipulate the duplicate record groups for which
merge/purge rules are not defined

Fig. 8.17 The complete Intelliclean strategy

- *Merge-purge rules*, specifying how duplicate records are to be handled. An example is "Only the tuple with the least number of empty fields is to be kept in a group of duplicate tuples, and the rest are to be deleted."

The complete Intelliclean strategy is shown in Fig. 8.17. The procedure can be seen as an improvement over the SNM presented in Sect. 8.7.1, where the improvement mainly regards the adoption of rules and a more effective transitive closure strategy.

From step 2.1 of Fig. 8.17, we observe that rules are extracted from domain knowledge by domain experts; therefore the approach can be classified as domain dependent. The selection of precise, expressive, and efficient rules is a crucial activity to achieve effectiveness of the cleaning process, i.e., maximize recall and precision (see Sect. 8.9). Step 2.3 is motivated by the fact that transitive closure in the multi-pass sorted neighborhood algorithm tends to increase false matches. As we have seen in the example, in Intelliclean a *certainty factor* (CF) is applied to each duplicate identification rule. During the computation of the transitive closure, we compare the resulting certainty factor of the merged group to a user-defined threshold. This threshold represents how tight or confident we want the merges to be. Any merges that result in a certainty factor less than the threshold will not be executed.

As an example, let us assume we perform step 2.3 on the following pairs of tuples: (A, B) with CF = 0.9; (B, C) with CF = 0.85; (C, D) with CF = 0.8; threshold = 0.5. The groups (A, B) and (B, C) will be firstly considered, as these groups have higher CFs. They will be merged to form (A, B, C) with

CF = 0.9 x 0.85 = 0.765. Then, this group is merged with (C,D) to form (A,B,C,D) with CF = 0.765 x 0.8 = 0.612, still greater than the threshold; however, if the threshold were set at 0.7, (A,B,C) and (C,D) would remain separate, as the resulting CF of the merged group, equal to 0.612, would be less than the threshold.

8.8.3 Learning Methods for Decision Rules: Atlas

In Intelliclean, discussed in the previous section, rules are extracted from the domain knowledge by experts, and no specific learning process is conceived for their generation. In this section, we discuss Atlas, a technique, presented in [605], that improves the knowledge-based approach in the following directions:

1. The rules include a wide set of domain-independent transformations, as possible mappings between textual strings, such as <World Health Organization, WHO> which transforms a string of three items into the string made of the initials of the items. Examples of transformations are shown in Fig. 8.18. <World Health Organization, WHO> is an example of the *acronym* transformation.
2. Structural information on rules can be obtained first from an analysis performed on tuples in the input, in order to extract knowledge on recurrent similarities between the different pairs of attributes of objects to be matched.
3. Rules can be obtained through a learning process on a training set, with or without active expert user involvement.

In order to explain in more detail the overall strategy of Atlas, consider the pair of one-tuple relations shown in Fig. 8.19.

In the figure, the two relations have four attributes in common, LastName, Address, Region, and Telephone. We assume that the two tuples refer to the

1. Soundex converts an item into a Soundex code. Items that sound similar have the same code
2. Abbreviation replaces an item with corresponding abbreviation (e.g., third → 3rd)
3. Equality compares two items to determine if each item contains the same characters in the same order
4. Initial computes if one item is equal to the first character of the other.
5. Prefix computes if one item is equal to a continuous subset of the other starting at the first character
6. Suffix computes if one item is equal to a continuous subset of the other starting at the last character
7. Abbreviation computes if one item is equal to a subset of the other (e.g., Blvd, Boulevard)
8. Acronym computes if all characters of one item string are initial letters of all items from the other string

Fig. 8.18 Examples of transformations

Relation1

LastName	Address	City	Region	Telephone
Ngyo	Mombsa Boulevard	Mutu	MM	350-15865

Relation2

LastName	Address	Region	Telephone
Ngoy	Mombasa Blvd.	Masai Mara	350-750123

Fig. 8.19 Two relations

same real-world object. The items in the two tuples have several differences, whose nature depends on the attribute. More specifically:

1. Values of `LastName` differ, probably due to typing Errors.
2. Values of `Address` differ, both for a character in the first item and for "distance abbreviation transformation" in the second item.
3. Values of `Region` differ in distance "acronym transformation."
4. Values of `Telephone` match only in the area code, probably due to a different currency.

The four attributes show different behaviors with respect to the differences appearing in the corresponding items. In order to precompute candidate mappings between tuples, *similarity scores* are computed for each couple of fields of tuples. They measure:

1. Local distances between each pair of attributes, based on a composition of applications of transformation and edit distance, applying the cosine similarity measure (see Sect. 8.5.3).
2. A global distance, where different weights are assigned to attributes in local distances; weights measure the selectivity of the attribute, to reflect the idea that we are more likely to believe matching between attributes in which values are rarer (for definitions and formulas, see [605]).

At this point, mapping rules have to be constructed. Looking at Fig. 8.19, an example of mapping rule is

```
If Address > threshold1 ∧ Street > treshold2
Then matching
```

The *mapping rule learner* determines which attributes or combinations of attributes are most effective for mapping objects, with the final goal of determining the most accurate mapping rules, given threshold values. *Accuracy of mapping rules* is seen as their ability in dividing a given set of training examples in matched/unmatched. This is performed by two methods:

1. *Decision trees* is an inductive learning technique, where attributes (and thresholds) are tested one at a time in the tree to discriminate between matching and unmatching pairs of tuples. Once an "optimal" decision tree is created, it is

converted into the corresponding mapping rule. In general, this method requires a large number of training examples.

2. An *active learning procedure*, where a committee of decision tree learners that vote is created in order to choose the most informative examples for the user to classify as matching or unmatching.

Once mapping rules are chosen, they are applied to candidate mappings to determine the set of mapped objects.

8.9 Quality Assessment

In Sect. 8.4, *search space reduction*, *choice of comparison function*, and *comparison decision* were identified as relevant steps in the object identification process. In this section, we first introduce metrics used to evaluate specific steps of object identification techniques (Sect. 8.9.1). Then, we describe a detailed comparison on two sets of techniques: (1) techniques that are mainly concerned with efficiency issues, i.e., search space reduction methods (Sect. 8.9.2) and comparison functions (Sect. 8.9.3), and (2) techniques that are mainly focused on effectiveness, i.e., decision methods (Sect. 8.9.4). Finally, in Sect. 8.9.5, we comment on some experimental results.

8.9.1 Qualities and Related Metrics

The decision on actual matching M or unmatching U of two records can give rise to two types of errors, *false positives* FPs (also called *false matches* in the chapter) for records declared as M while actually being U and *false negatives* FNs (*false unmatches*) for records declared as U while actually being M. *True positives* TPs (*true matches*) are the correctly identified M and *true negatives* TN (*true unmatches*) are the correctly identified U. Figure 8.20 summarizes such different cases. It follows

Fig. 8.20 Notation on matching decision cases

M	Actual match w.r.t. real world
U	Actual non match w.r.t. real world
FP	Declared match while actual non match
FN	Declared non-match while actual match
TP	Declared match while actual match
TN	Declared non match while actual non match

from definitions that the following equalities hold:

$$M = TP + FN$$

$$U = TN + FP$$

Several metrics to evaluate effectiveness of object identification techniques have been proposed, combining such criteria. The most typical metrics are *recall* and *precision*. *Recall* measures how many true positives are identified in relation to the total number of actual matches. It is given by:

$$recall = \frac{TP}{M} = \frac{TP}{TP + FN}.$$

The aim of an object identification technique is of course to have a high recall. *Precision* measures how many true matches are identified in relation to the total number of declared matches, including erroneous ones (i.e., FPs):

$$precision = \frac{TP}{TP + FP}.$$

The aim is to have a high precision. Recall and precision are often conflicting goals in the sense that if one wants to have a greater number of true positives (i.e., to increase recall level), usually more false positives are also found (i.e., precision decreases). Besides recall and precision, other metrics that have been used are *false negative percentage* and *false positive percentage*. False negative percentage considers how many undetected matches are present relative to the number of actual matches:

$$\text{false negative percentage} = \frac{FN}{M} = \frac{FN}{TP + FN}.$$

False positive percentage considers how many wrongly detected matches are present, relative to the number of actual matches:

$$\text{false positive percentage} = \frac{FP}{M} = \frac{FP}{TP + FN}.$$

In order to combine recall and precision, *F-measure* has also been proposed. It corresponds to the harmonic mean of recall and precision. More specifically, *F*-measure is given by

$$F\text{-measure} = \frac{2RP}{P + R}.$$

Besides these specific metrics, traditional time complexity metrics are used to evaluate the efficiency of the object identification process; an example is the *number of comparisons* to be performed during the process.

8.9.2 Search Space Reduction Methods

As already described, given two sets of records A and B we want to compare for identifying the same objects belonging to both of them, the search space is the cartesian product A × B. In order to reduce such space, we have seen that three principal methods exist, blocking, sorted neighborhood, and pruning.

Typically, pruning is used in most empirical techniques, either in conjunction with blocking or in conjunction with sorted neighborhood; in the following we will examine blocking and sorted neighborhood. In [193], a comparison of blocking and sorted neighborhood is reported. The two methods are compared considering (1) the blocking method for different values of the block key length and (2) the SNM for different values of the window size. Blocking and sorted neighborhood are evaluated on the basis of the effectiveness of the matching process, measured by the F-measure metric. The experiments show that the F-measure values for blocking and sorted neighborhood are comparable for appropriate choices of the blocking key length and the window size.

Furthermore, when comparing the time complexity of the two methods, a comparable behavior is similarly exhibited. Indeed, as already shown in Sect. 8.5.2, the total time complexity of blocking is $O(h(n) + n^2/b)$, where $h(n) = n\log n$ if blocking is implemented using sorting, which is comparable to the total time complexity of the sorted method, that is, $O(n\log n + wn)$.

8.9.3 Comparison Functions

Various empirical analyses have been done to discover which comparison functions perform better. In [193] a comparison is reported between 3 grams, bigrams, edit distance, and Jaro algorithm. The experiment considers the behavior of the functions on a set of name pairs, some of which are the same names, but misspelled, while others are different or swapped. The result of the experiment is that Jaro outperforms for the same name misspelled and known to be different, while bigram outperforms for names swapped. In [673], Jaro is again compared with edit distance and bigram, and it is shown that it is superior, especially when transpositions are present.

8.9.4 Decision Methods

We now characterize the decision methods adopted by the object identification techniques described in this chapter. For each decision method, we report:

- *Input parameters* required by the method. Note that some techniques also provide methods for computing such parameters.
- *Output* provided by the method.

- *Objective*, which summarizes the main goal to be achieved by the decision method.
- *Human interaction*, representing the steps of the object identification process that require the involvement of an expert.
- *Selection-construction of a representative* (this last step also called *fusion*) for the matching records, showing which methods explicitly include the selection or construction of a record that represents a specific cluster obtained in the matching process.

The techniques are represented in Fig. 8.21.

Looking at the input column, the decision rules that are used by the method can be specified at attribute and at tuple levels for structured data types. For the techniques that consider relational hierarchies, such as Delphi or XML documents, e.g., DogmatiX, thresholds are specified according to the various elements of the adopted data model. Specifically, in Delphi, thresholds are specified by the comparison between tuples and their children sets; in DogmatiX, the objects to be compared need to be explicitly identified in the XML documents, and thresholds are defined for such objects.

In the output column, observe that the probabilistic techniques typically partition records into three sets, match, unmatch, and possible match, at given error rates. Conversely, both the empirical and knowledge-based techniques are used to partition records into two sets, match and unmatch. The underlying assumption of such techniques is that of completely automated decision methods, not requiring any human review on possible matches (consider also the human interaction column).

The objective column summarizes the objective of the decision method. The probabilistic techniques rely on formal models explicitly including such an objective. The Fellegi and Sunter model is formulated to minimize possible matches, while the cost-based model has the objective of minimizing the cost of errors. The empirical and knowledge-based methods instead are all validated against the precision-recall performance, namely, how effective the decision method is in detecting true positives (precision) and not detecting false positives (recall).

In the human interaction column, for all methods but Delphi, there is the need of human-defined thresholds. Indeed, Delphi introduces a technique to dynamically determine thresholds, based on standard outlier detection methods, considering that a duplicate has an outlier-like behavior referred to given similarity metrics.

The representative of a cluster of matched records is actually constructed/selected only by Intelliclean. The concept of cluster representative is proposed also within the SNM and the priority queue method, but with a different scope, reducing the number of pairwise comparisons to detect duplicates. In contrast, Intelliclean identifies a strategy and appropriate rules for building cluster representatives.

Technique	Input	Output	Objective	Human interaction	Selection/Construction of a representative for the matching records
Fellegi&Sunter	γ vector of comparison functions Estimation of Tμ and Tλ m- and u-probabilities	For each record pair, decision on match, non-match, possible match with given error rates	Low error rates (false match and false non-match) Minimization of possible matches	Clerical Review of possible matches	No
Cost Based	Matrix of costs of decision rules m- and u- probabilities	For each record pair, decision on match, non-match, possible match with given error rates	Minimization of cost of errors (false match and false non-match)	Clerical Review of possible matches Matrix of costs of decision rules	No
SNM	Declarative rules encoding domain knowledge (for tuple level decision) Comparison functions (for attribute value decision) Threshold (for attribute value decision)	For each record pair, decision on match or non-match	Precision/Recall tradeoff	Choice of the matching key Threshold Specification Decision Rules	No (only for incremental SNM)
Priority-Queue	Smith Waterman comparison function Threshold (for tuple value decision)	For each record pair, decision on match or non-match	Precision/Recall tradeoff	Threshold Specification	No
Delphi	Textual Comparison Function Co-occurrence metric Set of thresholds (dynamically updated)	For each record pair, decision on match or non-match	Precision/Recall tradeoff	None	No
DogMatrix	XML Threshold similarity (object level)	For each XML element pair, decision on match or non-match	Precision/Recall tradeoff	Selection of candidates Threshold Specification	No
IntelliClean	Duplicate Identification Rules (for tuple decision) Merge Purge Rules (for tuple decision) Set of thresholds (for attribute comparison and for tuple merging)	For each record pair, decision on match or non-match Merged Result for matching records	Precision/Recall tradeoff User controlled confidentiality for merging	Duplicate Identification,Merge/Purge Rules Specification Threshold Specification Human verification for merging duplicates when rules are not specified	Yes
Atlas	Learnt Decision rules Set of domain independent transformations Thresholds	For each record pair, decision on match or non-match	Precision/Recall tradeoff	Mapping rule learning	No

Fig. 8.21 Comparison of decision methods

Technique	Metrics	Synthetic/ Real Data	Results
SNM	Precision False Positive Percentage	Synthetic	Precision 50%-70% on independent pass Precision close to 90% with transitive closure False Positive Percentage not significant (0.05 -0.2%)
	Precision False positive Percentage False negative Percentage	Real	Not significant False Negatives Percentage Not significant False Positive Percentage
Priority-Queue	Precision Efficiency (Number of comparisons)	Synthetic	Precision similar to SNM Efficiency : 5 times less than SNM
	Efficiency (Number of comparisons)	Real	Precision not provided as for real data difficult to identify actual duplicate s EffiNumber of reduced comparisons similar to the one for the synthetic data set
Delphi	False Positive Percentage False Negative Percentage	Real	False Positive Percentage less than 25% False Negative Percentage around 20%
DogmatiX	Precision Recall	Real	For similarity measure: Experiment 1: Precision 70-100% Experiment 1: Recall: 2%-35% Experiment 2: Precision 60-100%
IntelliClean	Precision	Real	Experiment 1: Precision 80% Experiment 1: Less than 8% Recall Experiment 2 :Precision: 100% Experiment 2 :Recall:100%
Atlas	Precision (accuracy)	Real	Experiment 1: Precision 100% Experiment 2: Precision 99%

Fig. 8.22 Metrics used to evaluate object identification by empirical techniques and related results

8.9.5 Results

The table in Fig. 8.22 describes the results obtained by the different decision methods and the features of the datasets used for the experiments. For each technique, we report the metrics addressed, the type of data used in the experiments (synthetic vs. real), and the provided results in terms of the different metrics, as claimed by the authors of each technique.

The first row of Fig. 8.22 refers to the SNM. Results of experiments are reported for both the synthetic and the experimental datasets. Note that such results depend on a specific parameter, namely, the size of the sliding window: intervals of values shown in the figure correspond to different sizes of the window. For the priority queue algorithm, the result of an efficiency test is shown, measured by the number of comparisons that the algorithm performs. The results for Delphi concern the first level of the hierarchy (see Sect. 8.7.3). For DogmatiX the reported results concern primarily the similarity measure included in the approach. The intervals of the metrics refer to the variability of the threshold used for the measure.

The experimental datasets, as well as the experimental conditions and assumptions, are different, and therefore it is not possible to actually compare the different techniques. Nevertheless, the figure's utility is in its summarizing the features of the experimental validation and testing performed on each technique.

8.10 Summary

In this chapter we have described several techniques proposed for the most relevant IQ activity, object identification. Due to heterogeneous schemas and to possible errors in data entry and update processes, objects happen to have different representations and values in distinct databases. As a consequence, a *loss* of a clear identity may affect objects, thus compromising the possibility of reconstructing information sparse in distinct sources. Object identification techniques aim at repairing this loss of identity, using context information available on the similarity of objects' representations in terms of tuples, hierarchical relations, and XML files. The concepts of "context information available" and "similarity" are formalized in different ways in probabilistic, empirical, and knowledge-based techniques. Moreover, techniques proposed in the three areas can be differently characterized with respect to the level of adoption, their efficiency, and their effectiveness. The probabilistic techniques emerge as the most adopted ones, due to their relative maturity and the experiences gained from their application. The empirical techniques have the efficiency as a major objective and thus are particularly suitable for time critical applications. The knowledge-based techniques have the best potential effectiveness, due to the explicit modeling of domain knowledge. Comparisons between techniques, described in Sect. 8.9, as well as criteria adopted by specific techniques, provide the reader elements for choosing the most effective technique according to the context. We will discuss these issues in more depth in Chap. 12.

Chapter 9
Recent Advances in Object Identification

9.1 Introduction

Research on *object identification* has been producing several significant results in the last years, in different areas of computer science. As observed in [140], it is well known that in data mining projects, a large proportion of effort (20–30 % reported in [566]) is spent for understanding data and 50–70 % for data preparation. Governmental organizations need to reconcile and integrate their huge and heterogeneous data assets; statistical agencies routinely link survey and administrative data, in the health sector historical data on patients; and analyses are to be linked for improving effectiveness of operation and policies [80]; security agencies increasingly rely on the ability to correlate files referring to a single individual; data linkage can help in bioinformatics to relate known genome sequences to a new unknown sequence. Due to such increasing interest in object identification, in this chapter, we pay attention to the main trends and results in the area with a focus on the latest results.

We have first attempted to find a correspondence between the terminology adopted in our previous book [37] and the prevalent terminology in the recent literature. About 60 % of surveyed papers adopt the term *record linkage*, while 40 % adopt the term *object identification* or the term *entity resolution*, with this percentage increasing in the last years. As to phases of object identification, *preprocessing* is also called *standardization*, while *search space reduction* is also called *blocking* and *indexing*, and the terms *comparison & decision* are widely adopted. For the sake of a better cohesion, we decided to keep in this chapter the same general terminology of the previous one, with some exceptions chosen case by case to prefer understandability of described frameworks.

To have a picture at a glance of the main recent contributions in the literature of the last years, see the traditional life cycle of object identification (*OID* in the following) represented in the left-hand side of Fig. 9.1 (where an example extraction step has been highlighted whose goal is to identify a sample and label matching and

© Springer International Publishing Switzerland 2016
C. Batini, M. Scannapieco, *Data and Information Quality*, Data-Centric Systems
and Applications, DOI 10.1007/978-3-319-24106-7_9

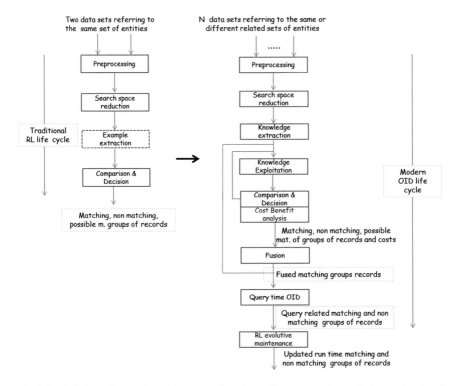

Fig. 9.1 Evolution of research on object identification and corresponding evolution of the object identification life cycle

not matching pairs in the sample), while recent advancements in the life cycle are shown in the right-hand side.

In order to understand the innovations in *OID*, we observe that until the end of the last century, *OID* was considered an off-line activity that was conducted when both (1) the cost of management of a set of heterogeneous databases representing the same or overlapping sets of objects and (2) the loss in effectiveness in their usage were considered unbearable. In modern *OID*, the life cycle (see Fig. 9.1, right-hand side) is much richer and spans at least on other two activities in the information system life cycle, namely, (a) the run time execution of queries, when the user is interested to apply *OID* only to data involved in the query, and (b) the dataset maintenance, when updates on data and on integrity constraints change the dataset and its semantics, leading to conceive techniques that operate on data at maintenance time. Furthermore, the high cost of certain steps of the *OID* activity has suggested to conceive pay-as-you-go strategies, where *OID* is performed only to the extent in which a certain cost benefit-ratio is achieved. Finally, fusion of data has been frequently considered in the past as a separate activity with respect to *OID*; instead, to fasten and improve the quality of the *OID* process, in several modern approaches, the result of fusion is incrementally exploited during the comparison & decision activity.

Another issue investigated in the last years concerns the improvements in quality and efficiency that arise from (automatically) gathering and exploiting knowledge on data that have to be linked, e.g., knowledge on the relationships of data with other known data. Some first examples as [23, 660] are discussed in Chap. 8.

As a final remark, we consider important to explore *OID* for types of information different from relational data and XML semistructured information, especially maps and images, where comparison and fusion activities are also called *conflation*.

The chapter is organized as follows. In Sect. 9.2, we focus on systematizations of qualities and metrics for the modern *OID* process. Section 9.3 deals with preprocessing techniques. Section 9.4 discusses evolution of techniques for reducing the search space, so to increase efficiency without losing in quality. As to subsequent steps in Fig. 9.1, papers in the literature usually do not focus on a single activity; so in Sect. 9.5, we investigate techniques that span over one or more steps among the following: (a) knowledge extraction, (b) knowledge exploitation, (c) comparison and decision, (d) cost-benefit analysis, (e) fusion, (f) run time *OID*, and (g) *OID* evolutionary maintenance. In the last three sections of the chapter, we address other important issues related with *OID*: domain specificity, different information types, and privacy. In particular, Sect. 9.6 considers the problem of identification in specific domains, such as names in general, names of persons and names of businesses. The idea is that considering *OID* in specific domains should improve the effectiveness and efficiency of the process. In the spirit of the book, Sect. 9.7 discusses object identification in types of information different from relational tables, namely, the linkage of maps with orthoimages representing the same or overlapping network of roads. Finally, Sect. 9.8 addresses a problem of increasing importance, techniques for performing *OID* on data that are subject to privacy constraints.

9.2 Quality Assessment

In Sect. 8.9.1, we have addressed the issue of quality assessment, and we have introduced several metrics and discussed results of experiments on the basis of them. In this section, we extend metrics with new ones, both for search space reduction (simply *reduction* in the rest of the chapter)—see Sect. 9.2.1—and for comparison & decision (see Sect. 9.2.2), where we shortly recall metrics for comparison and decision defined in the previous chapter. In Sect. 9.2.3 we resume recommendations to be considered in experiments on quality evaluation for reduction, while in Sect. 9.2.4, we discuss surveys and frameworks for comparing evaluation techniques in the area of object identification. Among papers dealing with qualities, we refer to [140]. The assumption in [140] is that the linkage classifier has a single threshold parameter so that record pairs are classified as matches and unmatches. Furthermore, the two datasets to be linked are assumed without duplicates.

9.2.1 Qualities for Reduction

Two measures that quantify the efficiency and quality of reduction techniques are:

1. *Reduction ratio* [193] is measured as $rr = 1 - \frac{N_b}{|A| \times |B|}$, with N_b being the number of record pairs produced by the reduction technique (i.e., the number of record pairs not removed by reduction). The reduction ratio does not take into account the quality of the reduction, i.e., how many record pairs from the not matching and matching sets are removed from reduction.
2. *Pairs completeness* [193, 280] is measured as $pc = \frac{N_m}{|M|}$ with N_m being the number of correctly classified truly matched record pairs in the reduced comparison space and $|M|$ being the total number of true matches. Pairs completeness is analogous to recall.

9.2.2 Qualities for the Comparison and Decision Step

In the following, we call A and B the two datasets that have to be matched and A_e and B_e the two sets of entities of the real world that are represented in A and B, respectively. $M_e = A_e \cap B_e$ is the intersection set of matched entities that appear (as records) both in A_e and in B_e, and U_e is the set of unmatched entities that appear in either A_e or B_e, but not in both. The space described by A_e, B_e, M_e, and U_e is termed *entity space*. As an example (taken from [140]), assume the set A_e contains 5 million entities and set B_e contains 1 million entities, with 700,000 entities present in both sets (i.e., the cardinality of $M_e = 700,000$). The number of unmatched entities in this situation is $U_e = 4,600,000$, which is the sum of the entities in both sets (6 million) minus twice the number of matched entities (as they appear in both sets A_e and B_e). The goal of an object identification process is to classify pairs of records in A and B as matches and unmatches in the two disjoint spaces of (a) true matches (M in the following) and (b) true unmatches (U in the following). M and U are defined as in Sect. 8.9.1.

Assuming that no reduction is applied and that all pairs of records in A and B are compared, the total number of comparisons equals $|A| \times |B|$, which is much larger than the number of entities in A_e and B_e together. The space of record pair comparisons is called the *comparison space*. In the example, the comparison space consists of $5,000,000 \times 1,000,000 = 5 \times 10^{12}$ record pairs, with $|M| = 700,000$ and $|U| = 5 \times 10^{12} - 700,000 = 4.9999993 \times 10^{12}$ record pairs.

To conclude with the notation, TP, true positives; FP, false positives; TN, true negatives; and FN, false negatives, are in Sect. 8.9. As to the number of TN entities in the comparison space, it is

$$|TN| = |A| \times |B| - |TP| - |FN| - |FP| .$$

Since TP, FP, and FN are limited by the number of records in A and B, we conclude that usually the value of TN is significantly higher than the three other measures.

The first three qualities referred to comparison and decision have been mentioned in Sect. 8.9: they are *recall* (R), interpreted as true-positive rate, also known as *sensitivity* [696]; *precision* (P) also called *positive predictive value*; and the *F-measure*. An aggregate value for the *F*-measure is *maximum F-measure*, the maximum value of the *F*-measure over a varying threshold.

Two figures that allow to both visually and synthetically esteem the relationship between precision and recall are:

1. *Precision-recall graph*, a two axes diagram created by plotting precision values on the vertical axis and recall values on the horizontal axis. As we observed in Chap. 8, there is a trade-off between precision and recall, in that higher precision can normally only be achieved at the cost of lower recall values and vice versa.
2. *Precision-recall break-even point* is the value where precision becomes equal to recall. This measure is a single number.

Other qualities that are proposed in the literature and critically discussed in [140] are:

- *Accuracy* (see [545]) is measured as $acc = \frac{TP+TN}{TP+FP+TN+FN}$. As this measure includes the number of TN, it is affected by their large number when used in the comparison space. For example, erroneously classifying all matches as unmatches will still result in a very high accuracy value. Accuracy is therefore considered in [140] not a good quality measure for *OID* and deduplication and should not be used.
- *Specificity* [696] (which can be interpreted as the true-negative rate) is frequently used in epidemiological studies (see [696]) and is measured as $spec = \frac{TN}{TN+FP}$. As it includes the number of TN, it suffers from the same problem as accuracy and should not be used for *OID*.
- *False-positive rate* is measured as $fpr = \frac{FP}{TN+FP}$. Note that $fpr = 1 - spec$; so, the false-positive rate has a very low value and suffers from the complementary problem with respect to accuracy and specificity.
- *ROC curve* (receiver operating characteristic curve) is plotted as the recall on the vertical axis against the false-positive rate on the horizontal axis for a varying threshold. For an introduction to ROC graphs , see [226]. One advantage of ROC graphs is that they enable visualizing and organizing decision performance without regard to class distributions or error costs. This ability becomes very important when investigating learning with skewed distributions or cost-sensitive learning. The problem with ROC graphs is the same as highlighted before, the number of true negatives, which only appears in the false-positive rate. This rate will be calculated too low, resulting in optimistic ROC curves.

As to our example, let us assume that for a given threshold, the decision technique has classified in the comparison space 900,000 record pairs as matches and the rest $= 5 \times 10^{12} - 900,000$ as unmatches. Of these 900,000 matches, 650,000 were TPs

Metric	Entity Space	Comparison Space
Precision	72,2%	72,2%
Recall	92,8%	92,8%
F-measure	81,2%	81,2%
Accuracy	94,3%	99,9%
Specificity	94,5%	99,95
False positive rate	5,4%	0.000005%

Fig. 9.2 Comparison of quality measures in the entity space and in the comparison space

and 250,000 are FPs. The number of FNs is 50,000, and the number of TNs is $5 \times 10^{12} - 950,000$. When looking at the entity space, the number of not matched entities is $4,600,000 - 250,000 = 4,350,000$. Figure 9.2 shows the resulting quality measures for this example in both the comparison and the entity spaces.

While all quality measures presented so far assume a binary classification without possible matches, a measure has been proposed [280] that aims to quantify the proportion of possible matches within a traditional probabilistic *OID* system. The measure $pp = \frac{N_{P,M} + N_{P,U}}{TP + FP + TN + FN}$ is proposed, where $N_{P,M}$ is the number of true matches that have been classified as possible matches and $N_{P,U}$ is the number of true unmatches that have been classified as possible matches. Low pp values are desirable, as they correspond to less manual clerical review.

A final quality of the *OID* process is *scalability* that expresses the process computational effort and can be measured in terms of computational complexity with the O-notation [488] that is expressed in terms of a given measure of the number n of records; e.g., $O(\log n)$ represents logarithmic complexity and $O(n)$ linear complexity.

9.2.3   General Analyses and Recommendations

When different techniques are compared on the same problem class, as observed in [140], some care has to be taken to make sure that the achieved quality results are statistically valid. One mentioned pitfall is the *multiplicity effect* [544], meaning that, when comparing techniques on the same data, because of the lack of independence of the data, the chances of erroneously achieving significance on a single test increases. Independent researchers using the same datasets can suffer from this problem as well.

From the discussion in [75, 544], the following general recommendations can be provided:

- The quality of techniques varies depending on the nature of the datasets the techniques are applied to. Therefore, results should be produced from datasets which are broadly available to researchers and practitioners in the field. However, this does not preclude research on private datasets.

- Ideally, a suite of datasets should be collected and made publicly available for the *OID* process, and they should encapsulate as much variation in types of data as feasible.
- As to comparison and decision techniques, due to the problem of the number of true negatives in any comparison, quality measures that use that number should not be used.
- When comparing techniques, precision-versus-recall or *F*-measure graphs provide an additional dimension to the results. For example, if a small number of highly accurate links is required, the technique with higher precision for low recall should be preferably chosen.
- As to reduction, since in general it removes record pairs from the set of true matches, it is recommended that if computationally feasible, for example, in an empirical study using small datasets, all quality measurement results be obtained without the use of reduction. If this is not possible, it is worthwhile to publish the two reduction measures introduced above, reduction ratio and pairs completeness, and to make the reduced dataset available for analysis and comparison to other researchers.

9.2.4 Hints on Frameworks for OID Techniques Evaluation

Comparison and decision techniques both with and without using machine learning are also compared in [378]. State-of-the-art commercial *OID* implementations are considered. Results indicate significant quality and efficiency differences between approaches. It is also shown that some tasks such as matching product entities from online shops are not sufficiently solved with conventional approaches based on the similarity of attribute values.

Brizan and Tansel [94] is an overview of some similarity measures and reduction/decision methods. Elmagarmid et al. [197] deal with reduction techniques, comparison functions, and decision models, distinguishing between (a) probabilistic models and supervised, semisupervised, and unsupervised learning, (b) active learning techniques, (c) distance-based techniques, and (d) rule-based approaches. Getoor and Machanavajjhala [262] address both single set and multiple set of entities methods, with specific attention to efficiency. Open research directions are highlighted.

Among evaluation environments, Tailor [193] is worth to be mentioned, being a framework designed in an extensible way to interface with existing (at the date, 2002) and future *OID* models and allowing for comparison of classification methods that span from supervised to unsupervised to hybrid. In Fig. 9.3, the architecture of the evaluation environment is shown. The flow is coherent with the general process discussed in Chap. 8.

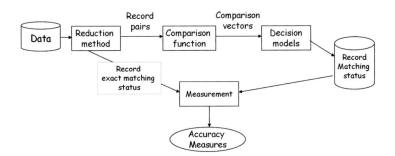

Fig. 9.3 Architecture of Tailor

Goiser and Christen [268] compare several string comparison and decision methods, on real-world data and synthetic data, providing figures and discussing motivations for the different method behaviors. Hassanzadeh et al. [301] compare several clustering algorithms of different types, such as (a) single pass, (b) star clustering, (c) cut clustering, (d) articulation point clustering, and (e) Markov clustering and others.

The study in [377] aims at exploring the current state of the art in research prototypes of entity matching frameworks. The paper considers both frameworks that do and do not utilize training data to semiautomatically find an entity matching strategy to solve a given match task; furthermore, it considers support for reduction and the combination of different match algorithms. Several criteria are considered for comparison:

- Type of test: test may involve real-world data sources or may be artificially generated
- Number of domains/sources/tasks: how many domains, sources, and match tasks are considered
- Semantic entity types: kinds of match problems that have been solved
- Minimum/maximum number of entities involved in a match task
- Minimum/maximum number of attributes (features) used for solving a match task
- Used similarity functions
- Number of training examples used for training
- Blocking performance quality measures considered
- Quality of entity matching measures considered
- Efficiency measures considered

9.3 Preprocessing

Preprocessing activities have been discussed in Chap. 8 as appropriate in order to
harmonize records in the two datasets to be linked so to maximize the effectiveness
of the comparison and decision step.

Recent literature on preprocessing has focused on the possibility to automatize as
far as possible activities related to standardization; more specifically, some attention
has been dedicated to items' transformations such as "JFK Airport" → "John
Fitzgerald Kennedy Airport." Such transformations, and their automatic learning,
have been recently investigated with notable results. Consider the examples in
Fig. 9.4 from [25] related to citation domain string matching.

A number of transformations are relevant to this matching task. These include:

1. Conference and journal abbreviations (VLDB → Very Large Data Bases)
2. Subject-related abbreviations (Soft → Software)
3. Date-related variations (Nov → November)
4. Number-related abbreviations (8th → Eighth)

and a large number of variations that do not fall into any particular class (e.g., pp →
pages, eds → editors).

It is evident that this list is a miscellanea of many kinds of transformations, hence
manually compiling it is a challenging task. For some popular domains such as
addresses, there are standard precompiled sets of transformations made available
by several national postal systems. While these (and others) sources are indeed
valuable sources, they are rarely comprehensive for a given record linkage task.
As an example, while the precompiled set of transformations provided by, e.g.,
the US Postal System covers variations relating to street name endings (e.g., Ave
→ Avenue), it does not cover variations relating to street names (e.g., Univ →
University and 5th → Fifth). Furthermore, when comparing a pair of strings of items

Id	Left	Right
1	Katayama,T., 2A hierarchical and functional software process description and its enaction", Proc. 11th ICSE, IEEE, 1989, pp.343-352	T. Katayama, "A hierarchical and functional software process description and its enaction," In: Proceedings of the Eleventh Int. Conf. On Soft. Eng. Pages: 343{352, IEEE Computer Society Press, Pittsburgh, PA, Jan 1989.
2	Knuth, D., The art of Computer Programming, Vol. III, Addison-Wesley, (1973).	8. D. Knuth, The art of Computer Programming, Volume 3: Sorting and Searching, Addison-Wesley, Reading, MA, 1973.
3	[ESWARAN76] Eswaran, K. P., J. N. Gray, R. A. Lorie, I. L. Traiger, \The notions of consistency and predicate locks in a database system", Communications of the ACM, Vol. 19, No. 11, November, 76	[14] K. P. Eswaran, J. N. Gray, R. A. Lorie, and I. L. Traiger, \The notions of consistency and predicate locks in a database system," Commun. Assoc. Comput. Mach., Vol. 19, No. 11, Nov. 1976

Fig. 9.4 Examples of citation domain string matching from [25]

such as citations in Fig. 9.4, several transformations coexist, making the problem
hard to solve.

The first proposals to automatically recognize sets of transformations in a given
domain appear in [442], where different techniques are proposed for incorporating
a priori knowledge of variations into the *OID* process. Exploiting variations learned
by such techniques can significantly improve the quality of *OID*. The limit of such
works is that they do not address how to identify suitable transformations in a
specific *OID* setting. A contribution in this direction is provided by Michelson
and Knoblock [438] and Arasu et al. [24]. The approach followed starts from
the observation that a transformation introduces textual differences between two
matching records. Informally, the difference between two strings is part of one string
that is not present in the other and vice versa. Consider, for example, the pair of
strings

$$< 60460\textbf{Highway}50OlatheCO > \text{ and } < 60460\textbf{Hwy}50OlatheCO > .$$

The difference between the two strings is highlighted in bold and corresponds to
the transformation Highway $\rightarrow$ Hwy. In general, a high number of transformation
could contribute to differences between two matching strings. For example, many
transformations such as (Proc $\rightarrow$ Proceedings), (11th $\rightarrow$ Eleventh), and (pp $\rightarrow$
Pages) contribute to the differences between the first pair of strings in Fig. 9.4.

In order to learn meaningful transformations, Arasu et al. [24] analyze a large
number of matching strings and seeks a concise set of syntactic rules (candidate
transformations) of the form $x \rightarrow y$ that can be used to account for a large part of
the differences between each pair of matching strings. Informally, a rule such as
Proc $\rightarrow$ Proceedings is likely to be in such a concise set, since we expect it to occur
in a large number of matching strings. On the other hand, a rule such as 11th $\rightarrow$
Eleventh, is unlikely to be part of such a concise set since we expect it to occur in
few matching strings.

The *rule learning problem* presented in [24] is a formalization of the above
ideas and has connections to the *minimum description length principle* [279]. As
stated in [24], the candidate rules considered in [438] are entire differences between
matching strings. For example, the candidate rule for matches in the first pair of
Fig. 9.4 would be

$$\text{Proc. 11th ICSE} \ldots \rightarrow \text{In: Proceedings of the Eleventh} \ldots .$$

In other words, Michelson and Knoblock [438] do not consider the option of
accounting for differences between matches using multiple transformations. Arasu
et al. [24] argue that most of the technical complexity of the proposed algorithm
formulation arises precisely due to this component. The reader is addressed for the
details to mentioned papers.

9.4   Search Space Reduction

The main source for this section is [139], which provides a thorough survey of techniques for reduction and criteria for their comparison. The paper discusses six techniques (with a total of 12 variations of them) and provides a theoretical analysis of their complexity and an empirical evaluation of techniques within a common framework of datasets. After an initial introductory section, we will describe some of the techniques discussed in [139] and will complement the discussion with other recent contributions referred to methods for dynamic selection of reduction techniques.

9.4.1   Introduction to Techniques for Search Space Reduction

The performance bottleneck in an *OID* system is usually the expensive comparison of attribute values between records. Assuming there are no duplicate records in the datasets to be matched (i.e., one record in A can only be a true match to one record in B and vice versa), it is intuitive to conclude that the maximum possible number of true matches will correspond to min $(|A|, |B|)$. Therefore, while the number of pair comparisons increases quadratically with the number n of records of A and B, the number of potential true matches increases only linearly in the size of the datasets. The aim of the reduction step is to reduce this large number of potential comparisons by removing as many record pairs as possible that correspond to unmatches.

9.4.2   Indexing Techniques

In the following, we first consider traditional blocking, some evolution of sorted neighborhood, and suffix-based techniques and then provide some details on other types of techniques.

9.4.2.1   Traditional Blocking

As remarked in Chap. 8, one of the techniques for the search space reduction activity adopted in traditional OID is *blocking*, which splits the datasets into nonoverlapping blocks, such that only records within each block are compared with each other. A blocking criterion, called in the following a *blocking key* (BK), whose values are called *blocking key values* (BKV), is either based on a single record field (attribute) or on the concatenation of values from several fields.

a

Identifier	Surname	BK (Soundex encoding)
R1	Smith	S530
R2	Miller	M460
R3	Peters	P362
R4	Smyth	S530
R5	Millar	M460
R6	Miller	M460

b

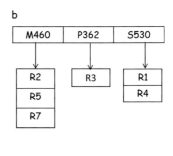

Fig. 9.5 Example of traditional blocking (here and in the following section examples are inspired by Christen [139]). (**a**) Record table with Soundex encodings used as BKVs. (**b**) Inverted index structure

In Fig. 9.5, an example is shown where a Soundex encoding is chosen for the BK, and blocking is implemented using an inverted index.

Several issues need to be considered when record fields are selected to be used as blocking keys, including:

1. The quality of the values in the BK influences the quality of the generated candidate record pairs. Fields containing the fewest errors, variations, or missing values should be chosen. Any error in a field value used to generate a BKV will potentially result in records being inserted into the wrong block, thus leading to missing true matches. One approach used to overcome errors and variations is to generate several blocking keys based on different record fields, so that records that refer to true matches have hopefully at least one BKV in common and will therefore be inserted into the same block.
2. The frequency distribution of the values in the fields used for blocking keys will impact the size of the generated blocks. If m records in database A and n records in database B have the same BKV, then $m \times n$ candidate record pairs will be generated from the corresponding block. The largest blocks generated in the blocking step will dominate execution time of the comparison step, because they will contribute with the larger portion of the total number of candidate record pairs. Therefore, if possible, it may be profitable to use fields that contain uniformly distributed values.

9.4.2.2   Sorted Neighborhood Indexing

This technique in its basic version [308] together with two extensions have been described in Chap. 8, to which we refer. In Fig. 9.6, we show an example of application for a window size equal to 3, where surname is the chosen BK.

Window position	BK (Surname)	Identifier
1	Millar	R6
2	Miller	R2
3	Miller	R8
4	Myler	R4
5	Peters	R3
6	Smith	R1
7	Smyth	R5
8	Smyth	R7

Window range	Candidate record pairs
1-3	(R6,R2), (R6,R8), (R2,R8)
2-4	(R2,R8), (R2,R4), (R8,R4)
3-5	(R8,R4), (R8,R3), (R4,R3)
4-6	(R4,R3), (R4,R1), (R3,R1)
5-7	(R3,R1), (R3,R5), (R1,R5)
6-8	(R1,R5), (R1,R7), (R5,R7)

a. Records table with BKVs and window positions   b. Record pairs in windows

Fig. 9.6 Example of traditional sorted neighborhood with window size $w = 3$

Window position	BK (Surname)	Identifier
1	Millar	R6
2	Miller	R2, R8
3	Myler	R4
4	Peters	R3
5	Smith	R1
6	Smyth	R5,R7

Window range	Candidate record pairs
1-3	(R6,R2), (R6,R8), (R6,R4), (R2,R8), (R2,R4), (R8,R4)
2-4	(R2,R8), (R2,R4), (R8,R4), (R8,R4),(R8,R3),(R4,R3)
3-5	(R4,R3), (R4,R1), (R3,R1)
4-6	(R3,R1), (R3,R5), (R3,R7), (R1,R5), (R1,R7), (R5,R7)

a. Records table with inverted index   b. Record pairs in windows

Fig. 9.7 Example of sorted neighborhood based on inverted index

An alternative approach [142] for the sorted neighborhood technique is the *inverted index-based approach*, which instead of a sorted array makes use of an inverted index similar to traditional blocking. In Fig. 9.7, we see an example with the same BK as the previous one.

Other variants of sorted neighborhood techniques are described in [183, 685]. An adaptive approach to dynamically set the window size is proposed in [685], while [183] discusses a combined blocking and sorted neighborhood approach, which allows the specification of the desired overlap between the two techniques.

9.4.2.3   Suffix Array-Based Blocking

The basic idea of this technique presented in [14] is, once the BK is chosen, to insert the BKVs and their suffixes into a suffix array-based inverted index. A *suffix array* contains strings or sequences and their suffixes in an alphabetically sorted order. See in Fig. 9.8 an example, where BKVs are variants of the given name Catherine. The two tables on the right-hand side show the resulting sorted suffix array. The

Identifier	BK (Given Name)	Suffixes
R1	Catherine	Catherine, atherine, therine, herine, erine, rine
R2	Katherina	Katherina, atherina, therina, herina, erina, rina
R3	Catherina	Catherina, atherina, therina, herina, erina, rina
R4	Catrina	Catrina, atrina, trina, rina
R5	Katrina	Katrina, atrina, trina, rina

Suffix	Identifier	Suffix	Identifier
atherina	R2,R3	herine	R1
atherine	R1	katherina	R2
atrina	R4,R5	katrina	R5
catherina	R3	rina	R2,R3,R4,R5
catherine	R1	rine	R1
catrina	R4	therina	R2,R3
erina	R2,R3	therine	R1
erine	R1	trina	R4,R5
herina	R2,R3		

a. Records table with BK and suffixes   b. Sorted suffix-array

Fig. 9.8 Example of suffix array-based blocking

block with suffix value "rina" will be removed because it contains more than a given threshold (here equal to 3) of record identifiers. Indexing based on suffix arrays has successfully been used on both English and Japanese bibliographic databases.

An improvement upon the suffix array-based blocking technique has been proposed in [171]. In this technique, the inverted index lists of suffix values that are similar to each other in the sorted suffix array are merged, where similarity is measured according to a distance function discussed in [136].

9.4.2.4   Other Techniques

Other techniques mentioned in [139] are:

- *Q-gram-based blocking.* This technique produces an index such that records that have a similar, not just the same, BKV are inserted into the same block. Assuming the BKVs are strings, the basic idea is to create variations for each BKV using q-grams (substrings of length q) and to insert record identifiers into more than one block. Each BKV is converted into a list of q-grams, and sublist combinations of these q-gram lists are generated down to a certain minimum length. These sublists are then converted back into strings and used as the actual key values in an inverted index.
- *Canopy clustering.* It is based on the idea of using a computationally cheap clustering approach to create high-dimensional overlapping clusters from which blocks of candidate record pairs can be generated [145]. Clusters are created by calculating the similarities between BKVs using measures such as the Jaccard distance.
- *String-map-based indexing.* It is based on mapping BKVs (assumed to be strings) to objects in a multidimensional Euclidean space, such that the distances between pairs of strings are preserved. Any string similarity measure that is a distance function can be used in the mapping process. Groups of similar strings are then generated by extracting objects in this space that are similar to each other.

Previous techniques are experimentally evaluated in [139] and compared using the two blocking qualities discussed in Sect. 9.2, namely, reduction ratio and pairs completeness; for a discussion on the comparison we refer to [139].

9.4.3   Learnable, Adaptive, and Context-Based Reduction Techniques

All previously discussed reduction techniques require manually constructing an index. Since an effective reduction strategy can be highly domain dependent, the ad hoc construction and manual tuning of blocking techniques makes this task nontrivial. Several papers propose machine learning techniques for automatically constructing reduction functions that are efficient and accurate.

Bilenko et al. [76] formulates the problem of learning an optimal blocking function as the task of finding a combination of blocking predicates that captures all or nearly all coreferent object pairs (namely, pairs that refer to the same entity in the real world) and a minimal number of noncoreferent pairs. The approach is general in the sense that no restrictions are placed on the similarity predicates computed on instance pairs selected by blocking, such as requiring them to correspond to a distance metric.

Examples of blocking predicates for different domains are shown in Fig. 9.9.

More formally, a blocking predicate corresponds to an indexing function that is applied to a field value and generates one or more keys for the field value.

Each general blocking predicate can be instantiated for a particular field (or a combination of fields) in a given domain, resulting in a set of specific blocking predicates for the domain. Figure 9.10a shows a sample record and the table in Fig. 9.10b shows a set of blocking predicates (column 1 of the table), and for each predicate the values produced by their indexing functions for the value fields of the record.

Two types of blocking functions are considered: disjunctions of blocking predicates and predicates combined in disjunctive normal form, that is, a normalization of a logical formula which is a disjunction of conjunctive clauses. For the two types of blocking functions, predicate-based formulations of learnable blocking functions are described in the chapter. The effectiveness of the proposed techniques is demonstrated on real and simulated datasets, on which they prove to be more accurate than nonadaptive blocking methods.

A machine learning approach based on the multipass approach presented in Chap. 8 is proposed in [437]. The general idea of the multipass approach is to

Fig. 9.9 Examples of blocking predicates from [76]

Domain	Blocking Predicate
Census data	Same first three chars in Last Name
Product normalization	Common token in Manufacturer
Citations	Publication Year same or off-by-one

Author	Year	Title	Venue	Other
Freund, Y.	(1995)	Boosting a weak learning algorithm by majority	Information and computation	(121(2), 256-285

a. Sample record

Predicate	Author	Title	Venue	Year	Other
Contain common token	(freund, y)	(boosting, a, weak, learning, algorithm, by, majority)	(information, computation)	(1995)	(121,2,256,285)
Exact match	("freund y")	("Boosting a weak learning algorithm by majority")	("information and computation)	("1995")	("121 2 256 285")
Same 1st three Chars	(fre)	(boo)	(inf)	(199)	(121)
Contain same or off-by-one integer	-	-	-		(120_121, 121_122, 1_2, 2_3,,255_256, 256_257, 284_285,285_286)

b. Blocking predicates and key sets produced by their indexing functions for the record

Fig. 9.10 Blocking key values for a sample record from [76]

generate candidate matches using different attributes and techniques across independent runs. The paper presents a machine learning approach to discovering which attributes and which techniques generate a small number of candidate matches while covering as many true matches as possible, fulfilling both goals for blocking.

Other methods for blocking exploit the context in which (relational) data are defined, where the context are the relationships among data established by keys and foreign keys. Nin et al. [473] proposes a new family of blocking techniques that substitute the blocking or sorting key used by typical blocking methods by another type of block building technique based on the context. This *semantic graph blocking* proposed in [473] is based on the capabilities that collaborative graphs offer in order to extract the information about the relationship between the records in the source files. *Collaborative graphs* are a common method for representing the relationships among a set of entities. Nodes represent the entities to be matched, and edges capture the relationships between entities. Figure 9.11 shows an example of collaborative graph; on the left-hand side three tables related by foreign keys are represented, while on the right-hand side the corresponding collaborative graph is represented. A block can be constructed starting from an entity and associating all neighbors up to a given distance. In Fig. 9.11, from [473] we see within a closed line the block of nodes corresponding to author "Smith, John" up to distance two. Experiments discussed in the paper show that the technique improves the recall and reduces the amount of expert review process with respect to previous techniques.

The technique described in [685] is an example of the adaptive blocking technique. The reference technique is the traditional sorted neighborhood described in the previous section. Here the adaptivity refers to the window size, which is dynamically adapted by exploiting an idea similar to how people watch videos, i.e., if two subsequent scenes are similar, people press fast-forward to skip frames to arrive at new scenes quickly and press rewind to go back if too many frames are

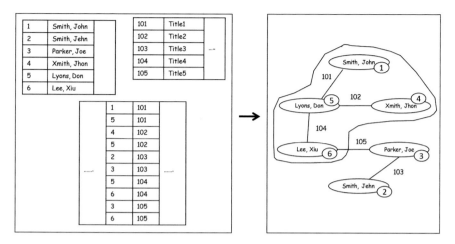

Fig. 9.11 Example of semantic blocking from [473]

skipped. Similarly, by monitoring how close or far two neighboring entities are, the sliding window can be extended or shrunk adaptively.

In the chapter, such an idea is adopted measuring if records within a small neighborhood are close/sparse and if there are rooms to grow/shrink in the window; in this case, the window size is increased/decreased dynamically. In order to measure the record distribution within a window, one has to measure the distances between all the records in the window. The approach adopts an heuristic that measures the distance between the first and last record in the window and uses this distance to approximate the overall record distribution within the window.

9.5   Comparison and Decision

In this section, we address all the new steps in the life cycle of the *OID* problem shown in Fig. 9.1. Section 9.5.1 is focused on extensions of the Fellegi and Sunter probabilistic model. Section 9.5.2 analyzes knowledge exploitation on comparison functions. Section 9.5.3 discusses how the context can be exploited to improve the quality and efficiency of the comparison and decision techniques that can be classified in terms of (a) techniques adopting the model of the input datasets (Sect. 9.5.3.1) and (b) techniques based on a model transformation (Sect. 9.5.3.2). Section 9.5.4 focuses on types of knowledge different from context, namely, (a) constraints, (b) behavior, and (c) crowd sourcing, while Sect. 9.5.5 discusses techniques that adopt an incremental strategy in *OID*, leveraging intermediate results for improving subsequent matching choices; a distinction is made between techniques that span only on the decision step, techniques that span on both decision and fusion (Sect. 9.5.5.1), and techniques whose main goal in the incremental approach is efficiency (Sect. 9.5.5.2). Section 9.5.6 considers decision models based on multiple techniques. The above classification is not orthogonal among techniques, e.g., several techniques are both contextual and incremental; we have chosen to describe techniques in the section where the related characteristic is prevalent. Section 9.5.7 deals with techniques that can be used at query time, while Sect. 9.5.8 discusses *OID* at maintenance time.

9.5.1   Extensions of the Fellegi and Sunter Probabilistic Model

A contribution that addresses an extension of the Fellegi and Sunter probabilistic model is [536] that allows $k > 2$ input datasets. Also previous literature allowed for $k > 2$ files to be matched but with ad hoc procedures for each pair of datasets and not guaranteeing the transitivity of the linkage decisions (see, e.g., [29]). In the generalization proposed in [536], possible agreement paths among k records belonging to k datasets are the set of parts of k; e.g., for $k = 3$, the five agreement patterns of three records are shown in Fig. 9.12. The vertexes representing records are connected if corresponding records match, unconnected otherwise.

A different extension of the Fellegi-Sunter model is discussed in [580], where it is observed that while the model treats all pairs of candidate matches as independent and identically distributed, this is clearly not the case in general, since each entity may appear in multiple pairs of candidate matches. This interdependency offers the opportunity to improve the decision step, by taking into account information that was previously ignored. This is done in [580] proposing a simple and mathematically sound formulation of the *OID* problem that incorporates the above point and that can be viewed as a generalization of the Fellegi-Sunter model. In particular, a Markov logic is proposed, an evolution of a first-order logic enriched with a Markov network, which provides a model for the joint probability distribution of a set of variables [526].

Reformulating the *OID* problem in terms of Markov logic allows formal representation and management of a wide variety of knowledge, mainly domain dependent, in terms of distance functions and rules/constraints on data.

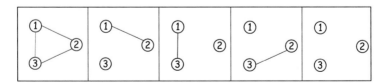

Fig. 9.12 Possible paths of agreement for three datasets in [536]

9.5.2   Knowledge in the Comparison Function

A first set of adaptive techniques for the decision activity is presented in [145, 553], both focused on data integration applications. In [145], the term *adaptive* is used to mean that the quality of the technique can be improved by training on specific domains. Adaptive matching is implemented by learning an appropriate *pairing function* that indicates if two records should be matched. A first algorithm proposed in the paper generates from all pairs a training set of matched pairs and then trains a classification learner. A second more efficient and accurate algorithm exploits similarities in the textual names used for objects in different datasets and relies on the ability to take a record name and efficiently find all nearby names according to some approximate distance metric. In learning, two issues must be addressed: how to represent pairs of records and which learning algorithm to use. Several different classification learning systems and different feature sets are explored. Examples of the features used to encode a pair are shown in Fig. 9.13.

Bilenko and Mooney [75] observe that certain words can be informative when comparing two strings for equivalence, while others can be ignored. For example, ignoring the substring "Street" may be acceptable when comparing addresses, but not when comparing, e.g., newspapers (e.g., "Wall Street Journal"). Thus, accurate similarity computations require adapting string similarity metrics for each field of the database with respect to the particular data domain. Rather than hand-tuning a distance metric for each field, Bilenko and Mooney [75] propose to use trainable similarity measures that can be learned from small corpora of labeled examples and thus adapt to different domains. Two string similarity measures are presented: the first one is character based and utilizes the expectation-maximization (EM) algorithm, and the second similarity measure employs support vector machines (SVM) [622] to obtain a similarity estimate based on the vector-space model of text. The character-based distance is best suited for shorter strings with minor variations, while the measure based on vector-space representation is more appropriate for fields that contain longer strings with more global variations. The overall process of training and matching resulting from the above techniques is shown in Fig. 9.14.

The problem of learning a record matching decision classifier in an active learning setting is considered in [26]. In active learning, the learning algorithm picks the set of examples to be labeled, unlike more traditional passive learning

Name of Feature	Description
SubstringMatch	true iff one of the two strings is a substring of the other
PrefixMatch	true iff one of the two strings is a prefix of the other
StrongNumberMatch	true iff the two strings contain the same number
Edit distance	usual meaning
Jaccard distance	usual meaning

Fig. 9.13 Examples of features in [145]

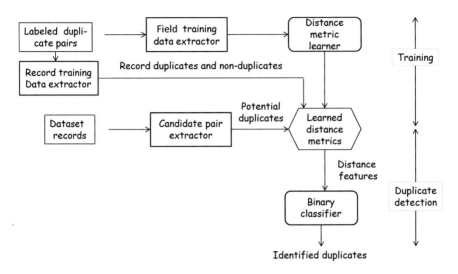

Fig. 9.14 Phases of knowledge extraction and exploitation in [75]

settings where a user selects the labeled examples. The authors observe that a crucial problem in *OID* is the imbalance between the number of unmatches and the number of matches, as also mentioned in previous sections in this chapter. Prior works (e.g., [75] above discussed) propose using a filter based on textual similarity to eliminate a large number of unmatches followed by sampling to pick examples. In [26], it is shown that while this approach mitigates the problem described above, it does not eliminate it, since it introduces the additional problem of picking a good filter. Motivated by these considerations, Arasu et al. [26] explore the use of active learning where the learning algorithm itself picks the examples to be labeled. The idea here is that the algorithm can exploit this additional flexibility to pick examples that are most informative for the learning task.

The proposed algorithms cover decision trees and linear classifiers (which include SVM) and allow a user to specify a precision threshold as input. The learned classifier is guaranteed to have a precision greater than this threshold and (under certain reasonable assumptions) to have a recall close to the best possible given the precision constraint. The algorithms also differ from previous algorithms in that they are designed from scratch for record matching and do not just invoke a known learning algorithm as a black box.

Structured neural networks are proposed in [505] for object identification. A structured neural network is a neural network [287] whose architecture is constrained to bias its learning (e.g., see [391]) as well as to facilitate knowledge extraction. Structured neural networks are used in [505] in the context of pedigree-based *OID*, where similarity is considered between both individuals and their relatives. In pedigree datasets, a composite similarity measure benefits from being weighted in at least two complementary ways:

1. Across two individuals, where the attributes are likely to carry different weights when considering overall similarity between individuals. For example, it seems reasonable that matching surnames may be more relevant in determining an overall match of individuals than would be matching birthplaces.
2. Across two pedigrees, where the similarities between corresponding individuals (e.g., grandmothers) are likely to carry different weights when considering overall similarity between pedigrees. For example, it seems reasonable that similarity between mothers may be more relevant in determining an overall match than would be similarity between great-grandfathers.

The approach in [505] is to learn the weights from sample labeled data using a structured neural network.

A two-step approach to unsupervised record pair matching is presented in [137, 138]. In the first step, example training data of high quality is generated automatically, and in the second step, these examples are used to train a binary classifier. To explain the approach, look at Fig. 9.15, where weights are associated to single fields of record pairs; weights are numerical values expressing the similarity between corresponding values.

In the first step of the technique, weight vectors are selected as training examples that with high likelihood correspond to true matches and true unmatches. For example, in Fig. 9.15, considering weighted vectors WRs, WV(R1, R2) is an example of true match and WV(R1, R3) is an example of true unmatch. In the second step, these training examples are used to train a classifier, which is then employed to classify all weight vectors into matches and unmatches.

With reference to the first step, two different approaches are mentioned in [138] on how to select training examples: *threshold* or *nearest based*. In the first approach, weight vectors that have all their vector elements within a certain distance to the exact similarity or total dissimilarity values, respectively, will be selected. The second approach sorts weight vectors according to their distances from the vectors containing only exact similarities and only total dissimilarities, respectively, and then selects the nearest vectors, respectively. Experiments in [137] show that

a							b
Record	Name			Address			WV(R1,R2): [0.9, 1.0, 1.0, 1.0, 0.9]
R1	Christine	Smith	42	Main	Street		WV(R1,R3): [0.0, 0.0, 0.0, 0.0, 0.0]
R2	Christina	Smith	42	Main	St.		WV(R1,R4): [0.0, 0.0, 0.5, 0.0, 0.0]
R3	Bob	O'Brian	11	Smith	Rd		WV(R2,R3): [0.0, 0.0, 0.0, 0.0, 0.0]
R4	Robert	Bryee	12	Smythe	Road		WV(R2,R4): [0.0, 0.0, 0.5, 0.0, 0.0]
							WV(R3,R4): [0.7, 0.3, 0.5, 0.7, 0.9]

Fig. 9.15 Example of weight vectors from [138]. (**a**) Four record examples. (**b**) Corresponding weight vectors

the nearest-based approach generally outperforms threshold-based selection. One
reason is that nearest-based selection allows explicit specification of the number of
weight vectors to be included into training example sets for matches and unmatches;
this feature allows to take into account that weight vector classification is a very
imbalanced problem, where the number of true unmatches is often much larger than
the number of true matches, as we discussed in Sect. 9.2.

In the second step, the training sets are used to train a binary SVM classifier.
This choice is made because such technique can handle high-dimensional data and
is known to be robust to noisy data.

9.5.3 Contextual Knowledge in Decision

Contextual knowledge exploited in *OID* techniques refers to knowledge related to
the context of records to be merged, namely, other information to which records
are semantically linked, or properties of specific domains modeled by records that
can be exploited in the decision activity. In Chap. 8, Sect. 8.7.3, we discussed a first
technique that exploits knowledge on context made up of dimensional hierarchies
among records. In the following, we first discuss techniques that take decisions
within the model of the input datasets and subsequently techniques that perform
a model transformation.

9.5.3.1 Within the Same Model

Contextual *OID* in the setting of the authors-papers domain is discussed in [66, 67].
Suppose that we have two different papers and we are trying to determine if there
are any authors in common between them. We can perform a string similarity
match between the author names, but often references to the same person vary
significantly. Bhattacharya and Getoor [66, 67] propose to make use of additional
context information in the form of coauthor relationships. More generally, we can
assume to have a collection of references R, where each reference corresponds
to a unique entity, and conversely each entity corresponds in general to a set of
references. References are members of links (where the set of links is L); each link
is a collection of references, and a reference appears in only one link. In the example
in Fig. 9.16, each author is a reference, the list of author names for a paper form a
link, and the entities are the true authors. Given R and L, the problem is to correctly
determine both the entities and the mapping from references to entities.

The problem of author resolution is likely to be an iterative process; as we identify common authors, this will allow us to identify additional potential coreferences.
We can continue in this fashion until all of the entities have been resolved.

A distance between two references is defined as a weighted combination between
the distance between the attributes of the entities and the distance measure between
link sets of references. The similarity of two links is defined as the ratio of the

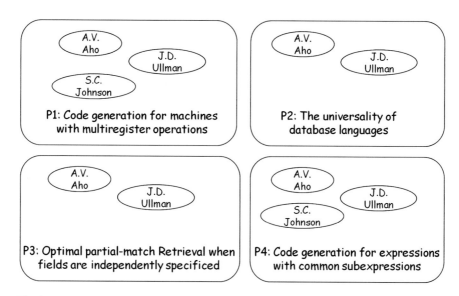

Fig. 9.16 An example Author/Paper resolution problem from [66]. Each *box* represents a paper reference (in this case unique), and each *oval* represents an author reference

```
Person (name, email, *coAuthor, *emailContact)
Article ( title, year, pages, *authoredBy, *publishedIn)
Conference (name, year, location)
Journal (name, year, volume, number)
```

Fig. 9.17 Example of exploitation of context information in [179]

number of duplicates they share and the length of the longer link. An algorithm is proposed that performs entity deduplication through recursive evaluation of distance and similarity formulas on the network of references and links.

Several innovative issues are introduced in [179] to the above entities/references/links framework that can be discussed using the relational database example of Fig. 9.17. In the example, the attributes that express associations between and within tables are denoted with the symbol "*." As an example, the Person table has two association attributes, emailContact and coAuthor, whose values are links to other Person instances.

Innovative features in [179] are:

- Context knowledge exploitation—extensive use of context knowledge (the associations between references) is made to provide evidence for reconciliation decisions and design new methods for reference comparison. For example, given two references to persons, their coauthors and e-mail contacts are considered (knowledge exploitation) to help decide whether to reconcile them.
- Reconciliation propagation—information on reconciliation (matching) decisions are propagated to accumulate positive and negative evidences. For example, when two papers are reconciled, additional evidence is obtained for reconciling

the person references to their authors. This, in turn, can further increase the confidence in reconciling other papers authored by the reconciled persons.
• Reference enrichment—to address the lack of information in each reference, references are gradually enriched by merging attribute values. For example, when two person references are reconciled, the different representations of the person's name are gathered, different e-mail addresses are collected, and his or her list of coauthors and e-mail contacts is enlarged. This enriched reference can later be reconciled with other references where previously, information for the reconciliation was lacked.

9.5.3.2   With Model Transformation

In previous papers, techniques for comparison and decision do not change the model of the dataset, working instead with such a model assuming it as "given." With the goal of improving efficiency, the techniques described in the following adopt a graph model. Kalashnikov and Mehrotra [353] are concerned with the problem of *reference disambiguation*, related though distinct with respect to the *OID* problem. While *OID* consists of determining when two records correspond to the same real-world entity, reference disambiguation corresponds to ensuring that references in a dataset point to the correct entities. When the model of the dataset is the relational model, references correspond to *referential integrity constraints* or *foreign keys*.

Authors of [353] observe that given the tight relationship between the two problems, existing approaches to *OID* can be adapted for reference disambiguation. In particular, feature-based similarity methods that analyze similarity of record attribute values can be used to determine if a particular reference corresponds to a given entity or not. The quality of disambiguation can be significantly improved by exploring the context of entities, represented by relationships/connections between records. The example from [353] reproduced in Fig. 9.18 helps to understand the novelties presented in the paper.

The two datasets represent authors (Fig. 9.18a) and publications (Fig. 9.18b). The goal of the matching problem is to identify for each paper the correct authors it refers

a

Window position	BK (Surname)	Identifier
1	Millar	R6
2	Miller	R2, R8
3	Myler	R4
4	Peters	R3
5	Smith	R1
6	Smyth	R5, R7

b

Window range	Candidate record pairs
1-3	(R6,R2), (R6,R8), (R6,R4), (R2,R8), (R2,R4), (R8,R4)
2-4	(R2,R8), (R2,R4), (R8,R4), (R8,R4),(R8,R3),(R4,R3)
3-5	(R4,R3), (R4,R1), (R3,R1)
4-6	(R3,R1), (R3,R5), (R3,R7), (R1,R5), (R1,R7), (R5,R7)

Fig. 9.18 Related records and corresponding Entity Relationship schema as adapted from [353]. (**a**) Records table with inverted index. (**b**) Record pairs in windows

to. Feature-based similarity techniques allow us to resolve almost every reference matching in the example. For instance, such techniques would identify that "Sue Grey" reference in P2 refers to A3 "Susan Grey." The only exception are "D. White" references in P2 and P6 that could match either A1 ("Dave White") or A2 ("Don White"). We can disambiguate the references "D. White" by analyzing relationships among entities. As an example, author "Don White" has coauthored a paper (P1) with "John Black" who is at MIT, while the author "Dave White" does not have any coauthored papers with authors at MIT. We can use this observation to disambiguate between the two authors. In particular, since the coauthor of "D. White" in P2 is "Susan Grey" of MIT, there is a higher likelihood that the author "D. White" in P2 is "Don White."

The above example can be generalized if we transform relational tables into the corresponding Entity Relationship graph of instances, whose schema is represented in Fig. 9.18c. The approach proposed in [353] exploits the graph representation of data, viewing the underlying dataset D as an Entity Relationship graph of instances, wherein the nodes represent the entities in D and the edges represent the relationships among the entities (other approaches exploiting ER graphs appear in [424, 441]). For any two entities, the coreference decision is made not only based on the entity features but also based on the inter-entity relationships, including indirect ones that may exist among the two representations.

A concept of *connection strength* that represents what we can intuitively call the "intensity" of connections established by references is proposed in the paper. The technique, described in a nutshell, first discovers connections between the entity in the context of which the reference appears and the matching candidates for that reference. Then, it measures the connection strength of the discovered connections in order to give preference to one of the matching candidates. In [353], the above approach is formalized in terms of the concepts of Entity Relationship graph, context attraction principle, connection strength, and weight/based model.

Authors of [126] acknowledge that the model adopted in [353] for connection strength is based on intuition, so it might not be adequate for particular application domains or might lead to only minor quality improvements. To overcome this problem, in [126], they present an algorithm that makes the overall approach self-adaptive to the data being processed, leading to an improvement of the quality and efficiency of the technique.

The above approach is extended in [476], where another adaptive connection strength model is proposed that learns the connection strength from past data, leading to significant quality improvement over the previously described models. The approach minimizes the domain analyst's effort by adapting the connection strength measure automatically to the given domain using past data instead of requiring the analyst to decide which model is more suitable for the given domain and how to tune its parameters.

A technique that is both incremental and contextual is presented in [68]. Within such a technique, called *collective object identification*, entities related to co-occurring references to be matched are determined jointly rather than independently.

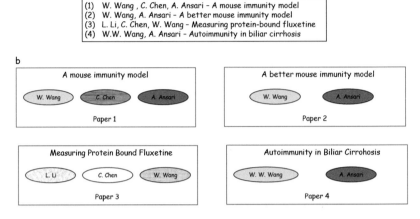

Fig. 9.19 Bibliographic example from [68]. (**a**) A set of four papers. (**b**) References to the same author are identically shaded

A relational clustering algorithm is proposed that uses both feature and contextual information to identify the underlying matching references.

The example considered in the paper is shown in Fig. 9.19. The goal here is to find out, given the four papers represented in the box in Fig. 9.19a, which of the author names refer to the same author entities. In Fig. 9.19b, we provide a graphical representation of the four papers in which references (authors) to the same entity are identically shaded.

In this example, assume there are six underlying author entities, which we may call *Wang1* and *Wang2*, *Chen1* and *Chen2*, *Ansari*, and *Li*. The three references with the name *A*. Ansari correspond to the author *Ansari*; however, the two references with name C. Chen map themselves to two different authors *Chen1* and *Chen2*. Similarly, the four references with names W. Wang and W.W. Wang map to two different authors. The aim of the technique presented in the paper is to make use of the relationships that hold among the observed references to find matching and unmatching references. This is done by means of the following steps:

1. Relationships among authors and papers are represented as a graph where the vertexes represent the author references and the hyperedges represent the coauthor relationships that hold between them in the dataset. Figure 9.20a shows the reference graph for the example. Given this graph representation, the goal is to take the hyperedges into account to better partition the references into entities. In addition to the similarity of the attributes of the references, relationships are considered as well. In terms of the graph representation, two references that have similar attributes are more likely to be the same entity if their hyperedges connect to the same entities as well.
2. The identity of a reference depends on those of its collaborators, and in turn, the identity of the collaborators depends on the identity of the reference itself.

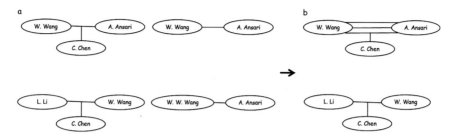

Fig. 9.20 (**a**) Reference graph and (**b**) entity graph for the author resolution example in [68]

PublID	Author	Title	Venue	VenueID	Year
0	X.Li	Predicting the stock market	KDD	10	2010
1	X.Li	Predicting the stock market	Int'l Conference on Knowledge Discovery	20	2010
2	J.Smith	Semi-Definite Programming for Link Prediction	KDD	30	2011
3	J.Smith	Semi-Definife Programing for Link Prediction	Conference on Knowledge Discovery	40	2011

Fig. 9.21 Motivating example in [159]

So where do we begin? The matching process proposed in the paper starts with the matchings that we are most confident about. For instance, two references with the name *A.* Ansari are more likely to be the same because Ansari is an uncommon name in contrast to references with common names such as Chen, Li, or Wang. This then provides additional evidence for merging other references. After consolidating the Ansari's, the Wang's references from papers 1, 2, and 4 have a common coauthor which provides evidence for consolidating them. Figure 9.20b shows the resulting entity graph after all references have been matched.

In [68], the impact that different relational similarity measures have on *OID* quality is investigated. Furthermore, the collective entity matching algorithm is evaluated on real-world databases, and it is shown that it improves entity matching performance over both attribute-based techniques and over algorithms that consider relational information but do not resolve entities collectively.

Bibliographical databases are also considered in [159], this time in terms of the relationship between papers and venues. Focusing on relational databases, Culotta and McCallum [159] observe that whereas nearly all previous approaches have merged records of different types independently, the technique presented in the paper models these interdependencies explicitly to collectively and incrementally deduplicate records of multiple types. A conditional random field model of dedupli-cation is proposed that captures these relational dependencies, and then a relational partitioning algorithm is employed to jointly deduplicate records.

We exemplify the technique using the *motivating example* from [159] reproduced in Fig. 9.21, referring to research papers, with author, title, venue, and year.

Here, the task is to deduplicate the various mentions of these records into unique entities. Papers 0 and 1 and papers 2 and 3 should be merged; all the venues should be merged. The paper proposes an agglomerative deduplication technique which begins by assuming each record is unique. Suppose the system first considers merging papers 0 and 1. Although the venues do not match, all the other fields are exact matches, so we can tentatively match the two records. After merging papers 0 and 1, the system also merges the corresponding venues 10 and 20 into the same cluster, since the venues of duplicate papers must themselves be duplicated.

Imagine the technique next merges venues 10 and 30 because they are identical strings. The technique must now decide if papers 2 and 3 are duplicates. Treated in isolation, a system may have a hard time correctly detecting that 2 and 3 are duplicates: the authors are highly similar, but the title contains two misspellings, and the venues are extremely dissimilar. However, the system described so far has more information at its disposal. It has already merged venues 10 and 20, which are highly similar to venues 30 and 40. By consulting its database of deduplicated venues, it could determine that 30 and 40 are in fact the same venue. With this information at hand, we may assign minor relevance to the spelling mistakes in the title, finally merging papers 2 and 3 correctly. This example illustrates the concept that the identity of an object is dependent on the identity of related objects.

In the technique presented in [159], relational tables are transformed into graphs, and a conditional random field model (see [384]) is adopted that jointly models the conditional probability of multiple deduplication decisions. The resulting relational graph partitioning algorithm not only ensures that deduplication decisions made for different record types are consistent but also allows the decisions from one record type to inform the decisions for other record types.

9.5.4 Other Types of Knowledge in Decision

Besides knowledge on context, recent techniques for *OID* exploit other types of knowledge, such as knowledge on constraints, behavioral knowledge, and knowledge based on crowdsourcing. We examine the three types of knowledge in the following.

9.5.4.1 Constraints-Driven

Contextual knowledge exploited in [121] corresponds to a particular type of integrity constraints that can be defined in a relational table, namely, *aggregate constraints* that, instead of being defined on single tuples, are defined over groups of tuples in the table. Such constraints often arise when integrating multiple sources of data, so they can be leveraged to enhance the quality of the *OID* process. Let us consider Fig. 9.22, which refers to a `Parks` company that manages several parks; individuals can enroll as members in different of these parks. An example

Member	Fees stored	Fees derived
John Doe	100	130
J. Doe	40	10
....	.....	.....

First scenario

Member	Fees stored	Fees derived
John Doe	100	100
J. Doe	40	10
....	.....	.....

Second scenario

Fig. 9.22 Example of aggregate constraint in [121]

of constraint is that the total monthly fee for each member is calculated by adding up the monthly fees for each park in which the member is enrolled.

In Fig. 9.22, we assume that each park maintains a separate registration table, while there is a central billing repository containing information about all members and the total amount they are billed. Suppose that we are interested in deduplicating the member entities in the two scenarios in the figure, where in both of them Fees stored is the total fees for the member as stored in the Billing database, while Fees derived represents the total fee as computed by aggregating the data across the parks.

The figure shows that we have two members "John Doe" and "J. Doe." These strings may or may not refer to the same person. An aggregate constraint may state that adding all amounts in Fees stored and in Fees derived referring to the same person must lead to obtain the same total amount. In Scenario 1, there is a mismatch between the stored and derived fees in the same tuple, while collapsing the two tuples fixes this mismatch. In Scenario 2, there is no mismatch between the stored and derived fees for the string "John Doe," while collapsing the tuple with "J. Doe" creates a mismatch. We can use the aggregate constraint to merge the two tuples in Scenario 1, whereas in Scenario 2, we do not.

The class of aggregate constraints is formalized in the paper, and it is shown that techniques attempting satisfaction of constraints in the whole search space is semantically challenging and leads to computational intractability. An algorithm exploring a restricted search space is proposed. Furthermore, experiments show that leveraging aggregation constraints substantially improves the quality of deduplication.

9.5.4.2 Behavior-Driven

A highly innovative approach to *OID* is presented in [683], where the knowledge on behavior, namely, a log of tuple updates, is considered when matching entities. The behavior information for each candidate pair of entities to be matched is merged. If the two behaviors seem to complete one another, in the sense that well-recognized behavioral patterns become detectable after the merge, then this is a strong indication that the two entities are the same. The gain in recognizing a behavior before and after merging the entities transactions is evaluated, and this

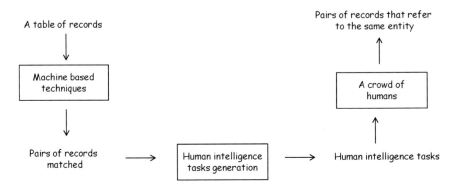

Fig. 9.23 Example of hybrid human-machine workflow proposed in [642]

gain is used as a matching score. An extensive experimental study on real-world datasets demonstrates the effectiveness of the approach to enhance the *OID* quality.

9.5.4.3   Crowdsourcing Exploitation

Crowdsourcing is the kind of knowledge exploit in [642]. The traditional *OID* process based on automatic techniques is enriched (see Fig. 9.23) with the generation of tasks performed by humans, named *human intelligence tasks*. Compared to algorithmic techniques, people are much slower and more expensive. Based on this idea, the workflow shown in Fig. 9.23 first uses machine-based techniques to compute for each pair of records the likelihood that they refer to the same entity. Then, only those pairs whose likelihood exceeds a specified threshold are sent to the crowd. Experiments show that by specifying a relatively low threshold, the number of pairs that need to be verified is dramatically reduced with only a minor loss of quality. Given the set of pairs to be sent to the crowd, the next step is to generate human intelligence tasks so that people can check them for matches. Human intelligence tasks correspond to groups of individual records rather than pairs, thus allowing a significant increase in efficiency. Finally, generated human intelligence tasks are sent to the crowd for processing, and the answers are collected.

9.5.5   *Incremental Techniques*

Techniques reported in this section see the process of *OID* as incremental and use strategies that exploit intermediate results of the *OID* process to make more efficient and effective subsequent matching decisions. The incremental feature of these techniques leads to iterate the execution of comparison and decision activities and in some cases, also of fusion activities. In Sect. 9.5.3, we have discussed techniques that exploited context through iteration of comparison and decision on related record types. In this section, we focus on techniques that iterate on both comparison and decision and on fusion; see Sect. 9.5.5.1. Subsequently, in Sect. 9.5.5.2, we introduce techniques where the main goal is achieving efficiency, through monitoring and optimizing costs of *OID*.

9.5.5.1 Incremental Techniques in Decision and Fusion Activities

An incremental technique that iteratively performs decision and fusion activities is presented in [284], where the *OID* process is investigated on datasets with uniqueness constraints and erroneous values. In the paper, it is observed that when merging different heterogeneous sources using *OID* techniques, there are often attributes that satisfy a uniqueness constraint, where each real-world entity (or most entities) has a unique value for the attribute; examples include contact phone and e-mail address of businesses, cell-phone number, and so on. However, data may not satisfy such constraints, either because some sources provide erroneous values or because there can be a small number of exceptions in the real world. Traditional techniques handle this case in two steps: first, the decision step and then the fusion step that merges the matched records and decides the correct values for each result entity in the presence of conflicts. In [284], it is claimed that such techniques have at least two problems, illustrated in the example of Fig. 9.24, where ten sources are considered.

1. Erroneous values may prevent correct linking. In the example, careless decision may merge the "MS Corp." record from S10 with the "Macrosoft" records, as they share phone and address, while failing to merge them with the "MS Corp." records from S7 and S8; if we realize that S10 confuses between Microsoft and Macrosoft and provides wrong values, we are more likely to obtain the correct matching results.
2. Techniques can fall short when exceptions to the uniqueness constraints exist. In the example, enforcing uniqueness can miss, e.g., the correct number "9400" for Microsoft.

Resolving conflicts locally for matched records may overlook important global evidence. In the example, suppose we have correctly merged all "MS Corp." records with other Microsoft records; then the fact that "0500" is provided by several sources for *Macrosoft* provides further evidence that it is incorrect for *Microsoft*.

The key idea of the technique proposed in [284] is to incrementally merge the matching step and the fusion step so to be able to identify incorrect values and differentiate them from alternative representations of the correct value from the beginning, obtaining in such a way better linkage results. As a second point, the technique makes global decisions based on sources that associate a pair of values in the same record, so to obtain better fusion results. Finally, although the solution relies on uniqueness constraints to detect erroneous values, a small number of violations to capture real-world exceptions are allowed.

a

Source	Name	Phone	Address
S1	Microsofe Corp.	xxx-1255	1 Microsoft Way
	Microsofe Corp.	xxx-9400	1 Microsoft Way
	Macrosoft Inc.	xxx-0500	2 Sylvan W.
S2	Microsoft Corp.	xxx-1255	1 Microsoft Way
	Microsofe Corp.	xxx-9400	1 Microsoft Way
	Macrosoft Inc.	xxx-0500	2 Sylvan Way
S3	Microsoft Corp.	xxx-1255	1 Microsoft Way
	Microsoft Corp.	xxx-9400	1 Microsoft Way
	Macrosoft Inc.	xxx-0500	2 Sylvan Way
S4	Microsoft Corp.	xxx-1255	1 Microsoft Way
	Microsoft Corp.	xxx-9400	2 Sylvan Way
	Macrosoft Inc.	xxx-0500	1 Microsoft Way
S5	Microsoft Corp.	xxx-1255	1 Microsoft Way
	Microsoft Corp.	xxx-9400	1 Microsoft Way
	Macrosoft Inc.	xxx-0500	2 Sylvan Way
S6	Microsoft Corp.	xxx-2255	1 Microsoft Way
	Macrosoft Inc.	xxx-0500	2 Sylvan Way
S7	MS Corp.	xxx-1255	1 Microsoft Way
	Macrosoft Inc.	xxx-0500	2 Sylvan Way
S8	MS Corp.	xxx-1255	1 Microsoft Way
	Macrosoft Inc.	xxx-0500	2 Sylvan Way
S9	Macrosoft Inc.	xxx-0500	2 Sylvan Way
S10	MS Corp.	xxx-0500	2 Sylvan Way

b

Name	Phone	Address
Microsofe Corp., Microsofe Corp, MS Corp.	xxx-1255 Xxx-9400	1 Microsoft Way
Microsoft Inc.	xxx-0500	2 Sylvan Way, 2 Sylvan W.

Fig. 9.24 Example proposed in [284]. (**a**) Data sources. (**b**) Real-world entities

The technique reduces the problem into a *k-partite graph clustering problem*. The clustering technique considers both similarity of attribute values and the set of sources that associate values in the same record, thus performing global merging and fusion simultaneously. Furthermore, soft uniqueness is considered for capturing possible exceptions of the constraints.

The issue of considering decision and fusion together within an incremental algorithm is central also in [54]. We show this incremental feature of the algorithm by means of the example shown in Fig. 9.25.

Suppose that the decision function works as follows: the function compares the name, phone, and e-mail values of the two records. If the names are very similar

Fig. 9.25 Example from
[54]. (**a**) An instance of
persons representing persons.
(**b**) A new record generated
by merging

a

	Name	Phone	E-mail
r1	JohnDoe	235-2635	jdoe@yahoo
r2	J.Doe	234-4358	
r3	JohnD.	234-4358	jdoe@yahoo

b

	Name	Phone	E-mail
r4	John Doe	234-4358 235-2635	jdoe@yahoo

(above some threshold), the records are said to match. The records also match if the
phone and e-mail are identical. For matching records, the merge function combines
the names into a "normalized" representative and performs a set-union on the e-
mails and phone numbers.

In the example, the black-box comparison function determines that records r1
and r2 match, but record r3 does not match either r1 or r2. For instance, the function
finds that "JohnDoe" and "J.Doe" are similar, but finds "JohnD." not similar to
anything (e.g., because John is a frequent first name). Thus, records r1 and r2 are
decided to match and are fused into a new record r4, shown in Fig. 9.25, where the
two phone numbers are simply juxtaposed.

Notice that r4 now matches r3 since the same phone and e-mail appear in both
records. The combination of the information in r1 and r2 led us to discover a new
match with r3, therefore yielding an initially unforeseen merge.

9.5.5.2 Efficiency Driven

Besides considering together matching and fusion, the fundamental concern in [54]
is the efficiency of the entity resolution process, without considering other qualities.
The assumption is to take a generic approach for solving entity resolution, i.e., no
internal details of the functions used to compare and fuse records are investigated.
Some further assumptions are made, namely:

- Functions to match and fuse records operate on two records at a time.
- Numeric similarity values or confidences are not considered. Carrying confidences in the *OID* computations could in principle lead to more accurate
  decisions but complicates processing significantly.
- Records are assumed to contain all the information that pertains to each entity,
  and relationships between records are discarded.

Notwithstanding the above limitations, the authors claim that the *OID* variant
they address can still be very expensive to compute. For this reason, they list four
desirable properties of initial records and of merged records that lead to efficient
OID: idempotence, commutativity, associativity, and representativity. Idempotence,

commutativity, and associativity have the same meanings as in the algebra of sets. The meaning of the representativity property is that a record r3 obtained from merging records r1 and r2 represents the original records, in the sense that any record r4 that matches r1 or r2 will also match r3. The authors conceive several algorithms, respectively:

- G-Swoosh, the four properties do not hold
- R-Swoosh, the four properties hold and comparisons are performed at the granularity of records
- F-Swoosh, the four properties hold and feature level comparisons are performed

In the paper, it is shown that avoidance in F-Swoosh of redundant comparisons potentially performed in R-Swoosh significantly results in a more efficient algorithm than R-Swoosh. It is also shown that R-Swoosh and F-Swoosh can be used even when the four properties do not hold, if an "approximate" result is acceptable.

The efficiency of the *OID* process is the most influencing issue in [664], with a different point of view, called pay-as-you-go approach to *OID*. Figure 9.26 clarifies such point of view.

The horizontal axis represents the amount of work performed in the decision activity, say the number of record pairs that are compared (using expensive application logic). The vertical axis shows the number of pairs that have been found to match (i.e., to represent the same entity). The bottom curve in the figure (running mostly along the horizontal axis) illustrates the behavior of a typical non-incremental *OID* technique: it only yields its final answer after it has done all the work. The center solid line represents a typical incremental *OID* technique that reports results as it proceeds. This technique is preferable when we do not have time for the full resolution. The dotted line in Fig. 9.26 shows the type of technique the authors propose in the paper: instead of comparing records in random order, it looks for matches in the pairs that are most likely to match; hence, it gets good efficiency since the early stage of the algorithm execution.

Fig. 9.26 Pay-as-you-go approach in [664]

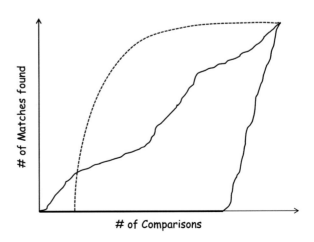

# of Matches found

# of Comparisons

To identify the most profitable work to do early on, the technique performs some pre-analysis (the initial flat part of the curve). The pre-analysis yields what in the paper are called *hints* that are used by the subsequent decision phase to identify profitable work. Hints are in essence heuristics; three types of hints are proposed: (a) a sorted list of record pairs, ranked by the likelihood that the pairs match, (b) a hierarchy of likely record partitions, and (c) an ordered list of records. We provide some details on the first hint.

In the paper, it is assumed that the *OID* algorithm uses either a distance or a match function. The *distance function* $d(r, s)$ quantifies as in Chap. 8 the differences between records r and s: the smaller the distance, the more likely it is that r and s represent the same real-world entity. A *match function* $m(r, s)$ evaluates to true if it is deemed that r and s represent the same real-world entity. Note that a match function may use a distance function. For instance, the match function may be of the form "if $d(r, s) \leq T$ and other conditions hold, then true," where T is a threshold.

The paper also assumes the existence of an estimator function $e(r, s)$ that is much less expensive to compute than both $m(r, s)$ and $d(r, s)$. The value of $e(r, s)$ approximates the value of $d(r, s)$, and if the *OID* algorithm uses a match function, then the smaller the value of $e(r, s)$, the more likely it is that $m(r, s)$ evaluates to true. As to the hint, conceptually it will be the list of all record pairs, ordered by increasing value of the estimator function. In practice, the list may not be explicitly and fully generated. For instance, the list may be truncated after a fixed number of pairs or after the estimates reach a given threshold. Another alternative is to generate the pairs "on demand": the *OID* algorithm can request the next pair on the list; at that point, such a pair is computed.

Coming to the use of the hint, two general principles can be exploited:

- If there is flexibility on the order in which functions $d(r, s)$ and $m(r, s)$ are called, evaluate these functions first on (r, s) pairs that are higher in the pair list. This approach will hopefully let the algorithm identify matching pairs earlier than if pairs are evaluated in random order.
- Do not call the d or m functions on pairs of records that are low on the pair list, assuming instead that the pair is "far" (pick some large distance as default) or does not match.

Furthermore, the hint may provide useful optimizations for specific techniques or domains. For example, if the distance function computes the geographic distance between people records, we may estimate the distance $e(r, s)$ using zip codes: if two records have the same zip code, we say they are close; else we say they are far. If the distance function computes and combines the similarity between many of the record attributes, the estimate can only consider the similarity of one or two attributes, perhaps the most significant.

Many other heuristics are introduced and experimented in [664], where also the potential gains of the pay-as-you-go approach compared to running *OID* without using hints are illustrated.

An adaptive progressive approach to relational *OID* is presented in [16] that aims to generate a high-quality result using a limited resolution budget. To achieve adaptivity, the approach continually reassesses how to solve two key challenges: (a) the parts of the dataset to resolve next?" and (b) how to resolve them?". For that, it divides the decision process into phases called in the paper *resolution windows* and analyzes the decision progress at the beginning of each window to generate a decision plan for the current window. Furthermore, the approach associates with each identified pair of entities a workflow that expresses the order in which to apply the similarity functions on the pair. Such an order plays a significant role in reducing the overall cost, because applying the first few functions in this order might be sufficient to resolve the pair.

In [16], it is claimed that the presented technique must be implemented carefully so that the benefits obtained are not overshadowed by the associated overheads of adaptation. This is achieved in the paper by designing efficient algorithms, appropriate data structures, and a benefit cost model relying on statistics that gathers and chooses methods that do not impose high overheads.

9.5.6 Multiple Decision Models

A final issue discussed in this section concerns the joint application of multiple decision models. Chen et al. [127] observe that often no single *OID* technique always performs the best, consistently outperforming other *OID* techniques in terms of quality. Instead, different *OID* techniques perform better in different contexts.

Various techniques drawn from statistical pattern recognition, machine learning, and neural networks are applied in [695] for the comparison and decision activity, together with a variety of ways to combine multiple classifiers for improved decision quality. Several empirical results are reported that demonstrate performance improvement by combining multiple classifiers. While in [695] the classifiers need to know the details of the features of records in the datasets and the similarity functions as well, the approach in [127] takes the outputs of the techniques without the need to know the details of the algorithms and the features of the datasets.

The paper presents a framework represented in Fig. 9.27. The framework learns a mapping of the matching decisions of the base-level *OID* techniques, together with the local context, into a combined clustering decision. More precisely, the process is divided into (a) training and (b) application. During training, the base-level systems are applied to the training dataset, generating for each pair of matching records j the decision feature d_j and, after reduction, the context feature f_j for selected pairs. Both features are used to train the combining model given the ground truth matching clusters. In the application phase, the vector of all combinations of d_j and f_j is used to predict the matching/unmatching status of the related pair j, and finally, the output cluster is created. The paper empirically studies the framework by applying it to different domains.

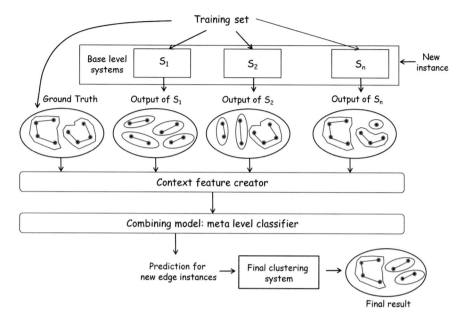

Fig. 9.27 The framework presented in [127]. The ground truth cluster is used only for training

9.5.7 Object Identification at Query Time

As observed in [17], a typical usage of *OID* is when creating a data warehouse prior to making it available to analysis, where *OID* is used as a preprocessing step. Performing *OID* on the entire data warehouse, however, requires a considerable amount of time and significant computing resources. Hence, such an approach is often suboptimal for many modern query-driven applications that need to analyze only small portions of the entire dataset and produce answers "on the fly" and in real time. There are several key perspectives that motivate a query-driven approach, e.g., in the context of streaming (Web) data, from social media such as tweets from Twitter where the continuous storage can be not feasible or practical.

To describe the approach in [17], let us consider a user searching Google Scholar for bibliographic information of a researcher named "Alon Halevy," the results of which are shown in Fig. 9.28.

We assume that all the publications are written by the same author, but some of the returned publications could be duplicates. In Fig. 9.28, publications (P1; P7), (P2; P3; P4), and (P5; P6) are duplicates and refer to the same real-world entities (papers). Hence, we know that they should be clustered into three clusters C1, C2, and C3 by an entity resolution algorithm.

Suppose that the user is actually not interested to all the papers of Alon Halevy, but only to the best-cited ones, e.g., those with a citation count above or equal to 45.

P_id	P_title	Cited	Venue	Authors	Year
P1	Towards efficient entity resolution	65	Very Large Data Bases	Alon Halevy	2000
P7	Towards efficient ER	45	VLDB	Alon Halevy	2000
P2	Entity Resolution on dynamic data	25	ACM SIGMOD	Alon Halevy, Jane Doe	2005
P3	ER on dynaminc data	20	Proc of ACM SIGMOD Conf	A.Y. Halevy, J. Doe	2005
P4	Entity Resolution for dynamic data	15	SIGMOD Conf.	A. Halevy, Jane D.	2005
P5	Entity Resolution for Census data	10	ICDE Conf.	Alon Halevy	2002
P6	ER on census data	5	Proc of ICDE Conf	Alon Y. Halevy	2002

Fig. 9.28 Example from [17]

The following query represents the user's area of interest:

Query 1. SELECT * FROM R WHERE Cited $\geq$ 45

When Query 1 is issued on the table prior to cleaning it, the results are publications P1 and P7, corresponding to cluster C1. This is incorrect since the second paper cluster C2 has a citation count equal to $60 \geq 45$ and should also be returned.

The standard way to answer Query 1 is to first deduplicate relation R to create merged profiles of each paper and then compute the query over this clustering. We assume that the algorithm uses a pairwise decision function to compare records and a pairwise fusion function to consolidate two matching records. The result of entity resolution is shown in Fig. 9.29; Query 1 on such table returns clusters C1 and C2.

A *query-driven approach* is described in [17] that incrementally executes the query performing a minimal number of matching steps that are only necessary to answer a given selection query correctly. A key concept steering the query-driven approach is that of *vestigiality*. A cleaning step (i.e., a call to a decision function for a pair of records) is called *vestigial* (redundant) if the query-driven approach can guarantee that it can still compute a correct final answer without knowing the outcome of this decision. The concept of *vestigiality* is formalized in the context of a large class of SQL selection queries and techniques developed to identify vestigial matching steps.

Query time entity resolution is also addressed in [69] with the same motivations mentioned before. The authors adapt a previous approach to collective resolution

Cluster	P_id	P_title	Cited	Venue	Authors	Year
C1	P1, P7	Towards efficient entity resolution	110	Very Large Data Bases	Alon Halevy	2000
C2	P2, P3, P4	Entity Resolution on dynamic data	60	Proc of ACM SIGMOD Conf	Alon Halevy, Jane Doe	2005
C3	P5, P6	Entity Resolution for Census data	15	ICDE Conf. Proc of ICDE Conf	Alon Halevy	2002

Fig. 9.29 Relation R after being clustered using an entity resolution algorithm

discussed previously in Sect. 9.5.3.2 of this chapter [68]. This is done with the following contributions:

1. The *OID* approach is based on a relational clustering algorithm.
2. For collective *OID* using relational clustering, an analysis is presented of how the accuracy of different decisions depends on each other and on the structural characteristics of the data. The notion of precision and recall for individual entities is presented, and it is shown how they follow a geometric progression as neighbors at increasing distances are considered and resolved.
3. For resolving a query collectively, a two-phase "expand and resolve" algorithm is presented. It first extracts the related records for the query using two novel expansion operators and then resolves the query by only considering the extracted records.
4. The algorithm is further improved using an adaptive approach that selectively considers only the "most informative" ones among the related records for a query. This enables collective resolution at query time without compromising query accuracy.

9.5.8 OID *Evolutive Maintenance*

As underlined in [278], in the Big Data era, the velocity of data updates is often high, quickly making previous *OID* activities obsolete. The paper presents an end-to-end framework that can incrementally and efficiently update matching results in a dataset when new updates are made on the dataset. The algorithms not only allow merging updated records with existing clusters but also allow leveraging new evidence from the updates to fix previous matching errors.

To explain the approach, look at Fig. 9.30 that shows a set D0 of ten business records that represent five businesses. Pairwise similarity is computed comparing (a) name, (b) street address excluding house number, (c) house number in street address, (d) city, and (e) phone; the similarity is set to 1 if all five values are the same, 0.9 if four are the same, 0.8 if three are the same, and 0 otherwise. Figure 9.30b shows the similarity graph between the records, where each node represents a record and each edge represents the pairwise similarity. It also shows the matching results of a correlation clustering technique. Note that it wrongly clusters r4 with (r1,r3) because of the wrong phone number from r4 (in italics); it fails to match r5 and r6 because of the missing information in r6; and it wrongly matches r9 with (r7,r8) instead of with r10, because r9 appears similar to (r7,r8) while r10 does not (different name, different house number, and missing phone).

Now consider four updates D1 to D4 in Fig. 9.31 that together insert records r11 to r17. The paper shows the updated similarity graph and the results of the aforementioned naive approach. It creates a new cluster for r11 as it is different from any existing record and adds the rest of the inserted records to existing clusters.

	BizId	Id	Name	Street address	City	Phone
	B1	r1	Starbucks	123 MISSION ST STE ST1	SAN FRANCISCO	4155431510
	B1	r2	Starbucks	123 MISSION ST	SAN FRANCISCO	4155431510
	B1	r3	Starbucks	123 Mission St	SAN FRANCISCO	4155431510
	B2	r4	Starbucks Coffee	340 MISSION ST	SAN FRANCISCO	4155431510
D0	B3	r5	Starbucks Coffee	333 MARKET ST	SAN FRANCISCO	415534786
	B3	r6	Starbucks	MARKET ST	San Francisco	
	B4	r7	Starbucks Coffee	52 California St	San Francisco	4153988630
	B4	r8	Starbucks Coffee	52 CALIFORNIA ST	SAN FRANCISCO	4153988630
	B5	r9	Starbucks Coffee	295 California St	SAN FRANCISCO	415986234
	B5	r10	Starbucks	295 California ST	SF	

a. Original business listings

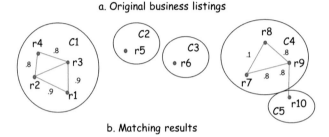

b. Matching results

Fig. 9.30 Original business listings and object identification results in [278]

	BizId	Id	name	Street address	city	phone
D1	B6	r11	Starbucks Coffee	201 Spear Street	San Francisco	4159745077
D2	B3	r12	Starbucks Coffee	MARKET STREET	San Francisco	4155434786
	B3	r13	Starbucks	333 MARKET ST	San Francisco	4155434786
D3	B1	r14	Starbucks	123 MISSION ST STE	SAN FRANCISCO	4155431510
	B1	r15	Starbucks	ST1	San Francisco	4155431510
D4	B5	r16	Starbucks Starbucks	295 CALIFORNIA ST	SAN FRANCISCO	4155431510
	B4	r17		52 California St	SF	4153988630

Fig. 9.31 New updates in [278]

However, a more careful analysis of the inserted nodes allows fixing some previous mistakes and obtaining a better clustering, also shown in the paper. First, because (r12,r13) are similar both to r5 and to r6, they provide extra evidence to merge r5 and r6. Second, when we consider (r1,r4), (r14,r15) jointly, we find that (r1,r3) and (r14,r15) are very similar, but r4 is different from most of them, suggesting moving r4 out. Third, with (r16,r17), r9 appears to be more similar to r10 and r16 than to (r7,r8), suggesting moving r9 from C4 to C5.

In the paper, three types of update operations are considered, insert, delete, and change, that are collectively called *increment*. In the paper, every increment is valid. The incremental linkage (in the terminology adopted in this book, incremental *OID*) is defined in the paper as follows. Let D be a set of records and I be an increment to D. Let M be the actual matching of records in D. Incremental linkage clusters records in $D + I$ based on M. The incremental linkage method proposed in the paper is denoted by f and the result of applying f is denoted as $f(D, I, M)$. The goal for incremental linkage is twofold, (a) to be much faster than conducting batch linkage, especially when the number of increments is small, and (b) to obtain results that are of similar quality to batch linkage.

Gruenheid et al. [278] present a set of algorithms that can incrementally conduct *OID* when new records are inserted and when existing records are deleted or changed. In particular, an end-to-end solution for incremental *OID* is presented that maintains a similarity graph for the records and conducts incremental graph clustering, resulting in clusters of records that refer to the same real-world entity. Further, as to incremental graph clustering, the paper proposes two optimal algorithms that apply clustering on subsets of the records rather than to all records. Then, a greedy approach is designed that conducts matching incrementally in polynomial time by merging and splitting clusters connected to the updated records and moving records between those clusters. The two clustering methods *correlation clustering* and *DB-index clustering* do not require the knowledge of the number of clusters a priori. Experiments on real-world data sets show that algorithms run significantly faster than batch linkage while obtaining similar results.

The problem of keeping the result of entity resolution up-to-date when the *OID* comparison and decision logic or data evolve frequently is addressed in [662, 663]. A naive approach that reruns *OID* from scratch may not be tolerable for resolving large datasets. Whang and Garcia-Molina [663] investigate when and how previous "materialized" *OID* results can instead be exploited to save redundant work with evolved logic and data. Algorithm properties are introduced that facilitate evolution and apply efficient rule, and data evolution techniques are proposed for three *OID* models:

- Match-based clustering (records are clustered based on Boolean matching information)
- Distance-based clustering (records are clustered based on relative distances)
- Pairs decision (the pairs of matching records are identified)

To explain the approach focusing on rules, consider the example in Fig. 9.32. The initial set of records S is shown in Fig. 9.32a. The first rule B1 (see Fig. 9.32b)

a

Record	Name	Zip	Phone
r1	John	54321	123-4567
r2	John	54321	987-6543
r3	John	11111	987-6543
r4	Bob	null	121-1212

Records to match

b

Comparison Rule	Definition
B1	P_{name}
B2	P_{name} AND P_{zip}
B3	P_{name} AND P_{phone}

Evolving from rule B1 to rule B2

Fig. 9.32 Records to match and evolving rules in [663]

says that two records match (represent the same real-world entity) if predicate *pname* evaluates to true. Predicates can in general be quite complex, but for this example, predicates simply perform an equality check. The decision algorithm uses B1 to compare records and groups together records with name "John" producing the partition (r1, r2, r3, r4).

Assume that users are not satisfied with this result, so a data administrator decides to refine B1 by adding a predicate that checks zip codes. Thus, the new rule is B2 shown in Fig. 9.32b. The naive option is to run the same entity resolution algorithm with rule B2 on set S to obtain the partition (r1, r2), (r3, r4). Only records r1 and r2 have the same name and same zip code. This process repeats some unnecessary work: for instance, we would need to compare r1 with r4 to see whether they match on name and zip code, but we already know from the first run that they do not match on name (B1), so they cannot match under B2.

The second problem addressed in the papers is incremental *OID* on new data. This time, the rule remains the same, but new records may now have to be resolved in addition to the original records. For example, after resolving the four records in Fig. 9.32a, we could have to match two more records r5 and r6. While matching the additional records, we would like to avoid redundant record comparisons as much as possible.

The main contributions of [663] are as follows:

- An *OID* technique is defined that clusters records and formalizes evolution for Boolean comparison rules.
- Two desirable properties of *OID* techniques (*rule monotonic* and *context free*; for their treatment, see the paper) are identified that enable efficient evolution.
- Efficient rule and data evolution techniques are proposed that use one or more of the above properties.
- Two variations of the evolution problem are explored: (a) the comparison rule is a distance function instead of a Boolean function and (b) an *OID* technique that returns pairs of matching records instead of a partition.

The rule and data evolution algorithms for the different clustering-based *OID* techniques are experimentally evaluated, and the results show scenarios where rule evolution can be faster than the naive approach by up to several orders of magnitude.

9.6   Domain-Specific Object Identification Techniques

It is frequently observed in the *OID* literature that comparison functions have different behaviors according to the domain of features they apply to. Furthermore, knowing in advance the reasons of most frequent errors can be useful to understand the mix of formulas that optimize the decision phase. For all these reasons, part of the literature investigates more in-depth specific domains, analyzing how the heterogeneities and variants from one side, and the most frequent errors on the other side influence the quality of distance measures. Most frequently analyzed domains are names in general, personal names, names of businesses, and addresses. Among others, [75] analyzes names in general, [136, 523] focus on personal names, [319] deals with personal names in lists of research publications, and [674] spans over personal names, business names, and addresses. In other cases, the domain does not concern the shape of data to be compared but else an area of human activity such as crime identity detection in [500]. We will consider the first type of domain, focusing in particular on [136, 674], and about names, on names of persons and names of businesses.

9.6.1 Personal Names

As observed in [523], names of persons are of great importance in a variety of areas like population registries, libraries, research, genealogy, administration, and business. Therefore, it is not surprising that there are many datasets that deal with personal names. Christen [136] underlines that even when only considering the English-speaking world, a name can have several different spelling forms for a variety of reasons. In the Anglo-Saxon region and most other Western countries, a personal name is usually made of a given name, an optional middle name, and a surname or family name. For Asian names, there exist several transliteration systems into the Roman alphabet, the surname traditionally appears before the given name, and frequently a Western given name is added. Hispanic names can contain two surnames, while Arabic names are often made of several components and contain various affixes that can be separated by hyphens or white spaces.

Studies on spelling errors provide figures for general words and for personal names that are not convergent. Experiments referred in [160] report that over 80 % of errors were single errors, such as a letter was deleted, an extra letter was inserted, a letter was substituted for another letter, or two adjacent letters were transposed. Substitutions were the most common errors, followed by deletions, then insertions, and finally transpositions, followed by multiple errors in one word. Patient names in hospitals are investigated in [247], where experiments show that the most common errors, with a percentage of 36 %, were insertion of an additional name word, initial, or title, followed in 14 % of errors by several different letters in a name due to nicknames or spelling variations. Single errors in this study accounted for 39 % of all errors, only around half compared to the 80 % reported in [160]. Thus, there seem to be significant differences between general text and personal names, which have to be considered when name matching algorithm are being developed and used.

The most common name variations are categorized in [385] as:

- Spelling variations (like "Meier" and "Meyer") due to typographical errors that do not affect the phonetical structure of a name but still pose a problem for matching
- Phonetic variations (like "Sinclair" and "St. Clair") where the phonemes are modified and the structure of a name is changed substantially

- Compound names (like "Hans-Peter" or "SmithMiller") that might be given in full, one component only, or components swapped
- Alternative names (like nicknames, married names, or other deliberate name changes)
- Initials only (mainly for given and middle names)

Types of errors are related in [382] with the nature of the data entry, leading to the following conclusions:

- When handwritten forms are scanned and optical character recognition (OCR) is applied, the most likely types of errors will be substitutions between similar-looking characters.
- Manual keyboard-based data entry can result in wrongly typed neighboring keys.
- Data entry over the telephone (e.g., as part of a survey study) is a confounding factor to manual keyboard entry. The person doing the data entry might not request the correct spelling, but rather assume a default spelling which is based on the person's knowledge and cultural background.
- Limitations in the maximum length of input fields can force people to use abbreviations, initials only, or even disregard some parts of a name.
- People themselves sometimes report their names differently depending upon the organization they are in contact with or deliberately provide wrong or modified names.

A first conclusion in [136] is that while there is only one correct spelling for most general words, there are often no wrong name spellings, just several valid name variations. For this reason, in many cases, it is not possible to disregard a name as wrong if it is not found in a dictionary of known names. When matching names, the challenge is in distinguishing between two sources of variation, namely, (a) legitimate name variations (which should be preserved and matched) and (b) errors introduced during data entry and recording (which should be corrected). The challenge lies in distinguishing between these two sources of variations.

Comparison functions investigated in [75] for generic names and in [136] for personal names extend those functions considered in Chap. 8. In [136], they are classified into:

1. Pattern matching, including edit distance, q-grams, and Jaro algorithm mentioned among others in Chap. 8. Among them, [136] considers the Winkler algorithm [512] that improves upon the Jaro algorithm by applying ideas based on empirical studies [512], showing that fewer errors typically occur at the beginning of names. The Winkler algorithm increases the Jaro similarity measure for agreeing person names initial characters (up to four).
2. Phonetic encoding, such as soundex and phonex, that tries to improve the encoding quality by preprocessing names according to their English pronunciation before the encoding.
3. Combined techniques that combine phonetic encoding and pattern matching with the aim to improve the matching quality. Among them, we mention the *syllable*

alignment pattern searching [532], based on the idea of matching two names syllable by syllable, rather than character by character.

Several experiments on precision, recall, *F*-measure, and timing results are reported in [75] for generic names and in [136] for personal names; for details, we refer to the papers. Such experiments give rise in [136] to several suggestions, among them:

1. It is important to know the type of names to be matched and if these names have been properly parsed and standardized.
2. For names parsed into separate fields, the Jaro and Winkler techniques seem to perform well for both given names and surnames, as do unigrams and bigrams.
3. If speed is important, it is imperative to use techniques with time complexity linear in the string length (like q-grams, Jaro, or Winkler), as otherwise, name pairs made of long strings (especially unparsed full names) will slow down matching.
4. If additional personal information is available besides names, for example, addresses and dates of birth, then proper techniques [674] should be applied rather than basic name matching techniques.

9.6.2   Businesses

Business lists are typically more difficult to match than person lists because of the variants of names and the variants of addresses [670]. If a register is not maintained effectively, undetected duplication may increase by 1 % or more per year. A case study documented in [674] shows that in a list of businesses consisting of entities selling petroleum products, a turnover of 20 % per year in the names and addresses has been found. In some situations, a small company may have gone out of business. In many other situations, the company may have changed its address to that of its accountant or changed from a location address to an owner address. Winkler [674] observes that the duplicates among names of businesses would inflate estimates in different industrial categories. The duplicates could also cause the number of individuals employed in a set of different firms to be overestimated.

Combinations of business names and person names for the purpose of studying employment and labor dynamics are investigated in [6]. In the paper, it is observed that the effect of very small amounts of error in identifiers can have small effects of some estimates and relatively large effects on other estimates. For instance, in a file of a billion records representing quarterly employment in the state of California for 20 years, the number of erroneous social security numbers (SSNs) has been approximately 1–2 % per quarter.

One conclusion in [670] is that often the best information for improving the linkage of two files of businesses may come from a large business population register. If the government has expended substantial resources in creating the register, then it can be used as a bridging file for linking other business lists.

Another observation in [670] confirms that the maturity in the field has not been achieved when a question is posed: if an agency maintains a large business register, how useful is it to maintain multiple versions of the name, addresses, and contact individuals associated with enterprises or company locations? The final conclusion in [670] is that business list matching is a major problem.

9.7   Object Identification Techniques for Maps and Images

Geospatial dataset object identification (term seldom used for geospatial datasets; terms more used are linkage, fusion, matching, integration, and *conflation*; in the following we will also use the term matching) is a complex process that may utilize work from a broad range of disciplines that include geographical information systems, cartography, computational geometry, graph theory, image processing, pattern recognition, and statistical theory. Geospatial datasets have two physical representations that deeply influence the nature of matching:

- *Vector representation* corresponds to the use of geometrical primitives such as points, lines, curves, and shapes or polygons to represent maps or images.
- *Raster representation* is a dot matrix data structure representing a generally rectangular grid of pixels or points of color.

In general, based on the types of geospatial datasets dealt with, matching techniques can be categorized into the following three groups:

- Vector-to-vector matching: for example, the integration of two road networks with different accuracy levels
- Vector-to-raster matching: for example, the integration of road network and imagery or road network and raster maps
- Raster-to-raster matching: for example, the integration of two images with different resolutions or the integration of raster maps and imagery

As the above examples show, in geospatial matching, datasets may be of the same type, for example, two maps, or of different types, for example, a map and an image. Furthermore, datasets may pertain to specific representation domains of the territory, being the road network domain the most frequent investigated domain. In addition, knowledge exploited in the matching process may refer to locations (when available) of entities to be matched (e.g., streets in a city) or to their features, corresponding to entity names, types, and properties (e.g., one-way vs. two-way streets).

In the following, we address first matching based on the location of entities being them points or polylines; see Sect. 9.7.1; then in Sect. 9.7.2, we discuss location- and feature-based matching. We consider at this point the two most investigated cases among those ones listed above, represented by (a) vector road maps and orthoimages in Sect. 9.7.3.1 and (b) raster road maps and orthoimages in Sect. 9.7.3.2. In

Sect. 9.7.4, digital gazetteer matching is discussed, where a gazetteer is a spatial dictionary of named and typed places in some environment.

9.7.1 Map Matching: Location-Based Matching

9.7.1.1 Matching of Points

Authors of [50] observe that since location is the only property that is always available for spatial objects, they are interested to investigate location-based matching. The assumption is made in [50] that each dataset has at most one object per real-world entity and locations are given as points.

Several are the reasons that make the location-based matching not a trivial task [50]:

1. Measurements introduce errors, and the errors in different datasets are independent of each other.
2. Each organization has its own approach and requirements and hence uses different measurement techniques and different scales. For example, one organization might represent buildings as points, while another could use polygonal shapes for the same purpose.
3. Displacements may occur due to cartographic generalizations (on cartographic generalization, see Sect. 3.3.2 of Chap. 3).

The model adopted in [50] sees a geographic dataset as a set of spatial objects, each object representing a single real-world geographic entity. An object has associated spatial and nonspatial attributes. Locations of objects are recorded as points, the simplest form of location representation. More complex forms of recording locations (e.g., polygons) can be approximated by points. The two datasets are $A = (a_1, a_2, \ldots, a_m)$ and $B = (b_1, b_2, \ldots, b_n)$. One of the oldest methods for entity matching is the *one-sided nearest-neighbor join*, commonly used in commercial geographic-information systems, also discussed in [440]. This method associates to an object a in A the object b in B that is the closest object to a among all the objects in B (called nearest B-neighbor of a). The one-sided nearest-neighbor join of a dataset B with a dataset A produces all sets, called fusion sets $(a; b)$, such that a is in A and b is in B and b is the nearest B-neighbor to a. Note that this method is not symmetric, since several objects in A may correspond to the same object in B. It can be shown that the one-sided nearest-neighbor join is likely to produce good approximation only when the dataset A is *covered* by B, namely, every real-world entity that is represented in A is also represented in B, while the performance is poor when the overlap between the two datasets is small; in fact, every object of A is matched with some object of B, even if B has objects that should not be matched with any object of A.

In [50], two other techniques are presented: the mutually nearest technique and the probabilistic technique. Both of them compute a confidence value for every fusion set; for both of them, the final result is produced by choosing the fusion sets that have a confidence value that is above a given threshold value. The difference among the methods is:

- In the *mutually nearest* method, the confidence is a formula where also the second nearest B-neighbor is considered. The main advantage of the mutually nearest method over the traditional one-sided nearest-neighbor join is lower sensitivity to the degree of overlap between the two datasets.
- In the probabilistic method, it is not enough to consider only the nearest and the second nearest B-neighbors of a in A, since there could be several objects that are close to a. In the method, the confidence of a fusion set $(a; b)$ depends on the probability that b is the object that corresponds to a and that probability depends inversely on the distance between a and b.

In [51], the concept of join set is introduced as a generalization of the fusion set to n input datasets. Furthermore, previous techniques are generalized to any number of datasets with two different approaches. In the first approach, a join algorithm for two datasets is applied sequentially; in the latter, all the integrated datasets are processed simultaneously.

The paper [539] integrates the above approaches. Furthermore, a new technique is presented, the normalized-weights technique, where for each possible join set, a weight is computed. This weight indicates how likely it is for the join set to be correct. For computing the weights, probability functions are assigned to all the pairs and all the singletons. Probability functions are considered as initial weights. Then, the algorithm performs an iterative process of normalizing sets of at most n objects.

The interested reader is referred to [50, 51, 539] for formal definitions, properties, and examples.

9.7.1.2 Matching of Polylines

Matching polylines is in the category of vector to vector matching; it is a problem significantly more complex than matching locations. As recalled in [538], one of the first papers on matching of polylines [231] applies a point-matching algorithm as the first step and then uses the topology of polylines to propagate the matching. Finally, the average distance between the lines is used to estimate the relative compatibility of the lines. In [251], a polyline from one source is augmented with a buffer. When a polyline from the other source is completely contained in that buffer, the two polylines are considered a matching pair.

Safra et al. [538] propose an algorithm for the matching of polylines in the domain of road maps that improves the efficiency of the matching of previous approaches. The novelty of the approach is in matching roads based merely on locations of endpoints of polylines rather than trying to match whole lines.

The algorithm receives as input two datasets consisting of polylines. The output is an approximate matching of the polylines. Computing the matching is a four-step

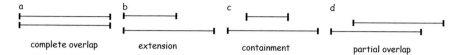

Fig. 9.33 Possible relationships between polylines

process. In the first step, the algorithm finds the topological nodes, corresponding to intersections where two or more roads meet or road ends where roads terminate without intersecting another road. Then the algorithm generates all pairs consisting of a node and a polyline, such that the node is an endpoint of the polyline. In the third step, a matching of the nodes is computed. Finally, the matching of the polylines is generated. In the final step, four types of spatial relationships between polylines are considered (see Fig. 9.33), (a) complete overlap, (b) extension, (c) containment, and (d) partial overlap.

The matching of the polylines according to the above four relationships is computed by the technique *Match-Lines*. The reader is referred to the paper for details on the technique.

All of the above techniques address map matching at design time or else at a certain point of the life cycle of the geographical information system. In such cases, the matching can be done without strict time constraints. As noticed in [540], in many scenarios, it is required to integrate road maps for a specific run time user need, such scenarios are called in [540] *ad hoc integration*; let us notice here some similarity with issues addressed in Sect. 9.5.7 on *OID* at query time. In ad hoc integration, the matching is done in real time (no more than a few seconds) and with almost no preprocessing. A typical scenario of ad hoc integration is when a small fragment of a road network has to be matched with a larger network. In [540], a method for ad hoc integration of two vectorial road networks, whereby polylines are matched according to the locations of their endpoints, is presented. Essentially, the method is a two-stage process. Initially it finds the endpoints of the polylines in the two sources and computes a partial matching between them. Then, it finds a partial matching between polylines, according to the matching of the endpoints. So, the major novelty of the approach is in using only the locations of the endpoints of the polylines rather than trying to match the whole lines.

9.7.2 Map Matching: Location- and Feature-Based Matching

A typical geospatial database contains heterogeneous features such as location name, spatial coordinates, location type, and demographic information. Other features correspond to neighbors of a location, similarly to what we have commented in previous sections for links among data in datasets.

The use of all of the abovementioned features in techniques for geospatial matching is investigated in [558]. The approach learns to combine the different features to perform accurate matching. Location name matching is performed with the same techniques described in Chap. 8. Coordinate matching can be performed with methods discussed in Sect. 9.7.1. Location-type matching is evaluated in [558], computing the location type similarity based on co-occurrence. Two positive and negative training sets are constructed, and the similarity between two location types is set equal to the number of positive training samples where location types co-occur ratio the total number of instances containing these location types. Several combinations of previous similarities are proposed and experimented in [558]. One way to combine similarities is by putting a threshold on one while using the other as a secondary filter. A second measure takes into account the relation between spatial and nonspatial features, where weight is learned from ground truth data consisting of matching locations. Experiments for the above similarities and also for usage of only the spatial or else the nonspatial component for finding matching are reported.

Linear programming is used in [400] for matching objects in spatial datasets. Based on a modified assignment problem model, an objective function is formulated that can be solved by an optimization model that takes into account all potentially matched pairs simultaneously by minimizing the total distance of all pairs in a similarity space. Experiments are conducted over street network data in Goleta CA, USA, created under different standards by two agencies. Data represent approximately the same streets in a neighborhood of Goleta. Experiments show that the strategy consistently improves global matching quality.

With the proliferation of location-based services and the increasing amount of geographic data, many issues arise related to the integration of spatial data and their visualization. Berjawi [58] observes that there are many providers in the market (in 2015, Google Maps, OpenStreetMap, Tomtom TeleAtlas, etc.), each of them using its own concepts, models, data, legends, and background maps. As a consequence, customers obtain different and conflicting answers from one provider to another for the same query. Berjawi [58] investigates techniques that allow integration of services offered by multi-providers in the context of touristic points of interests.

9.7.3   Map and Orthoimage Matching

As noticed in [123], a large amount of geospatial data are now readily available on the Web. Furthermore, a wide variety of maps are available from various government agencies, such as property survey maps and maps of resources such as railways or oil and natural gas fields [122]. Satellite imagery and aerial photography have been utilized to enhance real estate listings, military intelligence applications, and other applications. By integrating these spatial datasets, one can support a rich set of analyses that lead to better decisions and cost savings for many applications, such as city, region, and state planning, or integration of diverse datasets for emergency response. However, integrating these geospatial data from different data sources is a challenging task, because spatial data obtained from various data sources may cover different areas and have different projections and different accuracy levels.

The integration of maps and images representing a portion of the territory needs for different techniques depending on the types of maps and the types of images. In the next two sections, we deal with images that have been orthorectified, called orthoimagery or *orthoimages*, i.e., the image is altered from original photos so that it has the geometric properties of a map. As to maps, we consider maps that represent networks of roads, in the two cases of *vector maps*, that are formed by a network of polylines and the more general case of *raster maps*, where the map is made of an array of pixels.

9.7.3.1   Vector Road Map and Orthoimage Matching

Figure 9.34 shows an example of combining a road network and an image; in the two cases in which map and image are and are not aligned, clearly our target is the aligned integration of the road map and the image.

The literature on vector map and imagery matching is rich of contributions that differ on the strategy to extract useful knowledge from the map/imagery to allow their accurate integration. For example, in [232], first all, edges such as road and building edges are detected from the imagery, then edges extracted are compared with vector map data to identify road edges, and finally the two sets of road edges are matched. Fortier et al. [242] find all the junction points of all detected lines in the imagery, then match the junction points of the road vector with the image junctions, and finally match the two sets of road edges.

a   b

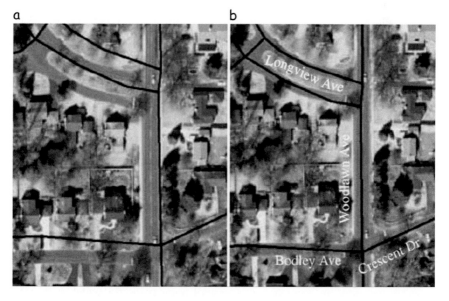

Fig. 9.34 Matching between road vector map and orthoimagery, from [123], Geoinformatica ©Springer 2006. (**a**) Map and image not aligned. (**b**) Map and image aligned

Lat / Long

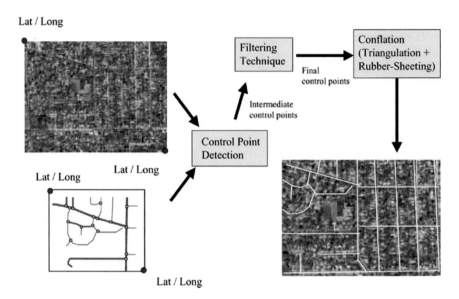

Fig. 9.35 The approach presented in [123], Geoinformatica ©Springer 2006

In the following, we describe the approach to vector map/imagery alignment proposed in [123], whose phases, represented in Fig. 9.35, are:

- Control point detection—Control points represent the knowledge extracted from maps/imagery that is subsequently used for matching control point pairs. Road intersections are good candidates for being control points, because road intersections are salient points to capture the major layouts of road network and the road shapes around intersections are often well defined. We describe the process for vector data; the process is divided into two steps. First, the system examines all line segments in the vector data to label the endpoints of each segment as the candidate points. Second, the connectivity of these candidate points is examined to determine if they are intersection points, namely, each candidate point is verified to see if there are more than two line segments connected at the point. For imagery, a Bayes classifier is used (see [123] for details).
- Filtering control points—Due to the complexity of natural scene in the imagery, the technique adopted in the previous step may still misidentify intersections as control points. In this step, a filter is used to eliminate misidentified intersections and only keep the accurately identified ones, hence improving the precision with the cost of reducing recall. The filter adopted is *vector median filter*, which is a popular filter to perform noise removal in image processing.
- Matching imagery and vector data—After filtering the control point pairs, the system identifies an accurate set of control point pairs, for which it may be assumed that each point of the control point pair from the vector data and imagery

indicates the same position. To align all other points, suitable transformations are calculated from the control point pairs. For example, to achieve overall alignment of imagery and vector data, vector data must be adjusted locally to conform to the imagery. The system aligns the two datasets based on local adjustments, because small changes in one area usually do not affect the geometry at long distances [123]. The Delaunay triangularization (see [534]) is especially suited for vector matching systems.

The interested reader is invited to read [123] for further details.

9.7.3.2   Raster Road Map and Orthoimage Matching

This case is made more complex than the vector map to imagery by the absence of a reference system for maps. Since the geocoordinates of many online street maps are unknown, the localized image processing techniques adopted in [123] to find intersection points on maps cannot be adopted. We present the approach in [124]; the overall set of activities is shown in Fig. 9.36 and is made of three phases (we simplify here the approach, made of four phases), described in the following.

1. Detect intersection points on the map—In order to deal with the more general scenario, in which the geocoordinates of many online street maps are unknown, automatic map processing and pattern recognition algorithms are needed for identifying intersection points. Points could be extracted by simply detecting road lines. However, due to the varying thickness of lines on diverse maps,

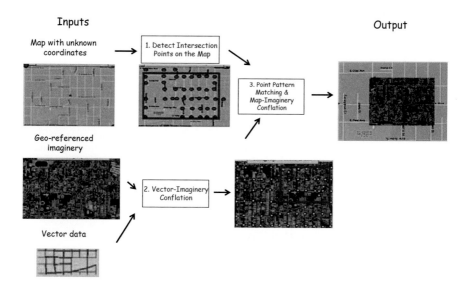

Fig. 9.36 The approach and example presented in [124], Geoinformatica ©Springer 2008

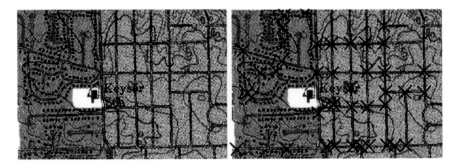

Fig. 9.37 Intersection points automatically detected on a map in [124], Geoinformatica ©Springer 2008

accurate extraction of intersection points from maps is difficult [457], due to noisy information, such as symbols and alphanumeric characters or contour lines on the map, which make hard to accurately identify the intersection points. To overcome these problems, road intersection from maps are detected, performing first a preprocessing in terms of various image processing techniques, such as determining the road widths and text/graphics separation techniques. Algorithms mentioned in [124] allow computing the number of road segments that meet at an intersection (called the degree of an intersection) and the directions of those segments. This additional information can help to improve the subsequent point pattern matching algorithm. Figure 9.37 shows an example from [124].

2. Vector-imagery conflation—Identifying intersections in imagery assumes that existing road network vector datasets are utilized as part of the prior knowledge. The approach for automatic conflation of georeferenced road vector data with georeferenced imagery (Step 2) has been described in the previous section.

3. Point pattern matching and map-imagery conflation—To achieve generation and matching of control points by pattern matching, the basic idea is to find the transformation between the layout (with relative distances) of the intersection point set on the map and the intersection point set on the imagery. Three algorithms are described in [124] to this goal: (a) a naive brute force algorithm, (b) an enhanced point pattern matching algorithm, and (c) an improvement of the brute force algorithm by exploiting information on direction and distances available from the vector sets and maps; the interested reader is addressed to [124] for a detailed discussion.

9.7.4 Digital Gazetteer Data Matching

A digital gazetteer is a spatial dictionary of named and typed places in a given environment, typically the near surface of the earth [302]. A familiar kind of gazetteer is the index in an atlas, for which the maps themselves supply the georeference. The utility of a digital gazetteer is the correspondence created between systems of place referencing, i.e., between the ad hoc names and type classifications assigned to places, on the one hand, and quantitative locations for them, on the other. A number of desirable gazetteer properties are proposed in [364], which include (a) accessing multiple data sources, (b) exploiting volunteered data sources, (c) maintaining mechanisms to assess trust in resources, and (d) developing an agreed high-level domain ontology. Frequently, it is necessary to consult and combine results from multiple sources of gazetteer data; thus, a fundamental challenge with digital gazetteers is merging gazetteer data so that place identity is preserved.

A fundamental item described in gazetteer are toponyms. Several string similarity measures for toponyms in different languages are compared in [518]; 21 different measures on datasets containing Romanized toponyms from 11 different countries (see Fig. 9.38) are compared. Best-performing measures reported in [518] vary widely across datasets but are highly consistent within country and within language.

A mediation framework to access and integrate distributed gazetteer resources is presented in [582], with the goal of building a meta-gazetteer that generates augmented versions of place name information. The approach combines different aspects of place name information from multiple gazetteer sources that refer to the same geographic place and employs several similarity metrics to identify equivalent toponyms. The paper introduces a toponym ontology, which in combination with Web services and data mediation functionality enables access to multiple resources in response to a query on the ontology. The main purposes of the toponym ontology are (1) to find toponym data that match a given input string representing a place name and (2) to retrieve georeferenced place names given a spatial footprint as an input.

The technique presented in [302] has the goal of automatically integrating digital gazetteer information. The technique makes use of a computational approach

Country	Languages
China	Standard Chinese (Mandarin), Cantonese, Shangainese, Fozhou, Hokkinen-Taiwanese, Xiang, Gan, Hakka dialects, and others
France	French, regional dialects
Germany	German
Italy	Italian, German, French, Slovene
Japan	Japanese
Mexico	Spanish, indigenous languages (Mayan, Nauhatl, and others)
Saudi Arabia	Arabic
Spain	Castilian Spanish, Catalan, Galician, Basque
Taiwan	Mandarin Chinese, Taiwanese, Hakka dialects
United Kingdom	English, Scots, Scottish Gaelic, Welsh, Irish, Cornish
Yemen	Arabic

Fig. 9.38 Countries and languages investigated in [518]

modeled on human behavior, focusing first on place geometries (assuming that disjoint places cannot be the same), second on their type categories, and finally on their names. Related metrics mimic the human cognitive process that is complemented with operational procedures for automated matching of digital gazetteer information.

9.8 Privacy Preserving Object Identification

Privacy preserving object identification (PPOID) (frequently called privacy preserving record linkage) has been in recent years an intensive research area, the reason being the explosion of the use of personal information in a vast number of applications and services. Examples of personal information are found in financial information, health information, e-mails, and tweets, while examples of applications are health information systems, customer relationship management, crime and fraud detection, and national security [248, 682].

To understand the difference between a traditional *OID* environment and a *PPOID* environment, look at Figs. 9.39 and 9.40 inspired to [623]. In Fig. 9.39, we see represented the typical workflow of an *OID* process, with blocks representing the preprocessing, reduction, and comparison and decision steps.

In Fig. 9.40, we see the novelties that are introduced in a PPOID environment. Here we have two (or more, in general) parties that are interested to submit their own dataset to be linked with another dataset, under the condition that the only information disclosed to the other party are the matched records, or even only part of them, while all other information and phases must remain private.

Notice that because preprocessing can be conducted independently at each data source, it is not part of the privacy preserving context. All other phases must be conducted in such a way to avoid disclosure of information to the other party, so they have to be managed as private processes. The same for data flows from one step to another. Furthermore, notice that the evaluation is challenging, because in PPOID the access to the actual record values is not possible as this would reveal private information.

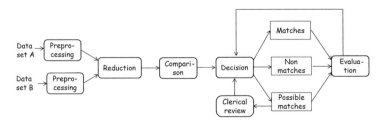

Fig. 9.39 Classical object identification process

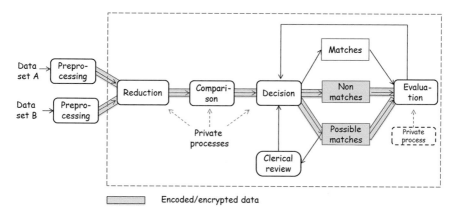

Fig. 9.40 Privacy preserving object identification (inspired to [623])

Several surveys on PPOID have been published recently [187, 290, 354, 613, 623, 627]. Four techniques are compared in [613]; techniques analyzed in [627] range from classical techniques for *OID* enhanced with privacy features to native PPOID techniques, and [187] analyzes six comparators that can be used in PPOID, while [290] is mainly focused on reduction and comparison steps; furthermore, prominent unsolved challenges are discussed. The most comprehensive survey on PPOID is [623], paper on which the following of the section is mainly based.

Fifteen dimensions of applications and techniques developed for PPOID are categorized in [623]. They are summarized in the following in four areas, namely, privacy requirements, matching techniques, theoretical analysis and evaluation, and practical aspects.

9.8.1 Privacy Requirements

The privacy requirements of PPOID among organizations refer to the number of parties, the adversary model, and the privacy techniques.

1. Number of parties—Solutions may be classified into (a) those that require a third party (also named *third-party protocols*) and (b) those that do not (*two-party protocols*). Two-party protocols are more secure than third-party protocols, because there is no possibility of collusion between one of the dataset owners and the third party; at the same time, they are characterized by higher complexity.
2. Adversary model—An adversary model is a representation of an adversary behavior that the technique must take into account and be able to oppose. Two adversary models are considered.

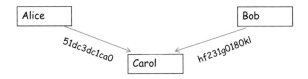

First Name	Surname	Compound string	Hash string
peter	christen	peterchristen	51dc3dc1ca0
pete	christen	petechristen	h231g0180kl

Fig. 9.41 Secure hash encoding

- *Honest-but-curious behavior*, where parties are curious, i.e., they follow the protocol but try to find out information about the other party's data.
- *Malicious behavior*, where parties can behave arbitrarily.

3. Privacy technique—Ten types of techniques are discussed in [623]; among them we introduce the following ones:

(a) *Secure hash encoding*, one-way hash encoding functions [555], convert a string value into a hash code (for instance, "carlo" into "73tg46t76n9") such that having access to only one hash code will make it nearly impossible with current computing technology to learn its original string value. A major limit of this technique is that only exact matches can be found [188]. An example of application of this technique is shown in Fig. 9.41.

(b) *Secure multi-party computation*, where a computation is secure if at its end no party knows anything except its own input and the final results. Secure multi-party computation techniques employ some form of encryption schemes to allow secure computation.

(c) *Embedded space*, based on the idea of mapping-based blocking (see Sect. 9.4.2). Attribute values are embedded (mapped) into a metric space, and the mapping is such that the distances between values are preserved [550].

(d) *Generalization techniques*, where data are perturbed through a process of generalization in such a way that re-identification from the perturbed data is not possible. A type of generalization is k-anonymity that is defined for tables in relational databases. Said *quasi-identifier* an attribute that can be used to identify individual entities, a table satisfies the k-anonymity criteria if every combination of quasi-identifier attributes is shared by at least k tuples; see an example for $k = 2$ in Fig. 9.42. Dataset owners k-anonymize their datasets with the same anonymization technique and send the encrypted dataset to the third party. The third party constructs buckets corresponding to the combination of k-anonymous values.

(e) *Random values* that consists of adding random noise in the form of extra records to the datasets (this is called a *data perturbation technique* [355]).

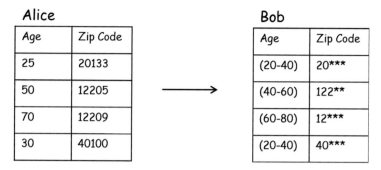

Fig. 9.42 *k*-Anonymized tuples as used in [323]

(f) *Differential privacy*, a recent technique [324] that allows parties to interact with each other's datasets using statistical queries. Random noise is added to each query result to preserve data privacy. Only the perturbed results of statistical queries are disclosed to other parties.

For other privacy aspects related to pseudo random functions, phonetic encoding, reference values, and Bloom filters, we refer the reader to [623].

9.8.2   Matching Techniques

Techniques used in the different phases of the PPOID process are considered here.

1. Reduction—Techniques employed in the reduction step become more challenging in PPOID, since here the trade-off involves, besides accuracy and efficiency, also privacy. Four blocking techniques are proposed in [15]:

   (a) *Simple blocking* arranges hash signatures in blocks where the similarity of a pair can be computed more than once if they are in more than one common block.
   (b) *Record-aware blocking* uses an identifier with every hash signature.
   (c) *Frugal third-party blocking* uses a secure set intersection.
   (d) *Secure multi-party computation protocol* that before transferring datasets to the third party identifies common hash signatures.

   For more details, we address the reader to [15, 623].

2. Comparison—The main challenge with these techniques is how the similarity between pairs of strings values can be calculated such that no private information is revealed to parties.

3. Decision—Here the challenge is to keep high quality in terms of recall and precision, while at the same time preserving the privacy of records that are not part of the matching pairs (see Fig. 9.40). Details of decision techniques used in PPOID are found in [623].

9.8.3   Analysis and Evaluation

Theoretical analysis makes reference to scalability, linkage quality, and privacy vulnerabilities. Scalability has been considered among qualities in Sect. 9.2.2; the novelty of PPOID is that we have also to take into account communication costs between parties. Matching quality is analyzed in terms of fault tolerance of the matching technique to data errors. Fault tolerance to errors can be addressed by using approximate matching or preprocessing techniques; the reader is addressed to [623] for examples. Assuming that true matching status of data is available (which is frequently not the case in PPOID applications), the linkage quality can be assessed using any of the measures discussed in Sect. 9.2.2. Main privacy vulnerabilities include frequency attack, dictionary attack, and collusion between parties. Privacy evaluation can be performed with various measures; we mention two of them:

1. Entropy, information gain and relative information gain—Entropy measures the amount of information contained in a message X. The information gain assesses the possibility of inferring the original message Y, given its enciphered version X. The relative information gain measure normalizes the scale of information gain to the interval [0,1], providing a scale for comparison and evaluation.
2. Security/simulation proof—The proof of privacy can be evaluated by simulating the solutions under different adversary models. If under a certain adversary model a party learns no information except its input and output, the technique can be proven to be secure and private.

9.8.4   Practical Aspects

Practical aspects include implementation of techniques, datasets available for experiments, and application areas. Some techniques provide only theoretical evaluation; other techniques have been implemented to conduct experiments, but only some of them provide details about the implementation. As to datasets, due to the difficulties to obtain real-world data with personal information, synthetically generated datasets are commonly used, and several tools are available; see, e.g., [141]. As to application areas, the main targeted areas include healthcare, census, e-commerce, and finance applications.

   All previous dimensions are considered in [623] in the comparison of 29 techniques that are also described in the paper.

9.9   Summary

The last years have seen an explosion of research on *OID*, leading to the extension of the life cycle of *OID* to new phases such as *OID* at query time and *OID* at maintenance time, covering all phases of the life cycle of an information system.

As to traditional phases, such as preprocessing, reduction, and comparison and decision, the inherent complexity of the *OID* process, the increasing size of datasets, the need to reduce human intervention, and the pressure for quality improvement led to the development of knowledge/learning-based techniques that exploit the context of entities to be matched and other types of knowledge.

Other areas that have been investigated concern the enrichment of the decision process, from one side to take into account intermediate results of the matching activity, extend the decision to the fusion step, and take advantage of such intermediate decisions to incrementally improve the efficiency and quality of the process and, from the other side, to increase the cost-benefit ratio of the process in the early matching decisions and monitor costs to orient incremental decisions.

In the spirit of the book, which extends the investigation on quality from data to a wide spectrum of types of linguistic and perceptual information, in the chapter, we have also discussed matching techniques for geospatial information, such as map matching and map/orthoimage matching.

Chapter 10
Data Quality Issues in Data Integration Systems

10.1 Introduction

In distributed environments, data sources are typically characterized by various kinds of heterogeneities that can be generally classified into (1) technological heterogeneities, (2) schema heterogeneities, and (3) instance-level heterogeneities. *Technological heterogeneities* are due to the use of products by different vendors, employed at various layers of an information and communication infrastructure. An example of technological heterogeneity is the usage of two different relational database management systems like IBM's DB2 vs. Microsoft's SQLServer. *Schema heterogeneities* are principally caused by the use of (1) different data models, such as one source that adopts the relational data model and a different source that adopts the XML data model, and (2) different data representations, such as one source that stores addresses as one single field and another source that stores addresses with separate fields for street, civic number, and city. *Instance-level heterogeneities* are caused by different, conflicting data values provided by distinct sources for the same objects. This type of heterogeneity can be caused by quality errors, such as accuracy, completeness, currency, and consistency errors; such errors may result, for instance, from independent processes that feed the different data sources.

Today, there are many examples of scenarios in which data residing at different sources must be accessed in a unified way, overcoming such heterogeneities. *Data integration* is a major research and business area that has the main purpose of allowing a user to access data stored by heterogeneous data sources through the presentation of a unified view of this data. Though data integration must face all the types of heterogeneities listed above, in this chapter we focus particularly on instance-level heterogeneities, where data quality issues become very significant. Indeed, instance-level heterogeneities can strongly affect query processing in data integration systems (DISs). Specifically, the query processing activity can be performed by considering that different data sources may exhibit different quality levels. Hence, answering algorithms can be executed to provide the optimal quality

© Springer International Publishing Switzerland 2016
C. Batini, M. Scannapieco, *Data and Information Quality*, Data-Centric Systems and Applications, DOI 10.1007/978-3-319-24106-7_10

results for the final user. We will describe some approaches to such *quality-driven query processing*. Furthermore, when collecting data as answers to queries, possible conflicts must be solved, by means of a specific *instance-level conflict resolution* activity; otherwise, the whole integration process cannot be correctly terminated.

Quality-driven query processing and instance-level conflict resolution can be seen as two complementary approaches that deal with instance-level heterogeneities. Specifically, it is possible to consider:

1. Only-quality-driven query processing (without conflict resolution)
2. Only conflict resolution (without quality-driven query processing)
3. Both approaches used complementarily

Quality-driven query processing modifies the query answering semantics in order to take into account varying quality of source data. It can assume (case 1) that instance-level conflicts are not solved, but metadata are available in the system to return the best quality answer (see [463]). Instance-level conflict resolution can focus on solving conflicts between sources independently of the query processing (case 2), for example, by operating not at query time but at a different phase of the data integration process, such as the population of a data warehouse (see [462]). Alternatively (case 3), conflict resolution techniques can be performed at query time, within the quality-driven query answering process itself (see [548]).

In [81], data fusion is described as a step of a data integration process, following both the *schema mapping* step and the *duplicate detection* step (in the terminology adopted in the book, this is the object identification step). Data fusion deals indeed with contradictory values in a data integration process. A possible classification of data fusion (also called conflict handling) strategies is presented in [81] and is shown in Fig. 10.1. Conflict-ignoring strategies do not take any decision with respect to conflicting data, possibly not even being aware of data conflicts. Conflict-avoiding strategies take conflicts into account, but not in the sense of detecting and

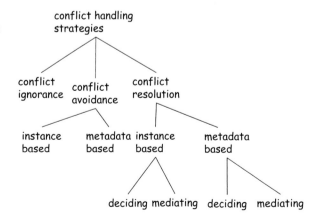

Fig. 10.1 Data fusion (conflict handling) strategies in [81]

solving single conflicts. Instead, they handle them by applying a unique decision to all data, such as preferring data from a special source. Conflict resolution strategies, in contrast, do deal with all data and metadata to resolve conflicts. They can be subdivided into deciding and mediating strategies, in the former case choosing a value from existing ones (deciding) and in the latter case choosing a value that does not necessarily exist among the conflicting values (mediating).

The remaining of the chapter is organized as follows: First we describe some basic concepts on DISs (Sect. 10.2). Then, we provide an overview of existing proposals to deal with quality-driven query processing (Sect. 10.3). In Sect. 10.4, we will show several techniques that perform conflict resolution, adopting either deciding or mediating strategies or both of them. Finally, we give some insights into theoretical proposals to address inconsistent query answering in DISs (Sect. 10.5).

10.2 Generalities on Data Integration Systems

Two main approaches to data integration can be identified, based on the actual location of data stored by sources to be integrated:

- *Virtual data integration*, where the unified view is virtual and data reside only at sources. A reference architecture for virtual data integration is the mediator-wrapper architecture [666].
- *Materialized data integration*, where the (unified view of) data is materialized, for instance, in a data warehouse.

In this chapter, we will refer mainly to *virtual* data integration. When describing quality-driven query processing, we will essentially focus only on virtual DISs. In contrast, the concepts related to instance-level conflict resolution techniques can be applied in both virtual and materialized data integration scenarios.

In the following section, we will describe the major features of a virtual DIS. As already discussed in the introduction, data integration is the problem of combining data residing in different sources, providing the user with a unified view of this data, called *global schema*. A DIS is composed of three elements: (1) a *global schema*; (2) a set of *source schemas*, including schemas of all sources; and (3) a *mapping* between the global schema and the source schemas, which specifies the relationships between the concepts expressed in the global schema and the concepts in the source schemas.

Virtual data integration typically assumes a mediator-wrapper architecture, depicted in Fig. 10.2. Wrappers have the main task of providing a uniform data model to the mediator. The mediator has the task of decomposing the global query into queries on the schemas of data sources. Furthermore, the mediator must combine and reconcile the multiple answers coming from wrappers of local data sources.

Fig. 10.2 Mediator-wrapper
architecture

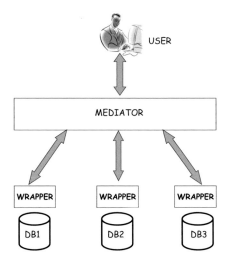

Two basic approaches have been proposed to specify the mapping [397]. The first approach, called *global-as-view* (GAV) mapping, requires the global schema to be expressed in terms of queries (or views) over the data sources. The second approach, called *local-as-view* (LAV) mapping, requires each data source to be expressed in terms of queries over the global schema. A third approach is called *global-local-as-view* (GLAV) mapping, and it is a mixture of the two; it combines the GAV and LAV approaches in such a way that queries over the sources are put into correspondence with queries over the global schema.

10.2.1   Query Processing

Irrespective whether the mapping is GAV or LAV (or GLAV), query processing in data integration requires a reformulation step: the query posed over the global schema has to be reformulated in terms of a set of queries over the sources. Nevertheless, the actual realization of query processing in DISs is strictly dependent on the method used for the specification of the mapping.

Query processing in GAV can be based on a simple *unfolding* strategy: given a query q over the alphabet of the global schema A_G, every element of A_G is substituted with the corresponding query over the sources, and the resulting query is then evaluated on data stored by local sources. Query processing in GAV is reduced to unfolding (and is therefore not complex), if there are no integrity constraints on the global schema. Conversely, if integrity constraints are present, data retrieved from the sources may or may not satisfy such constraints. If constraints are violated, the parts of data that do not violate the constraints may still be of interest, and the query answering process should allow their return as a result. Therefore, introducing integrity constraints in GAV implies dealing with issues related to query answering in the presence of incomplete information and to query answering in the presence of inconsistent information [105]. However, typically, query answering in GAV has the advantage of leading to simpler query answering mechanisms.

Conversely, in the LAV approach, it is easier to add or remove sources from the system, while generally requiring more sophisticated query answering techniques. Specifically, since in the LAV approach sources are modeled as views over the global schema, the problem of processing a query is called *view-based query processing*. There are two approaches to view-based query processing: view-based query rewriting and view-based query answering.

View-based query rewriting consists of reformulating the query into a possibly equivalent expression that refers only to the source structures. Once the rewriting of the query has been computed, it can be directly evaluated over the sources to obtain the answer to the query.

View-based query answering is more direct: besides the query and the mapping definitions, we are also given the extensions of the views over the global schema. The goal is to compute the set of tuples that is the answer set of the query in all databases consistent with the information on the views.

More details on query processing and on the definition of a formal framework for data integration are described in Sect. 10.5.1. In the following, we provide an example to show how the mapping can be specified and used for query processing. Let us consider a global schema consisting of the following relations:

- `Book(Title, Year, Author)`, representing books with their titles, their years of publication, and their authors
- `Award(Title, Prize)`, representing titles of and prizes won by the books
- `NonProfessional(Author)`, storing names of authors whose main profession is not writing books

Let us suppose there are two sources: S_1`(Title, Year, Author)`, storing information on books since 1930 by nonprofessional authors, and S_2`(Title, Prize)`, storing information on awards won by books since 1970. A global query could ask for "title and prize of books published after 1980," corresponding to the Datalog formulation (see [614]):

$$\text{Book}(\text{T};\ 1980;\ \text{A})\ \wedge\ \text{Award}(\text{T};\ \text{P}),$$

where the query is expressed as the conjunction of two atomic formulas with arguments that are variables (`T`, `A`, `P`) and constants (`1980`). A GAV mapping would define the global concepts in terms of the sources by means of the following rules:

- `Book(T; Y; A)` ← S_1`(T; Y; A)`
- `NonProfessional(A)` ← S_1`(T; Y; A)`
- `Award(T; P)` ← S_2`(T; P)`

The global query `Book(T; 1980; A)` ∧ `Award(T; P)` is processed by means of unfolding, i.e., by expanding the atoms according to their definitions until we come up with source relations. Therefore, in this case, the unfolding process leads to the following query, expressed in terms of source schemas:

$$S_1 (T;\ 1980;\ A)\ \wedge\ S_2 (T;\ P).$$

Conversely, in the case of an LAV mapping, rules define the concepts in the local source schemas in terms of the global schema as follows:

- S_1`(T; Y; A)` ← `Book(T; Y; A)` ∧ `NonProfessional(A)` ∧ `Y` ≥ `1930`
- S_2`(T; P)` ← `Book(T; Y; A)` ∧ `Award(T, P)` ∧ `Y` ≥ `1970`

The query on the global schema is processed by means of an inference mechanism aiming to reexpress the atoms of the global view in terms of atoms at the sources. Therefore, in this case, the inference process leads to the following query, expressed in terms of source schemas:

$$S_1 (T;\ 1980;\ A)\ \wedge\ S_2 (T;\ P).$$

This is the same query derived as a result of the unfolding process; but an inference procedure has been used instead.

10.3   Techniques for Quality-Driven Query Processing

In this section we provide an overview of several proposals to perform quality-driven query processing, which returns an answer to a global query, by explicitly taking into account the quality of data provided by local sources; however, several other techniques are present in the literature, e.g., [61, 62].

10.3.1   The QP-alg: Quality-Driven Query Planning

In this section, we describe the approach presented in [463], which we will refer to as QP-alg in the following. The mapping between local sources and the global schema is specified by means of *query correspondence assertions* (QCAs) that have the general form

$$MQ \leftarrow Si.vj \leftarrow WQ,$$

where (1) MQ is the mediator query and is a conjunctive query, (2) Si.vj denotes an arbitrary view vj on the source Si, and (3) WQ is the wrapper query. The mapping can be classified GLAV, as a query on the global schema is defined in terms of a query on the sources.

Three classes of data quality dimensions, called *information quality criteria* (IQ criteria), are defined:

- *Source-specific criteria*, defining the quality of a whole source. Examples of such criteria are *reputation* of the source, based on users' personal preferences, and *timeliness*, measured by the source update frequency.
- Quality correspondence assertions—specific criteria (*QCA-specific criteria*), defining the quality of specific QCAs. An example of such criteria is *price*, i.e., the price to be paid for the query.
- *User-query-specific criteria*, measuring the quality of the source with respect to the answer provided to a specific user query. An example of such criteria is *completeness*, based on the fullness of source relations.

Some IQ criteria metrics are predetermined, others are dynamically calculated, and the result is a set of IQ criteria vectors to be used to rank sources and plans. Note that, in a DBMS, given a query, query plans are constructed that are equivalent in terms of the query result provided; they are then ranked and selected on the basis of a cost model. Conversely, the plans built according to the QP-alg's approach produce different query results, though they are checked to be semantically correct. The phases of QP-alg are shown in Fig. 10.3.

The first phase consists of a pruning of the source space by filtering out low-quality sources on the basis of source-specific criteria. In order to classify sources on the basis of IQ criteria vectors, a multiattribute decision-making method is used, namely, the data envelopment analysis [119].

The second phase creates plans by exploiting the fact that QCAs are actually views over the mediator schema, and thus basic data integration results for query answering using views can be exploited [399].

The third phase first evaluates the quality of QCAs (step 1 in plan selection in Fig. 10.3). Specifically, QCA-specific criteria and user-query-specific criteria are calculated for each QCA. Then, the quality of a plan is evaluated (step 2 in plan selection in Fig. 10.3) by relying on a procedure similar to cost models for DBMSs. A tree is built for each plan, with QCAs as leaves and join operators as inner nodes. The IQ vector is recursively calculated for a node, starting from its children nodes. A set of "merge" functions for each quality criterion is defined in order to combine IQ vectors. As an example, the merge function for the price criterion is defined as the sum of both the right child and the left child of a given node, meaning that both queries must be made. In Fig. 10.4, an example is shown, detailing how the price of a plan P_i is computed.

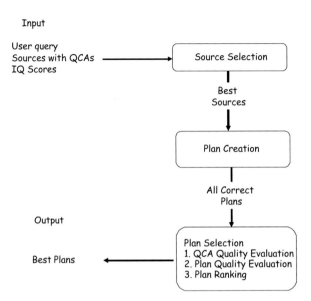

Fig. 10.3 Phases of the QP-alg approach

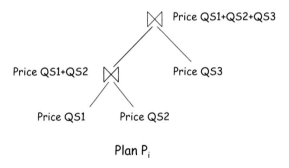

Fig. 10.4 Example of price computation for the plan P_i

Then, plan ranking is performed by means of the simple additive weighting (SAW) method (step 3 in plan selection in Fig. 10.3). Specifically, the final IQ score for a plan is computed as the weighted sum of scaled criteria, where weights represent the "importance" of each criterion to the user. Finally, the best plans, according to the performed ranking, are returned.

10.3.2   DaQuinCIS Query Processing

The DaQuinCIS system, described in [548], is a framework for dealing with data quality in cooperative information systems. A module of the system, the *data quality broker*, is a DIS. In this section we focus on the proposed query answering process, which is one of the functionalities of the data quality broker.

The main idea of the DaQuinCIS approach is to make cooperating organizations export not only data that they intend to exchange with other organizations but also metadata that characterize their quality level. To this extent, a specific semistructured data model is proposed, called D^2Q. The model is extensively described in Chap. 6. On the basis of such quality characterization of exported data, user queries are processed so that the "best quality" answer is returned as a result.

Queries on the global schema are processed according to the GAV approach by unfolding, i.e., by replacing each atom of the original query with the corresponding view on local data sources. When defining the mapping between concepts of the global schema and concepts of the local schemas, while the extension of global-level concepts can be retrieved by multiple sources, the mapping is actually defined to retrieve the union of local source extensions. Such a mapping definition stems directly from the assumption that the same concept can have different extensions at a local source level due to data quality errors. Therefore, when retrieving data, they can be compared and a best quality copy can be either selected or constructed.

More specifically, query processing in DaQuinCIS is performed by the following sequence of steps:

1. *Query unfolding.* A global query $\mathcal{Q}$ is unfolded according to a static mapping that defines each concept of the global schema in terms of the local sources; this mapping is defined in order to retrieve all copies of the same data that are available, i.e., exported by the cooperating organizations according to the D^2Q model. Therefore, the query $\mathcal{Q}$ is decomposed into $\mathcal{Q}_1, \ldots, \mathcal{Q}_k$ queries to be posed over local sources. Such queries are then executed to return a set of results $\mathcal{R}_1, \ldots, \mathcal{R}_k$ (see Fig. 10.5).
2. *Extensional checking.* In this step, a record matching algorithm is run on the set $\mathcal{R}_1 \cup \mathcal{R}_2 \cup \cdots \cup \mathcal{R}_k$. The result of the running of the record matching algorithm is the construction of a set of clusters composed by records referring to the same real-world objects $\mathcal{C}_1, \ldots, \mathcal{C}_z$ (see Fig. 10.5, middle).
3. *Result building.* The result to be returned is built by relying on a *best quality default semantics.* For each cluster, a best quality representative is either selected or constructed. Each record in the cluster is composed of couples in which a quality value q is associated with each field value f. The best quality record for each cluster is selected as the record having the best quality values in all fields, if such a record exists. Otherwise, a best quality record is constructed by composing the fields that have the highest quality from records within the same cluster. Once representatives for each cluster have been selected, the result $\mathcal{R}$ is constructed as the union of all cluster representatives (see Fig. 10.5, right). Each quality value q is a vector of quality values corresponding to the different quality dimensions. For instance, q can include values for accuracy, completeness, consistency, and currency. These dimensions have potentially different scales; therefore, a scaling step is needed. Once scaled, those vectors need to be ranked. Therefore a ranking

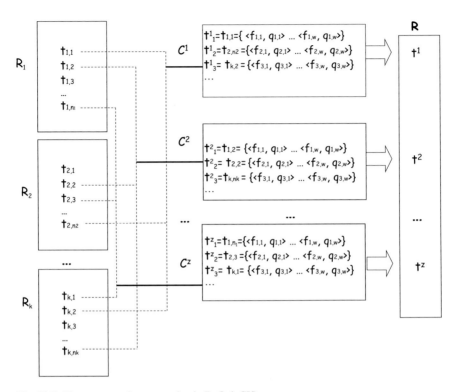

Fig. 10.5 The query result construction in DaQuinCIS

method must also be applied. Both scaling and ranking problems have well-known solutions, e.g., multiattribute decision-making methods, like AHP [535].

10.3.3 Fusionplex Query Processing

Fusionplex [454] models a DIS by (1) a relational global schema D; (2) a set of relational local sources (D_i, d_i), where d_i is the instance of the local schema D_i; and (3) a set of schema mappings (D, D_i). The mapping definition is GLAV, i.e., views on the global schema are put in correspondence with views on schema of the local sources. In Fusionplex, it is assumed that the *schema consistency assumption* holds, meaning that there are no modeling errors at the local sources, but only modeling differences. Instead, it is assumed that the *instance inconsistency assumption* holds, meaning that the same instance of the real world can be represented differently in the various local sources due to errors. In order to deal with such instance-level inconsistencies, Fusionplex introduces a set of metadata, called *features*, about the sources to be integrated. As better detailed in Sect. 10.4.2.3, source features include time stamp, availability, and accuracy. The data integration framework definition presented above is extended by including features into the definition of schema mappings. Specifically, the mappings are triples consisting of a global schema view D, a local schema view D_i, and, in addition, the features associated with the local view. Fusionplex includes an extension of the relational algebra that takes into account the association of a set of features $F = \{F_1 \ldots F_n\}$ with source relations. For instance, the extended cartesian product concatenates the database values of the participating relations, but fuses their feature values. The fusion method depends on the particular feature. Therefore, the availability value of the new tuple is the product of the availability values of the input tuples; the time stamp is the minimum of the input time stamps; and so on. In this setting, query processing is performed in several steps:

1. Given a query Q, the set of *contributing views* is identified. First, the sets of attributes of the query and each contributing view are intersected. If the intersection is empty, the contributing view is not relevant. Next, the selection predicates of the query and the contributing view are joined. If the resulting predicate is true, then the contributing view is considered relevant to the query.
2. Once relevant contributing views are identified, *query fragments* are derived as the unit of information suitable for populating the answer to the query. A query fragment results from the removal from the contributing view of all tuples and attributes that are not requested in the query and from the addition of null values for the query attributes that are missing from the contributing view. As an example, in Fig. 10.6, two contributing views, C_1 and C_2, and the corresponding query fragments, QF_1 and QF_2, are shown.
3. From each relevant contributing view, a single query fragment is constructed, where some of these fragments may be empty. The union of all nonempty query fragments is termed a *polyinstance* of the query. Intuitively, a polyinstance includes all the information derived from the data sources in response to a user query.

In order to provide a unique answer to the query Q for the user, instance-level conflicts present in the polyinstance must be solved. Once polyinstances have been constructed, a strategy for conflict detection and resolution is applied, as described in Sect. 10.4.2.3.

Fig. 10.6 Example of query fragment construction from contributing views

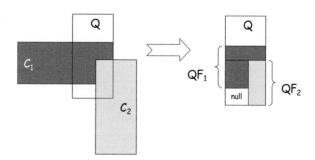

Techniques	Quality Metadata	Granularity of Quality Characterization	Type of Mapping	Quality Algebra Support
QP-alg	YES	Source, Query Correspondences Assertions, User Queries	GLAV	Preliminary
DaQuinCIS Query Processing	YES	Each data element of a semistructured data model	GAV	No
FusionPlex Query Processing	YES	Source	GLAV	Preliminary

Fig. 10.7   Comparison of quality-driven query processing techniques

10.3.4   Comparison of Quality-Driven Query Processing Techniques

In Fig. 10.7, a comparison of the query processing techniques described is shown. The techniques are compared according to the following features:

- *Quality metadata*, showing that each technique is based on a set of metadata that support the query processing activity.
- *Granularity of the quality model* that represents data elements quality metadata can be associated with. QP-alg associates quality metadata not only with sources but also with qQCAs and user queries. DaQuinCIS exploits the flexibility of a semistructured data model for quality association at various granularity levels. Fusionplex allows association only at a source level.
- *Type of mapping*, showing that both QP-alg and Fusionplex have a GLAV approach to the mapping definition, while DaQuinCIS has a GAV approach.
- *Support to quality algebra*, meaning that quality values associated with local source data need to be "combined" by means of specific algebraic operators. As described in Chap. 7, Sect. 7.3, there are some research proposals in this direction, but it is still an open problem. Some attempts toward the algebraic manipulation of quality values are present in the merge functions of QP-alg and in the extension of the relational operators of Fusionplex.

10.4   Instance-Level Conflict Resolution

Instance-level conflict resolution is a major activity in DISs. No DIS can return answers to user queries if these types of conflicts are not solved. As data integration typically deals with heterogeneous and autonomous sources, instance-level conflicts are very common and frequent. Unfortunately, most of the existing data integration solutions have simplifying assumptions regarding conflicts on data values.

In this section, after a classification of these conflicts (Sect. 10.4.1), we describe some of the existing proposals of instance-level conflict resolution techniques (Sect. 10.4.2), and we conclude with a comparison between techniques (Sect. 10.4.3).

10.4.1 Classification of Instance-Level Conflicts

As already mentioned in Sect. 10.1, in order to integrate data coming from distinct data sources, problems caused by technological, schema, and instance-level heterogeneities need to be solved. In the following section, we briefly describe conflict originating from schema heterogeneities, called *schema-level conflicts*, while the latter part is devoted to the description of conflicts due to instance-level heterogeneities, called *instance-level conflicts*.

Schema-level conflicts have been extensively studied (see [366]) and include:

- *Heterogeneity conflicts*, occurring when different data models are used.
- *Semantic conflicts*, regarding the relationship between model element extensions. For instance, a `Person` entity may have different extensions in different sources that may be disjoint, partially overlapping, including one into another, or completely overlapping.
- *Description conflicts*, concerning the description of concepts with different attributes. These conflicts include different formats, different attribute types, and different scaling. These conflicts are on the boundary between schema-level conflicts and instance-level conflicts; for instance, in [224], such conflicts are classified as data value conflicts. We prefer to consider description conflicts at a schema-level because they are actually caused by different design choices of data schemas, though such choices certainly have an impact on values to be integrated.
- *Structural conflicts*, regarding different design choices within the same model. For instance, such conflicts may occur if one source represents an `Address` as an entity and another source represents it as an attribute.

In contrast with schema-level conflicts, instance-level conflicts have received much less attention, and only recently has the importance of these types of conflicts increased, due to the primary role they play in the data integration processes. Instance-level conflicts are due to poor quality of data; they occur because of errors in the data collection process or the data entry process or because sources are not updated.

According to the granularity of the model element, instance-level conflicts can be distinguished into *attribute conflicts* and *key conflicts*, also called *entity* or *tuple conflicts*. Some works, e.g., [405], also consider *relationship conflicts* that are particularly meaningful at a conceptual level. In the following, we will focus on attribute and key conflicts, as they are the principal conflict types involved in data integration processes.

Let us consider two relational tables, $S_1(A_1, \ldots, A_k, A_{k+1}, \ldots, A_n)$ and $S_2(B_1, \ldots, B_k, B_{k+1}, \ldots, B_m)$, where $A_1 = B_1 \ldots A_k = B_k$. Let the same real-world entity be represented by the tuple t_1 in S_1 and by the tuple t_2 in S_2, and let $A_i = B_i$; the following conflicts can be defined:

- An *attribute conflict* occurs iff

$$t_1.A_i \neq t_2.B_i.$$

- Let us further suppose that A_i is a primary key for S_1 and B_i is a primary key for S_2. A *key conflict* occurs iff

$$t_1.A_i \neq t_2.B_i \text{ and } t_1.A_j = t_2.B_j,$$

for all j ranging from 1 to k, and $i \neq j$.

In Fig. 10.8, several examples of both attribute and key conflicts are shown. In the figure, two relations, `EmployeeS1` and `EmployeeS2`, represent information about employees of a company. Notice that we assume there is no schema-level conflict, i.e., the two relations have exactly the same attributes and the same extension. Nevertheless, they present instance-level conflicts. Two attribute value conflicts are shown, concerning the `Salary` of the employee `arpa78` and the `Surname` of the employee `ghjk09` in the two relations. A key-level conflict is also shown between the employee `Marianne Collins`, as identified in the relation `EmployeeS1` and as identified in relation `EmployeeS2`, assuming that the two tuples represent the same real-world object.

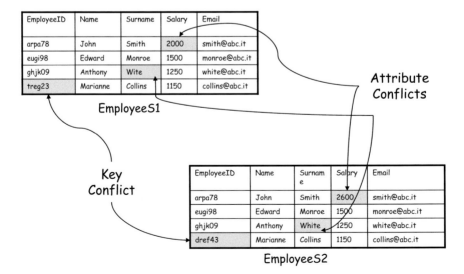

Fig. 10.8 An example of key- and attribute-level conflicts

Instance-level conflicts can be present in both virtual and materialized integration. In virtual data integration, a theoretical formulation of the problem has been proposed. Specifically, the cited key and attribute conflicts have been formally specified as a violation of integrity constraints expressed over the global schema representing the integrated view. More details on the theoretical perspective on inconsistencies in data integration are provided in Sect. 10.5.2.

In the next section, we will describe several techniques proposed in order to solve instance-level conflicts.

10.4.2 Overview of Techniques

Techniques that deal with instance-level conflicts can be applied in two different phases of the life cycle of a DIS, namely, at *design time* and at *query time*. In both cases, the actual conflicts occur at query time; however, the design time approaches decide the strategy to follow for fixing conflicts before queries are processed, i.e., at the design stage of the DIS. The techniques operating at query time incorporate the specification of the strategy to follow within query formulation.

A proposal for solving conflicts at design time can be found in [167]. The main idea is to resolve attribute conflicts by means of aggregation functions to be specified for each attribute that may involve conflicts during query execution time.

Design time techniques have a major optimization problem, as outlined in [684]. Let us consider the example shown in Fig. 10.8, and suppose that it is specified at design time, for the `Salary` attribute, that in the case of conflicts, the minimum salary must be chosen. Given a global schema, `Employee(EmployeeID, Name, Surname, Salary, Email)`, let us consider the following query:

```
SELECT  EmployeeID, Email
FROM    Employee
WHERE   Salary < 2000
```

Since the `Salary` attribute is involved in the query, all employees must be retrieved in order to compute the minimum salary, not only employees with `Salary < 2000`, even if no conflicts on salary occur. Therefore, conflict resolution at design time may be very inefficient.

Query time conflict resolution techniques have been proposed to overcome such performance inefficiencies. Furthermore, query time techniques are characterized by greater flexibility, since, as we will see, they allow those who formulate the query to indicate a specific strategy to adopt for conflict resolution. Given a user query posed on the global schema, query time techniques deal with key and/or attribute conflicts that may occur on the data retrieved as results.

Key conflicts require the application of object identification techniques, described in detail in Chaps. 8 and 9. With reference to the example shown in Fig. 10.8, object identification techniques will match the tuple `treg23` from `EmployeeS1` with the tuple `dref43` from `EmployeeS2` by comparing the attribute values of the two tuples in order to determine whether the "Marianne Collins" represented in the two sources is the same person. After a positive matching decision, the tuples referring to "Marianne Collins" will be considered a single tuple, and a unique key will be chosen to identify the tuple, thereby solving the key conflict. If the matching decision is negative, no key conflict occurs.

With respect to attribute conflicts, several techniques for solving them have been proposed:

- SQL-based conflict resolution [462]
- Aurora [684]
- Fusionplex [454]
- DaQuinCIS [549]
- FraSQL-based conflict resolution [552]
- OO_{RA} [405]

In the following we describe the details of such techniques; however, several other proposals are present in the literature, including [250, 489]. Before providing the detailed description, we illustrate which are the "abstract" steps to be followed for solving attribute-level conflicts.

Let us consider again the example in Fig. 10.8, and let us suppose the following query is formulated over the global schema `Employee(EmployeeID, Name, Surname, Salary, Email)`:

```
SELECT  Salary
FROM    Employee
WHERE   Name = "John" AND Surname = "Smith"
```

In order to return a result to this type of query, the attribute conflict between the two values for John Smith's salary stored in the relations `EmployeeS1` and `EmployeeS2` must be solved.

A solution to this problem is to *declaratively* specify how to deal with such conflicts. A declarative specification consists of:

- A set of conflict resolution functions that, on the basis of the specific attributes involved in the conflict, can select the most appropriate value
- A set of strategies to deal with conflicts, corresponding to different tolerance degrees
- A query model that can take into account possible conflicts directly, i.e., with specific extensions, such as ad hoc functions dealing with conflicts, or indirectly, i.e., without specific extensions

A *resolution function* takes two (or more) conflicting values of an attribute as input and outputs, a value that must be returned as the result to the posed query. Common resolution functions are `MIN` and `MAX`. To these, resolution functions

Function	Attribute Type	Description
COUNT	any	Counts number of conflicting values
MIN	any	Minimum value
MAX	any	Maximum value
RANDOM	any	Random non null value
CHOOSE(Source)	any	Chooses most reliable source for the particular attribute
MAXIQ	any	Value of highest information quality
GROUP	any	Groups all conflicting values
SUM	numerical	Sums all values
MEDIAN	numerical	Median value, namely having the same number of higher and lower values
AVG	numerical	Arithmetic mean of all values
VAR	numerical	Variance of values
STDDEV	numerical	Standard Deviation of values
SHORTEST	non-numerical	Minimum length value, ignoring spaces
LONGEST	non-numerical	Maximum length value, ignoring spaces
CONCAT	non-numerical	Concatenation of values
ANNCONCAT	non-numerical	Annotated concatenation of values, whose purpose is to specify the source, before the actual returned value

Fig. 10.9 Resolution functions as proposed in [462]

that are specific to some attribute types can be added. For instance, for numerical attribute types, SUM and AVG can be used. For nonnumerical attributes, further resolution functions can be identified, such as CONCAT. In [462], a resolution function MAXIQ is proposed. Assuming the presence of a data quality model that associates quality values to model elements (e.g., attributes), the resolution function MAXIQ returns the value with the highest quality. In Fig. 10.9, conflict resolution functions are summarized, as proposed in [462]. Some functions are the usual aggregation functions; others serve the specific purpose of resolving conflicts.

The *tolerance strategies* allow the user to define the degree of conflict permitted. For example, it is possible to specify that on a specific attribute no conflicts are admitted. This means that all values returned by the sources on that attribute must be aligned. As another example, it may be possible to specify that in the case of conflicts, a randomly chosen value among the conflicting ones be proposed as the result. As another tolerance strategy, a threshold value may be specified for distinguishing tolerable conflicts from intolerable ones. For instance, a conflict on two values for the Name attribute such as Michael and Maichael, which have a reciprocal edit distance of one character, can be tolerated since it is very easy to transform Maichael into Michael, by deleting simply one character. In contrast, for a numerical attribute like Salary, even a one-digit distance may be intolerable.

With respect to the *query model*, it is possible to appropriately use SQL to specify how to solve conflicts [462] or to use ad hoc extensions such as the ones proposed in [405, 684].

The next sections will describe several techniques for conflict resolution that instantiate the abstract steps presented.

10.4.2.1   SQL-Based Conflict Resolution

The approach proposes formulating queries in SQL, exploiting the capabilities of current database systems. Three possible strategies are discussed, based on three SQL operations:

- *Group*, whereby using the `Group by` SQL statement, a query is specified that groups tuples on the basis of one or more group attributes. Then, an aggregated function is specified to select conflicting values appropriately. For instance,

```
SELECT    EmployeeId, min(Salary)
FROM      Employee
GROUP BY EmployeeId
```

The main disadvantage of this approach is that only the aggregation functions supported by SQL can be used.

- *Join*, which considers the union of two sources and partitions it into three sets: the intersection of the two sources, the tuples only in the first source, and the tuples only in the second source. Then, the merging query is expressed on each of these parts, and finally, the results are merged. The first query is expressed on the intersection:

```
SELECT EmployeeID, min(Employee1.Salary,
Employee2.Salary)
FROM    Employee1, Employee2
WHERE   Employee1.EmployeeId = Employee2.EmployeeId
```

This query has the advantage that the resolution is no longer an aggregate function, but a scalar one. This extends the possibility of using user-defined functions, thereby enlarging the spectrum of possible resolution functions while continuing to be compliant with most database systems that allow user-defined scalar functions. The following query selects the tuples of the first source that are not in the second:

```
SELECT EmployeeId, Price
FROM    Employee1
WHERE   Employee1.EmployeeId NOT IN
        (SELECT EmployeeID
         FROM Employee2)
```

The query to select the tuples of the second source that are not in the first source is similar to the above one. The query to merge is simply the combination of the results of all queries through the `UNION` operator. The main disadvantage of this approach is the complexity of the queries, because the number of partitions increases exponentially with the number of sources. The length and complexity of queries may become prohibitive.

- *Nested Join*, an improvement over the previous method, which can be performed when resolution functions are associative. Given *N* sources to be merged, the idea is to first merge two, then merge this with a third, and so on. With this approach, queries grow linearly, but still remain complex.

10.4.2.2   Aurora

Aurora is a mediation-based DIS. The approach proposes a conflict-tolerant query model for conflict resolution at a desired degree. The conflict-tolerant query model has the following features:

- Two operators, for attribute conflict resolution, called *resolve attribute-level conflict* (RAC), and for tuple conflict resolution, called *resolve tuple-level conflict* (RTC). The operators take a resolution function as parameter. For example, consider the global population of the relation Employee, shown in Fig. 10.10, which represents the global instance resulting from the integration of the two relations EmployeeS1 and EmployeeS2 shown in Fig. 10.8. An example of how the operator RAC works is reported in Fig. 10.11, where the specified resolution functions are MIN for Salary, LONGEST for Surname, and ANY for EmployeeID. An example for the RTC operator is shown in Fig. 10.12, where the resolution function is ANY, and the tuple conflicts are solved choosing tuple dref43.
- Three strategies for conflict resolution, namely, HighConfidence, RandomEvidence, and PossibleAtAll. These strategies allow the user to define the degree of conflicts permitted and are used in conjunction with the previously described operators when formulating queries. HighConfidence allows us to specify that no conflicts on a specific attribute are admitted. This means that all values returned by the sources on that attribute must be aligned. RandomEvidence specifies that in the case of conflicts, a runtime function

TupleID	EmployeeID	Name	Surname	Salary	Email
t_1	arpa78	John	Smith	2000	smith@abc.it
t_2	eugi98	Edward	Monroe	1500	monroe@abc.it
t_3	ghjk09	Anthony	Wite	1250	white@abc.it
t_4	treg23	Marianne	Collins	1150	collins@abc.it
t_5	arpa78	John	Smith	2600	smith@abc.it
t_6	eugi98	Edward	Monroe	1500	monroe@abc.it
t_7	ghjk09	Anthony	White	1250	white@abc.it
t_8	dref43	Marianne	Collins	1150	collins@abc.it

Fig. 10.10 Instance of the global relation Employee

TupleID	EmployeeID	Name	Surname	Salary	Email
t_1	arpa78	John	Smith	2000	smith@abc.it
t_2	eugi98	Edward	Monroe	1500	monroe@abc.it
t_3	ghjk09	Anthony	White	1250	white@abc.it
t_4	treg23	Marianne	Collins	1150	collins@abc.it

RAC(Employee,Salary(MIN), Surname(Longest), EmployeeID(Any))

Fig. 10.11 Resolution of attribute conflicts

TupleID	EmployeeID	Name	Surname	Salary	Email
t_1	arpa78	John	Smith	2600	smith@abc.it
t_2	eugi98	Edward	Monroe	1500	monroe@abc.it
t_3	ghjk09	Anthony	Wite	1250	white@abc.it
t_4	dref43	Marianne	Collins	1150	collins@abc.it

RTC(Employee,ANY)

Fig. 10.12 Resolution of tuple conflicts

has to select a value to be returned. `PossibleAtAll` returns all values that correctly answer the query, independently of conflicts.

The conflict-tolerant query model is built on tuple-level conflicts only, but the user is allowed to specify attribute-level conflict resolution. Some examples of conflict-tolerant queries are as follows:

- Q1: `SELECT  EmployeeID, Name (ANY), Salary[MIN]`
       `FROM    Employee`
       `WHERE   Salary>1800`
       `WITH    HighConfidence`
- Q2: `SELECT  [ANY]EmployeeID, Name, Salary`
       `FROM    Employee`
       `WHERE   Salary>1800`
       `WITH    RandomEvidence`

Both queries select employees with `Salary` greater than 1800 euros. If there is a conflict, Q1 selects employees whose `Salary` value is greater than 1800 in all sources. Therefore, based on Fig. 10.10, the tuples t_1 and t_5 are selected. Then, applying the resolution function `MIN` on `Salary`, the returned tuple will have the `Salary` value of t_1, namely, 2000. Q2 selects a random `Salary` value, and if it is greater than 1800, it is returned as a result. Then, the `ANY` tuple resolution function is applied as specified in the selection clause. Based on Fig. 10.10, a random value between the `Salary` values of t_1 and t_5 is returned.

10.4.2.3 Fusionplex and DaQuinCIS

The two approaches to conflict resolution adopted in the Fusionplex and DaQuinCIS systems are similar. They both resolve attribute conflicts on the basis of metadata associated with data of local sources.

Fusionplex proposes the following metadata, called *features*:

- *Time stamp*, representing the time the source was validated in the system
- *Cost*, which can be transmission time over the network, or money to be paid for information, or both
- *Accuracy*, evaluated according to a probabilistic approach
- *Availability*, probability that the information is randomly available
- *Clearance*, corresponding to the clearance level needed to access the information

In Fusionplex, the features are associated with sources as a whole, with the restrictive assumption that data in sources are homogeneous with respect to a specific feature.

DaQuinCIS proposes the following metadata, referred to as *dimensions*:

- *Accuracy*, concerning the syntactical accuracy of data values
- *Currency*, considering the degree of up-to-dateness of values
- *Consistency*, measuring intrasource integrity constraints
- *Completeness*, counting the number of null values

The D^2Q data model, described in detail in Chap. 6, is semistructured and permits the association of metadata with data elements of different granularity and, therefore, with single values, as well as with attributes and all other model elements.

An example of the extended SQL statements that can be defined in Fusionplex is

```
SELECT  EmployeeID, Salary
FROM    EmployeeS1, EmployeeS2
WHERE   EmployeeS1.EmployeeID=EmployeeS2.EmployeeID
USING   cost>0.6
WITH    timestamp as 0.5
```

Considering an XML-based representation of the two relations `EmployeeS1` and `EmployeeS2`, an example of a DaQuinCIS query, expressed in XQuery [82], is

```
FOR     $i in input()//EmployeeS1
FOR     $j in input()//EmployeeS2
WHERE   ($i/EmployeeID=$j/EmployeeID) and
        quality($i/Salary)>0.7 and quality
        ($j/salary)>0.7
RETURN  ($i/Name,$i/Salary)
```

As described, attribute conflict resolution is based on metadata in both Fusion-plex and DaQuinCIS. Also, both systems have a step in which, upon issuing a user query, all the significant instances answering the query are collected and grouped into clusters of different copies of the same objects. Then, in both systems, a resolution policy is applied in order to produce selected tuples to be included in the result.

The two systems differ in the process for building the final result. In Fusionplex, as described in Sect. 10.3.3, the phase in which results are collected from local sources terminates with the construction of a polyinstance, upon which a conflict resolution strategy is applied. Conflict resolution is performed in two phases: in the first phase, a utility function is used to take user preferences into account, while in the second phase, the actual fusion is performed.

With reference to the first phase, users can specify the importance they assign to each feature. Then, an overall utility function consisting of the weighted sum of the feature values of a source is calculated, and a first pruning of sources is done on the basis of a fixed utility threshold.

With respect to the second phase, resolution of inconsistencies can be done either on the basis of their features, called *feature-based resolution*, or on the basis of the data, called *content-based resolution*.

A resolution policy consists of the sequential selection of:

- *Elimination functions*, which can be feature based or selection based. Examples of elimination functions are MIN and MAX; MAX(timestamp) and MIN(cost) are examples of feature-based elimination functions, while MAX(Salary) is an example of a content-based elimination function.
- *Fusion functions*. Fusion functions are always content based; examples are ANY and AVERAGE.

Note that the resolution policy is completely specified by users according to their specific requirements. Moreover, Fusionplex admits three tolerance levels: no reso-lution, pruning of polytuples, and selective attribute resolution. The no resolution policy allows an answer with conflicts to be returned to the user. The pruning of polytuple policy removes tuples that either do not satisfy the feature selection predicate or are below the utility threshold. The selective attribute resolution forces resolution on some attributes only.

In the DaQuinCIS system, the reconciled result is produced according to the process described in Sect. 10.3.2, and it is completely based on quality values associated with data on the basis of the D^2Q model.

10.4.2.4 FraSQL-Based Conflict Resolution

The approach proposes an extension of a multidatabase query language, called *FraSQL*, which provides operations for transformation and integration of hetero-geneous data. The main idea is to use grouping for duplicate elimination and aggregation for conflict resolution. For conflict resolution, FraSQL provides both *user-defined aggregation* and *user-defined grouping*. User-defined aggregation is useful for conflict resolution, allowing for the selection of a representative value from a group of values corresponding to the same real-world object. The grouping of values is performed by means of user-defined grouping. User-defined grouping can be of two types: (1) *context-free* and (2) *context aware*. Context-free grouping is the usual approach, as in SQL standards, with, in addition, the possibility of using external functions. The following query shows the usage of a context-free user-defined grouping [552]:

```
SELECT   avg (Temperature),rc
FROM     Weather
GROUP BY regionCode(Longitude,Latitude) AS rc
```

where `regionCode` is an external function that computes the region from its geographical position.

Context-aware grouping is proposed in order to overcome some limitations of the current SQL standardized group by operator. Indeed, SQL standardized group by operator works one tuple at a time, not considering possible relationships between grouping tuples. Therefore, in order to have a more flexible grouping, similarity criteria can be introduced that split or merge the group conveniently. As an example, consider the query:

```
SELECT EmployeeID,Salary
FROM    EmployeeS1
GROUP   maximumDifference(Salary,diff=150)
BY CONTEXT
```

The query considers the relation EmployeeS1 shown in Fig. 10.8 and groups the tuples as shown in Fig. 10.13, generating three sets corresponding to tuples for which the `Salary` values differ by at most 150.

Fig. 10.13 Result of the context-aware query as applied to the table EmployeeS1 of Fig. 10.8

EmployeeID	Salary
arpa78	2000

EmployeeID	Salary
eugi98	1500

EmployeeID	Salary
ghjk09	1250
treg23	1150

10.4.2.5   OO$_{RA}$

Though in the following we focus only on attribute-level conflicts, the model also considers key conflicts and relationship conflicts (see [405] for more details on these two conflict types). The approach distinguishes two types of attribute conflicts, namely, *tolerable conflicts*, which can be automatically solved, and *intolerable conflicts*, which have to be solved with human intervention. The two types of conflicts are separated by means of a threshold. An extended object-oriented data model, called OO$_{RA}$, is proposed to handle attribute-level conflicts. The main features of the model with respect to attribute conflict resolution are:

- The possibility of specifying thresholds and resolution functions for attribute-level conflict resolution
- The representation of original and resolved attribute values

With respect to the threshold specification and resolution functions, the following three different combinations are considered for a given attribute: (i) threshold predicate and resolution function both unspecified, (ii) specified threshold predicate and unspecified resolution function, and (iii) threshold predicate and resolution function both specified. In case (i), no conflict is tolerated, so if a conflict arises, the resolved attribute value is null. In case (ii), a conflict can arise and can be acceptable, but if it arises, the returned value is NULL. In case (iii), there can be tolerable conflicts, and the returned value is computed by the resolution function.

With respect to conflicting values representation, the OO$_{RA}$ approach for every non-identifier attribute represents a triple: original value, resolved value, and conflict type. Conflict type is NULL if there is no conflict, RESOLVABLE if there is an intolerable conflict, and ACCEPTABLE if there is a tolerable conflict. For example, let us consider the following threshold predicate and resolution function applied to the global relation described in Fig. 10.10:

```
DEFINE Salary.threshold@EMPLOYEE(s1,s2) = (abs(s1-s2)
<=1000)
DEFINE Salary.resolution@EMPLOYEE(s1,s2) = MIN(s1,s2)
```

In this case, the conflict between t_1 and t_5 is tolerable, as the differences between the two values for salary are within the specified threshold. The conflict is solved by choosing the value for salary present in tuple t_1.

As another example, let us consider the following threshold predicate and resolution function, also applied to the relation in Fig. 10.10:

```
DEFINE Surname.threshold@EMPLOYEE(s1,s2)
= (editDistance(s1,s2)<=1)
DEFINE Surname.resolution@EMPLOYEE(s1,s2)
= LONGEST(s1,s2)
```

Still, the conflict between t_3 and t_7 is tolerable, and the value for Surname stored by tuple t_7 is returned as a result. In contrast, supposing that the Surname value for t_3 were `Wie` and the edit distance between t_3.`Salary` and t_7.`Salary` greater than 1, an intolerable conflict would have occurred.

10.4.3   Comparison of Instance-Level Conflict Resolution Techniques

In Fig. 10.14, the different declarative techniques for the resolution of inconsistencies are compared with respect to permitted tolerance strategies and query models. Reviewing the tolerance strategies column, Aurora, Fusionplex, and OO_{RA} propose a degree of flexibility that can be selected once conflicts occur. We recall that the three degrees of flexibility proposed by Aurora are (1) high confidence, meaning that no conflict is tolerated; (2) random evidence, meaning that in the case of conflicts, a runtime function will select the value to be returned; and (3) possible at all, meaning that all values that correctly answer the query must be returned. Similar to Aurora, Fusionplex admits three tolerance levels: no resolution, pruning of polytuples, and selective attribute resolution. The no resolution policy corresponds to PossibleAtAll; in both approaches, the answer with conflicts is returned to the user. The pruning of polytuple policy, which removes tuples not satisfying the feature selection predicate or the utility threshold, is a more specific case of the RandomEvidence policy and it shares the threshold concept with OO_{RA}. The selective attribute resolution involves leaving some (or all) attributes unresolved; it is a specific case of the no resolution policy with higher granularity.

Reviewing the query model column, we see that the SQL-based conflict resolution can rely on SQL. However, it has inefficiencies due to the fact that resolution functions were not considered for the native SQL. Therefore, computing aggregation and expressing SQL statements for them can become very onerous. Both DaQuinCIS and OO_{RA} deal with models that are different from the relational model, namely, with the XML data model and the object-oriented data model, respectively.

Techniques	Tolerance Strategies	Query Model
SQL-Based Conflict Resolution	NO	SQL
Aurora	High Confidence, RandomEvidence, PossibleAtAll	Ad-hoc Conflict Tolerant Query Model
Fusionplex	No resolution strategy, selective attribute resolution	Extended SQL
DaQuinCIS	NO	Extended XML
FraQL-Based Conflict Resolution	NO	Ad-hoc FraQL
OO_{RA}	Thresholds for tolerable and intolerable conflicts	Ad hoc Object Oriented Extension (OO_{RA})

Fig. 10.14 Conflict resolution techniques

10.5   Inconsistencies in Data Integration: A Theoretical Perspective

In this section, we first provide several basic definitions that formally specify a DIS (Sect. 10.5.1). Then, we discuss an example of what inconsistency means on the basis of such formal specifications and give some hints on specific semantics that have been defined for dealing with inconsistencies (Sect. 10.5.2).

10.5.1   A Formal Framework for Data Integration

A *DIS* [397] can be formally defined as a triple (G, S, M) where:

- G is the global schema, expressed in a language L_G over an alphabet A_G.
- S is the source schema,[1] expressed in a language L_S over an alphabet A_S.
- M is the mapping between G and S, constituted by a set of assertions of the forms

$$q_S \rightsquigarrow q_G \text{ and}$$

$$q_G \rightsquigarrow q_S,$$

where q_G and q_S are two queries of the same arity, respectively, over the global schema G and the source schema S. Queries q_S are expressed in a query language $L_{M,S}$ over the alphabet A_S, and queries q_G are expressed in a query language $L_{M,G}$ over the alphabet A_G.

In Sect. 10.2, we provided some examples on how mapping assertions can be specified.

Given a DIS $I = (G, S, M)$, a *semantics* to it can be assigned by specifying the information content of the global schema G. Let D be a source database for I, i.e., a (set of) database that conforms to the source schema S and satisfies all constraints in S. On the basis of D, we can define the information content of the global schema G. We call *global database* for I any database for G. A global database B is said to be *legal with respect to* D if:

- B is legal with respect to G, i.e., B satisfies all the constraints of G.
- B satisfies the mapping M with respect to D.

An important notion to be introduced is that of *certain answers*. Given a source database D for I, the answer $q_{I,D}$ to a query q in I with respect to D is the set of

---

[1]The source schema in [397] is a collective name that indicates the *set* of source schemas, as introduced in Sect. 10.2.

tuples t of objects such that t ∈ q_B for every global database B that is legal for I with respect to D.

The meaning of the sentence "B satisfies the mapping M with respect to D" depends on how to interpret the assertions.

In the LAV case, where mapping assertions have the form $s \rightsquigarrow q_G$, the following cases have been identified:

- *Sound views.* When a source s is *sound*, its extension provides any subset of the tuples satisfying the corresponding view q_G.
- *Complete views.* When a source s is *complete*, its extension provides any superset of the tuples satisfying the corresponding view.
- *Exact views.* When a source s is *exact*, its extension is exactly the set of tuples of objects satisfying the corresponding view.

In the GAV case, a similar interpretation of mapping assertions can be given, and hence, sound, complete, and exact views can correspondingly be defined. In the following section, we see the role that sound, complete, and exact views can play when dealing with inconsistent answers.

10.5.2 The Problem of Inconsistency

In a DIS, beyond the inconsistency problems that are local to sources, inconsistency may arise due to integrity constraints that are specified on the global schema.

Integrity constraints on the global schema represent a fundamental knowledge, as they actually allow one to capture the semantics of the reality. Sources in a DIS are autonomous and independent; indeed, DISs can be seen as a particular case of cooperative information systems, where the cooperation is actually realized by means of data sharing among the distinct sources (see Chap. 1, Sect. 1.5). Each source in a DIS locally checks for the satisfaction of its own integrity constraints. As a component of a DIS, each source has to check further if it violates the integrity constraints specified over the global schema. If this happens, it is necessary to set how to deal with such inconsistencies. More specifically, it is not admissible that the whole DIS does not provide any answer to a user query if consistency violation occurs. Instead, specific techniques need to be introduced in order to deal with such inconsistencies. In the following, an example of integrity constraint violation is described, and different problems that arise are introduced.

Let us consider a global schema consisting of two relations, representing movies and the actors who have acted in these movies: Movie(Title, Director) and Actor(Name, Surname, Movie). Let us assume that a foreign key constraint exists between the attribute Movie of Actor and the attribute Title of Movie. Let us further assume that a GAV mapping is defined.

We first consider the case in which both the relations are defined by exact views on the sources, i.e., all and only all the data retrieved from the sources satisfy the global schema. Let us assume we retrieve the following instances:

```
1 <actor(Audrey, Hepburn, Roman Holidays)>
2 <movie(Roman Holidays, Wyler)>
3 <actor(Russel, Crowe, The Gladiator)>
```

Tuple 3 violates the foreign key constraint; therefore, a query asking for all movies would provide no answer, though tuple 2 could be provided as an answer.

If we do not consider exact views but instead consider sound or complete views, it is possible to provide answers. Recall that a view is sound in a GAV mapping if the provided data are a subset of the data satisfying the global schema. A view is complete if it provides a superset of the data satisfying the global schema.

As a second case, we consider the relation Actor defined as a complete view and Movie as a sound view. In this case, a query asking for all movies would have tuple 2 as an answer, because it is possible to delete some tuples of actors due to soundness and it is possible to add a tuple <movie(The Gladiator, α)>, where α is a placeholder for the director's value.

Also in the case of sound or complete views, there are cases in which no answer can be provided. Indeed, if Actor were defined by a complete view and Movie by a sound view, the foreign key constraint could not be satisfied.

In order to provide consistent answers, when inconsistent databases are retrieved, it is necessary to introduce different semantics for the DISs that take into account the possibility of adding or deleting tuples to reinstate consistency. Some works in the direction of defining a semantics for DISs in the presence of inconsistencies have been proposed in the literature. All such works are based on the notion of repair, introduced in the setting of inconsistent databases in [27]. Given an inconsistent database, a repair is a database consistent with the integrity constraint which "minimally" differs from the original database, where minimality depends on the semantic criteria adopted to define an ordering among consistent databases (e.g., based on set containment [27, 106, 277] or cardinality [406]). Other works (see, e.g., [92, 107]) generalized this notion to the context of DISs, properly taking into account the role of the mapping. The work presented in [259, 260] brings together two crucial activities in data integration and data quality, i.e., transforming data using schema mappings and fixing conflicts and inconsistencies using data repairing. In [259], a new semantics for schema mappings and data repairing in scenarios where they are jointly considered is proposed, as well as a chase-based algorithm to compute solutions and a scalable implementation of the chase algorithm. Geerts et al. [260] present the LLUNATIC mapping and cleaning system implementing such an approach to support data cleaning activities in data integration scenarios.

Finally, some works have considered the problem for DISs in the presence of preferences specified on the data sources. In [169], there is the proposal of a semantics for taking preference criteria into account when trying to solve inconsistencies between data sources in an LAV setting. *Preference criteria* are actually quality criteria specified on data sources. First, a maximally sound semantics is introduced. Given a DIS $I = (G, S, M)$, the defined semantics considers those interpretations that satisfy G and satisfy the mapping assertion in M *as much as possible* with respect to a source model D for I. Then, the concept of source preference is added, so that among maximally sound models, only those that refer to sources that are *best* with respect to quality preferences are selected. In [276], a different semantics is introduced, based on the repair of data stored at sources in the presence of a global inconsistency. This choice is an alternative to the choice of repairing global database instances constructed on the basis of the mapping. The semantics introduced in [276] refers to the GAV mapping.

10.6   Summary

Data integration and data quality are two interrelated concepts. On the one hand, data integration can benefit from data quality. Quality-driven query processing techniques have the purpose of selecting and accessing data of the highest quality, thus deriving the maximum benefits from a context with multiple sources with varying quality of their data assets.

On the other hand, it is intuitive that most data quality problems become evident when data in one source are compared with similar data stored in a different source. Once they are detected, there is the need for appropriate mechanisms that allow a DIS to perform the query processing function. These techniques are the conflict resolution techniques, which play the significant role of supporting query processing in virtual DISs. Note that the choice of solving conflicts at query time is an alternative to the more expensive choice of cleaning data sources *before* they are actually integrated. This would indeed require a data quality improvement activity performed independently by each source, and hence the complexity and the cost would grow.

In materialized data integration, e.g., in data warehouses, a cleaning activity is performed when populating the global schema. As instances gathered by disparate sources typically present instance-level conflicts, conflict resolution techniques can be also effectively applied for the purpose of producing a consistent materialized global instance. In [490], a framework to estimate the effort necessary to cleaning and mapping activities in a data integration setting is proposed, as a support to the management of data integration projects.

Chapter 11
Information Quality in Use

11.1 Introduction

We have seen in the Preface that the amount of information exchanged in the
Web doubles every one year and a half. Besides the Web, to make a whole
picture of the multitude of information used every day, we have to consider the
information managed in information systems of organizations, the information
exchanged by organizations, and the information used in everyday life by all of us.
Organizations and single persons make use of information for different purposes,
among such purposes, we are interested in those related to (1) taking decisions
and (2) doing actions. Decisions and actions in organizations are of different nature
according to the type of organization; in public administrations, they are the result
of administrative processes, which are executed to provide services to citizens and
communities; for private companies, they are the result of business processes, which
produce goods or services to be sold in the market.

Figure 11.1 from [510] shows the evolution of the labor force in the United States
from 2,000,000 years ago to year 2050, for the hunt, agriculture, manufacture, and
service sectors, where the service sector is distinguished into informative services
and other types of services. This impressive figure shows that in modern economies,
services based on information represent the principal sector as source of labor.

We focus in the following on information used for two different purposes:

- As a *production factor* in business processes of private organizations; notice that
  many of the arguments we discuss can be applied to public administrations and
  individuals.
- In *decision making*, where an organization or an individual has to take a decision
  that, according to its outcome, may lead to different possible utilities.

With reference to business processes, private companies produce and sell goods
and services leveraging on information and information technologies to get revenues
that exceed production costs, leading to profits. In order to get profits, business

© Springer International Publishing Switzerland 2016   309
C. Batini, M. Scannapieco, *Data and Information Quality*, Data-Centric Systems
and Applications, DOI 10.1007/978-3-319-24106-7_11

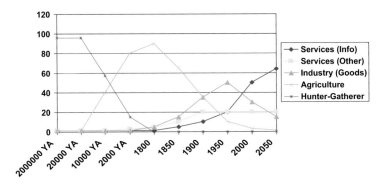

Fig. 11.1 Evolution of US Labor Percentages by Sector in the last 2,000,000 years

processes have to be organized in such a way to produce better goods and services at lower costs with respect to competing companies. Business processes using human, technological, and other types of resources transform those resources that are input to the production chain into an output made of goods or services. Among the various types of resources such as finance, human resources, logistics, etc., we are interested in this book to focus on the information resource. We have seen in Chap. 6 that the IP-MAP model describes effectively information used and transformed by business processes. In this chapter, we aim to investigate the relationship between the quality of information and the quality of the processes output (or, simply, the process quality) that make use of information to be produced. Since processes are made of decisions and actions, we aim in turn to relate information quality with the quality of actions and decisions that make use of information.

According to another point of view, also decision making and its effectiveness is intuitively related to information and its quality. A utility is associated to a decision; as the decision, among other factors, is influenced by the accuracy, completeness, currency, etc., of the available information; its final utility is indeed influenced by the quality of information.

In short, in this chapter, we want to deepen our understanding on how the information processor, be it a human being or an automated process, can manage the fitness for use of the information consumed. In the context of IQ, the term *fitness for use* has been used first in [646] to underline the characteristics of information quality not considered in an abstract environment, but else when information is used for some goal, and one wants to predict the influence of quality on the outcome, namely, the degree of achievement of the goal.

In this chapter, we also examine the relationship between IQ and information utility, where utility corresponds to the achievement of an advantage by the agent that makes use of the information; the advantage (or benefit) can be economic, social, physiological, cultural, or emotional. Here, we have to raise a terminological issue, noticing that the concepts of utility, benefit, and value are frequently adopted with similar meanings. In this chapter, we consider *utility* (or *benefit*) as the advantage obtained in general, while when we strictly refer to the economic utility of information, we adopt the term *value*.

The relationship between quality, utility, and value of information is discussed in the following under different perspectives:

- We first consider (Sect. 11.2) the relationship between IQ and utility under a historical perspective both in business processes and in decision making.
- Starting from Sect. 11.3, we focus on business processes; in Sect. 11.3, we discuss models proposed for utility and for the utility assessment process, discovering that the definitions themselves of quality dimensions and metrics are deeply influenced by utility. Indeed, besides dimensions and their metrics discussed in previous chapters that will be called *objective*, we have to define other dimensions and metrics whose definition and process of measurement inherently depend on the context of use of information, resulting in the new class of *subjective* dimensions and metrics.
- Then (Sect. 11.4), we move to the economic perspective, defining and comparing proposed classifications for costs/benefits of IQ.
- The economic perspective in the area of information system projects related to IQ improvement is examined in Sect. 11.5, where we discuss the methodologies proposed in the literature for the net benefit optimization of the information resource; here, the optimization corresponds to the maximization of economic benefits in comparison with costs of IQ management. The materials of Sects. 11.4 and 11.5 will be reused in Chap. 12 on methodologies.
- Section 11.6 is an extension of Sect. 11.3, where the focus is on utility and value of information in customer relationship management, by considering in particular the currency dimension.
- Finally, in Sect. 11.7, we discuss the relationship between IQ and decision making (Sect. 11.7.1), the usage of IQ in the decision process (Sect. 11.7.2), the consequences of information overload on decision making (Sect. 11.7.3), and value-driven decision making (Sect. 11.7.4).

11.2   A Historical Perspective on Information Quality in Business Processes and Decision Making

The relationship between IQ and process quality is a wide area of investigation, due to the relevance and diversity of characteristics of business processes in organizations. The different impacts of IQ at the three typical organizational levels, namely, *operational*, *tactical*, and *strategic level*, are analyzed in [520] reporting results of ad hoc interviews and outcomes of several proprietary studies. Information quality and its relationship with the quality of services, products, business operations, and consumer behaviors is investigated in very general terms in [572] and [571]. The symmetric problem of investigating how improving information production processes positively influences IQ is analyzed in [200].

The influence of IQ on processes in the presence of extreme settings, such as disasters, is investigated in [234]. Flaws in accuracy, completeness, consistency, and timeliness are considered in decision making, for example, for the 1986 NASA space shuttle Challenger accident, which killed seven people, and the US Navy cruiser Vincennes firing at an Iranian Airbus, which brought 290 people to their death.

One of the first authors to deal with the relationship between decision quality and IQ is [591], in which it is observed that to make high-quality decisions, it is crucial to have access to information that is as complete and relevant to decision tasks as possible, rather than just having a high volume of information.

A qualitative investigation of the relationship between decision quality and IQ is performed in [350], where the IQ conceptual framework proposed in [645] (mentioned also in Chap. 2) is adopted, in which IQ is classified in terms of intrinsic, contextual, representational, and accessibility dimensions. As to contextual dimensions, it is observed that decision-makers could benefit from contextual information by increasing the efficiency and effectiveness of both retrieval processes and of information interpretation. As to representational dimensions, Vessey [628] suggests that a decision-maker's processing task would be more efficient and effective when there is a cognitive match between the information emphasized in the representation type and that required by the task type. With reference to accessibility information, Jung [350] mentions navigation aids in the Web as tools to improve the quality of the decision.

11.3 Models of Utility and Objective vs. Contextual Metrics

Quantitative evaluation of quality dimensions such as accuracy, currency, or completeness has been based in previous chapters on objective characteristics of information. Ballou and Pazer [33] identify this approach as *structural*, while other authors use the term *objective*, emphasizing the intrinsic character of the quality measurement. Other approaches, proposed in [211, 212, 214, 656] consider, as criteria for the measurement, the usage of data and the relevance of administrative/business processes that adopt it, assuming a measurement of IQ focused on utility.

The concept of *information utility* considered independently from the quality perspective has been long investigated in the literature on management of information systems; see, e.g., [11, 12]. One of the first papers that systematically analyzes

a

ID	Date	Customer code	Product code	Quantity	Price	Amount
1	June 7, 2015	C	X	20	€ 5.000	€ 100.000
2	June 7, 2015	B	Y	3	€ 1.000	€ 3.000
3	June 8, 2015	A	Y	1	€ 1.000	€ 1.000
4	June 8, 2015	B	Z	5	€ 3.000	€ 15.000

b

ID	Date	Customer code	Product code	Quantity	Price	Amount
1	June 7, 2015	C	X	20	€ 5.000	€ 100.000
2	June 7, 2015	B	Y	3	€ 1.000	€ 3.000
3	June 8, 2015	A	Y	1	€ 1.000	€ 1.000
4	June 8, 2015	B	Z	5	€ 3.000	€ 15.000

Fig. 11.2 Sales transactions example from [211]. (**a**) Illustrative sale transaction dataset. (**b**) Dataset actually delivered

the relationship between information utility and IQ is [211], which provides a conceptual measure of the information value, called *intrinsic value* (i.e., in this case, synonym of utility). The information type considered in the formalization of the intrinsic value is the relational table. A single tuple represents an atomic portion of business activities; the intrinsic value of a table dataset is a relative measurement that reflects the business value that the table represents for business activities. Consider a table with M attributes and N tuples. To fix the ideas, make use of the sales transaction dataset in Fig. 11.2a.

The following definitions are provided in [211]. We have first to characterize the uneven business value of the different attributes in tuples in terms of a scaling factor that rescales the intrinsic value to the desired numeric scale; it is defined as:

$$\text{Tuple Value Scaling Factor as } K = \Sigma^{M}_{m=1} K_m$$

where K_m is the value for the attribute m. For example, in the table in Fig. 11.2, Price and Amount have intuitively more value than Date for a marketing campaign.

The *Intrinsic tuple value* represents the relative business value captured by a tuple. Two approaches can be considered:

- *Fixed intrinsic tuple value*: if tuples T_i are assumed equally valuable with a fixed intrinsic value V' scaled by K, then $V_i = KV'$.
- *Factored intrinsic tuple value*: in this case, we assume that business processes assign different relevance to different tuples, based on attributes acting as weight factor, scaled by K; $V_i = KM_i$ where M_i is the value of an attribute k of the tuple, assumed as value weight factor.

With reference to the whole dataset, the *intrinsic dataset value*, namely, the table business value, is the sum of the intrinsic tuple values; more specifically, for the two approaches, fixed and factored, introduced above, it holds:

- *Fixed intrinsic dataset value*: $V = \Sigma_{n=1}^{N} KV'$
- *Factored intrinsic dataset value*: $V = K \Sigma_{n=1}^{N} M_n$

Assume now that the sales transaction table of the company is the simplified table of Fig. 11.2a. Assuming a record scaling factor of $K = 1$, the different methods for calculating the intrinsic value are as follows.

- *Fixed intrinsic (dataset) value*: assigning a fixed value per record (e.g., $V' = 1$); the intrinsic value is $V = N * K * V' = 4 * 1 * 1 = 4$.
- *Amount-factored intrinsic value*: Using Amount in the table as a scaling factor, the intrinsic value is

$$V = K * \Sigma_{n=1}^{N} M_n = 1 * (100,000 + 3,000 + 1,000 + 15,000) = 119,000.$$

- *Customer-factored intrinsic value*: Using Customer Code as a scaling factor and assigning relative value contribution to each customer (e.g., 1 to A, 2 to B, and 5 to C, based on their customer lifetime value), the intrinsic value is

$$V = K * \Sigma_{n=1}^{N} M_n = 1 * (1 + 2 * 2 + 5) = 10.$$

The above example shows that the intrinsic value can, but does not necessarily, reflect monetary values. The intrinsic value is important and useful as a factor that underlies the calculation of content-based quality measurement. Such a content-based quality measurement is discussed in [211] for several dimensions, namely, completeness, validity, accuracy, and currency; in the following for showing the approach, we just focus on completeness.

Consider again the dataset illustrated in Fig. 11.2a. Assume that the first record was corrupted and the data contained in it is unreadable; Fig. 11.2b shows the dataset that is actually delivered. What is the completeness of the delivered dataset? Recalling the previous discussion, we can consider completeness according to multiple points of view (refer to Chap. 2 for a discussion on objective completeness metrics).

1. *Structural completeness*: the number of items that should have been delivered is 28 (4 tuples, 7 attributes per tuple). The actual number of items delivered is 21; hence, the completeness in this case is $C = 21/28 = 0.75$.
2. *Completeness based on fixed intrinsic value*: assigning a fixed value per record (e.g., $V' = 1$), completeness can be computed as

$$C = 1/KN \; \Sigma_{n=1}^{N} \Sigma_{m=1}^{M} K_m \; C_{n,m}$$

In this case, being $C_{n,m}$ identical for all attributes within a tuple, $C = 0.75$.

3. *Completeness based on amount-factored intrinsic value*: when the `Amount`
   attribute is used as scaling factor

$$C = (\Sigma_{n=1}^{N}M_n\Sigma_{m=1}^{M}K_mC_{n,m})/(K * \Sigma_{n=1}^{N}M_n) \text{ leading to}$$

$$C = 19{,}000/119{,}000 = 0.16.$$

4. *Completeness based on customer-factored intrinsic value*: under the assumption
   that value contributions are assigned as 1 to A, 2 to B, and 5 to C, the
   completeness is C = 0.5.

The conclusion is that in a contextual approach, the completeness values to be
applied depend on the data used. The structural completeness score best represents
the *purely technical perspective*; namely, given that one tuple out of four is missing,
we get a contextual completeness equal to 75 %. From the *accounting perspective*,
the amount-driven completeness score is more relevant since the biggest sale
transaction is missing from the database; hence, the quality is perceived to be quite
poor (16 %). If the purpose is tracking the activity of key clients, the customer-driven
completeness (50 %) appears quite relevant, since the missing transaction represents
a relatively significant customer.

A more general model for utility-driven quality assessment is investigated in
[212]. This study addresses the quality assessment and improvement of dimensional
data in a data warehouse, whose quality is critical in decision support environments.
For example, database marketing experts use sales data to analyze consumption
behavior and manage promotion campaigns that target specific customers and
products at specific locations: maintaining the associated dimensional data (i.e.,
customers, products, and locations) at a high quality is critical; otherwise, campaigns might fail to reach the right target. Even and Shankaranarayanan [212]
explore a methodology that evaluates the presence of quality defects (an objective
perspective) and their impact on utility degradation (a contextual perspective); it
adopts a generalization of the model previously described in this section, in which
aggregated formulas for quality are provided that range along different dimensions,
each reflecting a specific quality defect. Furthermore, quantitative characterizations
for quality are provided both for objective measures that reflect a ratio between
the counts of perfect items and total items in the dataset and for contextual utility-
driven measures, where the contribution to the utility of each tuple and attribute is
considered.

In [212], a case study is discussed based on an alumni example; two datasets are
considered, `Profiles` and `Gifts`. We show here the schema of the `Profiles`
dataset:

`Profiles (`<u>`Profile ID`</u>`, Graduation Year, Update Year, School,`
`Gender, Marital, Income, Ethnicity, Religion, Contact`
`information)`

where all attribute names have a clear meaning except `Update Year`, which
corresponds to the year the generic `Profiles` tuple was last updated.

Utility-driven quality assessment is based on two utility measures, namely, a. *inclination*, a binary variable that reflects a person's inclination to make a gift, and b. *amount*, the total amount of gifts made. A detailed calculation methodology in terms of formulas is provided in [212]; we here discuss the results on a qualitative basis.

The assessment includes three steps:

1. Objective quality assessment, where measurements, which are based on item counts, are used to evaluate objective dimension metrics. The types of considered errors (with the corresponding quality dimension) are (a) missing values (completeness), (b) invalid data (validity), (c) out-of-date data (currency), and (d) inaccuracies (accuracy).
2. Utility-driven quality assessment: the quality assessment is repeated, using utility measurements as scaling factors; e.g., for the `Gifts` table, we evaluate two utility measurements per profile, (1) inclination and (2) amount. These two utility measurements reflect different potential usages; inclination, for example, is likely to be observed for pledge campaigns that target a large donor base. Amount, on the other hand, is more useful for targeting specific donors who can potentially make very high contributions.
3. Analysis: evaluating and comparing the results of objective and utility-driven quality assessments leads to useful insights and has some important implications for developing IQ management policies.

An illustrative alumni profile example in which only attributes `Gender`, `Marital`, and `Income` of `Profiles` are considered is shown in Fig. 11.3.

Here, two out of four records have the value for gender missing; hence, objective completeness with respect to this attribute is 0.5. Similarly, objective completeness with respect to marital status is 0.75 (one out of four missing) and 0.25 with respect to income level (three out of four missing). For all attributes combined, the objective completeness is 0.5 (6 out of 12 missing). For tuple-level completeness calculated along the absolute rank, three out of the four records have missing values (at least one attribute); hence, completeness is 0.25. Using the grade rank, the tuple-level completeness (i.e., the average tuple grade) is 0.5.

ID	Gender	Marital Status	Income Level	Record Complete (Absolute)	Record Complete (Grade)	Last Update	Recent Update	Up-to-date rank	Inclination	Amount
A	Male	Married	Medium	1	1	2015	1	1	1	200
B	Female	Married	NULL	0	0.667	2012	0	0.47	1	800
C	NULL	Single	NULL	0	0.333	2013	0	0.78	0	0
D	NULL	NULL	NULL	0	0	2005	0	0.08	0	0
								Total	2	1,000

Fig. 11.3 Alumni profile example from [212]

For utility-driven completeness measurement, only two out of the four profile tuples (namely, A and B) are associated with utility, and inclination and amount are used as scaling factors. With respect to gender and marital status, none of the two utility-contributing tuples have missing values; hence, the utility-driven completeness is 1. With respect to income level, one utility-contributing record (B) is missing the value. Factoring by inclination, the table completeness is $(1*1+1*0)/2=0.5$, and factoring by amount, the table completeness is $(1*200+0*800)/1000=0.2$. Factoring the grade rank by inclination yields $(1*1+0*0.667)/1.667=0.6$ and by amount $(1*200+0.667*800)/1000=0.733$.

We omit further steps on the analysis of data. Besides, we list the most relevant results mentioned in [212]:

- Higher objective quality (less defects, more recent updates) is associated with higher utility.
- Inclination to donate has a significantly strong association with almost all objective indicators.
- Most utility-driven IQ measurement scores are higher than their corresponding objective measurement scores.
- Utility-driven completeness measurements, at the attribute level and at the tuple level, are relatively consistent along the four utility metrics. This implies that, when assessing the completeness of alumni profile data, calculating utility-driven measurements along multiple utility metrics does not grant a significant advantage over measuring it along a single metric.
- Analyzing impact of missing values at the tuple level by itself is insufficient.

As a conclusion, we can comment two claimed limitations of the approach, namely, (a) the assessment procedure considers a single dataset, a dimension table in a data warehouse, and (b) the value utility measurements are very specific to the customer relationship management domain.

The above approach is extended in [219], introducing analytical tools for modeling and quantifying inequality in the distribution of utility and demonstrating their application for assessing inequality in a large information repository. The distribution of utility and the magnitude of inequality are shown to have important implications for information management such as impacting the design and administration of the information resource and prioritizing quality improvement efforts.

Here, the dataset is, as before, a relational table made of N tuples; the utility of tuples is represented by the random variable u, with a known *probability density function* $f(u)$. To assess the variation in utility, the proportion R of highest-utility records is defined as a [0,1] ratio of the $N*$ tuples of highest utility (i.e., the top $N*$ when ranked in descending order). This model is applied to the same alumni case study considered before; the interested reader is addressed to the paper for the definition of the statistical model. The conclusions are:

- The magnitude of inequality in a table should impact how the dataset is designed and implemented. When the inequality is low, one either chooses to implement the entire table or not to implement it at all.

- For tables with high-utility inequality, depending on utility/cost trade-offs, the designer may wish to exclude low-utility tuples or manage them separately in a cheaper or less accessible storage. A typical example of such differentiation is archiving older data. Older records are often excluded from actively used tables. Associating utility with the recency of tuples and assessing their inequality accordingly can help identify the economically optimal time span of data to be included in the table.
- Differentiating utility can help define superior measurements for IQ dimensions (e.g., completeness and accuracy) that reflect quality assessment in context.
- Differentiating the tuples based on utility contribution can help prioritize and make quality management efforts more efficient. Fixing all missing values (and/or correcting all errors in existing ones) may be expensive. To improve cost/effectiveness, we may consider fixing only attributes that can better predict contribution. Pending further analysis, such attributes may need to be fixed only for high-utility records.

To conclude, we see in this approach a first example of model managing the utility/cost trade-off, which we will discuss extensively in Sect. 11.5.

A final issue we consider in this section is the contribution in [110], grounded in the phenomenon we have highlighted in Fig. 11.1, the explosion of *information as a service* as a relevant part of the labor force and gross domestic product in developed countries. Cappiello and Comuzzi [110] observe that in the information age, enterprises base or enrich their core business activities with the provision of informative services. For this reason, organizations are becoming increasingly aware of IQ issues, which concern the evaluation of the ability of a data collection to meet users' needs and therefore refer, in the terminology introduced above, to contextual dimensions and metrics.

The paper adopts the point of view that, when considering IQ, the users' perspective should always be considered fundamental. As a consequence, from one side, providers should adapt, and consequently improve, their service offerings in order to completely satisfy users' demands. On the other side in service provisioning, providers are subject to restrictions, stemming, for instance, from cost and benefit assessments. The paper considers the need for a conciliation of provider and user quality targets in defining the optimal IQ level of an informative service. The definition of such a balance is considered a complex issue since each type of user accessing the service may define different utilities regarding the provided information. Considering this scenario, the paper presents a utility-based model of the providers' and customers' interests developed on the basis of multi-class offerings. The model is exploited to analyze the optimal service offerings that allow the efficient allocation of quality improvement activities for the provider.

11.4   Cost-Benefit Classifications for Data Quality

In this section, we start to discuss how an organization can analyze whether it is economically convenient or not to engage IQ improvement campaigns. In other words, we will discuss how quantifying (1) the costs of current poor IQ, (2) the costs of IQ initiatives to improve it, and (3) the benefits that are gained from such initiatives. Cost-benefit analysis is an arduous task in many cost domains, and it is more arduous in the IQ area due to the less consolidated nature of the discipline. The existing proposals range from classifications provided for costs and benefits to methodologies for performing the cost-benefit analysis process. Classifications are either generic or specific, e.g., for the financial domain. The advantages of generic classifications (see also [203]) range from establishing clearer terminology to providing consistent measurement metrics. They can be used as checklists during the cost-benefit analysis activity. We discuss in this section issues related to generic classifications and postpone to Chap. 12 the discussion on methodologies. In the following, we distinguish the differences between cost issues and benefit issues.

11.4.1   Cost Classifications

Three very detailed classifications for costs appear in English [202], Loshin [413], and Eppler and Helfert [203]. We first present the three classifications, discussing their original issues; then, we propose a common classification framework to compare them all.

The English classification is shown in Fig. 11.4. Information quality costs correspond to costs of business processes and information management processes due to poor IQ. Costs for information quality assessment or inspection measure IQ dimensions to verify that processes are performing properly. Finally, process improvement and defect prevention costs involve activities to improve the quality of information, with the goal of eliminating, or reducing, the costs of poor IQ. Costs due to poor IQ are analyzed in depth in the English approach, shown in Fig. 11.4, and are subdivided into three categories:

1. *Process failure costs* result when poor quality information causes a process not to perform properly. As an example, inaccurate mailing addresses cause correspondence to be misdelivered.
2. *Information scrap and rework.* When information is of poor quality, it requires several types of defect management activities, such as reworking, cleaning, or rejecting. Examples of this category are (here we adopt the original term "data" instead of information):

   • Redundant data handling—if the poor quality of a source makes it useless, time and money has to be spent to collect and maintain data in another dataset.

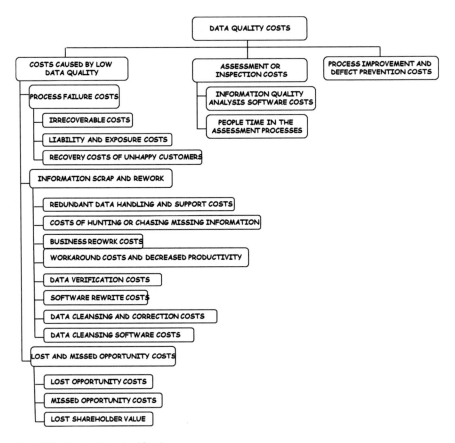

Fig. 11.4 The English classification

- Business rework costs—due to re-performing failed processes, such as resend-ing correspondence, as in the previous example.
- Data verification costs—when information users do not trust the information, they have to perform their own quality inspection, to remove low-quality data.

3. *Loss and missed opportunity costs* correspond to the revenues and profits not realized because of poor IQ. For example, due to low accuracy of customer e-mail addresses, a percentage of customers already acquired cannot be reached in periodic advertising campaigns, resulting in lower revenues, roughly propor-tional to the decrease of accuracy in addresses.

The Loshin classification is shown in Fig. 11.5. Loshin analyzes the costs of low IQ, classifying it in different domain impacts, on the following:

- The operational domain, which includes the components of the system used for processing information and the costs of maintaining the operation of the system

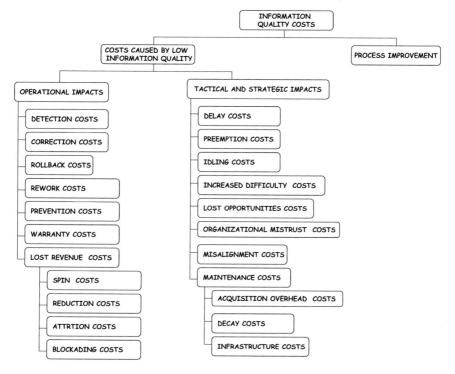

Fig. 11.5 The Loshin classification

- The tactical domain, which attempts to address and solve problems before they arise
- The strategic domain, which stresses the decisions affecting the longer term

For both the operational impact and tactical/strategic impact, several cost categories are introduced. Here, we describe some of the operational impact costs:

- Detection costs are incurred when an IQ problem provokes a system error or processing failure.
- Correction costs are associated with the actual correction of a problem.
- Rollback costs are incurred when work that has been performed needs to be undone.
- Rework costs are incurred when a processing stage must be repeated.
- Prevention costs arise when a new activity is implemented to take the necessary actions to prevent operational failure due to a detected IQ problem.

Examples of tactical/strategic costs are (1) delay, due to inaccessible information resulting in a delayed decision process that, in turn, may cause productivity delays; (2) lost opportunities, i.e., the negative impact on potential opportunities in strategic initiatives; and (3) organizational mistrust, due to the decision of managers,

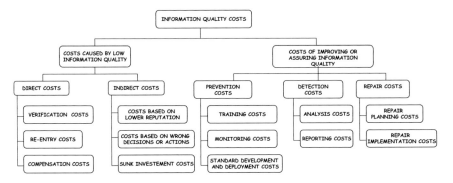

Fig. 11.6 The EpplerHelfert classification

unsatisfied by inconsistencies in information, to implement their own decision support system, resulting in redundancies and inconsistencies due to frequent use of the same sources.

The EpplerHelfert classification is shown in Fig. 11.6. EpplerHelfert derives its classification with a bottom-up approach; first, it produces a list of specific costs that have been mentioned in the literature, such as higher maintenance costs and information re-input costs. Then, it generates a list of direct costs associated with improving or assuring information quality, such as training costs of improving IQ know-how. At this point, it puts together the two classifications corresponding to the two major classes of costs, namely, cost due to poor IQ and improvement costs. Costs due to poor information quality are categorized in terms of their measurability or impact, resulting in direct vs. indirect cost classes. *Direct costs* are those monetary effects that arise immediately from low IQ, while *indirect costs* arise from the intermediate effects. Improvement costs are categorized within the IQ process.

For the purpose of producing a new classification that allows for the integration of the three classifications discussed above, we use a second classification proposed by Eppler and Helfert in [203]; such a classification produces a conceptual framework that can be used in the cost-benefit analysis of IQ programs. It is based on the information production life cycle approach, which distinguishes between *data entry*, *information processing*, and *information usage* costs. The iterative attribution of all the cost categories of the three previous classifications to this new high-level classification leads to the comparative classification of Fig. 11.7; the different background patterns used for the English, Loshin, and EpplerHelfert classification items are shown in the legend. When comparing the three classifications, we notice that they have only one item in common, namely, costs *caused by low data quality*, different items common among two classifications, and the two most similar classifications are the English and Loshin ones.

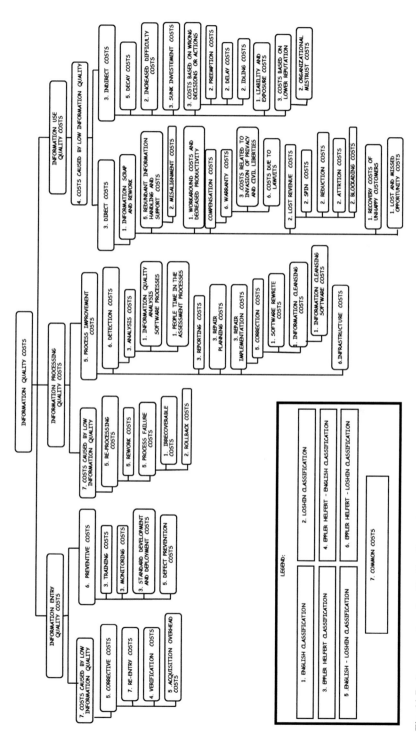

Fig. 11.7 A comparative classification for costs

11.4.2   Benefits Classification

Benefits are typically classified into three categories:

1. *Monetizable*, when they correspond to values that can be directly expressed in terms of money. For example, improved IQ results in terms of increased monetary revenues.
2. *Quantifiable*, when they cannot be expressed in terms of money, but one or more indicators exist that measure them, they are expressed in a different numeric domain. For example, improved IQ in government-to-business relationships can result into a reduced wasted time by businesses, which can be expressed in terms of a time indicator; we will see a clear example of this issue in Chap. 12. Observe that in several contexts, a quantifiable benefit can be expressed in terms of a monetizable benefit if a reasonable and realistic conversion function is found between the quantifiable domain and money. In our example, if the time wasted by business is productive time, the "wasted time" quantifiable benefit can be translated in terms of the monetizable benefit "unproductively spent money."
3. *Intangible*, when they cannot be expressed by a numeric indicator. A typical intangible benefit is the loss of image of an agency or a company due to inaccurate information communicated to customers, e.g., requests to citizens for undue tax payments from the revenue agency.

Figure 11.8 shows the English and Loshin items represented together, corresponding to benefits in the three categories. With regard to monetizable benefits, the two classifications agree in the indication of economic issues related to revenue increase and cost decrease, while in quantifiable and intangible benefits, the English classification is richer; among the intangible benefits, the reference to service

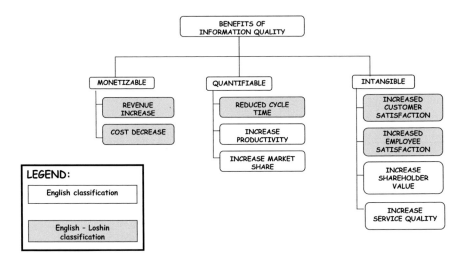

Fig. 11.8 A comparative classification for benefits

quality is relevant. In Chap. 12, we will see examples of applications of the above classifications in a real case study.

11.5 Methodologies for Cost-Benefit Management of Information Quality

In this section, we consider utility from an economic point of view, discussing approaches that put in practice the classifications seen in the previous section on costs and benefits of IQ, providing models and methodologies for cost-benefit management. A framework for guiding accounting-related IQ research is presented in [468], based on four major research topics: people and decision making, governance, operations, and technology. The field of *accounting* is concerned with representing the financial status of an organization, and the accuracy and reliability of the resulting financial statements allow stakeholders to make informed decisions. Two critical components of any accounting information system are the quality of the information residing within the system as well as in the outputs of the system. In the paper, it is observed that the dimensions of accuracy, reliability, relevance, and understandability of information are of critical importance in accounting. However, depending on the context, other dimensions can be similarly important. In some cases, timely information is imperative, e.g., for demand data or stock prices; in others, investors require accurate financial statements. Furthermore, dimensions often require trade-offs; we refer the reader to the discussion on trade-offs among dimensions in Chap. 2.

Several laws that link (1) information seen as an organizational asset to (2) its value (with a meaning similar to the concept of economic utility) and (3) other characteristics such as number of users, level of integration, and quality are addressed in [449]. Such laws are expressed through functions over a two-dimensional space, where the y-coordinate represents the value of information and the x-coordinate is the related characteristic. Three of the seven laws refer to quality. They are discussed in the following.

The third law (see Fig. 11.9) states that "information is perishable," namely, the value of information depreciates over time.

Fig. 11.9 Law 3: Information is perishable, from [449]

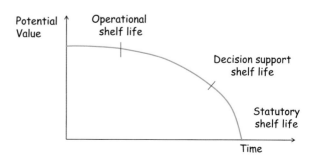

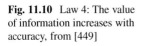

Fig. 11.10 Law 4: The value of information increases with accuracy, from [449]

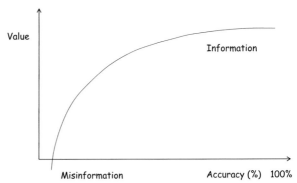

Fig. 11.11 Law 5: More is not necessarily better, from [449]

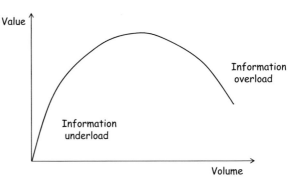

As an example, a flight ticket with a penalty has high value only before the flight is operational; its value decreases due to the penalty if we have to delay the flight; its marginal value after the flight has occurred refers to its usage in legal disputes that have a deadline after a given time.

The fourth law states that "the value of information increases with accuracy" (Fig. 11.10). As an example, having inaccurate addresses of customers in customer relationship management systems reduces the potential effectiveness of marketing campaigns, since related customers are not reachable (see more on this point in Sect. 11.6).

The fifth law states that "more is not necessarily better," namely, the value of information is influenced by the volume that, in case of excessive flow of information, may result in information overload (Fig. 11.11). We will discuss this law in more detail in Sect. 11.7 in the context of a discussion on the influence of information overflow in decision making.

Several approaches provide full-fledged models that allow to evaluate the costs and the economic benefits of IQ projects. One of the first proposals in this direction appears in [32], where a general model to assess the impact of information and process quality on the outputs of information-decision systems is presented. The model provides a representation of possible errors in intermediate and final outputs in terms of input and process error functions.

While [32] is limited to the analysis of poor IQ on processes, in [34], a conceptual model is provided for evaluating economic issues related to enhancing IQ in data warehouse environments. The following issues are modeled:

- Organizational activities supported by the data warehouse, such as, e.g., production planning and sales
- Datasets, such as inventory information, historical sales information, and promotional information
- IQ dimensions such as accuracy and timeliness
- Possible IQ projects

An optimization model is proposed whose inputs and related parameters are the following:

1. Current quality, as a function of datasets and quality dimensions
2. Required quality, function of organizational activities, datasets and quality dimensions
3. Target quality, function of datasets, quality dimensions, and information quality projects
4. Priority of organizational activity
5. Cost of IQ improvement, function of IQ project
6. Value added modeled as utility, function of organizational activities, datasets, IQ dimensions, and IQ projects

The integer programming formulation is shown in Fig. 11.12, where the following index notation is used:

- I. Index for organizational activities supported
- J. Index for datasets
- K. Index for data quality attributes or dimensions
- L. Index for possible data quality projects

Each project L is associated with a weight and a set of utilities, whose weighted sum produces an overall value associated to L. The optimization model includes an objective function that is the sum of values of all selected processes. Several constraints are stated in addition to the objective function. The resource constraint

Fig. 11.12 Integer programming formulation proposed in [34]

$$\text{Value of Project } L = \sum_{\text{All I}} \text{Weight(I)} \sum_{\text{ALL J}} \sum_{\text{All K}} \text{Utility(I,J,K;L)}$$

Maximize: Total Value from all projects

$$\sum_{\text{All L}} X(L) * \text{Value}(L)$$

Resource Constraint: $\sum_{L} X(L) * \text{Cost}(L) \leq \text{Budget}$

Exclusiveness Constraint: $X(P(1)) + X(P(2)) + \ldots + X(P(S)) \leq 1$

Interaction Constraint: $X(P(1)) + X(P(2)) + X(P(3)) \leq 1$

Integer Constraints: 1 if project L is selected; 0 otherwise

$$X(L) = \left\{ \begin{array}{c} 0 \\ 1 \end{array} \right.$$

asserts that the sum of the cost of all project selected cannot exceed the budget.
In case some projects are mutually exclusive, the exclusiveness constraint leads to
select at most one such project. The interaction constraint disciplines the selection
of one among three projects that share various aspects.

Going back to the fourth law proposed in [449], several models are provided in
the literature that detail the law and extend to dimensions different from accuracy.
Several generic functions are shown in [213] to represent qualitatively the effect
of completeness and accuracy on utility, cost, and net benefit. As to completeness,
as we have seen in Sect. 11.3, depending on the information content, some tuples
offer higher utility (in that paper called value) than others do (e.g., tuples that
refer to higher sales amount of more valuable customers are likely to contribute
higher utility within certain usages); concerning this issue, it is assumed that the
designer may deliberately exclude lower sales amount or else less recent records,
thus reducing the completeness of the table. So, the effect of completeness quality
degradation is assumed as due to a *deliberate choice*. Instead, degradation in
accuracy is seen as due to *random hazards*, such as manual data entry errors,
inconsistencies between information sources, or miscalculations. In Fig. 11.13, we
consider the relationship between utility, cost, and completeness; for accuracy, see
[213].

Figure 11.13a shows the uneven trend of utility for the different tuples, where
the contribution of each tuple tends to decrease. Figure 11.13b shows the functional

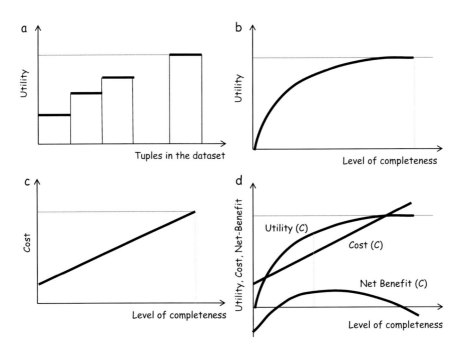

Fig. 11.13 The effect of relation completeness on utility (**a** and **b**), cost (**c**), and net benefit (**d**)

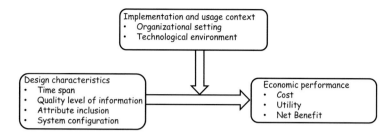

Fig. 11.14 Net-benefit maximization framework in [216]

relation between utility and completeness, approximated as a continuous curve. Assuming a fixed cost per tuple for recovering missing tuples, the overall cost (see Fig. 11.13c) is the sum of a fixed component which is independent of completeness and a variable cost which is proportional to the number of tuples included while increasing completeness. Finally, Fig. 11.13d shows utility, cost, and net benefit, namely, the difference between utility and cost in their relationship with completeness. The net-benefit curve, depending on the dataset, may have an optimal completeness point, at which the net benefit is the maximum.

The most relevant contribution to a mature definition of the area comes from the papers of Even and Shankaranarayanan [210, 215, 216, 220], and [218]. In [216], a comprehensive model is proposed in the context of data warehouses. It is observed that in previous approaches, the design of a data warehouse had been considered from a technical perspective; see, e.g., [367]. The paper considers, instead, the data warehouse design process from an organizational and economic perspective.

In Fig. 11.14, the proposed framework is shown. As to design characteristics, the time span is the time interval considered for the information acquisition in the data warehouse. Intuitively, the larger the time span, the richer is the information set that can be used in the analysis of information and the utility in the decision process. The quality level is also positively correlated with utility. Attributes to be potentially chosen as analysis dimensions are not necessarily equally important; a smaller set simplifies information acquisition and processing and leads to lower storage and administration costs but might also fail to capture relevant aspects of the phenomenon and preclude more extended analyses reducing the utility. System configuration includes the choice of hardware, database server, etc.

Utility of a dataset measures the contribution of the dataset to business value. It is measured monetarily. Assuming I possible usages, the overall utility can be expressed as $U(X) = \Sigma_{i=1}^{I} U_i(X)$, where X is the vector of design characteristics and U_i is the utility of usage i.

Utility grows with time span T and quality Q; for the corresponding formulas, see [216]. Overall costs too can be expressed with the formula $C(X) = \Sigma_{j=1}^{J} C_j(X)$ where J is the total number of cost components and $C_j(X)$ is the cost for component j; detailed formulas relating costs, time span, and quality are found in the paper. Net benefit is $B(X) = \Sigma_{i=1}^{I} U_i(X) - \Sigma_{j=1}^{J} C_j(X)$.

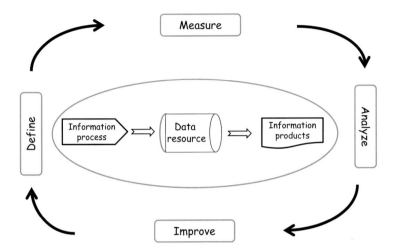

Fig. 11.15 A framework for the assessment/improvement IQ life cycle

Closed form solutions are obtained for optimizing T or Q or both, assuming a given set of attributes chosen as dimensions.

In the paper, it is recognized that economic performance could be affected by many technical characteristics (e.g., ICT infrastructure, process configuration, information delivery methods), as well as business characteristics such as commitments to clients, adherence to quality standards, information privacy, legal constraints, and/or competition versus collaboration; all such factors are considered as open problems.

A more general framework for assessing economic trade-offs in an IQ information production process is proposed in [210]; see Fig. 11.15.

Following previous research, the framework models information environments as multistage processes with information product outcomes. The framework links economic benefits (conceptualized as utility) to the use of information products and costs to the production process and IQ improvement efforts. The framework is further developed into a microeconomic model that permits quantitative assessment of IQ decisions, based on maximizing the net benefit, the difference between utility and cost. The model adopted in the framework to represent the information environment is based on several assumptions, among them are the following:

- The object for IQ improvement is a single dataset.
- The IQ level of the dataset at the beginning of a period $t - 1$ is subject to a temporal decline d, indicating that, in average, a percentage d of the dataset becomes defected within period t.
- The utility U_t a company can gain from the considered dataset at the end of period t depends on the IQ level Q_t. $U_t(Q_t)$ is a monotonically increasing function.

- Improving IQ by ΔQ_t incurs implementation costs $C_t(\Delta Q_t)$ in period t. $C_t(\Delta Q_t)$ is a strictly monotonically increasing function.
- The company would aim at maximizing the net benefit B_t from IQ improvement, given an interest rate r per period.

The above economic model is defined for a single iteration of the IQ improvement cycle. As IQ improvement is typically an iterative process, the model can however be extended to address IQ improvement over several periods. Based on the above assumptions, a net present value formula is defined as the objective function of a company.

The above model is extended and specialized in [218, 220] in the domain of customer relationship management, considering two quality dimensions particularly relevant in such domain, namely, completeness and currency. The following extensions are made:

- All tuples and attributes are retained, but possibly under different IQ management policies, while in previous approaches, less useful records and attributes are discarded entirely. Retaining some information without quality maintenance, rather than discarding it, is considered a more realistic scenario in marketing databases, especially if the information, albeit unimproved, are still of reasonably high quality.
- The model permits the setting of different quality levels for different tuples, as opposed to the more limiting situation of simply choosing how much information to retain and optimizing the quality of the entire remaining dataset, without allowing optimal quality to vary by tuple.

The above two arguments prompt authors to adopt an entirely new approach with respect to optimization at the attribute level. The assumptions that all attributes are retained and each attribute can be assigned a different level of targeted quality support the understanding and development of more detailed and fine-tuned IQ management policies.

The above approaches do not consider the effect of adoption of ICT technologies that can improve IQ from one side and, from the other side, can enable processing new valuable information, increasing in such a way the utility of the system. A unified model relating the concepts of IQ, capacity, utility, and value is proposed in [44] and [42]; see Fig. 11.16. The determinants that influence in Fig. 11.16 information capacity, utility, and value are the following:

- An information structure, made of:
  1. A set of databases and corresponding application loads in terms of queries and transactions.
  2. Information integration technologies that can be used for enhancing the level of integration among the input databases. Among technologies, virtual data integration (VDI in the following) technologies are considered (data integration has been discussed in Chap. 10).

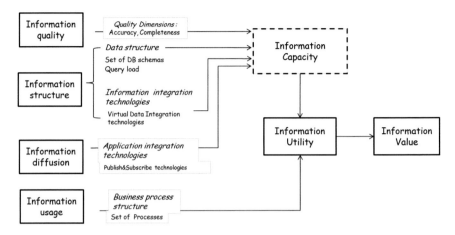

Fig. 11.16   A unified model of information quality, capacity, utility, and value

- Information quality, modeled by two IQ dimensions, accuracy and completeness.
- Application integration technologies focusing on publish and subscribe technologies that allow coordinated updates of the same data in different heterogeneous databases.
- Information usage, expressed by a matrix BP × Q, where BP are business processes and Q is the list of queries in the query load, that represents business processes bp_i making use of queries q_j in the query load.

Central concepts in the model are information capacity, information utility , and information value. The idea underlying information capacity is that the introduction of virtual data integration technologies in a heterogeneous database setting leads to the possibility of formulating new queries that can be issued by business processes; the net amount of queries results in an increment in capacity, seen as the incremental intensional knowledge that can be extracted within such a setting. We show an example of this concept from [46]. See in Fig. 11.17 the conceptual schemas of the two databases DB1 and DB2 of a furniture company, where a graphical formalism adapted from the entity relationship graphical model is used; names represent entities and unlabeled lines represent relationships among entities.

The integration of the two schemas results in the integrated schema in Fig. 11.18a. Several queries can be performed on the VDI architecture that could not previously be performed (or could be performed only with ad hoc applications) on the two schemas. We show two of them and the corresponding query paths in Figs. 11.18a and b.

Publish and subscribe technologies enable coordinated updates on autonomous databases that increase the coherence of tuples and consequently the quality of information used by business processes, resulting in higher amounts of tuples that can be linked in joins. This corresponds to incremental capacity at the extensional

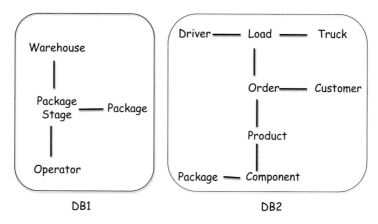

Fig. 11.17 Two distinct databases of a furniture company

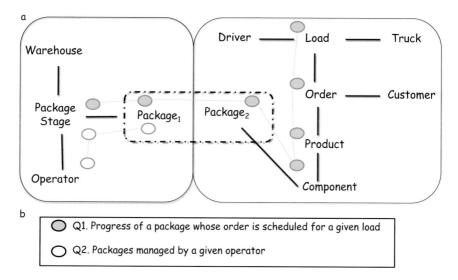

Fig. 11.18 Integrated schema and new queries that can be performed on it. (**a**) Integrated schema. (**b**) Queries with higher utility

level (tuples). Increased capacity leads to higher value for processes, measured globally using the matrix BP × Q introduced above.

The overall economic utility is increased by a factor that depends on the specific atomic utilities that new queries (enabled by VDI technologies) and higher-quality data (enabled by publish and subscribe technologies) bring to business processes. Finally, the information value corresponds to the net utility in previous approaches. The interested reader is addressed to [42, 44, 46] for case studies and numerical evaluations of the information capacity, utility, and value.

11.6 How to Relate Contextual Quality Metrics with Utility

In previous approaches, IQ dimensions and metrics have been contextualized to the utility of business processes and thus considered from an economic perspective. However, a poor consideration is dedicated in the described approaches to:

- The design process that, starting from general requirements, produces as output the dimensions and metrics for utility evaluation relevant for the problem at hand
- The quality of such a process

The two issues are discussed together in [305–307], papers that inspire this section. Let us consider first the second issue above, the quality of metrics.

Several contributions in the literature (see, e.g., [245]) underline the highly subjective character of the choice of IQ metrics. Heinrich et al. [307] list six properties of metrics:

1. *Normalization*: a normalization is necessary to assure that the values of the metrics are comparable.
2. *Interval scale*: the metrics have to be interval scaled to support the monitoring of their usage over time.
3. *Interpretability*: the quantification of the IQ metrics must be easy to interpret by users.
4. *Aggregation*: the metrics shall enable a flexible application through different aggregations in higher-level metrics.
5. *Adaptivity*: the metrics need to be adaptable to the context of a specific application.
6. *Feasibility*: the metrics should be based on input parameters that are determinable.

We discuss the approach proposed in the three mentioned papers, making use of an example, taken from [305], where a real-life business environment is investigated within the campaign management of a major mobile service provider (though presenting a simplified version of the example). The campaign is focused on customers with, e.g., tariff Mobile100. In the past, existing IQ problems often prohibited a correct and individualized customer addressing in mailing campaigns and led to lower campaign success rates. This problem occurred especially with prepaid contracts, since they do not guarantee customer contact at regular intervals (e.g., sending bills). Hence, the mobile service provider cannot easily verify whether these customers' contact information are still up-to-date. We assume that the provider aims to submit an offer to the prepaid customers (namely, paying the tariff Mobile100) in order to make them switch to postpaid tariffs. We start our analysis from the following Customer table:

Customer(ID, Surname, First Name, Birth Date, Place of Birth, Address, Current Tariff, Phone Number)

For what concerns IQ dimensions, the considered ones are accuracy and timeliness (this term, used in [305], corresponds to *currency* in this book). In the paper, it is observed that it is very time-consuming using metrics for accuracy, since the address of each single customer must be verified before mailing an offer. In contrast, the metric for timeliness can be formulated, giving a probability that indicates whether the address of a customer is still up-to-date, having in such a way the advantage of not knowing under certainty whether the address is indeed still correct. Hence, we focus on metrics for timeliness.

Moreover, the relevant attributes and their importance within the campaign have to be determined. The attributes Surname, First Name, and Address are considered important for delivering the offer to the customer by mail. Moreover, the customers' Current Tariff is essential, since it corresponds to the selection criterion within the campaign. So we focus on the table Customer(Surname, First Name, Address, Current Tariff).

In addition, we have to assign weights to attributes according to their relevance within the campaign; see Fig. 11.19. Since only those customers with the tariff Mobile100 should be addressed, the attribute Current Tariff is stated as most important, and the weight 1 is assigned. The attribute Address is considered the most important following the tariff, since without the address, the offer cannot be delivered to the customer. Address is given a weight 0.9, since parts of the address as, e.g., an up-to-date house number are not indispensable for the delivery of the offer. The attribute Surname is weighted 0.9, since this attribute is important to the delivery as well, and if the surname changes (e.g., after a marriage), the old surname might in some cases still be known to the postal service. In contrast, the first name is considered less important. The attribute First Name is nevertheless assigned the weight 0.2, since the mobile service provider does not want to affect existing customer relationships.

Now we have to express the *decline rate* decline(A_i) of quality metrics for attributes A_i, indicating how many values of the considered attribute become out-of-date in percentage within, say, 1 year. Decline(A_i) has to be specified for each attribute selected in the previous step, which can be done by comparison with external sources or else based on available statistics on historical information. Regarding the attributes Surname and Address, empirical information from the National Statistical Offices considering marriages/divorces and the frequency of relocation can be taken into account. Thereby, decline rates of 0.02 for the attribute

Attribute$_i$	Surname	First Name	Address	Current Tariff
relevance$_i$	0.9	0.2	0.9	1.0
decline(Ai) [1/year]	0.02	0.0	0.1	0.4
age(Ai) [year]	0.5	0.5	2	0.5
Q$_{timeliness}$ (Ai)	0.99	1.00	0.82	0.82

Fig. 11.19 Evaluation of relevance and timeliness for the attributes in the table

Surname (i.e., on average, 2 % of all customers change their surname in a year)
and 0.1 for the attribute Address can be fixed. If no such third-party information
is available, the decline rate of the attribute Address can be estimated by means of
internal (historical) information or samples. For example, in the case of frequency of
relocation, it would be possible to draw a sample of the customer base. After having
surveyed the average duration of validity of the customer addresses in the sample
(i.e., how long does a customer live in the same house on average?), the parameter
decline(A) of the metric for timeliness can be set by means of an unbiased estimator
equal to $\frac{1}{\text{average duration of validity of the addresses}}$ calculated on the probability distribution
of the duration of validity.

The decline rate of the attribute First Name is assumed as 0.0 since the first
name usually remains the same. In contrast, the decline rate of Current Tariff
is estimated, based on historical information from the mobile service provider as
0.4.

With the final goal of evaluating the timeliness, we have now to estimate for an
example tuple the age(A_i) of each attribute, which corresponds to the time lapse
between (a) the instant when IQ is quantified and (b) the instant of information
acquisition, which is stored as meta-information in the records; see Fig. 11.19. The
value of timeliness for the four attributes of an example tuple can be determined
with the formula

$$Q_{\text{Timeliness}}(A_i) = \exp(-\text{decline}(A_i) * \text{age}(A_i)).$$

Figure 11.19 sums up the relevant values.

In [305], it is shown that all the above choices are coherent with the quality
criteria for metrics introduced at the beginning of the section.

The value of the metric at the level of tuples is computed by aggregation of the
results at the level of attribute values, considering the weights relevance$_i$:

$$Q_{\text{Timeliness}}(T, A_1, \ldots, A_4) = \frac{0.99 \times 0.9 + 1 \times 0.2 + 0.82 \times 0.9 + 0.82 \times 1}{0.9 + 0.2 + 0.9 + 1} = 0.882$$

In order to decide how to use the above figures, a similar campaign where customers
had been offered a tariff switching is analyzed; such a campaign was performed
a few months earlier. The metric for timeliness is computed for all customers
addressed in the former campaign, and the function relating campaign success rates
and value of timeliness is evaluated; see the results in Fig. 11.20.

At this point, the results of the previous campaign are projected on the future
campaign, and it is possible to evaluate the mailing costs and the expected additional
revenues for each group of customers in the ten timeliness intervals. In particular:

- costs for each group = mailing cost x number of users
  in the group
- revenues for each group = success-rate x single
  revenue x number of users in the group

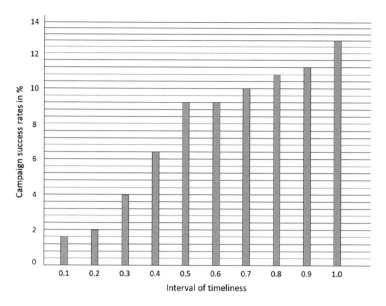

Fig. 11.20 Success rate of a former campaign

The final finding is that the break-even point for the economic convenience of the campaign was for value of timeliness greater than 0.3.

11.7   Information Quality and Decision Making

The quality of information used in a decision process has a crucial role in the outcome of decision making, since the final decision can be severely influenced by the poor quality of available information, and the decision outcome may result in different levels of utility depending on the quality of available information. Several papers in the literature address the above problem; they will be analyzed and discussed in Sects. 11.7.1 and 11.7.2. In Sect. 11.7.3, we will focus on another issue relating quality of information and quality of a decision, the case in which too much information is provided to the decision-maker, and the decision process is affected by information overload. Finally in Sect. 11.7.4, we will investigate proposals to enhance utility of information in the decision process.

11.7.1   Relationships Between Information Quality and Decision Making

We show in Fig. 11.21 the main papers that investigate the relationships between data and information quality and decision making.

Information quality characteristics are considered as the independent variable, while decision-making characteristics are the dependent variable. With reference to IQ characteristics, IQ dimensions are the most frequent; other characteristics concern IQ categories introduced in [645] and discussed in Chap. 2. With reference to dimensions, the most investigated are accuracy and completeness and besides them, relevance, usability, timeliness, and others. In two of the papers listed in

Paper	Independent variable	Measured as	Dependent variable	Modeled as	Domain
Jarvenpaa 1985	IQ dimensions	- Intepretation accuracy - Measurement validity - Consistency	Decision performance	- Display format - Task complexity	Managerial decision
Gonzales 1997	IQ dimension	Clarity of the animation	Decision quality	% of correct answers	- Rental decision - Fluidynamics problem
Ahituv 1998	IQ dimension	Completness	Decision efficiency	Number of enemy aircrafts hits	Reaction to an hostile air attack
Raghunathan 1999	IQ dimension	Accuracy	Decision quality	- Closeness of beleif output - Probability of output	
Chengalur-Smith 1999	- IQ metrics - Experience - Time	Reliability of information	Decision making outcome	Choice of best apartment	- Apartment selection - Restaurant site selection
Fisher 2003	Metadata on IQ	Present/ not present	Decision making outcome	- Complacency - Consensu - Consistency	- Apartment selection - Job transfer
Jung 2005	- IQ category - IQ dimensions	- Contextual quality - Completness/ Relevance/Aggregation	Decision quality	# of correct answers	Restaurant site selection
Ge 2006	IQ dimensions	- Accuracy - Completness	Decision quality → Decision effectiveness	% of right decisions	Investment decision
Shankarana-rayan 2006	- Metadata on data processing - Quality assessment	Accuracy, completness, currency, consistencym, relevance	Decision making outcome	Perceived usefullness	Allocation of advertising budget
Letzring 2006	IQ dimension	- Relatistic accuracy - Completness and Relevance of information on personality	Decision quality	Realistic accuracy	Personality judgment
Kerr 2007	IQ dimensions	Accuracy, Timeliness, Comparability, Usability, Relevance, Privacy	Decision quality	Intelligence density	New Zeland health information systems
Ge 2009	- IQ categories - IQ dimensions	- Intrinsic, contextual, representational - Accuracy, completness, consistency	Decision quality	Inventory optimization Cost minimization	Inventory management
Ge 2013	IQ dimensions	2.Accuracy, completness, consistency	Decision quality	Cost minimization	Inventory management

Fig. 11.21 Main papers addressing the relationship between information quality and decision making

Fig. 11.21, IQ is considered as provided through metadata on information or else process metadata.

Decision-making characteristics concern, in the majority of cases, decision quality, which is anyway intended differently in the papers, as highlighted by the column "modeled as." Other papers refer to the outcome of the decision process; in this case, the investigation concerns how the decision-maker has been influenced by the quality of information in making the decision and choosing the outcome. We see that investigation domains vary from apartment or restaurant site selection to inventory management, in one case a psychological domain, personality judgment, health information systems, and also a military domain such as decision in case of a hostile attack.

We now consider in more detail papers that provide most relevant contributions, grouping them according to the two main targets analyzed in decision making, usage of IQ information in the decision, and relationship between IQ and decision quality. In this section, we deliberately add to references the first authors to make easy the link to papers mentioned in Fig. 11.21.

11.7.2   Information Quality Usage in the Decision Process

An experiment that explores the consequences of providing information regarding the quality of information used in decision making is presented in Chengalur-Smith et al. [129]. The quality dimension considered is accuracy of information available for the decision, which is measured through reliability. This meta-information was made available to the subjects, along with the actual information, in three forms: (a) none, (b) two-point ordinal (i.e., above average, below average), and (c) interval scale. Two decision strategies were explored: conjunctive and weighted linear additive. *Conjunctive decision making* assumes that the decision depends upon a known and specified set of criteria; for each of these criteria, a minimum acceptable level is established. *Weighted additive decision making* also assumes that various criteria upon which the decision is based have been identified; in addition, a weight is assigned to each criterion to capture the criterion's relative importance. Two decision environments were used: a simple environment and a relatively complex environment. Hypotheses investigated are expressed in terms of two criteria (a third criterion, consistency, is outside the scope of this summary; the interested reader is addressed to the paper for a detail on that):

- *Complacency*, a measure of the degree to which information on IQ is ignored
- *Consensus*, a measure of the level of agreement within a group with respect to a preferred choice

We report some of the results:

- The level of complacency varied dramatically across the experiments. The smallest level of complacency, corresponding to the greatest impact of information on

IQ, existed for the simple task when groups with interval scaled information on IQ were compared to groups with no information on IQ. This was true for both the conjunctive and the weighted additive strategies. A different pattern emerged for the complex scenario.
- In a situation where subjects were confronted with clearly differentiated alternatives, the inclusion of information on IQ impacted the selection of the preferred alternative while maintaining group consensus.
- The interval format, clearly the one that presents the most detailed information on IQ, was more fully utilized in relatively simple task rather than in one characterized by a substantial level of complexity. The authors observe that while the results are not conclusive, they are strongly suggestive of an impact of information overload, an issue that will be considered in more detail in Sect. 11.7.3.

Also, Fisher et al. [235] are focused on how the available information on IQ is used in decision making, extending the investigation to the experience of the decision-maker and the influence of the available processing time. Results indicate the increasing use of information on IQ when experience levels progress through the stages from novice to professional. The conclusion is that information on IQ should be made available to managers without domain-specific experience. From this, it follows that information on IQ should be incorporated into data warehouses used by managers on an ad hoc basis.

Previous studies on the influence of available information on IQ in decision making are extended in Shankaranarayanan et al. [564], which considers the provision of process metadata, consisting in an abstracted description on how datasets are acquired, processed, stored, and delivered, as a mechanism that influences the end-user assessment of IQ. An exploratory test suggests that both IQ perceptions and the associated process metadata have beneficial effects on outcomes, when mediated by decision-making process efficiency. For large complex datasets, the human ability to detect IQ problems is limited. In such cases, information quantity and complexity exceed the limited capability of users, who can consequently benefit from the provision of IQ metadata.

11.7.2.1 Information Quality and Decision Quality

Generic methodological issues in experimental information system research are investigated in Jarvenpaa et al. [344], observing that despite a vast practice with experimentation, available studies suffer from methodological problems, such as:

- Lack of underlying theory
- Inappropriate research design
- Diversity of experimental tasks
- Proliferation of measuring instruments

With reference to this last problem, [344] introduces the *interpretation accuracy* dimension, which corresponds to (a) the accuracy with which information values displayed in different formats can be estimated or (b) the magnitude of errors found in interpretation tasks. Furthermore, as observed in [344], the literature on presentation modes does not usually indicate whether instruments have been tested for adequate reliability and validity.

The paper presents an interpretation accuracy test whose purpose is to appraise how accurately information was understood by subjects when displayed in a graphical form. Interpretation accuracy is considered as a prerequisite to a correct problem comprehension and improved decision quality. The result obtained in an experiment in the case of a low complexity problem-solving task is that subjects using grouped bar charts perform better than subjects using simple bar charts.

A framework to investigate the efficacy of animation in user interfaces designed for decision support systems is investigated in Gonzalez et al. [271]. One of the characteristics of animation considered in the paper refers to being realistic or abstract, corresponding in such a way to investigating the clarity/readability information dimensions. The conclusion of one of the experiments is that decision quality is significantly greater for subjects that use realistic as opposed to abstract images.

The analysis of the relationship between IQ and decision quality is extended in [515], considering also decision-maker quality; the quality dimension considered is accuracy. Both decision-maker quality and decision quality are analyzed in terms of a decision-making process, simulated through a belief network [495], in such a way that:

- IQ of input i to the decision-making process is modeled as the probability that the value of i believed by the decision-maker is the actual value.
- Decision-maker quality refers to the decision-making process and is measured in terms of the distance between conditional beliefs of the decision-maker and conditional probabilities.
- Decision quality refers to the quality of the decision made by the decision-maker, corresponding to the absolute difference between the probability and the belief of output values.

The analysis shows that the decision-maker quality, in addition to IQ, affects the decision quality significantly. In problems characterized by exact relationships among problem variables, the decision quality is positively correlated with information quality when decision-makers have accurate knowledge of the relationships. However, the decision quality degrades with higher information quality for decision-makers that do not have sufficiently accurate knowledge of the relationships. When exact relationships among problem variables do not exist, IQ does not have any impact on the decision quality.

Ahituv et al. [13] describe an experiment consisting of simulation sessions conducted in order to examine the effects of time pressure and completeness of information on the performance of top Israeli Air Force commanders. The variables examined were:

- Display of complete versus incomplete information
- Time-constrained decision making versus unlimited decision time
- The difference in performance between top strategic commanders and mid-level field commanders

Results show that complete information usually improved performance. However, field commanders (as opposed to top strategic commanders) did not improve their performance when presented with complete information under pressure of time.

Jung et al. [351] investigate in an experimental study the relationships between contextual IQ, task complexity and decision performance and effectiveness. Task complexity is defined as the degree of cognitive load or mental effort required to identify and/or solve a problem, so it can be seen as a function of the number of acts that must be executed and the number of information cues that must be processed when performing a task. Information quality dimensions that are considered relevant to the investigation are relevancy, accuracy, and completeness of information. Decision qualities considered in the study are decision performance, measured as the solution time, and decision effectiveness, measured by the number of correct answers for the correct solutions. The decision task consisted of a selection of a site for the construction of a Chinese restaurant. While the complex task asked respondents to select a site among five alternative sites in which to locate a Chinese restaurant, the simple task asked respondents to select a site among three alternative sites.

The respondents were supported with an appropriate amount of aggregated information in the form of tables, with varying degrees of relevance and completeness. The subjects considered as being assigned to the treatment of low-quality contextual information used irrelevant and incomplete information. For example, a pair of numbers in the dataset given to the respondents was missing. Therefore, they had to go through extra steps to infer the information necessary to make decisions. The analysis of responses confirmed the following hypotheses:

- *Decision efficiency vs. quality of information*—Regardless of the levels of task complexity, respondents with high-quality contextual information require less time than those with low-quality contextual information.
- *Decision effectiveness vs. quality of information*—Regardless of the levels of task complexity, problem solving with high-quality contextual information will lead to an increase in problem-solving accuracy compared to problem solving with low-quality contextual information.
- *Decision efficiency vs. task complexity*—Regardless of the levels of contextual IQ, subjects with a simple task will require less time than subjects with a complex task.

While the following hypothesis was disconfirmed:

- *Task complexity vs. information quality*—Regardless of the levels of contextual IQ, subjects with a simple task will make more accurate decisions than subjects with a complex task.

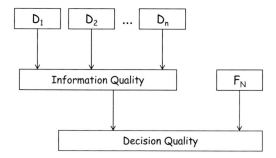

Fig. 11.22 General approach to factors influencing decision quality proposed in [257]

A decision-support framework is proposed in Shankaranarayanan et al. [564], which allows decision-makers to gauge quality both in an objective and in a context-dependent manner. The framework is based on the information product approach and uses the information product map; see Chap. 6; the dimension considered is completeness. A decision-support tool for managing IQ that incorporates the proposed framework is also described.

The objective of Ge et al. [257] is very ambitious, involving the investigation of a general approach to decision quality and IQ dimensions and factors that have influence on it; see Fig. 11.22, where D_i represent the value of dimension i and F_n represent other factors influencing decision quality, such as decision-makers' subjective preference or experience.

Dimensions investigated are accuracy and completeness. Functional relationships with decision quality are formulated for them, such as the one in Fig. 11.23 that shows several decision quality contours, where different combinations of completeness and accuracy achieve the same decision quality. An experiment based on an investment decision shows evidence of an almost linear relationship between completeness of information and decision quality.

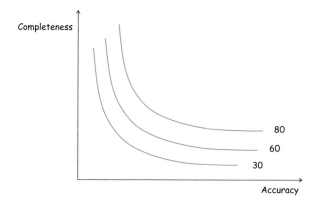

Fig. 11.23 Decision quality contours as a function of completeness and accuracy

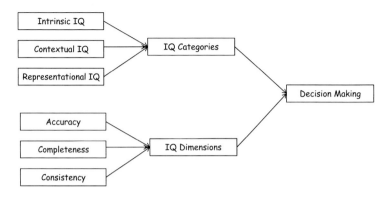

Fig. 11.24 Model proposed in [256]

	Order Complexity	Objective	Optimal Decision
Scenario 1	•One identical brand of beer over 10 weeks •One decision in each week	Minimize inventory	Zero inventory
Scenario 2	•Order 10 different brands of beer •Make one decision for each brand	Minimize total costs	Minimal total costs

Fig. 11.25 Scenarios proposed in [256] and [258]

The objective of Ge et al. [256, 258] is to systematically analyze the effects of IQ on decision making. In order to achieve this objective, a model is proposed (see Fig. 11.24) that considers both classes of dimensions as introduced in [646] and atomic dimensions as independent variables to be related to decision quality.

Scenarios experimented (see Fig. 11.25) are based on a management game, the Beer Game, a role-playing simulation that involves managing supply and demand in a beer supply chain. In Scenario 1, one identical brand of beer is ordered in 10 weeks and a decision is taken in each week; in this scenario, the objective of the inventory control policy is to minimize inventory, and the optimal decision is zero inventory. In the second scenario, of greater complexity, the policy leads minimize total costs.

Results show that the categories of intrinsic and contextual IQ are positively related to decision quality, while decision quality is not significantly affected by representational IQ. It is also found that in contrast to consistency, increasing information accuracy and completeness can significantly improve decision quality.

Above results are extended in Ge et al. [258] that, following a multidimensional view of IQ, investigate the effects of information accuracy, completeness, and consistency on decision making. Results confirm that information accuracy and completeness affect decision quality significantly. Although the effect of information consistency on decision quality appears to be nonsignificant, consistency of information could intensify the contribution of accuracy, indicating that information accuracy and consistency influence decision quality jointly.

An example of investigation in a quite different research area, namely, personality
and social psychology, appears in Letzring et al. [398]. Every day, people make
personality judgments on other people. These judgments differ in how accurate they
are, because they are made on the basis of varying degrees of acquaintance and
information that diverge in how relevant they are to personality. These two aspects
of the information available to a judge are referred to as information quantity, the
sheer amount of information that is available, and information quality that in [398] is
defined as the degree to which the available information is relevant to personality, so
pertains to relevance. The concept of information quantity is straightforward in that
it assumes that judges who have access to more information about the personality
of the target will make more accurate judgments of personality. The concept of
IQ refers to the likelihood that even when information quantity is held constant,
different contexts of acquaintanceship might vary in the degree to which personality
relevant information becomes available on them.

Decision quality is modeled in [398] through *realistic accuracy* that refers
to the level of agreement between a personality judgment and what a target is
really like. The paper states that this construct cannot be directly measured by any
single personality or behavior rating, as any single rating is highly uncertain as an
indicator of what a person is really like. Instead, the ideal of realistic accuracy can
be approached to the degree that multiple methods of measurement are used and
combined to form a broad-based accuracy criterion for each target of judgment.
Results supported the hypothesis that information quantity and quality are positively
related to objective knowledge about the targets and realistic accuracy. The same
holds for a second indicator of decision quality, consensus, which we encountered
when summarizing Shankaranarayanan [564].

The healthcare domain in New Zealand is examined in Kerr et al. [362]. The issue
of the relationship between IQ and decision quality is discussed within the wider
objective of establishing and applying an IQ strategy in healthcare information
systems. The study notes that the absence or incomplete availability of information
affects decision-making processes. For example, a decision on devolving services
from the Ministry of Health to healthcare providers ran into problems because it was
not supported with access to historical information on service provision. Equally
difficult was the need to make decisions using out-of-date information.

The IQ dimensions chosen for the study are accuracy, relevancy, timeliness,
comparability, usability, security, and privacy. Decision quality and more in general
the quality of what in the paper is called intelligent enterprise (see also [173] on this
issue) is modeled in terms of *intelligence density*, defined as the amount of useful
decision support information that a decision-maker gets from using organizational
tools and methods.

An IQ strategy is claimed by the authors to increase intelligence density in several
ways. Firstly, by design, inaccuracies and inconsistencies that decrease the value
and utility of decision support information are subject to improvement activities.
In addition, the co-availability with information of the metadata that define context
minimizes errors of interpretation. Where context is historical, metadata increase
information longevity, so that decision-makers can use information from historical

collections even when the processes and procedures used to capture information have changed over time.

11.7.3 *Decision Making and Information Overload*

A number of studies have tested the relationships between information overload, information processing, and decision quality, leading to different results. As an example, [579] finds no significant changes in decision quality at different information load levels, while [574] reports an inverted curve for the relationship between information overload and decision quality. A similar generic curve is reported in [449].

Both [329] and [320] investigate the relationship between information load and decision quality in two experiments, the first within a structured task and the latter within a highly unstructured task, namely, bankruptcy studies. In [329], decision quality is modeled in terms of (a) decision accuracy and (b) time needed for decision. The concept of information load is subdivided in terms of (1) quantity of repeated dimensions (namely, redundant information) and (2) quantity of different dimensions that models the complexity of information. The results can be summarized as follows:

- The relationship between the quantity of repeated dimensions and accuracy is an inverted U curve, but such property holds only for the fall in the curve.
- The relationship between the quantity of repeated dimensions and time is an inverted U curve, but such property does hold only for the raising part of the curve.

The approach of Iselin [329] is applied in [320] to firm bankruptcy studies. In this case, decision quality is measured as *prediction accuracy*, defined as the ratio of the number of correct predictions to the number of firms in the sample. Two indicators are considered for modeling information load, namely:

- *Information diversity*, defined as the number of different financial ratios used in the experiment
- *Information repetitiveness* calculated as the number of information cues minus information diversity

Results indicate that both information dimensions have a negative impact on decision quality: provision of either diverse or repeated information can be detrimental to prediction accuracy.

The effect of information overload on how consumers evaluate and purchase products is investigated among others in [360]. Authors observe that one major concern of policy makers and researchers interested in how consumers use available information is the determination of the maximum amount of information that a consumer can effectively process before experiencing decreased accuracy in assessing the value (utility) of available choice alternatives. Keller and Staelin [360]

investigate the effects of both quality and quantity of information on decision effectiveness that corresponds to the perceived utility. Several hypothesized correlations
are experimented; conclusions can be summarized as follows:

- Decision effectiveness is adversely affected by increases in the quantity of
  information made available (holding quality fixed) and fostered by increases in
  the quality level, at least up to a point (holding quantity levels fixed).
- Decision effectiveness first increases and then decreases as the amount of
  information available increases, holding fixed the average quality level of the
  informational environment.
- Higher levels of IQ are associated with higher relative amounts of attribute
  information used, holding quantity of available information fixed. Relating usage
  of attribute information to choice accuracy, it appeared that subjects were more
  likely to reach the correct choice when they used most but not all of the available
  information.

In the same area, [390] investigates the effect of information overload on
customer choice quality in an online environment. In an experiment, consumers
were asked to choose the best (dominant) CD player in a given set, varying
the number of alternatives and attributes (traditional measure) and attribute level
distribution across alternatives (structural measure). Results show that the number
of attributes and attribute level distribution are good predictors of the effect of
information overload on consumer choice. In addition, the study finds that online
information overload results in less satisfied, less confident, and more confused
consumers.

In [230], it is observed that in cognitive psychology and decision-making
research, the amount of information is considered to be a function that cannot
take negative values. Adaptive decision making requires that contingencies between
decision options and their relative assets be assessed accurately and quickly. The
research addresses the challenging notion that contingencies may be more visible
from small than from large samples of observations. An algorithmic evidence
for such a seemingly paradoxical effect is offered within a satisficing-choice
framework. The conclusion after experiments is that contingencies are more visible
from small than from large samples of observations. Across a broad range of
parameters, the resulting small-sample advantage in terms of hits is stronger than
their disadvantage in false alarms. Computer simulations and experiments support
the model predictions.

Several papers address the issue of how to contrast the effect of information
overload. Solutions introduced in [360] to reduce information overload are:

- A reduction in the duplication of information
- The adoption of personal information management strategies, together with the
  integration of software solutions such as push technology working by pushing
  notices of preselected information sources alerting users to new and updated
  information
- The provision of value-added information

The effectiveness of using graphs as decision aids to reduce the adverse effects of information overload on decision quality is discussed in [116]. The results obtained from an experiment simulating a real business prediction task indicated that prediction accuracy deteriorated under information overload. However, the mode of presentation format alone did not have any significant impact on prediction accuracy nor did the interactions of information load and the mode of presentation format. Authors suggest that to improve the performance of business managers, information systems professionals should focus more on determining the optimal amount of information that should be provided to users, instead of indiscriminately offering graphs for all figures.

An original contribution to the investigation of the effects of information overload appears in [376] where it is stated that a lack of structure, not the amount, is the reason for the growing inability to cope with information today. Four structuring dimensions are proposed:

- Selection of information to be filtered for users by professional information providing bodies.
- Time; each type of information, such as weather forecasts or else Wikipedia, has its own life cycle, so additional methods of time positioning and information aggregation and abstraction have to be found.
- Hierarchy, both in terms of quality and level of detail.
- Sequence that corresponds to classification and ordering of information.

We have to observe that the paper was published in 1995, and so does not take into account the evolution of research raising from the phenomenon of big data; see Chap. 14.

11.7.4 Value-Driven Decision Making

In [217, 374, 375], it is observed that business intelligence (BI) systems and tools are broadly adopted in modern organizations, supporting activities such as information analysis, managerial decision making, and business performance measurement. Such papers investigate the integration of value-based recommendation mechanisms into business intelligence solutions. Recommendation mechanisms are textual, visual, and/or graphical cues that are embedded into front end BI tools and guide the end user to consider using certain data subsets and analysis functionalities. The research focuses on recommendation mechanisms based on assessment of previous usage and the associated value gain; it incorporates a methodology that exploits value-driven metadata for tracking and communicating the usage of information, linked to a quantitative assessment of the value gained. Furthermore, a high-level architecture is presented for supporting the collection, storage, and presentation of metadata and a quantitative method for assessing it; see Fig. 11.26.

In [375], it is observed that tracking the usage of information objects (e.g., tables, attributes, and records) is identified in the decision-making literature and

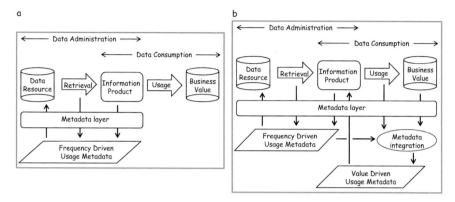

Fig. 11.26 (**a**) Frequency driven vs. (**b**) value-driven usage metadata

applications as an important form of metadata. Usage tracking utilities are offered by some specialized commercial solutions and, to an extent, by DBMS and BI platforms. Such an approach is named in [375] *frequency-driven usage metadata*; see Fig. 11.26a. In the paper, it is claimed that such a framework has to evolve toward value-driven usage metadata; see Fig. 11.26b. The following example explains the new approach.

Consider a database made of the unique table Customers in Fig. 11.27. We assume that the query load is made of four queries, all having a similar structure based on a selection made over a subset of attributes; see the queries table in Fig. 11.27, where attributes and tuples involved are shown for each query. Frequency metadata on tuples and attributes can be evaluated based on the queries table and assuming for simplicity that queries have the same frequency conventionally set to 1.

A potential risk when basing information management decisions solely on frequency-driven metadata is a possible loss of opportunity to benefit from tuples and attributes that information consumers have neglected to use so far, which may permit new forms of information usage, thus increasing potential information utility. In the paper, it is claimed that, beyond the benefit offered to information administration, collecting quantitative assessment of the business-value gained as a form of metadata can improve information consumption as well. Business value can be measured, for example, in terms of decision outcomes (e.g., production increase, customers' purchase intent), revenues and profitability. In [375], a method is proposed based on the assumption that each query has led to a certain promotion campaign in which a group of customers has been approached. Customers may have responded to the campaign by making certain purchases, and the overall value attributed to a query is the total purchase amount; see in Fig. 11.28 attribute Total value of table Queries. We see in the figure that this value can significantly vary among queries. The above value index for queries can be used to assess the relative

Customers

#	Customer	Gender	Income	Children	Status	Frequency
1	James	Male	High	0	Single	1
2	Sarah	Female	Low	1	Married	2
3	Isaac	Male	Medium	2	Married	1
4	Rebecca	Female	Low	0	Single	1
5	Jacob	Male	Medium	3	Married	1
6	Lea	Female	High	2	Married	3
7	Rachel	Female	Low	4	Single	0
Frequency		3	1	2	1	

Queries

WHERE Condition	Attributes Used	Tuples Retrieved
Gender = "Male" and Children > 0	Gender, Children	[3], [5]
Gender = "Female" and Children < 3	Gender, Children	[2], [4], [6]
Gender = "Female" and Status = "Married"	Gender, Status	[2], [6]
Income = "High"	Income	[1], [6]

Fig. 11.27 Example from [375] and frequency driven usage metadata

value of each attribute and of each tuple. The formula proposed in [375] is

$$V_{n,m} = \Sigma_{q=1}^{Q} V_{n,m}^{q} = \Sigma_{q=1}^{Q} V^{q} / (\Sigma_{n=1}^{N} \Sigma_{m=1}^{M} R_{n}^{q} R_{m}^{q})$$

where

- $V_{n,m}$ is the value of attribute m in tuple n.
- V^{q} is the above value of query q.
- R_{n}^{q} and R_{m}^{q} are binary indicators of the participation of tuple n and attribute m in query q.

Corresponding aggregated values for each tuple and for each attribute are shown in Fig. 11.28, table Customers, respectively, in the last column and in the last row.

In [375], it is claimed that important insights can be gained by analyzing the value distribution, along with the assessment of frequency of use. For example, the Income attribute, which was not frequently used, is associated with the highest value, while the Children attribute, which was more frequently used, is associated with lower value. Such kind of insights can be transformed into valuable recommendations for a future marketing campaign.

Customers

#	Customer	Gender	Income	Children	Status	......	Value
1	James	Male	High	0	Single		1
2	Sarah	Female	Low	1	Married		2
3	Isaac	Male	Medium	2	Married		1
4	Rebecca	Female	Low	0	Single		1
5	Jacob	Male	Medium	3	Married		1
6	Lea	Female	High	2	Married		3
7	Rachel	Female	Low	4	Single		0
....							
Value		515	2.000	60	500		

Queries

WHERE Condition	Attributes Used	Tuples Retrieved	Total Value
Gender = "Male" and Children > 0	Gender, Children	[3], [5]	100
Gender = "Female" and Children < 3	Gender, Children	[2], [4], [6]	30
Gender = "Female" and Status = "Married"	Gender, Status	[2], [6]	1000
Income = "High"	Income	[1], [6]	2000

Fig. 11.28   Value-driven usage metadata from [375]

11.8   Summary

In this chapter, we have faced several economic and managerial issues related to information quality when information is used in business processes and decision making. We have seen that when the quality has to be related to the efficiency or effectiveness of processes or decisions, we have to adopt metrics that are to be contextualized to the problem at hand. This is a fundamental change of perspective in comparison to objective dimensions and metrics considered so far, and a significant challenge for future research in information quality, also considering that case studies investigated so far refer specifically to the marketing domain. We have also seen that in the information system life cycle, when the issue of improving quality of managed information becomes relevant, we have to adopt first of all cost and benefit classifications discussed and compared in the chapter.

The economic issues have been discussed in the chapter both from the point of view of costs of poor quality and of quality improvement projects and from the point of view of the value that quality information provides to processes and decisions that make use of it. We have also seen that the value of information can be enhanced when integration technologies, discussed in Chap. 10, are adopted to reconcile heterogeneities present in a group of datasets.

To extend our analysis on value of information, we have finally addressed a topic that is collateral with respect to information quality, namely, value-driven decision making, trying to show that quality and value are two complementary faces of that versatile and powerful resource represented by information. Considering quality and value of information together provides powerful capabilities that researchers just started to understand in depth.

Chapter 12
Methodologies for Information Quality Assessment and Improvement

12.1 Introduction

Measuring and improving information quality in a single organization or in a set of cooperating organizations is a complex task. In previous chapters, we discussed relevant activities for improving information quality (Chap. 7) and corresponding techniques (Chaps. 7–10). Several methodologies have been developed in the last few years that provide a rationale for the optimal choice of such activities and techniques. In this chapter, we discuss methodologies proposed in the research and professional literature for information quality assessment and improvement from multiple perspectives.

We address the issue of methodologies with a top-down perspective. Section 12.2 provides, in terms of classifications, typical inputs and outputs, strategies addressed, and typical phases of methodologies.

Section compares, according to several general criteria, 13 methodologies that have been proposed in the literature for information quality assessment and improvement. Section 12.4 describes and compares in more detail three of the most relevant general purpose methodologies addressed in Sect. 12.3. Section 12.5 deals with assessment methodologies and describes in detail one of them, the methodology for the Quality Assessment of Financial Data (QAFD).

In Sect. 12.6, we propose the Complete Data Quality Methodology (CDQM), focused mainly on structured relational data that at the same time is complete, flexible, and simple to apply; in Sect. 12.7 CDQM is applied to a case study. Section 12.8 extends CDQM to other types of information, providing a case study in which the new type of information considered is semistructured information.

In this chapter, more than in other chapters, it is hard to be coherent with respect to the issue addressed in the preface on the data/information and data quality/information quality terminology. The large majority of methodologies for information quality assessment and improvement focuses on structured data and semistructured information; some methodologies, while providing case studies

© Springer International Publishing Switzerland 2016
C. Batini, M. Scannapieco, *Data and Information Quality*, Data-Centric Systems and Applications, DOI 10.1007/978-3-319-24106-7_12

Section	Topic	Types of information	Terminology adopted
2.	Methodologies in general	Information in general	Information & Information Quality
3.	Comparison of 13 methodologies	Different types of information	Information & Information Quality
4.	Detailed comparison of three methodologies: TDQM, TIQM, Istat	Different types of information	Information & Information Quality
5.	Assessment methodologies: Description of QAFD	Structured relational data	Data and Data Quality
6.	Assessment & improvement methodologies: the CDQM Methodology	Structured relational data	Data and Data Quality
7.	Case study on CDQM application	Structured relational data	Data and Data Quality
8.	Extension of CDQM	Structured relational data & Semistructured information	Information & Information Quality

Fig. 12.1 Terminologies adopted in chapter sections

mainly or exclusively based on structured data and databases, include phases and steps that can be applied to information in general. Other methodologies, while adopting in their short name the term data, make indeed reference to information in general in their detailed descriptions (Fig. 12.1).

12.2 Basics on Information Quality Methodologies

We define an IQ methodology as a set of guidelines and techniques that, starting from the input information concerning a given reality of interest, defines a rational process for using the information to assess and improve IQ of an organization through given phases and decision points. In the rest of the section, we focus on knowledge in input and on produced output (Sect. 12.2.1), classifications of methodologies (Sect. 12.2.2), typical strategies adopted (Sect. 12.2.3), and finally typical steps of assessment and measurement phases (Sect. 12.2.4).

12.2.1 Inputs and Outputs

The different types of input knowledge to an IQ methodology in the most general case are shown in Fig. 12.2, where arrows represent generalization hierarchies among concepts; e.g., *collections of data* can be *internal groups* or *external sources*, and internal groups can be *data flows* or *databases*.

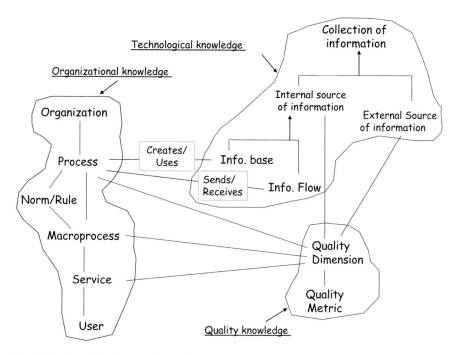

Fig. 12.2 Knowledge involved in the IQ measurement and improvement process

The main types of knowledge are:

1. The *organization* or the set of organizations involved in the processes, with related organizational structures, functions, norms, and rules.
2. The business *processes* performed in the organization and the *macroprocesses*, i.e., processes that executed together produce services or goods for users, customers, and businesses.
3. The *services* delivered by processes and the *segments of users* requesting services.
4. The *norms/rules* that discipline the execution of processes and macroprocesses.
5. The *quality of processes, macroprocesses, and services*, e.g., the time of execution of a process, the usability of a service, and the accuracy of information provided by a data service. For a detailed treatment of this point, we refer the reader to [631].
6. The *collections of information*, corresponding to all sources of information internal and external to the organization which are of some interest to the organization. As to references to internal sources, we distinguish between:

   • *Information bases*, and among them specifically databases that are information stored permanently and organized logically and physically in such a way to be easily accessed and managed

- *Information flows*, namely, information that is exchanged between different organizational units

Both types of information, "motionless" information and "moving" information, have to be considered, since:

- Errors can affect and be propagated by both.
- Depending on their quality, they can positively or negatively influence the quality of processes.

The *external sources of information* are often more critical than internal information for their quality, since there is little or no control over their production process and previous origin.

7. The *information quality dimensions* and corresponding *metrics* are defined previously in Chaps. 2–5, and also in forthcoming Chap. 14, a large set of them is concerned with the improvement process.

Besides the types of knowledge described, other relevant elements involved in an IQ methodology are:

- The *information quality activities*, which is the whole set of activities introduced in Chap. 7 that can be performed to improve the quality of information
- *Costs and benefits* discussed in Chap. 11: (1) costs associated with processes due to poor information quality, (2) costs of the improvement process, (3) and benefits (savings and/or increased revenues) resulting from the use of better quality information

Based on the knowledge involved in the IQ measurement and improvement process, the input/output structure of a general-purpose methodology for IQ is shown in Fig. 12.3.

Inputs refer to all types of knowledge described in Fig. 12.2, plus the available budget, if known. The outputs concern (1) the activities to be performed and the techniques to be applied; (2) the business processes that have to be controlled and/or reengineered; (3) the optimal improvement process, i.e., the sequence of activities that achieve the target quality dimensions with the minimum cost; (4) the information bases and information flows respecting new target quality dimensions; and (5) costs and benefits.

Fig. 12.3 Inputs and outputs of an IQ measurement and improvement methodology

12.2.2 Classification of Methodologies

Information quality methodologies can be classified according to several criteria:

1. *Information driven vs. process driven.* This classification is related to the general strategy chosen for the improvement process. *Information-driven* strategies are based on using information sources exclusively to improve the quality of information; they make use of the information quality activities introduced in Chap. 7. In *process-driven* strategies, the information production process is analyzed and possibly modified to identify and remove the root causes of quality problems. We analyze this classification in more detail in Sect. 12.2.3. As we will see in Sect. 12.3, general-purpose methodologies can adopt both information-driven and process-driven strategies, with different depth according to the specific methodology.

2. *Assessment* vs. *improvement.* Methodologies are needed for measuring/assessing the quality of information, or to improve their quality. Assessment and improvement activities are closely interrelated, since only when IQ measurements are available is it possible to conceive techniques to be applied and priorities to be established. As a consequence, the boundary between the methodologies for measurement and improvement is sometimes vague. In the following, we will use the term *measurement* when we address the issue of measuring the values of a set of IQ dimensions in a information base (or a set of information bases). We use the term *assessment* or *benchmarking* when such measurements are compared to reference values, to enable a diagnosis of the quality of the information base. The usual term adopted will be assessment. Assessment methodologies will be discussed in Sect. 12.5.

3. *General purpose vs. special purpose.* A *general-purpose* methodology covers a wide spectrum of phases, dimensions, and activities, while a *special purpose* methodology is focused on a specific activity (e.g., measurement, object identification), on a specific information domain (e.g., a census, a registry of addresses of persons), or on specific application domains (e.g., biology). Three of the most relevant general-purpose methodologies will be discussed in Sect. 12.4.

4. *Intraorganizational vs. interorganizational.* The measurement and improvement activity concerns a specific organization, or a specific sector of the organization, or even a specific process or information base. Otherwise, it concerns a group of organizations (e.g., a group of public agencies) cooperating for a common goal (e.g., in the case of public agencies, providing better services to citizens and businesses).

12.2.3   Comparison Among Information-Driven and Process-Driven Strategies

In this section, we compare information-driven and process-driven strategies. Among information-driven strategies, we distinguish for simplicity three major strategies, using three distinct IQ activities discussed in Chap. 7:

1. New information acquisition from the real world. When information representing a certain reality of interest is inaccurate, incomplete, or out-of-date, a possible way for improving its quality may be to again observe the reality of interest and perform the activity called in Chap. 7 *new information acquisition*. For example, if in a registry of employees, the DateOfBirth is known only in 30 % of the cases, we could request employees' missing information. Intuitively, if the information acquisition campaign is performed effectively, this strategy immediately improves certain quality dimensions such as completeness, accuracy, and currency, since the data exactly represent the most recent reality of interest; we however note that errors can be introduced by the measurement activity.
2. Object identification or, more generally, the comparison of information whose quality dimensions have to be improved with other information in which the quality is known to be good. As an example, let us consider a structured database of addresses of clients that have been collected for a long period of time in a supermarket through forms, in order to provide clients with a fidelity card. After a while, certain quality dimensions, such as accuracy of home addresses, tend to worsen. We could decide to perform a record matching activity to compare client records with an administrative database, known to be updated with the most recent data.
3. Use of data edits/integrity constraints, in which (1) we define a set of integrity constraints against which data have to be checked, (2) we discover inconsistencies among data, and (3) we correct the inconsistent data by means of error localization and correction activities.

Process-driven strategies focus on processes. Consequently, they need to acquire knowledge from information bases and information flows in inputs only to a limited extent. Conversely, they focus mainly on measuring the quality of processes and formulating proposals for process improvement. Two main phases characterize process-driven strategies:

- *Process control*, which inserts checks and control procedures into the information production process when (1) new information is inserted from internal or external sources, (2) information sources accessed by the process are updated, or (3) new information sources are involved in the process. In this way, a reactive strategy is applied to information modification events, to avoid information degradation and error propagation.
- *Process redesign*, where we avoid improving the actual process. We redesign the production processes in order to remove the causes of bad quality and introduce

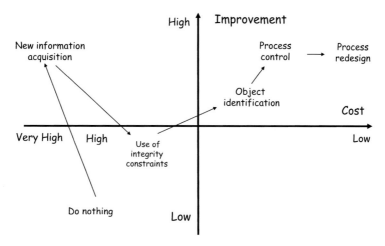

Fig. 12.4 Improvement and cost of information-/process-driven strategies: comparison in the long term

new activities that produce information of better quality. In the case in which the change in the process is radical, this strategy corresponds to the activity called *business process reengineering* (see [293] and [592] for a comprehensive introduction to this issue).

We compare now information- and process-driven strategies according to two coordinates of analysis: (1) the improvement the strategy is potentially able to produce on quality dimensions and (2) the cost of its implementation. This comparison can be performed both in the short term and in the long term. In the following (see Fig. 12.4), we compare improvement and costs in the long term; optimal target objectives are high improvement and low cost.

The simplest and most trivial strategy is to *do nothing*. In this case, information is neglected and abandoned; certain quality dimensions, such as completeness and currency, tend to worsen in the long term. The consequence is that information progressively deteriorates the quality of business processes and the cost of lost quality increases over time.

A better strategy is *new information acquisition*; in the short term, the improvement is relevant, since information is current, complete, and accurate. However, as time goes by, we are obliged to periodically repeat the process, and the cost becomes intolerable.

The strategy that uses integrity constraints leads to much lower costs, but at the same time it is less effective, since only the errors related to constraints can be checked. Errors can be corrected only to a certain extent, as we have seen in Chap. 7.

The strategy performing *object identification* has even lower costs and even more improvements, since many techniques have been developed and implemented, as we saw in Chaps. 8 and 9. A relevant part of the work can be done automatically. Furthermore, once the records corresponding to the same object have been identified, high-quality values can be chosen for the different attributes from the higher-quality source.

In order to be effective, previous strategies that belong to the class of information-driven strategies have to be repeated, leading to costs that increase in the long term. Only when we move to process-driven methods can we optimize at the same time effectiveness and costs: *process control* activities and, above all, *process redesign* activities can get to the root of the problem and solve the problem once and for all. Their costs are mainly the fixed costs related to the one-shot control or redesign activity, plus variable process maintenance costs distributed over a time period.

The above considerations are valid for the long term. For the short term it is well known that process redesign can be very costly. As a consequence, information-driven strategies become more competitive. We refer the reader to [519] for a complete discussion on these issues.

12.2.4 Basic Common Phases Among Methodologies

Basic common *phases* can be obtained by abstracting from specific notations adopted in the specific approaches. We distinguish between assessment and improvement processes.

12.2.4.1 Assessment

Common phases for the assessment process are:

- *Analysis*, which examines information bases and databases, schemas, and meta-data available on them and performs interviews to reach a complete understanding of information and related architectural and management rules.
- *IQ requirements analysis*, which surveys the opinion of information users and administrators to identify quality issues and set new quality targets.
- *Identification of critical areas*, which selects the most relevant information bases and flows to be assessed quantitatively.
- *Process modeling*, which provides a model of the processes producing or updating information.
- *Measurement of quality*, which selects the quality dimensions affected by the quality issues identified in the IQ requirements analysis step and defines corresponding metrics. Measurement can be *objective*, when it is based on quantitative metrics, or *subjective*, when it is based on qualitative evaluations by information/data administrators and users.

Each of the above activities can be performed both as a global step on the whole set of organizational units of an interorganizational information system and as a specific step performed autonomously by a local organizational unit in an intraorganizational information system.

Notice that in all the steps of the assessment phase, a relevant role is played by *metadata* that store complementary information for a variety of purposes, including information quality. Metadata often provide the knowledge needed to understand information and/or assess it.

12.2.4.2 Improvement

The steps of the improvement phase are:

- *Evaluation of costs*, which estimates the direct and indirect costs of information quality
- *Assignment of process responsibilities*, which identifies the process owners and defines their responsibilities on information production and management activities
- *Assignment of responsibilities*, which identifies the information owners and defines their data management responsibilities
- *Identification of the causes of errors*, which identifies the causes of quality problems
- *Selection of strategies and techniques*, which identifies all the information improvement strategies and corresponding techniques that comply with contextual knowledge, quality objectives, and budget constraints
- *Design of information improvement solutions*, which selects the most effective and efficient strategy and related set of techniques and tools to improve information quality
- *Process control*, which defines checkpoints in the information production processes, to monitor quality during process execution
- *Process redesign*, which defines the process improvement actions that can deliver corresponding IQ improvements
- *Improvement management*, which defines new organizational rules for information quality
- *Improvement monitoring*, which establishes periodical monitoring activities that provide feedback on the results of the improvement process and enables its dynamic tuning

Also in the case of improvement activities, methodological phases can involve a whole organization, or a group of organizations, or a specific organizational unit.

12.3 Comparison of Methodologies

This section compares 13 methodologies based on the classification criteria discussed in the previous section. Other methodologies have been proposed and are currently used. Redman [519] describes a significant number of guidelines and experiences to be applied in IQ projects; they will not be discussed as a distinct

Table 12.1 Methodologies compared in this section

Acronym	Extended name	Main reference
TDQM	Total Data quality Management	Wang 1988
DWQ	The Datawarehouse Quality Methodology	Jarke 1999
TIQM	Total Information Quality Management	English 1999
AIMQ	A Methodology for information quality assessment	Lee 2001
CIHI	Canadian Institute for Health Information Methodology	Long 2005
DQA	Data Quality Assessment	Pipino 2002
IQM	Information Quality Measurement	Eppler 2002
ISTAT	ISTAT Methodology	Falorsi 2003
AMEQ	Activity Based Measuring and Evaluating of Product Information Quality Methodology	Su 2004
COLDQ	Cost Effect of Low Data Quality Methodology	Loshin 2004
DaQuinCIS	Data Quality in Cooperative Information Systems	Scannapieco 2004
QAFD	Methodology for the Quality Assessment of Financial Data	De Amicis 2004
CDQ	Comprehensive Methodology for Data Quality Management	Batini 2006

methodology. The study of Jarke et al. [342] is worth mentioning as a methodology for building data warehouses considering data quality aspects; the methodology adapts the goal-question-metric approach from software quality management to a data management environment.

Table 12.1 shows the list of the methodologies considered in this section identified by acronyms together with the extended name of the methodology and the main reference. The acronym will be used to identify each methodology in the remainder of this section.

We anticipate that three of the methodologies, namely, TDQM (Total Data Quality Methodology), TIQM (Total Information Quality Methodology), and Istat (Istituto Nazionale di Statistica), will be compared with greater detail in Sect. 12.4, while CDQM will be analytically described in Sect. 12.6 and applied in a case study in Sect. 12.7.

The above methodologies have been compared in [41] over a wide set of criteria and are also discussed in this chapter (Fig. 12.5).

12.3.1   Assessment Phase

Table 12.2 compares the steps followed by different methodologies in the assessment phase.

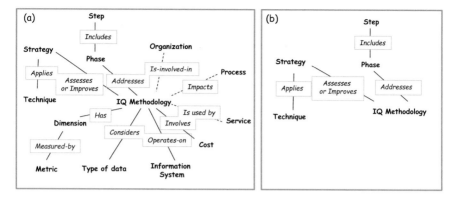

Fig. 12.5 (**a**) Criteria adopted in [41] and (**b**) criteria considered in this section

Table 12.2 Methodologies and assessment steps

Step/ Meth Acronym	Analysis	IQ Requirement Analysis	Identification of Critical Areas	Process Modeling	Measurement of quality	Extensible to other dimensions and metrics
TDQM	+		+	+	+	Fixed
DWQ	+	+	+		+	Open
TIQM	+	+	+	+	+	Fixed
AIMQ	+		+		+	Fixed
CIHI	+		+			Fixed
DQA	+		+		+	Open
IQM	+				+	Open
ISTAT	+				+	Fixed
AMEQ	+		+	+	+	Open
COLDQ	+	+	+	+	+	Open
DaQuinCIS	+		+	+	+	Open
QAFD	+	+			+	Fixed
CDQ	+	+	+	+	+	Open

The most commonly addressed steps of the assessment phase are *analysis* and *measurement of quality*. However, they are performed according to different approaches. For example, the *measurement of quality* step is performed with questionnaires in AIMQ, with a combination of subjective and objective metrics in DQA, or with statistical analyses in QAFD. Different measurement approaches meet the specific requirements of different organizational contexts, processes, users, or services. Only a few methodologies consider the *IQ requirements analysis* step, identifying IQ issues and collecting new target quality levels from users. This step is particularly relevant to evaluate and solve conflicts in target IQ levels from different stakeholders. For example, QAFD recommends the collection of target quality levels from different types of experts, including business experts and financial operators, but does not help the reconciliation of incompatible IQ levels. A few methodologies support *process modeling*. Note that with the exception of AMEQ, the methodologies supporting process modeling also adopt a process-driven strategy for the improvement phase (see next section).

The last column of Table 12.2 specifies whether the methodology allows extensibility to dimensions (and metrics) other than those explicitly dealt with in the methodology.

Note that the methodologies that address both the *process modeling* and *measurement of quality* steps are based on the "fitness for use" approach; see Chap. 11. They evaluate the quality of information along the processes in which they are used and, thus, mainly provide subjective measures.

12.3.2 Improvement Phase

Tables 12.3 and 12.4 compare the improvement steps of different methodologies.

The *identification of the causes of errors* is the most widely addressed improvement step. DQA emphasizes the importance of the *identification of the causes of errors* step, but it does not discuss its execution. Similarly, DWQ refers to a mathematical model based on the concept of dependency to support the *identification of the causes of errors* step, but the definition of the model is presented as on-going work and is not provided.

Only six methodologies address multiple improvement steps, as confirmed in Table 12.5. Improvement activities are mostly based on *process redesign*, with the exception of the DWQ methodology, which provides an extension of the goal-question-metric [104] initially proposed in the software engineering field. The *cost evaluation* step is usually mandatory in IQ methodologies. This step is considered critical to measure the economic advantage of improvement solutions and to choose the most efficient improvement techniques. In contrast, the *management*

Table 12.3 Methodologies and improvement steps—part 1

Step/ Meth. Acronym	Evaluation of costs	Assignment of process responsibilities	Assignment of data responsibilities	Selection of strategies and techniques	Identification of the causes of errors
TDQM	+	+	+	+	+
DWQ	+		+	+	+
TIQM	+	+	+	+	+
DQA					+
ISTAT				+	+
AMEQ					+
COLDQ	+			+	+
DaQuinCIS				+	+
CDQ	+	+	+	+	+

Table 12.4 Methodologies and improvement steps—part 2

Step/Meth. Acronym	Process control	Process re-design	Improvement management	Improvement monitoring
TDQM		✦	✦	✦
DWQ			✦	
TIQM		✦		✦
DQA				
ISTAT		✦		
AMEQ				✦
COLDQ	✦	✦		✦
DaQuinCIS				
CDQ	✦	✦		

Table 12.5 Methodologies, strategies, and techniques

Strategy/ Meth. Acronym	Data-driven	Process-driven
TDQM		Process Redesign
DWQ	Data and schema integration	
TIQM	Information cleansing Normalization Error localization and correction	Process Redesign
ISTAT	Standardization Object Identification	Process Redesign
COLDQ	Cost optimization	Process Control Process Redesign
DaQuinCIS	Source trustworthiness Object Identification	
CDQ	Standardization Object Identification Data and schema integration Error localization and correction	Process Control Process Redesign

of the improvement solution step is explicitly performed only by TDQM. Other methodologies refer to the broad range of management techniques and best practices available from the change management field [365]. Furthermore, it is possible to repeat the assessment phase of the methodology in order to evaluate the results of the improvement phase. As an example, DQA explicitly recommends the application of previous methodological steps to evaluate the effectiveness of improvement.

12.3.3   Strategies and Techniques

Table 12.5 shows the strategies and techniques adopted by different methodologies. A methodology is associated with a strategy if it provides guidelines to select and design corresponding techniques.

Notice that the column labeled *process driven* in Table 12.5 provides the same information as columns *process control* and *process redesign* in Table 12.4. The column labeled *data driven* explicitly mentions the data-driven techniques implicitly considered in Tables 12.3 and 12.4.

Table 12.5 shows that four IQ methodologies adopt mixed strategies, variously combining data-driven and process-driven techniques. The methodology applying the wider range of data- and process-driven techniques is TIQM. Conversely, TDQM provides guidelines to apply process-driven strategies by using the information manufacturing analysis matrix [31], which suggests when and how to improve data. A wider analysis of strategies and techniques can be found in [40].

12.3.4   Comparison of Methodologies: Summary

The detailed comparison of methodologies discussed in the previous sections clearly indicates that methodologies tend to focus on a subset of IQ issues. The broad differences in focus across methodologies can be recognized at a glance by classifying methodologies into four categories, as shown in Fig. 12.6:

- Complete methodologies, which provide support to both the assessment and improvement phases and address both technical and economic issues
- Audit methodologies, which focus on the assessment phase and provide limited support to the improvement phase
- Operational methodologies, which focus on the technical issues of both the assessment and improvement phases, but do not address economic issues
- Economic methodologies, which focus on the evaluation of costs

It should be noted that audit methodologies are more accurate than both complete and operational methodologies in the assessment phase; they identify all types of issues, irrespective of the improvement techniques that could or should be applied. AIMQ and QAFD methodologies, for instance, describe in detail how objective and subjective assessments can be performed and provide guidelines to interpret results. DQA discusses the operating definitions that can be used to measure the different DQ dimensions, to evaluate aggregate measures of DQ for databases and generic information sources. As a final example, AIMQ (see Fig. 12.7) classifies dimensions into *sound*, *useful*, *dependable*, and *usable*, according to their positioning in quadrants related to "product quality/service quality," and "conforms to specifications/meets or exceeds consumer expectations" coordinates. The goal of the

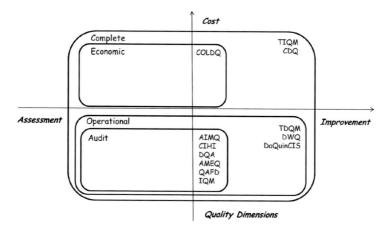

Fig. 12.6 A classification of methodologies

	Conforms to specifications	Meets or exceeds consumer expectations

Product quality	Sound
	
	Dimensions:
	  Free of error
	  Coincise representation
	  Completeness
	  Consistent representation
		Useful
		
		Dimensions:
		  Appropriate amount
		  Relevancy
		  Understandability
		  Intepretability
		  Objectivity

Service quality	Dependable
	
	Dimensions:
	  Timeliness
	  Security
		Usable
		
		Dimensions:
		  Believability
		  Accessibility
		  Ease of operation
		  Reputation

Fig. 12.7 Classification of dimensions in [392] for assessment purposes

classification is to provide a context for each individual's IQ dimension and metric and for consequent assessment.

Operational methodologies on IQ assessment focus on identifying the issues for which their improvement approach works best. One of the main contributions is the identification of a set of relevant dimensions to improve and the description of a few straightforward methods to assess them. For example, DWQ analyzes the data warehouse context and defines new quality dimensions tailored to the architecture of a data warehouse. The list of relevant dimensions represents an important starting point for the improvement process, since it supports companies in the identifications of the IQ issues affecting their data warehouse.

Note that the assessment procedures are described more precisely in operational methodologies that focus on a specific context, rather than in general-purpose methodologies. Thus, the specialization of operational methodologies reduces their completeness and applicability if compared with complete methodologies, but increases the efficiency of the proposed techniques. As an example, if IQ issues are related to the accuracy and completeness of personal data, improvement methodologies can be more straightforward in targeting record linkage techniques; this is the case of the DaQuinCIS and Istat methodologies that use record linkage to integrate different sources, by providing domain specific similarity algorithms for the discovery of duplicate records. For example, in the Istat methodology, deduplication of names of streets is performed in bilingual regions, such as the "Alto Adige" region in Italy, adopting similarity functions specialized to paradigmatic errors such as imputing "u" instead of "Äu" that is typical of the Austrian lexicon.

Complete methodologies are helpful in providing a comprehensive framework to guide large IQ programs in organizations that process critical data and attribute to IQ a high strategic priority, such as banks and insurance companies. On the other hand, they show the classical trade-off between the applicability of the methodology and the lack of personalization to specific application domains or technological contexts. Being high level and rather context independent, complete methodologies are only marginally affected by the evolution of ICT technologies and, over time, have been revised to encompass the variety of data types, sources, and flows that are part of modern information systems. We will see an example of this issue referring to TDQM in the next section.

Economic methodologies complement other methodologies and can be easily positioned within the overall framework provided by any complete methodology. Most audit and improvement methodologies have a cost evaluation step. However, they mostly focus on the cost of IQ initiatives, while a complete cost-benefit analysis should also consider the cost of "doing nothing," i.e., the cost of poor data quality, which is typically of organizational nature. Economic methodologies focus on both aspects. In particular, COLDQ focuses on the evaluation of the cost associated with poor data quality, characterizing the economic impact based on the ultimate effects of bad data. The result is the so-called data quality scorecard, which can be used as a tool to find the best solutions for improvement.

12.4   Detailed Comparative Analysis of Three General-Purpose Methodologies

In this section we deepen the analysis of three methodologies only generically compared in Sect. 12.3. The methodologies are:

1. The Total Data Quality Methodology (TDQM) (see [563]), initially conceived as a research activity and subsequently widely used in several application domains.

2. The Total Quality data Methodology (TQdM), described in [202], was devised for consultancy purposes and is particularly suited for managers. The TQdM has subsequently been renamed as Total Information Quality Methodology (TIQM); we have adopted this latter acronym in the previous section.
3. The Istat methodology, developed in the context of an Italian project, conceived by the Italian National Institute of Statistics (Istituto Nazionale di Statistica, whose acronym is Istat) and the former Authority for Information Technologies in Public Administration. The methodology concerns interorganizational information systems; it was conceived for the public administration domain and was first specialized for address data in databases (see [222]).

12.4.1 The TDQM Methodology

The TDQM proposed in [563] can be seen as an extension of total quality management to data, which was originally proposed for manufacturing products. Several enrichments of TDQM have been proposed, including the languages IP-MAP and IP-UML described in Chap. 6, leading, in this second case, to a new methodology. We describe the organization in phases of the original TDQM and the IP-UML methodological extension in Fig. 12.8, within the common definition framework proposed in the previous section. Terminological differences for the IP-UML extension are highlighted.

The process underlying TDQM considers four phases as necessary for managing information products: definition, measurement, analysis, and improvement. These phases are iteratively executed, thus constituting a cycle. The *definition* phase includes the identification of data quality dimensions and related requirements. The *measurement* phase produces quality metrics that provide feedback to data quality management and allow for the comparison of the effective quality with predefined quality requirements. The *analysis* phase identifies the roots of quality problems and studies their relationships. The *improvement* phase devises quality improvement activities.

1. Definition
   Data quality requirements analysis (named Quality Analysis in the IP-UML extension)
2. Measurement
   Perform measurement (part of Quality Analysis in IP-UML)
3. Analysis
   Data Analysis (the same name in IP-UML)
   Model the processes (less relevant in IP-UML)
4. Improvement (Quality improvement in IP-UML)
   Design improvement solutions on data and processes (Quality verification in IP-UML)
   Re-design processes (only in IP-UML, named Quality improvement)

Fig. 12.8 TDQM description

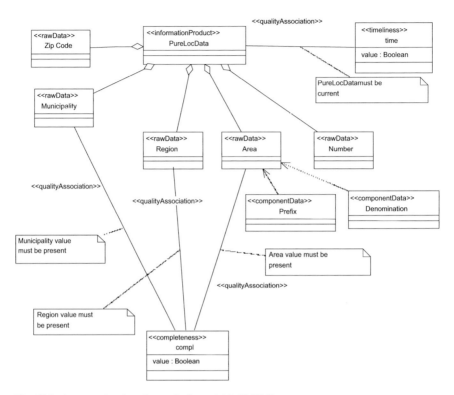

Fig. 12.9 An example of quality analysis model in IP-UML

Phases defined in IP-UML are data analysis, quality analysis, and quality improvement design. Quality improvement design is composed of quality verification and quality improvement. In the *data analysis* phase, information products are identified and modeled. As a second step, in the *quality analysis* phase, the quality dimensions are defined, along with the requirements on the information product and on its constituents. It distinguishes between the requirements for raw data and component data. In Fig. 12.9, an example of a quality analysis model is shown, referring to quality requirements of location data of citizens. A timeliness constraint is expressed on the information product PureLocationData, and completeness constraints are expressed on attributes Municipality, Region, and Area.

The *quality verification* phase focuses on the identification of areas that are critical and on the quality checks to be introduced in the data flows of the information production process. Finally, the *quality improvement* phase investigates a reengineering of processes aimed at improving the quality of data. An example of a quality improvement model is shown in Fig. 12.10, where the process of transfer of a citizen from one to another municipality is considered. Municipality A, where the citizen transfers from, notifies the transfer event to Municipality B, where the

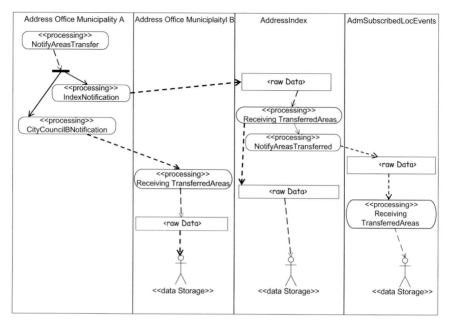

Fig. 12.10 An example of a quality improvement model in IP-UML

citizen transfers to, and to all other organizations involved in such an event. In this way, location data are kept current and accurate in all databases.

The quality requirements specified in the quality analysis model are the drivers of the redesign performed in this phase. The concept of *data steward*, i.e., person, role, or organization that is responsible for data involved in the process, is introduced. In our example in Fig. 12.9, the data steward of the raw data `PureLocationData` is assumed to be the Municipality A the citizen has transferred from, and therefore Municipality A is in charge of starting the event notification.

12.4.2   The TIQM

The TIQM (see [202]) was initially designed for data warehouse projects, but its broad scope and its level of detail characterize it as a general-purpose IQ methodology. In a data warehouse project, one of the most critical phases concerns the activity of off-line consolidation of operational data sources into a single, integrated database, used in all types of aggregations to be performed. In the consolidation phase, errors and heterogeneities present in sources have to be discovered and solved, or we will suffer from data warehouse corruption and failure.

The orientation of TIQM toward data warehouses results in a prevalent information-driven character of the methodology. The general strategy of TIQM

1. Assessment
   Data analysis
      Identify information groups and stakeholders
      Assess consumer satisfaction
   DQ requirements analysis
   Measurement
      Identify data validation sources
      Extract random samples of data
      Measure and intepret data quality
   Non quality evaluation
      Identify business performance measures
      Calculate non quality costs
   Benefit evaluation
      Calculate information value
2. Improvement
   Design solution improvement
      On data
         Analyse data defect types
         Standardize data
         Correct and complete data
         Match, transform and consolidate data
      On processes
         Check effectiveness of improvement
3. Management of improvement solutions – organizational perspective
   Assess the organization's readiness
   Create a vision for information quality improvement
   Conduct a customer satisfaction survey of the information stakeholders
   Select a small and payoff area to conduct a pilot project
   Define the business problem to be solved
   Define the information value chain
   Perform a baseline assessment
   Analyze customer complaints
   Quantify costs due to quality problems
   Define information stewardship
   Analyze the systematic barriers to DQ and recommend changes
   Establish a regular mechanism of communication and education with senior managers

Fig. 12.11 TIQM description

is synthesized in Fig. 12.11. The areas in which TIQM is original and more comprehensive when compared to other methodologies are cost-benefit analysis and managerial perspective. TIQM provides extensive guidelines for evaluating costs of loss of quality, costs of the process of information improvement, and benefits and savings resulting from information quality improvement. We notice here that another methodology, specifically focused on costs and savings, is described in [413], while [34] describes an integer linear programming formulation of a quality improvement process that optimizes costs. We focus now on the managerial issues of TIQM.

12.4.2.1   Management of Improvement Solutions

The main issue discussed in TIQM concerns the managerial perspective, i.e., the strategy that has to be followed in an organization in order to make technical choices effective. The alternatives are in terms of IQ activities to be performed, information collections and flows to be considered, and adopted techniques. In the final stage of

TIQM, the focus is moved from technical to managerial aspects. The extent of the steps, shown in Fig. 12.11, provides evidence of the attention devoted to this issue. Specific tasks of the managerial perspective concern:

1. Assessment of organization readiness in pursuing IQ processes.
2. Survey of customer satisfaction, in order to discover problems at the source, i.e., directly from service users.
3. Initial focus on a pilot project, in order to experiment with and tune the approach and avoid the risk of failure in the initial phase, which is typical of large-scale projects performed in one single phase. This principle is inspired by the well-known motto "think big, start small, scale fast."
4. Definition of information stewardship, i.e., the organizational units and their managers who, with respect to the laws (in public administrations) and rules (in private organizations) that govern business processes, have specific authority on information production and exchange.
5. Following the results of the readiness assessment, the analysis of the main barriers in the organization to the IQ management perspective in terms of resistance to change processes, control establishment, information sharing, and quality certification. In principle, every manager thinks that his or her information is of very high quality, and he or she is reluctant to accept controls, respect standards and methods, and share information with other managers. This step concerns a well-known habit of managers to consider information as a form of power.
6. Establishment of a specific relationship with senior managers, in order to get their consensus and active participation in the process.

Before concluding this section on TIQM, we mention a second set of major managerial principles inspired by [161]:

- Principle 1. Since information is never what it is supposed to be, check and recheck schema constraints and business rules every time fresh information arrives. Immediately identify and send discrepancies to responsible parties.
- Principle 2. Maintain a good and strict relationship with the information owners and information creators, to keep up with changes and to ensure a quick response to problems.
- Principle 3. Involve senior management willing to intervene in the case of uncooperative partners.
- Principle 4. Data entry, as well as other processes, should be fully automated in such a way that data can be entered only once. Furthermore, data should only be entered and processed coherently with schema and business specifications.
- Principle 5. Perform continuous and end-to-end audits to immediately identify discrepancies; the audits should be a routine part of information processing.
- Principle 6. Maintain an updated and accurate view of the schema and business rules; use proper software and tools to enable this.
- Principle 7. Appoint an information steward who owns the entire process and is accountable for the quality of information.
- Principle 8. Publish the information where it can be seen and used by as many users as possible, so that discrepancies are more likely to be reported.

12.4.3   The Istat Methodology

The Istat methodology (see [222] and [223]) has been designed for Italian public administrations. Specifically, it concerns address data of citizens and businesses. The Istat methodology is explicitly focused on databases and data flows made of structured data. Notwithstanding the domain limitation, it is characterized by a rich spectrum of strategies and techniques that allow for its adaptation to many other domains. The principal reason for this is the complexity of the structure of the Italian public administration, which is characterized by at least three tiers of agencies:

1. *Central agencies*, located close to each other, usually in the capital city of a country.
2. *Peripheral agencies*, corresponding to organizational structures distributed through the territory, hierarchically dependent on central agencies.
3. *Local agencies*, which are usually autonomous from central agencies and correspond to districts, regions, provinces, municipalities, and other smaller administrative units. Sometimes they are functionally specialized, e.g., hospitals.

The above is an example of the organizational structure of a public administration sector, which have many variants in different countries. However some common aspects include:

- Its complexity, in terms of interrelations, processes, and services in which they are involved, due to the fragmentation of competencies among agencies. This frequently involves information flows exchanged between several agencies at the central and local level.
- Agencies' autonomy, which makes it difficult to enforce common rules.
- The high heterogeneity of meanings and representations that characterize databases and data flows and the high overlapping of usually heterogeneous records and objects.

Improving IQ in such a complex structure is usually a very large and costly project, needing an activity that may last several years. In order to solve the most relevant issues related to data quality, in the Istat methodology, attention is primarily focused on the most common type of data exchanged between agencies, namely, address data. When compared to previously examined methodologies, this methodology is innovative since it addresses all the coordinates introduced in Sect. 12.2, specifically, data vs. process driven and intraorganizational vs. interorganizational. A synthetic description of the Istat methodology is shown in Fig. 12.12, where the three main phases are represented, together with the information flows between them.

The assessment made in Phase 1 identifies the most relevant activities to be performed in the improvement process. These activities are:

- Phase 2, activities on databases locally owned by agencies under their responsibility. Tools were distributed for performing these types of activities autonomously, and courses were offered for learning more on IQ issues.

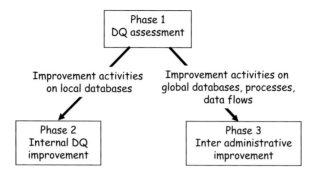

Fig. 12.12   General view of the Istat methodology

1. Global assessment and improvemement
1.1 Global assessment
    DQ Requirements analysis – Isolate from a general process analysis relevant qualities
    for address data: accuracy, completeness.
    Find critical areas, using statistical techniques
        Choose a national database
        Choose a representative sample
        Find critical areas
        Find potential causes of errors
  Communicate results of assessment to single agencies
1.2 Global improvement
    Design improvement solutions on data
      Perform record linkage between relevant national databases
      Establish a national data owner for specific fields
    Design improvement solutions on processes – Use the results of the global assessment
    to decide specific interventions on processes
    Choose tools and techniques – Make or buy, and adapt, tools for most relevant
    DQ activities to deliver to agencies
2. Internal DQ improvement (for each agency, autonomous initiative)
    Design improvement solutions on processes
        Standardize acquisition format
        Standardize internal exchange format using XML
    Perform specific local assessments
    Design improvement solutions on data and processes in critical areas
        Use the results of the global assessment and local assessment to decide specific
        interventions on internal processes
        Use the results of the global assessment and the acquired tools to decide specific
        interventions on data, e.g. perform record linkage between internal databases
3. DQ improvement of inter administrative flows
        Standardize inter administrative flows format using XML
        Redesign exchange flows, using a public and subscribe event-driven architecture

Fig. 12.13   Detailed description of the Istat methodology

- Phase 3, activities that concern the overall cooperative information system of
  administrations, in terms of exchanged data flows, and central databases set up
  for possible coordination purposes. These activities are centrally planned and
  coordinated.

A more detailed description of the methodology is shown in Fig. 12.13; the
innovative aspects concern:

- The assessment phase, initially performed on central databases, with the goal
  of detecting a priori critical areas. For example, as previously discussed within
  addresses of some regions, such as New Mexico in the United States or Alto

Adige in Italy, the names of streets are bilingual or they have different spellings in their original and official languages, leading to errors. In our example, the original languages are, respectively, Spanish and German, and the official languages are English and Italian. New Mexico and Alto Adige are potentially critical areas for the assessment phase.

- The application of a variety of simple but effective statistical techniques in quality measurement steps.
- The definition of data owners at a very detailed granularity level, corresponding to single attributes, such as `MunicipalityCode` and `SocialSecurityNumber`.
- The arrangement of techniques and tools for the most relevant cleaning activities; the aim has been to produce and distribute techniques and tools to single agencies, assisting them in tailoring the activities to specific territorial or functional issues.
- The standardization of address data formats and their expression in a common XML schema, implemented to minimize internal changes to agencies and to allow interoperability in flows between agencies.
- The redesign of exchanged data flows, using a publish and subscribe event-driven technological architecture, an example of which we will see in the case study in Sect. 12.6.

12.5 Assessment Methodologies

The goal of assessment methodologies is to provide a precise evaluation and diagnosis of the state of the information system with regard to IQ issues. Therefore, the principal outputs of assessment methodologies are (1) measurements of the quality of information bases and information flows, (2) costs to the organization due to the present low quality, and (3) a comparison with IQ levels considered acceptable from experience, or else a benchmarking with best practices, together with suggestions for improvements. The usual process followed in assessment methodologies has three main activities:

1. Relevant dimensions and metrics are initially chosen, classified, and measured.
2. Subjective judgments of experts are performed.
3. Objective measurements and subjective judgments are compared.

In the following we describe the methodology proposed in [168] in detail, which was tailored for the financial domain (see the main phases in Fig. 12.14) (we will present another assessment methodology in Chap. 13). For an example of benchmarking in the financial domain, see [431]. Here, we adopt the statistical term *variable* for attributes whose quality is to be measured.

Phase 1, *variables selection*, concerns the identification, description, and classification of primary variables of financial registries, which correspond to the main information attributes to be assessed. The most relevant variables in financial

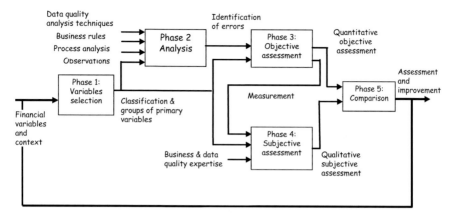

Fig. 12.14 The main phases of the assessment methodology described in [168]

information bases are identified. Then, they are characterized according to their meaning and role. The possible characterizations are *qualitative/categorical*, *quantitative/numerical*, and *date/time*.

In phase 2, *analysis*, information dimensions and integrity constraints to be measured are identified. Simple statistical techniques are used for the inspection of financial information. Selection and inspection of dimensions is related to process analysis. It has the final goal of discovering the main causes of erroneous information, such as unstructured and uncontrolled information loading and information updating processes. The result of the analysis on selected dimensions leads to a report with the identification of the errors.

In phase 3, *objective/quantitative assessment*, appropriate indices are defined for the evaluation and quantification of the global IQ level. The number of erroneous observations for the different dimensions and the different information attributes is first evaluated with statistical and/or empirical methods and, subsequently, normalized and summarized. An example of quantitative assessment is shown in Fig. 12.15, where the three variables considered, typical of the financial domain, are:

1. Moody's rating. Moody's Investors Service is a leading provider of risk analysis, offering a system of ratings of the relative creditworthiness of securities.
2. Standard and Poor's rating, from another leading provider.
3. Market currency code, e.g., EUR.

The values associated with quality dimensions represent the percentages of erroneous information by IQ dimension. Internal consistency refers to the consistency of an information value item within the same set of financial information; external consistency refers to the consistency of an information value item in different information sources.

Phase 4 deals with *subjective/qualitative assessment*. The qualitative assessment is obtained by merging three independent evaluations from (1) a business expert,

	Variables		
Quality dimensions	Moody's Rating	Standard's & Poor Rating	Market Currency Code
Syntactic Accuracy	1.7	1.5	2.1
Semantic Accuracy	0	0.1	1.4
Internal Consistency	2.7	3.2	1.3
External Consistency	1.6	1.1	0.1
Incompleteness	3.5	5.5	8.1
Currency	0	0	0
Timeliness	8.6	9.2	2
Uniqueness	4.9	4.9	9.3
Total (average)	3.6	3.2	3.0

Fig. 12.15 Example of objective quantitative assessment

	Rating Moody's	Rating S&P	Market Currency Code
Syntactic Accuracy	H	H	H
Semantic Accuracy	H	H	M
Internal Consistency	H	H	H
External Consistency	H	H	M
Incompleteness	L	L	L
Currency	H	H	H
Timeliness	M	M	H
Uniqueness	H	H	H
Total	H	H	H

Fig. 12.16 Example of subjective quantitative assessment

who analyzes information from a business process point of view; (2) a financial operator (e.g., a trader), who uses daily financial information; and (3) an IQ expert, who has the role of analyzing information and examining its quality. See Fig. 12.16 for a possible result of this phase, where domain values are High, Medium, and Low.

Finally, a comparison between objective and subjective assessment is performed. For each variable and quality dimension, we calculate the distance between:

1. The percentages of erroneous observations obtained from quantitative analysis, mapped in the discrete domain [High, Medium, Low]
2. The quality level defined by the judgment of the three experts

Discrepancies are analyzed by the IQ expert, to detect causes of errors and to find alternative solutions to correct them.

Phase 1: State reconstruction
1. Reconstruct the state and meaning of most relevant databases and data flows exchanged between organizations, and build the *database + dataflow/organization matrixes*.
2. Reconstruct most relevant business processes performed by organizations, and build the *processes /organizations matrix*.
3. For each process or group of processes related in a macroprocess, reconstruct the norms and organizational rules that discipline the macroprocess and the service provided.
   Phase 2: Assessment
4. Check the major problems related with the services provided with the internal and final users. Fix these drawbacks in terms of process and service qualities, and identify the causes of the   drawbacks due to low data quality.
5. Identify relevant DQ dimensions and metrics, measure data quality of databases and data flows, and identify their critical areas.
   Phase 3: Choice of the optimal improvement process
6. For each database and data flow, fix the new DQ levels that improve process quality and reduce costs under a required threshold.
7. Conceive process re-engineering activities and choose DQ activities, that may lead to DQ improvement targets set in step 6, relating them in the *data/activity matrix* to clusters of databases and data flows involved in DQ improvement targets.
8. Choose optimal techniques for the DQ activities.
9. Connect crossings in the *data/activity matrix* in reasonable candidate improvement processes
10. For each improvement process defined in the previous step, compute approximate costs and benefits, and choose the optimal one, checking that the overall cost-benefit balance meets the targets of step 6.

Fig. 12.17 Phases and steps of CDQM

12.6   The CDQM

Now we discuss an original methodology, characterized by a reasonable balance between completeness on one side and a practical feasibility of the data quality improvement process on the other side. The methodology is explicitly focused on structured data in databases. Besides this limitation, the methodology deals with all types of knowledge described in Fig. 12.2; for this reason, we will call it *Complete Data Quality Methodology (CDQM)* . The phases and steps of CDQM are shown in Fig. 12.17.

The overall strategy of CDQM sees the measurement and improvement activities as being deeply related to the business processes and to the costs of the organization. In phase 1 all the most important relationships between organizational units, processes, services, and data, if not known, are reconstructed. Phase 2 sets new target quality dimensions which are needed to improve process qualities and evaluates reduced costs and new benefits. Phase 3 finds the optimal improvement process, i.e., the sequence of activities that has the optimal cost-effectiveness. In this section we examine the specific steps. The next section will provide a detailed case study.

12.6.1   Reconstruct the State of Data

Similar to what happens in information system planning methodologies, at the beginning of the IQ process, we reconstruct a model of the most relevant relationships between organizations or organizational units and data used and exchanged. This information is important, since it provides a picture of the main uses of data,

Database/ Organization	Database 1	Database 2	....	Database n
Organization 1	Creates	Uses		Uses
Organization 2		Uses		
....				
Organziation m		Creates		Creates

Fig. 12.18 The database/organization matrix

Dataflow/ Organization	Dataflow 1	Dataflow 2	....	Dataflow n
Organization 1	Provider	Consumer		Consumer
Organization 2		Consumer		Provider
....				
Organization m	Consumer	Provider		Consumer

Fig. 12.19 The data flow/organization matrix

of providers, and of consumers of data flows. We can represent these relationships with two matrices:

1. The *database/organization matrix* (see Fig. 12.18), where, for the most relevant databases, we represent organizations that create data and organizations that use data. This matrix could be refined, representing single entities (or tables), but in order to make its size reasonable, we set the granularity at the database level.
2. The *data flow/organization matrix* (see Fig. 12.19), similar to the previous one, in which we represent the provider and consumer organizations of the most relevant data flows.

12.6.2   Reconstruct Business Processes

In this step, we focus on processes and their relationships with organizational units. *Processes* are units of work performed in the organization and related to the production of goods or services. For every process we have to find the organizational unit, that is, its owner, and the units that participate in the execution of the process:

Fig. 12.20 The process/
organization matrix

Process/ Organization	Process 1	Process 2	....	Process n
Organization 1	Owner	Participates		
Organization 2		Participates		Owner
....				
Organization m	Participates	Owner		Participates

the whole set of cross-relationships is represented in the *process/organization matrix*, an example of which is given in Fig. 12.20. Distinguishing the owner of the process is important in IQ issues, so that we can assign precise responsibilities in data-driven and process-driven improvement activities.

12.6.3 Reconstruct Macroprocesses and Rules

In this step, we analyze two aspects in depth: the structure and the final objectives of the processes in the organization, i.e., how they are related and linked in the production of goods/services (denoted in the following for simplicity as services) and the legal and organizational rules that discipline and specify this structure. The relevant characteristics of processes are described in the *macroprocess/norm-service-process matrix* (see Fig. 12.21), where the following aspects are represented:

- The *macroprocess*, i.e., the set of processes that are all together involved in service provision
- *Services* provided, identified by a name and, possibly, by the class of users of the service, their characteristics, and the organization responsible for service provision
- *Norms* that discipline the high-level specification of the process

Reconstructing the macroprocesses is an important activity, since modeling processes independently provides only a fragmented view of the activities of the organization. On the contrary, we need an integrated view to make decisions related to the possible restructuring of processes and information flows. At the same time, especially in public organizations, the knowledge of norms related to the macroprocesses is relevant to precisely understand (1) the area at our disposal for "maneuvers" in process-driven activities, (2) the extent to which we are free to restructure processes, and (3) the norms or organizational rules to be repealed, changed, or modified.

Macroprocess	Macroprocess1	Macroprocess2	....	Macroprocess m
Norm/organiza-tional rule	Norm 1	Norm 2		Norm3 and Norm4
Service(s)	S1 and S5	S2 and S5		S3 and S4
Process 1	X			
Process 2		X		
Process 3	X			
Process 4	X			
...				
Process n				X

Fig. 12.21 The macroprocess/norm-service-process matrix

Notice in Fig. 12.21 that macroprocesses are represented as a set of processes. This model is very simple and could be enriched using a process specification language (see example in [2]).

12.6.4 Check Problems with Users

The goal of this step is to identify the most relevant problems, in terms of causes of poor data quality. Focusing initially on services, they can be identified by interviewing internal and final users and by understanding the major burdens and negative effects of poor data quality on the activities of internal users and on the satisfaction of final users. Then, the analysis goes back to processes to find the causes, in terms of quality and the nature of processes, that produce such burdens and negative effects. As an example, taxpayers of a district are bothered, if they receive erroneous notices of assessment from the revenue agency. It may be discovered that tax files for that district are not accurate, due to delayed or incorrect updates.

12.6.5 Measure Data Quality

In previous steps, we have identified main problems that lead to poor data quality; here, we have to select, among the set of dimensions and metrics discussed in Chap. 2, the most relevant ones for our problem; for such dimensions, we have to choose metrics to provide a quantitative evaluation of the state of the system. For example, if the major burden perceived by final users is the time delay between an information service request and service provision, we have to focus on the currency dimension and organize a process to measure it.

Another relevant aspect of this step is locating critical areas, mentioned in the discussion on the Istat methodology. Since the improvement activities are complex and costly, it is advisable to focus on the parts of databases and data flows that reveal major problems. This activity can be performed in two ways:

- Analyzing problems and causes and trying to identify the data whose poor quality is more negatively influenced by them. In the taxpayer example, we focus on one specific district, since complaints come prevalently from that area.
- Analyzing statistics on data quality metrics selected according to different properties of data and determining where poor quality is located. We have seen this case in the example on names of streets discussed in Sect. 12.4.3.

12.6.6   Set New Target IQ Levels

In this step, we set new target IQ levels, evaluating the economic impact of the improvement in terms of (hopefully) reduced costs and improved benefits. We have discussed in Chap. 11 some classifications of costs and benefits and proposed a new one. The idea in this step is to use such classifications as a checklist; for each item in the classification, or in a subset of it, we collect data that allow some approximate estimate of the costs, savings, and other benefits associated with the item. Some items are easily calculated, such as the cost of equipment involved in data cleaning activities. Other items need an estimate. For example, we may have perceived that a significant cost item is related to the time spent by clerks in looking for unmatched citizens, or for missing businesses in a registry. In the former case, we (1) estimate the number of clerks involved in the activity in terms of person-months per year and (2) multiply this number by the average of the gross salary. Some cost items are difficult or even impossible to estimate. In this case, we identify a proxy cost item that provides an indirect evaluation of the item that cannot be estimated.

Other aspects to be addressed concern the so-called intangible benefits, which are difficult to express in monetary terms and have to be possibly considered on a qualitative basis. Finally, the calculation of return on investment is useful to help senior management make a decision about the level of commitment to the data quality program.

The last issue to be dealt with in this step is the establishment of a relationship between costs, benefits, and quality levels. For instance, we assume that presently 10 % of customer addresses are not correct, and such poor quality reduces potential revenues of sales campaigns by 5 %. We have to identify, at least qualitatively, the functions that relate (1) costs of processes, (2) savings, and (3) the cost of the improvement program for accurate addresses. Then, we have to superimpose the three functions, to find the optimal balance between cost and savings and the corresponding target quality level to be achieved.

12.6.7   Choose Improvement Activities

This step is perhaps the most critical one for the success of the methodology. The goal here is to understand which process-driven activities and which data-driven activities lead to the most effective results for quality improvement of databases and data flows. In this choice we can group databases and data flows or split them, in order to examine only critical areas or specific parts that are relevant in an activity.

With regard to process-driven activities, business process reengineering activity (see [293, 592], and [458] for a comprehensive discussion) is composed of the following steps:

- Map and analyze the *as-is process*, in which the objective is typically to describe the actual process.
- Design the *to-be process*, producing one or more alternatives to the current process.
- Implement a reengineered process and improve continuously.

Data-driven activities have been described in great detail in previous chapters. To choose from them, we have to start the analysis from causes and problems, discovered in step 4. We discuss a few cases:

1. If a relational table has low accuracy and another source represents the same objects and common attributes with higher accuracy, we perform an *object identification* activity on the table and the source. Then, we select the second source for values of common attributes.
2. Assume that a table exists used mainly for statistical applications and characterized by low completeness. We perform an *error correction* activity that changes null values to valid values, keeping the statistical distribution of values unchanged.
3. Assume that a certain data flow is of very poor quality; in this case, we perform a source selection activity on data conveyed by the data flow. The goal of a *source selection* activity is to change the actual source, selecting one or more data sources that together provide the requested data with better quality. Source selection can be seen as a particular case of quality-driven query processing, discussed in Chap. 10.

At the end of the step, we should be able to produce a *data/activity matrix* like the one shown in Fig. 12.22, where we put a cross for every pair of (1) activity and (2) groups of databases or data flows to which it applies.

12.6.8   Choose Techniques for Data Activities

In this step, we have to choose the best technique and tool for each data activity in the *data/activity matrix*. To choose the technique, starting from the available

Data/Activity	DB1+DB2	DB1+DB3	DB4	DB5	DF1+DF2	DF3
DQ Activity 1	X		X			
DQ Activity 2		X				X
DQ Activity 3		X		X	X	
Process Re-engineering Activity 1	X		X			X
Process Re-engineering Activity 1		X	X		X	
Process Re-engineering Activity 1	X	X		X	X	

Fig. 12.22 The data/activity matrix

knowledge domain, we use all the arguments and comparative analysis dealt with in Chaps. 7–9. Here, we need to look at the market to check which techniques, among the chosen ones, are implemented in commercial IQ tools. We have to compare their costs and technical characteristics; therefore, the choice of the technique is influenced by the market availability of the tools. With reference to the object identification activity, many commercial tools or open source tools have initially adopted empirical techniques, while more recent tools adopt probabilistic techniques. If the tool is extensible, it can be chosen and then adapted to specific requirements. For instance, assume that we have performed in the past a deduplication activity on citizens of a country, in which last names are typically very long; now we have to perform the same activity on citizens of another country where last names are shorter. If in the past we have used a probabilistic technique with given distance functions for the attributes `Name`, `LastName`, and `Address`, we could modify the technique, adapting the decision procedure to the changed context, by changing, for instance, for the attribute `LastName`, the distance function and weights as discussed in Chap. 8.

12.6.9   Find Improvement Processes

We now have to link crosses in the data/activity matrix in order to produce possible candidate improvement processes, with the objective of achieving completeness, i.e., all databases and data flows involved in the improvement program are covered. Linking crosses in the data/activity matrix can be performed in several ways and gives rise to many candidate processes, two or three of them usually sufficient to cover all possible relevant choices. In Fig. 12.23 we see one of them, in a context in which we have chosen object identification, error correction, and data integration as data-driven activities and business process reengineering as the process-driven one.

Fig. 12.23 An example of improvement process

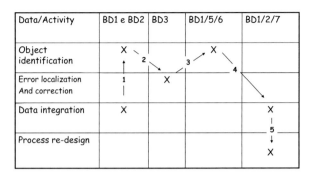

Data/Activity	BD1 e BD2	BD3	BD1/5/6	BD1/2/7
Object identification	X	2	X 3	4
Error localization And correction	1	X		
Data integration	X			X 5
Process re-design				X

12.6.10   Choose the Optimal Improvement Process

We are close to the solution; we now have to compare the candidate improvement processes from the point of view of the cost of the improvement program. For instance, anticipating a business process reengineering activity may lead to a more efficient object identification activity, and anticipating an object identification activity results in simpler error correction.

Items to be considered in cost evaluation include cost of equipment, cost of personnel, cost of licenses for tools and techniques, and cost of new custom software to be realized for ad hoc problems. Once the costs are evaluated and compared, we choose the most effective improvement process. At this point, it is important to compare again the costs of the selected improvement process with net savings (hopefully) resulting from the set new IQ levels step; the net final balance should be positive; otherwise, it is better to do nothing!

12.7   A Case Study in the e-Government Area

In this section we apply CDQM to a real-life case study, described in detail in [65], typical of Government-to-Business relationships in many countries. Businesses, in their life cycle, have to interact with several agencies to request administrative services. The interactions are needed for several business events. Examples of such events and related services are:

- Starting a new business or closing down a business, which involves registering the business, e.g., with the chamber of commerce
- Evolving a business, which includes variations in legal status, board composition and senior management, and number of employees, as well as the launching of a new location and the filing for a patent
- Other services concern territorial marketing, i.e., providing thematic information on the territory in order to facilitate the creation of business networks and extend product markets

- Security (e.g., issue of smart cards for service access, authentication, and authorization) and general enquiry services used by businesses

In their interaction with businesses, agencies manage both agency-specific information, such as employee social insurance taxes, tax reports, balance sheets, and information common to all the businesses, typically including the following:

- Attributes that characterize the business, including one or more identifiers, headquarters and branch addresses, legal structure, main economic activity, number of employees and contractors, and information about the owners or partners
- Milestone dates, including date of business start-up and date of cessation

Each agency usually makes different use of pieces of the common information. As a consequence, each agency enforces different types of quality control, which are deemed adequate for local use of the information. Since every business reports independently to each agency, the copies have different levels of data accuracy and currency. As a consequence, similar information about one business is likely to appear in multiple databases, each autonomously managed by different agencies that historically have never been able to share their data about the businesses. The problem is aggravated by the typical large number of errors contained in databases, which cause mismatches between the different records that refer to the same business. One major consequence of having multiple disconnected views for the same information is that businesses experience severe service degradation during their interaction with the agencies.

Because of the abovementioned complications, a project is launched that follows two main strategies, aimed at improving the state of existing business data and at maintaining correct record alignment for all future data:

1. Extensive object identification and data cleaning should be performed on existing business information, resulting in the reconciliation of a large amount of business registry entries.
2. A "one-stop shop" approach is followed to simplify the life of a business and to ensure the correct propagation of its data. In this approach, a single agency is selected as a front-end for all communication with the businesses. Once the information received by a business is certified, it is made available to other interested agencies through a publish/subscribe event-driven infrastructure.

Now, we apply CDQM assuming for simplicity that we deal with three agencies, namely, the social security agency, the accident insurance agency, and chambers of commerce. Chambers of commerce in many countries are a form of business network, whose goal is to promote the interests of businesses.

Database/ Organization	SocialSecurity Registry of businesses	Accident Insurance Registry of businesses	Chambers of Commerce Registry of businesses
SocialSecurity	Creates/Uses		
Accident Insurance		Creates/Uses	
Chambers of Commerce			Creates/Uses

Fig. 12.24 The database/organization matrix

Dataflow/ Organization	Dataflow 1: Information for service request	Dataflow 2: Information related to service provision
SocialSecurity	Consumer	Provider
Accident Insurance	Consumer	Provider
Chambers of Commerce	Consumer	Provider
Businesses	Provider	Consumer

Fig. 12.25 The data flow/organization matrix

12.7.1   Reconstruct the State of Data

In Figs. 12.24 and 12.25, we report the present situation of the databases managed
by the three agencies and data flows between agencies and businesses. Each agency
has its own registry of businesses; no shared database exists. Concerning flows, each
agency receives information from businesses for service requests and sends back to
businesses information related to service provision.

12.7.2   Reconstruct Business Processes

We focus on interactions between businesses and agencies where businesses
have to inform agencies of a large set of variations in their status according to
existing administrative rules. This covers change of address of the registered office,
headquarters, and branches and updates to main economic activity. In Fig. 12.26
we show three of these processes that have the common feature of involving (in

Process/ Organization	Update registered office info	Update branches info	Update main economic activity info
SocialSecurity	X	X	X
Accident Insurance	X	X	X
Chambers of Commerce	X	X	X

Fig. 12.26 The process/organization matrix

distinct threads) all three agencies. As evident from the figure, coordination does not presently exist between agencies in the management of common information.

12.7.3 Reconstruct Macroprocesses and Rules

We assume that every interaction between a business and an agency that informs the agency of a variation of status is ordered by a law or as more frequent by organizational rules specific to each agency. Examples of these rules are:

1. The business can be represented by an agent, but in this case the agent should have been accredited in advance by the agency.
2. When the update is made, a specific form has to be used.
3. The agency has to be informed of the variation within 60 days after the corresponding event.

With regard to macroprocesses, as we stated we assume a very fragmented situation of administrative activities, in which interactions with businesses are completely independent of each other. In this case, macroprocesses consist of the chain of activities related to the update, which consists of (1) entering information into the database, (2) if necessary, providing a receipt to the business or intermediary, (3) and sending a message to the business if inconsistencies have occurred.

Other processes concern, for example, the payment of pensions or insurance contributions. In some countries, they are deducted from wages and paid directly by businesses. For these processes the macroprocess is much more complex. It includes transactional activities such as collection and registration of payments, correctness checks, and other related processes such as discovery of and contribution evasion recovery.

12.7.4 Check Problems with Users

We now have to interact with the internal and final users of the data and analyze their perception of the quality of data they use (internal users) or get from the agencies. We assume that the results of interviews can be summarized as follows:

1. Internal users are frustrated by the fact that businesses contacted frequently complain about multiple letters, messages, or telephone calls. This is a sign of the presence of duplicate objects in the databases.
2. Internal users involved in tax frauds do not succeed in matching businesses when they perform cross-queries on several databases. For example, taxes paid and energy consumption are not found among the three databases of agencies in cross-queries searching for tax evaders. This is an indication of loose matching of records in databases.
3. Final users (businesses) contacted by phone interviews are burdened by the fact that for a long time after the communication of variations, e.g., of the address ("several months" is typical), they do not receive letters or messages from agencies at the new address. Conversely internal users receive a huge amount of messages back from addresses that correspond to unknown businesses. This in an indication of the lengthy period it takes to perform updates in the database.
4. Final users are very unhappy about the long lines at counters, the time lost in providing variation information, and the long delays in administrative procedures.

From the results of interviews and a qualitative analysis of processes described in step 2, we conclude that we have to focus on the following quality dimensions and metrics:

- Presence of duplicate objects in single databases, classified in Chap. 2 as inaccuracy
- Presence of unmatching objects in the three databases, again classified as inaccuracy
- Delay in the registration of updates, a case of low currency

Apart from accuracy and currency, other quality dimensions, e.g., completeness of databases, result in similarly relevant problems. Furthermore, we could consider also the quality resulting from item 4 of the previous list, i.e., the burden for the business resulting from long lines corresponds to time lost in the interaction with the agency and the service time spent by the agency; these are not data quality dimensions, but, in any case, they are important qualities that need to be improved on in the project. In a data quality improvement project, a larger set of problems and improvement objectives have to be addressed, in addition to those about the quality of data. These aspects are related to the quality of processes and the quality of the services.

12.7.5 Measure Data Quality

In the previous step, we identified the quality dimensions to focus on. Now we have to choose related metrics and organize a process to measure the actual values. With reference to previous dimensions:

- Accuracy can be measured with the percentage of duplicates and the percentage of unmatching objects.
- Currency can be measured as the average delay between the time t_1, at which the information "enters" the agency, and the time t_2, at which it is registered in the system

The measurement process for accuracy (and for completeness if considered) can be performed on a sample of the database. In the choice of samples, a set of tuples must be selected that are representative of the whole universe, in which the overall size is manageable. Methodologies for choosing suitable samples are described in [202]. For time dimension measurements, we interview internal or final users, in order to get a better estimate of their rough perception of the delay. Otherwise, for the time spent by the agency in performing the administrative process, we make a more precise evaluation: starting from the same sample chosen for accuracy, we measure time spent as the time interval between process start and process end. This is made easy by the presence of a workflow tool that traces interaction events in input and output to and from the agency. At the end of the measurement process, we should be able to fill in the table shown in Fig. 12.27.

Quality dimension/ Database	Duplicate objects	Matching objects	Accuracy of names and addressed	Currency
SocialSecurityDB	5%	--	98%	3 months delay
Accident Insurance DB	8%	--	95%	5 months delay
Chambers of Commerce DB	1%	--	98%	10 days delay
The three databases together	--	80%	--	--

Fig. 12.27 Actual quality levels

12.7.6   Set New Target Data Quality Levels

New data quality levels have to be correlated with the desired benefits, in terms of cost savings and other measurable benefits. Cost savings estimation needs to evaluate actual costs and reduced costs due to the data quality improvement.

Two cost drivers that are a direct consequence of the misalignment can be chosen as more relevant: the heterogeneity and the poor accuracy of names and addresses at the agencies. First, we assume that agencies, conscious of the misalignment and inaccuracy of addresses, spend an estimated 10 million Euros a year to correct and reconcile records using clerical review, for example, to manually trace businesses that cannot be correctly and unequivocally identified. Second, because most tax fraud prevention techniques rely on cross-referencing records over different agencies, misalignment results in undetected tax fraud; this phenomenon is made more critical by the practical impossibility of reaching businesses whose addresses are incorrect or not current. Tax fraud can be roughly estimated as a percentage, depending on the country, between 1 and 10 % of the gross domestic product. A country with a gross domestic product equal to 200 billion Euros, assuming a (conservative) percentage of 1.5 %, has reduced revenues equal to at least 300 million Euros.

In a broader sense, we investigate other costs involved with the low quality of processes and services. In the traditional, nonintegrated setting, the burden of business transactions is shared between the businesses and the agencies. The costs to businesses, in terms of personnel involved and fees to intermediaries, can be estimated on the basis of the number of events per year. If, for example, we assume 2 million events per year and three person-hours spent for each event, we estimate a loss of 200 million Euros per year. On the agency side, the cost of handling a single transaction is about 5 Euros, equivalent to 20–25 person-minutes devoted to the internal bookkeeping associated with a single business event. Overall, the cost for a single agency to handle the inefficiency, considering its own events, is no less than 10 million Euros per year. Assuming that the records of each business appear in the databases of at least ten agencies, this brings the total cost per year to 100 million Euros or more.

We come to the conclusion that in order to make the use of the publish and subscribe infrastructure effective and to reduce tax evasion with the consequence of increasing revenues, we need to set the following targets (see Fig. 12.28):

1. 1 % of duplicates in the different databases, except for the chambers of commerce, where we start with good quality and set a higher target, i.e., 0.3 %
2. 3 % of businesses that do not match in the three databases
3. 1 % inaccuracy of addresses
4. An acceptable delay of 3–4 days in the update of information in the three databases

These targets are a qualitative balance between the "100 % quality" ideal (and unreachable) objective and the present situation. The increased revenues can be

Quality dimension/ Database matrix	Duplicate objects	Matching objects	Accuracy of names and addressed	Currency
SocialSecurityRegis try	1%	--	99%	3-4 days delay
Accident Insurance Registry	1%	--	99%	3-4 days delay
Chambers of Commerce registry	0.3%	--	99%	2-3 days delay
The three registries together	--	97%	--	--

Fig. 12.28 New quality targets

estimated assuming that tax fraud decreases proportionally with the number of businesses that can be matched or reached. Other savings will be estimated after having a more precise view of the new ICT infrastructure, provided in the next section.

12.7.7   Choose Improvement Activities

We distinguish between process-driven and data-driven activities. First, we consider process-driven activities. While the present interaction between agencies and businesses involves multiple transactions against the proprietary interfaces of the agencies, a strategic decision of the project is to enable agencies to offer the front-office services with a common infrastructure. Such an interface provides a coherent view of the agencies and a single point of access to their business functions. A back-office infrastructure is introduced into the architecture to hide the heterogeneity of the proprietary interfaces as well as their distribution. The approach followed to improve the interaction between administrations is based typically on a *cooperative architecture* that, with some variants, follows the general structure shown in Fig. 12.29.

We now provide some comments on the back-office layers. Besides the *connectivity infrastructure*, a *cooperation infrastructure* is shown, including application protocols, repositories, gateways, etc., in which the main goal is to allow each agency to specify and publish a set of cooperative interfaces that include data and application services made available to other agencies. On top of this layer, an *event notification infrastructure* is placed, in which the goal is to guarantee synchronization between update events. This layer can be used by an agency when receiving an update from a business. It is published in the cooperative infrastructure; then the information can be subscribed to by all other agencies interested in the

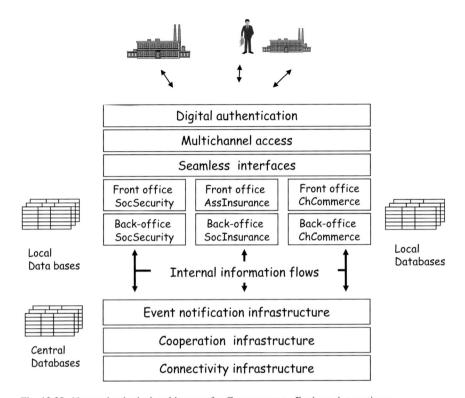

Fig. 12.29 New technological architecture for Government-to-Business interactions

update. A number of administrative processes can be reengineered in order to take advantage of this architecture. Specific agencies can be selected as front-end entry points to businesses for specific types of information. In our example, the chambers of commerce can be involved in updates related to administrative information, while social security can manage information related to the workforce, assuming that one of its missions is to collect insurance contributions.

With regard to data-driven activities, in order to make effective reengineered business processes, we need to restructure the data architecture. The two extreme possibilities are:

- Create a central database in which all types of managed information on businesses are integrated from the three existing databases.
- Create a light central database in which the records result from the linkage of the identifiers of related business records managed by individual agencies. This new database, which we call *Identifiers database*, is needed to achieve object (business) identification between agencies and allows for the readdressing of information in the event notification infrastructure.

Data/Activity	Type of activity	The three databases together	New flows between agencies	The new Identifiers database
Object identification	Data driven	X		
Process Reengineering on update processes	Process driven	X	X	X

Fig. 12.30 The data/activity matrix

The first solution cannot be put into practice because of the autonomy of the agencies. Thus, we choose the second solution. The creation of the Identifiers database requires the object identification activity on the social security, accident insurance, and chamber of commerce registries. At the end of the step, we draw the data/activity matrix (see Fig. 12.30). In the databases and data flows, we include the new Identifiers database and the new data flows generated by the event notification infrastructure. We also include the process reengineering activity and the object identification activity discussed above.

We observe that the adoption of the new infrastructure leads to significant savings in costs of interactions. First, we deal with the costs handled by businesses. If businesses reduce interactions by a 3:1 ratio, we estimate that their costs decrease to 70 million Euros a year. With regard to the costs of agencies, in the original system configuration, three front-office transactions were required for each business-originated update (e.g., change of address), one for each of the three agencies involved in the project; given a cost of 5 Euros for each front-office transaction, the total cost is $5 \times 3 = 15$ Euros. After reengineering, the new update process involves only one front-office transaction, plus two new back-office transactions to propagate the change. The cost of one back-office transaction is 2 Euros, estimated as the sum of fixed costs amortized over the current life of the new system, plus variable costs, considering that initially only one-third of the business events may currently benefit from the new system. Hence, the total cost to the agency goes from 15 Euros to 9 Euros and can further decrease to a limit cost of 6 Euros as more events are included in the system. Furthermore, if more agencies join the cooperative system, fixed costs will be distributed even further. Finally, provisions can be made to reduce the front office costs, by moving to an entirely paperless and certified submission process for the businesses, with improved up-front validation of the input data. This brings the 5 Euros down significantly. Fixing the cost realistically to 6 Euros, we have a decrease in costs from 100 million Euros to 40 million Euros a year.

12.7.8   Choose Techniques for Data Activities

We now have to address the problem of choosing the best techniques for object identification, that is, the main data activity to be performed. Several scenarios can be drawn.

First, we assume that in the past few years, partial record linkage activities have been performed between two or all of the three agencies. This is reasonable in the case in which the agencies have a relevant amount of interaction. Consequently, we assume that in previous years they tried to remove, at least partially, errors and misalignments. In this case we have precious knowledge available, consisting of records previously matched and not matched. We take advantage of this knowledge, choosing a probabilistic technique, including a learning activity on frequencies of matching and mismatching.

A second scenario assumes that no previous activity has been performed; but we know that one of the three databases is more accurate than others in certain fields. For instance, one of the agencies is responsible, by law, to certify data related to the names and addresses of businesses. In this case we use the bridging file method.

A third scenario assumes that knowledge is available concerning the behavior of businesses interacting with agencies. For instance, we assume that from data mining tools it has been discovered that specific types of companies, e.g., small family companies, have different part-time activities, changing during different seasons. Consequently, they tend to declare different types of activities to the different agencies, choosing each time the most convenient solutions from an administrative point of view. Among them, certain patterns could be particularly frequent in pairs of records, e.g., <ice-cream vendor, doorkeeper>. In this case, it is worthwhile to adopt a knowledge-based technique with a rule-based system that includes these types of patterns.

12.7.9   Find Improvement Processes

The analysis performed in previous steps simplifies the identification of improvement processes. We have a unique improvement process (see Fig. 12.31) in which we perform the process reengineering activity in parallel, building the publish and subscribe infrastructure and the object identification on the stock. The two activities have to be synchronized at the moment at which the new system becomes operational. Other possibilities, such as data integration, have been excluded in step 8 (choose improvement activities). Note that we do not need a periodic object identification, since business process reengineering, once performed, aligns information hence in the three agencies.

Data/Activity	The three DataBases together	New flows between agencies	The new Identifiers DB
Object identification	Perform object identification on the stock and consequent deduplication on the three DBs		
Process Reengineering on update processes	Update first the Chambers ofCommerce DB	Use the P&S Infrastructure toUpdate SocSec DB and SocIns DB	Create the DB and use it in the new interagency update process

Fig. 12.31 An improvement process

12.7.10   Choose the Optimal Improvement Process

In this case, we have to consider only one improvement process. We have to check for this process to which extent benefits, especially cost savings, exceed the actual cost of quality plus the cost of the project. We apply a simple methodology where we do not consider issues related to investment analysis and actualization of costs (see [202] and [413]). Concerning actual costs and future cost savings, we have to consider (see the classification provided in Chap. 11) the following major items: (1) costs due to poor data quality, in terms of clerical alignment costs and reduced revenues, and (2) other costs to businesses and to agencies.

Concerning costs of the data quality improvement project, we have to consider costs related to (1) the object identification activity, in terms of software application and clerical costs, and (2) the reengineering of the process, related to setup and maintenance of the publish and subscribe infrastructure.

Reasonable estimates are reported in Fig. 12.32. We have estimated some items of the figure in previous sections. With regard to the cost of the improvement project, considering the different subitems, we conclude that the cost of the application architecture is 5 million Euros and estimate 20 % of maintenance costs a year. Object identification is estimated by analogy with previous projects. Finally, increased revenues are estimated on the basis of the percentage of irregular businesses that can be selected with the new target matching values.

In conclusion, if we consider a 3-year period, the overall savings and increased revenues come to about 1.2 billion Euros, against a cost of the project that can be considered negligible. If we limit the balance to only data quality-related costs and savings, we obtain a net balance of 600 million Euros; the data quality improvement project is extremely worthwhile.

Costs and benefits	Once for all	Yearly
Actual costs due to poor data quality		
Clerical alignement costs		10 MI
Reduced revenues (prudential)		300 MI
Other costs		
For businesses		200 MI
For agencies		100 MI
Costs of the improvement project		
Object identification - automatic	800.000	
Object identification - clerical	200.000	
Application architecture – set up	5MI	
Application architecture – maintenance		1MI
Future costs and savings due to improved data quality		
Increased revenues (prudential)		200MI
Clerical alignement costs		0
Other savings		
For businesses		130MI
For agencies		60MI

Fig. 12.32 Costs and savings of the data quality improvement process

12.8   Extension of CDQM to Heterogeneous Information Types

In the description of the CDQM, we have assumed that all information sources were made of structured data, namely, tables in databases. As we have seen in the preface, information systems of organizations manipulate data and information that have different heterogeneous representations, from tables to XML documents, Excel sheets, loosely structured documents, and images. In Chaps. 2–5, we have systematically proposed quality dimensions for several information types. In this section we discuss how to extend the methodology CDQM to take into account sources made of heterogeneous information types. We will consider semistructured information, but the approach can be followed also for other information types. The main idea underpinning this extended methodology is to map the information resources used in an organization to a common conceptual representation and then to assess the quality of information considering such homogeneous conceptual representation.

We notice that the above mapping can be fully performed for information types such as semistructured information or maps, which have an underlying conceptual schema that captures at least part of the information semantics, while for other types, such as images, it can be performed at a macro level. For example, if we have a registry of hospital patients and a registry of their medical exams, e.g., their radiographies, the contribution of the radiography to the integrated schema could be made of a single entity `Radiography`, related to the entity `Patient`, or else specify properties of the set of the represented body organs.

As a result of the above choices, we achieve two goals: On one hand, we reach the flexibility and modularity that is needed when coping with users of different departments (e.g., a salesman and an IT developer) and levels (e.g., an IT project manager and the CEO). On the other hand, by assessing information quality on each organizational (information) resource and composing IQ values at the level of the common concepts represented, we provide organizations with a wider selection of improvement strategies they can be undertaken to achieve their quality targets. For instance, provided that the overall quality of the information regarding customers must increase by, say, 5 % (resulting in less costs and higher potential revenues), the methodology encompasses methods to choose what information resources referring to customers should be improved first or more intensively and how the objective should be reached. In the following we resume main issues addressed in [43]; the interested reader can refer to the paper for details.

The new methodology extends CDQM in the following new steps:

- New step in the state reconstruction phase: build an integrated conceptual schema of information types in sources.
- New step in the improvement phase: measure a weighted value of quality for each information type in sources and a global value for each entity in the integrated schema.

We show now the new two steps, using as case study the one adopted in [43] and synthesized in Fig. 12.33.

The three most relevant information sources representing customers are:

- A White Page Directory (WPD) that is created starting from the information streams coming from profiling providers; WPD represents, besides customers, their locations, information on businesses, and their owners
- An Agent-Customer Spreadsheet (ACS) file that is partly derived from the WPD and contains some further fields to be added in the field of work referring to agents and their remarks and installations, products and solutions
- A Corporate Database, which consolidates information on customers and solutions and links them to orders and invoices

Instances of the three information collections are shown in Fig. 12.34.

The new state reconstruction step results in building an integrated conceptual schema of information types in sources. This can be done by first reverse engineering the information collections to produce corresponding local conceptual schemas (a methodology for this step is described in [38]); then, the three schemas can be integrated (also for this step, see [38]). We show in Fig. 12.35 the integrated conceptual schema built from the three input schemas; such schemas are also highlighted in the figure.

•The core business of a private firm is to develop innovative systems for wireless hand-held order entry systems. These systems are used by waiters to collect orders from patrons at their tables and communicate with the kitchen in real time through a wireless connection. As the majority of businesses, the main entities to be managed are those of Customer and Supplier. In this example, we will concentrate on the Customer entity.

•The Marketing Department (MD) and its network of commercial agents are supposed to either seek new customers or propose new solutions and upgrades to old ones. MD agents need to have very precise information on the profile of potential customers as this can be acquired form specific vendors and aggregated along several dimensions, like region, turnover, and cuisine.

•The Technical Department (TD) is supposed to monitor the well running of sold installations and provide both ordinary and extraordinary maintenance upon on it. TD members must then rely on information about customers regarding systems purchased, and where they are located.

•Lastly, the Accounts Department (AD) needs accurate and up-to-date administrative information for invoice drawing and accounting.

Fig. 12.33   Requirements of the case study

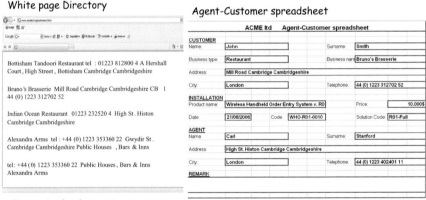

White page Directory

Agent-Customer spreadsheet

Corporate database

ID_Customer	Name	Surname	Business Type	Business Name	ID_Installation	ID_Solution
001	John	Smith	Restaurant	Bruno's Brasserie	WHO-R01-0010	R01-Full
002	Simon	Kent	Restaurant	India Ocean	WHO-R01-0011	R01-Full
003	Paul	Buck	Restaurant	Bottisham Tandoori	WHO-R01-0010	R01-Full

Fig. 12.34   The three information collections input to the process

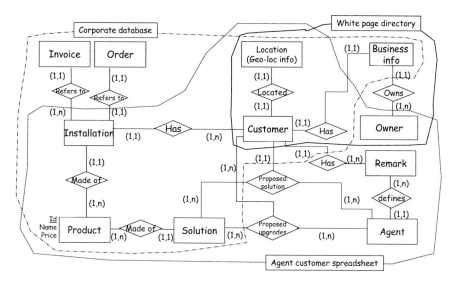

Fig. 12.35 The integrated schema and the three input schemas

Data set → Dimension	WPD	ACS	CDB
Actual currency	12 days delay	6 days delay	16 days delay
Optimal currency	1 day delay	1 day delay	1 day delay
Normalized currency	7%	16%	6%

Fig. 12.36 Currency assessment

We assume now to focus on the Customer entity and on the currency dimension. First we have to fix a metrics for currency that normalizes the different values of currency of Customer in the three information bases. We introduce a concept of normalized currency calculated as

$$\text{Normalized currency (information base)} = \frac{\text{optimal currency}}{\text{actual currency (information base)}}.$$

We see in Fig. 12.36 the values of the normalized currency for the three information bases.

Assuming that the three information bases have the same relevance for business processes that make use of them, we can first compose the three normalized currencies into a global value by simply calculating the average value (step 1 in Fig. 12.37). Now we can define the global target value of normalized currency, and fix it at the value 50 % (step 2).

As the third step, we fix the new values of normalized currency, suitably increasing previous values, with the constraint that the global value is 50 %. Notice

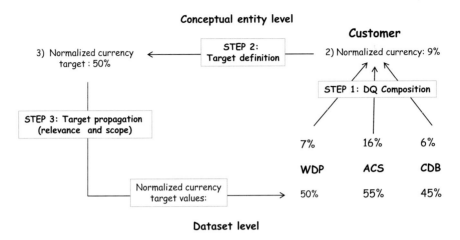

Fig. 12.37 Composition of currency values

that the same procedure could have been followed for other types of information considered in the book.

12.9 Summary

Methodologies in general, and, therefore, also information quality methodologies, may be seen as providing common sense reasoning. Their role is to guide in the complex decisions to be made and to understand the knowledge that has to be acquired. At the same time, they have to be adapted to the application domain. A typical error made by designers is to interpret a methodology as an immutable and absolute set of guidelines that have to be applied as they are, without critical examination. The experience gained in working in different domains instructs on how to adapt general guidelines. Furthermore, it is more effective to see the guidelines, phases, tasks, activities, and techniques, which together form a methodology, as a toolbox, where single pieces are to be used in connection and/or in sequence, according to circumstances and to specific characteristics of the application domain involved in the process.

Another critical issue in IQ methodologies concerns the knowledge available for performing the measurement and improvement defined by the methodology. Sometimes, acquiring the knowledge needed can be very costly and even impossible. In these cases, the methodology has to be simplified and adapted to knowledge available; otherwise, it is refused by management and users, who are bothered by dozens of questions to which they are not able to reply and whose purpose they do not understand.

Chapter 13
Information Quality in Healthcare

Federico Cabitza and Carlo Batini

13.1   Introduction

In this chapter, we will shortly frame information quality in healthcare as a matter of study or concern. Being aware that such a vast topic cannot be covered in one single book chapter, here we will at least orient interested readers to resources that could be consulted to get further information on this broad field of study and practice. To this aim, we will proceed as follows: firstly, we will define the kind of data or information whose quality is under consideration and possibly at stake; then, we will try to convey the importance to focus on this area of interest within the broader information quality field; lastly, we will try to consider how health practitioners see this area and how this can inform programs of quality assessment and improvement from a practice-oriented perspective. Short conclusions will summarize the main points outlined in this chapter. The chapter is organized as follows: in Sect. 13.2, we will recall some of the oft-mentioned definitions of the concepts related to the heading of this chapter. In Sect. 13.3, we outline the main challenges that are posed by the healthcare domain to those willing to address the task of improving the related information, while Sect. 13.4 provides the core notions to orient those practitioners by extracting from the relevant literature references to the main dimensions, methodologies, and initiatives where those methods and the related techniques have been applied with some success. Section 13.5 discusses the most recent trends in research on information quality in healthcare. Finally, Sect. 13.6 aims to motivate the serious practitioners and scholars to devote more efforts in the development of further tools and techniques for the clear impact that IQ can have on health outcomes, costs, and long-term sustainability of healthcare.

© Springer International Publishing Switzerland 2016
C. Batini, M. Scannapieco, *Data and Information Quality*, Data-Centric Systems and Applications, DOI 10.1007/978-3-319-24106-7_13

13.2   Definitions and Scopes

In what follows, we will consider both *healthcare data*, i.e., "items of knowledge about an individual patient or a group of patients" [678] that have been either produced or consumed during the provision of health-related services, and *health data*, which is any representation of facts related to the health of single individuals or entire populations and that is suitable for communication, interpretation, or processing by manual or electronic means [4]. Both these definitions try to grasp an important aspect of health(care) data: they can refer to individuals and be collected at the single patient level, the so-called unit level data [361], and they can also be aggregated when they result from the processing (often just the sum) of unit level data. Individual data are intended to represent the characteristics of single patients, their health conditions (often categorized in terms of some illness), and of the healthcare interventions and processes that they have undergone in order to support proper care and decision making at the point of care [190]. Aggregated data, for instance, on the basis of gender, age, diagnosis, treatment, or residence, can result from an anonymization process that prevents the identification of patients (health-related data are considered sensitive data by many privacy regulations in the world, among which is the Data Protection Directive (95/46/EC) of the European Union) and gives information on either the prevalence and distribution of diseases in a population or on the efficacy of an intervention of procedure [396].

In light of these definitions, we will use the term *health information* to denote health(care) data (i.e., either healthcare data or health data) that, irrespective of the level they pertain to (i.e., either individual or aggregated), "have been organized into a meaningful format, that is in such a way that [these data] can be understood and retrieved when needed" [165]. Since the concept of health information includes both kinds of health-related data, such an expression is purposely intended to be broad enough to capture any kind of information regarding the health of people, including what any person can report about his or her own symptoms or conditions in a written exchange with his or her caregivers or post as comment or reply into a vertical social networking site that is specialized in health conditions, like PatientsLikeMe.[1] Coherently with the terminology introduced in the Preface, the term "meaningful format," referred to health information, concerns any format that has been discussed in this book [576]: long unstructured narratives, any-length and any-structure texts (e.g., unstructured yet well-formatted reports, semistructured forms, structured tables), multi-type numerical values (e.g., physiological parameters), recorded (time-dependent) signals (e.g., electrocardiograms), still pictures (e.g., X-rays), and audio and video recordings (e.g., ultrasound examinations).

---

[1]http://www.patientslikeme.com. Accessed on the 5th of January 2015.

13.3   Inherent Challenges of Healthcare

Notwithstanding any endeavor to pinpoint health information with unambiguous definitions, framing health information quality (HIQ) is a recognized tough task [7, 288, 361], let alone considering all of the feasible approaches and techniques for HIQ monitoring and continuous improvement [363]. If this can be said for many organizational domains (or yet for all the domains), in fact, healthcare exhibits a heterogeneity that has been observed by most of the researchers that have directed their attention to this concern. First of all, healthcare is characterized by highly complex labor- and skill-intensive services where the actors involved still rely primarily on paper tools, their own cognition (competencies and memory), and other traditional methods [288]. This could be shallowly associated with some sort of conservationism and inertia to change of health practitioners [387, 475], but it is more a matter of the (sometimes overlooked) qualities of traditional means [236, 296], the ad hoc and often actually not to be planned nature of healthcare processes [297], and also the inherent difficulties in representing medical knowledge formally, let alone computationally [57], to support the practice effectively [237, 658]. These factors could also be behind the current lag between investments in information technology of healthcare organizations with respect to other industries (less than the half, approximately 3.5–4.5 % vs. 10 %) [288] and the fact that full adoption of electronic records in hospitals is still low to support care practice (between 1 and 8 % according to what "full adoption" actually means) [348].

Then, as hinted at above, HIQ regards both *primary data* coming from a broad range of sources and *secondary data* that are produced from the primary data [4] at various levels of aggregation: from individuals—both patients and caregivers—to hospitals, primary care facilities, and health authorities, both at regional, national, and international levels [525, p. 323]. For this reason, health information is said to "encompass the organization of a limitless array and combination of possible data items" [165], and in [196], a set of interdependent and heterogeneous health information systems is called a *patchwork* (see Fig. 13.1). This is reflected by the fact that HIQ concerns multiple levels at the same time:

- The level of single measures or data elements
- The level of aggregation of single patient data (both on the transversal, i.e., multi-facility, and longitudinal, i.e., temporal, dimensions)
- The level of multi-patient applications

Consequently criteria to assess HIQ span from data element definitions to the coding of episodes and interventions, the adoption of nationally standardized (core) data and measure sets, and audit methodologies, as we will see below.

Fig. 13.1 The patchwork of medical records and health information systems "in the wild" (a radiological outpatient office)

13.3.1 Multiple Uses, Users, and Applications

Healthcare and health are broad application domains, or better yet, they are collections of different organizational and inter-organizational domains, that encompass, e.g., primary care, acute care, mental health, rehabilitation, continuing care, and home care from the clinical side, and health spending, community health monitoring, and health system resources planning, with respect to the administrative side [525]. These and other domains encompass multiple sources of data that are used by different users for different purposes (see Table 13.1 to have an idea of the heterogeneity of the health information spectrum).

In particular, health information sources include:

- Facility-specific electronic records [482] (what is usually called electronic patient record, which is often the aggregation of a patient- and hospital-specific medical record and the corresponding nursing record)
- Clinical trial databases [459] and case report forms [621]
- Administrative health data registries [28], including billing records and the applications that organize and present these data to patients and practitioners over the Web, like electronic health records which give online access to all the health data pertaining to the single citizens enrolled in a national health system and personal health records, which are considered to be a sort of evolution of the electronic health record platforms but more (or totally) in control of single patient with regard to content and interactions [103, 581]

Table 13.1 Users, scopes and types of health information

Users	Type of information	Level	Scope
World health officials Policy makers Researchers and research institutions Lawmakers	General health status and health-related needs of individual nations	Aggregate	World wide
Policy makers Researchers Lawmakers Insurers	Trend in incidence, prevalence, outcomes, and costs by region, by diagnosis, by type of provider	Aggregate	Nationwide
Analysts Researchers Quality auditors and managers Public health officials	Comparison of treatments, outcomes, and costs by locality and by provider. Incidence and prevalence of diagnosis by region	Aggregate	Community/ region wide
Top managers Administrators Researchers and research institutions Accreditation bodies Quality auditors and managers	Costs of care by category of patient. Number of patients admitted with specific diagnosis, volume of tests, procedures and interventions, outcomes for patients grouped by diagnosis	Aggregate	Funder/provider organisation wide
Care givers Researchers (for case reports) Provider organisation departments Insurers QA personnel Patients and relatives (informal care givers)	Patient specific data e.g. assessments, diagnosis, interventions, diagnostic test results, procedures, treatments, outcomes. Used to provide most appropriate care	Individual	Provider organisation wide and patient specific

Adapted from [361]

- The unstructured information that patients can reach through e-health and monitoring applications [529, 639], vertical Web sites [101, 597], and health-related social media [8], as well as, most recently, mobile *apps* [577, 588] that all provide users with information about common illnesses and symptoms, drugs, self-care treatments, diet regimens, and workout programs

The last elements that take into account e-health [79], m-health [357] and the Web 2.0 resources [221] broaden the scope of health information (and consequently of the HIQ) significantly and not without important consequences related to the reliability, understandability, and timeliness of the information found on the Web [79, 456]; however, this looks necessary nowadays, in times when 80 % of Internet users (approximately 60 % of all adults) look online routinely for information about health topics such as a specific diseases or treatments [244].

Moreover, as rightly noted in [363], health data repositories can seldom be considered as *monads*, that is, independent units whose data can be monitored, assessed, and cleansed with local and circumscribed initiatives: "data move with the patients they refer to," and this creates "reciprocal dependences between healthcare organizations [that can result] in one organization adversely and incrementally affecting other organizations and the quality of care a patient receives" (p. 259).

This diversity of data sources and processes that contribute in shaping HIQ is a phenomenon that must be coupled with another important twofold characteristic of health information that differentiates it from information produced and consumed in other domains: reuse, both the intended reuse, e.g., [261, 661], and the unintended one. Reuse simply refers to the fact that data are produced by someone for some specific purpose (e.g., care) and then are also used by some other agent for completely different aims (e.g., billing). As unintended data reuse is a notorious source of problems that is difficult to cope with for the almost total lack of control and monitoring means [479, p. 27], here, we focus on the intended reuse, which relates to the importance of every piece of health information, potentially.

Indeed, health information is most of the times generated by doctors, nurses, and health practitioners at the *point of care* [190], mainly *for*, and *during*, care: this obviously encompasses understanding what a patient suffers (*diagnosis*) and treating the hypothesized condition (*therapy*) but also other phases of the so-called illness trajectory of patients [596], as well as of their lifelong chronic conditions. As plain as this can seem, health information is then also used for a number of other aims, which are often more related with the administrative processing of the case, like reimbursement. In the specialist literature, this potential clash of purposes is referred as the "primary vs. secondary use" of health information [102, 425], which would be simplistic to downsize to a clinical vs. administrative tension.

The primary purpose of health information is to support direct patient care both by aiding medical decision making and by ensuring continuity of care by all providers, that is, both interpretation of medical signs for decision making (see also Chap. 11) and coordination among the actors involved around the patient [56].

On the other hand, secondary purposes regard other uses of the same information collected for the primary purpose: first of all, the legal one as health information is used to secure the legal rights of both the patient and the clinicians involved. First, health information is supposed to represent the faithful and neutral account of all the activities the patient has gone through, even the faulty ones. Second, this information must also allow to reconstruct the context in which clinicians had to take life-saving decisions, so as to release them from hindsight liabilities.

Besides the medicolegal purposes for the patient, the doctor, and the healthcare service, clinical records must also support healthcare service management and scientific research: the clinical record is in fact the main basis for billing and reimbursement and it is the main source of information both within a hospital (e.g., for care quality evaluation, resource planning, and cost management) and outside any caring setting for a large number of scopes, like enabling research surveys, performing epidemiology studies and healthcare statistics, allowing for practitioner training and continuous education, post-marketing surveillance of drugs, public policy making, and the working out of staffing requirements and the planning of healthcare services.

13.4   Health Information Quality Dimensions, Methodologies, and Initiatives

The variation and complexity described above is probably inherent in the general consensus that can be found in the specialist healthcare literature about the contextual nature of HIQ, in terms of "fitness for purpose/use" that has been discussed in Chap. 11, what in the specialist literature is referred to as *appropriateness* of health interventions and processes. Although the healthcare domain would not add other IQ dimensions to the number of dimensions already considered in previous chapters as well as in many contributions focusing on the organizational domain (e.g., [521, 641]), in what follows, we recall the dimensions that are mentioned more often in the medical and medical informatics literature (cf., e.g., [4, 678]) , also to allow the reader notice the affinities with those presented in dimension clusters of Chap. 2:

- Accuracy (also mentioned as validity)—health data represent the truth and what actually happened.
- Currency—data are recorded at the time of observation and are up-to-date.
- Completeness—all required data to make an informed decision should be available.
- Readability (also mentioned as legibility)—all data whether written, handwritten, transcribed, and/or printed should be understandable.
- Reliability— data are consistent and information generated is understandable.
- Usefulness—only data that are useful for care and secondary purposes should be collected "for specified, explicit and legitimate purposes and not further processed in a way incompatible with those purposes."[2]
- Cost-effectiveness—the cost (also not monetary, as the patient's discomfort) of collecting and disseminating information must not exceed its value.
- Confidentiality—data are available to authorized persons when and where needed.

In regard to accuracy and completeness , a number of assessment methods have been described in the literature (the reader can refer to [661] for more details to this regard): paper-based records are usually taken as the "gold standard" [113], that is, the reference information taken (and often assumed) to be true and against

---

[2]Cf. the 6th Article of the European Union data protection directive (Council of the European Union, 1995).

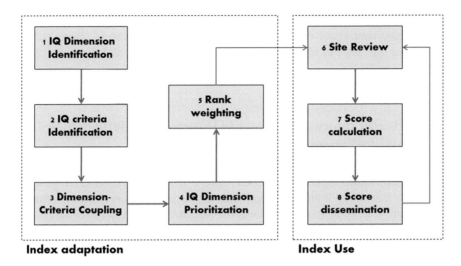

Fig. 13.2 A stepwise methodology for the assessment of HIQ in the domain of unstructured (Web) content, adapted from [101]

which compare digital information. Other gold standards are information supplied by patients, review of data by the patients involved, clinical encounters with patients, information presented by trained standard patients, information requested from the treating physician, and alternative data sources from which the information was abstracted. All these means to evaluate HIQ can be expensive (if not organizationally infeasible in any practical sense), especially when sampling from a population of cases would not be considered sufficiently reliable for the variability at hand.

In Fig. 13.2, it is depicted a simple stepwise methodology to assess HIQ in the domain of unstructured information and, more specifically, in the Web domain, which has been validated in the domain of the complementary and alternative medicine. With respect to other methodologies, from which it borrows the main structure, this exhibits a task of prioritization of HIQ dimensions (step 4), which is accomplished by qualitative means involving either domain experts or consumers, and the review of accessible content by matching it with the guidelines and criteria detected at step 2.

Moving to HIQ assessment, even assuming it as a cost-effective procedure, a number of problems have been observed in actual initiatives of HIQ improvement. Therefore, overcoming problems related to information quality has been considered a challenging task for the following reasons (the full list is discussed in [678]).

- Lack of uniformity of information types
- Poorly designed data collection forms
- Limitations to doctors' capacity to record and communicate information (including the extensive use of nonstandard abbreviations and handwritten notes for the sake of efficiency and convenience in coping with frantically busy schedules)

- Limitations to information transfer between different teams (handovers), departments of the same facility, and between different healthcare organizations
- Limited education of processing staff (both clinical and administrative), especially with respect to knowledge of the consequences of poor HIQ
- Lack of HIQ-related planning by administrative staff
- No single record or repository
- Information inconsistencies

These difficulties notwithstanding [59], addressing and improving HIQ is generally perceived as an urging task [4]: a growing number of institutions and national bodies are implementing quality management programs to improve care processes [363], both in terms of performance (efficiency) and outcomes (effectiveness), and to comply with quality standards of worldwide accrediting agencies, like the Joint Commission (formerly known as the Joint Commission on Accreditation of Healthcare Organizations), the Joint Commission International, the Australian Council on Healthcare Standards, and the Accreditation Canada, just to mention the most important bodies that are represented by the International Society for Quality in Health Care. This is an organization that in 2014 spanned approximately 100 countries and five continents.

Healthcare and hospital accreditation is a way to gain visibility and trust in a more and more competitive market of healthcare-oriented services; moreover, it is also often a legal obligation for healthcare providers to be enrolled in the national health system and get service reimbursement. For this reason, accreditation is becoming an increasingly important driver for the improvement of IQ in healthcare organizations [415] as many of the guidelines that accredited organizations must apply in their services and processes regard data, mainly in terms of proper documenting and coding[3] (see Fig. 13.3). This focus on data is so important that it has been epitomized that "the quality of health care is measured by the quality of the data in the medical records" [678, p. 19].

One common way to improve the quality of primary data is by adopting a standard coding and enacting it in digital records and through their forms. In particular, coding in healthcare is proposed for two main aims: as a way to facilitate the sharing and exchange of health information between departments, health agencies, and health workers [316] and as a way to allow the design of systems capable of extracting information from coded records, aggregate and analyze this information in many ways [317], and reason on the basis of it to support experts in decision making and planning [317]. For these reasons, coding has received much attention from scholars and many efforts from the involved organizations under the promises to minimize variation due to individual interpretation.

---

[3] And this has also been considered a limit of those guidelines, that of being circumscribed to paper work, so to say, and fail to address patient safety in real situations; see, e.g., [311].

IM.7.5.1	Records of emergency visits contain time and means of arrival.
IM.7.5.2	Records of emergency visits contain conclusions at end of treatment, including final disposition, condition and instructions for follow-up.

The clinical record contains sufficient information to identify the patient, support the diagnosis, justify the treatment, document the course and results of treatment, and promote continuity of care among health care providers (MOI.2.1 JCIASH).

Measurable elements of MOI.2.1 include:
1. patient clinical records contain adequate information to identify the patient;
2. patient clinical records contain adequate information to support the diagnosis;
3. patient clinical records contain adequate information to justify the care and treatment;
4. patient clinical records contain adequate information to document the course and results of treatment;
5. patient clinical records promote continuity of care; and
6. the specific content of patient clinical records has been determined by the organization.

The intent of this standard is that the clinical record of each patient needs to present sufficient information to support the diagnosis, justify the treatment provided, and document the course and results of treatment. A standardized format and content of a patient's clinical record helps promote the integration and continuity of care among the various providers of care to the patient.

Fig. 13.3 Examples of standards issued by the Joint Commission (2000). Adapted from [678]

In particular, the Health Level 7 (HL7), the Digital Imaging and COmmunications in Medicine (DICOM), and the Systematized Nomenclature of Medicine (SNOMED) have so far emerged as significant international standards for health data serialization and messaging [55] that include reference models to represent HI, as well as comprehensive sets of rules and requirements to define and classify health terms against which information repositories can be challenged to assess their quality.

This notwithstanding standard classifications are not a panacea and cannot guarantee the achievement of high HIQ by themselves: first of all, the categorizing of codes, especially to denote diagnoses and interventions, is in continuous change; the clinical picture for diseases gets new definitions as medical knowledge advances, and new interventions are introduced once validated at community level [196]. For instance, the International Classification of Diseases (ICD) is one of the most important international standards "for epidemiology, health management, and clinical purposes" and since its first versions, issued in the nineteenth century, has changed several times: the current version (the 10th) was developed in 1992 especially to track health statistics, and a new version (the 11th) is planned for 2017. However, many countries have modified the official standard to fit their local needs, also extensively; for instance, while the ICD-10 counts 14,400 different codes to classify disease-related information, the US clinical modification version (US ICD-10 CM), which is adopted in many other countries and their national health systems, encompasses some 68,000 codes. Moreover, also the intrinsically local and socially constructed nature of any taxonomy [589] and of any coding practice should be taken into account [675, 676].

13.5 The Relevance of Information Quality in the Healthcare Domain

The attention to HIQ can be related to a number of reasons. A first reason refers to concern about information quality which could have been transferred from the information system and information technology discourses and communities to healthcare during the pervading digitization of the healthcare processes and of the artifacts used therein (i.e., documents, forms, records); although this process of digitization is proving itself to be harder in reaching the initial promises than expected [57, 189, 296, 297, 356], it is a fact that the health sector is increasingly characterized by the efficient provision of information-driven services, and these latter ones, as discussed in Chap. 1, are inextricably linked to the use of information systems [361], where information quality has always been an important factor to be considered; see, e.g., [37].

In this conceptual strand, almost all of the authors that in the last 25 years have contributed to the growth of the health informatics discipline and scholarly field [146, 316] agree on the assumption that problems with "data quality, account-ability, and integrity" (often acronymized as "DQAI issues") have a potential to deeply impair the capability to measure outcomes and performance (as observed in [537, p. 321] where "high-quality health information is [said to be] critical for quality health care and for effective and efficient management of the heath care system"). In addition to that, in the last 20 years or so, several studies have shed light on the fact that HIQ is far from being of the desired level, e.g., [638][4]: information quality is reported to be poor in about 5 % of records regularly maintained in health organizations [265, 318, 403].

This consideration puts the healthcare domain among those with the worst baseline IQ, if the estimation mentioned in [519, p. 303] is correct that from 1 to 5 % of data found in organizations are of poor quality. This fact, if taken from a secondary purpose perspective, would urge for important and strong interventions aimed at improving HIQ. For instance, a study analyzing Medicare data [155] found that almost 3 % of the nearly 12 million records in the database of this US social insurance program (i.e., approximately 321,300 records) contained coding errors. These errors surely impacted insurance reimbursement of facilities, clinicians, and patients but could also be related to additional time to be spent correcting the errors and hence to other economic losses. While IT practitioners have generally devoted more interest in this kind of consequences of HIQ, it has been the primary purpose

---

[4]We are aware that this claim is somehow flimsy according to the contextual nature of health information recalled above. That notwithstanding, taking an IT-oriented perspective, IQ levels detected in healthcare repositories are among the lowest ones in the organizational domain, broadly meant. In particular, it is probably a matter of high expectations: in [201], it is sustained that healthcare should aim to achieve the highest degree of IQ maturity, stage 5 (IQ certainty); this is the stage where practitioners involved can rightly claim that they *know why they do not have problems with Information Quality* (p. 78).

of healthcare information that has attracted most of the interest from the medical literature, and hence the (hospital-specific) medical record and its content.

In their review of the HIQ-related literature produced from 1990 to 2000 [28], the authors focused on two IQ dimensions, mainly for their popularity: accuracy, which they defined as "the extent to which registered data are in conformity to the truth" (p. 603), and completeness, defined as "the extent to which all necessary data that could have been registered have actually been registered"; moreover, they distinguished between the quality of data directly imputed into computerized systems, e.g., Electronic Patient Records (incompleteness: 4 %), and then transferred to a central registry (incompleteness: 6 %; inaccuracy: 2 %) and the quality of data that are imported into computerized systems (like a central registry database) from paper-based records and forms (incompleteness: 5 %; inaccuracy: 4.6 %).

In their more recent review of the literature produced in the following decade (2000–2010), [403] reviewed a significantly bigger body of works (245) and added to accuracy and completeness a comprehensive list of definitions also for the dimensions of "correctness, consistency, and timeliness" and for the methods to assess HIQ along those dimensions, e.g., [135, 314]. However, quite surprisingly the authors in 2013 reiterated the observation made by their colleagues also in 2002 that HIQ still "lacks a consensus conceptual framework and definition."

Also in the recent review (230 articles) reported in [661], it has been found that there is little consistency or potential generalizability in the methods used to assess HIQ in medical records. The lack of a general consensus (often even at regional level) on the definitions of data quality, data quality attributes, and the ways to measure it must not be underestimated [411], in that standards are necessary to compare data quality among research registries or within a registry at different points in time [608] and their absence can undermine intended reuse [661] (see above) and lead to very high variability: for instance, in the literature review reported in [314], the authors found that the correctness ranged between 44 and 100 % and completeness between 1 and 100 %, depending on the clinical concepts under consideration. In [608], values of sensitivity are reported ranging from 26 to 100 %, and in [115], completeness (of blood pressure recordings) has been found to range between 50 and 99.01 % in a transversal study across multiple institutions. Likewise, most of the studies reviewed in [403] reported "a range of deficiencies in the routinely collected electronic information for clinical, e.g., [421, 447], or health promotion [265, 585] purposes in hospital [402] and general practice [404] settings"; however, the HIQ picture they take is not uniform as data for administrative purposes (rather than clinical ones) were found of better quality, e.g., [514], so as prescription data (rather than diagnostic or lifestyle data) [404, 608].

Evidence of the effectiveness of HIQ assessment and improvement initiatives have to be found in anecdotal reports or reports of circumscribed experiences and initiatives. For instance, in [525], it has been recently reported a number of case studies from the Canadian experience with the Canadian Institute for

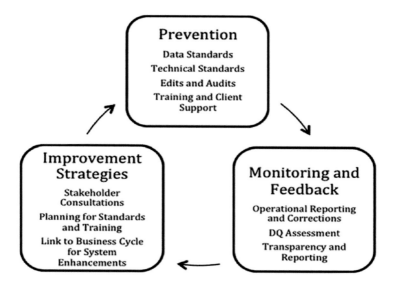

Fig. 13.4   The CIHI continuous data quality improvement process. Taken from [525]

Health Information (CIHI) data quality program that has been considered as one of the methodologies compared in Chap. 12; this program, which has also been discussed in [41], encompasses strategies for the continuous improvement of the HIQ in Canadian healthcare organizations through specific actions of IQ problem prevention, IQ level monitoring, and feedback actions to close the loop on the data quality cycle (see Fig. 13.4). Within the monitoring strategies, the CIHI Data Quality Framework Assessment Tool articulates HIQ in terms of five dimensions, i.e., accuracy, timeliness, comparability, usability, and relevance; and for each dimension, the tool expands it in terms of a set of characteristics and criteria for the dimension assessment (e.g., usability is expanded in terms of accessibility, documentation, and interpretability).

Another review, which focused on the program implemented at the beginning of the century by the UK Audit Commission [3], found significant improvements to levels of data quality in the UK National Health System. This review also detected corporate leadership as a necessary factor for success, although not sufficient alone. Moreover, the commission found that one of the biggest factors leading to poor IQ was the lack of understanding among end users and practitioners of the reasons for IQ-oriented practices and of the benefits of the high-quality HIQ they contribute to collect and process.

However, meta-reviews assessing the effectiveness of some specific methodology or approach (e.g., CIHI, TDQM) by comparing favorable and negative reports (and taking into account possible *file drawer* effects), as it is done in the evidence-based medicine literature, are still lacking (if feasible at all). Consequently, a growing number of contributions that review HIQ management programs in single facilities advocate this kind of meta-review [90, 311, 575]. This lack notwithstanding, the effective initiatives reported so far in the literature seem to include some (or all) of the following actions [625]:

- The standardization of data entry fields and in the processes for entering data, e.g., [266, 606]
- The implementation of real-time quality checking procedures, including the use of validation and feedback loops, e.g., [420, 511]
- The careful design data element and their holding structures to avoid errors, which in some cases have been observed to be introduced by the "bad" design of the data entry interfaces [379]
- The development of (and adherence to) guidelines for the proper documentation of the care provided to the patient [625]
- The review and continuous evolution of automated billing software
- The strong commitment of top and middle management toward the improvement of the human capital, including training programs and awareness-raising campaigns, and also of the benefits of organizational change, process innovation, and total quality management programs

Although interested readers could refer to the literature reviews undertaken in [28, 115, 403, 466, 516, 524, 529], it should be understood that these are all partial reviews (notwithstanding their sectorial comprehensiveness): a systematic literature review of the general topic denoted above as HIQ would be probably impossible to accomplish (and to our knowledge it is still to be) because health information is simply articulated in too many strands, scopes, and aims. Suffice to say that in PubMed, which is one of the most complete search engines indexing articles on life sciences and biomedical topics, more than 600 papers had either "Data Quality" or "Information Quality" in their titles, and almost 4000 had either these two phrases in their abstract[5]; in Google Scholar, a Web search engine whose coverage spans across an enormous array of publishing formats and disciplines, resources having the abovementioned phrases in their titles, along with some other health-related terms, are more than 17,000.[6] As said above, HIQ regards a too broad domain to be easily grasped within a unified framework and methodology, as often scholars would like to as a way to tame complex systems.

---

[5]These are the numbers of results returned on the 16th of May 2014 using the following query "('information quality' [Title/Abstract]) OR 'data quality' [Title/Abstract]."

[6]Results retrieved on the 22nd of May 2014 using the following query "intitle: ('data quality' OR 'information quality') AND intitle: ('heathcare' OR 'health' OR 'hospital' OR 'medical' OR 'clinical')."

13.5.1 Health Information Quality and Its Consequences on Healthcare

In the medical literature, problems with HIQ are almost never seen as a problem per se (as it is for the IT practitioner for obvious professional reasons); rather, poor HIQ is seen as a *hazard*, that is, a factor or facilitating condition that can (but does not necessarily) lead to erroneous interpretations of the reality—which is misrepresented by the data—and, for the same reason, to wrong decisions [130, 362] and medical errors [503]. Medical errors in their turn can lead to *adverse events*, i.e., when the patient is either harmed, damaged (also permanently), or even killed [630].

Indeed, the relationship between information quality and care quality, which is usually measured along both the dimensions of performance (i.e., efficiency) and outcome (i.e., effectiveness), looks as an easy guess especially in a Donobedian perspective, where resources, processes, and outcomes are recognized as being deeply intertwined [178]. Some studies, e.g., [182, 583] have recently claimed to have clearly detected a link between poor quality data (in medical registries and databases) and medical errors and subsequent poor quality of care.

For instance, poor quality of identification of patient data [120] is an oft-cited hazard that can lead to serious adverse events [439, 480, 503, 507] (e.g., when these problems can lead to get the wrong person for a certain treatment) or to relatively important privacy concerns [361], and also other cases have been reported like the case of false negatives in Down's syndrome screening and the omissions in cervical screening reported in [528]. These examples notwithstanding, a causal and, above all, direct relationship between poor IHQ and adverse events is far from having been demonstrated objectively, e.g., [358, 362], but this link is rather often postulated, e.g., [4], to give strong motivations that could underlie costly interventions of data cleaning and HIQ monitoring programs.[7]

Indeed, since the famous report of the Institute of Medicine [373] and its widely discussed (and also contested [590]) estimate of between 44,000 and 98,000 deaths due to medical errors in hospitals alone (resulting in an additional 17–29 billion of dollars in annual healthcare costs), medical errors have been a topic of passionate debate, especially for the call to actions that various authors make to change the gloomy situation.

Many of these actions can be rubricated under the Total (Data) Quality Management movement [363, 643]. Although there is a general awareness that the idea to transfer the achievements of manufacturing industries due to Total Quality

---

[7]This can look as an either weird or provocative point to make to an IT scholar or practitioner. However, the reason why the relationship between medical errors and inaccurate/incomplete/obsolete/…data should not be taken for granted lies in the simple fact that most clinicians are actually *trained to expect* errors in the data they consult on a daily basis, mainly because they are aware of how these are usually collected (sometimes also in virtue of well-meant workarounds [147]. Therefore, they rely first and foremost on the living body of the patient they somehow observe and manipulate [625], rather than on the written record.

Management initiatives into the much less structured (and structurable, as argued above) domain of hospital work, let alone healthcare (broadly meant), would be overambitious, some early endeavors are promising: for instance, a study on child mental health services showed that 58 % of the patients had improved outcomes after a data quality improvement project had been instituted [471], cited in [625].

However, an analysis of the benefits and costs of these programs in healthcare, in the mold of the best known analyses of this kind (e.g., [203]), is still lacking. Indeed, in the best and only (to date) scholarly source addressing the relationship between HIQ and medical errors explicitly, [503] raised a call on the need to devote more research on this interesting (and potentially far-reaching) topic, but their appeal seems to have remained unheeded. In this short review, we relaunch their original contribution, i.e., the notion of *information error*, which we see as a potential bridging concept that could make the IT community and the medical community converge on a common field of research and contributions.

> Information error: The state of the information such that its measurement, collection, storage, maintenance, retrieval (or lack thereof), its transmittal (or lack thereof), its visualization, or its use, create an environment that enables actions that, in turn, contribute directly or indirectly to intermediate or final adverse outcomes.

This notion looks sufficiently socio-technical, i.e., encompasses data and both its human and social contexts of production, use, and communication, to require a genuinely multidisciplinary approach that could beyond simplistic easy triumphalism and critical fatalism [237], in order to frame HIQ at complementary levels in the next quality-oriented agendas in the next health systems to come: the technological, ergonomic, organizational, and cultural levels. Considering also the human and cultural aspects related to health, information production and use is important, if not necessary, because the first step in HIQ management, i.e., data entry, is deemed to cause the three-fourths of all errors [625], and this will necessarily involve human beings for still a very long time to come. Thus, these aspects should be taken into consideration both to properly conceive improvement initiatives that are aimed also at changing the mindset and attitudes of people toward data recording [475] and to understand if those initiatives are really necessary or worth the trouble [297].

13.6 Summary

In this chapter, we have not had the pretension to address the multifaceted topic of information quality in healthcare with an ambition of comprehensiveness; however, we have given elements to understand why we could not proceed differently. The fact that HIQ is not merely IQ in an extremely heterogeneous domain, but rather a socio-technical *wicked problem* [530], could be the main reason why HIQ has received relatively little coverage in the specialist IQ literature and in the main books that have recently focused on data and information quality. Rather than further summarizing the already succinct outline performed in the previous sections, in these last remarks, we aim to advocate more studies tackling this wicked problem with a multiplicity of approaches and perspectives, possibly by using our contribution as a starting point to understand what we have achieved so far.

This seems desirable and beneficial also to fill in an apparent gap in the existing literature. Indeed, among the most recent books regarding IQ, HIQ is treated to some extent only in [537], whereas in [525], the authors report on the strategies and programs that the Canadian Institute for Health Information (CIHI) have aimed at supporting quality health information across the healthcare continuum (pp. 321–346). Important books on information quality like [37, 204, 430, 479, 557], and [451] did not address HIQ at all. Some years ago, in [202], English mentions the healthcare sector in an enumeration of cases of high costs related to low-quality data and cites a US local newspaper claiming that in the late 1990s, "approximately $23 billion, or 14 percent of the healthcare dollar, is wasted in fraud or inaccurate billing" (p. 8). Ten years later, the same author in [201] mentions HIQ in regard to inaccurate food labels that would "cause health problems" (p. 18). One of the most recent books focusing on IQ devotes just two pages (out of 275) on HIQ [233, pp. 7–9]; in this book, Fisher cites only one source [412] focusing on how shortcomings in coding and the lack of widely adopted standards of classification resulted in misreporting and therefore also in inappropriate decisions and interventions.

Even recently in [414], Loshin claims that "there can be serious health risks associated with incorrect data," but he or she does not assert that such an association does have a casual nature; indeed, the only case he or she mentions resulted in a single "botched heart-lung transplant." Thus, he or she concludes admitting that "disagreements about the number of critical events that are attributable to medical errors" (notably not IQ-related errors) exist but "discrepancies related to incorrect or invalid information are often identifiable as the root cause."

In another recent work on HIQ [100], its authors advocate future studies investigating whether better information quality leads to better healthcare quality and which IQ dimensions, like accuracy and timeliness, might affect different aspects of healthcare quality more, such as appropriateness, effectiveness, and sustainability.

However, this lie of the land is not highlighted as a criticism of past and current research on the application of the IQ discourse to healthcare. Rather, it can be seen as a call to devote greater efforts in this area at the intersection between IT and healthcare. This chapter represents a contribution in that direction.

Chapter 14
Quality of Web Data and Quality of Big Data: Open Problems

Monica Scannapieco and Laure Berti

14.1 Introduction

In this chapter we discuss some open issues related to two typologies of information sources that nowadays are particularly significant, namely, Web data and Big Data.

Searching and using the information stored on billions of Web pages poses significant challenges, because this information and related semantics are usually more complex and dynamic than the information that traditional database management systems store [304, 506]. As an evolving collection of interrelated files on one or more Web servers, Web data is extremely rich and diverse, combining multiple types of media and data.

The vision of the semantic Web aims to make use of semantic representations on the Web at the largest possible scale. Large knowledge bases such as DBpedia (http://dbpedia.org/), GovTrack (http://www.govtrack.us/), and OpenCyc (http://www.cyc.com/platform/opencyc) are freely available as linked data and SPARQL endpoints (see Chap. 3 for a systematic introduction to linked data). However, users of such large semantic Web knowledge bases are often facing three important problems:

- Limited access, due to the lack of high-quality keyword-based searches and the lack of deep Web access [423, 506]: users can hardly know which identifiers are used and are available for the construction of their queries. Furthermore, domain experts might not be able to express their queries in a structured form, although they have a very precise idea of what kind of results they would like to retrieve [599, 600, 679].
- Limited knowledge of the various IQ problems existing in the Web data: for example, data extracted from semistructured or even unstructured sources, such as DBpedia or Yahoo Finance (http://finance.yahoo.com/), often contain inconsistencies as well as misrepresented, redundant, obsolete, inaccurate, or

© Springer International Publishing Switzerland 2016
C. Batini, M. Scannapieco, *Data and Information Quality*, Data-Centric Systems
and Applications, DOI 10.1007/978-3-319-24106-7_14

incomplete information [401] the users may even not be aware of. They usually do not have appropriate tools to evaluate, control, or monitor IQ.

- Dissatisfaction and misuse of the available Web data or services: depending on the level of quality required, retrieved data or accessed services may not fit for the intended use. For example, in Wikipedia, it may happen, though in relatively few cases, that some information or some facts are missing or incomplete for general information purposes. But for self-medication, the same quality level may be completely insufficient. To date, some Web-based e-commerce service systems, such as amazon.com and expedia.com, register every user's past traversal or purchase history and build customer profiles from that data. Based on a user's profile and preferences, these sites select appropriate sales promotions and recommendations, thereby providing better quality of service than sites that do not track and store this information. Although a personalized Web service based on a user's traversal history could help recommend appropriate services, a system usually cannot collect enough information about a particular individual to warrant high-quality recommendations [497].

As a consequence, one of the most important challenges is to determine the quality of Web data—created with HTML and XML or generated dynamically by underlying Web database service engines—and make this quality information fully and relevantly usable and exploitable.

Two relevant paradigms for characterizing the quality of Web data are trustworthiness and provenance. Trustworthiness can be characterized on the basis of three dimensions, namely, *believability*, *verifiability*, and *reputation*. Provenance is a rather complex concept that has been being investigated since several years and that recently, with the advent of the Web of data, has become even more important. In Sect. 14.2 we will characterize and describe both paradigms, as well as relevant tools and techniques for dealing with them.

Ensuring IQ is obviously a substantial challenge in Web data management as it involves a set of autonomously evolving data sources that need to be monitored and possibly cleaned for data integration. To the purpose a very relevant task is object identification that aims at identifying pairs of data objects that represent the same real-world object and that has been discussed in the context of well-grounded types of data in Chaps. 8 and 9. When objects are Web data, some relevant features must be taken into account, namely, Web data can be highly time-dependant and their quality must be assessed. In Sect. 14.3 we will describe some relevant issues related to object identification of Web data, and we will also describe possible techniques solving such issues.

The second part of the chapter will deal with Big Data. In Sect. 14.4 after a general characterization of Big Data sources, we will describe issues in characterizing the quality of such data. In particular, we will outline that Big Data involves very different types of sources, and hence their quality characterization does need to be source specific. In this direction, an overview of approaches for quality characterization of sensor data will be presented in Sect. 14.5 as an example of how a source-specific quality characterization of Big Data can be carried out.

Specification of Big Data quality can also be dependent on specific application domains, i.e., it is domain specific. In this respect, in Sect. 14.6 we will provide an example of quality issues in dealing with Big Data that come from the Official Statistics domain.

14.2 Two Relevant Paradigms for Web Data Quality: Trustworthiness and Provenance

14.2.1 Trustworthiness

In the following we first define concepts related to trust, and then we discuss their interrelationships.

Trust is a level of subjective and local probability with which an agent assesses that another agent will perform a particular action. *Trustworthiness* is the objective probability that the trustee performs a particular action on which the interests of the truster depend. In other words, trustworthiness is the assurance that a system will perform as expected. Though trust and trustworthiness are two distinct concepts, when dealing with techniques for assessing them, the two concepts play often a single role; hence in the following the two terms will be used interchangeability unless needing specific characterizations.

Thirunarayan et al. [609] provide a comprehensive ontology to capture trust-related concepts as well as a detailed comparative analysis of trust models and metrics in diverse contexts. They classify the approaches into *direct trust* referring to trust determined using firsthand experiences over a period of time and *indirect trust* referring to trust determined using experiences of others via referrals. They describe and compare Bayesian approaches to direct trust and trustworthiness in reputation-based processes.

Recent work on performing trust analysis based on the data provided by multiple sources has been proposed. Yin et al. [688] introduced a heuristic fact-finder algorithm *TruthFinder* which performs trust analysis on a providers' facts network. This work was followed by various fact-finder algorithms in the context of trust propagation [634] and truth discovery analysis [181]. The goal is to find the truth about some questions or facts given multiple conflicting sources. The proposed approaches differ in the factors taken into account to estimate *source accuracy* and *trustworthiness*, e.g., the difficulty of the questions [252], the type of errors [694], the applications (Wikipedia or collection of Web documents), [634] or some potential dependence (through copying relationships) between sources [181].

According to [634], a general approach to trust assessment uses (1) domain-dependent properties for determining trustworthiness based on content and on external metadata and (2) domain-independent mapping to trust levels through quantification and classification. For example, Wikipedia articles can be assessed based on domain-dependent content-based quality factors such as references to peer-reviewed publications, proportion of paragraphs with citation, article size, and also metadata-based credibility factors such as author connectivity, edit pattern and development history, revision count, proportion of reverted edits, mean time between edits, and mean edit length. Another example is the estimation of a Web site's trustworthiness based on the levels of sensitivity of exchanged information with highly trusted sites (e.g., for identity and banking information exchanges).

14.2.1.1   Trustworthiness Dimensions

There are three dimensions for characterizing trustworthiness, namely, *believability*, *verifiability*, and *reputation* that are displayed along with their respective metrics in Table 14.1. The reference for each metric is provided in the table.

In the following, a detailed characterization of the three dimensions is provided.

14.2.1.2   Believability

Believability refers to the extent to which information is regarded as true and credible. Believability can also be defined as the subjective measure of a user's belief that the data is "true" [336]. Believability is measured as follows (see also Table 14.1):

- Compute the trustworthiness of RDF statements based on provenance information and on the opinion of other information consumers: the system applies a trust function which assigns a trust value which can be a value in the interval $[-1, 1]$ where 1 is the absolute belief, -1 the absolute disbelief, and 0 the lack of belief/disbelief. The trust functions that compute a trust value are based on user-based ratings and provenance-based or opinion-based method.
- Compute the trustworthiness of an entity, namely, an object or a resource: an objective trust measure for each entity is provided a priory by a trusted third party which provides information such as citation count or global reputation. Once each entity has been given its trust value, then it is possible to make trust inference on the new arriving entities.
- Compute the trust between two entities by using a combination of (1) a propagation algorithm which utilizes statistical techniques for computing trust values between two entities through a path and (2) an aggregation algorithm based on a weighting mechanism for calculating the aggregate value of trust over all paths.
- Acquiring content trust from users: based on associations that transfer trust from entities to resources.
- Detection of trustworthiness, reliability, and credibility of a data source: use of trust annotations made by several individuals to derive an assessment of the sources' trustworthiness, reliability, and credibility.

Table 14.1 Comprehensive list of IQ metrics for trust dimensions

Dimension	Subdimension	Description
Believability	Computing the trustworthiness of RDF statements	Computing a trust value based on user-based ratings or opinion-based method [298]
	Computing the trust of an entity	Construction of decision networks informed by provenance graphs [254]
	Accuracy of computing the trust between two entities	By using a combination of (1) propagation algorithm which utilizes statistical techniques for computing trust values between two entities through a path and (2) an aggregation algorithm based on a weighting mechanism for calculating the aggregate value of trust over all paths [569]
	Acquiring content trust from users	Based on associations that transfer trust from entities to resources [263]
	Detection of trustworthiness, reliability, and credibility of a data source	Use of trust annotations made by several individuals to derive an assessment of the sources' trustworthiness, reliability, and credibility [264]
	Assigning trust values to data/sources/rules	Use of trust ontologies that assign content-based or metadata-based trust values that can be transferred from known to unknown data [336]
	Determining trust value for data	Using annotations for data such as (1) blacklisting, (2) authoritativeness, and (3) ranking and using reasoning to incorporate trust values to the data [84]
	Meta-information about the identity of information provider	Checking whether the provider/contributor is contained in a list of trusted providers [78]
Verifiability	Verifying publisher information	Stating the author and his or her contributors, the publisher of the data and its sources [238]
	Verifying authenticity of the dataset	Whether the dataset uses a provenance vocabulary, e.g., the use of the provenance vocabulary [238]
	Verifying correctness of the dataset	With the help of unbiased trusted third party [78]
	Verifying usage of digital signatures	Signing a document containing an RDF serialization or signing an RDF graph [238]
Reputation	Reputation of the publisher	Survey in a community questioned about other members [263]
	Reputation of the dataset	Analyzing references or page rank or by assigning a reputation score to the dataset [436]

- Assigning trust values to data sources/rules: use of trust ontologies that assign content-based or metadata-based trust values that can be transferred from known to unknown data.
- Determining trust value for data: using annotations for data such as (1) blacklisting, (2) authoritativeness, and (3) link-based ranking.

- Meta-information about the identity of information provider: checking whether the provider/contributor is contained in a list of trusted providers.

Another method proposed by Tim Berners-Lee was that Web browsers should be enhanced with an "Oh, yeah?" button to support the user in assessing the believability of data encountered on the Web.[1] Pressing of such a button for any piece of data or an entire dataset would contribute toward assessing the believability of the dataset.

According to the last three points in the listing given before, we can point out that believability is measured by checking whether the contributor is contained in a list of trusted providers. There exists an interdependency between the data provider and the data itself. On the one hand, data is likely to be accepted as true if it is provided by a trustworthy provider. On the other hand, the data provider is trustworthy if it provides true data.

14.2.1.3   Verifiability

Verifiability refers to the degree by which a data consumer can assess the correctness of a dataset.

Verifiability is described as the "degree and ease with which the information can be checked for correctness" [78]. Similarly, in [238] the verifiability criterion is used as the means a consumer is provided with, which can be used to examine the data for correctness. Without such means, the assurance of the correctness of the data would come from the consumer's trust in that source. It can be observed here that on the one hand the authors in [78] provide a formal definition, whereas the author in [238] describes the dimension by providing its advantages and metrics.

Verifiability can be measured either by an unbiased third party, if the dataset itself points to the source or by the presence of a digital signature (see Table 14.1).

As an example, if we assume that a flight search engine crawls information from arbitrary airline Web sites, which publish flight information according to a standard vocabulary, there is a risk for receiving incorrect information from malicious Web sites. For instance, such a Web site publishes cheap flights just to attract a large number of visitors. In that case, the use of digital signatures for published RDF data could allow to restrict crawling only to verified datasets.

Verifiability is an important dimension when a dataset includes sources with low believability or reputation. This dimension allows data consumers to decide whether to accept provided information. One means of verification in linked data is to provide basic provenance information along with the dataset, such as using existing vocabularies like SIOC, Dublin Core, provenance vocabulary, the OPMV,[2]

---

[1] http://www.w3.org/DesignIssues/UI.html.

[2] http://open-biomcd.sourceforge.net/opmv/ns.html.

or the recently introduced PROV vocabulary.[3] Yet another mechanism is the usage of digital signatures [112], whereby a source can sign either a document containing an RDF serialization or an RDF graph. Using a digital signature, the data source can vouch for all possible serializations that can result from the graph, thus ensuring the user that the data he or she receives is in fact the data that the source has vouched for.

14.2.1.4   Reputation

Reputation is a judgment made by a user to determine the integrity of a source. It can be associated with a data publisher, a person, organization, group of people, or community of practice, or it can be a characteristic of a dataset (see Table 14.1).

The authors in [263] associate reputation of an entity (i.e., a publisher or a dataset) either as a result from direct experience or recommendations from others. They propose the tracking of reputation through a centralized authority or, in alternative, via decentralized voting.

Reputation is usually a score, for example, a real value between 0 (low) and 1 (high). There are different possibilities to determine reputation and can be classified into human-based or (semi)automated approaches. The human-based approach is via a survey in a community or by questioning other members who can help to determine the reputation of a source or by the person who published a dataset. The (semi)automated approach can be performed by the use of external links or page ranks.

The provision of information on the reputation of data sources allows conflict resolution. For instance, several data sources report conflicting prices (or times) for a particular flight number. In that case, a search engine can decide to trust only the source with higher reputation.

Reputation is a social notion of trust [269]. Trust is often represented in a web of trust, where nodes are entities and edges are the trust values based on a metric that reflects the reputation one entity assigns to another [263]. Based on the information presented to a user, he or she forms an opinion or makes a judgment about the reputation of the dataset or the publisher and the reliability of the statements.

14.2.2   Provenance

Representing and analyzing provenance is a topic of research since a decade [299, 602]. Bunemann et al. [98] identify several open issues for data provenance of Web data such as (1) obtaining provenance information, (2) citing components of a data resource that may be (components of) another resource in another context, and (3) ensuring integrity of citations under the assumption that cited data resources evolve.

---

[3]http://www.w3.org/TR/prov-o/.

Not knowing the exact provenance used to produce a published dataset often renders the dataset useless (and not only from a scientific point of view). While there has been substantial work on database and workflow provenance, the two problems have generally been examined in isolation. Database provenance, which has been investigated in Chap. 6 , is fine-grained and captures precise—why, where, and how—dependencies [128] between data and queries. These dependencies are used to formally analyze and improve the quality of data and query results. In contrast, workflow provenance is represented at a coarser level and reflects the functional model of workflow systems which is stateless (each computational step derives a new artifact). Workflow provenance is mainly used to achieve reproducibility of workflow executions.

On the positive side, capturing provenance information is facilitated by the widespread use of workflow tools for processing scientific data and more recently open data. The workflow process describes all the steps involved in producing a given dataset and hence captures its lineage. Efficiently deriving [19, 87] storing and querying [22] provenance information is still an important research issue in both database and workflow environments.

For Web data, we are confronted with several challenging issues concerning provenance information management. The first challenge addresses the problem of keeping track of Web data lineage from its origin to its final uses and consists in defining and implementing tools for capturing and querying provenance information of data-centric workflows. These tools have to combine database and workflow provenance techniques [132] that specialize general data-oriented transformations, such as the ones specified for warehousing systems [158].

The second challenging issue addresses the problem of building and increasing confidence in the data and consists in using provenance information for capturing and improving the quality of data manipulated by SPARQL queries [176]. The goal is to define appropriate abstract provenance models that capture the relationship between query results and source data by taking into account the employed query operators [607].

With the development of the linked data initiative [407], the provenance of that data becomes an important factor for developing new semantic Web applications. A dedicated W3C group, the Provenance Working Group, part of the W3C Semantic Web Activity [636], developed a set of documents, collectively named as the PROV Family of documents [635], with the purpose of promoting and enabling representation and interchange of provenance information using widely available formats such as RDF and XML. The following section describes some interesting outcomes of this W3C standardization activity.

14.2.2.1   Provenance on the Web

Provenance of a resource is a record of metadata containing descriptions of the entities and activities involved in producing and delivering or otherwise influencing a given object. The main usage of provenance are related to (1) understanding where

Fig. 14.1 Key concepts of
the PROV Family of
documents

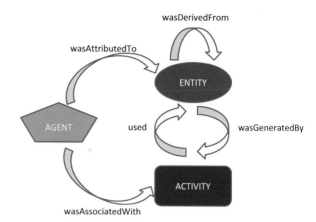

data come from, (2) identifying ownership and rights over a resource, (3) making judgments about a resource to determine whether to trust it, (4) verifying that the process used to obtain a result complies with given requirements, and reproducing it.

Three different perspectives on provenance can be considered:

- *Agent-centered provenance*, that is, what people or organizations were involved in generating or manipulating a resource. For example, in the provenance of a picture in a news article, it is possible to capture the photographer who took it, the person that edited it, and the newspaper that published it.
- *Object-centered provenance*, by tracing the origins of portions of an entity, i.e., an object or a resource, to other entities.
- *Process-centered provenance*, capturing the activities and steps taken to generate a resource. For example, some statistical data are the result of a data collection phase that involved a certain sample, of a data correction phase that involved specific imputation techniques, and of a data estimation phase, performed according to defined methods.

The relationships among the different perspectives are shown in Fig. 14.1. Key dimensions concerning provenance are shown in Table 14.2 and are *content*, *management*, and *use*. The four dimensions characterizing the content dimension aim to take into account who provided the content (*attribution*), how the content was generated (*process*), how it evolved in time (*evolution* and *versioning*), notes on the content (*justification for decision*), and the content it was derived from (*entailment*). Management is instead described by the availability of provenance

Table 14.2 Dimensions of provenance of Web data

Category	Dimension	Description
Content	Attribution	Provenance as the sources or entities that were used to create a new result
		Responsibility: knowing who endorses a particular piece of information or result
		Origin: recorded vs. reconstructed, verified vs. non-verified, asserted vs. inferred
	Process	Provenance as the process that yielded an artifact
		Reproducibility (e.g., workflows, mash-ups, text extraction)
		Data access (e.g., access time, accessed server, party responsible for accessed server)
	Evolution and versioning	*Republishing* (e.g., re-tweeting, re-blogging)
		Updates (e.g., a document with content from various sources and that changes over time)
	Justification for decisions	Includes argumentation, hypotheses, why-not questions
	Entailment	Given the results to a particular query, what axioms or tuples led to those result
Management	Publication	Making provenance information available (expose, distribute)
	Access	Finding and querying provenance information
	Dissemination control	Track policies specified by creator for when/how an artifact can be used
		Access control: incorporate access control policies to access provenance information
		Licensing: stating what rights the object creators and users have based on provenance
		Law enforcement (e.g., enforcing privacy policies on the use of personal information)
	Scale	How to operate with large amounts of provenance information
Use	Understanding	End user consumption of provenance
		Abstraction: multiple levels of description, summary
		Presentation, visualization
	Interoperability	Combining provenance produced by multiple different systems
	Comparison	Finding what is in common in the provenance of two or more entities (e.g., two experimental results)
	Accountability	The ability to check the provenance of an object with respect to some expectation
		Verification of a set of requirements
		Compliance with a set of policies

(continued)

Table 14.2 (continued)

	Trust	Making trust judgments based on provenance
		Information quality
		Reputation, reliability
	Imperfections	Reasoning about provenance information that is not complete or correct
		Incomplete provenance
		Uncertain, probabilistic provenance
		Erroneous provenance
		Fraudulent provenance
	Debugging	Using provenance to detect bugs or failures of processes

information (*publication*) as well as its accessibility (*access*) and by nonfunctional provenance requirements like control policies (*dissemination control*) and performance (*scale*). Finally, the use dimension is characterized by usability aspects (*understanding*), integration aspects (*interoperability* and*comparison*), provenance verifiability (*accountability* and *trust*), and error management issues (*imperfection* and *debugging*).

The PROV Family of documents collectively consists of eleven documents. Each document can be classified according to the specific type of audience it is intended for, namely:

- Users that want to understand PROV and use applications that support PROV
- Developers that want to develop or build applications that create and consume provenance using PROV
- Advanced that want to create validators, new PROV serializations, or other advanced provenance-based systems

Table 14.3 lists the PROV framework documents according to the different types of users, namely, *users*, *developers*, and *advanced*. While the set of documents related to the developers view is of immediate practical usage for provenance publishers, the set of documents that is apart of the advanced view is more intended to be used for both (1) formal definition of the framework's concepts and (2) provision of specifications for developers of tools that can support provenance publication and validation.

Among the documents shown in Table 14.3, the PROV-O document is particularly relevant that defines an OWL2 ontology, enabling the representation of provenance information for linked open data. In this respect, it provides both a data model and a technical solution to associate provenance information to linked open data.

Table 14.3 Dimensions of provenance of Web data

Audience	Document name	Description
Users	Prov-Primer	It is the entry point to PROV offering an introduction to the provenance data model. This is where you should start and for many may be the only document needed
Developers	Prov-O	It defines a lightweight OWL2 ontology for the provenance data model. This is intended for the linked data and semantic Web community
	Prov-XML	Defines an XML schema for the provenance data model. This is intended for developers who need a native XML serialization of the PROV data model
	Prov-AQ	Defines how to use Web-based mechanisms to locate and retrieve provenance information
	Prov-DC	Defines a mapping between Dublin Core and PROV-O
	Prov-Dictionary	Defines constructs for expressing the provenance of dictionary style data structures
Advanced	Prov-DM	It defines a conceptual data model for provenance including UML diagrams. PROV-O, PROV-XML, and PROV-N are serializations of this conceptual model
	Prov-N	Defines a human-readable notation for the provenance model. This is used to provide examples within the conceptual model as well as used in the definition of PROV-CONSTRAINTS
	Prov-CONSTRAINTS	Defines a set of constraints on the PROV data model that specifies a notion of valid provenance. It is specifically aimed at the implementors of validators
	Prov-Sem	Defines a declarative specification in terms of first-order logic of the PROV data model
	Prov-LINKS	Defines extensions to PROV to enable linking provenance information across bundles of provenance descriptions

14.3   Web Object Identification

We have seen in Chaps. 8 and 9 that the scope of object identification (OID) is very huge, going from structured data to images (image matching) and to completely unstructured information like documents (document matching).

The focus of this section is restricted to Web data, which is a huge category as well. From an OID perspective, Web data can be characterized by some relevant features, listed in the following:

- Time variability, considering the time dependency of most of Web data
- Quality, in terms of its characterizing IQ dimensions

In the following, for each of the above-listed features, we will illustrate the impact on the OID process and some examples of research works that address the OID problem with respect to the specific feature under analysis.

14.3.1 Object Identification and Time Variability

In Chap. 1, we introduced the concept of time variability of data and of its impact on data and information quality. When considering specifically Web data, the relationship with time has two main aspects. The first one is data volatility, i.e., a temporal variability of the information the data are meant to represent: there are data that are highly volatile (e.g., stock options), others which exhibit some degree of volatility (e.g., product prices), and some which are not volatile at all (e.g., birth dates). The second aspect is more generally related to the time features of the data generating mechanism. For instance, some Web data spring up and get updated in an almost unpredictable fashion, so that their time dimension is not available in a direct way, but does need to be reconstructed, if wishing to use those data in any meaningful analysis.

14.3.1.1 Need for Fully Automated Methods

From an OID perspective, the data volatility aspect has the direct implication that manual tasks are not anymore possible (or at least are hard to be executed) during the OID process, that is, the process should be fully automated. Decision models for OID are often supervised or semi-supervised, or, in other words, selected record pairs (typically the more difficult to classify) are sent to be clerically reviewed and training set of prelabeled record pairs can be prepared. Implementations of the Fellegi and Sunter model [229] (see also Chap. 8 for an introduction to the model) are often classified as unsupervised methods for learning the status of matching or unmatching of object pairs. However, such implementations are not actually fully automated, as it would be necessary in an OID process on Web data. As an example, several implementations of Fellegi and Sunter rely on the expectation-maximization (EM) algorithm [174] for the estimation of the parameters of the model. However, in these techniques, manual intervention is required due to (1) the need of setting thresholds for identifying matching and unmatching pairs and (2) possible unsuccessful parameter estimation via the EM algorithm (which may happen, for instance, if the size of the search space is too huge or too much limited).

An example of fully automated technique that can fit the fully automation
requirement of Web data is provided in [690], where a statistical approach based
on *mixture models* is adopted. More specifically, OID methods rely on distance
(or similarity) measures between object pairs. Due to the stochastic nature of
every real-world data generating process, such pairwise distances can be seen as
(realizations of) a random variable. Thus, the intuition behind the use of mixture
models is that the observed distances arise from a superposition of two distinct
probability distributions: the one stemming from the subpopulation of matches and
the other from that of unmatches. The ultimate aim of this statistical perspective
is to exploit the mixture model for classification purposes, i.e., to bring to light
the hidden grouping of the pairs in the underlying M and U classes. To such a
scope, the distance is viewed as an observable auxiliary random variable that can
be used to make inference on a latent interest random variable, namely, the class
membership indicator of the pairs. The whole picture is founded upon the hypothesis
that the probability distribution of the distance is significantly different inside the
M and U classes (see also Chap. 9, where Sect. 9.2 focuses on the impact that the
different distributions have on OID metrics). Luckily this is almost always the case
in real application scenarios, because typically errors affect data at moderate rates.
Whenever such condition holds, the shapes of the M and U distance densities are
indeed very different: (1) unmatches tend to be concentrated at higher distances
than matches, which furthermore generally exhibit their own distinctive peak at
zero distance; (2) M and U densities show only a relatively small overlap. These
qualitative features are so general that one can rightly consider them as a piece
of prior knowledge about the underlying (unknown) M and U distance probability
distributions: we refer to it as PK1.

Besides PK1, another piece of prior knowledge is readily available in OID
applications, namely, that matches are rare as compared to unmatches. We refer
to this second kind of prior knowledge as PK2. In Fig. 14.2, the distribution of
distances for a real dataset (the restaurant dataset of the riddle online repository)
is shown. The paper [691] presents a system called MAERLIN (the acronym stands
for Mixture-based Automated Effective Record LINkage) that implements the novel
suite of methods proposed in [690] and shows how to exploit PK1 and PK2 when
facing practical OID tasks. MAERLIN represents the probability density function of
the distance as a two-component beta mixture. The system structures the decision
phase of an OID process into two consecutive tasks, as schematically depicted in
Fig. 14.3. First, it finds (constrained) maximum likelihood estimates for the mixture
parameters by fitting the model to the observed distance measures between pairs.
Then, it obtains a probabilistic clustering of the pairs into matches and unmatches
by exploiting the fitted model.

The fitting phase is the crucial one, as it implicitly determines the quality of
the subsequent clustering results. However, it represents a very hard task; indeed,
the problem of fitting a mixture model is always difficult, but it is even more
severe in OID applications. This is due to the huge class skew inherent in OID
problems, where the very few (and unidentified) distance measures stemming from

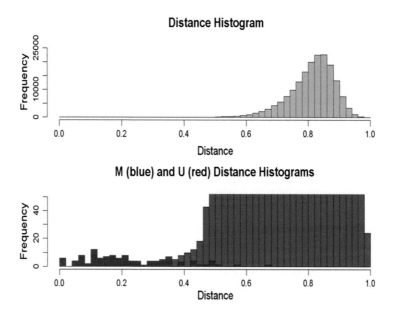

Fig. 14.2 Distance histogram and matches and unmatches histograms: the unmatches *red* histogram in the *lower panel* has been cut to allow the detection of the very small matches distribution (*blue*)

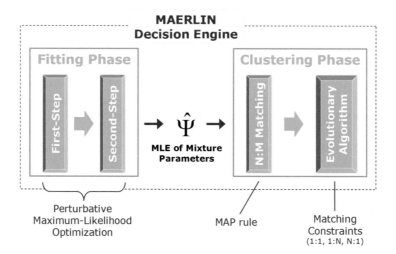

Fig. 14.3 MAERLIN decision engine

matches risk to be completely overwhelmed by the bulk of those stemming from
unmatches. To overcome this difficulty, MAERLIN exploits an original fitting
technique inspired by perturbation theory (see, e.g., [53]) and designed to take
advantage from both PK1 and PK2. The technique is coded as a two-step algorithm,
with the M class mixing weight playing the role of the perturbative expansion
parameter. The first step concentrates on the U component mixture parameters and is
specifically aimed at "factorizing" the leading contribution arising from unmatches.
The second step strives to increase the likelihood achieved in the previous step
by using the remaining mixture parameters in a smart way; that is, M density
parameters are tuned in such a way as to better fit the behavior of the distance
distribution exactly in those regions where, thanks to PK1, values stemming from
matches are more likely to be found.

In the clustering phase, MAERLIN searches an optimal classification rule such
that each pair can be assigned, based on its observed distance value, either to the M
or to the U class. The system can minimize either the probability of classification
error (maximum likelihood objective) or, alternatively, the expected classification
cost (minimum cost objective), while satisfying arbitrary matching constraints
among the two sets of objects to be matched (1:1, 1:n, n:1, or n:m). If no constraints
are imposed (i.e., for n:m matching), the applied classification rules depend in a
quite straightforward way on posterior estimates of class membership probabilities
and reflect classical decision theory results (see, e.g., [185]). For instance, the
maximum likelihood objective leads to the well-known maximum a posteriori
(MAP) rule; see Fig. 14.3. When, on the contrary, matching constraints are imposed,
MAERLIN faces directly the full-complexity constrained optimization problem by
means of a purposefully designed evolutionary algorithm [690].

14.3.1.2   Need for Time-Aware Techniques

Let us consider the second aspect related to OID and time dependence, i.e., the
possible availability of a time stamp for Web data. The OID matching process does
need to be aware of this specific kind of information, and indeed there are some
preliminary works that actually take explicitly into account the temporal information. As an example, in [496], an approach that leverages temporal information
with linkage is presented. The approach takes into account cases in which as time
elapses, values of a particular entity may evolve; for example, a researcher may
change affiliation or email. On the other hand, different objects are more likely to
share the same value(s) with a long time gap. Thus the concept of *decay* is defined,
with which the penalty for value disagreement is reduced and, at the same time,
the reward for value agreement over a long period is reduced as well. Moreover,
temporal clustering algorithms are proposed that explicitly consider time order of
records in order to improve linkage results.

14.3.2 Object Identification and Quality

When considering OID of Web data, quality becomes a fundamental issue: the greater the complexity of the process, the poorer the quality of data. Assessing the quality of Web data is a current research activity and is of course highly dependent on the specific Web source. In the following, we give two examples that show that, unfortunately, the overall quality of Web data appears to be dramatically poor.

A first example is related to social media data, such as Twitter data. As reported in [89] Twitter has been used to examine a wide variety of patterns such as mood rhythms, media event engagement, political uprisings, etc. However,

> Twitter does not represent "all people", and it is an error to assume "people" and "Twitter users" are synonymous: they are a very particular sub-set. Neither is the population using Twitter representative of the global population. Nor can we assume that accounts and users are equivalent. Some users have multiple accounts, while some accounts are used by multiple people. Some people never establish an account, and simply access Twitter via the Web. Some accounts are "bots" that produce automated content without directly involving a person.

Twitter data are characterized for being highly unstructured and often not accompanied by metadata. This means that high percentages of these data cannot be simply used by automated processes, as they are "pointless babbles" [88]. To get an effective use of this kind of data, it is necessary to investigate methods for automatic generation of the right metadata to describe the data under review.

The second example of Web quality assessment is related to deep Web data. Deep Web indicates that part of the Web that is not directly indexed by standard search engines. A huge amount of information on the Web is sunk on dynamically generated sites, and traditional search engines cannot access this information as those pages do not exist until they are created dynamically as the result of a specific search. Most Web sites are interfaces to databases, including e-commerce sites, flight companies sites, online bibliographies, etc. The deep Web includes all these sites and thus it is estimated that its size is several orders of magnitude larger than the surface Web [506].

In [401], an assessment of the quality of deep Web data from stock (55 sources) and flight (38 sources) domains is presented. The results of the assessment report a bad quality in terms of inconsistency (for 70 % of data items, more than one value is provided) and of correctness (only 70 % correct values are provided by the majority of the sources).

Interestingly, the work [401] provides a specific definition of quality metrics for Web data. Such set of metrics is described in the following and represents one of the first attempts to define a quality assessment framework for Web data.

First, the *redundancy* of data is evaluated, specifically: (1) redundancy on objects, i.e., the percentage of sources that provide a particular object, and (2) redundancy on data items, i.e., the percentage of sources that provide a particular data item.

The further considered dimension is *consistency* of the data, defined according to three measures:

- Number of values. By denoting as $V(d)$ the set of values provided by various sources on d, the number of values reports the number of different values provided on d, that is, the size of $V(d)$.
- Entropy. By denoting as $S(d)$ the set of sources that provide data on item d and $S(d; v)$ the set of sources that provide value v on d, the entropy is

$$\sum_{v \in V(d)} \frac{|S(d, V)|}{|S(d)|} \log \frac{|S(d, V)|}{|S(d)|}.$$

Intuitively, the higher the inconsistency, the higher the entropy.
- Deviation. For numerical values, by defining as v_0 the dominant value, i.e., the one with the largest number of providers given by $\mathrm{argmax}_{v \in V(d)} |S(d, V)|$, the deviation from d is

$$D(d) = \sqrt{\frac{1}{|V(d)|} \sum_{v \in V(d)} (\frac{v - v_0}{v_0})^2}.$$

Finally, accuracy is evaluated according to two measures, namely:

- Source accuracy: we compute accuracy of S as the percentage of its provided values that are consistent with the given gold standard.
- Accuracy deviation: computed as the standard deviation of the accuracy of a source over a period of time. Given that $\mathcal{T}$ is the set of time points in a period, $A(t)$ is the accuracy of the source at time $t \in \mathcal{T}$, and $\bar{A}$ is the mean accuracy over $\mathcal{T}$, the variety is computed by $\sqrt{\frac{1}{|\mathcal{T}|} \sum_{t \in \mathcal{T}} (A(t) - \bar{A})^2}$.

The final results of the assessment activity performed according to such measures are quite poor, namely:

- For the stock domain, there is a very high redundancy at the object level, namely, each source provides over 90 % of the stocks; for the flight domain, object-level redundancy is lower, namely, only 36 % of the sources cover 90 % of the flights. It is observed that there is large redundancy on data items, over various domains: on average each data item has a redundancy of 66 % for stock and 32 % for flight.
- There is a quite high inconsistency of values on the same data item: for stock and flight, the average entropy is 0.58 and 0.24, and the average deviation is 13.4 and 13.1, respectively. The inconsistency can vary from attributes to attributes. By choosing dominant values as the true value, precision is 0.908 for stock and 0.864 for flight for the two domains, respectively.
- Accuracy of the sources can vary a lot: on average the accuracy is about 0.86 for stock and 0.80 for flight.

14.4   Quality of Big Data: A Classification of Big Data Sources

The term Big Data (BD) is used for identifying structured or unstructured datasets that are impossible to store and process using common software tools (e.g., relational databases), regardless of the computing power or the physical storage at hand. The size of data, typically spanning dimensions of tera and peta byte orders of magnitude, is not the only aspect that make data "Big." Indeed, the problem of feasibility in treating data increases when datasets grow continuously over time, while a timely processing is necessary for producing business value [551]. According to a classification proposed by UNECE (United Nations Economic Commission for Europe) (see [616]), there are three main types of data sources that can be viewed as Big Data:

1. Human-sourced information sources
2. Process-mediated sources
3. Machine-generated sources

Type 1 sources include a vast amount of data types such as (a) social networks (Facebook, Twitter, LinkedIn, etc.), (b) blogs and comments, (c) Internet searches on search engines (Google, etc.), (d) videos loaded in the Internet (YouTube, etc.), (e) user-generated maps, (f) picture archives (Instagram, Flickr, Picasa, etc.), (g) data and contents from mobile phones (text messages, etc.), (h) e-mails, and so on.

Type 2 sources can consist of (a) data produced by public bodies and institutions (medical records, etc.) and (b) data produced by the private sector (commercial transactions, banking/stock records, e-commerce, credit cards, etc.).

Among type 3 sources, we can distinguish (a) data from fixed sensors (home automation, weather/pollution sensors, traffic sensors/Web cameras, scientific sensors, security/surveillance videos/images, etc.); (b) data from mobile sensors, i.e., for tracking or analysis purposes (satellite images, GPS, mobile phone location, car devices, etc.); and (c) data from computer systems (log files, Web logs, etc.).

Big Data is gaining more and more attention both in academic and business contexts. Nowadays, the main unmatched challenges in Big Data management concern the so-called 3V:

- *Variety*, referring to the heterogeneity of data acquisition, data representation, and semantic interpretation. As to BD representations, we have introduced in the Preface two evolution coordinates for information types, the perceptual coordinate and the linguistic coordinate.
- *Volume*, referring to the size of the data. Worldwide information volume is growing at a rate of 60 % annually, and 90 % of data in the today world has been created during the last 2 years.
- *Velocity*, referring to the data provisioning rate and to the time in which it is necessary to act on them. Every minute 400,000 tweets on Tweet are posted, 200 million e-mails are sent, and 2 million Google search queries are submitted [460].

Given that BD involves so many different sources and business domains, a quality characterization of them should be *source specific* and *domain specific*.

Source specificity is very much evident when considering the heterogeneous nature of some sources. For instance, sensor network's data streams can be quality characterized by the fact that data is often missing, and when not missing they are subject to potentially significant noise and calibration effects. In addition, because sensing relies on some form of physical coupling, the potential for faulty data is high. Depending on where a fault occurs in the data reporting, observations might be subject to unacceptable noise levels (for example, due to poor coupling or analog-to-digital conversion) or transmission errors (packet corruption or loss). In Sect. 14.5.1 we will discuss in detail quality issues in sensor data sources.

Conversely, for social media data, data are highly unstructured and often not accompanied by metadata. This means that high percentages of these data cannot be simply used by automated processes as they are affected by high percentages of noise. In other cases, however, dedicated and often expensive activities of semantic extraction must be performed.

Domain specificity is the other relevant dimension for the specific characterization of quality of Big Data. Depending on the domain, it is necessary to focus on some aspects of Big Data quality rather than others. In Sect. 14.6 we will see the example of the Official Statistical domain for which the representativeness or selectivity of Big Data sources is a particularly relevant feature. Indeed, statistical production processes do have to seriously take into account such a feature in order to produce reliable estimates.

14.5   Source-Specific Quality Issues in Sensor Data

Big Data sources of type 3 include sensors and sensor networks (S&SN). In this section, we first discuss the evolution of the S&SN technology and the most relevant applications. Then, we consider the most usual fault events and phenomena that affect IQ. We also analyze quality dimensions that are characteristic of this technology, and some techniques proposed for quality assessment and improvement.

14.5.1   Information Quality in Sensors and Sensor Networks

Sensor networks can be defined as large-scale ad hoc networks of homogeneous or heterogeneous, compact, and mobile or immobile sensor nodes that are randomly deployed in an area of interest [253]. Different types of data are collected by the sensor nodes, e.g., application-specific environmental parameters, meteorological, or Global Positioning System. These data can be in different forms, digital or analog, spatial or temporal, alphanumeric or image, and fixed or moving. The measurements taken by the sensor nodes in SN are discrete samples of physical phenomena that are subject to review of their accuracy dependent on location. General causes of errors in sensor data include (a) noise from external sources, (b) hardware noise, (c) inaccuracies and impressions in sampling methods and derived data, and (d) environmental effects. In addition, corruption of functioning can result from (e) adverse weather conditions, (f) faulty equipment, or (g) human error.

Klein and Lehner [371] observe that the underlying measurement process as well as sensor failures or malfunctions may lead to falsified, wrong, or missing values. To extract complex knowledge, sensor data are merged, transformed, and aggregated by applying traditional data stream queries, complex signal analysis, or numerical operators. During the data stream processing task, the initial sensor-inherent errors may be amplified. Additionally, new errors may be introduced.

For [346], "dirty data" in receptor data manifest themselves in three general forms: (a) missed readings (for example, RFID readers often capture only 60–70 % of the tags in their vicinity), (b) unreliable readings (often, individual sensor readings are imprecise and/or unreliable), and (c) variance in errors due to the environment.

When data are collected in S&SN, their quality can deeply impact on decisions to be taken, e.g.:

- Data may not be readily available for analysis and interpretation.
- Problems with the equipment, such as battery voltage, high differences between the temperature of the instrument and the external temperature, and dark current drifts, might be difficult to identify.
- As the complexity of the equipment increases, so does the difficulty to determine the cause of equipment malfunctions.

Besides general descriptions of quality of information in S&SN, in the following we report two proposals of quality dimensions:

- Sha and Shi [562], detailing S&SN quality dimensions as subtypes of consistency
- Manzoor et al. [427], linking quality of S&SN to the notion of *quality of context (QoC)*

Sha and Shi [562] define several subtypes of consistency, shown in Table 14.4, together with their definitions and an identification whether the dimension refers to individual data or data streams. At a macro level, three types of consistency are considered, namely, numerical, temporal, and frequency consistency: numerical consistency is equivalent to accuracy; temporal consistency is meant to be a degree of up-to-dateness; frequency consistency focuses on abnormal changes in data provisioning.

Manzoor et al. [427] observe that diverse sources of context information, ranging from physical and logical sensors to user interfaces and applications on mobile devices, affect the quality of context data. QoC sources are the information about the sources that collect context information, the environments where that context information is collected, and the entities about which the context information is collected. Examples of QoC sources are source location, measurement time, source state, sensor data accuracy, etc.

Table 14.4 Various types of consistency as defined in [562]

Types of consistency	Numerical/ Temporal/ Frequency	Individual data/ Data streams/ Both	Definition
Numerical	Numerical	Individual data	Collected data should be accurate
Temporal	Temporal	Individual data	Data should be delivered to the sink before or by the time it is expected
Frequency	Frequency	Both	Controls the frequency of dramatic data changes and abnormal readings of data streams
Absolute numerical	Numerical	Both	Sensor reading is out of the normal range, which can be preset by the application
Relative numerical	Numerical	Both	Error between the real field reading and the corresponding data at the sink
Hop	Numerical	Individual data	Data should keep consistency at each hop
Single path	Numerical and temporal	Individual data	Consistency holds when data are transmitted from the source to the sink using a single path
Multiple path	Numerical and temporal	Individual data	Consistency holds when data are transmitted from the source to the sink using multiple paths
Strict	Numerical and temporal	Data streams	Differs from hope consistency because it is defined on a set of data and requires no data loss
Alpha-loss	Numerical and temporal	Data streams	Similar to strict consistency except that alpha-data loss is accepted at the sink
Partial	Numerical and temporal	Data streams	Similar to alpha consistency except that temporal consistency is released
Trend	Numerical and temporal	Data streams	Similar to partial consistency except that numerical consistency is released
Range frequency	Frequency	Data streams	The number of abnormal readings exceed a certain number preset by the application
Change frequency	Frequency	Data streams	Changes of sensor readings exceed preset threshold

Table 14.5 Clusters, quality of context dimensions, definitions in [427], and related sources of context data

Cluster	Dimension in cluster	Definition	Sources of QoC used in the evaluation
Accuracy	Up-to-dateness	Degree of rationalism to use a context object for a specific application at a given time	Measurement time Current time
Accuracy	Precision	–	–
Completeness	Completeness	Quantity of information that is provided for a specific object	Ratio of number of attributes filled to the total number of attributes
Completeness	Significance	Worth or preciousness of the context information in a specific situation	Critical value
Redundancy	Conciseness	–	–
Consistency	Representation consistency	–	–
Trustworthiness	Trustworthiness	Belief that we have in the correct information in a given context object	Source location information entity location sensor data accuracy

QoC parameters are derived from QoC sources and are represented in a form that is suitable for use by an application. QoC parameters can be divided into generic and domain-specific parameters. Generic QoC parameters are those parameters which are required by most applications, such as up-to-dateness, trustworthiness, completeness, representation consistency, and precision. Domain-specific QoC parameters are those parameters that are important for some specific application domains. Table 14.5 summarizes the main concepts introduced in [427]: on one side dimensions with clusters they belong to and their definitions and on the other side related QoC sources.

14.5.2 Techniques for Data Cleaning in Sensors and Sensor Networks

A variety of techniques are currently investigated for IQ management in S&SN.

Jeffery et al. [346] observe that the nature of the errors in receptor data is not easily corrected by traditional data cleaning. Receptor data demands different techniques that address the nature of its errors (i.e., missed and unreliable readings). These data tend to be strongly correlated in both time and space; the readings observed at one time instant are highly indicative of the readings observed at the next time instant, as are readings at nearby devices. To provide a simple and flexible means of programming cleaning tools, Jeffery et al. [347] propose to specify cleaning stages using high-level declarative queries over relational data streams; the system then translates the queries into the appropriate low-level operations necessary to produce cleaned results.

As to dimensions and techniques for specific sensor technologies such as RFID, Jeffery et al. [347] observe that one of the primary factors limiting the widespread adoption of RFID technology is the unreliability of the data streams produced by RFID readers. To face with such an issue, a temporal "smoothing filter" is proposed, namely, a sliding window over the reader's data stream that interpolates for lost readings from each tag within the time window. The goal is to reduce or eliminate dropped readings by giving each tag more opportunities to be read within the smoothing window. Unlike conventional techniques, the technique does not expose the smoothing window parameter to the application; instead, it determines the most appropriate window size automatically and continuously adapts it over the lifetime of the system based on observed readings. Rao et al. [517] discuss the issue of dealing with anomalies in RFID reads, where each application specifies the detection and the correction of relevant anomalies using declarative sequence-based rules.

The contributions of [125] concern spatial redundancy (and consequent spatial inconsistency), where an object is detected by multiple readers in its neighborhood, and temporal redundancy (and consequent temporal inconsistency), where an object is detected multiple times by a single reader over time.

Finally, as to IQ and the new frontier of participatory sensing in social networks, Burke et al. [99] observe that mobile devices are increasingly capable of capturing, classifying, and transmitting image, acoustic, location, and other data, interactively or autonomously. They could act as sensor nodes and location-aware data collection instruments. Burke et al. [99] introduces the concept of *participatory sensing*, which asks everyday mobile devices, such as cellular phones, to form interactive, participatory sensor networks that enable public and professional users to gather, analyze, and share local knowledge.

14.6   Domain-Specific Quality Issues: Official Statistics

In this section we discuss Big Data quality issues in the Official Statistics (OS) domain.

The main purpose of Official Statistics is well defined by Principle 1 of the Fundamental Principles of Official Statistics, as provided by the UN Statistics Division [177]:

> Official statistics provide an indispensable element in the information system of a demo-
> cratic society, serving the Government, the economy and the public with data about the
> economic, demographic, social and environmental situation.

The quality of data resulting from OS production by National Statistical Institutes is therefore a primary issue. National Statistical Institutes started investigating the roles that Big Data can have in Official Statistics usage either for its own or in combination with more traditional data sources such as sample surveys and administrative registers [267]. Recently, the Scheveningen memorandum [435], which has the role of providing strategic guidelines to European national offices, clearly stated that, given the opportunities that Big Data offer to OS, National Statistical Institutes are encouraged to undertake initiatives to examine the potential of Big Data sources in that regard. In the following, we first define the concept of quality of Big Data of OS (Sect. 14.6.1), then, in Sect. 14.6.2 we describe a case study showing examples of quality issues that can emerge when conducting a Big Data project in the OS domain.

14.6.1 On the Quality of Big Data for Official Statistics

There are a number of issues that are specific of the OS domain, mainly:

- Selectivity and representativeness: populations covered by Big Data sources are not typically the target populations of OS and are often not explicitly defined. Moreover, given that the Big Data generating mechanisms are not under OS control, data deriving from Big Data sources can be selective, i.e., not representative of the target population. Dealing with these issues is not easy, especially because it is not always feasible to assess the relationships between the covered population and the target population, on one side, and to estimate the bias to control, on the other side.
- Data processing: this issue is concerned with three different aspects that are very important for dealing with Big Data in OS, namely: (i) data preparation, (ii) data filtering, and (iii) data reconciliation. With respect to (i), big sources are typically event based rather than unit based, as it traditionally happens for OS survey data (or for administrative data). Hence a first preparation step is needed in order to deal with such new types of data. With respect to (ii) Big Data are often affected by "noise" with respect to the analysis purpose that must be filtered.

  On one side, this noise is related to the fact the data generation process is not under a direct control of the statistician that cannot apply a "design" to the data collection phase. On the other side, the noise can be related to particular nature of some sources, like unstructured information sources (e.g., Twitter data). With respect to (iii), even when some schema or metadata information is present in Big Data sources, such metadata need to be reconciled with metadata driving the statistical production; hence a reconciliation step is needed. As a further observation, due to the great variety of schema information that can derive from Big Data sources (e.g., Internet data), the reconciliation step can be very hard due to the sparsity/incompleteness of Big Data source schemas.

- Quality of estimates: this issue is related to the major paradigm shift in the analysis activities caused by the usage of Big Data. In particular, data analysis approaches traditionally used within OS may not be directly applied to Big Data analysis. Methodologies that proceed by exploratory analysis, like those based on data mining and machine learning, could be, instead, more appropriately applied. However, they are new for OS: though they are currently successfully applied in specific domains (e.g., customer profiling), their usage in the OS domain has still to be properly investigated.
- Integration with traditional data sources: this issue is related to the usage of Big Data sources integrated with survey-based data or administrative data sources. However, several problems have been identified: (1) linking Big Data is hard because of privacy issues that prevent Big Data vendors to release data that are identifiable, (2) integration task requires to have a precise and explicit structural metadata representation (schema information) that is often not available for Big Data, and (3) even when schema information is available, it will need to be reconciled with traditional source schemas.

In the following we describe a case study showing a concrete usage of Big Data for official statistics by focusing on quality-related issues.

14.6.2   A Case Study

Among the different possible types of Big Data sources, Internet data are surely among the most at hand and promising; Internet As a Data source (IaD) has been more and more emerging as a paradigm that concretely allows to complement or substitute traditional statistical sources that, for official statistics, are either resulting from survey questionnaires or from administrative sources.

In this section, we describe an experimental project conducted by Istat, the Italian National Institute of Statistics, adopting IaD for collecting data. The project has been carried out within the Istat sampling survey on "ICT in enterprises" that aims at producing information on the use of ICT and in particular on the use of Internet by Italian enterprises for various purposes (e-commerce, e-recruitment, advertisement, e-tendering, e-procurement, e-government). To do so, data are collected by means of the traditional instrument of the questionnaire.

Istat started to explore the possibility to use Web scraping techniques, associated in the estimation phase with text and data mining algorithms, in order to substitute traditional instruments of data collection and estimation or to combine them in an integrated approach. Hence, in the project, the 8600 Web sites, indicated by the 19,000 respondent enterprises, have been scraped; acquired texts were processed in order to estimate information which is currently collected via questionnaires.

As described in [543], the overall process consisted of the following phases:

- *Web scraping*: aimed at transforming the (unstructured) information in each Web site into indexed documents that can be stored and analyzed

- *Terms extraction and normalization*: targeted to identify those terms that could provide information on the Internet usage by enterprises
- *Inference activity*: aimed at estimating some classification models in order to come up with estimated answers to questionnaires, derived from enterprises' Web sites

The inference activity of the process is particularly relevant for the quality aspects and is described in the following as reported in [35]. The input to the inferential activity was a document/term matrix, where each row represents a Web site, each column is referred to an influent word, and the intersection indicates the presence or the absence of the word in the Web site.

In order to choose the best instruments useful to build the inference system, in this exploratory phase, several tools were tested, namely:

- Data mining learners, applicable to this text mining problem: *classification trees*; *ensemble learners (random forest, adaptive boosting, bootstrap aggregating)*; *neural networks, maximum entropy, and support vector machines; and latent Dirichlet allocation* [338]
- A text mining learner: *naïve Bayes* [386].
- The approach followed in the *content analysis* [315]

As usual, available data have been partitioned into a training set and a test set: each model, fitted using the training set, has been applied to the test set in order to evaluate its performance, by comparing observed and predicted values for the target variables, both at individual and aggregate levels. In general, the proportion between the two sets was determined in 75/25, but a sensitivity analysis has been performed for naïve Bayes and content analysis defining nine different levels for the training set (from 10 to 90 %). Experiments have been carried out considering the four different subsets of words defined accordingly to their chi-square, and the most favorable in terms of performance has been retained. Performance has been measured by considering the following indicators: (1) *precision* (number of correctly classified cases on the total number of cases), (2) *sensitivity* (rate of correctly classified positive cases), (3) *specificity* (rate of correctly classified negative cases), and (4) the *proportion of predicted positive cases* (which was introduced, as it corresponds to the final estimates needed and whose accuracy was important to maximize).

From such a comparative analysis, the best method among those considered resulted to be naïve Bayes. This method was applied in order to estimate other suitable variables in the questionnaire, obtaining the results reported in Table 14.6.

The final obtained results can be considered satisfiable. Interestingly, in some cases it was possible to verify by manual inspection that some enterprises answering *no* to the Web sales do provide instead Web sales, i.e., the answer was probably due to a misunderstanding of the question. In these cases, the automatic approach even outperforms the traditional one with respect to quality of the answers. Anyway, an issue related to the quality of estimates is there: the adoption of machine learning

Table 14.6 Results of the application of naïve Bayes to the complete set of questions related to Web sales

Question	Precision	Sensitivity	Specificity	Proportion Web sales = yes (observed)	Proportion Web sales = yes (predicted)
Web sales functionality	0.78	0.50	0.86	0.21	0.21
Orders tracking	0.82	0.49	0.85	0.18	0.11
Description and price list of goods	0.62	0.44	0.79	0.48	0.32
Personalized content for regular visitors	0.74	0.41	0.781	0.09	0.23
Possibility to customize online goods	0.86	0.53	0.87	0.05	0.14
Privacy policy statement	0.59	0.57	0.64	0.68	0.51
Online job application	0.69	0.521	0.78	0.35	0.33

approaches, not typically used in OS, poses the issue to verify the reliability of the results. The study described in this section is a step toward such kind of verification. Once this alternative approach will be proved to offer a quality of obtainable estimates higher than that of the traditional approach, the new process could become an important part of the survey on "ICT in enterprises." It will also be possible to consider not only an improvement of the accuracy of already available estimates but also to produce new estimates related to additional information currently not covered by the survey. Finally, in order to detect erroneous values in the survey data, predicted values could be used in the editing phase of the current production process.

14.7   Summary

In order to exploit the enormous range of opportunities deriving from using Web data, it is really important to have a quality characterization of them. Trustworthiness and provenance, as discussed in this chapter, have a prominent role in such a characterization. Web data often need to be integrated with more traditional data sources that are typically used in business processes. To the scope, activities like matching Web data objects assume a particularly important role.

The discussion on issues and techniques related to Web information quality as performed in this chapter has been complemented with consideration on Big Data quality. This is a huge and hot issue: on one side, at this stage, the use of Big Data as a source of information seems really mandatory, on the other side it is necessary to characterize the quality of Big Data properly, in order to make a correct use of it. As shown by the examples on the quality of sensor data and on quality issues in Official Statistics, however, the way to well-defined methods and approaches has been just taken and is still a bit long to go.

Erratum to: Data and Information Quality: Dimensions, Principles and Techniques

Carlo Batini and Monica Scannapieco

Erratum to:

C. Batini, M. Scannapieco, *Data and Information Quality*, Data-Centric Systems and Applications, DOI 10.1007/978-3-319-24106-7

The affiliation of the author Monica Scannapieco has been incorrectly captured in Page IV and the correct affiliation is as follows:

Istituto Nazionale di Statistica-Istat, Rome, Italy.

The names of co-authors have been missed in the Chapter opening pages of Chapters 4 (page 87), 5 (page 113), 13 (page 403) and 14 (page 421). The correct information is as follows:

Chapter 4 has been written by Anisa Rula, Andrea Maurino, and Carlo Batini.
Chapter 5 has been written by Gianluigi Ciocca, Silvia Corchs, Francesca Gasparini, Carlo Batini, and Raimondo Schettini.
Chapter 13 has been written by Federico Cabitza and Carlo Batini.
Chapter 14 has been written by Monica Scannapieco and Laure Berti.

The online version of the updated book can be found under
DOI 10.1007/978-3-319-24106-7

© Springer International Publishing Switzerland 2016   E1
C. Batini, M. Scannapieco, *Data and Information Quality*, Data-Centric Systems and Applications, DOI 10.1007/978-3-319-24106-7_15

References

1. Mittal A, Moorthy AK, Bovik AC (2012) No-reference image quality assessment in the spatial domain. IEEE Transactions on Image Processing 21(12):4695–4708
2. van der Aalst WMP, ter Hofstede A (2005) YAWL: yet another workflow language. Information Systems 30(4):245–275
3. AAVV (2004) Information and data quality in the NHS. Technical report, UK Audit Commission, London, URL http://archive.audit-commission.gov.uk/auditcommission/SiteCollectionDocuments/AuditCommissionReports/NationalStudies/20040330dataquality.pdf
4. Abdelhak M, Grostick S, Hanken MA (eds) (2012) Health Information: Management of a Strategic Resource, 4th edn. Elsevier Saunders, St. Louis
5. Abiteboul S, Buneman P, Suciu D (2000) Data on the Web: From Relations to Semistructured Data and XML. Morgan Kaufmann, Los Altos
6. Abowd JM, Vilhuber L (2005) The sensitivity of economic statistics to coding errors in personal identifiers. Journal of Business & Economic Statistics 23(2)
7. Adams S, Berg M (2004) The nature of the net: constructing reliability of health information on the web. Information Technology & People 17(2):150–170, DOI 10.1108/09593840410542484, URL http://www.emeraldinsight.com/10.1108/09593840410542484
8. Adams SA (2010) Revisiting the online health information reliability debate in the wake of web 2.0: an inter-disciplinary literature and website review. International Journal of Medical Informatics 79(6):391–400
9. Agnoloni T, Francesconi E (2011) Modelling semantic profiles in legislative documents for enhanced norm accessibility. In: ICAIL, pp 111–115
10. Agrawal R, Gupta A, Sarawagi S (1997) Modeling multidimensional databases. In: Gray A, Larson P (eds) Proceedings of the 16th International Conference on Data Engineering (ICDE 2000). IEEE Computer Society, Birmingham, April 7–11, 1997, pp 232–243
11. Ahituv N (1980) A systematic approach toward assessing the value of an information system. MIS Quarterly 4(4):61–75
12. Ahituv N (1987) Assessing the Value of Information: Problems and Approaches. Faculty of Management, The Leon Recanati Graduate School of Business Administration, Tel Aviv University
13. Ahituv N, Igbaria M, Sella A (1998) The effects of time pressure and completeness of information on decision making. Journal of Management Information Systems 15(2):153–172

© Springer International Publishing Switzerland 2016

451

C. Batini, M. Scannapieco, *Data and Information Quality*, Data-Centric Systems and Applications, DOI 10.1007/978-3-319-24106-7

14. Aizawa A, Oyama K (2005) A fast linkage detection scheme for multi-source information integration. In: Proceedings of the International Workshop on Challenges in Web Information Retrieval and Integration, 2005 (WIRI'05). IEEE, New York, pp 30–39

15. Al-Lawati A, Lee D, McDaniel P (2005) Blocking-aware private record linkage. In: Proceedings of the 2nd International Workshop on Information Quality in Information Systems. ACM, New York, pp 59–68

16. Altowim Y, Kalashnikov DV, Mehrotra S (2014) Progressive approach to relational entity resolution. Proceedings of the VLDB Endowment 7(11):999–1010

17. Altwaijry H, Kalashnikov DV, Mehrotra S (2013) Query-driven approach to entity resolution. Proceedings of the VLDB Endowment 6(14):1846–1857

18. Aluisio S, Specia L, Gasperin C, Scarton C (2010) Readability assessment for text simplification. In: Proceedings of the NAACL HLT 2010 Fifth Workshop on Innovative Use of NLP for Building Educational Applications. Association for Computational Linguistics, pp 1–9

19. Amann B, Constantin C, Caron C, Giroux P (2013) Weblab prov: computing fine-grained provenance links for xml artifacts. In: EDBT/ICDT Workshops, pp 298–306

20. Amat G, Laboisse B (2005) B.d.q.s. une gestion opérationnelle de la qualité de données. In: First Data and Knowledge Quality Workshop, Paris, 18th January 2005. In Conjunction with ECG

21. Amsterdam AU (2001) The role of verification in improving the quality of legal decision-making. In: Legal Knowledge and Information Systems: JURIX 2001: The Fourteenth Annual Conference. IOS Press, Amsterdam, vol 70

22. Anand MK, Bowers S, Ludscher B (2010) Techniques for efficiently querying scientific workflow provenance graphs. In: International Conference on Extending Database Technology (EDBT), pp 287–298

23. Ananthakrishna R, Chaudhuri C, Ganti V (2002) Eliminating Fuzzy duplicates in data warehouses. In: Proceedings of VLDB 2002, Hong Kong, pp 586–597

24. Arasu A, Chaudhuri S, Kaushik R (2008) Transformation-based framework for record matching. In: IEEE 24th International Conference on Data Engineering (ICDE 2008). IEEE, New York, pp 40–49

25. Arasu A, Chaudhuri S, Kaushik R (2009) Learning string transformations from examples. Proceedings of the VLDB Endowment 2(1):514–525

26. Arasu A, Götz M, Kaushik R (2010) On active learning of record matching packages. In: Proceedings of the 2010 ACM SIGMOD International Conference on Management of data. ACM, New York, pp 783–794

27. Arenas M, Bertossi LE, Chomicki J (1999) Consistent Query Answers in Inconsistent Databases. In: Proceedings of the PODS'99

28. Arts DG, De Keizer NF, Scheffer GJ (2002) Defining and improving data quality in medical registries: a literature review, case study, and generic framework. Journal of the American Medical Informatics Association 9(6):600–611

29. Asher J, Fienberg SE, Stuart E, Zaslavsky A (2003) Inferences for finite populations using multiple data sources with different reference times. In: Proceedings of Statistics Canada Symposium 2002: Modelling Survey Data For Social and Economic Research. Statistics Canada, Ottawa, vol 385

30. Atzeni P, de Antonellis V (1993) Relational Database Theory. The Benjamin/Cummings Publishing Company, Inc., Menlo Park

31. Ballou DP, Wang R, Pazer HL, Tayi G (1998) Modeling information manufacturing systems to determine information product quality. Management Science 44(4):462–484

32. Ballou DP, Pazer HL (1985) Modeling data and process quality in multi-input, multi-output information systems. Management Science 31(2):150–162

33. Ballou DP, Pazer HL (2003) Modeling completeness versus consistency tradeoffs in information decision contexts. IEEE Transactions on Knowledge Data Engineering 15(1):240–243

34. Ballou DP, Tayi GK (1999) Enhancing data quality in data warehouse environments. Communications of the ACM 42(1):73–78

35. Barcaroli G, Nurra A, Scarno M, Summa D (2014) Use of web scraping and text mining techniques in the istat survey on information and communication technology in enterprises. In: Proceedings of Quality Conference 2014 (Q2014), Wien
36. Bartleson C (1982) The combined influence of sharpness and graininess on the quality of color prints. Journal of Photographic Science 30(2):33–38
37. Batini C, Scannapieco M (2006) Data Quality: Concepts, Methodologies and Techniques (Data Centric Systems and Applications). Springer, New York
38. Batini C, Ceri S, Navathe S (eds) (1992) Conceptual Data Base Design: An Entity Relationship Approach. Benjamin and Cummings, Menlo Park
39. Batini C, Barone D, Cabitza F, Ciocca G, Marini F, Pasi G, Schettini R (2008) Toward a unified model for information quality. In: Proceedings of the International Workshop on Quality in Databases and Management of Uncertain Data, Auckland, August 2008, pp 113–122
40. Batini C, Cabitza F, Cappiello C, Francalanci C (2008) A comprehensive data quality methodology for web and structured data. International Journal of Innovative Computing and Applications 1(3):205–218
41. Batini C, Cappiello C, Francalanci C, Maurino A (2009) Methodologies for data quality assessment and improvement. ACM Computing Surveys (CSUR) 41(3):16
42. Batini C, Grega S, Maurino A (2010) Optimal enterprise data architecture using publish and subscribe. In: Proceedings of the 19th ACM International Symposium on High Performance Distributed Computing. ACM, New York, pp 541–547
43. Batini C, Barone D, Cabitza F, Grega S (2011) A data quality methodology for heterogeneous data. International Journal of Database Management Systems 3(1)
44. Batini C, Cappiello C, Francalanci C, Maurino A, Viscusi G (2011) A capacity and value based model for data architectures adopting integration technologies. In: A Renaissance of Information Technology for Sustainability and Global Competitiveness. 17th Americas Conference on Information Systems (AMCIS 2011), Detroit, August 4–8 2011
45. Batini C, Palmonari M, Viscusi G (2012) The many faces of information and their impact on information quality. In: Proceedings of the 17th International Conference on Information Quality (IQ 2012), pp 212–228
46. Batini C, Castelli M, Comerio M, Viscusi G (2014) Value of integration in database and service domains. In: 2014 IEEE 7th International Conference on Service-Oriented Computing and Applications (SOCA). IEEE, New York, pp 161–168
47. Batini C, Nardelli E, Tamassia R (April 1986) A Layout Algorithm for Data Flow Diagrams. IEEE Transactions on Software Engineering
48. Bauer F, Kaltenböck M (2011) Linked Open Data: The Essentials. Edition mono/monochrom, Vienna
49. Beckett D (2004) RDF/XML Syntax Specification (Revised). Technical report, World Wide Web Consortium, http://www.w3.org/TR/2004/REC-rdf-syntax-grammar-20040210/
50. Beeri C, Kanza Y, Safra E, Sagiv Y (2004) Object fusion in geographic information systems. In: Proceedings of the Thirtieth International Conference on Very Large Data Bases. VLDB Endowment, vol 30, pp 816–827
51. Beeri C, Doytsher Y, Kanza Y, Safra E, Sagiv Y (2005) Finding corresponding objects when integrating several geo-spatial datasets. In: Proceedings of the 13th Annual ACM International Workshop on Geographic Information Systems. ACM, New York, pp 87–96
52. Belin TR, Rubin DB (1995) A method for calibrating false matches rates in record linkage. Journal of American Statistical Association 90:694–707
53. Bender C, Orszag S (1999) Advanced Mathematical Methods for Scientists and Engineers: Asymptotic Methods and Perturbation Theory. Springer, New York
54. Benjelloun O, Garcia-Molina H, Menestrina D, Su Q, Whang SE, Widom J (2009) Swoosh: a generic approach to entity resolution. The VLDB Journal, The International Journal on Very Large Data Bases 18(1):255–276
55. Benson T (2010) Principles of Health Interoperability HL7 and SNOMED. Springer, New York

56. Berg M (1999) Accumulating and coordinating: occasions for information technologies in medical work. Computer Supported Cooperative Work, The Journal of Collaborative Computing 8(4):373–401
57. Berg M, Toussaint P (2003) The mantra of modeling and the forgotten powers of paper: a sociotechnical view on the development of process-oriented ICT in health care. International Journal of Medical Informatics 69(2):223–234
58. Berjawi B (2013) Introduction to the Integration of Location-Based Services of Several Providers
59. Berndt DJ, Fisher JW, Hevner AR, Studnicki J (2001) Healthcare data warehousing and quality assurance. Computer 34(12):56–65
60. Berners-Lee T (2006) Design issues: Linked data
61. Berti-Équille L (2004) Quality-adaptive query processing over distributed sources. In: Proceedings of the 9th International Conference on Information Quality (IQ 2004), pp 285–296
62. Berti-Équille L (2001) Integration of biological data and quality-driven source negotiation. In: Proceedings of the ER 2001, Yokohama, pp 256–269
63. Berti-Equille L, Batini C, Srivastava D (eds) (2005) Exploiting Relationships for Object Consolidation. ACM, New York
64. Bertolazzi P, Santis LD, Scannapieco M (2003) Automatic record matching in cooperative information systems. In: Proceedings of the ICDT'03 International Workshop on Data Quality in Cooperative Information Systems (DQCIS'03), Siena
65. Bertoletti M, Missier P, Scannapieco M, Aimetti P, Batini C (2005. Shorter version also in ICIQ 2002) Improving government-to-business relationships through data reconciliation and process re-engineering. In: Wang R (ed) Information Quality - Advances in Management Information Systems-Information Quality Monograph (AMIS-IQ) [Monograph, Sharpe ME]
66. Bhattacharya I, Getoor L (2004) Deduplication and group detection using links. In: KDD Workshop on Link Analysis and Group Detection
67. Bhattacharya I, Getoor L (2004) Iterative record linkage for cleaning and integration. In: Proceedings of the 9th ACM SIGMOD Workshop on Research Issues in Data Mining and Knowledge Discovery. ACM, New York, pp 11–18
68. Bhattacharya I, Getoor L (2007) Collective entity resolution in relational data. ACM Transactions on Knowledge Discovery from Data (TKDD) 1(1):5
69. Bhattacharya I, Getoor L, Licamele L (2006) Query-time entity resolution. In: Proceedings of the 12th ACM SIGKDD International Conference on Knowledge Discovery and Data Mining. ACM, New York, pp 529–534
70. Bhattacharya S, Sukthankar R, Shah M (2011) A holistic approach to aesthetic enhancement of photographs. ACM Transactions on Multimedia Computing, Communications, and Applications 7S:21:1–21:21
71. Biagioli C, Francesconi E, Spinosa P, Taddei M (2003) The nir project: Standards and tools for legislative drafting and legal document web publication. In: Proceedings of ICAIL Workshop on e-Government: Modelling Norms and Concepts as Key Issues, pp 69–78
72. Biagioli C, Cappelli A, Francesconi E, Turchi F (2007) Law making environment: perspectives. In: Proceedings of the V Legislative XML Workshop, pp 267–281
73. Bianco S, Ciocca G, Marini F, Schettini R (2009) Image quality assessment by preprocessing and full reference model combination. In: Image Quality and System Performance VI. SPIE, vol 7242, pp 1–9
74. Bibliographic Center for Research CDP Digital Imaging Best Practices Working Group (2008) Digital Imaging Best Practices, Version 2.0. Bibliographic Center for Research, URL http://books.google.it/books?id=vjeEXwAACAAJ
75. Bilenko M, Mooney RJ (2003) Adaptive duplicate detection using learnable string similarity measures. In: Proceedings of the Ninth ACM SIGKDD International Conference on Knowledge Discovery and Data Mining. ACM, New York, pp 39–48
76. Bilenko M, Kamath B, Mooney RJ (2006) Adaptive blocking: learning to scale up record linkage. In: Sixth International Conference on Data Mining, 2006 (ICDM'06). IEEE, New York, pp 87–96

77. Bitton D, DeWitt D (1983) Duplicate record elimination in large data files. ACM Transactions on Databases Systems 8(2):255–262
78. Bizer C (2007) Quality-driven information filtering in the context of web-based information systems. PhD thesis, Freie Universität Berlin
79. Black AD, Car J, Pagliari C, Anandan C, Cresswell K, Bokun T, McKinstry B, Procter R, Majeed A, Sheikh A (2011) The impact of eHealth on the quality and safety of health care: a systematic overview. PLoS Medicine 8(1):e1000387
80. Blakely T, Salmond C (2002) Probabilistic record linkage and a method to calculate the positive predictive value. International Journal of Epidemiology 31(6):1246–1252
81. Bleiholder J, Naumann F (2008) Data fusion. ACM Computing Surveys
82. Boag A, Chamberlin D, Fernandez MF, Florescu D, Robie J, Simèon J (2003) XQuery 1.0: An XML Query Language. http:///www.w3.org/TR/xquery
83. Böhm C, Naumann F, Abedjan Z, Fenz D, Grütze T, Hefenbrock D, Pohl M, Sonnabend D (2010) Profiling linked open data with prolod. In: ICDE Workshops. IEEE, New York, pp 175–178
84. Bonatti PA, Hogan A, Polleres A, Sauro L (2011) Robust and scalable linked data reasoning incorporating provenance and trust annotations. Journal of Web Semantics 9(2):165–201
85. Bouzeghoub M, Peralta V (2004) A framework for analysis of data freshness. In: Proceedings of the International Workshop on Information Quality in Information Systems, Paris, June 18th 2004
86. Bovee M, Srivastava RP, Mak BR (2001) A conceptual framework and belief-function approach to assessing overall information quality. In: Proceedings of the 6th International Conference on Information Quality (IQ 2001), pp 311–328
87. Bowers S, McPhillips T, Ludscher B (2012) Declarative rules for inferring fine-grained data provenance from scientific workflow execution traces. In: International Provenance and Annotation Workshop (IPAW), pp 1–15
88. Boyd D (2009) Twitter: pointless babble or peripheral awareness + social grooming? Technical report, Apophenia Inc., URL http://www.zephoria.org/thoughts/archives/2009/08/16/twitterpointle.html
89. Boyd D, Crawford K (2012) Critical questions for big data: provocations for a cultural, technological, and scholarly phenomenon. Information, Communication, & Society 15(5)
90. Bradley EH, Herrin J, Mattera JA, Holmboe ES, Wang Y, Frederick P, Roumanis SA, Radford MJ, Krumholz HM (2005) Quality improvement efforts and hospital performance: rates of beta-blocker prescription after acute myocardial infarction. Medical Care 43(3):282–292
91. Brandao T, Queluz MP (2008) No-reference image quality assessment based on dct domain statistics. Signal Processing 88(4):822–833
92. Bravo L, Bertossi LE (2003) Logic Programming for Consistently Querying Data Integration Systems. In: Proceedings of the IJCAI 2003, pp 10–15
93. Brickley D, Guha RV (2004) RDF vocabulary description language 1.0: RDF schema. Technical report, W3C, http://www.w3.org/TR/2004/REC-rdf-schema-20040210/
94. Brizan DG, Tansel AU (2006) A survey of entity resolution and record linkage methodologies. Communications of the IIMA 6(3):41–50
95. Bruni R, Sassano A (2001) Errors detection and correction in large scale data collecting. In: Proceedings of the 4th International Conference on Advances in Intelligent Data Analysis, pp 84–94
96. Buechi M, Borthwick A, Winkel A, Goldberg A (2003) ClueMaker: a language for approximate record matching. In: Proceedings of the 7th International Conference on Information Quality (ICIQ 2003), Boston, pp 207–223
97. Buneman P (1997) Semistructured data. In: Proceedings of the 16th ACM Symposium on Principles of Database Systems (PODS 1997), Tucson, pp 117–121
98. Buneman P, Khanna S, Tan WC (2001) Why and where: a characterization of data provenance. In: Proceedings of the 8th International Conference on Database Theory (ICDT)

99. Burke J, Estrin D, Hansen M, Parker A, Ramanathan N, Reddy S, Srivastava MB (2006) Participatory sensing. In: Proceedings of the Workshop on World-Sensor-Web (WSW) at ACM Conference on Embedded Networked Sensor Systems (SenSys 2006), Boulder, pp 417–418

100. Byrd LW, Byrd TA (2012) Developing an instrument for information quality for clinical decision making. In: 2012 45th Hawaii International Conference on System Science (HICSS). IEEE, New York, pp 2820–2829, DOI 10.1109/HICSS.2012.210, URL http://ieeexplore.ieee.org/lpdocs/epic03/wrapper.htm?arnumber=6149169

101. Cabitza F (2013) An information reliability index as a simple consumer-oriented indication of quality of medical web sites. In: Pasi G, Bordogna G, Lakhmi J (eds) Quality Issues in the Management of Web Information, Intelligent Systems Reference Library. Springer, Berlin/Heidelberg, vol 50, pp 159–177

102. Cabitza F, Simone C (2012) "Whatever works": making sense of information quality on information system artifacts. In: Viscusi G, Campagnolo GM, Curzi Y (eds) Phenomenology, Organizational Politics, and IT Design: The Social Study of Information Systems. IGI Global, pp 79–110, URL 10.4018/978-1-4666-0303-5.ch006

103. Cabitza F, De Michelis G, Simone C (2014) User-driven prioritization of features for a prospective interpersonal health record: perceptions from the Italian context. Computers in Biology and Medicine DOI 10.1016/j.compbiomed.2014.03.009, URL http://linkinghub.elsevier.com/retrieve/pii/S0010482514000729

104. Caldiera VRBG, Rombach HD (1994) Goal question metric paradigm. Encyclopedia of Software Engineering 1:528–532

105. Cali A, Calvanese D, De Giacomo G, Lenzerini M (2002) On the role of integrity constraints in data integration. IEEE Data Engineering Bulletin 25(3):39–45

106. Calì A, Lembo D, Rosati R (2003) On the decidability and complexity of query answering over inconsistent and incomplete databases. In: Proceedings of the PODS 2003, pp 260–271

107. Calì A, Lembo D, Rosati R (2003) Query rewriting and answering under constraints in data integration systems. In: Proceedings of the IJCAI 2003, pp 16–21

108. Callet P, Autrusseau F (2005) Subjective quality assessment IRC-CyN/IOVC database. http://www.irccyn.ec-nantes.fr/ivcdb/

109. Calvanese D, De Giacomo G, Lenzerini M (1999) Modeling and querying semi-Structured data. Networking and Information Systems Journal 2(2):253–273

110. Cappiello C, Comuzzi M (2009) A utility-based model to define the optimal data quality level in IT service offerings. In: 17th European Conference on Information Systems (ECIS 2009), Verona, pp 1975–1986

111. Carnec M, Callet PL, Barba D (2008) Objective quality assessment of color images based on a generic perceptual reduced reference. Signal Processing: Image Communication 23(4):239–256

112. Carroll J (2003) Signing rdf graphs. Technical report, HPL-2003-142, HP Labs

113. Carroll JG (2004) The gold standard: the challenge of evidence-based medicine and standardization in health care. Quality Management in Healthcare 13(2):150–151

114. Chall JS (1995) Readability Revisited: The New Dale-Chall Readability Formula. Brookline Books, Cambridge, vol 118. Brookline Books, Cambridge

115. Chan KS, Fowles JB, Weiner JP (2010) Review: electronic health records and the reliability and validity of quality measures: a review of the literature. Medical Care Research and Review 67(5):503–527

116. Chan SY (2001) The use of graphs as decision aids in relation to information overload and managerial decision quality. Journal of Information Science 27(6):417–425

117. Chandler D, Hemami S (2007) A57 image database. http://foulard.ece.cornell.edu/dmc27/vsnr/vsnr.html

118. Chandler DM (2013) Seven challenges in image quality assessment: past, present, and future research. ISRN Signal Processing

119. Charnes A, Cooper W, Rhodes E (1978) Measuring the efficiency of decision making units. European Journal of operational research 2

120. Chassin MR, Becher EC (2002) The wrong patient. Annals of Internal Medicine 136(11):826–833
121. Chaudhuri S, Das Sarma A, Ganti V, Kaushik R (2007) Leveraging aggregate constraints for deduplication. In: Proceedings of the 2007 ACM SIGMOD International Conference on Management of Data. ACM, New York, pp 437–448
122. Chen CC, Knoblock CA, Shahabi C, Chiang YY, Thakkar S (2004) Automatically and accurately conflating orthoimagery and street maps. In: Proceedings of the 12th Annual ACM International Workshop on Geographic Information Systems. ACM, New York, pp 47–56
123. Chen CC, Shahabi C, Knoblock CA, Kolahdouzan M (2006) Automatically and efficiently matching road networks with spatial attributes in unknown geometry systems. In: Proceedings of the Third Workshop on Spatio-Temporal Database Management (Co-located with VLDB2006), Seoul, pp 1–8
124. Chen CC, Knoblock CA, Shahabi C (2008) Automatically and accurately conflating raster maps with orthoimagery. GeoInformatica 12(3):377–410
125. Chen H, Ku W, Wang H, Sun M (2010) Leveraging spatio-temporal redundancy for rfid data cleansing. In: Proceedings of SIGMOD 2010, Indianapolis, pp 51–62
126. Chen Z, Kalashnikov DV, Mehrotra S (2007) Adaptive graphical approach to entity resolution. In: Proceedings of the 7th ACM/IEEE-CS Joint Conference on Digital Libraries. ACM, New York, pp 204–213
127. Chen Z, Kalashnikov DV, Mehrotra S (2009) Exploiting context analysis for combining multiple entity resolution systems. In: Proceedings of the 2009 ACM SIGMOD International Conference on Management of Data. ACM, New York, pp 207–218
128. Cheney J, Chiticariu L, Tan W (2007) Provenance in Databases: Why, How, and Where. Foundations and Trends in Databases 1:379–474
129. Chengalur-Smith IN, Ballou DP, Pazer HL (1999) The impact of data quality information on decision making: an exploratory analysis. IEEE Transactions on Knowledge and Data Engineering 11(6):853–864
130. Chengalur-Smith IN, Ballou DP, Pazer HL (1999) The impact of data quality information on decision making: an exploratory analysis. IEEE Transactions on Knowledge and Data Engineering 11(6):853–864, DOI http://dx.doi.org/10.1109/69.824597
131. Chikkerur S, Sundaram V, Reisslein M, Karam L (2011) Objective video quality assessment methods: a classification, review, and performance comparison. IEEE Transactions on Broadcasting 57(2):165–182
132. Chirigati F, Freire J (2012) Towards integrating workflow and database provenance. In: 4th International Provenance and Annotation Workshop (IPAW 2012), pp 11–23
133. Chiticariu L, Tan W, Vijayvargiya G (2004) An annotation management system for relational databases. In: Proceedings of the 30th Very Large Databases Conference (VLDB)
134. Cho J, Garcia-Molina H (2003) Estimating frequency of change. ACM Transactions on Internet Technology 3(3):256–290, DOI 10.1145/857166.857170, URL http://doi.acm.org/10.1145/857166.857170
135. Choquet R, Qouiyd S, Ouagne D, Pasche E, Daniel C, Boussaid O, Jaulent MC (2010) The information quality triangle: a methodology to assess clinical information quality. Studies in Health Technology and Informatics 160(Pt 1):699–703
136. Christen P (2006) A comparison of personal name matching: techniques and practical issues. In: Sixth IEEE International Conference on Data Mining Workshops, 2006 (ICDM Workshops 2006). IEEE, New York, pp 290–294
137. Christen P (2007) A two-step classification approach to unsupervised record linkage. In: Proceedings of the Sixth Australasian Conference on Data Mining and Analytics. Australian Computer Society, Inc., vol 70, pp 111–119
138. Christen P (2008) Automatic record linkage using seeded nearest neighbour and support vector machine classification. In: Proceedings of the 14th ACM SIGKDD International Conference on Knowledge Discovery and Data Mining. ACM, New York, pp 151–159
139. Christen P (2012) A survey of indexing techniques for scalable record linkage and deduplication. IEEE Transactions on Knowledge and Data Engineering 24(9):1537–1555

140. Christen P, Goiser K (2007) Quality and complexity measures for data linkage and dedupli-cation. In: Quality Measures in Data Mining. Springer, New York, pp 127–151
141. Christen P, Pudjijono A (2009) Accurate synthetic generation of realistic personal infor-mation. In: Advances in Knowledge Discovery and Data Mining. Springer, New York, pp 507–514
142. Christen P, et al (2007) Towards parameter-free blocking for scalable record linkage. Australian National University, Canberra
143. Ciancio A, da Costa A, da Silva E, Said A, Samadani R, Obrador P (2009) Objective no-reference image blur metric based on local phase coherence. Electronics Letters 45(23):1162–1163
144. Codd EF (1970) A relational model of data for large shared data banks. Communications of the ACM 13(6):377–387
145. Cohen WW, Richman J (2002) Learning to match and cluster large high-dimensional data sets for data integration. In: Proceedings of the Eighth ACM SIGKDD International Conference on Knowledge Discovery and Data Mining. ACM, New York, pp 475–480
146. Coiera E (2003) Guide to Health Informatics. CRC Press, Boca Raton
147. Collins SA, Fred M, Wilcox L, Vawdrey DK (2012) Workarounds used by nurses to overcome design constraints of electronic health records. In: NI 2012: Proceedings of the 11th International Congress on Nursing Informatics. American Medical Informatics Association, vol 2012
148. Consiglio Regionale della Toscana (2003) Indice di qualita': Percorso e metodologia (in Italian)
149. Corchs S, Gasparini F, Marini F, Schettini R (2011) Image quality: a tool for no-reference assessment methods. Image Quality and System Performance VIII 7867(1):786712
150. Corchs S, Gasparini F, Marini F, Schettini R (2012) A sharpness measure on automatically selected edge segments. Image Quality and System Performance IX 8293(1):82930A
151. Corchs S, Gasparini F, Schettini R (2014) No reference image quality classification for jpeg-distorted images. Digital Signal Processing 30:86–100
152. Corchs S, Gasparini F, Schettini R (2014) Noisy images-jpeg compressed: subjective and objective image quality evaluation. In: IS&T/SPIE Electronic Imaging. International Society for Optics and Photonics
153. Corner BR, Narayanan RM, Reichenbach SE (2003) Noise estimation in remote sensing imagery using data masking. International Journal of Remote Sensing 24(4):689–702
154. Correndo G, Salvadores M, Millard I, Shadbolt N (2010) Linked timelines: Temporal representation and management in linked data. In: Hartig O, Harth A, Sequeda J (eds) Proceedings of the First International Workshop on Consuming Linked Data, Shanghai, November 8, 2010. CEUR-WS.org, CEUR Workshop Proceedings, vol 665, URL http://ceur-ws.org/Vol-665/CorrendoEtAl_COLD2010.pdf
155. Cottrell C (2000) Medicare data study spotlights coding errors. Journal of AHIMA/American Health Information Management Association 71(8):58
156. Crosby P (1979) Quality Is Free. McGraw-Hill, New York
157. Crossley SA, Greenfield J, McNamara DS (2008) Assessing text readability using cognitively based indices. Tesol Quarterly 42(3):475–493
158. Cui Y, Widom J, Wiener JL (2000) Tracing the Lineage of View Data in a Warehousing Environment. ACM Transactions on Database Systems 25(2):179–227
159. Culotta A, McCallum A (2005) Joint deduplication of multiple record types in relational data. In: Proceedings of the 14th ACM International Conference on Information and Knowledge Management. ACM, New York, pp 257–258
160. Damerau FJ (1964) A technique for computer detection and correction of spelling errors. Communications of the ACM 7(3):171–176
161. Dasu T, Johnson T (2003) Exploratory Data Mining and Data Cleaning. J. Wiley Series in Probability and Statistics. Wiley, New York
162. Data Warehousing Institute (2005) Data Quality and the Bottom Line: Achieving Business Success Through a Commitment to High Quality Data. http://www.dw-institute.com/

163. Datta R, Joshi D, Li J, Wang JZ (2006) Studying aesthetics in photographic images using a computational approach. In: Proceedings of the ECCV, pp 7–13
164. Davis GB, Olson MH (1984) Management Information Systems: Conceptual Foundations, Structure, and Development, 2nd edn. McGraw-Hill, New York
165. Davis NA (2014) Health Information Technology, 3rd edn. Elsevier/Saunders, Amsterdam/London
166. Davis R, Strobe H, Szolovits P (1993) What is knowledge representation. AI Magazine 14(1):17–33
167. Dayal U (1985) Query processing in a multidatabase system. In: Query Processing in Database Systems. Springer, New York, pp 81–108
168. De Amicis F, Batini C (2004) A Methodology for Data Quality Assessment on Financial Data. Studies in Communication Sciences
169. De Giacomo G, Lembo D, Lenzerini M, Rosati R (2004) Tackling inconsistencies in data integration through source preferences. In: Proceedings of the IQIS 2004 (SIGMOD Workshop), pp 27–34
170. De Michelis G, Dubois E, Jarke M, Matthes F, Mylopoulos J, Papazoglou MP, Schmidt J, Woo C, Yu E (1997) Cooperative information systems: a manifesto. In: Papazoglou M, Schlageter G (eds) Cooperative Information Systems: Trends & Directions. Academic, London
171. De Vries T, Ke H, Chawla S, Christen P (2009) Robust record linkage blocking using suffix arrays. In: Proceedings of the 18th ACM Conference on Information and Knowledge Management. ACM, New York, pp 305–314
172. Dejaeger K, Hamers B, Poelmans J, Baesens B (2010) A novel approach to the evaluation and improvement of data quality in the financial sector. In: Proceedings of the 15th International Conference on Information Quality
173. Delic KA, Dayal U (2002) The rise of the intelligent enterprise. Ubiquity 2002(December):6
174. Dempster A, Laird N, Rubin D (1977) Maximum likelihood from incomplete data via the EM algorithm. Journal of Royal Statistical Society 39:1–38
175. Demter J, Auer S, Martin M, Lehmann J (2012) LODStats – an extensible framework for high-performance dataset analytics. In: EKAW. Lecture Notes in Computer Science. Springer, New York, pp 353–362
176. Dividino R, Sizov S, Staab S, Schueler B (2009) Querying for provenance, trust, uncertainty and other meta knowledge in RDF. Web Semantics: Science, Services and Agents on the World Wide Web 7:204–219
177. Division UNS (February 2015) http://unstats.un.org/unsd/methods/statorg/FP-English.htm (accessed)
178. Donabedian A (1980) The definition of quality and approaches to its management. Health Administration Press, Ann Arbor, MI
179. Dong X, Halevy A, Madhavan J (2005) Reference reconciliation in complex information spaces. In: Proceedings of the 2005 ACM SIGMOD International Conference on Management of Data. ACM, New York, pp 85–96
180. Dong X, Halevy AY, Madhavan J (2005) Reference reconciliation in complex information spaces. In: Proceedings of the SIGMOD 2005, pp 85–96
181. Dong XL, Berti-Equille L, Srivastava D (2009) Truth discovery and copying detection in a dynamic world. PVLDB 2(1):562–573
182. Dovey S, Meyers D, Phillips R, Green L, Fryer G, Galliher J, Kappus J, Grob P (2002) A preliminary taxonomy of medical errors in family practice. Quality and Safety in Health Care 11(3):233–238
183. Draisbach U, Naumann F (2009) A comparison and generalization of blocking and windowing algorithms for duplicate detection. In: Proceedings of the International Workshop on Quality in Databases (QDB), pp 51–56
184. DuBay WH (2004) The Principles of Readability [Online Submission]
185. Duda R, Hart P, Stork D (2000) Pattern Classification. Wiley, New York
186. Dunn HL (1946) Record linkage. American Journal of Public Health 36:1412–1416

187. Durham E, Xue Y, Kantarcioglu M, Malin B (2012) Quantifying the correctness, computational complexity, and security of privacy-preserving string comparators for record linkage. Information Fusion 13(4):245–259

188. Dusserre L, Quantin C, Bouzelat H (1994) A one way public key cryptosystem for the linkage of nominal files in epidemiological studies. Medinfo 8:644–647

189. Dykstra RH, Ash JS, Campbell E, Sittig DF (2009) Persistent paper: the myth of "going paperless". In: AMIA Annual Symposium Proceedings, 2009, pp 158–162

190. Ebell M (1999) Information at the point of care: answering clinical questions. The Journal of the American Board of Family Practice 12(3):225–235

191. Eckbert M, Bradley A (1998) Perceptual quality metrics applied to still image compression. Signal Processing 70(3):177–200

192. Eckerson W (2002) Data Quality and the Bottom Line: Achieving Business Success through a Commitment to High Quality Data. Technical report, The Data Warehousing Institute

193. Elfeky MG, Verykios VS, Elmagarmid AK (2002) Tailor: a record linkage toolbox. In: Proceedings of the 18th International Conference on Data Engineering, 2002. IEEE, New York, pp 17–28

194. Elhadad N, Sutaria K (2007) Mining a lexicon of technical terms and lay equivalents. In: Proceedings of the Workshop on BioNLP 2007: Biological, Translational, and Clinical Language Processing. Association for Computational Linguistics, pp 49–56

195. Ell B, Vrandečic D, Simperl E (2011) Labels in the web of data. In: Proceedings of the 10th International Conference on the Semantic Web - Volume Part I (ISWC'11). Springer, Berlin/Heidelberg, pp 162–176, URL http://dl.acm.org/citation.cfm?id=2063016.2063028

196. Ellingsen G, Monteiro E (2003) A patchwork planet integration and cooperation in hospitals. Computer Supported Cooperative Work, The Journal of Collaborative Computing 12(1):71–95

197. Elmagarmid AK, Ipeirotis PG, Verykios VS (2007) Duplicate record detection: a survey. IEEE Transactions on Knowledge and Data Engineering 19(1):1–16

198. Elmasri R, Navathe S (1994) Foundamentals of Database Systems, 5th edn. Addison-Wesley, Reading

199. Engeldrum PG (2001) Psychometric scaling: avoiding the pitfalls and hazards. In: IS&T's 2001 PICS Conference Proceedings, pp 101–107

200. English L (2002) Process management and information quality: how improving information production processes improves information (product) quality. In: Proceedings of the 7th International Conference on Information Quality (IQ 2002), pp 206–209

201. English L (2009) Information Quality Applied: Best Practices for Improving Business Information, Processes, and Systems, 1st edn. Wiley, Indianapolis

202. English LP (1999) Improving Data Warehouse and Business Information Quality. Wiley, New York

203. Eppler M, Helfert M (2004) A classification and analysis of data quality costs. In: ICIS'04: Proceedings of the International Conference on Information Quality, pp 311–325

204. Eppler MJ (2006) Managing information quality: increasing the value of information in knowledge-intensive products and processes. Springer, New York

205. Erling O (2012) Virtuoso, a hybrid rdbms/graph column store. IEEE Data Engineering Bulletin 35(1):3–8

206. European Parliament (2003) Directive 2003/98/EC of the European Parliament and of the Council of 17 November 2003 on the Re-use of Public Sector Information. Official Journal of the European Union

207. European Parliament (2013) Revision of the directive 2003/98/ec of the European parliament and of the council on the re-use of public sector information

208. EUROSTAT (accessed 2014) http://ec.europa.eu/eurostat/web/quality/quality-reporting

209. EUROSTAT (accessed 2015) http://epp.eurostat.cec.eu.int/pls/portal/

210. Even A, Kaiser M (2009) A framework for economics-driven assessment of data quality decisions. In: AMCIS, p 436

211. Even A, Shankaranarayanan G (2005) Value-driven data quality assessment. In: IQ

212. Even A, Shankaranarayanan G (2007) Understanding impartial versus utility-driven quality assessment in large datasets. In: ICIQ, pp 265–279

213. Even A, Shankaranarayanan G (2007) Utility-driven configuration of data quality in data repositories. International Journal of Information Quality 1(1):22–40

214. Even A, Shankaranarayanan G (2009) Dual assessment of data quality in customer databases. Journal of Data and Information Quality (JDIQ) 1(3):15

215. Even A, Shankaranarayanan G (2009) Utility cost perspectives in data quality management. Journal of Computer Information Systems 50(2):127–135

216. Even A, Shankaranarayanan G, Berger PD (2007) Economics-driven data management: an application to the design of tabular data sets. IEEE Transactions on Knowledge and Data Engineering 19(6):818–831

217. Even A, Kolodner Y, Varshavsky R (2010) Designing business-intelligence tools with value-driven recommendations. In: Global Perspectives on Design Science Research. Springer, New York, pp 286–301

218. Even A, Shankaranarayanan G, Berger PD (2010) Evaluating a model for cost-effective data quality management in a real-world crm setting. Decision Support Systems 50(1):152–163

219. Even A, Shankaranarayanan G, Berger PD (2010) Inequality in the utility of customer data: implications for data management and usage. Journal of Database Marketing & Customer Strategy Management 17(1):19–35

220. Even A, Shankaranarayanan G, Berger PD (2010) Managing the quality of marketing data: cost/benefit tradeoffs and optimal configuration. Journal of Interactive Marketing 24:209–221

221. Eysenbach G (2008) Medicine 2.0: social networking, collaboration, participation, apomediation, and openness. Journal of Medical Internet Research 10(3)

222. Falorsi PD, Scannapieco M (eds) (2006) Principi Guida per la Qualità dei Dati Toponomastici nella Pubblica Amministrazione (in Italian). ISTAT, serie Contributi, vol. 12. Available at: http://www.istat.it/dati/pubbsci/contributi/Contr_anno2005.htm

223. Falorsi PD, Pallara S, Pavone A, Alessandroni A, Massella E, Scannapieco M (2003) Improving the quality of toponymic data in the Italian public administration. In: Proceedings of the DQCIS 2003 (ICDT Workshop)

224. Fan W, Lu H, Madnick S, Cheungd D (2001) Discovering and reconciling value conflicts for numerical data integration. Information Systems 26(8):635–656

225. Farr JN, Jenkins JJ, Paterson DG (1951) Simplification of flesch reading ease formula. Journal of Applied Psychology 35(5):333

226. Fawcett T (2004) Roc graphs: notes and practical considerations for researchers. Machine Learning 31:1–38

227. Fellbaum C (1999) WordNet. Wiley Online Library

228. Fellegi IP, Holt D (1976) A systematic approach to automatic edit and imputation. Journal of the American Statistical Association 71(353):17–35

229. Fellegi IP, Sunter AB (1969) A theory for record linkage. Journal of the American Statistical Association 64

230. Fiedler K, Kareev Y (2006) Does decision quality (always) increase with the size of information samples? Some vicissitudes in applying the law of large numbers. Journal of Experimental Psychology: Learning, Memory, and Cognition 32(4):883

231. Filin S, Doytsher Y (2000) Detection of corresponding objects in linear-based map conflation. Surveying and Land Information Systems 60(2):117–128

232. Filin S, Doytsher Y (2000) A linear conflation approach for the integration of photogrammetric information and gis data. International Archives of Photogrammetry and Remote Sensing 33(B3/1; PART 3):282–288

233. Fisher C, Lauria E, Chengalur-Smith S, Wang R (2011) Introduction to Information Quality. AuthorHouse, Bloomington

234. Fisher CW, Kingma BR (2001) Criticality of Data Quality as Exemplified in Two Disasters. Information Management 39:109–116

235. Fisher CW, Chengalur-Smith I, Ballou DP (2003) The impact of experience and time on the use of data quality information in decision making. Information Systems Research 14(2):170–188

236. Fitzpatrick G (2000) Understanding the paper health record in practice: implications for EHRs. In: Proceedings of Health Informatics Conference HIC'2000, Adelaide

237. Fitzpatrick G, Ellingsen G (2012) A review of 25 years of CSCW research in healthcare: contributions, challenges and future agendas. Computer Supported Cooperative Work (CSCW), DOI 10.1007/s10606-012-9168-0, URL http://www.springerlink.com/index/10.1007/s10606-012-9168-0

238. Flemming A (2011) Qualitätsmerkmale von Linked Data-veröffentlichenden Datenquellen. Diplomarbeit (Quality Criteria for Linked Data Sources), https://cs.uwaterloo.ca/~ohartig/files/DiplomarbeitAnnikaFlemming.pdf

239. Flemming, Annika (accessed 2014) Basel Committee on Banking Supervision, http://www.ots.treas.gov

240. Flesch R (1948) A new readability yardstick. Journal of Applied Psychology 32(3):221

241. Floridi L (2005) Semantic conceptions of information

242. Fortier MFA, Ziou D, Armenakis C, Wang S (2000) Automated updating of road information from aerial images. In: American Society Photogrammetry and Remote Sensing Conference, pp 16–23

243. Fowler M (2004) UML Distilled: A Brief Guide to the Standard Object Modeling Language. Pearson Education

244. Fox S, Jones S (2009) The social life of health information. Pew Internet & American Life Project, Washington, DC, pp 2009–12

245. Francalanci C, Pernici B (2004) Data quality assessment from the user's perspective. In: Proceedings of the 2004 International Workshop on Information Quality in Information Systems. ACM, New york, pp 68–73

246. Frey F, Reilly J, of Technology Image Permanence Institute RI (1999) Digital Imaging for Photographic Collections: Foundations for Technical Standards. Image Permanence Institute, URL http://books.google.it/books?id=75QrAQAAMAAJ

247. Friedman C, Sideli R (1992) Tolerating spelling errors during patient validation. Computers and Biomedical Research 25(5):486–509

248. Fung B, Wang K, Chen R, Yu PS (2010) Privacy-preserving data publishing: a survey of recent developments. ACM Computing Surveys (CSUR) 42(4):14

249. Fürber C, Hepp M (2011) Swiqa - a semantic web information quality assessment framework. In: ECIS

250. Fuxman A, Fazli E, Miller RJ (2005) ConQuer: efficient management of inconsistent databases. In: Proceedings of the SIGMOD 2005, pp 155–166

251. Gabay Y, Doytsher Y (2000) Features-an approach to matching lines in partly similar engineering maps. Geomatica 54(3):297–310

252. Galland A, Abiteboul S, Marian A, Senellart P (2010) Corroborating information from disagreeing views. In: WSDM, pp 131–140

253. Gallegos I, Gates A, Tweedie C (2010) Dapros: a data property specification tool to capture scientific sensor data properties. In: Proceedings of ER Workshops. Vancouver, BC, pp 232–241

254. Gamble M, Goble C (2011) Quality, trust, and utility of scientific data on the web: towards a joint model. In: ACM WebScience, pp 1–8

255. Gangadharan GR, Weiss M, D'Andrea V, Iannella R (2007) Service license composition and compatibility analysis. In: ICSOC, pp 257–269

256. Ge M (2009) Information quality assessment and effects on inventory decision-making. PhD thesis, Dublin City University

257. Ge M, Helfert M (2006) A framework to assess decision quality using information quality dimensions. In: ICIQ, pp 455–466

258. Ge M, Helfert M (2013) Impact of information quality on supply chain decisions. Journal of Computer Information Systems 53(4)

259. Geerts F, Mecca G, Papotti P, Santoro D (2014) Mapping and cleaning. In: IEEE 30th International Conference on Data Engineering (ICDE 2014), Chicago, March 31–April 4, 2014, pp 232–243
260. Geerts F, Mecca G, Papotti P, Santoro D (2014) That's all folks! LLUNATIC goes open source. PVLDB 7(13):1565–1568
261. Geissbuhler A, Safran C, Buchan I, Bellazzi R, Labkoff S, Eilenberg K, Leese A, Richardson C, Mantas J, Murray P, De Moor G (2013) Trustworthy reuse of health data: a transnational perspective. International Journal of Medical Informatics 82(1):1–9, DOI 10.1016/j.ijmedinf. 2012.11.003, URL http://linkinghub.elsevier.com/retrieve/pii/S138650561200202X
262. Getoor L, Machanavajjhala A (2012) Entity resolution: theory, practice & open challenges. Proceedings of the VLDB Endowment 5(12):2018–2019
263. Gil Y, Artz D (2007) Towards content trust of web resources. Web Semantics 5(4):227–239
264. Gil Y, Ratnakar V (2002) Trusting information sources one citizen at a time. In: ISWC. Springer, New York, pp 162–176
265. Gillies A (2000) Assessing and improving the quality of information for health evaluation and promotion. Methods of Information in Medicine 39(3):208–212
266. Gissler M, Hemminki J, Teperi J, Merilainen J (1995) Data quality after restructuring a national medical registry. Scandinavian Journal of Social Medicine 23:75–80
267. Glasson M, Trepanier J, Patruno V, Daas P, Skaliotis M, Khan A (2013) What does Big data mean for official statistics? Technical report, UNECE, URL http://www1.unece.org/stat/ platform/pages/viewpage.action?pageId=77170622
268. Goiser K, Christen P (2006) Towards automated record linkage. In: Proceedings of the Fifth Australasian Conference on Data Mining and Analytics. Australian Computer Society, Inc., vol 61, pp 23–31
269. Golbeck J (2004) Inferring reputation on the semantic web. In: WWW
270. Gonzales RC, Woods R (2008) Digital Image Processing. Prentice Hall, Englewood Cliffs
271. Gonzalez C, Kasper GM (1997) Animation in user interfaces designed for decision support systems: the effects of image abstraction, transition, and interactivity on decision quality. Decision Sciences 28(4):793–823
272. Gostojić S, Milosavljević B, Konjović Z (2013) Ontological model of legal norms for creating and using legislation. Computer Science and Information Systems 10(1):151–171
273. Graesser AC, McNamara DS (2011) Computational analyses of multilevel discourse comprehension. Topics in Cognitive Science 3(2):371–398
274. Graesser AC, McNamara DS, Louwerse MM (2003) What do readers need to learn in order to process coherence relations in narrative and expository text. In: Rethinking Reading Comprehension, pp 82–98
275. Graesser AC, McNamara DS, Louwerse MM, Cai Z (2004) Coh-metrix: analysis of text on cohesion and language. Behavior Research Methods, Instruments, & Computers 36(2):193–202
276. Greco G, Lembo D (2004) Data integration with preferences among sources. In: Proceedings of the ER 2004, pp 231–244
277. Greco G, Greco S, Zumpano E (2003) A logical framework for querying and repairing inconsistent databases. Transactions on Knowledge and Data Engineering 15(6):1389–1408
278. Gruenheid A, Dong XL, Srivastava D (2014) Incremental record linkage. PVLDB 7(9):697–708
279. Grünwald PD (2007) The Minimum Description Length Principle. MIT Press, Cambridge
280. Gu L, Baxter RA (2004) Adaptive filtering for efficient record linkage. In: SDM. SIAM, Philadelphia, pp 477–481
281. Gu L, Baxter R, Vickers D, Rainsford C (2003) Record Linkage: Current Practice and Future Directions. Technical Report 03/83, CMIS 03/83
282. Guéret C, Groth P, Stadler C, Lehmann J (2012) Assessing linked data mappings using network measures. In: ESWC
283. Gunning R (1952) The Technique of Clear Writing. McGraw Hill International Book, New York

284. Guo S, Dong XL, Srivastava D, Zajac R (2010) Record linkage with uniqueness constraints and erroneous values. Proceedings of the VLDB Endowment 3(1–2):417–428
285. Guptil C, Morrison J (1995) Elements of Spatial Data Quality. Elsevier Science Ltd, Oxford
286. H Tang NJ, Kapoor A (2011) Learning a blind measure of perceptual image quality. In: IEEE Conference on Computer Vision and Pattern Recognition (CVPR), pp 305–312
287. Hagan MT, Demuth HB, Beale MH, et al (1996) Neural Network Design, vol 1. PWS, Boston
288. Haines M (2010) Information quality research from the healthcare perspective. In: Proceedings of the Fourth MIT Information Quality Industry Symposium, July 14–16, 2010
289. Hall PA, Dowling G (1980) Approximate string comparison. ACM Computing Surveys 12(4):381–402
290. Hall R, Fienberg SE (2011) Privacy-preserving record linkage. In: Privacy in Statistical Databases. Springer, New York, pp 269–283
291. Halliday M, Hasan R (1976) Cohesion in English. English Language Series, Longman, URL http://books.google.it/books?id=zMBZAAAAMAAJ
292. Halpin H, Hayes P, McCusker JP, McGuinness D, Thompson HS (2010) When owl:sameas isn't the same: an analysis of identity in linked data. In: Proceedings of the 9th International Semantic Web Conference (ISWC), vol 1, pp 53–59
293. Hammer M, Champy J (2009) Reengineering the Corporation: Manifesto for Business Revolution, A. Collins Business Essentials, HarperCollins, URL http://books.google.it/books?id=mjvGTXgFl6cC
294. Han J, Kamber M (2000) Data Mining: Concepts and Techniques. Morgan Kaufmann, Los Altos
295. Härle P, Heuser M, Pfetsch S, Poppensieker T (2010) Basel iii. What the draft proposals might mean for european banking. Online verfügbar unter http://wwwmckinseycom/clientservice/Financial_Servicvices/Knowledge_Highlights/~/media/Reports/Financial_Services/MoCIB10_Basel3 ashx, zuletzt geprüft am 30:2011
296. Harper RHR, O'Hara KPA, Sellen AJ, Duthie DJR (1997) Toward the paperless hospital? A case study of document use by anaesthetists. British Journal of Anaesthesia 78:762–767
297. Harrison MI, Koppel R, Bar-Lev S (2007) Unintended consequences of information technologies in health care - an interactive sociotechnical analysis. Journal of the American Medical Informatics Association 14(5):542–549
298. Hartig O (2008) Trustworthiness of data on the web. In: STI Berlin and CSW PhD Workshop, Berlin
299. Hartig O (2009) Provenance information in the web of data. In: Proceedings of the Linked Data on the Web (LDOW'09), Workshop of the World Wide Web Conference (WWW)
300. Hasler D, Süsstrunk SE (2003) Measuring colorfulness in natural images. Human Vision and Electronic Imaging VIII 5007:87–95
301. Hassanzadeh O, Chiang F, Lee HC, Miller RJ (2009) Framework for evaluating clustering algorithms in duplicate detection. Proceedings of the VLDB Endowment 2(1):1282–1293
302. Hastings J (2008) Automated conflation of digital gazetteer data. International Journal of Geographical Information Science 22(10):1109–1127
303. Hayes P (2004) RDF Semantics. Recommendation, World Wide Web Consortium, http://www.w3.org/TR/2004/REC-rdf-mt-20040210
304. Heath T, Bizer C (2011) Linked Data: Evolving the Web into a Global Data Space. Morgan & Claypool
305. Heinrich B, Kaiser M, Klier M (2007) How to measure data quality - a metric based approach. In: Appraisal for: International Conference on Information Systems, pp 1–15
306. Heinrich B, Kaiser M, Klier M (2008) Does the eu insurance mediation directive help to improve data quality? - a metric-based analysis. In: Golden W, Acton T, Conbo K, van der Heijden H, Tuunainen V (eds) Conference Proceedings/ECIS 2008, 16th European Conference on Information Systems, Galway, June 9th–11th 2008, pp 1871–1882
307. Heinrich B, Klier M, Kaiser M (2009) A procedure to develop metrics for currency and its application in crm. Journal of Data and Information Quality (JDIQ) 1(1):5

308. Hernández MA, Stolfo SJ (1995) The merge/purge problem for large databases. In: ACM SIGMOD Record. ACM, New York, vol 24, pp 127–138
309. Hernandez MA, Stolfo SJ (1998) Real-world data is dirty: data cleansing and the merge/purge problem. Journal of Data Mining and Knowledge Discovery 1(2)
310. Herzfeld T, Weiss C (2003) Corruption and legal (in) effectiveness: an empirical investigation. European Journal of Political Economy 19(3):621–632
311. Hinchcliff R, Greenfield D, Moldovan M, Westbrook JI, Pawsey M, Mumford V, Braithwaite J (2012) Narrative synthesis of health service accreditation literature. BMJ Quality & Safety 21(12):979–991, DOI 10.1136/bmjqs-2012-000852, URL http://qualitysafety.bmj.com/lookup/doi/10.1136/bmjqs-2012-000852
312. Hogan A, Harth A, Passant A, Decker S, Polleres A (2010) Weaving the pedantic web. In: LDOW
313. Hogan A, Umbrich J, Harth A, Cyganiak R, Polleres A, Decker S (2012) An empirical survey of linked data conformance. Journal of Web Semantics
314. Hogan WR, Wagner MM (1997) Accuracy of data in computer-based patient records. Journal of the American Medical Informatics Association 4(5):342–355
315. Hopkins D, King G (2010) A method of automated nonparametric content analysis for social science. American Journal of Political Science 54(1):229–247
316. Hovenga EJ (2010) Health Informatics: An Overview. IOS Press, vol 151
317. Hristovski D, Rogac M, Markota M (2000) Using data warehousing and OLAP in public health care. In: Proceedings of the AMIA Symposium. American Medical Informatics Association, p 369
318. Huaman MA, Araujo-Castillo RV, Soto G, Neyra JM, Quispe JA, Fernandez MF, Mundaca CC, Blazes DL (2009) Impact of two interventions on timeliness and data quality of an electronic disease surveillance system in a resource limited setting (peru): a prospective evaluation. BMC Medical Informatics and Decision Making 9(1):16
319. Huang J, Ertekin S, Giles CL (2006) Efficient name disambiguation for large-scale databases. In: Knowledge Discovery in Databases: PKDD 2006. Springer, New York, pp 536–544
320. Hwang MI, Lin JW (1999) Information dimension, information overload and decision quality. Journal of Information Science 25(3):213–218
321. I3A (2007) Fundamentals and review of considered test methods. CPIQ Initiative Phase 1 White Paper
322. Imatest (2010) Digital Image Quality Testing. http://www.imatest.com
323. Inan A, Kantarcioglu M, Bertino E, Scannapieco M (2008) A hybrid approach to private record linkage. In: IEEE 24th International Conference on Data Engineering, 2008 (ICDE 2008). IEEE, New York, pp 496–505
324. Inan A, Kantarcioglu M, Ghinita G, Bertino E (2010) Private record matching using differential privacy. In: Proceedings of the 13th International Conference on Extending Database Technology. ACM, New York, pp 123–134
325. International Conference on Information Quality (IQ/ICIQ) (accessed 2015) http://www.iqconference.org/
326. International Monetary Fund (accessed 2014) http://dsbb.imf.org/
327. International Organization for Standardization (accessed 2014) http://www.iso.org
328. INTERPARES Project (accessed 2014) http://www.interpares.org
329. Iselin ER (1988) The effects of information load and information diversity on decision quality in a structured decision task. Accounting, Organizations and Society 13(2):147–164
330. ISO-25012 (2008) ISO/IEC 25012:2008 software engineering – software product quality requirements and evaluation (SQuaRE) – data quality model
331. ISO (2000) Quality Management and Quality Assurance. Vocabulary. ISO 84021994. International Organization for Standardization, 1994
332. ISO (2005) Image Technology Colour Management - Architecture, Profile Format and Data Structure - Part 1: Based on ICC.1:2004-10. ISO 15076-1. ISO, 2005

333. ISO (accessed February 09, 2012) Information technology – Multimedia content description interface – Part 1: Systems. URL http://www.iso.org/iso/iso_catalogue/catalogue_tc/catalogue_detail.htm?csnumber=34228

334. ITU (2002) Methodology for the subjective assessment of the quality for television pictures. Technical report, ITU-R Rec. BT. 500-11

335. Jaccard P (1901) Etude comparative de la distribution florale dans une portion des Alpes et du Jura. Impr. Corbaz

336. Jacobi I, Kagal L, Khandelwal A (2011) Rule-based trust assessment on the semantic web. In: International Conference on Rule-Based Reasoning, Programming, and Applications Series, pp 227–241

337. Jain AK (2001) Corruption: a review. Journal of Economic Surveys 15(1):71–121

338. James G, Witten D, Hastie T, Tibshirani R (2013) An Introduction to Statistical Learning with Applications in R. Springer Texts in Statistics. Springer, New York

339. Janssen T (2001) Computational Image Quality. SPIE Press

340. Janssen T, Blommaert F (2000) A computational approach to image quality. Displays 21:129–142

341. Jarke M, Lenzerini M, Vassiliou Y, Vassiliadis P (eds) (1995) Fundamentals of Data Warehouses. Springer, New York

342. Jarke M, Jeusfeld MA, Quix C, Vassiliadis P (1999) Architecture and quality in data warehouses: an extended repository approach. Information Systems

343. Jaro MA (1985) Advances in record linkage methodologies as applied to matching the 1985 Cencus of Tampa, Florida. Journal of American Statistical Society 84(406):414–420

344. Jarvenpaa SL, Dickson GW, DeSanctis G (1985) Methodological issues in experimental is research: experiences and recommendations. MIS Quarterly 9(2)

345. Jayaraman D, Mittal A, Moorthy A, Bovik A (2012) Objective quality assessment of multiply distorted images. In: Proceedings of the of the Asilomar Conference on Signals, Systems and Computers, pp 1693–1697

346. Jeffery S, Alonso M Gand Franklin, Hong W, Widom J (2005) A Pipelined Framework for Online Cleaning of Sensor Data Streams. Technical report, Computer Science Division (EECS), University of California, uCB/CSD-5-1413

347. Jeffery S, Garofalakis M, Franklin M (2006) Adaptive cleansing for rfid data streams. In: Proceedings of Very Large Database Conference (VLDB 2006), Seoul, 2006, pp 163–174

348. Jha AK, DesRoches CM, Kralovec PD, Joshi MS (2010) A progress report on electronic health records in U.S. hospitals. Health Affairs 29(10):1951–1957, DOI 10.1377/hlthaff.2010.0502, URL http://content.healthaffairs.org/cgi/doi/10.1377/hlthaff.2010.0502

349. Johnson S, Kaufmann D, Zoido-Lobaton P (1998) Regulatory discretion and the unofficial economy. American Economic Review 88(2):387–392

350. Jung W (2004) A review of research: an investigation of the impact of data quality on decision performance. In: Proceedings of the 2004 International Symposium on Information and Communication Technologies. Trinity College, Dublin, pp 166–171

351. Jung W, Olfman L, Ryan T, Park YT (2005) An experimental study of the effects of contextual data quality and task complexity on decision performance. In: IEEE Conference on Information Reuse and Integration, 2005 (IRI-2005). IEEE, New York, pp 149–154

352. Juran J (1988) Juran on Planning for Quality. The Free Press, New York

353. Kalashnikov DV, Mehrotra S (2006) Domain-independent data cleaning via analysis of entity-relationship graph. ACM Transactions on Database Systems (TODS) 31(2):716–767

354. Karakasidis A, Verykios VS (2010) Advances in privacy preserving record linkage. In: E-Activity and Intelligent Web Construction: Effects of Social Design, pp 22–29

355. Kargupta H, Datta S, Wang Q, Sivakumar K (2003) On the privacy preserving properties of random data perturbation techniques. In: Third IEEE International Conference on Data Mining, 2003 (ICDM 2003). IEEE, New York, pp 99–106

356. Karsh BT, Weinger MB, Abbott PA, Wears RL (2010) Health information technology: fallacies and sober realities. Journal of the American Medical Informatics Association 17(6):617–623

357. Kay M, Santos J, Takane M (2011) mHealth: New Horizons for Health Through Mobile Technologies. World Health Organization, Geneva
358. Kazley AS, Ozcan YA (2008) Do hospitals with electronic medical records (EMRs) provide higher quality care? an examination of three clinical conditions. Medical Care Research and Review 65(4):496–513
359. Keelan BW (2002) Handbook of Image Quality: Characterization and Prediction. CRC Press, Boca Raton
360. Keller KL, Staelin R (1987) Effects of quality and quantity of information on decision effectiveness. Journal of Consumer Research 200–213
361. Kerr K, Norris T (2008) Improving health care data quality: a practitioner's perspective. International Journal of Information Quality 2(1):39, DOI 10.1504/IJIQ.2008.019562, URL http://www.inderscience.com/link.php?id=19562
362. Kerr K, Norris T, Stockdale R (2007) Data quality information and decision making: a healthcare case study. In: 18th Australasian Conference on Information Systems, Toowoomba, pp 5–7
363. Kerr KA, Norris T, Stockdale R (2008) The strategic management of data quality in healthcare. Health Informatics Journal 14(4):259–266, DOI 10.1177/1460458208096555, URL http://jhi.sagepub.com/cgi/doi/10.1177/1460458208096555
364. Keßler C, Janowicz K, Bishr M (2009) An agenda for the next generation gazetteer: geographic information contribution and retrieval. In: Proceedings of the 17th ACM SIGSPA-TIAL International Conference on Advances in Geographic Information Systems. ACM, New York, pp 91–100
365. Kettinger W, Grover V (1995) Special section: toward a theory of business process change management. Journal of Management Information Systems 12(1):9–30
366. Kim W, Seo J (1991) Classifying schematic and data heterogeneity in multidatabase systems. IEEE Computer 24(12):12–18
367. Kimball R (1998) The Data Warehouse Lifecycle Toolkit: Expert Methods for Designing, Developing, and Deploying Data Warehouses. Wiley, New York
368. Kincaid JP, Fishburne Jr RP, Rogers RL, Chissom BS (1975) Derivation of new readability formulas (automated readability index, fog count and flesch reading ease formula) for navy enlisted personnel. Technical report, DTIC Document
369. Kitson HD (1921) The Mind of the Buyer: A Psychology of Selling. Macmillan, New York, vol 21549
370. Klare GR (1974) Assessing readability. Reading Research Quarterly 62–102
371. Klein A, Lehner W (2009) Representing data quality in sensor data streaming environments. Journal of Data and Information Quality 1(2)
372. Koda K (2005) Insights into Second Language Reading: A Cross-Linguistic Approach. Cambridge University Press, Cambridge
373. Kohn LT, Corrigan JM, Donaldson MS (eds) (2000) To Err Is Human: Building a Safer Health System. Institute of Medicine (IOM)
374. Kolodner Y (2009) Enhancing business-intelligence tools with value-driven recommendations. PhD thesis, Ben-Gurion University of the Negev
375. Kolodner Y, Even A (2009) Integrating value-driven feedback and recommendation mechanisms into business intelligence systems. In: ECIS, pp 1987–1998
376. Königer P, Janowitz K (1995) Drowning in information, but thirsty for knowledge. International Journal of Information Management 15(1):5–16
377. Köpcke H, Rahm E (2010) Frameworks for entity matching: a comparison. Data & Knowledge Engineering 69(2):197–210
378. Köpcke H, Thor A, Rahm E (2010) Evaluation of entity resolution approaches on real-world match problems. Proceedings of the VLDB Endowment 3(1–2):484–493
379. Koppel R, Metlay JP, Cohen A, Abaluck B, Localio AR, Kimmel SE, Strom BL (2005) Role of computerized physician order entry systems in facilitating medication errors. Journal of the American Medical Association 293:1197–1203

380. Krawczyk H, Wiszniewski B (2003) Visual GQM approach to quality-driven development of electronic documents. In: Proceedings of the 2nd International Workshop on Web Document Analysis (WDA2003), pp 43–46

381. Krötzsch M, Speiser S (2011) Sharealike your data: self-referential usage policies for the semantic web. In: International Semantic Web Conference (1), pp 354–369

382. Kukich K (1992) Techniques for automatically correcting words in text. ACM Computing Surveys (CSUR) 24(4):377–439

383. Kusuma T, Zepernick HJ (2003) A reduced-reference perceptual quality metric for in-service image quality assessment. In: Joint First Workshop on Mobile Future and Symposium on Trends in Communications (SympoTIC '03), pp 71–74

384. Lafferty JD, McCallum A, Pereira FCN (2001) Conditional random fields: probabilistic models for segmenting and labeling sequence data. In: Proceedings of the Eighteenth International Conference on Machine Learning (ICML '01). Morgan Kaufmann, San Francisco, pp 282–289, URL http://dl.acm.org/citation.cfm?id=645530.655813

385. Lait A, Randell B (1996) An assessment of name matching algorithms. Technical Report Series-University of Newcastle Upon Tyne Computing Science

386. Lantz B (2013) Machine Learning with R. Packt Publishing Ltd

387. Lapointe L (2006) Getting physicians to accept new information technology: insights from case studies. Canadian Medical Association Journal 174(11):1573–1578, DOI 10.1503/cmaj. 050281, URL http://www.cmaj.ca/cgi/doi/10.1503/cmaj.050281

388. Larsen MD, Rubin DB (1989) An iterative automated record matching using mixture models. Journal of American Statistical Association 79:32–41

389. Larson EC, Chandler DM (2010) Most apparent distortion: full-reference image quality assessment and the role of strategy. Journal of Electronic Imaging 19(1):011006-1–011006-21

390. Lee BK, Lee WN (2004) The effect of information overload on consumer choice quality in an on-line environment. Psychology & Marketing 21(3):159–183

391. Lee C, Rey T, Mentele J, Garver M (2005) Structured neural network techniques for modeling loyalty and profitability. In: Proceedings of SAS User Group International (SUGI 30), pp 082–30

392. Lee YW, Strong DM, Kahn BK, Wang RY (2002) AIMQ: a methodology for information quality assessment. Information and Management 40(2):133–146

393. Lehmann J, Gerber D, Morsey M, Ngonga Ngomo AC (2012) DeFacto - deep fact validation. In: ISWC. Springer, Berlin/Heidelberg

394. Lehti P, Fankhauser P (2005) Probabilistic iterative duplicate detection. In: OTM Conferences (2), pp 1225–1242

395. Lei Y, Uren V, Motta E (2007) A framework for evaluating semantic metadata. In: 4th International Conference on Knowledge Capture (K-CAP '07). ACM, New York, no. 8, pp 135–142

396. Leiner F, Gaus W, Haux R, Leiner F, Gaus W, Haux R (2003) Medical Data Management. Springer, New York

397. Lenzerini M (2002) Data integration: a theoretical perspective. In: Proceedings of the PODS 2002, pp 233–246

398. Letzring TD, Wells SM, Funder DC (2006) Information quantity and quality affect the realistic accuracy of personality judgment. Journal of Personality and Social Psychology 91(1):111

399. Levy AY, Mendelzon AO, Sagiv Y, Srivastava D (1995) Answering queries using views. In: Proceedings of the PODS 1995, pp 95–104

400. Li L, Goodchild M (2012) Automatically and accurately matching objects in geospatial datasets. Advances in Geo-Spatial Information Science 10:71–79

401. Li X, Dong XL, Lyons K, Srivastava D (1999) Truth finding on the deep web: is the problem solved? In: PVLDB

402. Liaw S, Chen H, Maneze D, Taggart J, Dennis S, Vagholkar S, Bunker J (2011) Health Reform: Is Current Electronic Information Fit for Purpose. Emergency Medicine Australasia
403. Liaw S, Rahimi A, Ray P, Taggart J, Dennis S, de Lusignan S, Jalaludin B, Yeo A, Talaei-Khoei A (2013) Towards an ontology for data quality in integrated chronic disease management: a realist review of the literature. International Journal of Medical Informatics 82(1):10–24, DOI 10.1016/j.ijmedinf.2012.10.001, URL http://linkinghub.elsevier.com/retrieve/pii/S1386505612001931
404. Liaw ST, Taggart J, Dennis S, Yeo A (2011) Data quality and fitness for purpose of routinely collected data – a general practice case study from an electronic practice-based research network (ePBRN). In: AMIA Annual Symposium Proceedings. American Medical Informatics Association, vol 2011, p 785
405. Lim EP, Chiang RH (1998) A global object model for accommodating instance heterogeneities. In: Proceedings of the ER'98, Singapore, pp 435–448
406. Lin J, Mendelzon AO (1998) Merging databases under constraints. International Journal of Cooperative Information Systems 7(1):55–76
407. Linked Open Data (LOD) (2006) http://linkeddata.org/
408. Liu L, Chi L (2002) Evolutionary data quality. In: 7th International Conference on Information Quality, Boston
409. LIVE video (2009) Live video quality database. URL http://live.ece.utexas.edu/research/quality/live_video.html
410. Lohningen H (1999) Teach Me Data Analysis. Springer, New York
411. Lorence D, Jameson R (2001) Adoption of information quality practices in US healthcare organisations. A national assessment. International Journal of Quality and Reliability Management 19(6):737–756
412. Lorence DP (2003) The perils of data misreporting. Communications of the ACM 46(11):85–88
413. Loshin D (2004) Enterprise Knowledge Management - The Data Quality Approach. Morgan Kaufmann Series in Data Management Systems
414. Loshin D (2011) The Practitioner's Guide to Data Quality Improvement. Morgan Kaufmann, Burlington, MA
415. Lovern E (2000) Accreditation gains attention. Modern Healthcare 30(47):46
416. Low W, Lee M, Ling T (2001) A knowledge-based approach for duplicate elimination in data cleaning. Information Systems 26(8):586–606
417. Lundstrom C (2006) Technical report: Measuring digital image quality. Tech. rep., Linkoping UniversityLinkoping University, Visual Information Technology and Applications (VITA), The Institute of Technology
418. Lupo C, Batini C (2003) A federative approach to laws access by citizens: the "normeinrete" system. In: Electronic Government. Springer, New York, pp 413–416
419. Lupo C, De Santis L, Batini C (2005) Legalurn: a framework for organizing and surfing legal documents on the web. In: Challenges of Expanding Internet: E-Commerce, E-Business, and E-Government. Springer, New York, pp 313–327
420. de Lusignan S, Stephens PN, Adal N, Majeed A (2002) Does feedback improve the quality of computerized medical records in primary care? Journal of the American Medical Informatics Association 9(4):395–401
421. de Lusignan S, Khunti K, Belsey J, Hattersley A, van Vlymen J, Gallagher H, Millett C, Hague NJ, Tomson C, Harris K, Majeed A (2010) A method of identifying and correcting miscoding, misclassification and misdiagnosis in diabetes: a pilot and validation study of routinely collected data. Diabetic Medicine 27(2):203–209, DOI 10.1111/j.1464-5491.2009.02917.x, URL http://doi.wiley.com/10.1111/j.1464-5491.2009.02917.x
422. MacDonald L, Jacobson R (2006) Assessing image quality. In: Digital Heritage: Applying Digital Imaging to Cultural Heritage. Elsevier Butterworth-Heinemann
423. Madhavan J, Ko D, Kot L, Ganapathy V, Rasmussen A, Halevy AY (2008) Google's deep web crawl. PVLDB 1(2):1241–1252

424. Malin B (2005) Unsupervised name disambiguation via social network similarity. In: Workshop on Link Analysis, Counterterrorism, and Security, vol 1401, pp 93–102
425. Mann R, Williams J (2003) Standards in medical record keeping. Clinical Medicine. Journal of the Royal College of Physicians 3(4):329–332
426. Mann WC, Thompson SA (1988) Rhetorical structure theory: toward a functional theory of text organization. Text 8(3):243–281
427. Manzoor A, Truong H, S D (2008) On the evaluation of quality of context. In: European Conference on Smart Sensing & Context (EuroSSC), Zurich, pp 140–153
428. Martinez A, Hammer J (2005) Making quality count in biological data sources. In: IQIS '05: Proceedings of the 2nd International Workshop on Information Quality in Information Systems. ACM Press, New York, pp 16–27
429. Marziliano P, Dufaux F, Winkler S, Ebrahimi T (2002) A no-reference perceptual blur metric. In: IEEE 2002 International Conference on Image Processing, pp 57–60
430. Maydanchik A (2007) Data Quality Assessment. Data Quality for Practitioners Series. Technics Publications, Bradley Beach
431. McKeon A (2003) Barclays bank case study: using artificial intelligence to benchmark organizational data flow quality. In: Proceeding of the Eighth International Conference on Information Quality, pp 10–13
432. McKinsey Global Institute (2013) Open data: Unlocking innovation and performance with liquid information
433. McLaughlin GH (1969) Smog grading: a new readability formula. Journal of Reading 12(8):639–646
434. McNamara DS, Louwerse MM, Graesser AC (2002) Coh-metrix: automated cohesion and coherence scores to predict text readability and facilitate comprehension. Unpublished Grant proposal, University of Memphis, Memphis, Tennessee
435. Memorandum S (accessed 2014) http://epp.eurostat.ec.europa.eu/portal/page/portal/pgp_ess/0_DOCS/estat/SCHEVENINGEN_MEMORANDUM%20Final%20version_0.pdf
436. Mendes P, Mühleisen H, Bizer C (2012) Sieve: linked data quality assessment and fusion. In: LWDM
437. Michelson M, Knoblock CA (2006) Learning blocking schemes for record linkage. Proceedings of the National Conference on Artificial Intelligence 21(1):440
438. Michelson M, Knoblock CA (2007) Mining heterogeneous transformations for record linkage. In: Proceedings of the 6th International Workshop on Information Integration on the Web, pp 68–73
439. Mikkelsen G, Aasly J (2005) Consequences of impaired data quality on information retrieval in electronic patient records. International Journal of Medical Informatics 74(5):387–394
440. Minami M, et al (2002) Using arcmap. In: Using ArcMap, ESRI
441. Minkov E, Cohen WW, Ng AY (2006) Contextual search and name disambiguation in email using graphs. In: Proceedings of the 29th Annual International ACM SIGIR Conference on Research and Development in Information Retrieval. ACM, New York, pp 27–34
442. Minton SN, Nanjo C, Knoblock CA, Michalowski M, Michelson M (2005) A heterogeneous field matching method for record linkage. In: Fifth IEEE International Conference on Data Mining. IEEE, New York
443. Missier P, Batini C (2003) A model for information quality management framework for cooperative information systems. In: Proceedings of the 11th Italian Symposium on Advanced Database Systems (SEDB 2003), pp 191–206
444. Missier P, Batini C (2003) An information quality management framework for cooperative information systems. In: Proceedings of the International Conference on Information Systems and Engineering (ISE 2003)
445. Missier P, Batini C (2003) A multidimensional model for information quality in cooperative information systems. In: Proceedings of the 8th International Conference on Information Quality, pp 25–40

446. Missier P, Lack G, Verykios V, Grillo F, Lorusso T, Angeletti P (2003) Improving data quality in practice: a case study in the Italian public administration. Parallel and Distributed Databases 13(2):135–160
447. Mitchell J, Westerduin F (2008) Emergency department information system diagnosis: how accurate is it? Emergency Medicine Journal 25(11):784–784
448. Monge A, Elkan C (1997) An efficient domain independent algorithm for detecting approximate duplicate database records. In: Proceedings of the SIGMOD Workshop on Research Issues on Data Mining and Knowledge Discovery (DMKD'97), Tucson
449. Moody DL, Walsh P (1999) Measuring the value of information-an asset valuation approach. In: ECIS, pp 496–512
450. Moorthy A, Bovik A (2011) Visual quality assessment algorithms: what does the future hold? Multimedia Tools and Applications 51:675–696
451. Morbey G (2013) Data Quality for Decision Makers: A Dialog Between a Board Member and a DQ Expert. Springer, New York
452. Mostafavi M, G E, Jeansoulin R (2004) Ontology-based method for quality assessment of spatial data bases. In: International Symposium on Spatial Data Quality, vol 4, pp 49–66
453. Motik B, Patel-Schneider PF, Parsia B, Bock C, Fokoue A, Haase P, Hoekstra R, Horrocks I, Ruttenberg A, Sattler U, Smith M (2008) OWL 2 web ontology language: Structural specification and functional-style syntax. Last call working draft, W3C, http://www.w3.org/2007/OWL/draft/owl2-syntax/
454. Motro A, Anokhin P (2005) Fusionplex: Resolution of Data Inconsistencies in the Data Integration of Heterogeneous Information Sources. Information Fusion
455. Motro A, Ragov I (1998) Estimating quality of databases. In: Proceedings of the 3rd International Conference on Flexible Query Answering Systems (FQAS'98), pp 298–307
456. Murero M, Rice RE (2013) The Internet and Health Care: Theory, Research, and Practice. Routledge, London
457. Musavi MT, Shirvaikar MV, Ramanathan E, Nekovei A (1988) A vision based method to automate map processing. Pattern Recognition 21(4):319–326
458. Muthu S, Withman L, Cheraghi S (1999) Business process re-engineering: a consolidated methodology. In: Proceedings of the 4th Annual International Conference on Industrial Engineering Theory, Applications and Practice
459. Nahm ML, Pieper CF, Cunningham MM (2008) Quantifying data quality for clinical trials using electronic data capture. PLoS One 3(8):e3049, DOI 10.1371/journal.pone.0003049, URL http://dx.plos.org/10.1371/journal.pone.0003049
460. NASSCOM (2012) Big Data-The Next Big Thing. URL http://www.nasscom.in/sites/default/files/researchreports/softcopy/Big%20Data%20Report%202012.pdf
461. Naumann F (2002) Quality-Driven Query Answering for Integrated Information Systems. Lecture Notes in Computer Science. Springer, New York, vol 2261
462. Naumann F, Häussler M (2002) Declarative data merging with conflict resolution. In: 7th International Conference on Information Quality, pp 212–214
463. Naumann F, Leser U, Freytag JC (1999) Quality-driven integration of heterogenous information systems. In: Proceedings of the VLDB'99, pp 447–458
464. Naumann F, Freytag JC, Leser U (2004) Completeness of integrated information sources. Information Systems 29(7):583–615
465. Navarro G (2001) A guided tour of approximate string matching. ACM Computing Surveys 31:31–88
466. Ndabarora E, Chipps JA, Uys L (2014) Systematic review of health data quality management and best practices at community and district levels in LMIC. Information Development 30(2):103–120, DOI 10.1177/0266666913477430, URL http://idv.sagepub.com/cgi/doi/10.1177/0266666913477430
467. Nebel B, Lakemeyer G (eds) (1994) Foundations of Knowledge Representation and Reasoning. Lecture Notes in Artificial Intelligence Edition. Springer, New York, vol 810
468. Neely MP, Cook JS (2011) Fifteen years of data and information quality literature: developing a research agenda for accounting. Journal of Information Systems 25(1):79–108

469. Newbold N, Gillam L (2010) The linguistics of readability: the next step for word processing. In: Proceedings of the NAACL HLT 2010 Workshop on Computational Linguistics and Writing: Writing Processes and Authoring Aids. Association for Computational Linguistics, pp 65–72
470. Newcombe HB, Kennedy JM, Axford SJ, James APF (1959) Automatic linkage of vital records. Science 130
471. Nicholson R, Penney D (2004) Quality data critical to healthcare decision making. In: Proceedings of the 2004 American Health Information Management Association. American Health Information Management Association, Chicago
472. Nigam K, McCallum A, Thrun S, Mitchell T (2000) Text classification from labeled and unlabeled documents using EM. Machine Learning 39:103–134
473. Nin J, Muntes-Mulero V, Martinez-Bazan N, Larriba-Pey JL (2007) On the use of semantic blocking techniques for data cleansing and integration. In: 11th International Database Engineering and Applications Symposium, 2007 (IDEAS 2007). IEEE, New York, pp 190–198
474. Nishiyama M, Okabe T, Sato I, Sato Y (2011) Aesthetic quality classification of photographs based on color harmony. In: 2011 IEEE Conference on Computer Vision and Pattern Recognition (CVPR), pp 33–40
475. Nov O, Schecter W (2012) Dispositional resistance to change and hospital physicians' use of electronic medical records: a multidimensional perspective. Journal of the American Society for Information Science and Technology 63(4):648–656, DOI 10.1002/asi.22602, URL http://doi.wiley.com/10.1002/asi.22602
476. Nuray-Turan R, Kalashnikov DV, Mehrotra S (2013) Adaptive connection strength models for relationship-based entity resolution. Journal of Data and Information Quality (JDIQ) 4(2):8
477. Object Management Group (OMG) (2003) Unified Modeling Language Specification, Version 1.5
478. Office of Management and Budget (2002) Information Quality Guidelines for Ensuring and Maximizing the Quality, Objectivity, Utility, and Integrity of Information Disseminated by Agencies. http://www.whitehouse.gov/omb/fedreg/reproducible.html
479. Olson JE (2003) Data Quality: The Accuracy Dimension. Morgan Kaufmann, Los Altos
480. Ong MS, Coiera E (2010) Safety through redundancy: a case study of in-hospital patient transfers. Quality and Safety in Health Care 19(5):1–7
481. ORACLE (accessed 2014) http://www.oracle.com/solutions/business-intelligence
482. Orfanidis L, Bamidis PD, Eaglestone B (2004) Data quality issues in electronic health records: an adaptation framework for the Greek health system. Health Informatics Journal 10(1):23–36
483. Organization for Economic Co-Operation and Development (1994) Improving the quality of laws and regulations
484. Osservatorio Legislativo Interregionale, Italy (2007) Regole e suggerimenti per la redazione di testi normativi (in Italian)
485. Ostman A (1997) The specifications and evaluation of spatial data quality. In: Proceedings of the 18th ICA/ACI International Conference, pp 836–847
486. Ozsu T, Valduriez P (2000) Principles of Distributed Database Systems. Springer Science & Business Media, New York
487. Ozuru Y, Dempsey K, McNamara DS (2009) Prior knowledge, reading skill, and text cohesion in the comprehension of science texts. Learning and Instruction 19(3):228–242
488. Papadimitriou CH (2003) Computational Complexity. Wiley, New York
489. Papakonstantinou Y, Abiteboul S, Garcia-Molina H (1996) Object fusion in mediator systems. In: Proceedings of the VLDB 1996, pp 413–424
490. Papotti P, Naumann F, Kruse S (2015) Estimating data integration and cleaning effort. In: Proceedings of the 18th International Conference on Extending Database Technology (EDBT 2015), Brussels, March 23–27, 2015, pp 61–72

491. Parssian A, Sarkar S, Jacob V (1999) Assessing data quality for information products. In: Proceedings of the 20th International Conference on Information Systems (ICIS 99), pp 428–433

492. Parssian A, Sarkar S, Jacob V (2002) Assessing information quality for the composite relational operation join. In: Proceedings of the 7th International Conference on Information Quality (IQ 2002), pp 225–237

493. Parssian A, Sarkar S, Jacob V (2004) Assessing data quality for information products: impact of selection, projection, and Cartesian product. Management Science 50(7):967–982

494. Payne RS, McVay S (1971) Songs of humpback whales. Science 173(3997):585–597

495. Pearl J (1986) Fusion, propagation, and structuring in belief networks. Artificial Intelligence 29(3):241–288

496. Pei L, Dong XL, Maurino M, Srivastava D (2011) Linking temporal records. Frontiers of Computer Science

497. Perkowitz M, Etzioni O (2000) Adaptive web-sites. Communication of the ACM 43(8)

498. Pernici B, Scannapieco M (2003) Data quality in web information systems. Journal of Data Semantics

499. Pessoa A, Falcao A, e Silva A, Nishihara R, Lotufo R (1998) Video quality assessment using objective parameters based on image segmentation. In: Proceedings of the SBT/IEEE International Telecommunications Symposium (ITS '98), vol 2, pp 498–503

500. Phua C, Smith-Miles K, Lee V, Gayler R (2012) Resilient identity crime detection. IEEE Transactions on Knowledge and Data Engineering 24(3):533–546

501. Pierce E (2002) Extending ip-maps: incorporating the event driven process chain methodology. In: Proceedings of the International Conference on Information Quality, pp 268–278

502. Pinson M, Wolf S (2004) A new standardized method for objectively measuring video quality. IEEE Transactions on Broadcasting 50(3):312–322

503. Pipino L, Lee Y (2011) Medical errors and information quality: a review and research agenda. In: AMCIS'11: Proceedings of the Seventeenth Americas Conference on Information Systems, Detroit, August 4th–7th 2011

504. Pipino LL, Lee YW, Wang RY (2002) Data quality assessment. Communications of the ACM 45(4)

505. Pixton B, Giraud-Carrier C (2006) Using structured neural networks for record linkage. In: Proceedings of the Sixth Annual Workshop on Technology for Family History and Genealogical Research

506. Planet B (2000) The deep web: Surfacing hidden value. The Journal of Electronic Publishing

507. Plebani M (2009) Exploring the iceberg of errors in laboratory medicine. Clinica Chimica Acta 404(1):16–23

508. Poirier C (Rome, Italy, 2–4 June 1999) A functional evaluation of edit and imputation tools. In: UN/ECE Work Statistical Data Editing

509. Ponomarenko N, Lukin V, Zelensky A, Egiazarian K, Astola J, Carli M, Battisti F (2009) A database for evaluation of full reference visual quality assessment metrics. Advances of Modern Radioelectronics 10:30–45

510. Porat MU (1977) The Information Economy: Definition and Measurement. ERIC

511. Porcheret M (2003) Data quality of general practice electronic health records: the impact of a program of assessments, feedback, and training. Journal of the American Medical Informatics Association 11(1):78–86, DOI 10.1197/jamia.M1362, URL http://www.jamia.org/cgi/doi/10.1197/jamia.M1362

512. Porter EH, Winkler WE, et al (1997) Approximate string comparison and its effect on an advanced record linkage system. In: Advanced Record Linkage System. US Bureau of the Census, Research Report, Citeseer

513. Quality of laws Institute (accessed 2014) URL http://www.qualityoflaws.com

514. Quan H, Li B, Duncan Saunders L, Parsons GA, Nilsson CI, Alibhai A, Ghali WA (2008) Assessing validity of ICD-9-CM and ICD-10 administrative data in recording clinical conditions in a unique dually coded database. Health Services Research 43(4):1424–1441

515. Raghunathan S (1999) Impact of information quality and decision-maker quality on decision quality: a theoretical model and simulation analysis. Decision Support Systems 26(4):275–286

516. Rahimi B, Vimarlund V (2007) Methods to evaluate health information systems in healthcare settings: a literature review. Journal of Medical Systems 31(5):397–432, PMID: 17918694

517. Rao J, Doraiswamy S, Thakkar H, Colby L (2006) A deferred cleansing method for rfid data analytics. In: Proceedings of Very Large Database Conference (VLDB 2006), Seoul, pp 175–186

518. Recchia G, Louwerse M (2013) A comparison of string similarity measures for toponym matching. In: Proceedings of The First ACM SIGSPATIAL International Workshop on Computational Models of Place, pp 54–61

519. Redman TC (1996) Data Quality for the Information Age. Artech House

520. Redman TC (1998) The impact of poor data quality on the typical enterprise. Communications of the ACM

521. Redman TC (2001) Data Quality the Field Guide. The Digital Press, Belford

522. Renkema J (2001) Undercover research into text quality as a tool for communication management. Reading and writing public documents: problems, solutions and characteristics. John Benjamins Publishing Company, Amsterdam, pp 37–57

523. Reuther P, Walter B (2006) Survey on test collections and techniques for personal name matching. International Journal of Metadata, Semantics and Ontologies 1(2):89–99

524. Reynolds T, Painter I, Streichert L (2013) Data quality: a systematic review of the biosurveillance literature. Online Journal of Public Health Informatics 5(1)

525. Richards H, White N (2013) Ensuring the quality of health information: the Canadian experience. In: Handbook of Data Quality. Springer, Berlin/Heidelberg, pp 321–346

526. Richardson M, Domingos P (2006) Markov logic networks. Machine Learning 62(1–2):107–136

527. de Ridder H, Endrikhovski S (2002) Image quality is fun: reflections on fidelity, usefulness and naturalness. SID Symposium Digest of Technical Papers 33:986–989

528. Rigby M, Roberts R, Williams J, Clark J, Savill A, Lervy B, Mooney G (1998) Integrated record keeping as an essential aspect of a primary care led health service. British Medical Journal 317(7158):579

529. Risk A, Dzenowagis J (2001) Review of internet health information quality initiatives. Journal of Medical Internet Research 3(4)

530. Rittel HWJ, Webber MM (1973) Dilemmas in a general theory of planning. Policy Sciences 4(2):155–169

531. Rouse DM, Hemami SS (2008) Analyzing the role of visual structure in the recognition of natural image content with multi-scale SSIM. In: Proceedings of the SPIE: HVEI XIII, vol 6806, pp 1–14

532. Ruibin G, Tony K (2006) Syllable alignment: a novel model for phonetic string search. IEICE Transactions on Information and Systems 89(1):332–339

533. Rula A, Panziera L, Palmonari M, Maurino A (2014) Capturing the currency of dbpedia descriptions and get insight into their validity. In: Proceedings of the 5th International Workshop on Consuming Linked Data (COLD 2014) at the 13th International Semantic Web Conference (ISWC)

534. Saalfeld AJ (1993) Conflation: Automated map compilation. PhD thesis, University of Maryland at College Park, College Park, MD, USA, uMI Order No. GAX93-27487

535. Saaty TL (1980) The Analytic Hierarchy Process. McGraw-Hill, New York

536. Sadinle M, Fienberg SE (2013) A generalized fellegi–sunter framework for multiple record linkage with application to homicide record systems. Journal of the American Statistical Association 108(502):385–397

537. Sadiq S (ed) (2013) Handbook of Data Quality. Springer, Berlin/Heidelberg, URL http://link.springer.com/10.1007/978-3-642-36257-6

538. Safra E, Kanza Y, Sagiv Y, Doytsher Y (2006) Efficient integration of road maps. In: Proceedings of the 14th Annual ACM International Symposium on Advances in Geographic Information Systems. ACM, New York, pp 59–66

539. Safra E, Kanza Y, Sagiv Y, Beeri C, Doytsher Y (2010) Location-based algorithms for finding sets of corresponding objects over several geo-spatial data sets. International Journal of Geographical Information Science 24(1):69–106

540. Safra E, Kanza Y, Sagiv Y, Doytsher Y (2013) Ad hoc matching of vectorial road networks. International Journal of Geographical Information Science 27(1):114–153

541. Saha S, Vemuri R (2000) An analysis on the effect of image activity on lossy coding performance. In: Proceedings of the 2000 IEEE International Symposium on Circuits and Systems (ISCAS 2000), Geneva, vol 3, pp 295–298

542. Sala M (2006) Versions of the constitution for Europe: linguistic, textual and pragmatic aspects. Linguistica e filologia 22:139–167

543. Salamone S, Scannapieco, Scarno M (2014) Web scraping and web mining: new tools for official statistics. In: Proceedings of Societa Italiana di Statistica (SIS 2014), Cagliari, Sardegna

544. Salzberg SL (1997) On comparing classifiers: pitfalls to avoid and a recommended approach. Data Mining and Knowledge Discovery 1(3):317–328

545. Sarawagi S, Bhamidipaty A (eds) (Edmonton, Alberta, Canada, 2002) Interactive Deduplication Using Active Learning

546. Sazzad Z, Kawayoke Y, Horita Y (2000) Mict image quality evaluation database, http://mict.eng.u-toyama.ac.jp/mict/index2.html

547. Scannapieco M, Batini C (2004) Completeness in the relational model: a comprehensive framework. In: Proceedings of the 9th International Conference on Information Quality (IQ 2004), pp 333–345

548. Scannapieco M, Virgillito A, Marchetti C, Mecella M, Baldoni R (2004) The DaQuinCIS architecture: a platform for exchanging and improving data quality in cooperative information systems. Information Systems 29(7):551–582

549. Scannapieco M, Pernici B, Pierce EM (2005) IP-UML: a methodology for quality improvement based on IP-MAP and UML. In: Wang RY, Pierce EM, Madnick SE, Fisher CW (eds) Advances in Management Information Systems - Information Quality (AMIS-IQ) Monograph, Sharpe ME

550. Scannapieco M, Figotin I, Bertino E, Elmagarmid AK (2007) Privacy preserving schema and data matching. In: Proceedings of the 2007 ACM SIGMOD International Conference on Management of Data. ACM, New York, pp 653–664

551. Scannapieco M, Virgillito A, Zardetto D (2013) Placing big data in official statistics: a big challenge? In: Proceedings of 2013 New Techniques and Tools for Statistics (NTTS) Conference, Brussels

552. Schallehn E, Sattler KU, Saake G (San Jose, CA, 2002) Extensible and similarity-based grouping for data integration. In: Proceedings of the ICDE 2002, pp 277–277

553. Schapire WWCRE, Singer Y (1998) Learning to order things. In: Advances in Neural Information Processing Systems 10: Proceedings of the 1997 Conference. MIT Press, Cambridge, vol 10, p 451

554. Schettini R, Gasparini F (2009) A review of redeye detection and removal in digital images through patents. Recent Patents on Electrical Engineering 2(1):45–53

555. Schneier B (2007) Applied Cryptography: Protocols, Algorithms, and Source Code in C. Wiley, New York

556. Schober D, Barry S, Lewis ES, Kusnierczyk W, Lomax J, Mungall C, Taylor FC, Rocca-Serra P, Sansone SA (2009) Survey-based naming conventions for use in OBO foundry ontology development. BMC Bioinformatics 10(125):1–9

557. Sebastian-Coleman L (2013) Measuring Data Quality for Ongoing Improvement: A Data Quality Assessment Framework. Morgan Kaufmann, Waltham, MA

558. Sehgal V, Getoor L, Viechnicki PD (2006) Entity resolution in geospatial data integration. In: Proceedings of the 14th Annual ACM International Symposium on Advances in Geographic Information Systems. ACM, New York, pp 83–90
559. Senate M (2010) Legislative research and drafting manual
560. Senter R, Smith E (1967) Automated readability index. Technical report, DTIC Document
561. Seshadrinathan K, Bovik AC (2010) Motion tuned spatio-temporal quality assessment of natural videos. Transaction Imgage Processing 19(2):335–350
562. Sha K, Shi W (2008) Consistency-driven data quality management of networked sensor systems. Journal of Parallel and Distributed Computing 68(9):1207–1221
563. Shankaranarayan G, Wang R, Ziad M (2000) Modeling the manufacture of an information product with IP-MAP. In: Proceedings of the 5th International Conference on Information Quality (ICIQ'00), Boston
564. Shankaranarayanan G, Cai Y (2006) Supporting data quality management in decision-making. Decision Support Systems 42(1):302–317
565. Sharma G (2002) Digital Color Imaging Handbook. CRC Press, Boca Raton
566. Shearer C (2000) The crisp-dm model: the new blueprint for data mining. Journal of Data Warehousing 5(4):13–22
567. Sheikh H, Bovik A (2006) Image information and visual quality. IEEE Transactions on Image Processing 15(2):430–444
568. Sheikh HR, Wang Z, Cormack L, Bovik AC (2005) LIVE Image Quality Assessment Database Release 2
569. Shekarpour S, Katebi S (2010) Modeling and evaluation of trust with an extension in semantic web. Web Semantics: Science, Services and Agents on the World Wide Web 8(1):26–36
570. Shekhar S, Xiong H (2008) Encyclopedia of GIS. Springer, New York
571. Sheng Y (2003) Exploring the mediating and moderating effects of information quality on firm's endeavour on information systems. In: Proceedings of the Eight International Conference on Information Quality 2003 (ICIQ03), Boston, pp 344–352
572. Sheng Y, Mykytyn P (2002) Information technology investment and firm performance: a perspective of data quality. In: Proceedings of the Seventh International Conference on Information Quality 2002 (ICIQ02), Washington, DC, pp 132–141
573. Shi W, Fisher P, Goodchild MF (2003) Spatial Data Quality. CRC Press, Boca Raton
574. Shields MD (1983) Effects of information supply and demand on judgment accuracy: evidence from corporate managers. Accounting Review 284–303
575. Shortell SM, Jones RH, Rademaker AW, Gillies RR, Dranove DS, Hughes EF, Budetti PP, Reynolds KS, Huang CF (2000) Assessing the impact of total quality management and organizational culture on multiple outcomes of care for coronary artery bypass graft surgery patients. Medical Care 38(2):207–217
576. Shortliffe EH, Barnett GO (2001) Medical data: their acquisition, storage, and use. In: Medical Informatics. Springer, New York, pp 41–75
577. Siau K, Shen Z (2006) Mobile healthcare informatics. Informatics for Health and Social Care 31(2):89–99
578. Sikora T (2001) The MPEG-7 visual standard for content description-an overview. IEEE Transactions on Circuits and Systems for Video Technology 11(6):696–702
579. Simnett R (1996) The effect of information selection, information processing and task complexity on predictive accuracy of auditors. Accounting, Organizations and Society 21(7):699–719
580. Singla P, Domingos P (2006) Entity resolution with markov logic. In: Sixth International Conference on Data Mining, 2006 (ICDM'06). IEEE, New York, pp 572–582
581. Singleton P, Pagliari C, Detmer D (2009) Critical issues for electronic health records: considerations from an expert workshop. Technical report, Nuffield Trust
582. Smart PD, Jones CB, Twaroch FA (2010) Multi-source toponym data integration and mediation for a meta-gazetteer service. In: Geographic Information Science. Springer, New York, pp 234–248

583. Smith PC, Araya-Guerra R, Bublitz C, Parnes B, Dickinson LM, Van Vorst R, Westfall JM, Pace WD (2005) Missing clinical information during primary care visits. JAMA 293(5):565–571

584. Smith TF, Waterman MS (1981) Identification of common molecular subsequences. Molecular Biology 147:195–197

585. Soto CM, Kleinman KP, Simon SR (2002) Quality and correlates of medical record documentation in the ambulatory care setting. BMC Health Services Research 2(1):22

586. Soundararajan R, Bovik A (2012) Rred indices: reduced reference entropic differencing for image quality assessment. IEEE Transactions on Image Processing 21(2):517–526

587. Soundararajan R, Bovik A (2013) Video quality assessment by reduced reference spatio-temporal entropic differencing. IEEE Transactions on Circuits and Systems for Video Technology 23(4):684–694

588. Sriram J, Shin M, Kotz D, Rajan A, Sastry M, Yarvis M (2009) Challenges in data quality assurance in pervasive health monitoring systems. In: Future of Trust in Computing. Springer, New York, pp 129–142

589. Star SL, Bowker GC (1999) Sorting Things Out: Classification and Its Consequences. MIT Press, London, UK

590. Stelfox HT, Palmisani S, Scurlock C, Orav EJ, Bates DW (2006) The "To err is human" report and the patient safety literature. Quality & Safety in Health Care 15(3):174–178, DOI 10.1136/qshc.2006.017947, URL http://www.ncbi.nlm.nih.gov/pubmed/16751466, PMID: 16751466

591. Stephenson B (1985) Management by information. Information Strategy: The Executive's Journal 1(4):26–32

592. Stoica M, Chawat N, Shin N (2003) An investigation of the methodologies of business process reengineering. In: Proceedings of Information Systems Education Conference

593. Stolfo SJ, Hernandez MA (1995) The merge/purge problem for large databases. In: Proceedings of the SIGMOD 1995, pp 127–138

594. Storey V, Wang RY (2001) Extending the ER model to represent data quality requirements. In: Wang R, Ziad M, Lee W (eds) Data Quality. Kluwer Academic, Dordrecht

595. Storey VC, Wang RY (1998) An analysis of quality requirements in database design. In: Proceedings of the 4th International Conference on Information Quality (IQ 1998), pp 64–87

596. Strauss A, Fagerhaugh S, Suczek B, Wiener C (1985) The Social Organization of Medical Work. University of Chicago Press, New York

597. Stvilia B, Mon L, Yi YJ (2009) A model for online consumer health information quality. Journal of the American Society for Information Science and Technology 60(9):1781–1791, DOI 10.1002/asi.21115, URL http://doi.wiley.com/10.1002/asi.21115

598. Suthaharan S (2009) No-reference visually significant blocking artifact metric for natural scene images. Signal Processing 89(8):1647–1652

599. Talukdar PP, Jacob M, Mehmood MS, Crammer K, Ives ZG, Pereira F, Guha S (2008) Learning to create data-integrating queries. PVLDB 1(1):785–796

600. Talukdar PP, Ives ZG, Pereira F (2010) Automatically incorporating new sources in keyword search-based data integration. In: SIGMOD Conference 2010, pp 387–398

601. Tamassia R, Batini C, Di Battista G (1987) Automatic graph drawing and readability of diagrams. IEEE Transactions on Systems, Men and Cybernetics

602. Tan WC (2007) Provenance in databases: past, current, and future. IEEE Data Engineering Bulletin 30(4):3–12

603. Tarjan RE (1975) Efficiency of a good but not linear set union algorithm. Journal of the ACM 22(2):215–225

604. TASI (1979) Technical advisory service for images

605. Tejada S, Knoblock C, Minton S (2001) Learning object identification rules for information integration. Information Systems 26(8):607–633

606. Teperi J (1993) Multi method approach to the assessment of data quality in the finish medical birth registry. Journal of Epidemiology and Community Health 47(3):242–247

478

References

607. Theoharis Y, Fundulaki I, Karvounarakis G, Christophides V (2011) On provenance of queries on semantic web data. IEEE Internet Computing 15(1):31–39
608. Thiru K, Hassey A, Sullivan F (2003) Systematic review of scope and quality of electronic patient record data in primary care. British Medical Journal 326(7398):1070–1072
609. Thirunarayan K, Anantharam P, Henson C, Sheth A (2013) Comparative trust management with applications: Bayesian approaches emphasis. Future Generation Computer Systems
610. Thurstone LL (1927) A law of comparative judgement. Psychological Review 34:273–286
611. Torgerson W (1958) Theory and Methods of Scaling. Wiley, New York
612. Tourancheau S, Autrusseau F, Sazzad Z, Horita Y (2008) Impact of subjective dataset on the performance of image quality metrics. In: 15th IEEE International Conference on Image Processing (ICIP 2008), pp 365–368
613. Trepetin S (2008) Privacy-preserving string comparisons in record linkage systems: a review. Information Security Journal: A Global Perspective 17(5–6):253–266
614. Ullman JD (1988) Principles of Database and Knowledge-Base Systems. Computer Science Press, Rockville
615. Umbrich J, Hausenblas M, Hogan A, Polleres A, Decker S (2010) Towards dataset dynamics: change frequency of linked open data sources. In: 3rd Linked Data on the Web Workshop at WWW
616. UNECE (accessed 2014) http://www1.unece.org/stat/platform/display/bigdata/Classification+of+Types+of+Big+Data
617. Unit EI (2011) Big data: Harnessing a game-changing asset. A report from the economist intelligence unit sponsored by sas
618. US National Archives (accessed February 09, 2012) Technical guidelines for digitizing archival materials for electronic access: creation of production master files - raster images. URL http://www.archives.gov/preservation/technical/guidelines.html
619. US National Institute of Health (NIH) (accessed 2014) http://www.pubmedcentral.nih.gov/
620. Van Engers TM (2004) Legal engineering: a knowledge engineering approach to improving legal quality. In: eGovernment and eDemocracy: Progress and Challenges, pp 189–206
621. Vantongelen K, Rotmensz N, Van Der Schueren E (1989) Quality control of validity of data collected in clinical trials. European Journal of Cancer and Clinical Oncology 25(8):1241–1247, DOI 10.1016/0277-5379(89)90421-5, URL http://linkinghub.elsevier.com/retrieve/pii/0277537989904215
622. Vapnik VN, Vapnik V (1998) Statistical Learning Theory. Wiley, New York, vol 2
623. Vatsalan D, Christen P, Verykios VS (2013) A taxonomy of privacy-preserving record linkage techniques. Information Systems 38(6):946–969
624. Veregin H, Hargitai P (1995) An evaluation matrix for geographical data quality. In: Elements of Spatial Data Quality, pp 167–188
625. Verhulst S (2006) Background issues on data quality. Technical report, Markle Foundation, URL www.connectingforhealth.org
626. Verykios VS, Moustakides GV, Elfeky MG (2003) A Bayesian decision model for cost optimal record matching. The VLDB Journal 12:28–40
627. Verykios VS, Karakasidis A, Mitrogiannis VK (2009) Privacy preserving record linkage approaches. International Journal of Data Mining, Modelling and Management 1(2):206–221
628. Vessey I (1991) Cognitive fit: a theory-based analysis of the graphs versus tables literature*. Decision Sciences 22(2):219–240
629. Villata S, Gandon F (2012) Licenses compatibility and composition in the web of data. In: COLD
630. Vincent C, Neale G, Woloshynowych M (2001) Adverse events in British hospitals: preliminary retrospective record review. Bmj 322(7285):517–519
631. Viscusi G, Batini C, Mecella M (2010) Information Systems for eGovernment: A Quality of Service Perspective. Springer, New York
632. VQEG (2000) Final report from the video quality experts group on the validation of objective models of video quality assessment, URL http://www.vqeg.org/
633. VQEG (2000) Vqeg frtv phase 1 database, URL ftp://ftp.crc.ca/crc/vqeg/TestSequences/

634. Vydiswaran VGV, Zhai C, Roth D (2011) Content-driven trust propagation framework. In: KDD, pp 974–982
635. W3C (2013) An overview of the prov family of documents, http://www.w3.org/TR/prov-overview/
636. W3C (2013) W3c semantic web activity, URL http://www.w3.org/2001/sw/
637. W3C (accessed 2014) http://www.w3.org/WAI/
638. Wagner MM, Hogan WR (1996) The accuracy of medication data in an outpatient electronic medical record. Journal of the American Medical Informatics Association 3(3):234–244
639. Wagner S, Toftegaard TS, Bertelsen OW (2011) Increased data quality in home blood pressure monitoring through context awareness. In: 2011 5th International Conference on Pervasive Computing Technologies for Healthcare (PervasiveHealth). IEEE, New York, pp 234–237
640. Wand Y, Wang RY (1996) Anchoring data quality dimensions in ontological foundations. Communications of the ACM 39(11):86–95
641. Wand Y, Wang RY (1996) Anchoring data quality dimensions in ontological foundations. Communications of the ACM 39(11):86–95
642. Wang J, Kraska T, Franklin MJ, Feng J (2012) Crowder: crowdsourcing entity resolution. Proceedings of the VLDB Endowment 5(11):1483–1494
643. Wang RY (1998) A product perspective on total data quality management. Communications of the ACM 41(2):58–65
644. Wang RY, Madnick SE (1990) A polygen model for heterogeneous database systems: the source tagging perspective. In: Proceedings of the VLDB'90, pp 519–538
645. Wang RY, Strong DM (1996) Beyond accuracy: what data quality means to data consumers. Journal of Management Information Systems 12(4):5–33
646. Wang RY, Strong DM (1996) Beyond accuracy: what data quality means to data consumers. Journal of Management Information Systems 5–33
647. Wang RY, Storey VC, Firth CP (1995) A framework for analysis of data quality research. IEEE Transaction on Knowledge and Data Engineering 7(4):623–640
648. Wang RY, Lee YL, Pipino L, Strong DM (1998) Manage your information as a product. Sloan Management Review 39(4):95–105
649. Wang RY, Ziad M, Lee YW (2001) Data Quality. Kluwer Academic, Dordrecht
650. Wang RY, Chettayar K, Dravis F, Funk J, Katz-Haas R, Lee C, Lee Y, Xian X, S B (2005) Exemplifying business opportunities for improving data quality from corporate household research. In: Wang RY, Pierce EM, Madnick SE, Fisher CW (eds) Advances in Management Information Systems - Information Quality (AMIS-IQ) Monograph, Sharpe ME
651. Wang RY, Pierce E, Madnick S, Fisher C (2005) Information Quality, Advances in Management Information Systems. Sharpe ME, Vladimir Zwass Series
652. Wang Z, Simoncelli EP (2005) Reduced-reference image quality assessment using a wavelet-domain natural image statistic model. In: Proceedings of SPIE Human Vision and Electronic Imaging, vol 5666, pp 149–159
653. Wang Z, Bovik A, Evans B (2000) Blind measurement of blocking artifacts in images. In: Proceedings of the IEEE International Conference Image Processing, pp 981–984
654. Wang Z, Bovik AC, Sheikh HR, Simoncelli EP (2004) Image quality assessment: from error visibility to structural similarity. IEEE Transactions on Image Processing 13(4):600–612
655. Watson AB, Borthwick R, Taylor M (1997) Image quality and entropy masking. In: SPIE Human Vision and Electronic Imaging Conference, vol 3016, pp 2–12
656. Watts S, Shankaranarayanan G, Even A (2009) Data quality assessment in context: a cognitive perspective. Decision Support Systems 48(1):202–211
657. Wayne S (1983) Quality control circle and company wide quality control. Quality Progress 14–17
658. Wears RL, Berg M (2005) Computer technology and clinical work: still waiting for godot. Journal of the American Medical Association 293(10):1261–1263
659. Wee CY, Paramesran R, Mukundan R, Jiang X (2010) Image quality assessment by discrete orthogonal moments. Pattern Recognition 43(12):4055–4068

660. Weis M, Naumann F (2005) DogmatiX tracks down duplicates in XML. In: Proceedings of the SIGMOD 2005, pp 431–442
661. Weiskopf NG, Weng C (2013) Methods and dimensions of electronic health record data quality assessment: enabling reuse for clinical research. Journal of the American Medical Informatics Association 20(1):144–151
662. Whang SE, Garcia-Molina H (2010) Entity resolution with evolving rules. Proceedings of the VLDB Endowment 3(1–2):1326–1337
663. Whang SE, Garcia-Molina H (2014) Incremental entity resolution on rules and data. The VLDB Journal, The International Journal on Very Large Data Bases 23(1):77–102
664. Whang SE, Marmaros D, Garcia-Molina H (2013) Pay-as-you-go entity resolution. IEEE Transactions on Knowledge and Data Engineering 25(5):1111–1124
665. White C (2005) Data Integration: Using ETL, EAI, and EII Tools to Create an Integrated Enterprise, http://ibm.ascential.com
666. Wiederhold G (1992) Mediators in the architecture of future information systems. IEEE Computer 25(3):38–49
667. Wikipedia (accessed 2014) https://www.wikipedia.org/
668. Winkler W (1993) Improved decision rules in the Fellegi-Sunter model of record linkage. In: Proceedings of the Section on Survey Research Methods. American Statistical Association
669. Winkler WE (1988) Using the EM algorithm for weight computation in the Fellegi and Sunter modelo of record linkage. In: Proceedings of the Section on Survey Research Methods. American Statistical Association
670. Winkler WE (1995) Matching and record linkage. Business Survey Methods 1:355–384
671. Winkler WE (2000) Machine learning, information retrieval and record linkage. In: Proceedings of the Section on Survey Research Methods. American Statistical Association
672. Winkler WE (2001) Quality of Very Large Databases. Technical Report RR-2001/04, U.S. Bureau of the Census, Statistical Research Division
673. Winkler WE (2004) Methods for evaluating and creating data quality. Information Systems 29(7):531–550
674. Winkler WE (2006) Overview of record linkage and current research directions. In: Bureau of the Census, Citeseer
675. Winthereik BR (2003) We fill in our working understanding: on codes, classifications and the production of accurate data. Methods of Information in Medicine 42(4):489–496
676. Winthereik BR, Vikkels S (2005) ICT and integrated care: some dilemmas of standardising inter-organisational communication. Computer Supported Cooperative Work (CSCW) 14(1):43–67
677. Wiszniewski B, Krawczyk H (Dublin, Ireland, 2003) Digital document life cycle development. In: Proceedings of the 1st International Symposium on Information and Communication Technologies (ISICT 2003), pp 255–260
678. World Health Organization, Regional Office for the Western Pacific (2003) Improving data quality: a guide for developing countries. World Health Organization, Regional Office for the Western Pacific, Manila
679. Wu W, Yu CT, Doan A, Meng W (2004) An interactive clustering-based approach to integrating source query interfaces on the deep web. In: SIGMOD Conference, pp 95–106
680. Xanthaki H (2001) The problem of quality in eu legislation: what on earth is really wrong? Common Market Law Review 38:651–676
681. Xue W, Zhang L, Mou X, Bovik AC (2014) Gradient magnitude similarity deviation: a highly efficient perceptual image quality index. IEEE Transactions on Image Processing 23(2):684–695
682. Yakout M, Atallah MJ, Elmagarmid A (2009) Efficient private record linkage. In: IEEE 25th International Conference on Data Engineering, 2009 (ICDE'09). IEEE, New York, pp 1283–1286
683. Yakout M, Elmagarmid AK, Elmeleegy H, Ouzzani M, Qi A (2010) Behavior based record linkage. Proceedings of the VLDB Endowment 3(1–2):439–448

684. Yan LL, Ozsu T (1999) Conflict tolerant queries in AURORA. In: Proceedings of the CoopIS'99, pp 279–290

685. Yan S, Lee D, Kan MY, Giles LC (2007) Adaptive sorted neighborhood methods for efficient record linkage. In: Proceedings of the 7th ACM/IEEE-CS Joint Conference on Digital Libraries. ACM, New York, pp 185–194

686. Ye P, Doermann D (2012) No-reference image quality assessment using visual codebooks. IEEE Transactions on Image Processing 21(7):3129–3138

687. Yendrikhovskij S (1999) Image quality: between science and fiction. In: PICS, pp 173–178

688. Yin X, Han J (2007) Truth discovery with multiple conflicting information providers on the web. In: Proceedings of the 2007 ACM SIGKDD International Conference Knowledge Discovery in Databases (KDD'07)

689. Zakaluk BL, Samuels SJ (1988) Readability: Its Past, Present, and Future. ERIC

690. Zardetto D, Scannapieco M, Catarci T (2010) Effective automated object matching. In: Proceedings of the International Conference on Data Engineering (ICDE 2010), pp 757–768

691. Zardetto D, Valentino L, Scannapieco M (2011) MAERLIN: new record linkage methods at work. In: Proceedings of the 6th International Conference on New Techniques and Technologies for Statistics (NTTS 2011)

692. Zaveri A, Rula A, Maurino A, Pietrobon R, Lehmann J, Auer S (2016) Quality assessment for linked data: A survey. Semantic Web 7(1):63–93, DOI 10.3233/SW-150175, URL http://dx.doi.org/10.3233/SW-150175

693. Zhang X, Wandell BA (1997) A spatial extension of cielab for digital color-image reproduction. Journal of the Society for Information Display 5(1):61–63

694. Zhao B, Rubinstein BIP, Gemmell J, Han J (2012) A Bayesian approach to discovering truth from conflicting sources for data integration. PVLDB 5(6):550–561

695. Zhao H, Ram S (2005) Entity identification for heterogeneous database integration—a multiple classifier system approach and empirical evaluation. Information Systems 30(2):119–132

696. Zingmond DS, Ye Z, Ettner SL, Liu H (2004) Linking hospital discharge and death records—accuracy and sources of bias. Journal of Clinical Epidemiology 57(1):21–29

Index

Accessibility, 4, 23, 33, 82, 88, 99, 111
  cultural, 69, 75
Accessibility cluster, 23
Access image, 131
Accident insurance registry, 158
Accounting, 325
Accounting information system, 325
Accounting persective, 315
Accuracy, 4–6, 15, 21, 23–26, 39, 40, 43,
    57, 60, 79, 83, 88, 99, 138, 140,
    145, 146, 150, 159, 163, 164, 179,
    183, 195–197, 262, 266, 275, 279,
    287, 299, 310, 312, 316, 318, 320,
    325–328, 332, 335, 339, 341–345,
    355, 358, 384, 387, 390–392, 438,
    448
  absolute positional, 57
  attribute, 25
  cluster, 23
  color, 115
  database, 25
  interpretation, 341
  lexical, 64
  prediction, 126, 346, 348
  problem-solving, 342
  realistic, 345
  reference, 79
  referential, 81
  relation, 25
  relation accuracy, 163
  relative positional, 57
  semantic, 24, 57, 100, 110, 111
  semantic accuracy, 99
  sensor, 441
  source, 423
  strong accuracy error, 26
  structural, 24
  syntactic, 24, 57, 64, 99, 100, 111
  thematic, 60
  time related, 27
  tuple, 163
  weak accuracy error, 26
Action, 309
Active learning procedure, 209
Adaptivity, 334
Address, 13
Ad hoc-integration, 265
Administrative flow, 13
Administrative process, 309
Administrative source, 446
Adversary model, 273
  honest-but-curious behaviour, 274
  malicious behaviour, 274
Aesthetic, 116
Aggregate constraint, 244
Aggregated data, 150
Aggregation, 334
Aggregation function, 153
Agriculture, 309
Ambiguity, 80
Ambiguous representation, 38
Amount, 316
Amount-factored fixed intrinsic value, 314
Annotation, 142, 144
Application domain
  accident insurance, 158
  administrative processes, 179
  archival, 50
  biology, 14, 15
  census, 179

© Springer International Publishing Switzerland 2016
C. Batini, M. Scannapieco, *Data and Information Quality*, Data-Centric Systems
and Applications, DOI 10.1007/978-3-319-24106-7